PASTOR, CHURCH & LAW

V O L U M E   T W O

Church Property
& Administration

RICHARD R. HAMMAR
J.D., LL.M., CPA

YOUR CHURCH

CHRISTIANITY TODAY
INTERNATIONAL

ISBN-10: 0-917463-46-3
ISBN-13: 978-0-917463-46-4

Published by Your Church Resources
Christianity Today International
465 Gundersen Drive
Carol Stream, IL 60188
(630) 260-6200
www.ChristianityToday.com
www.YourChurch.net
www.ChurchLawToday.com

Edited by: Marian V. Liautaud
Cover design by: Dean Renninger
Interior design by: Mary Bellus

Printed in the United States of America

To my beloved wife Christine,
and our children.

PASTOR, CHURCH & LAW
Volume Two

TABLE OF CONTENTS

Preface

What is a church? While the answer may seem obvious, defining the term "church" is a surprisingly complex task. For example, does a church include a church-operated school or nursing home, a denomination, a religious organization that conducts commercial activities, a small group of persons who meet in a home for religious study, a parachurch ministry, or a religious publisher? These are but a few of the issues that have confronted the courts.

The term "church" appears several times in the Internal Revenue Code. However, the term is never precisely defined. Presumably, Congress fears that any definition will be either too expansive (and encourage tax fraud) or too restrictive (and hurt legitimate churches).

The IRS has attempted to fill this definitional vacuum by compiling a list of 14 "criteria" which supposedly characterize a church. Unfortunately, these criteria are so restrictive that many if not most bona fide churches fail to satisfy several of them. It has been noted that even the churches described in the New Testament Book of Acts would have failed to fill the IRS's litmus test. The problem arises in part because of the IRS's attempt to draft criteria that apply to both local churches and religious denominations.

Courts most often are called upon to define the term church in the context of tax exemptions and zoning ordinances. Does a particular organization qualify for an exemption from federal income taxes or state property or sales taxes? May an organization construct a new facility in an area zoned exclusively for residential and "church" use? These are the very kinds of issues that have generated heated litigation, pitting churches against government agencies.

Chapter 5 was intentionally placed at the beginning of Volume Two, which is concerned with the relationship between law and the church. Obviously, one must have a clear idea of what the church is before examining how it operates.

Chapter 6 provides an in-depth legal perspective on the organizational and administrative issues that significantly impact a church's effectiveness in ministry. It's one of the most important chapters in this entire four-volume set. The chapter begins with a review of both the unincorporated and incorporated forms of organization. Should a church be incorporated? What advantages are there? Are there any disadvantages?

Church records raise a number of important legal questions. For example, under what circumstances can church members inspect church records? What church records are subject to their inspection? Can the IRS inspect church records? If so, what protections are available to churches?

Churches also may have a number of reporting requirements under state and federal law, including the filing of an annual corporate report, applications for exemption from various taxes, payroll tax reporting obligations, and the annual certification of racial nondiscrimination (for churches that operate a preschool, or an elementary or secondary school).

The selection, authority, removal, and personal liability of church officers, directors, and trustees present complex legal questions. For example, who are the legal members of a church? Can members lose their church membership through non-attendance or lack of support? How may a church remove a director prior to the expiration of a term of office? When may church directors or trustees be personally liable for their actions on behalf of a church?

Each of these problems will be analyzed in detail, along with the topic of church business meetings. How should a church give notice of its business meetings? What is a quorum? Who can vote? What is the effect of procedural irregularities? What body of parliamentary law applies?

You also will study the nature and extent of a church's legal authority, and the procedures employed in merging, consolidating, and dissolving churches.

Chapter 7 covers another legal hotbed—ownership of church property. Assume that a schism occurs in a local church and a dispute arises over ownership of the church's property. How do the civil courts resolve such a case? Which group will be awarded ownership of the property? And what about the application of local zoning laws to religious congregations. Sometimes civil interests conflict with a church's desire to use property for church purposes. Similarly, most communities have enacted building codes. To what extent do they apply to church buildings? Many areas have enacted "landmarking" ordinances that prohibit historic properties from being demolished or modified without approval. Do such laws apply to historic church buildings? For example, assume that a city designates a church as an historic landmark, and rejects the church's request to expand its building to accommodate a growing membership. Does the city have this authority? What about the church's constitutional right to freely exercise its religion?

Most churches will face at least some of these issues, and so a familiarity with the topics covered in this book is critical. This volume of Pastor, Church & Law, 4th edition, will help you understand the relationship between the law and the church. At the beginning of each section in this book, you'll find Legal Briefs—a quick snapshot of the main points covered in each chapter. From there you can explore each topic thoroughly, and dig deeply into the comprehensive information you need.

Definitions

Legal Briefs

What is a church? While the answer may seem obvious, a definition of the term "church" is a surprisingly complex task. For example, does a church include a church-operated school or nursing home, a denomination, a religious organization that conducts commercial activities, a small group of persons who meet in a home for religious study, a parachurch ministry, or a religious publisher? These are but a few of the issues that have confronted the courts.

> "There is little doubt that the proliferation of 'mail order churches' has caused the courts and the IRS to interpret the term 'church' more narrowly."

The term "church" appears several times in the Internal Revenue Code. However, the term is never defined. Presumably, Congress fears that any definition will be either too expansive (and encourage tax fraud) or too restrictive (and hurt legitimate churches). There is little doubt that the proliferation of "mail order churches" has caused the courts and the IRS to interpret the term "church" more narrowly. The IRS has created a list of 14 criteria that characterize a church. As you will see, these criteria are extremely narrow, and would not apply to many legitimate churches (including the original churches described in the New Testament Book of Acts).

The definition of the term "church" is also relevant in the contexts of zoning and property tax exemptions. Can a church that is located in an area zoned for residential and church uses build a school on its property? Can it construct an activities building? A softball field? A radio station? Does a state law that exempts churches from property taxes apply to church schools? To a vacant lot owned by a church? To a church-owned religious camp ground? Such illustrations demonstrate the importance and complexity of the question addressed in this chapter. These are the very kinds of issues that have generated heated litigation, pitting churches against government agencies.

This chapter was intentionally placed at the beginning of Volume Two of the text, which is concerned with the relationship between law and the church. Obviously, one must have a clear idea of what the church is before moving on to the remaining chapters in Volume Two. Be sure you understand thoroughly the materials presented in this chapter before moving on to chapter 6.

Definitions

Since many state and federal laws use the term *church*, it is important to define the term with precision. To illustrate, the Internal Revenue Code uses the term *church* in many contexts, including the following:

1. charitable giving limitations[1]

2. church pension plans under the Employee Retirement Income Security Act of 1974 (ERISA)[2]

3. church "retirement income accounts"[3]

4. deferred compensation plans[4]

5. ineligibility of churches for using an "expenditure test" for determining permissible lobbying activities[5]

6. unrelated business taxable income[6]

7. unrelated debt-financed income[7]

8. exemption from the necessity of applying for recognition of tax-exempt status[8]

9. treatment of church employees for social security purposes if church waives employer FICA coverage[9]

10. unemployment tax exemptions[10]

11. exemption from filing annual information returns[11]

12. exemption from filing returns regarding liquidation, dissolution, or termination[12]

13. restrictions on the examination of financial records[13]

---

[1] I.R.C. § 170(b)(1)(A)(i).

[2] *Id.* at §§ 410(d), 414(e).

[3] *Id.* at § 403(b)(9).

[4] *Id.* at §§ 414 and 457.

[5] *Id.* at § 501(h).

[6] *Id.* at § 512.

[7] *Id.* at § 514.

[8] *Id.* at § 508(c).

[9] *Id.* at § 1402(j).

[10] *Id.* at § 3309(b)(1).

[11] *Id.* at § 6033(a)(2)(A).

[12] *Id.* at § 6043(b)(1).

[13] *Id.* at § 7605(c).

14. election to waive the employer's obligation to pay social security and Medicare taxes on nonminister employees[14]

The Internal Revenue Code occasionally uses the term *church* in connection with the term *minister*. For example, service performed by a duly ordained, commissioned, or licensed minister of a church is exempt from federal employment taxes,[15] unemployment taxes,[16] income tax withholding requirements,[17] and self-employment taxes (if a valid waiver has been timely filed).[18] Despite these many references to the term *church*, the Internal Revenue Code contains no adequate definition of the term.[19]

In addition, federal law (1) imposes penalties on anyone who "intentionally defaces, damages, or destroys" a church or who "intentionally obstructs, by force or threat of force, any person in the enjoyment of that person's free exercise of religious beliefs, or attempts to do so";[20] (2) prescribes the position and manner of display of the United States flag in church buildings;[21] (3) imposes penalties upon persons who cross state lines to avoid prosecution for damaging or destroying church buildings, or who refuse to testify in any criminal proceeding relating to such an offense;[22] (4) describes the benefits available to churches under the National Flood Insurance Act;[23] (5) exempts churches from the "price discrimination" provisions of the Robinson-Patman Act;[24] and (6) provides for the employment of chaplains and the conduct of religious services at military installation.[25]

Many state and local laws contain specific references to the term *church*. Examples include laws pertaining to zoning, nonprofit corporations, state and local revenue, the use of church buses, the desecration of church buildings, the sale of intoxicating liquors within a specified distance from a church, building codes, property ownership, workers compensation, and interference with church services.

---

[14] *Id.* at § 3121(w).

[15] *Id.* at § 3121(b)(8).

[16] *Id.* at § 3309(b)(2).

[17] *Id.* at § 3401(a)(9).

[18] *Id.* at § 1402(e).

[19] *See generally* Gaffney, *Governmental Definition of Religion: the Rise and Fall of the IRS Regulations on an "Integrated Auxiliary of a Church,"* 25 Val. U. L. Rev. 203 (1991); Whelan, *"Church" in the Internal Revenue Code: The Definitional Problems,* 45 Fordham L. Rev. 885 (1977); Worthing, *"Religion" and "Religious Institutions" under the First Amendment,* 7 Pepperdine L. Rev. 313 (1980); Note, *Toward a Constitutional Definition of Religion,* 91 Harv. L. Rev. 1056 (1978).

[20] 18 U.S.C. § 247. Damages to church property must exceed $10,000. The penalties for violating this section include fines and a prison sentence of up to life (if a death results), up to ten years (if "serious bodily injury" results), or up to one year in all other cases. Section 247(d) specifies that "no prosecution for any offense described in this section shall be undertaken by the United States except upon the notification in writing of the Attorney General or his designee that in his judgment a prosecution by the United States is in the public interest and necessary to secure substantial justice."

[21] 4 U.S.C. § 7(k).

[22] 18 U.S.C. § 1074.

[23] 42 U.S.C. § 4013(b)(1)(C).

[24] 15 U.S.C. § 13c.

[25] 10 U.S.C. § 6031.

Every law that uses the term *church* raises definitional questions. As one court observed:

> [The term *church*] can mean an organization for religious purposes. It can also have the more physical meaning of a place where persons regularly assemble for worship. . . . [I]f "church" is interpreted to mean a place where persons regularly assemble for worship, does this include merely sanctuaries, chapels, and cathedrals, or does it also include buildings adjacent thereto such as parsonages, friaries, convents, fellowship halls, Sunday schools, and rectories?[26]

The courts have attempted to define the term *church* in various ways. Some of the definitions include:

- A body or community of Christians, united under one form of government by the profession of the same faith, and the observance of the same rituals and ceremonies.[27]

- An organization for religious purposes, for the public worship of God.[28]

- The term [church] may denote either a society of persons who, professing Christianity, hold certain doctrines or observances which differentiate them from other like groups, and who use a common discipline, or the building in which such persons habitually assemble for public worship.[29]

- A church consists of its land and buildings, its trustees and its congregation (the people who more or less regularly attend its religious services), as well as of its faith, doctrine, ritual and clergy.[30]

- At a minimum, a church includes a body of believers or communicants that assembles regularly in order to worship. Unless the organization is reasonably available to the public in its conduct of worship, its educational instruction, and its promulgation of doctrine, it cannot fulfill this associational role.[31]

- Among some ten definitions of "church" given by the lexicographers, two have gotten into the law books generally. One is "A society of persons who profess the Christian religion." The other is "The place where such persons regularly assemble for worship."[32]

---

[26] Guam Power Authority v. Bishop of Guam, 383 F. Supp. 476, 479 (D. Guam 1974).

[27] McNeilly v. First Presbyterian Church, 137 N.E. 691 (1923).

[28] Bennett v. City of LaGrange, 112 S.E. 482 (1922).

[29] First Independent Missionary Baptist Church v. McMillan, 153 So.2d 337 (Fla. App. 1963), quoting Baker v. Fales, 16 Mass. 488 (1820).

[30] Eastern Orthodox Catholic Church v. Adair, 141 N.Y.S.2d 772 (1955).

[31] American Guidance Foundation v. United States, 490 F. Supp. 304 (D.D.C. 1980).

[32] Church of the Holy Faith v. State Tax Commission, 48 P.2d 777 (N.M. 1935).

• A church is a building consecrated to the honor of God and religion, with its members united in the profession of the same Christian faith.[33]

• A Christian youth organization having no official connection with any denominational church body was a church since it "proclaims Christianity, conducts services for the worship of the Christian God and provides for the administration of the Christian sacraments to its assembled members.[34]

• The ordinary meaning of the term contemplates a place or edifice consecrated to religious worship, where people join together in some form of public worship.[35]

• The word "church" . . . includes at a minimum any religious organization which, as the whole of its activities, advocates and teaches its particular spiritual beliefs before others with a purpose of gaining adherents to those beliefs and instructing them in the doctrine which those beliefs comprise.[36]

• The term "church" means a voluntary organization of people for religious purposes who are associated for religious worship, discipline and teaching and who are united by the profession of the same faith, holding the same creed, observing the same rites, and acknowledging the same ecclesiastical authority.[37]

• The "plain, ordinary, and popular meaning of the word *church* includes a building in which people assemble for the worship of God and for the administration of such offices and services as pertain to that worship, a building consecrated to the honor of God and religion, and a place where persons regularly assemble for worship."[38]

• The term church includes "a building consecrated to the honor of a religion would likewise include buildings in which people assemble for non-Christian worship, such as a mosque, a synagogue, or a temple."[39]

• A church . . . in general terms, is an assemblage of individuals who express their adherence to a religion.[40]

• Where a particular word employed in a statute is not defined, it will be accorded its common, ordinary, plain, everyday meaning. "Church" is defined as

---

[33] Wiggins v. Young, 57 S.E.2d 486 (Ga. 1950).

[34] Young Life Campaign v. Patino, 176 Cal. Rptr. 23 (Cal. App. 1981) (an excellent discussion of the definition of *church*).

[35] In re Upper St. Clair Township Grange, 152 A.2d 768 (Pa. 1959).

[36] Christian Jew Foundation v. State, 653 S.W.2d 607 (Tex. App. 1983) (an excellent discussion of the term *church*, rejecting a proposed definition by the state of Texas as unconstitutionally preferring some churches over others).

[37] State v. Lynch, 265 S.E.2d 491 (N.C. App. 1980).

[38] Calvary Baptist Church v. Coonrad, 163 Neb. 25, 77 N.W.2d 821 (1956).

[39] Latenser v. Intercessors of the Lamb, Inc., 553 N.W.2d 458 (Neb. 1996).

[40] The Way International v. Limbach, 552 N.E.2d 908 (Ohio 1990).

"a body or organization of religious believers."[41]

• The term "church" is defined as 1. a building for public worship and especially Christian worship; 2. the clergy or officialdom of a religious body; 3. a body or organization of religious believers, as the whole body of Christians, a denomination, or congregation; 4. a public divine worship; 5. the clerical profession.[42]

• A church is a place where "an act, process, or instance of expressing veneration by performing or taking part in religious exercises or ritual" occurs.[43]

Courts most often are called upon to define the term *church* in the context of tax exemptions and zoning ordinances. Does a particular organization qualify for an exemption from federal income taxes or state property or sales taxes? May an organization construct a new facility in an area zoned exclusively for residential and "church" use? The definitions the courts have given to the term *church* in these two contexts will be considered separately.

Tax Legislation—Federal
§ 5-01

Federal tax law uses many terms to describe religious organizations. It is important to understand the meaning of these terms in order to determine the applicability of various tax provisions. All of these terms are addressed below.

Churches
§ 5-01.1

Key point 5-01.1. *The IRS has adopted a 14-criteria test for use in determining whether or not a particular entity is a church for purposes of federal tax law. This test is theologically flawed, and is subject to challenge.*

As noted above, the Internal Revenue Code contains several references to the term *church*, but provides no adequate definition. This is understandable, since a definition that is too narrow potentially interferes with the constitutional guaranty of religious freedom, while a definition that is too broad will encourage abuses in the name of religion.

The United States Supreme Court has noted that "the great diversity in church structure and organization among religious groups in this country . . . makes it impossible, as Congress perceived, to lay down a single rule to govern all church-

---

41 Crooks v. Director, 2007 WL 2482637 (Ohio App. 2007), quoting *Merriam-Webster's Collegiate Dictionary (11th ed. 2004)*.

42 TE-TA-MA Truth Foundation-Family of URI, Inc. v. World Church of the Creator, 2002 WL 126103 (N.D. Ill. 2002), quoting *Merriam-Webster's Collegiate Dictionary (10th ed. 1999)*.

43 North Pacific Union Conference v. Clark County, 74 P.3d 140 (Wash. App. 2003), quoting *Webster's Third New International Dictionary (1969)*.

related organizations."[44] Nevertheless, the Code contains some limited attempts to define churches and related organizations.

Prior to 1970, the income tax regulations specified that the term *church* included

> a religious order or religious organization if such order or organization (a) is an *integral part* of a church, and (b) is engaged in carrying out the functions of a church, whether as a civil law corporation or otherwise. In determining whether a religious order or organization is an integral part of a church, consideration will be given to the degree to which it is connected with, and controlled by, such church. A religious order or organization shall be considered to be engaged in carrying out the functions of a church if its duties include the ministration of sacerdotal functions and the conduct of religious worship. . . . What constitutes the conduct of religious worship or the ministration of sacerdotal functions depends on the tenets and practices of a particular religious body constituting a church.[45]

Sacerdotal= priestly

This language implied that a church is an organization whose "duties include the ministration of sacerdotal functions and the conduct of religious worship."

Section 3121(w) of the Code, which permits churches and church-controlled organizations to exempt themselves from the employer's share of social security and Medicare taxes (if certain conditions are met), defines the term *church* as follows:

> For purposes of this section, the term "church" means a church, a convention or association of churches, or an elementary or secondary school which is controlled, operated, or principally supported by a church or by a convention or association of churches. For purposes of this subsection, the term "qualified church-controlled organization" means any church-controlled tax-exempt organization described in section 501(c)(3), other than an organization which—(i) offers goods, services, or facilities for sale, other than on an incidental basis, to the general public, other than goods, services, or facilities which are sold at a nominal charge which is substantially less than the cost of providing such goods, services, or facilities; and (ii) normally receives more than 25 per cent of its support from either (I) governmental sources, or (II) receipts from admissions, sales of merchandise, performance of services, or furnishing of facilities, in activities which are not unrelated trades or businesses, or both.[46]

---

[44] St. Martin Evangelical Lutheran Church v. South Dakota, 451 U.S. 772, 782 n.12 (1981).

[45] Treas. Reg. § 1.511-2(a)(3)(ii) (emphasis added).

[46] I.R.C. § 3121(w)(3).

In 1974, the IRS proposed, but never adopted, the following definition of a "church" as part of proposed regulations addressing charitable contributions:

> A church or convention or association of churches is . . . an organization of individuals having commonly held religious beliefs, engaged solely in religious activities in furtherance of such beliefs. The activities of the organization must include the conduct of religious worship and the celebration of life cycle events such as births, deaths and marriage. The individuals engaged in the religious activities of a church are generally not regular participants in activities of another church, except when such other church is a parent or subsidiary organization of their church.[47]

In the context of charitable contribution deductions, the Internal Revenue Code defines the term *church, or convention or association of churches* as a "church, or convention or association of churches."[48]

These definitions clearly are inadequate, and provide very little help in applying the many Internal Revenue Code sections pertaining to churches. The IRS has attempted to fill this definitional vacuum by compiling a list of 14 "criteria" which presumably characterize a church:

1. a distinct legal existence

2. a recognized creed and form of worship

3. a definite and distinct ecclesiastical government

4. a formal code of doctrine and discipline

5. a distinct religious history

6. a membership not associated with any other church or denomination

7. an organization of ordained ministers

8. ordained ministers selected after completing prescribed studies

9. a literature of its own

10. established places of worship

11. regular congregations

12. regular worship services

13. Sunday schools for religious instruction of the young

14. schools for the preparation of ministers

---

[47] Quoted in GCM 37116 (1977).

[48] Treas. Reg. § 1.170A-9(a).

No single factor is controlling, although all fourteen may not be relevant to a given determination.[49]

These criteria have been applied by the IRS and the courts in several cases, as noted below.

Case Studies

• *The first federal court to recognize the IRS "14 criteria" test involved a claim by a husband and wife that they and their minor child constituted a church. The family insisted that it was a church since the father often preached and disseminated religious instruction to his son; the family conducted "religious services" in their home; and the family often prayed together at home. A federal court agreed with the IRS that the family was not a church, basing its decision on the 14 criteria. In commenting upon the 14 criteria, the court noted that "[w]hile some of these are relatively minor, others, e.g., the existence of an established congregation served by an organized ministry, the provision of regular religious services and religious education for the young, and the dissemination of a doctrinal code, are of central importance. The means by which an avowedly religious purpose is accomplished separates a 'church' from other forms of religious enterprise." In concluding that the family was not a church, the court observed: "At a minimum, a church includes a body of believers or communicants that assembles regularly in order to worship. Unless the organization is reasonably available to the public in its conduct of worship, its educational instruction, and its promulgation of doctrine, it cannot fulfill this associational role."[50]*

• *The IRS ruled that a religious organization was properly exempt from federal income taxes as a "church." The organization in question was established to develop an ecumenical form of religious expression that would "unify western and eastern modes of religious practice" and place greater significance on the mystical aspects of religious truth. Some twenty or so persons met for an hour each week in the church's facilities, and were asked to pay dues of $3 each month and subscribe to the church's ten precepts. A "Sunday school" was provided for children of members and nonmembers, and literature was produced. The IRS concluded that this organization was properly exempt from federal income taxes as a church, since it satisfied a majority of the 14 criteria. The IRS observed that "the organization meets most of the 14 criteria . . . . It is fully incorporated and has a fully distinct legal existence. It has a creed and form of worship recognized by its members. Although it is still in a developing stage, it has a definite and distinct ecclesiastical government . . . . It has a formal code of doctrine and discipline as evidenced by the ten precepts . . . . While it has a history of only a few years because it is a relatively new organization, its members have documented its growth and major changes. It has what could be called an organization of ordained ministers . . . a literature of its own . . . an established place of worship . . . a regular congregation . . . and regular services including Sunday school." The IRS noted that the church did not have a "membership not associated with any other church or denomination" since members were*

---

49   The 14 criteria seem to have originated in a 1959 IRS ruling that found the Salvation Army to be a church. See Rev. Rul. 59-129, 1959-1 C.B. 58, and GCM 37116 (1977).

50   American Guidance Foundation v. United States, 490 F. Supp. 304 (D.D.C. 1980). *See also* Lutheran Social Service of Minnesota v. United States, 758 F.2d 1283 (8th Cir. 1985); Church of the Visible Intelligence that Governs the Universe v. Commissioner, 4 Cls. Ct. 55 (Ct. Cl. 1983).

not required to sever their ties with other churches. However, a failure to meet this factor was "overcome" by the presence of the remaining thirteen factors.[51]

• *A federal appeals court, in rejecting an individual's claim that he was exempt from federal taxes since he was a "church," relied directly on the 14 criteria. The individual maintained that after "much Bible study" he had concluded that "if you believe you are a church and you are practicing your religion to your point of view, then you can have tax exempt status because churches are exempt." He pointed out that the Internal Revenue Code contains no definition of the term church, and that churches are not required to file applications for exemption from federal income tax. The court, in rejecting the taxpayer's "tax-exempt" status, observed that "it is obvious that one person cannot free all his taxable income from all tax liabilities by the simple expedient of proclaiming himself a church and making some religious contributions. Common sense makes this clear." If this were not so, "there would likely be an overabundance of one-person churches paying no income taxes, and leaving to the rest of us the payment of their fair share of the expense of running the government. That attitude hardly seems like an act of churchly charity to one's neighbors." The court concluded its opinion by observing: "Every year with renewed vigor, many citizens seek sanctuary in the free exercise [of religion] clause of the First Amendment. They desire salvation not from sin or from temptation, however, but from the most earthly of mortal duties—income taxes. Any salvation sought from income taxes in this court is denied."*[52]

• *The United States Tax Court ruled that a religious organization formed to "spread the message of God's love and hope throughout the world" and to "provide a place in which those who believe in the existence of God may present religious music to any persons interested in hearing such" was not a church.*[53] *The organization maintained an outdoor amphitheater on its property, at which musical programs and an occasional "retreat" or "festival" were conducted about twelve times each year. No other regularly scheduled religious or musical services were conducted. Most of the musical events were held on Saturdays so that persons could attend their own churches on Sundays. Musical services consisted of congregational singing of religious music. A minister always opened and closed these events with prayer. While it did not charge admission to its events, there was a published schedule of "donations" that were similar to admissions charges. The organization also maintained a chapel on its property that was open to the public for individual prayer. The organization applied to the IRS for recognition of tax exempt status on the ground that it was a church. Eventually, the IRS rejected the organization's exemption application on the ground that it was not a church. In reaching its decision, the IRS noted that the organization failed most of the 14 criteria used by the IRS in identifying churches. The organization maintained that it met a majority of these criteria, and appealed to the Tax Court. The Tax Court agreed with the IRS, and ruled that the organization was not a church. Significantly, it refused to accept the 14 criteria as the only test for determining whether or not a particular organization is a church. It did concede, however, that the 14 criteria are helpful in deciding such cases. The court noted that the organization met at least a few of the 14 criteria, and that some would not be relevant to "a newly-created rural organization." On the other hand, the court noted that the*

---

[51] Technical Advice Memorandum 8833001.

[52] United States v. Jeffries, 854 F.2d 254 (7th Cir. 1988).

[53] Spiritual Outreach Society v. Commissioner of Internal Revenue, 58 T.C.M. 1284 (1990), *aff'd*, 927 F.2d 335 (8th Cir. 1991).

organization had no ecclesiastical government, formal creed, organization of ordained clergy, seminary, or Sunday school for the training of youth. Further, it did not produce its own religious literature (it sold literature produced by other religious organizations). The court concluded by noting that "[w]hile a definitive form of ecclesiastical government or organizational structure may not be required, we are not persuaded that musical festivals and revivals (even if involving principally gospel singing . . .) and gatherings for individual meditation and prayer by persons who do not regularly come together as a congregation for such purposes should be held to satisfy the cohesiveness factor which we think is an essential ingredient of a 'church.'" This case is significant, since it represents the first time that the Tax Court has acknowledged that the 14 criteria used by the IRS in identifying churches are not an exclusive test that must be used in all cases.

• A state supreme court ruled that "all 14 factors need not be answered affirmatively in favor of there being a church for a religious organization to be classified as a church. Neither must there necessarily be a numerical majority. Mechanical evaluation is not the process to be used. Rather, the facts of each case are to be considered in their respective context and considered in light of these factors . . . ."[54]

• The IRS ruled that a nondenominational missions agency was not a church. The agency's purpose, as set forth in its articles of incorporation, is "carrying on evangelical missionary work in . . . any other country among any other peoples, including the training and support of missionaries, the training and education of the peoples of such countries, the establishment of indigenous churches, the operation of such institutions as are necessary for this purpose and for other exclusively religious, charitable, educational and missionary purposes as its board of directors may from time to time designate." The agency has a doctrinal statement, but its governing documents do not describe its use of any traditional means of ecclesiastical discipline (e.g., confession, counseling, withholding of sacraments, excommunication) utilized by churches.

The agency insisted that it was a church because it met most of the criteria in the IRS 14-criteria test. The IRS noted that "these criteria are helpful in deciding what constitutes a church for federal tax purposes, but are not a definitive test." It acknowledged that the agency met several of the 14 criteria. For instance, "it has a distinct legal existence, a formal code of doctrine, a recognized creed, a distinct religious history, and literature of its own. It is also closely affiliated with several Bible schools and seminaries." However, the IRS noted that "these are not distinctive characteristics of a church, but are common to both churches and non-church religious organizations. Meeting these criteria is not sufficient to establish [the agency is] a church." The IRS noted that the agency's primary activity was "the establishment and support of new churches in [foreign lands]." And, while the agency "exercises oversight and authority over its missionary-ministers, it does not have any formal authority over the churches or their leaders, or even a formal affiliation with most of the churches." Further, the IRS noted that the agency had not shown evidence of having a code of discipline. For instance, its literature "did not describe its use of any traditional means of ecclesiastical discipline (e.g., confession, counseling, withholding of sacraments, excommunication) utilized by churches." The IRS conceded that the agency had established training requirements for the missionary-ministers it appoints and provided some training, but it pointed out that "it does not require them to be ordained or licensed. Nor does it ordain or license ministers of the local churches it establishes. Rather, its affiliate churches are responsible for ordaining their own ministers. Thus, it

---

[54]   Nampa Christian Schools, Foundation v. State, 719 P.2d 1178 (Idaho 1986).

is not an 'organization of ordained ministers.'"

Although the agency provides training for missionary children and helps its affiliate churches to establish Sunday school programs, "it has not established that it operates its own Sunday schools or comparable programs for the religious instruction of the young." Finally, the agency "does not identify itself publicly as a church. Neither its organizing documents, its website, nor any of its literature refers to it as a church. Rather, it describes itself as a 'non-denominational missions agency.' This undermines its contention that it is a church."

• The IRS concluded that the agency did not meet most of the criteria for classification as a church "that courts have recognized as being of central importance," including "the existence of an established congregation, the provision of regular worship services and religious education for the young, and the dissemination of a doctrinal code. Although the agency disseminates a doctrinal code, it does not meet the other central criteria. In particular, it does not have a regular, established congregation of members who meet together, as a church, for regular worship services and instruction of the young." Nor did the agency meet most of the other criteria the IRS considers in determining whether to classify an organization as a church. In particular, "it does not ordain ministers, operate Sunday schools for religious instruction of the young, or have a code of discipline, a distinct ecclesiastical government, an established place of worship, or a membership not associated with other local churches or denominations. Although its affiliate churches may meet most of the criteria for classification as a church, the agency itself is separate and distinct from those churches."[55]

• The IRS concluded that a missions agency was not a church for federal tax purposes. The missions agency (the "agency") was similar in most respects to the agency involved in the previous example, except that it amended its articles of incorporation to refer to itself as a church as well as a "global evangelistic ministry." However, the IRS concluded that this single factor was not relevant, since the agency "does not identify itself publicly as a church. Neither its website nor the literature it distributes to the public refers to it as a church. Rather, it describes itself as a missions agency, a missionary society, and an evangelistic agency, but not as a church. Its literature often distinguishes it, as a missions agency, from churches with which it partners. This undermines its contention that it is a church for federal tax purposes." The agency also stressed that its central office hosts semiweekly prayer meetings for 15–35 staff members and a periodic "Day of Prayer" for its office staff. Once again, the IRS concluded that these facts did not transform the agency into a church, since "these activities are incidental to the main activity of the central office, which is to exercise administrative, financial, and operational oversight over [the agency's] worldwide ministry. Its employees are paid to engage in these activities at its headquarters. . . . The conduct of devotional worship and prayer services does not convert an administrative office into a church. . . . Furthermore, staff members all belong to other local churches, and do not consider the agency to be their church."[56]

These examples demonstrate the continuing viability of the 14 criteria. Nevertheless, these criteria are troubling because they are so restrictive that many if not most bona fide churches fail to satisfy several of them. In part, the problem

---

[55] IRS Letter Ruling 200727021.

[56] IRS Letter Ruling 200712047. *Accord* IRS Letter Ruling 200712046.

results from the attempt by the IRS to draft criteria that apply to both local churches and religious denominations. To illustrate, few if any local churches would meet the seventh, ninth, and 14th criteria, since these ordinarily would pertain only to religious denominations. In addition, many newer, independent churches often will fail the first and fifth criteria and may also fail the second, third, fourth, sixth, and eighth. It is therefore possible for a legitimate church to fail as many as ten of the 14 criteria.

Key point. *The original Christian churches described in the New Testament Book of Acts would have failed a majority of the 14 criteria.*[57]

The 14 criteria clearly are vague and inadequate. Some apply exclusively to local churches, others do not. And the IRS does not indicate how many criteria an organization must meet in order to be classified as a church. The vagueness of the criteria necessarily means that their application in a particular case will depend on the discretionary judgment of a government employee. This is the very kind of conduct that the courts repeatedly have condemned in other contexts as unconstitutional. To illustrate, the courts consistently have invalidated municipal ordinances that condition the constitutionally protected interests of speech and assembly upon compliance with criteria that are so vague that decisions essentially are a matter of administrative discretion. The United States Supreme Court has held that "[it] is a basic principle of due process that an enactment is void for vagueness if its prohibitions are not clearly defined. . . . A vague law impermissibly delegates basic policy matters to [government officials] for resolution on an *ad hoc* and subjective basis with the attendant dangers of arbitrary and discriminatory application."[58]

This same reasoning also should apply in the context of other fundamental constitutional rights, such as the First Amendment right to freely exercise one's religion. The IRS should not be permitted to effectively limit the right of churches and church members to freely exercise their religion on the basis of criteria that are as vague as the 14 criteria listed above, and whose application in a particular case is essentially a matter of administrative discretion.

The criteria also are constitutionally suspect on the related ground of "overbreadth." The Supreme Court "has repeatedly held that a governmental purpose to control or prevent activities constitutionally subject to state regulation may not be achieved by means which sweep unnecessarily broadly and thereby invade the area of protected freedoms. The power to regulate must be so exercised as not, in attaining a permissible end, unduly to infringe the protected freedom. Even though the governmental purpose be legitimate and substantial, that purpose cannot be pursued by means that broadly stifle fundamental personal liberties when the end can be more narrowly achieved."[59] Congress and the IRS undoubtedly have the authority to identify those churches that are not qualified for the tax benefits afforded

---

[57] *See generally* S. Schlatter, The Church in the New Testament Period (P. Levertoff trans. 1955); R. Schneckenburg, The Church in the New Testament (1965); E. Schweizer, Church Order in the New Testament (1961); E. Schweizer, The Church as the Body of Christ (1964).

[58] Grayned v. City of Rockford, 408 U.S. 104, 108-09 (1972).

[59] N.A.A.C.P. v. Alabama, 377 U.S. 288, 307-08 (1964).

by federal law, but they may not do so on the basis of criteria that sweep so broadly as to jeopardize the standing of legitimate churches. The courts understandably find the task of defining the term *church* perplexing. But they should avoid referring to the 14 criteria as support for their conclusions, particularly in cases involving "mail-order churches" and other obvious shams for which the definitional question is not in doubt.

The IRS has successfully challenged a variety of tax-evasion schemes that have operated under the guise of a church. These schemes usually involve some or all of the following characteristics: An individual forms his own church, assigns all or a substantial part of his income to the church, takes a vow of poverty, declares himself to be the minister, retains control over all church funds and property, designates a substantial housing allowance for himself, and reports the income that he has assigned to his church as a charitable contribution deduction on his federal tax return. In most cases the church has no building other than the personal residence of the "minister," and it conducts few if any religious activities. Since the minister often purchases his credentials and church charter by mail, such schemes commonly are referred to as mail-order churches. The IRS consistently has refused to recognize such entities as entitled to exemption from federal income taxation. This determination often is based on the fact that the net earnings of the alleged church "inure" to the benefit of private individuals, not because the organization is not a church.

A number of federal courts have defined the term *church* without reference to the 14 criteria, and have concluded that the term may include a private elementary and secondary school maintained and operated by a church,[60] a seminary,[61] and conventions and associations of churches.[62]

The United States Supreme Court has held that some church-controlled organizations that are not separately incorporated may be regarded for tax purposes as part of the church itself.[63]

Case Studies

• The IRS ruled that an evangelistic association was not a church. The most prominent feature of the association's ministry was the series of religious meetings held in various cities around the world. Each meeting followed a pattern virtually identical to that of thousands of other Christian church services, including prayer, music, an offering, announcements regarding the association's ministry, and further meetings and readings from the Bible. Each service culminated with the message that those present should commit or recommit their lives to Christ, followed by an invitation.

---

[60] St. Martin Evangelical Lutheran Church v. South Dakota, 451 U.S. 772 (1981).

[61] EEOC v. Southwestern Baptist Theological Seminary, 651 F.2d 277 (5th Cir. 1981).

[62] De La Salle Institute v. United States, 195 F. Supp. 891 (N.D. Cal. 1961); Senate Report 2375, 81st Congress, 2d Session, p. 27.

[63] St. Martin Evangelical Lutheran Church v. South Dakota, 451 U.S. 772 (1981) (the Court declined to rule on the status of separately incorporated, church-controlled organizations). *See also* Treas. Reg. § 1.6033-2(g)(5)(iv), example 6; Lutheran Social Service of Minnesota v. United States, 758 F.2d 1283 (8th Cir. 1985).

All of those who made decisions for Christ in the meetings were encouraged to join a local church. The association published a variety of religious books and tracts in furtherance of its teaching ministry. The association asked the IRS to rule that it was a church or a convention or association of churches, and thereby exempt from filing annual information returns (Form 990) with the IRS. The IRS declined to do so. It observed that "the association is not a convention or association of churches as it is completely independent from and, to the best of our knowledge, has no continuing relationship with any other religious organizations." The IRS also concluded that the association was not a church. It reviewed several other rulings addressing the definition of a church, and concluded that there was "one common thread"—whether or not "the organization had (or did not have) a distinct congregation whose members did not maintain affiliation with other churches." While the IRS conceded that this one factor was not determinative, it did find it significant that the association did not have a distinct congregation and that those attending its services maintained or acquired affiliation with other churches. Further, the association was essentially interdenominational and did not "seek converts other than to the principles of Christianity generally." The IRS concluded: "While it has a distinct legal existence and arguably a recognized creed and form of worship, it does not have a definite and distinct ecclesiastical government, a formal code of doctrine and discipline, or a distinct religious history. While it has ordained ministers, the association apparently does not prescribe courses of study leading to their ordination and in fact does not ordain them itself. Of course, these ministers have no distinct congregations to which they minister. While the association does publish and distribute [a magazine, it] has no distinct scripture and no established place of worship. It does not conduct regular religious services as its conduct of such services is dependent on invitations from other religious organizations. Finally, it has no Sunday schools and no schools for the preparation of its ministers. We think it evident that the association has relatively few of the characteristics normally associated with a church."[64]

• The Tax Court ruled that an interdenominational organization that existed to perform dental work in foreign countries as a means of promoting "the Gospel of the Lord Jesus Christ, around the world, and the evangelization of the world on the basis of the principles of the Protestant Faith," was not a church. The organization conducted regular services in the United States and provided various churches with speakers and literature concerning its activities. The members of the organization were all trained in the Bible and church work. While many of its members were ordained ministers, the organization did not conduct a seminary or Bible School. All members were required to be licensed dentists. The court determined that a more limited concept was intended for the term "church" than that denoted by the term "religious organization." It stated that Congress did not intend "church" to be used in a generic or universal sense but rather in the sense of a "denomination" or "sect." The court added that a group need not necessarily have an organizational hierarchy or maintain church buildings to constitute a "church." In holding that the organization was not a church, the court emphasized that (1) the organization's individual members maintained their affiliation with various churches; (2) the organization was interdenominational and did not seek converts other than to the principles of Christianity generally; (3) the organization did not ordain its own ministers; and (4) the conducting of religious services by its members was not conclusive per se that the organization was a church.[65]

---

[64] GCM 37116 (1977).

[65] Chapman v. Commissioner, 48 T.C. 358 (1967).

• A federal court, in revoking the tax-exempt status of a religious organization because of its extensive lobbying activities, commented on the organization's status as a church. It noted that the organization was founded and administered by an ordained minister; that other ordained ministers were employed by the organization and were empowered to perform all sacerdotal functions on its behalf; that the organization conducted numerous religious revivals in various churches throughout the United States sponsored by local congregations, and it also held regular Sunday services; and, that it conducted annual conventions, leadership schools, and summer sessions for the young. Although the organization's status as a "church" was not in issue, the court noted that the organization's "structure, its practices, precepts, and activities provide all the necessary elements of and is legally defined a church in the ordinary accepted meaning of the term and as used in the Internal Revenue Code of 1954, its amendments and applicable regulations. . . . [The organization's] followers together with its ordained pastors constitute a congregation the same as any local church."[66]

• A federal district court interpreted the meaning of the term "church" in the context of the unrelated business income tax (prior to the application of this tax to churches). The court noted that the unrelated business income tax was imposed upon the income of religious corporations other than churches or conventions or associations of churches. It noted that every church or convention or association of churches was obviously a religious organization, but questioned whether the converse was true—whether every religious organization was a church. The court pointed out that Congress would in all probability not have drawn a new word into the statute unless it meant thereby to express a different idea. There could be no sound reason to use the term "church" in the statute, unless there was an intention to express a more limited idea than is conveyed by "religious organization." The court also pointed out that the legislative history underlying the unrelated business income tax "constantly drew the distinction between churches and religious organizations under church auspices and that not all religious activities tended to make an organization a church. Rather, the legislative history imparted a restrictive interpretation to the word "church." The court employed a "common sense" approach in determining whether a particular organization constituted a church: "To exempt churches, one must know what a church is. Congress must either define church or leave the definition to the common meaning and usage of the word; otherwise, Congress would be unable to exempt churches." The court concluded that an incorporated religious teaching order that performed no sacerdotal functions was not a church, and that the income derived by the order from the ownership and operation of a separately incorporated winery was not the income of a church, despite the fact that both corporations were formed under church auspices.[67]

---

[66] Christian Echoes National Ministry, Inc. v. United States, 470 F.2d 848 (10th Cir. 1972) (quoting from a district court opinion in the same case).

[67] De La Salle Institute v. United States, 195 F. Supp. 891 (N.D. Cal. 1961).

Mail Order Churches

§ 5-01.2

Key point 5-01.2. *A "mail order church" is a sham organization that is created in order to reduce or eliminate the founder's tax liability. Often, such organizations purchase a "church charter" through the mail from an organization that also offers ministerial "credentials." Such organizations are not recognized as "churches" by the IRS.*

In recent years, many taxpayers have attempted to exclude all or part of their income from federal taxation through the creation of a mail order church. The IRS *Internal Revenue Manual* addresses the subject of mail order churches as follows:

> The term "mail order church" refers to organizations set up pursuant to "church charters" purchased through the mail from organizations that claim that the charters and other "ministerial credentials" can be used to reduce or eliminate an individual's federal income tax liability. Although a "mail order church" is not precluded from exemption, because it is possible for one to be organized operated exclusively for religious purposes, Service experience, as reflected in numerous court decisions, has shown that many are operated for the private benefit of those who control the organization.[68]

The IRS has challenged the tax-exempt status of several mail order churches on the ground that they fail to meet one or more of the prerequisites of exempt status. The IRS often asserts that mail order churches are ineligible for tax-exempt status since they are not organized or operated exclusively for exempt purposes. This assertion often is based on the following provision in the income tax regulations:

> An organization is not organized or operated exclusively for one or more [exempt purposes] unless it serves a public rather than a private interest. Thus, to meet [this] requirement . . . it is necessary for an organization to establish that it is not organized or operated for the benefit of private interests such as designated individuals, the creator or his family, shareholders of the organization, or persons controlled, directly or indirectly, by such private interests.[69]

A church that exists primarily to serve the private interests of its creator is not serving a public interest and therefore is not organized or operated for exempt purposes. Such a finding will be made whenever a church exists primarily as a means for handling the personal financial transactions of its founder.

---

[68] IRS Internal Revenue Manual § 7.25.3.6.11 (1999).

[69] Treas. Reg. § 1.501(c)(3)-1(d)(i)(ii).

Case Study

• In Revenue Ruling 81-94,[70] the IRS denied exempt status to a mail order church founded by a nurse. Following a vow of poverty, the nurse had transferred all of her assets, including her home and automobile, to her church and assigned her secular income to the church's checking account. In return, all of her expenses, such as her home mortgage and all outstanding credit card balances, were assumed by the church. The nurse also was provided with a full living allowance sufficient to maintain her previous standard of living. The church permitted her to use the home and automobile for personal uses. While the church's charter stated that it was organized exclusively for religious and charitable purposes, including a religious mission of healing the spirit, mind, emotions, and body, the church conducted few if any religious services and performed virtually no religious functions. The IRS concluded that the church existed primarily as a vehicle for handling the nurse's personal financial transactions and thus it was operated for the private interests of a designated individual rather than for a public interest.[71]

The IRS often asserts that a mail order church is ineligible for exempt status since its net earnings inure to the benefit of private individuals. A church cannot be exempt from federal income taxes if any part of its net earnings inures to the benefit of a private individual (other than as reasonable compensation for services rendered). Prohibited inurement may be indicated by a number of circumstances, including the following: (1) compensation paid by an exempt organization is excessive in light of services rendered; (2) the value of services performed and of the corresponding compensation paid cannot be established objectively; (3) payments are not compensation for services rendered; (4) material benefits are provided in addition to regular wages; (5) compensation is based on a percentage of a church's gross receipts; (6) substantially all of a church's gross receipts come from its minister and are returned to him or her in the form of compensation and reimbursement of personal expenses; or (7) a church exists primarily to facilitate the personal financial transactions of its founder.

To illustrate, inurement has been found in the following contexts: church ministers received fees, commissions, royalties, loans, a personal residence, and a car, in addition to ordinary wages;[72] a church devised a formula for determining the percentage of its gross receipts that would be payable to its minister, under which formula the minister received 63 percent of the church's gross receipts in one year and 53 percent in the next;[73] a boilermaker was ordained and chartered as "a church

---

[70] Rev. Rul. 81-94, 1981-1 C.B. 330. The IRS has stated that its position regarding mail order churches is set forth in this ruling, and, that "numerous court cases have held that, in situations similar to that described in Rev. Rul. 81–94, an organization that serves the private interests of a designated individual rather than a public interest does not qualify for exemption under IRC 501(c)(3)." See IRS INTERNAL REVENUE MANUAL § 7.25.3.6.11 (1999).

[71] *See also* New Life Tabernacle v. Commissioner, 44 T.C.M. 309 (1982); Solander v. Commissioner, 43 T.C.M. 934 (1982); Self v. Commissioner, 41 T.C.M. 1465 (1981); Basic Bible Church v. Commissioner, 74 T.C. 846 (1980); Southern Church of Universal Brotherhood Assembled, Inc. v. Commissioner, 74 T.C. 1223 (1980).

[72] Founding Church of Scientology v. Commissioner, 412 F.2d 1197 (Ct. Cl. 1969), *cert. denied,* 397 U.S. 1009 (1970).

[73] People of God Community v. Commissioner, 75 T.C. 127 (1981). The court concluded that "paying over a portion of gross earnings to those vested with the control of a church organization constitutes private inurement . . . ."

personally" by a mail order organization, took a vow of poverty, continued to work full time in secular employment, assigned his salary to his church account over which he maintained complete control, paid all of his personal expenses out of the church account, and claimed the maximum charitable contribution deduction for the amounts he transferred to the church account;[74] a married couple was ordained by and received a church charter from a mail order organization, established a church in their home, conducted religious services for between 3 and 10 persons, paid all of their secular income to the church, and received such income back in the form of compensation and a housing allowance;[75] a married couple took a vow of poverty and established a religious order in which they and their children were the only members, assigned all of their secular income to the order, and claimed a charitable contribution deduction for the income assigned;[76] a taxpayer was ordained by and received a church charter from a mail order organization, established a church in his home, declared himself and two others to be its ministers, assigned all of his secular income to the church, and received substantially all of it back in the form of wages, a housing allowance, loans, and travel allowances;[77] a church made substantial cash grants to its officers without provision for repayment;[78] and a mail order church could not support substantial payments made to its founder.[79]

Predictably, standards that are comprehensive enough to deal effectively with the abuses of mail order churches may be sufficiently broad to affect adversely some legitimate churches. For example, the Tax Court denied exempt status to a church having 56 members that conducted regular evangelistic worship services, performed baptisms, communion services, weddings, and burials; whose beliefs included the infallibility of the Bible; and whose pastor testified that "we do not have a creed but Christ; no law but love, no book but the Bible."[80] The IRS contended that the

---

[74] Hall v. Commissioner, 41 T.C.M. 1169 (1981). *See also* McGahen v. Commissioner, 76 T.C. 468 (1981).

[75] Church of the Transfiguring Spirit v. Commissioner, 76 T.C. 1 (1981). In all of the following cases, individuals were ordained by and received a church charter from a mail order organization, established a church in their homes, conducted few if any religious services, assigned their secular income to the church checking account out of which they paid most of their personal expenses, and attempted to claim the maximum charitable contribution deduction allowable for the income assigned. An IRS finding of inurement was upheld in each case. Basic Unit Ministry of Schurig v. Commissioner, 670 F.2d 1210 (D.C. Cir. 1982); Solander v. Commissioner 43 T.C.M. 934 (1982); Riemers v. Commissioner 42 T.C.M. 838 (1981); Southern Church of Universal Brotherhood Assembled v. Commissioner, 74 T.C. 1223 (1980); Bubbling Well Church of Universal Love v. Commissioner, 74 T.C. 531 (1980); Rev. Rul. 81-94, 1981-12 I.R.B. 15.

[76] Greeno v. Commissioner, 42 T.C.M. 1112 (1981); Granzow v. Commissioner, 739 F.2d 266 (7th Cir. 1984).

[77] Unitary Mission Church v. Commissioner, 74 T.C. 507 (1980). Besides finding the amount of ministerial wages paid by the church to be excessive, the court observed that housing allowances also may be so excessive as to constitute unreasonable compensation. In either case, inurement occurs. The court rejected the church's argument that the First Amendment prohibits the courts from inquiring into the reasonableness of church salaries, at least where such inquiries involve no analysis of religious doctrine. *See also* Universal Life Church v. Commissioner, 83 T.C. 292 (1984); Church of Ethereal Joy v. Commissioner, 83 T.C. 20 (1984); Self-Realization Brotherhood, Inc. v. Commissioner, 48 T.C.M. 344 (1984).

[78] Church in Boston v. Commissioner, 71 T.C. 102 (1978).

[79] Bubbling Well Church of Universal Love v. Commissioner, 74 T.C. 531 (1980). *See also* Truth Tabernacle v. Commissioner, 41 T.C.M. 1405 (1981).

[80] Truth Tabernacle v. Commissioner, 41 T.C.M. 1405 (1981). *But cf.* Truth Tabernacle, Inc. v. Commissioner of Internal Revenue, T.C. Memo. 1989-451.

church was not entitled to exempt status since it had not established that (1) its charter or bylaws provided for the distribution of church property to another exempt organization upon dissolution, (2) it was operated exclusively for religious purposes, (3) it was operated for public rather than private interests, and (4) its net earnings did not inure to the benefit of private individuals. In another case, the Tax Court observed: "Until recent years, a mere declaration that an organization was a church was almost enough to assure its treatment as such under the revenue laws. The cynical abuse of the church concept for tax purposes in recent years, however, has made necessary the same critical analysis of organizations claiming exemption on that ground as organizations engaged in admittedly secular activities." [81]

Key point. *Churches, like any other exempt organization, have the burden of proving that they meet each of the prerequisites to exempt status. The burden of proof is not on the IRS to disprove eligibility for exempt status. Many mail order churches have been denied exempt status because they could not prove that they in fact were organized or operated exclusively for exempt purposes or that none of their net earnings inured to the benefit of private individuals.*

Many mail order church schemes involve the assignment of a founder's secular income to his church's checking account, and the founder's claiming the largest allowable charitable contribution deduction on his or her federal income tax return. Since a charitable contribution deduction is available only to donors who make contributions to an exempt organization, the deductibility of charitable contributions to mail order churches often is challenged by the IRS. Unless taxpayers can prove that their contributions were made to a church that satisfies the prerequisites to exempt status listed in section 501(c)(3) of the Internal Revenue Code, their deductions will be disallowed. Occasionally, the IRS challenges a charitable contribution to a mail order church on the ground that such a transfer does not constitute a contribution.

> "The burden of proof is not on the IRS to disprove eligibility for exempt status."

To illustrate, in Revenue Ruling 78-232,[82] the IRS disallowed a charitable contribution deduction for any part of a taxpayer's secular income that he assigned to his mail order church's checking account, since

> [s]ection 170 of the Code provides . . . a deduction for charitable contributions to or for the use of [exempt] organizations . . . . Section 170(c)(2) of the Code provides, in part, that the term "charitable contribution" means a contribution or gift to or for the use of a corporation organized and operated exclusively for religious or other charitable purposes, no part of the net earnings of which inures to the benefit of any private shareholder or individual.

---

[81] Church of Ethereal Joy v. Commissioner, 83 T.C. 20, 27 (1984). An excellent summary of the abuses of mail order churches is contained in the congressional history to the Church Audit Procedures Act.

[82] Rev. Rul. 78-232, 1978-1 C.B. 69 (citations omitted).

The term "charitable contribution," as used in section 170 of the Code, has been held to be synonymous with the word "gift." A gift for purposes of section 170 is a voluntary transfer of money or property that is made with no expectation of procuring a commensurate financial benefit in return for the transfer. It follows that if the benefits the donor can reasonably expect to obtain by making the transfer are sufficiently substantial to provide a quid pro quo for it, then no deduction under section 170 is allowable.

In the instant case the money deposited by the taxpayer in the . . . church account was used or available for use for the taxpayer's benefit. . . . Accordingly, the amount of the salary checks deposited by the taxpayer in the bank account maintained in the name of the . . . church is not deductible as a "charitable contribution" under section 170 of the Code.

Judicial Impatience

The Tax Court has observed that "our tolerance for taxpayers who establish churches solely for tax avoidance purposes is reaching a breaking point. Not only do these taxpayers use the pretext of a church to avoid paying their fair share of taxes, even when their brazen schemes are uncovered many of them resort to the courts in a shameless attempt to vindicate themselves."[83]

Similarly, a federal appeals court has lamented that "we can no longer tolerate abuse of the judicial review process by irresponsible taxpayers who press stale and frivolous arguments, without hope of success on the merits, in order to delay or harass the collection of public revenues or for other nonworthy purposes."[84] The court ordered a mail order church to pay the government's costs and attorneys' fees incurred in contesting the church's claim of exemption, and warned that in the future it would "deal harshly" with frivolous tax appeals involving mail order churches. Other courts have sustained additions to tax for negligence or intentional disregard of tax laws pursuant to section 6653(a) of the Code.[85]

---

[83] Miedaner v. Commissioner, 81 T.C. 272 (1982).

[84] Granzow v. Commissioner, 739 F.2d 265 (7th Cir. 1984).

[85] *See, e.g.,* Hall v. Commissioner, 729 F.2d 632 (9th Cir. 1984); Davis v. Commissioner, 81 T.C. 806 (1983).

There are many potentially adverse consequences that can befall the founder of a mail order church. These include civil fraud penalties, criminal penalties, sanctions and costs of up to $25,000 for claiming a frivolous position, and substantial understatement penalties.[86]

The IRS is strictly construing the requirements of section 501(c)(3) when assessing the eligibility of a mail order church for exempt status, and it is threatening criminal prosecution of taxpayers who persist in using these tax evasion schemes.

Mail order clergy encounter difficulties in other contexts as well. For example, they have been denied eligibility to conduct marriage ceremonies by some states.[87]

Other Religious Organizations §5-01.3

Key point 5-01.3. *Federal tax law refers to several kinds of religious organizations in addition to churches, including conventions or associations of churches, integrated auxiliaries of churches, integral parts of a church, and qualified church-controlled organizations. It is important to define these terms in order to determine whether or not special tax rules apply.*

The Internal Revenue Code, income tax regulations, and IRS rulings refer to a number of church-related organizations, including *conventions or associations of churches, integrated auxiliaries of a church, integral agencies of a religious organization, integral parts of a church, qualified church controlled organizations, religious and apostolic organizations,* and *religious orders.* These terms are defined in a companion text.[88]

There is little if any justification for the confusing number of terms employed by the Internal Revenue Code and the income tax regulations in describing church-related organizations. Such terminology suggests a confusion on the part of Congress and the IRS in dealing with church-related organizations. An even more troubling concern is the largely discretionary authority of the IRS to interpret these ambiguously defined or undefined terms.

In summary, there clearly is a need for Congress to (1) reduce the unnecessarily confusing number of terms used in the Internal Revenue Code to describe church-related organizations; (2) sufficiently clarify the remaining definitions to eliminate discretionary application by the IRS; and (3) demonstrate a greater deference to the legitimate perceptions of bona fide churches concerning those entities that are sufficiently related as to come within the definition of the term *church.*

---

[86] All of these penalties are discussed in R. HAMMAR, CHURCH AND CLERGY TAX GUIDE chapter 1 (published annually by the publisher of this text).

[87] See section 3-04, *supra.*

[88] R. HAMMAR, CHURCH AND CLERGY TAX GUIDE (published annually by the publisher of this text).

Tax Legislation—State

§ 5-01.4

Key point 5-01.4. *The term "church" is used in a number of state tax laws, including property tax exemption statutes. State courts have struggled to provide an adequate definition.*

Several state courts have attempted to define the term *church* in the process of interpreting state tax exemptions.[89] To illustrate, in one case a religious radio station argued that it was exempt from state sales and use taxes since it was a church.[90] The radio station's corporate purpose was "to exalt the Lord Jesus Christ and to maintain facilities for the worship of God and for the teaching and preaching of the Gospel." The station actively engaged in religious activities, including broadcasting of predominantly religious programming, missions promotion, child evangelism, establishment of Bible study groups, and personal counseling. In addition, the station owned an auditorium that was used frequently for interdenominational worship services and related programs.

The state tax commissioner challenged the station's exemption on the ground that it was not a church. In particular, the commissioner argued that the radio station could not be a church since it did not have a body of communicants gathered together in an order, or united under one form of government." The court, acknowledging that the term *church* "is not susceptible to a precise definition," summarily concluded that the radio station was entitled to the exemption since it "exhibited the essential qualities of a church," despite the fact that it did not have a definite congregation.

In another case,[91] a county tax assessor determined that a private residence was not a church, despite the homeowners' contention that monthly meetings of the eleven-member Ideal Life Church were held in the home and the church had received a charter from the mail-order Universal Life Church. The tax assessor's determination was upheld by the state supreme court, which quoted with approval the reasoning of a lower court in the same case:

> [T]he proper test for determination of a "church" depends upon an analysis of all the facts and circumstances of each particular case. In the present action the following factors . . . lead to the clear conclusion that Petitioner is not a "church" . . . .

> 1. In substance, the preconceived and primary, if not the sole motive behind petitioner's organization and operation was tax avoidance in favor of the private individuals who control the corporation . . . .

> 2. Petitioner's doctrine and beliefs, such as they are, are intentionally vague and non-binding upon its members.

---

[89] *Id.*

[90] Maumee Valley Broadcasting Assoc. v. Porterfield, 279 N.E.2d 863 (Ohio 1972). *But see* G.C.M. 38982.

[91] Ideal Life Church v. County of Washington, 304 N.W.2d 308 (Minn. 1981).

3. Petitioner's members freely continue to practice other religions.

4. Petitioner has no formally trained or ordained ministry.

5. Petitioner has no sacraments, rituals, education courses or literature of its own.

6. Petitioner has no liturgy, other than simple meetings which resemble mere social gatherings or discussion groups rather than religious worship.

7. Petitioner is not an institution which advances religion (as that term is commonly understood) as a way of life for all men.

8. Petitioner does not require a belief in any Supreme Being or beings.[92]

Another court upheld the property tax exemption of a 65-acre tract of land containing a religious hermitage and retreat center. While noting that the property was "not a church in the narrow sense," the court concluded that a church is more than merely an edifice affording people the opportunity to worship God. . . . To limit a church to being merely a house of prayer and sacrifice would, in a large degree, be depriving the church of the opportunity of enlarging, perpetuating and strengthening itself and the congregation."[93]

One court ruled that an evangelistic association was not a church and so was not exempt from unemployment insurance payroll taxes.[94] The court noted that the evangelistic association was exempt from federal income tax, was established for avowedly religious purposes, conducted worship services in cities throughout the country, had a mailing list in excess of 25,000 persons, and relied upon contributions for its support. However, the association could not be deemed a church since "there was no group of believers who had voluntarily bound themselves together in an organized association for the purpose of shared and regular worship." Another court ruled that an interdenominational Christian youth organization that conducted religious services and administered sacraments was a church and thus was exempt from payment of unemployment taxes.[95] The court concluded that a comprehensive definition of the term *church* was not possible. Instead, the court opted for a functional approach—if an organization performs church functions, such as the conduct of worship and the promulgation of a creed, it will be deemed a church.

---

[92] *Id.* at 315. *But see* State v. American Fundamentalist Church, 530 N.W.2d 200 (Minn. 1995), in which the Minnesota Supreme Court, while not overruling its 8-factor test, noted that it should be applied together with a "subjective" test that looks to the sincerity of an organization's religious belief to be sure that it is not "cloaking a secular enterprise with the legal protections of religion." The 8-factor test was rejected by the Wisconsin Supreme Court in Waushara County v. Graf, 480 N.W.2d 16 (Wis. 1992).

[93] Order of Conventuals v. Lee, 409 N.Y.S.2d 667, 669 (1978).

[94] Vic Coburn Evangelistic Assoc. v. Employment Division, 582 P.2d 51 (Ore. 1978). *See also* Alton Newton Evangelistic Assoc., Inc. v. South Carolina Employment Security Commission, 326 S.E.2d 165 (S.C. 1985).

[95] Young Life Campaign v. Patino, 176 Cal. Rptr. 23 (1981).

Case Studies

• *The Georgia Supreme Court ruled that a state property tax exemption for "all places of religious worship" applied to a church-owned vacant lot that was used for parking. The court concluded: "The words 'religious worship' import a concept of a congregation assembling in a place open to the public to honor the Deity through reverence and homage. [The lot in question] is the site of the church's auxiliary parking lot, not its actual sanctuary. However [the statute] is phrased in inclusive general terms of 'all places of religious worship,' and does not employ the terms 'house' or 'church' of religious worship, which, arguably, might have limited it to a building. If the presence of the omnipotent and omnipresent God cannot be restricted to a mere man made edifice, surely it was not intended to limit the worship of such a God to a building."[96]*

• *The Supreme Court of Ohio, in concluding that a religious organization was exempt from state sales tax as a church, observed: "It has adherents. It adopts the Bible as the main source of its dogma, it propagates a comprehensive set of religious objectives and beliefs which attempt to answer its adherents' religious concerns, and it conducts services . . . . It employs ministers who preside at sacramental ceremonies, operates schools to train ministers, and sends forth missionaries to spread its beliefs."[97]*

• *The Pennsylvania Supreme Court ruled that a church's parking lots were exempt from property taxation under a state law exempting "all churches, meeting-houses, or other actual places of regularly stated religious worship, with the ground thereto annexed necessary for the occupancy and enjoyment of the same." The court concluded: "In this day and age, parking lots may be a necessity for a church, rather than just a convenience. People and churches have both moved away from towns, and many people are no longer living within walking distance of their church. To attend, they are required to drive and park a vehicle. With no available parking, church-goers may be forced to seek religious expression elsewhere, causing a decrease in membership and impeding the ability of the church to exist. . . . The church has established its parking lot is entitled to an exemption because it is necessary for the occupancy and enjoyment of [the church]. . . . We do not hold all church parking lots are entitled to tax-exempt status. However, if a church proves its parking lots are a reasonable necessity to the existence of the church itself, those lots are entitled to such status."[98]*

Other state courts have ruled that (1) a separately incorporated religious school operated by a group of local churches was not a church for purposes of unemployment law;[99] and (2) a Christian foundation that propagated its beliefs through written publications and radio broadcasts rather than through face-to-face communications, and that was not affiliated with any church or denomination, were "churches" for purposes of a state unemployment law.[100]

---

[96] Marathon Inv. Corp. v. Spinkston, 644 S.E.2d 133 (Ga. 2007).

[97] The Way International v. Limbach, 552 N.E.2d 908 (Ohio 1990).

[98] Wesley United Methodist Church v. Dauphin County Bd. of Assessment Appeals, 889 A.2d 1180 (Pa. 2005).

[99] Nampa Christian Schools Foundation v. State Department of Employment, 719 P.2d 1178 (Ida. 1986). The court concluded that the school was exempt under another provision of the unemployment law which exempted an organization operated primarily for religious purposes and which is operated or principally supported by a church or group of churches.

[100] Christian Jew Foundation v. State, 653 S.W.2d 607 (Tex. App. 1983).

Zoning law

§ 5-02

The civil courts often have been called upon to define the term *church* in the context of zoning laws. There rarely is a question about the status of a building used by a congregation for regular worship services. However, many churches do much more than conduct worship services. Some operate a preschool, elementary or secondary school, homeless shelter, recreational building, camp, bookstore, counseling center, or radio station. Can these kinds of activities be conducted on property that is zoned for "church" use?

Churches

§ 5-02.1

Key point 5-02.1. *Local zoning laws generally allow "churches" in residential areas. The courts have struggled with the application of this term to various activities and organizations other than traditional congregations meeting in a building for regular worship services.*

Many other courts have been asked to decide whether various uses of church-owned property constitute a *church* under municipal zoning laws. The following uses have been found to be "churches":

• use of a home across the street from a church for women's fellowship meetings and religious education classes;[101]

• a single-family residence used by the United Presbyterian Church as a religious coffeehouse for university students;[102]

• a priest's home, convent, and parochial school;[103]

• a 24-acre tract of land containing a large mansion that was used as a synagogue and a meeting place for the congregation's social groups and youth activities;[104]

• a kindergarten, play area, and parochial school;[105]

• a 37-acre estate used by an Episcopal church as a religious retreat and center for religious instruction;[106]

---

[101] Twin-City Bible Church v. Zoning Board of Appeals, 365 N.E.2d 1381 (Ill. 1977).

[102] Synod of Chesapeake, Inc. v. Newark, 254 A.2d 611 (Del. 1969).

[103] Board of Zoning Appeals v. Wheaton, 76 N.E.2d 597 (Ind. 1948).

[104] Community Synagogue v. Bates, 154 N.Y.S.2d 15 (1956).

[105] Diocese of Rochester v. Planning Board, 154 N.Y.S.2d 849 (1956).

[106] Diocese of Central New York v. Schwarzer, 199 N.Y.S.2d 939 (1960), *aff'd*, 217 N.Y.S.2d 567 (1961).

- a church-owned day care center;[107]

- a church-owned facility housing pregnant teenagers and including extensive spiritual counsel and enrichment;[108]

- a religiously affiliated student center at a state university;[109]

- a monastery that contained 42 bedrooms, conference rooms, library, and dining hall;[110]

- a private school operated by a Baptist church.[111]

Other courts have concluded that certain uses of property do not constitute a church in the context of zoning laws. To illustrate, one court has held that an area restricted to residential and church uses could not accommodate temporary, open-air camp meetings.[112] The court observed that not every place in which religious services are conducted is a church. It inferred that a church at the least must consist of "a building set apart for public worship," and thus could not include camp meetings. Another court held that a dwelling of 16 bedrooms and 12 bathrooms occupied by 25 people comprising four different families, all members of the American Orthodox Catholic Church, was not a church or parish house even though religious instruction was given daily for one hour to the children and three times a week to the adults.[113] The court reasoned that "the principal use of the building . . . is that of a dwelling for residential purposes" and that "the incidental religious instruction provided to the families does not change this fact."

Other courts have held that the following activities were not *churches* under municipal zoning laws:

- a 28-acre tract used by a Jewish foundation for a conference center, leadership training center, and children's retreat;[114]

- a private school operated by a local Baptist church;[115]

- a religious school not operated or controlled by a church;[116]

---

[107] Noah's Ark Christian Child Care Center v. Zoning Hearing Board, 831 A.2d 756 (Pa. Common. 2003).

[108] Solid Rock Ministries v. Board of Zoning Appeals, 740 N.E.2d 320 (Ohio. App. 2000).

[109] Diocese v. Zoning Hearing Board, 899 A.2d 399 (Pa. Common. 2006).

[110] Committee to Protect Overlook, Inc. v. Town Zoning Board, 806 N.Y.S.2d 748 (N.Y. App. 2005).

[111] City of Concord v. New Testament Baptist Church, 382 A.2d 377 (N.H. 1978). *Accord* Alpine Christian Fellowship v. Pitkin County, 870 F. Supp. 991 (D. Colo. 1994).

[112] Portage Township v. Full Salvation Union, 29 N.W.2d 297 (Mich. 1947).

[113] People v. Kalayjian, 352 N.Y.S.2d 115 (1973). *See also* Heard v. Dallas, 456 S.W.2d 440 (Tex. 1970) (child care center operated in minister's residence held not to be a "church").

[114] State ex rel. B'Nai B'rith Foundation v. Walworth County, 208 N.W.2d 113 (Wis. 1973).

[115] Abram v. City of Fayetteville, 661 S.W.2d 371 (Ark. 1984).

[116] Chaminade College v. City of Creve Coeur, 956 S.W.2d 440 (Mo. App. 1997).

- camp meetings;[117]

- a parish house used for Sunday school, choir practice, and church committee meetings;[118]

- a religious retreat house;[119]

- a dwelling of sixteen bedrooms and twelve bathrooms occupied by twenty-five persons comprising four different families, all members of the American Orthodox Catholic church;[120]

- a child-care center operated in a minister's residence;[121]

- a single-family residence used for organized religious services;[122]

- a church-owned building used primarily for administration that contained a small sanctuary comprising six percent of the building;[123]

- a college.[124]

Similarly, when a farmers' organization purchased a church building for meetings promoting agriculture and "higher ideals of manhood, womanhood, and citizenship," a court concluded that the building no longer could be considered a church.[125] "A church," observed the court, "[is] a place or edifice consecrated to religious worship, where people join together in some form of public worship."

Case Studies

• A New York court ruled that a city zoning board acted improperly in denying a homeowner's application to use his home as a church. The court noted that "the inclusion of churches among uses permitted in the [residential] zoning district is tantamount to a legislative determination that the use is in harmony with the general zoning plan and will not be detrimental to the surrounding area. It is presumed that a religious use will have a beneficial effect in a residential area." However, this presumption may be "rebutted with evidence of a significant impact on traffic congestion, property values, municipal services

---

[117] Portage Township v. Full Salvation Union, 29 N.W.2d 297 (Mich. 1947).

[118] Newark Athletic Club v. Board of Adjustment, 144 A. 167 (N.Y. 1928).

[119] Independent Church of the Realization of the Word of God, Inc. v. Board of Zoning Appeals, 437 N.Y.S.2d 443 (1981).

[120] People v. Kalayjian, 352 N.Y.S.2d 115 (1973).

[121] Heard v. Dallas, 456 S.W.2d 440 (Tex. 1970).

[122] Grosz v. City of Miami Beach, 721 F.2d 729 (5th Cir. 1983); State v. Cameron, 460 A.2d 191 (N.J. App. 1983).

[123] North Pacific Conference v. Adventists v. Clark County, 74 P.3d 140 (Wash. App. 2003).

[124] Fountain Gate Ministries, Inc. v. City of Plano, 654 S.W.2d 841 (Tex. App. 1983).

[125] In re Upper St. Clair Township Grange No. 2032, 152 A.2d 768 (Pa. 1959).

and the like." The zoning board's refusal to allow the homeowner to use his home as a church was improper since it was "based on conclusory findings and not upon substantial evidence of significant adverse effects." [126]

• *The Arkansas Supreme Court concluded that the word "church" in a state law prohibiting the sale of liquor within 200 yards of a church "means the place where a body of people or worshipers associate together for religious purposes." This definition included a congregation of forty members, thirteen of whom were active, that met for religious services every Sunday morning.* [127]

• *A Connecticut court ruled that a convent and chapel constituted a "church" for purposes of zoning law despite the operation of a bookstore and audiovisual center on the premises. The court concluded that the convent and chapel, by themselves, clearly satisfied the definition of a church. The fact that a bookstore and audiovisual center were also operated on the premises did not affect this conclusion, since the books and materials were religious and educational in nature and were sold to support the order's missionary and instructional purposes. The court quoted from a 1943 decision of the United States Supreme Court: "The mere fact that religious literature is sold rather than donated does not transform evangelism into a commercial enterprise." Further, the court concluded that the definition of "church" must be "regarded broadly for zoning purposes in order to avoid serious constitutional questions." The court rejected the claim that the convent and chapel should not be allowed in a residential neighborhood since they "would be a detriment to the neighborhood by increasing traffic congestion." The court observed that the intersection where the order planned to construct the convent and chapel "carried a daily traffic volume of over 18,000 cars," and that the construction of the convent and chapel "would draw approximately twenty [additional] cars per day." This case will be of interest to the many churches that operate bookstores on their premises.* [128]

• *The use of a two-story residence and smaller buildings on the premises qualified as a church within the meaning of a zoning ordinance, when the use of the buildings included daily religious ceremonies, prayers, lectures, and a public feast held each Sunday.* [129]

• *A Catholic religious order was formed for the purpose of intercessory prayer. The order purchased a tract of land including a large home. The home contained a chapel which could accommodate as many as 50 worshippers. It was used to conduct seminars on prayer. These events usually involved between 20 and 30 participants. The home also was used for worship services, and as a residence for several members of the order. The tract was subject to a "restrictive covenant" that prohibited it from being used for any purpose other than a church and certain other uses. Neighbors filed a lawsuit, claiming that the order's use of the property was in violation of the restrictive covenant. A court agreed, concluding that the order was not using the property as a church. The court based its conclusion on ten factors: (1) the order did not have rules, regulations, or discipline; (2) there was no priest assigned to the order; (3) there was no regular public mass or worship on the grounds; (4) for the most part, the residents attended*

[126] Neddermeyer v. Ontario Planning Board, 548 N.Y.S.2d 951 (1989).

[127] Arkansas A.B.C. v. Person, 832 S.W.2d 249 (Ark. 1992).

[128] Daughters of St. Paul v. Zoning Board of Appeals, 549 A.2d 1076 (Conn. App. 1988).

[129] Marsland v. International Society for Krishna Consciousness, 66 Haw. 119, 657 P.2d 1035 (1983).

their own parishes for mass; (5) the grounds were not open to the public for mass and other related church activities on a regular basis; (6) the order had no parish lines or jurisdictional limits; (7) the order's name did not include the word "church"; (8) the IRS recognized the order as an educational organization and not as a church; (9) the Catholic Church does not ordain females as priests; and (10) the order did not have any official recognition within the Catholic Church. A state appeals court reversed the trial court's decision, and ruled that the order's use of its property constituted a church. The court noted that the "plain, ordinary, and popular meaning of the word church includes a building in which people assemble for the worship of God and for the administration of such offices and services as pertain to that worship, a building consecrated to the honor of God and religion, and a place where persons regularly assemble for worship." The court concluded that the order's use of its property "having a priest assigned to it living on its grounds and holding daily religious services open to the public, is, under any definition, a use consistent with the plain, ordinary, and popular meaning of a church or use incident to a church."[130]

• A North Carolina court ruled that a church-owned house used by a church for social events was not a "church" for purposes of a local zoning law. The zoning law permitted "churches" in a city's historic district. A church owned a house in the historic district that was used for such purposes as bridge club, social gatherings, community functions, and occasional choir practices and religious instruction. The church planned to sell the home to an individual who wanted to use the home for a "bed and breakfast" establishment. The city informed the purchaser that such a use would not be permitted. The purchaser argued that the church's use of the home was also a "nonconforming" use that was allowed by the city and that could be continued by future owners. A court agreed that the home, as used by the church, was "nonconforming" since it was not a church. The court noted that the term "church" is not defined in the zoning law. It continued: "The expression "church" ordinarily embraces three basic and related definitions: (1) a building set apart for public worship; (2) a place of worship of any religion; and (3) the organization of Christianity or of an association of Christians worshipping together." The city zoning commission insisted that the third definition applied in this case—a church is an organization for religious purposes. The commission claimed that the term "church" cannot be limited to a building where religious services are held, but must also include any building owned and used by a church. The court rejected this sweeping definition, noting that it "would produce the unreasonable result that every building owned by a church or 'organization for religious purposes' would qualify as a 'church' for purposes of the ordinance. . . . [W]e believe the plain and ordinary meaning of 'church' . . . to be 'a building set apart for public worship.'"[131]

• A Texas court concluded that a proposed building that was to devote 2,400 square feet to healing and prayer rooms but only 600 square feet to a "church proper" was not a church.[132]

---

[130] Latenser v. Intercessors of the Lamb, Inc., 553 N.W.2d 458 (Neb. 1996). *See also* City of Omaha v. Kum & Go, 642 N.W.2d 154 (Neb. 2002).

[131] Hayes v. Fowler, 473 S.E.2d 442 (N.C. App. 1996).

[132] Coe v. City of Dallas, 266 S.W.2d 181 (Tex. App. 1953).

• *A Texas court ruled that even though an Episcopal vicar conducted religious worship and training in his rectory, this did not change what was essentially a day nursery into a "church" exempt from zoning regulations.[133]*

• *A federal court in Texas ruled that a small area used for religious purposes in a prison was not a "church" for purposes of a local ordinance banning any sexually oriented business within 1,000 feet of a "church." The ordinance defined a church as "a building in which persons regularly assemble for religious worship and activities intended primarily for purposes connected with such worship or for propagating a particular form of religious belief." The court concluded that the space used for religious worship within the prison did not satisfy this definition since it was a very small area of the prison; it was not used exclusively for religious purposes; it occasionally was shifted to different locations within the facility; and did not constitute a "building" as required by the ordinance.[134]*

Accessory Uses

§ 5-02.2

Key point 5-02.2. *Local zoning laws generally allow "churches" in residential areas. The courts generally have extended this term to various "accessory uses" that are needed for a church to carry out its mission and purposes.*

Many zoning laws permit uses that are "accessory" to a permitted use. As one court has observed:

A church is more than merely an edifice affording people the opportunity to worship God. Strictly religious uses and activities are more than prayer and sacrifice and all churches recognize that the area of their responsibility is broader than leading the congregation in prayer. Churches have always developed social groups for adults and youth where the fellowship of the congregation is strengthened with the result that the parent church is strengthened. To limit a church to being merely a house of prayer and sacrifice would, in a large degree, be depriving the church of the opportunity of enlarging, perpetuating, and strengthening itself and the congregation.[135]

To illustrate, one court upheld a church's right to construct a recreational complex on property adjacent to its sanctuary despite the claim of neighboring landowners that the complex was not a church and thus should not be permitted in a residential district.[136] The court concluded that the term *church* "is broader than the church building itself"

---

[133] Heard v. City of Dallas, 456 S.W.2d 440 (Tex. App. 1970).

[134] Hooters, Inc. v. City of Texarkana, 897 F. Supp. 946 (E.D. Tex. 1995).

[135] Cash v. Brookshire United Methodist Church, 573 N.E.2d 692 (Ohio App. 1988).

[136] Corporation of the Presiding Bishop v. Ashton, 448 P.2d 185 (Ida. 1968).

and must be interpreted to include "uses customarily incidental or accessory to church uses . . . if reasonably closely related, both in distance and space, to the main church purpose." The court upheld the use of the recreational complex since the activities conducted on the field were an integral part of the church's overall program.

Other courts have found that the following uses were accessory to a permitted church use and therefore were appropriate in a residential district:

- a church activities building and playground;[137]

- a kindergarten play area;[138]

- a parking lot;[139]

- residential use of church buildings by members;[140]

- a home for parochial school teachers;[141]

- a school;[142]

- a commercial day-care center;[143]

- a neon sign constructed on church property to inform the public as to the time of worship services;[144]

- a center for performing arts;[145]

- a sanctuary or shelter for the homeless.[146]

Not every use of church property, however, will be so approved. The following uses of church property have been disallowed on the ground that they were not accessory to permitted church use:

---

[137] Board of Zoning Appeals v. New Testament Bible Church, Inc., 411 N.E.2d 681 (Ind. 1980).

[138] Diocese of Rochester v. Planning Board, 154 N.Y.S.2d 849 (1956).

[139] Mahrt v. First Church of Christ, Scientist, 142 N.E.2d 567 (Ohio 1955), aff'd, 142 N.E.2d 678 (Ohio 1955).

[140] Havurah v. Zoning Board of Appeals, 418 A.2d 82 (Conn. 1979).

[141] Board of Zoning Appeals v. New Testament Bible Church, Inc., 411 N.E.2d 681 (Ind. 1980).

[142] City of Concord v. New Testament Baptist Church, 382 A.2d 377 (N.H. 1978); Westbury Hebrew Congregation, Inc. v. Downer, 302 N.Y.S.2d 923 (1969); Diocese of Rochester v. Planning Board, 154 N.Y.S.2d 849 (1956).

[143] Noah's Ark Christian Child Care Center v. Zoning Hearing Board, 831 A.2d 756 (Pa. Common. 2003).

[144] Parkview Baptist Church v. Pueblo, 336 P.2d 310 (Colo. 1959).

[145] North Shore Hebrew Academy v. Wegman, 481 N.Y.S.2d 142 (1984).

[146] St. John's Evangelical Lutheran Church v. City of Hoboken, 479 A.2d 935 (N.J. App. 1983); Lubavitch Chabad House of Illinois, Inc. v. City of Evanston, 445 N.E.2d 343 (Ill. App. 1982); Greentree at Murray Hill Condominium v. Good Shepherd Episcopal Church, 550 N.Y.S.2d 981 (1989).

- parking of a church bus on church property;[147]

- a ritualarium constructed by a Jewish synagogue;[148]

- a 301-foot radio transmission tower that was more than ten times higher than neighboring residences;[149]

- a school.[150]

Case Studies

• *A federal appeals court ruled that a county did not violate a church's constitutional right to religious freedom by denying it a zoning variance to operate a homeless shelter on its premises. A church became concerned with the problem of homelessness in its community. Homeless people were living in vacant lots under unsanitary conditions. In response to this community crisis, the church converted a building on its premises into a shelter for the homeless. The shelter created considerable distress among some residents of the community who were concerned about health and safety problems associated with the shelter. A zoning board later ordered the church to close the shelter on the ground that it was not a permitted use of the church's property under the county zoning ordinance and the church had not been granted a variance. The church sued the county arguing that closing the shelter would violate its First Amendment right to freely exercise its religion. Specifically, the church argued that sheltering the homeless is an essential aspect of the Christian faith. A federal appeals court ruled that no constitutional rights had been violated by the county's action.[151]*

• *The Alabama Supreme Court ruled that a church could not create a parking lot on land located across the street from the church. A church purchased land across the street from the church building in order to expand its parking facilities. Neighboring landowners complained that such a use of the property was not permitted by local zoning law. A local zoning board ruled in favor of the church. It reasoned that churches were permitted uses in the area in question, and that a church parking lot should*

---

[147] East Side Baptist Church v. Klein, 487 P.2d 549 (Colo. 1971).

[148] Sexton v. Bates, 85 A.2d 833 (N.J. 1951), *aff'd*, 91 A.2d 162 (N.J. 1952).

[149] Gallagher v. Zoning Board of Adjustment, 32 Pa. D. & C.2d 669 (Pa. 1963).

[150] Damascus Community Church v. Clackamas County, 610 P.2d 273 (Ore. 1980), *appeal dismissed*, 450 U.S. 902 (1981).

[151] First Assembly of God v. Collier County, 20 F.3d 419 (11th Cir. 1994). The court relied almost entirely on a 1993 decision of the United States Supreme Court in which the Court struck down a municipal ordinance that prohibited ritualistic animal sacrifices by the Santeria religion. The Supreme Court observed: "In addressing the constitutional protection for free exercise of religion, our cases establish the general proposition that a law that is neutral and of general applicability need not be justified by a compelling governmental interest even if the law has the incidental effect of burdening a particular religious practice." Church of the Lukumi Babaluaye, Inc. v. City of Hialeah, 113 S. Ct. 2217 (1993). The federal appeals court concluded that the county zoning law that prohibited the operation of homeless shelters without a variance was a "neutral law of general applicability," and accordingly it was valid even if it burdened the church's exercise of its religion. *Accord* Daytona Rescue Mission, Inc. v. City of Daytona Beach, 885 F. Supp. 1554 (M.D. Fla. 1995). *But see* Capital City Rescue Mission v. City of Albany, 652 N.Y.S.2d 388 (N.Y. 1997).

be permitted as an "accessory use" by a church. The neighbors appealed to a state appeals court, which reversed the decision of the zoning board and prohibited the church from establishing the parking lot. The case was then appealed to the state supreme court, which agreed with the appeals court that the parking lot should not be allowed. The court noted that the local zoning ordinance defined an accessory use as a use "on the same lot with" the principal use or structure. The court concluded that "the definition of accessory use in the ordinance is consistent with the general rule that the accessory use must be located on the same lot as the building to which it is accessory." Since the proposed parking lot was across the street from the church, it was not "on the same lot" and accordingly could not be permitted as an accessory use.[152]

• A city enacted a zoning ordinance permitting only single-family dwellings, churches, schools, libraries, and farms in areas classified as "residential." A church purchased seven acres of undeveloped land in a residential zone and constructed a church building, parking lot, and recreational complex consisting of two softball diamonds. The softball diamonds were surrounded by banks of high-intensity electric lights, which made nighttime games possible. Several neighbors complained of the bright lights, noise, dust, traffic, and stray softballs. The city discontinued electrical service to the softball fields, defending its action on the ground that the lighted softball fields were not a permissible activity in a residential zone. The church sued the city, arguing that the softball fields were a legitimate extension of the church itself, and therefore were permissible. The court agreed with the church: "The activities conducted on this field are an integral part of the church program and are sufficiently connected with the church itself that the use of this property for recreational purposes is permissible." The court emphasized that "the term 'church' is broader than the church building itself" and must be interpreted to include "uses customarily incidental or accessory to church uses . . . if reasonably closely related, both in substance and in space, to the main church purpose."[153]

• The Missouri Supreme Court ruled that a church-run child care center is a permissible activity on church property zoned exclusively for church or residential purposes. The court acknowledged that the zoning ordinance did not allow child care facilities in the neighborhood in which the church was located, but it concluded that such an activity was a permissible "accessory" use. The court observed: "The day care program is subordinate to the principal use of the church. It was created by the governing body of the church and funded by the church. The governing body determined the curriculum for the program and hired a director. The record shows that the church operates the day care to attract new members to the church and accomplish its mission of preaching the gospel and serving the community. Similarly, the day care is subordinate in area to the principal building and use of the church. The day care service contributes to the comfort and convenience of the church parishioners by providing child care for them. The day care proper is located on the same lot as the church and it is located in the same zoning district." Accordingly, the child care center was an accessory use of the church under Missouri law and was a

---

[152] Ex parte Fairhope Board of Adjustments and Appeals, 567 So.2d 1353 (Ala. 1990).

[153] Corporation of the Presiding Bishop v. Ashton, 448 P.2d 185, 189 (Ida. 1968).

permissible use of church property. [154]

• *A New York state court ruled that a church could operate a homeless shelter despite the complaints of neighboring residents. In response to a citywide need for emergency shelters for thousands of homeless, a church in New York City opened its doors to groups of 10 homeless men for temporary emergency shelter 3 nights each week. The church was part of a network of some 380 churches and synagogues in the city that provide more than 400,000 individual nights of temporary shelter annually. The city provides the churches and synagogues with beds, linens, clothing, toiletries, and cleaning supplies, and inspects shelters for compliance with health and safety regulations. Homeless men are transported to the church from a "drop-in center," and arrive at 9:30 PM. They are picked up by bus the following morning at 6:00 AM. From the time of their arrival until their departure the next morning, the men are continually supervised and are not allowed to congregate in the street. The church's minister asserted that sheltering the homeless is an important part of the church's religious mission. Neighboring luxury condominium owners sought a court order preventing the church from continuing its homeless shelter. They complained that the shelter violated city zoning laws, and constituted a public nuisance. The court began its opinion by observing that the lawsuit "concerns the extent, if any, to which the court may or should be brought in as arbiter of a dispute involving the right of a church and its parishioners to exercise their religion and to practice Christian charity by temporarily sheltering the homeless, and the rights of some adjacent property [owners] who fear crime, drug sales, prostitution and a [decrease] in their property values." The court acknowledged that churches may only be used for religious and social purposes, but it noted that "it has long been held that a church or synagogue may be used for accessory uses and activities which go beyond just prayer and worship." The court concluded that a church's operation of a shelter for the homeless is a legitimate "accessory use" of a church, since it "is a use which is clearly incidental to, and customarily found in connection with," a church. Therefore, a church's operation of a homeless shelter did not violate the city's zoning laws.* [155]

• *An Ohio appeals court ruled that a church could use its property to conduct a "Little League" baseball program, despite the claim of a neighbor that such use violated local zoning law. The church maintained that one of its fundamental tenets was that worship involves not only religious services, but also reaching out to the community through sponsorship of activities such as scouting and Little League. The church property was located in a residential zone, which permitted churches and "church use." A trial court agreed with the neighbor that the operation of a baseball program on church property was not a permitted use of church property in an area zoned for "church use." A state appeals court reversed this decision and permitted the baseball program to continue. The court observed: "The trial court appears to suggest that a church is only a building and any use of the building or land adjacent must be necessary to the operation of that building as a church. We disagree." The Ohio court concluded that "activities*

---

[154] City of Richmond Heights v. Richmond Heights Presbyterian Church, 764 S.W.2d 647 (Mo. 1989). *Accord* Shim v. Washington Township Planning Board, 689 A.2d 804 (N.J. Super. 1997) ("What is clear from this modern trend is that a church's ministry is not confined to prayer or dissemination of its religious beliefs. Religious institutions consider day care centers as part of their spiritual mission, not necessarily in advancing their religious teachings, but by providing a valuable community service. Grounded on this broad-based commitment, we are persuaded that a church-operated day care center is . . . an incidental use of church facilities.")

[155] Greentree at Murray Hill Condominium v. Good Shepherd Episcopal Church, 550 N.Y.S.2d 981 (Sup. 1989).

such as sponsoring a Little League baseball program on land owned by, and adjacent to, the [church] are incidental to, and form a part of, the public worship program of [the church] and are permitted under the city zoning ordinances as a church use." The court emphasized that zoning ordinances must be construed "in favor of the property owner" (whose use of property is being questioned) and "in favor of the free use of property."[156]

• A Pennsylvania state court ruled that a local zoning board acted improperly in refusing to allow a church to use a portion of its property for counseling services. The church sought a permit allowing it to convert a building containing the church offices into a counseling center. The church offered extensive pastoral counseling services to members and non-members alike. A zoning board denied the church's request on the ground that professional counseling was not a permitted use in a residential district (in which the church was located). The board expressed the view that "the counseling sought to be offered was of a secular nature and not directly related to the church's function." The church challenged this ruling in court, and won. The court ruled that the church's properties could lawfully be used for counseling since "counseling is an integral part of the church's activities" and therefore was a permissible "church use."[157]

---

[156] Cash v. Brookshire United Methodist Church, 573 N.E.2d 692 (Ohio App. 1988). The court rejected the neighbor's claim that the property's ineligibility for a property tax exemption prevented it from being considered an accessory use of the church.

[157] Church of the Savior v. Zoning Hearing Board, 568 A.2d 1336 (Pa. Common. 1989). *See also* Needham Pastoral Counseling Center, Inc. v. Board of Appeals, 557 N.E.2d 43 (Mass. App. 1990).

Instructional Aids to Chapter 5

Key Terms

accessory use

church

convention or association of churches

integral agency

integrated auxiliary

qualified church-controlled organizations

religious or apostolic associations

religious orders

religious organizations

Learning Objectives

- Identify several references to the term *church* in the Internal Revenue Code.

- Summarize some of the more common judicial interpretations of the term *church*.

- Familiarity with the 14 characteristics of a church developed by the IRS.

- Recognize several other terms used in the Internal Revenue Code, including *conventions or associations of churches, integrated auxiliaries of a church, integral agencies of a religious organization, integral parts of a church, qualified church-controlled organizations,* and *religious orders.*

- Describe the importance of the definition of the term *church* in the context of zoning laws.

- Describe the importance of the definition of the term *church* in the context of state property tax exemption laws.

Short-Answer Questions

1. Mention five examples of the use of the term "church" in the Internal Revenue Code.

2. How does the Internal Revenue Code define the term "church"?

3. What is the test used by the IRS in deciding if an entity is a church for federal tax purposes?

4. Can a parachurch ministry satisfy the IRS definition of a church? Explain. What difference does it make?

5. Which of the criteria in the IRS definition of a church does the IRS consider most important?

6. List two potential legal challenges to the IRS definition of a church. Explain both.

7. T, an electrician, obtains ministerial credentials after completing several correspondence school courses. He begins a Bible study group in his home. The group meets twice weekly for religious instruction and worship. Offerings are taken which go directly to T. Is T's home a church for purposes of local zoning law? Explain.

8. J, an attorney, purchases ministerial credentials from a mail order organization. She declares her home to be a church, and begins to conduct weekly services before her family and a few friends. She contributes half of her income to the church as a charitable contribution, and excludes from her gross income a housing allowance. Will the IRS recognize J's home to be a church? Why or why not?

9. Define "mail order church."

10. What penalties may the IRS impose on mail order churches?

11. A church begins a private elementary school. The church separately incorporates the school. Is the school exempt from federal income taxes? Explain.

12. A tax assessor informs a church that it must pay property taxes on its parking lot. What arguments can the church make to support the exemption of its parking lot from taxation?

13. A tax assessor informs a church that it must pay property taxes on a two-acre tract of undeveloped land adjacent to the church. What arguments can the church make to support the exemption of its parking lot from taxation?

14. A church operates a child care program and an elementary school at its facility. Neighbors complain to the city that the neighborhood is not zoned for school or preschool activities (it is zoned only for residential and church uses). Do the church's child care and school activities come within the definition of the term *church*? Explain.

15. Explain the significance of the term *accessory use* in the context of zoning law.

16. A city official informs a church that its operation of a bookstore is in violation of the property's classification as a "church" under the municipal zoning ordinance. What arguments can the church make to support the continued operation of the bookstore on its premises?

17. A city official informs a church that its operation of a homeless shelter on its property is in violation of the property's classification as a "church" under the municipal zoning ordinance. What arguments can the church make to support the continued operation of the shelter on its premises?

Discussion Questions

1. The Internal Revenue Code uses the term church in many contexts, yet it contains no definition of the term. Why do you suppose that Congress (which drafted the Code) failed to provide a definition?

2. Refer to the criteria developed by the IRS for determining whether a particular organization is a church. Do you think that these criteria are reasonable? Can you think of legitimate churches that might not satisfy this test?

Organization & Administration

Legal Briefs

Chapter 6 is a study of the legal aspects of church organization and administration. It's one of the most important chapters in this entire four-volume set. The chapter begins with a review of both the unincorporated and incorporated forms of organization. Should a church be incorporated? What advantages are there? Are there any disadvantages? These are issues of fundamental importance.

Church records raise a number of important legal questions. For example, under what circumstances can church members inspect church records? What church records are subject to their inspection? Can the IRS inspect church records? If so, what protections are available to churches?

Churches also may have a number of reporting requirements under state and federal law, including the filing of an annual corporate report, applications for exemption from various taxes, payroll tax reporting obligations, and the annual certification of racial nondiscrimination (for churches that operate a preschool, or an elementary or secondary school). Chapter 6 addresses these reporting requirements.

> The selection,
> authority,
> removal,
> and personal
> liability of
> church officers,
> directors, and
> trustees present
> complex legal
> questions.

The selection, authority, removal, and personal liability of church officers, directors, and trustees present complex legal questions. For example, who are the legal members of a church? Can members lose their church membership through non-attendance or lack of support? How may a church remove a director prior to the expiration of a term of office? When may church directors or trustees be personally liable for their actions on behalf of a church?

Each of these problems will be analyzed in detail, along with the topic of church business meetings. How should a church give notice of its business meetings? What is a quorum? Who can vote? What is the effect of procedural irregularities? What body of parliamentary law applies?

You also will study the nature and extent of a church's legal authority, and the procedures employed in merging, consolidating, and dissolving churches.

Chapter 6 provides an in-depth legal perspective on the organizational and administrative issues that significantly impact a church's effectiveness in ministry. For this reason, it's worth spending a considerable amount of time studying its contents. Take the test at the end of the chapter to gauge your level of understanding.

More than one hundred years ago, the United States Supreme Court observed that "the right to organize voluntary religious associations to assist in the expression and dissemination of any religious doctrine . . . is unquestioned."[1] Generally, churches have organized themselves as either corporations or unincorporated associations. This chapter will explore the main features of both forms of organization, discuss the advantages and disadvantages of each, and summarize the incorporation process. This chapter also will address several issues of church administration, including reporting requirements; the protection of church names; the selection, authority, and personal liability of officers and directors; the selection and dismissal of church members; annual and special membership meetings; and dissolution.

Unincorporated Associations   § 6-01

In general, any church that is not a corporation is an unincorporated association. The term *unincorporated association* is defined as any group "whose members share a common purpose, and . . . who function under a common name under circumstances where fairness requires the group be recognized as a legal entity."[2] One court has observed:

> A church or religious society may exist for all the purposes for which it was organized independently of any incorporation of the body . . . and, it is a matter of common knowledge that many do exist and are never incorporated. For the promotion of religion and charity, they may subserve all the purposes of their organization, and generally, need no incorporation except incidentally to further these objects.[3]

Are Unincorporated Churches Free from Government Regulation?

A few ministers have claimed that their church is free from all government regulation, including compliance with federal payroll tax reporting obligations, because the church is unincorporated. This view has been summarily rejected by the courts, in some cases resulting in substantial penalties and liabilities for the church. To illustrate, one church stopped filing federal employment tax returns and withholding or paying federal employment taxes for its employees. Church leaders insisted that the government could not regulate an unincorporated "New Testament church." When IRS attempts to discuss the matter with church leaders failed, the IRS assessed $5.3 million in unpaid taxes and interest. The IRS asked a federal court to enter a judgment for the full $5.3 million and to foreclose on a tax lien the IRS had placed on the church's property.

---

[1]   Watson v. Jones, 80 U.S. (13 Wall.) 679 (1872).

[2]   Barr v. United Methodist Church, 153 Cal. Rptr. 322, 328 (1979), *cert. denied*, 444 U.S. 973 (1980).

[3]   Murphy v. Taylor, 289 So.2d 584, 586 (Ala. 1974), quoting Hundley v. Collins, 32 So. 575 (Ala. 1901).

Are Unincorporated Churches Free from Government Regulation?

The church claimed that the First Amendment guaranty of religious freedom prevented the IRS from applying payroll tax reporting requirements to churches opposed on religious grounds to complying with those requirements, and also prohibited the IRS from penalizing noncompliant churches for failing to comply.

The court rejected the church's position, noting that "neutral laws of general application that burden religious practices do not run afoul" of the First Amendment. Since federal employment tax laws are "neutral laws of general application" (they apply to a large class of employers and do not single out religious employers for less favorable treatment), they do not violate the First Amendment.

This case demonstrates that any attempt by a church to avoid compliance with federal payroll tax obligations (including the withholding and payment of income taxes and Social Security taxes) on the basis of the First Amendment will be summarily rejected by the civil courts. *Indianapolis Baptist Temple v. United States, 224 F.3d 627 (7th Cir. 2000).*

Characteristics

§ 6-01.1

Key point 6-01.1. *Unincorporated associations have no legal existence and as a result cannot sue or be sued, hold title to property, or enter into contracts. Some states have modified or eliminated some or all of these limitations.*

Traditionally, unincorporated associations had no legal existence. This had many important consequences. First, an association could not own or transfer property in its own name; second, an association could not enter into contracts or other legal obligations; and third, an association could not sue or be sued.

The inability to sue or be sued had many important ramifications. It meant, for example, that a church association could not sue its members. If a church member's negligence caused fire damage to a church building, neither the church nor the church's insurance company could sue the member.[4] It also meant that a church association could not be sued by its members. In one case, a church member who was injured because of the negligence of her church was denied recovery against the church on the ground that a member of an unincorporated church is engaged in a joint enterprise and may not recover from the church any damages sustained through the wrongful conduct of another member.[5]

---

[4]   Employers Mutual Casualty Co. v. Griffin, 266 S.E.2d 18 (N.C. 1980).

[5]   Goard v. Branscom, 189 S.E.2d 667 (N.C. 1972), *cert. denied,* 191 S.E.2d 354 (1972).

Case Study

- *A Pennsylvania court ruled that a member of an unincorporated church cannot sue the church for injuries sustained on church property.[6] A church member was injured when she slipped and fell while leaving Christmas services. She sued her church, alleging that the church board had been negligent in failing to provide adequate lighting, handrails, and stripes on the stairs where the accident occurred. In dismissing the lawsuit, The court observed: "The members of an unincorporated association are engaged in a joint enterprise, and the negligence of each member in the prosecution of that enterprise is imputable to each and every other member, so that the member who has suffered damages through the tortious conduct of another member of the association may not recover from the association for such damages." The court concluded: "[The victim] was a member of the association and thus any negligence of her fellow members is imputed to her and she cannot recover in tort. . . . [The victim] was a member of the church, an unincorporated association, at all times material to this case. As a member of the association . . . the decision not to place a handrail, lights, and stripes on the stairway is attributed to her. She cannot recover in tort because any negligence of the board is attributable to her.*

Such rulings may leave members of unincorporated churches without a legal remedy for injuries sustained because of the negligence of other members. This certainly is a matter that should be considered seriously by any church wishing to remain unincorporated. Such churches should apprise their members that if they are injured during any church activity because of the actions of another member, they may have no legal right to compensation or damages from the church or other members— even if the church maintains liability insurance that otherwise would be available.

The traditional legal disabilities associated with unincorporated status, particularly the potential personal liability of every member for the acts of other members in the course of the association's activities (discussed below), made the unincorporated association form of organization undesirable for churches and other charities. Many states have enacted laws that remove some or all of these traditional disabilities. To illustrate, several states have enacted the Uniform Unincorporated Nonprofit Association Act, and others are considering it.[7] The purpose of the Act was described as follows:

> At common law an unincorporated association, whether nonprofit or for-profit, was not a separate legal entity. It was an aggregate of individuals. . . . This approach obviously created problems. A gift of property to an unincorporated association failed because no legal entity existed to receive it. . . . Proceedings by or against an unincorporated association presented similar problems. If it were not a legal entity, each of the members needed to

---

[6]   Zehner v. Wilkinson Memorial United Methodist Church, 581 A.2d 1388 (Pa. Super. 1990). *See also* Crocker v. Barr, 367 S.E.2d 471 (S.C. App. 1988) ("a member of a voluntary unincorporated association . . . cannot maintain an action in tort against the association for injuries suffered by the member because of the negligence of fellow members").

[7]   At the time of publication, the Act had been enacted by Alabama, Arkansas, Colorado, Delaware, the District of Columbia, Hawaii, Idaho, North Carolina, Texas, West Virginia, Wisconsin, and Wyoming.

be joined as party plaintiffs or defendants. . . . Unincorporated associations, not being legal entities, could not be liable in tort, contract, or otherwise for conduct taken in their names. On the other hand, their members could be. . . . The unincorporated nonprofit association is now governed by a hodgepodge of common law and state statutes governing some of their legal aspects. No state appears to have addressed the issues in a comprehensive, integrated, and internally consistent manner. This Act deals with a limited number of the major issues relating to unincorporated nonprofit associations in an integrated and consistent manner.

One of the most important features of the Act is its treatment of the personal liability of members. The Act provides that members of an unincorporated association are not liable for the contracts of the association or for the wrongs of other members (or of the association itself), assuming that they did not participate personally. The key provision specifies:

A nonprofit association is a legal entity separate from its members for the purposes of determining and enforcing rights, duties, and liabilities in contract and tort. . . . A person is not liable for a breach of a nonprofit association's contract merely because the person is a member, is authorized to participate in the management of the affairs of the nonprofit association, or is a person considered to be a member by the nonprofit association. A person is not liable for a tortious act or omission for which a nonprofit association is liable merely because the person is a member, is authorized to participate in the management of the affairs of the nonprofit association, or is a person considered as a member by the nonprofit association. A tortious act or omission of a member or other person for which a nonprofit association is liable is not imputed to a person merely because the person is a member of the nonprofit association, is authorized to participate in the management of the affairs of the nonprofit association, or is a person considered as a member by the nonprofit association.[8]

Tortious= Injurious; wrongful

The Act also clarifies that individual members can "assert a claim against the nonprofit association." In other words, members of an unincorporated church are not barred from suing the church for injuries they sustain as a result of the church's negligence.

But, unless state law provides otherwise, unincorporated associations remain incapable of suing or being sued, holding or transferring title to property, and entering into contracts and other legal obligations. In those states where some or all of the traditional legal disabilities persist, an association generally may act only through its membership.[9]

---

[8] UNIFORM UNINCORPORATED NONPROFIT ASSOCIATION ACT § 6 (1996).

[9] See, e.g., Trinity Pentecostal Church v. Terry, 660 S.W.2d 449 (Mo. App. 1983) (unincorporated religious association was "without capacity to hold and pass title to real estate under Missouri law").

Case Studies

• *A federal court in the District of Columbia dismissed a discrimination lawsuit that had been brought against a Catholic church and school on the ground that they were unincorporated entities that could not be sued. An applicant (the "plaintiff") for the position of music director at a school operated by a Catholic church claimed that she was not considered for the job because of her disability (multiple sclerosis), which confined her to a wheelchair. She sued the church and school for discrimination in violation of the Americans with Disabilities Act. The plaintiff conceded that the church and school were unincorporated divisions of the Archdiocese of Washington (a corporation), but she insisted that the church and school were sufficiently independent of the Archdiocese to be sued separately. The court disagreed. It began its opinion by noting that the Archdiocese is made up of all of the Catholic parishes and related facilities within its jurisdiction, which encompasses the District of Columbia and five surrounding Maryland counties. Although the Roman Catholic Church views each parish as a separate entity for religious purposes, the parishes are not separately incorporated under civil law. The parish that was sued in this case was within the jurisdiction of the Archdiocese. It operates independently of other parishes within the jurisdiction. The Archdiocese owns all of the parish's property, which consists of a church, school, preschool, and convent. The court referred to several cases holding that "unincorporated divisions of a corporation lack legal capacity to be sued." It noted that the rationale for this position "arises out of an unincorporated division's lack of independent assets: because any judgment against it must be satisfied out of the corporation's assets, the corporation must be named, and adjudged liable, as a party. . . . Absent the ability to satisfy a judgment against the larger corporation, a plaintiff gains little by suing one of the corporation's unincorporated divisions." The court agreed with the plaintiff that the parish operates independently within the Archdiocese, but it did not find this independence relevant to the question of the capacity of the church and school to be sued.*[10]

• *A Georgia court ruled that a member of an unincorporated church could sue his church for injuries he sustained while participating in a construction project, and that the church could be liable for the member's injuries on the basis of its negligent hiring of an incompetent construction foreman. The church argued that members of an unincorporated church cannot sue their church under any circumstances. The court disagreed. It noted that the state legislature had enacted a law specifying that unincorporated associations may be sued "in any cause of action," and this meant that members of an unincorporated association are not barred from suing the association. The court also noted that the same statute provided that individual members of unincorporated associations cannot be personally liable for the association's liabilities unless they personally participated in the act that led to the liability.*[11]

• *The Indiana Supreme Court ruled that members of an unincorporated church can sue their church for injuries they suffer on church property or in the course of church*

---

[10] Equal Employment Opportunity Commission v. St. Francis Xavier Parochial School, 77 F. Supp.2d 71 (D.D.C. 1999). While the court acknowledged that unincorporated associations may sue and be sued in most states, it ruled that "unincorporated divisions" of a corporation cannot. This is an important conclusion, since many churches and denominational agencies have affiliates that could be classified as unincorporated "divisions."

[11] Piney Grove Baptist Church v. Goss, 565 S.E.2d 569 (Ga. App. 2002).

activities.[12] The court conceded that under the traditional rule a member of an unincorporated association may not sue the association itself for injuries suffered as a result of the acts of the association or its members. However, the court concluded that the traditional rule had to be abolished, and that members should be allowed "to bring tort actions against the unincorporated associations of which they are part." It listed the following considerations to justify its decision: "(1) it is inherently unfair to require an injured member, who is one of a number of equally faultless members, to bear a loss incurred as a result of the association's activities; (2) there is no reason to limit the availability of the insurance that associations can, and presumably often do, obtain to avoid unexpected liabilities of the members as a result of exposure to third party claims." The court cautioned that an injured member's right to sue his or her unincorporated church was subject to some important limits. Most importantly, "while a member may now sue an unincorporated association in tort, she may only reach the association's assets. If she wishes to reach the assets of any individual, she must name that individual as a party and prove that individual's fault, as always. As a result, individual members, including officers and trustees, may not be held vicariously liable for a judgment against the association."

• The South Carolina Supreme Court ruled that a church member could sue his unincorporated church for injuries sustained while repairing the church sound system. The member volunteered to enter the church attic to repair the sound system. While in the attic, he fell through the ceiling and landed on a concrete floor some ten feet below. The victim sued his church, alleging that its negligence was the cause of his injuries. The supreme court ruled that the injured member could sue the church, even though it was unincorporated.[13]

• The Texas Supreme Court ruled that a member of an unincorporated church could sue the church for injuries she sustained when she slipped and fell on a wet linoleum floor. The court acknowledged that the longstanding rule in Texas had been that the members of an unincorporated church could not sue the church for injuries inflicted by fellow church members. It noted that this historic rule was based on the notion that the members of unincorporated churches are engaged in a "joint venture" and that the negligence of one is imputed to all the others, including a fellow member who is injured by the negligence. The court repudiated this rule, noting that it had been abandoned by most other states. The court concluded: "Why should a church member be precluded from suing an association in tort when a paid workman would be allowed to maintain an action for the very same injury. . . ? We are unable to discern a defensible reply to this query. Consequently, we hold that a member of an unincorporated charitable association is not precluded from bringing a negligence action against the association solely because of the individual's membership in the association. Any assets of the unincorporated charitable association, held either by the association or in trust by a member of the association, may be reached in satisfaction of a judgment against the association."[14]

---

[12] Hanson v. Saint Luke's United Methodist Church, 704 N.E.2d 1020 (Ind. 1998).

[13] Crocker v. Barr, 409 S.E.2d 368 (S.C. 1992).

[14] Cox v. Thee Evergreen Church, 836 S.W.2d 167 (Tex. 1992). A dissenting justice noted that "a majority of jurisdictions follow the rule that a member of an unincorporated association injured due to the tortious conduct of another member cannot sue the association. . . . The court may have wrongly implied that the rule exempting unincorporated associations from liability is a waning doctrine. In fact, most jurisdictions still adhere to it."

Unincorporated Churches

Many churches are unincorporated. This may be due to one or more of several factors, including the following: (1) the church never incorporated; (2) the church incorporated, but its corporate status "lapsed" due to noncompliance with legal requirements (such as filing an annual report with the secretary of state); (3) the church was incorporated for a specified term of years, and the term expired; (4) the church incorporated, but later decided to change its legal status to that of an unincorporated association; or (5) the church is located in a state where churches are not permitted to incorporate (or were not permitted to do so in the past).

Whatever the reason for unincorporated status, an unincorporated church's leaders should know whether their state has adopted the Uniform Nonprofit Unincorporated Association Act, since this will have a direct bearing on the liability of leaders and members alike for (1) contracts executed by other members on behalf of the church, and (2) personal injuries inflicted by other members in the course of church activities. Unfortunately, few states have implemented the Act.

Personal Liability of Members §6-01.2

Key point 6-01.2. *The traditional rule is that members of an unincorporated association are personally liable for the acts of other members committed within the course of association activities. Some courts have modified or rejected this rule.*

Since an unincorporated association could not sue or be sued under the traditional rule, it was assumed that an association's members were personally responsible for the acts of other members committed in the course of the association's business. One court stated the general rule as follows:

> The members of an unincorporated association are engaged in a joint enterprise, and the negligence of each member in the prosecution of that enterprise is imputable to each and every other member, so that the member who has suffered damages to his person, property, or reputation through the tortious conduct of another member of the association may not recover from the association for such damage although he may recover individually from the member actually guilty of the tort.[15]

---

[15] Williamson v. Wallace, 224 S.E.2d 253, 254 (N.C. 1976).

As noted in the preceding section, the traditional rule regarding the personal liability of the members of unincorporated associations for the acts of other members has been eliminated by statute in some states.[16]

Case Studies

• *A Colorado court ruled that an officer of a nonprofit unincorporated association was not personally liable for compensation that the association had failed to pay to former employees, since the association was located in a state that had enacted the Uniform Nonprofit Unincorporated Association Act. The court explained: "The Act makes a nonprofit unincorporated association a legal entity separate and apart from its members. Therefore, logically, nonprofit unincorporated associations are more in the nature of corporations, limited partnerships, or limited liability companies. This basic and fundamental change has a considerable impact on the liability of members and others for the liabilities of nonprofit unincorporated associations." The court concluded that the Act makes it clear that an officer is not liable for the contracts of an unincorporated association merely because he had management responsibilities or negotiated the former employees' employment contracts.[17]*

• *A Connecticut appeals court ruled that individual members of an unincorporated association could be sued personally as a result of negligence or other misconduct of fellow members. The court observed: "Persons who associate together for some common nonbusiness purpose without a corporate franchise from the state are merely an aggregation of individuals, not a separate legal entity. . . . A voluntary association for tort liability purposes remains an aggregation of individuals who may be held personally liable in tort for certain of its activities."[18]*

• *An Illinois court ruled that members of an unincorporated association were not responsible for the alleged defamatory statements made by other members of the association, since they had not authorized or ratified the statements and the association was not organized for profit. The persons who claimed to have been defamed by certain members of the association claimed that all of the members of an unincorporated association are legally responsible for the acts of their fellow members, on the basis of both partnership and agency law. A state appeals court disagreed. It concluded that members of an unincorporated association can be liable for the acts of other members only if the association is a "for profit" entity. Since the association in this case was a nonprofit entity, the members could not be liable for the actions of other members. The court concluded that members of a nonprofit unincorporated association cannot be legally responsible for the misconduct of other members "without their direct participation, authorization, or subsequent ratification."[19]*

• *An Indiana appeals court ruled that the individual members of an unincorporated nonprofit association were personally responsible for a contract entered into by the association. The association rented a convention facility for a fund-raising banquet.*

---

[16] *See* note 8, *supra*, and accompanying text.

[17] Mohr v. Kelley, 2000 WL 177691 (Colo. App. 2000).

[18] Company v. Sena, 619 A.2d 489 (Conn. Super. 1992).

[19] Joseph v. Collins, 649 N.E.2d 964 (Ill. App. 1995).

The bill for the event came to $16,000, but the association paid only $2,000. The convention center sued two of the association's members personally for the balance. The members claimed that they could not be liable for the association's debts, but a state appeals court disagreed. The court observed: "The common law is well settled that a member of an association which does not conduct business for profit becomes liable for obligations incurred on behalf of the association within the scope of the authority of the agent attempting to create the liability." The court quoted with approval from a leading treatise on contract law: "Insofar as the obligation was created in a manner authorized by [the association's] articles of agreement or bylaws, the individual members are liable, presumably jointly." Williston on Contracts § 308. The court also quoted with approval from a legal encyclopedia: "[Members of unincorporated nonprofit associations] are jointly and severally liable as principals on contracts made by, from or in the name of, the association for the purpose of promoting its objects, to which they have given either assent or subsequent ratification." 6 American Jurisprudence 2nd, Associations and Clubs, § 46. The court noted that "other states have uniformly applied the common law" rule, as does Indiana. Accordingly, "members of a not-for-profit unincorporated association are liable for the obligations incurred by the association under a contract if the members authorize the contract or subsequently ratify its terms."[20]

• A Texas appeals court suggested that the members of an unincorporated church could be sued individually in a "class action" for the church's fraudulent acts. The church used property that was owned by another person. A portion of the property was subject to an unpaid tax liability which created a defect in the title. A church employee allegedly informed the owner that he would help her clear this title defect by representing her before the local taxing authorities and by informing her if and when the property was to be sold to satisfy the tax liability. Instead, the church allegedly bought the property at a tax foreclosure sale without communicating this fact to the owner. The owner immediately filed a lawsuit. Since the church was unincorporated, she claimed that the individual members of the church were personally responsible for the church's alleged breach of the rental contract and the misconduct of the church in purchasing the property at the foreclosure sale. The owner attempted to sue all of the church's members by filing a class action lawsuit naming all of the members as defendants. The appeals court began its opinion by observing, "An unincorporated association is a voluntary group of persons, without a charter, formed by mutual consent for the purposes of promoting a common enterprise. An unincorporated association is not liable on its contracts, which are regarded as the liability of the individuals who sign them. . . . Members of an unincorporated association are individually liable for tortious acts of agents or employees of the association if the tort is committed within the scope of their authority." Further, the personal liability of individual members was affected by the fact that state law permits unincorporated organizations to be sued directly. However, the court concluded that the owner had not met all of the procedural requirements for filing a class action lawsuit, and remanded the case to the trial court. In summary, while the court dismissed the owner's attempt to bring a class action lawsuit against the members of an unincorporated church, it did so on the basis of an easily corrected technicality.[21]

---

[20] Victory Committee v. Genesis Convention Center, 597 N.E.2d 361 (Ind. App. 3 Dist. 1992).

[21] Hutchins v. Grace Tabernacle United Pentecostal Church, 804 S.W.2d 598 (Tex. App. 1991).

• *The Texas Supreme Court ruled that the members of an unincorporated association are not necessarily responsible for the misconduct of their fellow members. A police officer was injured while attempting to carry away a protester at an abortion clinic. He later sued twelve other persons who were engaged in the protest. The supreme court ruled that the twelve protesters were not personally liable for officer's injuries. It noted that "even if the demonstrators constituted an unincorporated association, we have never held that they are automatically liable for the actions of other members of the association." The court further noted that "imposing liability on individuals on the sole basis that a member of the group to which they belong has committed a [wrong] in the pursuit of the group's goals would pose serious threats to the right of free association." The court concluded: "We believe that the liability of members of a group should be analyzed in terms of the specific actions undertaken, authorized or ratified by those members. Therefore, regardless of whether there was an unincorporated association here, we reject the lower court's intimation that the existence of such an association might alone form the basis for imposing tort liability on all members for the acts of some." Note, however, that the court did not grant members of unincorporated associations absolute immunity from personal liability. The court pointed out that members can be personally liable on the basis of "specific actions undertaken, authorized or ratified."*[22]

▶ *As noted later in this chapter, incorporation is a simple and relatively inexpensive process. Of course, it requires the assistance of an attorney. Unfortunately, many church leaders do not know if their church is incorporated. Many assume that it is. This can be a dangerous assumption if in fact the church is not incorporated, since it may mean that the members are personally responsible for the liabilities of the church. It is essential for church leaders to confirm whether or not their church is incorporated. This easily can be done by contacting the office of the secretary of state in your state capital. Representatives of the office of secretary of state ordinarily will tell you over the telephone whether or not your church is incorporated. If you are informed that your church is incorporated, then you may wish to ask for a certificate of good standing (the name of this document varies somewhat from state to state) that confirms the corporate status of your church. You also should request a certified copy of your charter (article of incorporation), to be sure that you have a copy of the document on file with the state.*

▶ *Calling the office of the secretary of state is important even if you think that your church is incorporated, since the corporate status of many churches has "lapsed" through failure to file annual reports with the state. In many states, church corporations must file relatively simple annual reports with the state. In a surprisingly large number of cases, churches do not file these reports. In some states, the failure to file these reports will cause the church's corporate status to lapse. As a result, it is a prudent practice for churches to confirm each year with the office of their secretary of state that they are in fact a corporation in good standing.*

---

[22] Juhl v. Airington, 936 S.W.2d 640 (Tex. 1996). In a case addressing the question of whether or not members of an unincorporated church can sue the church for injuries they sustain, the Texas Supreme Court avoided the issue of the personal liability of individual members of unincorporated churches for the negligence or misconduct of other members. It simply noted that this lawsuit had not named any individual church members as defendants and accordingly there was no need to address this broader issue. It did mention, however, that "protection is afforded by the simple act of incorporation." Cox v. Thee Evergreen Church, 836 S.W.2d 167 (Tex. 1992).

Creation and Administration §6-01.3

Key point 6-01.3. *A church is an unincorporated association if it is not a corporation in good standing under state law. This status can occur in a number of ways, including the following: (1) a church never was incorporated; (2) a church was incorporated, but the period of duration specified in its charter has expired; or (3) a church was incorporated, but its corporate status lapsed under state law because of its failure to submit annual reports to the office of the secretary of state.*

In general, an unincorporated association is created by the voluntary association of two or more individuals under a common name for a particular purpose. The creation of an unincorporated association ordinarily does not require compliance with state laws, although several states have enacted laws allowing associations to organize in a more formal way. Such laws typically confer many of the rights and privileges enjoyed by corporations upon associations that choose to formally organize.

It is customary and desirable for the members of an unincorporated association to adopt rules for the internal management of the affairs of the association. Although these rules usually are called bylaws, they occasionally are called articles of association, constitution, or charter. Such terminology is not important.[23] In this chapter, the rules and regulations of an unincorporated association will be referred to as bylaws. The bylaws of an unincorporated association typically contain provisions dealing with meetings; election, qualification, and tenure of officers and trustees; qualification and acceptance of members; the acquisition and transfer of property; the status of property upon the dissolution of the association; and the rights and duties of members among themselves and with the association.

The bylaws of an unincorporated association constitute a contract between the association and its members, and that the rights and duties of members, as between themselves and in their relation to the association in all matters affecting its internal government and the management of its affairs, are measured by the terms of such bylaws.[24] By becoming a member an individual agrees to be bound by the association's bylaws, and to have his rights and duties determined by them.[25]

The members of an unincorporated association may vote to incorporate their organization and transfer title to all properties to the new corporation. A minority of the unincorporated association's members are without authority to block such a transfer.[26]

Although the Internal Revenue Code restricts tax-exempt status to corporations, community chests, funds, and foundations organized and operated exclusively for religious and other charitable purposes,[27] the IRS construes the

---

[23] Cunningham v. Independent Soap & Chemical Workers, 486 P.2d 1316 (Kan. 1971).

[24] Savoca Masonry Co., Inc. v. Homes & Son Construction Co., Inc., 542 P.2d 817, 820 (Ariz. 1975).

[25] Libby v. Perry, 311 A.2d 527 (Me. 1973).

[26] Jacobs v. St. Mark's Baptist Church, 415 So.2d 251 (La. App. 1982).

[27] I.R.C. § 501(c)(3).

term *corporations* to include unincorporated associations.[28] The inclusion of unincorporated associations within the definition of the term *corporations* is a well-established principle of federal tax law. Section 7701(a)(3) of the Internal Revenue Code defines *corporation* to include associations, and the federal courts for many years have held that associations possessing at least three of the four principal corporate characteristics of centralized control, continuity, limited personal liability, and transferability of beneficial interests are to be treated as corporations.[29] The exemption available to religious and charitable corporations under the Internal Revenue Code accordingly should be available to most unincorporated associations that meet all of the other conditions for exempt status.

Corporations § 6-02

The legal disabilities connected with the unincorporated association form of organization persuade many churches to incorporate. Unlike many unincorporated churches, church corporations are capable of suing and being sued, entering into contracts and other legal obligations, and holding title to property. Perhaps most important, the members of a church corporation ordinarily are shielded from personal liability for the acts and obligations of other members or agents of the church.

Two forms of church corporation are in widespread use in the United States. By far the more common is the membership corporation, which is comprised of and controlled by church members. Several states also recognize trustee corporations. The trustees of a trustee corporation constitute and control the corporation. A few states also permit certain officers of hierarchical churches to form a *corporation sole*, which is a corporation consisting of a single individual.

Some church leaders maintain that churches should never incorporate since incorporation constitutes a "subordination" of a church to the authority of the state. Such a view reflects a fundamental misunderstanding regarding the legal status of corporations. The term *corporation* has been defined "as an association of persons to whom the sovereign has offered a franchise to become an artificial, juridical person, with a name of its own, under which they can act and contract, sue and be sued, and who have . . . accepted the offer and effected an organization in substantial conformity with its terms."[30] A corporation, then, is entirely distinct from its members and should not be confused with them. A church that incorporates is not "subordinating itself" to the state. Rather, it is subordinating merely the artificial corporate entity to the state, and it is free to terminate that entity at any time. Similarly, under some corporation laws, the state can terminate the corporate status of church corporations that fail to file annual reports. But the termination of the church corporation under such conditions certainly does not mean that the church itself is dissolved, for the church is completely independent

---

[28] Treas. Reg. § 1.501(c)(3)-1(b)(2); IRS Publication 557.

[29] *See, e.g.,* Smith's Estate v. Commissioner, 313 F.2d 724 (8th Cir. 1963).

[30] Mackay v. New York, N.H. & H.R. Co., 72 A. 583 (1909) (this definition is still frequently cited by the courts).

of the artificial corporate entity and survives its demise. On the contrary, many church corporations have been terminated by operation of law because of noncompliance with the annual reporting requirements, yet church leaders and members alike remain oblivious to the fact.

One court acknowledged that "a church does not lose its ecclesiastical function, and the attributes of that function, when it incorporates. It does not, by incorporating, lose its right to be governed by its own particular form of ecclesiastical government. *Incorporation acts merely to create a legal entity to hold and administer the properties of the church.*"[31] Another court has observed that "the law recognizes the distinction between the church as a religious group devoted to worship, preaching, missionary service, education and the promotion of social welfare, and the church as a business corporation owning real estate and making contracts. . . . The former is a matter in which the state or the courts have no direct legal concern, while in the latter the activities of the church are subject to the same laws as those in secular affairs."[32] The United States Supreme Court has ruled that the First Amendment guaranty of religious freedom assures churches "an independence from secular control or manipulation, in short, power to decide for themselves, free from state interference, matters of church government as well as those of faith and doctrine."[33]

One legal scholar has observed that "the distinctiveness of the corporate entity from the members . . . is inherent in and exemplified by other corporate attributes, which could not be conceded were they one and the same, e.g., the transfer of shares and change in membership without change in the corporation [and] the right to sue and be sued in the corporate name. . . ."[34] The distinctiveness of the corporate entity from its members is also the basis for the limitation of personal liability of members for the acts of the corporation. This limitation of personal liability is not an example of social irresponsibility that should be avoided by churches. On the contrary, it is a recognition of the fact that church members should not be personally responsible for the wrongdoing of other members or agents over which they had no control.

Key point. *Church leaders having theological opposition to church incorporation should consider letting the church membership determine whether or not to incorporate the church. Church members who are apprised of the potential personal liability they have for the obligations of their unincorporated church may not agree with their leaders' theology on this issue.*

In summary, churches wanting to avail themselves of the benefits of the corporate form of organization should not be dissuaded by unwarranted fears

---

[31] Providence Baptist Church v. Superior Court, 243 P.2d 112 (Cal. 1952).

[32] Gospel Tabernacle Body of Christ Church v. Peace Publishers & Co., 506 P.2d 1135 (Kan. 1973).

[33] Kedroff v. St. Nicholas Cathedral, 344 U.S. 94 (1952) (the Court ruled that a New York statute transferring control over Russian Orthodox churches in the United States from the Patriarch of Moscow to the governing authorities of the Russian Orthodox Church in America "violates our rule of separation between church and state"). *See also* People v. Wood, 402 N.Y.S.2d 726 (1978) ("The purpose of the Religious Corporations Law is not to determine the ecclesiastical jurisdiction . . . .").

[34] FLETCHER CYC. CORP. § 25 (perm. ed. 2008).

of governmental control. In the unlikely event that an incorporated church ever does believe that it is being "unduly controlled" by the state, it can easily and quickly rectify the problem by voluntarily terminating its corporate existence. A number of courts have specifically held that incorporation of a church under a state corporation law does not subject the church to any greater degree of civil scrutiny.[35]

"...churches wanting to avail themselves of the benefits of the corporate form of organization should not be dissuaded by unwarranted fears of governmental control."

The Incorporation Process

§ 6-02.1

Key point 6-02.1. *In many states, churches can incorporate either under the Model Nonprofit Corporation Act or under an alternative statute that was adopted prior to the enactment of the Act. Some alternative statutes involve the filing of a petition with a local court. Often, these alternative statutes contain far less detail than the model Act. Some states have enacted statutes that regulate the incorporation of specific religious organizations.*

Although procedures for the incorporation of churches vary from state to state, most states have adopted one or more of the following procedures:

1. Model Nonprofit Corporation Act

In General

The Model Nonprofit Corporation Act, which has been adopted in whole or in part by several states,[36] provides a uniform method of incorporation for several kinds of nonprofit organizations, including religious, scientific, educational, charitable, cultural, and benevolent organizations. The procedure consists of the following steps:

- preparation of duplicate articles of incorporation setting forth the corporation's name, period of duration, address of registered office within the state, name and address of a registered agent, purposes, and names and addresses of the initial board of directors and incorporators;

- notarized signature of the duplicate articles of incorporation by the incorporators; and

---

[35] *See, e.g.*, Bourgeois v. Landrum, 387 So.2d 611 (La. App. 1980), *rev'd on other grounds*, 396 So.2d 1275 (La. 1981).

[36] Fletcher Cyc. Corp. § 2.65, n.2 (perm. ed. 2008).

- submission of the prescribed filing fee and duplicate articles of incorporation to the secretary of state.

The secretary of state reviews the articles of incorporation to ensure compliance with the Act. If the articles of incorporation are satisfactory, the secretary of state endorses both duplicate copies, files one in his or her office, and returns the other along with a certificate of incorporation to the church.[37] The church's corporate existence begins at the moment the certificate of incorporation is issued.[38]

After the certificate of incorporation has been issued, the Act specifies that an organizational meeting of the board of directors shall be held at the call of a majority of the incorporators for the purpose of adopting the initial bylaws of the corporation and for such other purposes as may come before the meeting.[39]

The incorporators and directors can be the same persons in most states. Many states require at least three directors. Incorporators and directors must have attained a prescribed age and be citizens of the United States. They ordinarily do not have to be citizens of the state in which the church is incorporated.

The Model Nonprofit Corporation Act governs many aspects of a nonprofit corporation's existence. As one court has observed, "if a church or religious group elects to incorporate under the laws of this state, then the courts have the power to consider and require that the corporation thus formed comply with state law concerning such corporations."[40] Some of the issues addressed by the Act include

- meetings of members;

- notice of meetings;

- voting;

- quorum;

- number and election of directors;

- vacancies;

- selection, qualifications, and authority of officers;

- removal of officers;

- books and records;

- merger or consolidation with other organizations;

- dissolution

---

[37] MODEL NONPROFIT CORPORATION ACT § 30.

[38] Id. at § 31.

[39] Id. at § 32.

[40] Lozanoski v. Sarafin, 485 N.E.2d 669, 671 (Ind. App. 1985). See also Board of Trustees v. Richards, 130 N.E.2d 736, 739 (Ohio App. 1954) ("if the church law is repugnant to the specific statutory enactments, the church law must yield to the civil law").

In most of these matters, a corporation is bound by the Act's provisions only if it has not provided otherwise in its articles of incorporation or bylaws. In other words, most of the Act's provisions apply "by default." For example, a corporation may stipulate in its bylaws the percentage of members constituting a quorum, but if it fails to do so the Act provides that a quorum consists of ten percent of the voting membership.[41] Similarly, the Act provides that directors shall serve for one-year terms unless a corporation's articles of incorporation or bylaws provide otherwise.[42]

Key point. *One court observed that "in a conflict between the general procedures outlined in the [state nonprofit corporation law] and the specific procedures contained in the church bylaws, we must defer to the church bylaws."[43]*

Case Studies

• *The Alaska Supreme Court ruled that proxy voting had to be recognized in a church election since the Model Nonprofit Corporation Act required it and the church had not provided otherwise in its articles or bylaws. The court rejected the church's claim that requiring it to recognize proxy votes violated the constitutional guaranty of religious freedom. The court observed that a church could easily avoid the recognition of proxy votes by simply amending its charter or bylaws to expressly prohibit this form of voting.[44]*

• *The Arkansas Supreme Court ruled that the provisions of the state nonprofit corporation law could not be applied to a church if doing so would violate church doctrine. As part of what the court described as a dispute of "a longstanding, ongoing, and heated nature," certain church members sought to obtain various financial records of the church as part of a concerted effort to oust the current church leadership. When church elders rejected the members' request, the members incorporated the church under a state nonprofit corporation law making the "books and records" of a corporation subject to inspection "by any member for any proper purpose at any reasonable time." Church elders continued to reject the members' request for inspection, whereupon the members asked a state court to recognize their legal right to inspection under state corporation law. The elders countered by arguing that application of state corporation law would impermissibly interfere with the religious doctrine and practice of the church, contrary to the constitutional guaranty of religious freedom. Specifically, the elders argued that according to the church's "established doctrine," the New Testament "places within the hands of a select group of elders the sole responsibility for overseeing the affairs of the church," and that this authority is "evidenced by biblical admonitions to the flock to obey and submit to them that have rule over the flock."*

---

[41] *Id.* at § 16.

[42] *Id.* at § 18.

[43] Green v. Westgate Apostolic Church, 808 S.W.2d 547 (Tex. App. 1991).

[44] Herning v. Eason, 739 P.2d 167 (Alaska 1987). *See also* Frankel v. Kissena Jewish Center, 544 N.Y.S.2d 955 (1989), in which a New York court concluded that the state "Not-For-Profit Corporation Law" permits proxy voting unless prohibited by the corporation's charter or bylaws.

The Arkansas Supreme Court agreed that "application of our state corporation law would almost certainly impinge upon the doctrine of the church" as described by the elders, and accordingly would violate the constitutional guaranty of religious freedom. The court concluded that if the application of a state law would conflict with the "doctrine, polity, or practice" of a church, then the law cannot be applied to the church without a showing of a "compelling state interest." No such showing was made in this case, the court concluded, and therefore the state law giving members of nonprofit corporations the legal right to inspect corporate records could not be applied to the church.[45]

• An Ohio court ruled that a church's board of trustees had been properly ousted and replaced with a new board in a specially-called business meeting that was called in accordance with state nonprofit corporation law. The court noted that "the calling of meetings is regulated by statute," and quoted from the state nonprofit corporation law: "Meetings of voting members may be called by any of the following . . . (3) The lesser of (a) ten percent of the voting members or (b) twenty-five of such members, unless the articles or the regulations specify for such purpose a smaller or larger proportion or number, but not in excess of fifty per cent of such members." The court noted that the membership meeting had been called by forty-two members, and it concluded that since the church's bylaws did not modify the number of members required to call a special meeting pursuant to the nonprofit corporation law, the bylaws did not supersede the nonprofit corporation law and therefore the special business meeting was properly called because the requirements of the statute were met when forty-two members had called the special meeting.[46]

Certain provisions of the Act may not be altered by a corporation. For example, the Act mandates that corporations have a minimum of three directors.[47] Although a corporation may require more than three directors, it may not require less. The Act also prohibits corporations from making loans to officers or directors.[48]

Annual Report

The Act requires all nonprofit corporations to file an annual report with the secretary of state's office.[49] A few states have amended this provision to require reports less frequently, such as once every two years. The report is filed on a form provided by the secretary of state, and ordinarily sets forth the name of the corporation, the address of the corporation's registered office in the state of incorporation, the name of the registered agent at such address, the names and addresses of the directors and officers, and a brief statement of the nature of the affairs the corporation is actually conducting. A nominal fee must accompany the report.

States that have adopted the Act differ with regard to the penalties imposed upon corporations that fail to file the annual report by the date prescribed. The

---

[45] Gipson v. Brown, 749 S.W.2d 297 (Ark. 1988).

[46] North Dayton First Church of God v. Berger, 2000 WL 1597963 (Ohio App. 2000).

[47] *Id.* at § 18.

[48] *Id.* at § 27. This important topic is discussed in more detail in section F of this chapter.

[49] MODEL NONPROFIT CORPORATION ACT § 81.

Act itself imposes a nominal fine ($50) on corporations that fail to comply with the reporting requirement. Many states have followed this provision, but others call for the cancellation of a corporation's certificate of incorporation. Cancellation of a certificate of incorporation has the effect of terminating the existence of a corporation. This is an extraordinary penalty, generally available only after the secretary of state's office has sent the corporation a written notice of the impending cancellation. If a corporation fails to respond to the written notice, the secretary of state issues a certificate of cancellation, which is the legal document terminating both the certificate of incorporation and the corporation's legal existence. Many states permit reinstatement of terminated corporations. Reinstatement generally is available upon the filing of a formal application within a prescribed time. Because of the potentially adverse consequences resulting from a cancellation of a church's corporation charter, church leaders should periodically check with the office of their secretary of state to ensure that the church is a corporation in good standing. Many churches will find that they are not, either because they failed to file an annual return, or because their corporation was created for a specified period of time that has expired.

The Revised Model Nonprofit Corporations Act

In 1987, the American Bar Association's Subcommittee on the Model Nonprofit Corporations Law of the Business Law Section adopted the "Revised Model Nonprofit Corporation Act." The revised Act, which has been adopted by a few states, is based on the Revised Model Business Corporations Act. It likely will be adopted by many states in the years to come. One of the important features of the revised Act is the division of nonprofit corporations into three classifications—(1) public benefit corporations, (2) mutual benefit corporations, and (3) religious corporations.[50] Special rules apply to each classification. This is the first recognition of the unique status of religious corporations in a "model" nonprofit corporations law.

DID YOU KNOW?
Model Nonprofit Corporation Act (3rd Edition)

The American Bar Association, Section on Business Law, Committee on Nonprofit Corporations appointed a Task Force to Revise the Model Nonprofit Corporation Act. In 2008, the Task Force published a 450-page draft version of the third edition of the Model Nonprofit Corporation Act. At the time of publication of this text, the third edition of the Model Nonprofit Corporation Act had not been finalized or adopted by any state legislature.

---

[50] MODEL REVISED NONPROFIT CORPORATION ACT § 2.02(a).

Other features of the revised Act include the following:

(1) **Members.** The definition of "members" is clarified. A corporation is required to compile a listing of eligible voters in advance of each annual or special membership meeting, and this list must be available for inspection. However, the Act specifies that "the articles or bylaws of a religious corporation may limit or abolish the rights of a member . . . to inspect and copy any corporate record."[51]

(2) **Religious doctrine.** The revised Act specifies that "if religious doctrine governing the affairs of a religious corporation is inconsistent with the provisions of this Act on the same subject, the religious doctrine shall control to the extent required by the Constitution of the United States or the constitution of this state or both."[52]

(3) **Duration.** There is a presumption of perpetual duration unless the articles of incorporation specifically provide otherwise.[53]

(4) **Emergency actions of board.** The board of directors is empowered to act in an "emergency" though a quorum of the board is not present.[54]

(5) **Personal liability.** The Act specifies that "a member of a corporation is not, as such, personally liable for the acts, debts, liabilities, or obligations of the corporation."[55]

(6) **Removal of members.** Detailed procedures apply to the suspension or expulsion of members, but these procedures do not apply to religious corporations (they apply only to public benefit corporations and mutual benefit corporations).[56]

(7) **Delegates.** A corporation "may provide in its articles or bylaws for delegates having some or all of the authority of members."[57]

(8) **Court-ordered meetings.** Civil courts are empowered to call meetings of a corporation upon the application of any member if the corporation fails to conduct an annual or special meeting within a prescribed number of days after a specified meeting.[58] A court also may determine those persons who constitute members for purposes of any such meeting, and

---

[51] *Id.* at § 7.20.

[52] *Id.* at § 1.80. This is the same conclusion reached by the Arkansas Supreme Court in Gipson v. Brown, 749 S.W.2d 297 (Ark. 1988). *See* note 45, *supra*, and accompanying text.

[53] *Id.* at § 3.02.

[54] *Id.* at § 3.03. The Act specifies that "[a]n emergency exists for purposes of this section if a quorum of the corporation's directors cannot readily be assembled because of some catastrophic event."

[55] *Id.* at § 6.12.

[56] *Id.* at § 6.21.

[57] *Id.* at § 6.40.

[58] *Id.* at § 7.03.

may "enter other orders necessary to accomplish the purpose or purposes of the meeting."

(9) **Action of members without a meeting.** Unless prohibited by the corporate charter or bylaws, members are permitted to act without a meeting if 80 percent or more of the membership agrees to a proposed action in a signed writing. Similarly, members may act by "written ballot" without calling a meeting if such action is not prohibited by the corporate charter or bylaws.[59]

(10) **Notice of meetings.** The Act specifies that "unless one-third or more of the voting power is present in person or by proxy, the only matters that may be voted upon at an annual or regular meeting of members are those matters that are described in the meeting notice."[60]

(11) **At least three directors.** The board of directors must consist of at least three directors.[61]

(12) **Removal of directors.** The Act specifies a procedure for removing directors from office, but permits religious corporations to provide otherwise in their charters or bylaws.[62]

(13) **Duties of board members.** The Act imposes specific "standards of conduct" upon each officer and director of a nonprofit corporation. These include the performance of an officer's or director's official duties "in good faith, with the care an ordinarily prudent person in a like position would exercise under similar circumstances, and in a manner the director [or officer] reasonably believes to be in the best interests of the corporation."[63]

(14) **Indemnification.** The Act contains detailed indemnification rules.[64]

(15) **Inspection of records.** The Act gives each member the right to inspect (and copy) corporate records "at a reasonable time and location" if a member "gives the corporation written demand at least five business days before the date on which the member wishes to inspect and copy." Corporate records include the articles of incorporation, bylaws, board resolutions, minutes of membership meetings, all written communications to members within the preceding three years, a list of the names and addresses of directors and officers, and the current annual report submitted to the secretary of state. Some limitations apply. Further, the Act provides that "the articles or bylaws of a religious corporation may limit or abolish the right of a member under this section to inspect and

---

[59] *Id.* at §§ 7.04 and 7.08.

[60] *Id.* at § 7.22.

[61] *Id.* at § 8.03.

[62] *Id.* at §§ 8.08 and 8.10.

[63] *Id.* at §§ 8.30 and 8.42.

[64] *Id.* at §§ 8.50 through 8.58.

copy any corporate record."[65]

(16) **Membership list.** The Act specifies that "except as provided in the articles or bylaws of a religious corporation, a corporation upon written demand from a member shall furnish that member its latest annual financial statements . . . ."[66]

Some churches prefer not to incorporate under the Model Nonprofit Corporation Act (or the Revised Model Nonprofit Corporation Act). This decision ordinarily is based on one or more of four considerations:

First, churches do not want to be bothered with the annual reporting requirements. Although these requirements normally are not burdensome, they must be rigidly followed if a church is to avoid fines, and in some states, the loss of its corporate status.

Second, many churches regard the Model Nonprofit Corporation Act as too restrictive since it regulates virtually every aspect of corporate organization and administration. The Act does specify that most of its provisions are applicable only if a corporation has not provided otherwise in its articles of incorporation or bylaws. However, churches often are unwittingly controlled by the Act through their failure to adopt articles or bylaws dealing with particular aspects of organization and administration that are addressed in the Act. Some churches of course consider this to be an advantage, for it means that there will be authoritative direction on most questions of church administration.

Third, the Act was based largely on the Model Corporation Act for business corporations, and therefore fails to adequately recognize the substantial differences between nonprofit and for-profit enterprises.[67]

Fourth, some clergy maintain that churches should not incorporate as "nonprofit" organizations since this would suggest that they are "unprofitable" or of no social or spiritual benefit. In this regard, one court has observed that the term *not-for-profit* refers only to monetary profit and does not include "spiritual profit," and therefore a church properly can be characterized as "not-for-profit" even though it "receives some type of profit from its public works in the form of the feeling of achievement and satisfaction the contributors derive from their good work or the enhancement of the image of the organization and its members in the eyes of the community."[68]

Here is one additional point about incorporating under the Model Nonprofit Corporation Act or the Revised Model Nonprofit Corporation Act. Remember that many of the provisions of both laws apply "by default"—meaning that they will apply unless a church has provided otherwise in its articles of incorporation

---

[65] *Id.* at §§ 16.01 through 16.05.

[66] *Id.* at § 16.20.

[67] The Revised Model Nonprofit Corporation Act is based directly on the Revised Model Business Corporation Act, and uses the same numbering system. However, the revised Act in several places attempts to take into account the unique status of religious corporations.

[68] United States v. 564.54 Acres of Land, More or Less, 576 F.2d 983, 989 (3rd Cir. 1978). *See also* People ex rel. Meiresonne v. Arnold, 553 P.2d 79 (Colo. 1976).

or bylaws. Churches that are incorporated under either of these laws, or that are considering doing so, must carefully review the language of the law to be sure they understand the applicable provisions. Any desired changes must be made in the church's articles or bylaws.

Nonprofit vs. Tax-Exempt
It is important to distinguish between the terms *nonprofit* and *tax-exempt*. Nonprofit corporations generally are defined to include any corporation whose income is not distributable to its members, directors, or officers. The fact that an organization incorporates under a state's nonprofit corporation law does not in itself render the corporation exempt from federal, state, or local taxes. Exemption from tax generally is available only to those organizations that have applied for and received recognition of tax-exempt status.
In some cases the law recognizes the tax-exempt status of certain nonprofit organizations and waives the necessity of making formal application for recognition of exempt status. For example, "churches, their integrated auxiliaries, and conventions or associations of churches" are deemed to be exempt from federal income tax without the need for filing an application for exemption. [69]
In summary, unless a nonprofit corporation applies for and receives recognition of tax-exempt status or is expressly recognized by law to be exempt from tax without the necessity of making formal application, it will not be considered tax-exempt.

▶ *Churches need not be incorporated to be exempt from federal income tax. However, one court has observed that "while not a prerequisite for exemption, a showing that [an organization seeking a property tax exemption as a church] is incorporated as a church or religious association will lend credence to that organization's claim that it is a bona fide church or religious association."[70]*

2. Special Statutes

Several states have adopted statutes that pertain exclusively to the incorporation and administration of specific religious denominations. Such statutes typically apply only to churches affiliated with specified denominations or religions. Some of the states that provide for the incorporation of churches of specified denominations also have general nonprofit corporation laws. Churches generally can elect to incorporate under either the general nonprofit or the special religious corporation law.[71]

Such statutes have been upheld against the claim that they "entangle" the state in religious matters contrary to the "nonestablishment of religion clause" of

---

[69] I.R.C. § 508(c).

[70] Waushara County v. Graf, 480 N.W.2d 16 (Wis. 1992).

[71] Bible Presbyterian Church v. Harvey Cedars Bible Conference, 202 A.2d 455 (N.J. 1964); Rector, Church Wardens & Vestrymen v. Committee to Preserve St. Bartholomew's Church, 445 N.Y.S.2d 975 (1982).

the First Amendment to the United States Constitution.[72] The Supreme Court has upheld the validity of such statutes,[73] and has referred to them as a permissible way to resolve church property disputes.[74]

3. Court-Approved Corporations

Some states allow churches to incorporate by submitting articles of incorporation or articles of agreement to a local state court for approval. If the court determines that the church is organized for religious purposes and its objectives are consistent with the laws of the state, a certificate of incorporation is issued, which ordinarily is filed with the local recorder's office and with the secretary of state. This form of incorporation provides a minimum of state control over the operation of church corporations, since ordinarily no annual reporting is required, and the corporation law regulates only a few areas of corporate organization and administration.

4. Religious Corporation Laws

Many states have adopted general laws pertaining to the incorporation and administration of religious corporations without any specific reference to particular denominations or religions. Incorporation under such statutes ordinarily is simpler than incorporating under the general nonprofit corporation law. Typically, a church may incorporate under a general religious corporation statute by adopting articles setting forth the church's name, address, purposes, and the names and addresses of church officers and directors, and filing the articles with the county recorder, a court, or the secretary of state.

Churches are free to incorporate under either the Model Nonprofit Corporation Act or a general religious corporation law in those states where both forms of incorporation are available. One court rejected the claim that churches must incorporate under a state's general religious corporation law.[75] Obviously, a church that incorporates under the Model Nonprofit Corporation Act rather than under a general religious corporation law will be governed by the Model Act.

5. Corporations Sole

A corporation sole is a type of corporation that allows the incorporation of a religious office, such as the office of bishop. The IRS has described corporations sole as follows:

> A corporation sole enables a bona fide religious leader, such as a bishop or other authorized church or other religious official, to incorporate under state law, in his capacity as a religious official. One purpose of the corporation sole is to ensure the continuation of ownership of property

---

[72] Smith v. Church of God, 326 F. Supp. 6 (D. Md. 1971). Bennison v. Sharp, 329 N.W.2d 466 (Mich. App. 1982).

[73] Maryland and Virginia Eldership of Churches of God v. Church of God at Sharpsburg, 396 U.S. 367 (1970).

[74] Jones v. Wolf, 443 U.S. 595 (1979).

[75] Bible Presbyterian Church v. Harvey Cedars Bible Conference, Inc., 202 A.2d 455 (N.J. 1964).

dedicated to the benefit of a religious organization which may be held in the name of its chief officer. A corporation sole may own property and enter into contracts as a natural person, but only for the purposes of the religious entity and not for the individual office holder's personal benefit. Title to property that vests in the office holder as a corporation sole passes not to the office holder's heirs, but to the successors to the office by operation of law. A legitimate corporation sole is designed to ensure continuity of ownership of property dedicated to the benefit of a legitimate religious organization.[76]

Corporations sole are recognized in only the following 12 states: Alabama, Alaska, Arizona, California, Colorado, Hawaii, Montana, Nevada, Oregon, Utah, Washington, and Wyoming. A typical example of a corporation sole statute is section 10002 of the California Corporations Code (enacted in 1878), which provides:

> A corporation sole may be formed under this part by the bishop, chief priest, presiding elder, or other presiding officer of any religious denomination, society, or church, for the purpose of administering and managing the affairs, property, and temporalities thereof.

Section 10008 specifies that "every corporation sole has perpetual existence and also has continuity of existence, notwithstanding vacancies in the incumbency thereof."

These sections in the California Corporations Code illustrate the purpose of the corporation sole—to provide for the incorporation of an ecclesiastical office so that it is not affected by changes in the persons who occupy that office. The corporation sole is designed for use by an individual ecclesiastical officer and not by churches or other religious organizations.

Are corporations sole exempt from government laws?

Some persons are promoting the use of corporations sole by churches and church members as a lawful way to avoid all government laws and regulations, including income taxes and payroll taxes. Church leaders are informed that by structuring their church as a corporation sole, they will become an "ecclesiastical" entity beyond the jurisdiction of the government. Individuals are told that by becoming a corporation sole, they can avoid paying income taxes. The promoters, who often use e-mail and the Internet, make it all sound believable with numerous references to legal dictionaries, judges, and ancient cases. Such claims are false and should be ignored. Consider the following two points. First, a church cannot incorporate as a corporation sole. Only the presiding officer of a religious organization can do so. A church officer's decision to incorporate as a corporation sole has no effect on the relationship of the church with the government. Second, not one word in any corporation sole statute suggests that a corporation sole is an "ecclesiastical corporation" no longer subject to the laws or jurisdiction of the

---

[76] Revenue Ruling 2004-27.

government. In fact, most corporation sole statutes clarify that such corporations are subject to all governmental laws and regulations. A good example is the California Corporations Code, which specifies that "the articles of incorporation may state any desired provision for the regulation of the affairs of the corporation *in a manner not in conflict with law*" (emphasis added).

Similarly, the Oregon corporations sole statute specifies that such corporations differ from other corporations "only in that they shall have no board of directors, need not have officers and shall be managed by a single director who shall be the individual constituting the corporation and its incorporator or the successor of the incorporator." This is hardly a license to avoid compliance with tax or reporting obligations. Nothing in the corporation sole statutes of any state would remotely suggest such a conclusion.

In summary, a church officer who incorporates as a corporation sole will not exempt his or her church from having to withhold taxes from employees' wages, issue Forms W-2 and Forms 1099- MISC, file quarterly Forms 941 with the IRS, or comply with any other law or regulation. Further, an officer who incorporates as a corporation sole will not insulate his or her church from legal liability.

Can individuals avoid taxes by forming a corporation sole?

No. In fact, the IRS has issued a warning to persons who promote or succumb to such scams.[77] The IRS noted that participants in these scams are provided with a state identification number that can be used to open financial accounts. They claim that their income is exempt from federal and state taxation because this income belongs to the corporation sole, a tax-exempt organization. Participants may further claim that because their assets are held by the corporation sole, they are not subject to collection actions for the payment of federal or state income taxes or for the payment of other obligations, such as child support.

The IRS has noted that promoters, including return preparers, are recommending that taxpayers take frivolous positions based on this argument. Some promoters are marketing a package, kit, or other materials that claim to show taxpayers how they can avoid paying income taxes based on this and other meritless arguments. The IRS concluded:

> A taxpayer cannot avoid income tax or other financial responsibilities by purporting to be a religious leader and forming a corporation sole for tax avoidance purposes. The claims that such a corporation sole is described in section 501(c)(3) and that assignment of income and transfer of assets to such an entity will exempt an individual from income tax are meritless. Courts repeatedly have rejected similar arguments as frivolous, imposed penalties for making such arguments, and upheld criminal tax evasion convictions against those making or promoting the use of such arguments.

---

[77] *See* Revenue Ruling 2004-27.

6. "De Facto" Corporations

Even if a church fails to comply with one or more technical requirements of incorporation, it will be considered a *de facto corporation* if the following three requirements are satisfied:

(1) a special act or general law under which a corporation may lawfully exist, (2) a bona fide attempt to organize under the law and colorable compliance with the statutory requirements, and (3) actual use or exercise of corporate powers in pursuance of such law or attempted organization.[78]

To illustrate, when church trustees failed to sign a certificate of incorporation as required by state law, and the certificate was duly filed with the proper state authorities and remained on file without challenge for over thirty years, a court rejected the contention that the church was not a corporation.[79] Once the de facto status of a corporation is established, it may be attacked only by the state in a *quo warranto* proceeding.

Charters, Constitutions, Bylaws, and Resolutions §6-02.2

Key point 6-02.2. *Churches are subject to the provisions of their governing documents, which generally include a charter and a constitution or bylaws (in some cases both). A charter is the state-approved articles of incorporation of an incorporated church. Most rules of internal church administration are contained in a constitution or bylaws. Specific and temporary matters often are addressed in resolutions. If a conflict develops among these documents, the order of priority generally is as follows—charter, constitution, bylaws, and resolutions.*

It is important for church leaders to be familiar with the terms *charter, constitution, bylaws*, and *resolution*. The United States Supreme Court has observed that "all who unite themselves to [a church] do so with an implied consent to its government, and are bound to submit to it."[80] A church's "government" generally is defined in its charter, constitution, bylaws, resolutions, and practice. In addition, numerous courts have observed that the articles of incorporation and bylaws of a church constitute a "contract" between the congregation and its members.[81]

1. Charters and Articles of Incorporation

The application for incorporation that is filed with the secretary of state generally is called the *articles of incorporation* or *articles of agreement*. This document, when approved and certified by the appropriate government official, is

---

[78] Trustees of Peninsular Annual Conference of the Methodist Church, Inc. v. Spencer, 183 A.2d 588, 592 (Del. 1962).

[79] *Id.*

[80] Watson v. Jones, 80 U.S. 679 (1871).

[81] *See, e.g.,* Lozanoski v. Sarafin, 485 N.E.2d 669 (Ind. App. 1985).

commonly referred to as the corporate *charter*.[82] It is often said that the corporate charter includes by implication every pertinent provision of state law.[83]

Church charters typically set forth the name, address, period of duration, and purposes of the corporation; the doctrinal tenets of the church; and the names and addresses of incorporators and directors.

The income tax regulations require that the assets of a church pass to another tax-exempt organization upon its dissolution.[84] The IRS has stated that the following paragraph will satisfy this requirement if contained in a church corporation's articles of incorporation:

> Upon the dissolution of the corporation, assets shall be distributed for one or more exempt purposes within the meaning of section 501(c)(3) of the Internal Revenue Code, or the corresponding section of any future federal tax code, or shall be distributed to the federal government, or to a state or local government, for a public purpose. Any such assets not so disposed of shall be disposed of by a Court of Competent Jurisdiction of the county in which the principal office of the corporation is then located, exclusively for such purposes or to such organization or organizations, as said Court shall determine, which are organized and operated exclusively for such purposes.[85]

It would be very unusual for a church to use this suggested language without modification. Most churches prefer to specify the religious organization to which their assets will be distributed in the event of dissolution rather than leaving this determination to a judge's discretion. There is no assurance, under the suggested IRS language, that a dissolved church's assets would even go to another religious organization. For example, a judge could transfer a dissolved church's assets to a city or state government, or to a non-religious charitable organization, under the IRS language. Of course, churches wishing to designate a religious organization in their dissolution clauses should condition the distribution upon that organization's existence and tax-exempt status at the time of the distribution.

The Internal Revenue Manual and IRS Publication 557 both require that an appropriate dissolution clause appear in a church's articles of incorporation. However, the IRS has conceded that no dissolution clause is required if state law requires that the assets of a dissolved church corporation (or other charitable corporation) be distributed to another tax-exempt organization.[86] The IRS has stated that this special provision does not apply to unincorporated churches, since no state "provides certainty by statute or case law, for the distribution of assets

---

[82] FLETCHER CYC. CORP. § 164, n.21 (perm. ed. 2008).

[83] *Id.*

[84] Treas. Reg. § 1.501(c)(3)-1(b)(4).

[85] IRS Publication 557. An abbreviated version of this language, which also is acceptable to the IRS, appears in Rev. Proc. 82-2, 1982-1 C.B. 367.

[86] The instructions to IRS Form 1023 (Application for Recognition of Exemption) state that "if you are a corporation formed in the following states, then you do not need a specific provision in your articles of incorporation providing for the distribution of assets upon dissolution: Arkansas, California, Louisiana, Massachusetts, Minnesota, Missouri, Ohio, Oklahoma."

upon the dissolution of an unincorporated nonprofit association. Therefore, any unincorporated nonprofit association needs an adequate dissolution provision in its organizing document . . . ."[87]

The IRS also suggests that the following two paragraphs be placed in a church corporation's articles of incorporation:

> Said corporation is organized exclusively for charitable, religious, educational, and scientific purposes, including, for such purposes, the making of distributions to organizations that qualify as exempt organizations under section 501(c)(3) of the Internal Revenue Code, or the corresponding section of any future federal tax code.

> No part of the net earnings of the corporation shall inure to the benefit of, or be distributable to its members, trustees, officers, or other private persons, except that the corporation shall be authorized and empowered to pay reasonable compensation for services rendered and to make payments and distributions in furtherance of the purposes set forth in Article Third hereof. No substantial part of the activities of the corporation shall be the carrying on of propaganda, or otherwise attempting to influence legislation, and the corporation shall not participate in, or intervene in (including the publishing or distribution of statements) any political campaign on behalf of or in opposition to any candidate for public office. Notwithstanding any other provision of these articles, the corporation shall not carry on any other activities not permitted to be carried on (a) by a corporation exempt from federal income tax under section 501(c)(3) of the Internal Revenue Code, or the corresponding section of any future federal tax code, or (b) by a corporation, contributions to which are deductible under section 170(c)(2) of the Internal Revenue Code, or the corresponding section of any future federal tax code.[88]

Inclusion of the preceding paragraphs in a church's articles of incorporation helps to insure the continued recognition of its tax-exempt status.[89]

Key point. *Some churches define their exempt purposes to include charity and education in addition to religion, believing that this will accommodate a greater diversity of ministries. However, note that such an expansion of corporate purposes may also jeopardize various exemptions that are available to "religious" organizations. Church leaders should discuss this important issue with an attorney.*

The state law under which a church is incorporated will specify the procedure

---

[87] INTERNAL REVENUE MANUAL § 322.3(13).

[88] IRS Publication 557. The IRS states in Publication 557 that "if reference to federal law in articles of incorporation imposes a limitation that is invalid in your state, you may wish to substitute the following for the last sentence of the preceding paragraph: 'Notwithstanding any other provision of these articles, this corporation shall not, except to an insubstantial degree, engage in any activities or exercise any powers that are not in furtherance of the purposes of this corporation.'"

[89] *See* R. HAMMAR, CHURCH AND CLERGY TAX GUIDE chapter 11 (published annually by the publisher of this text).

to be followed in amending the corporate charter. Generally, a charter amendment must be filed with and approved by the state official who approved the charter.

Case Study

• *The Washington Supreme Court ruled that a church's board of elders was powerless to amend the church's articles of incorporation without the pastor's approval. The church's articles of incorporation specified that neither the articles nor the bylaws could be amended without the pastor's approval. After allegations of sexual misconduct on the part of the pastor surfaced, the board of elders decided to conduct hearings into the matter. At the conclusion of these hearings, the board adopted a resolution placing the pastor on "special status." This meant that he could resume his duties as pastor of the church, but he would not be permitted to be alone with any females. This decision was announced to the church congregation in a special meeting. The pastor refused to accept this special status or to honor the board's decision. Instead, he announced to the congregation that he was not under the authority of the elders and that he would resume his role of pastor without restriction. The board convened a meeting with the pastor in an attempt to reach a compromise. When it was clear that no agreement was possible, the board members voted to amend the articles by removing the provision requiring the pastor to approve all amendments to the articles. They also voted to remove the pastor from office because of his breach of his "fiduciary duties" to the corporation. The pastor immediately filed a lawsuit asking a civil court to determine whether or not the elders had the authority to amend the articles without his approval. The state supreme court ruled in favor of the pastor. It reasoned that the articles clearly specified that they could not be amended without the pastor's approval, and that as a result the elders' attempt to amend the articles without the pastor's approval was null and void. The court observed: "Neither of the parties has called to our attention any case holding that any corporation law in the country, profit or nonprofit, prohibits a provision in the articles of incorporation requiring the concurrence of a special individual to amend the articles." The court agreed that the church's articles "might well, in retrospect, be viewed by some as an improvident provision," but it concluded that "it is not the function of this court . . . to protect those who freely chose to enter into this kind of relationship."*[90]

2. Constitutions and Bylaws

Articles of incorporation rarely contain rules for the internal government of the corporation. For this reason, it is desirable and customary for churches to adopt rules of internal administration. One court observed:

It has been uniformly held that religious organizations have the right to prescribe such rules and regulations as to the conduct of their own affairs as they may think proper, so long as the same are not inconsistent with . . . the law of the land.[91]

---

[90] Barnett v. Hicks, 792 P.2d 150 (Wash. 1990).

[91] Ohio Southeast Conference of Evangelical United Brethren Church v. Kruger, 243 N.E.2d 781, 787 (Ohio 1968).

Such rules ordinarily are called bylaws, although occasionally they are referred to as a constitution or a "constitution and bylaws." The terms *bylaws* and *constitution* often are used interchangeably. Technically, however, the terms are distinguishable—*bylaws* referring generally to the rules of internal government adopted by a corporation, and *constitution* referring to the supreme law of a corporation.[92] Correctly used, the term *constitution* refers to a body of rules that is paramount to the bylaws. It may refer to the charter or to a document separate and distinct from both the charter and bylaws.

Church corporations that differentiate between a constitution and bylaws ordinarily do so on the basis of the relative importance of the provisions assigned to either document. Often, more important provisions are assigned to the constitution, which is made more difficult to amend because a greater majority vote is required than for amendments to the bylaws. Routine items are assigned to the bylaws, which is more easily amended because of a lesser voting requirement.

It makes no sense for a church corporation to have both a constitution and a separate set of bylaws unless the constitution is made superior to the bylaws either by express provision or by a more restrictive amendment procedure. Identifying a single body of rules as the "constitution and bylaws" without any attempt to distinguish between the two is a common but inappropriate practice. Obviously, the best practice would be to set forth the corporation's purposes and beliefs in the corporate charter, and to have a single body of rules for internal government identified as bylaws.

At a minimum, church bylaws should cover the following matters:

- qualifications, selection, and expulsion of members
- time and place of annual business meetings
- the calling of special business meetings
- notice for annual and special meetings
- quorums
- voting rights
- selection, tenure, and removal of officers and directors
- filling of vacancies
- responsibilities of directors and officers
- method of amending bylaws
- purchase and conveyance of property[93]

Other matters that should be considered for inclusion in a church's bylaws include:

---

[92] Fletcher Cyc. Corp. § 4167, n.21 (perm. ed. 2008).

[93] *See generally* the Model Nonprofit Corporation Act Bylaws.

• adoption of a specific body of parliamentary procedure

• a clause requiring disputes between church members, or between a member and the church itself, to be resolved through mediation or arbitration

• a clause specifying how contracts and other legal documents are to be approved and signed signature authority on checks

• "bonding" of officers and employees who handle church funds

• an annual audit by independent certified public accountants

• an indemnification clause

• specification of the church's fiscal year

• "staggered voting" of directors (a portion of the board is elected each year—to ensure year-to-year continuity of leadership).

The power to enact and amend bylaws is vested in the members, unless the charter or bylaws grants this authority to some other body. Occasionally, trustees or directors are given the authority to enact and amend bylaws. Procedures to be followed in amending the bylaws should be and usually are set forth in the bylaws. Such procedures must be followed.

Church bylaws often contain ambiguous language, and this can result in both confusion and internal disputes. It is essential for church bylaws to be reviewed periodically by the board, or a special committee, to identify ambiguities and propose modifications. Will the civil courts interfere in a church dispute over the meaning of ambiguous bylaw provisions? Generally, the civil courts have been willing to do so if no interpretation of doctrine is required. The same is true for ambiguous provisions in a church's articles of incorporation.

Case Studies

• An Arizona court agreed to interpret a clause in a church's bylaws specifying that "a pastor may be terminated by the church congregation . . . but only if . . . the vote equals or exceeds three-fourths of the voting members present." A church voted to oust its pastor at a duly called meeting by a vote of 18 of the 26 members present (the remaining 8 members did not vote). The pastor refused to acknowledge that the vote resulted in his dismissal, since less than "three-fourths of the voting members present" had voted to dismiss him (18 is only 70 percent of 26). Several disgruntled members of the congregation disagreed with this interpretation, and petitioned a court for a ruling recognizing that the congregational vote had resulted in the dismissal of the pastor. The members argued that the phrase "three-fourths of the voting members present" should be interpreted to mean three-fourths of the individuals who actually cast votes at the business meeting rather than three-fourths of all members actually present and eligible to vote. Since all 18 of the persons who actually voted at the meeting voted to dismiss the pastor, 100 percent of the votes were cast in favor of dismissal. A state appeals court ruled that the pastor had not been lawfully dismissed in the meeting in question. The court relied on Robert's Rules of Order, which had been adopted by the church (in its bylaws) as the governing body of parliamentary procedure, as support for its conclusion that the phrase "three-fourths of the voting

members present" means three-fourths "of the individuals present and eligible to vote." Accordingly, the pastor had not been dismissed by the congregational vote since less than three-fourths of the members present and eligible to vote had voted to dismiss him.[94]

• A Florida court ruled that a church board's attempts to amend the articles of incorporation were invalid because procedural requirements were not followed. The court concluded that the First Amendment religion clauses did not prevent it from resolving this dispute since the case "implicates neutral legal principles only" and "precedent supports judicial resolution of the parties' dispute over corporate assets, the corporation's religious purposes notwithstanding." It further observed: "The doctrine of either side is . . . of no moment here. The courts are not concerned with the articles of faith of either, nor with the question as to whether or not the articles of faith or the religious doctrines of either are respected and observed. The only question which is sought to be presented here which may be addressed to the courts is in regard to the right to control the church property. The parties have asked neither us nor the trial court to become entangled in essentially religious controversies or intervene on behalf of groups espousing particular doctrinal beliefs."[95]

• The Iowa Supreme Court suggested that it was barred by the First Amendment guaranty of religious freedom from resolving a dispute involving the interpretation of church bylaws.[96] A group of church members filed a lawsuit claiming that the pastor and other members had violated the church bylaws in several ways, including the following: (1) Placed some members on "probation" when no such status was recognized by the bylaws; (2) terminated longtime members without cause; (3) allowed the minister and his wife to take money from the church treasury and funds for their own personal and private use; (4) appointed members to leadership positions illegally; (5) refused to honor a proper request for a meeting of the congregation called for the purpose of exploring the relationship of the church and its minister; (6) leased church property to private individuals; (7) disposed of property belonging to the church to private individuals; (8) eliminated church committees; (9) held illegal meetings; (10) violated church spending limits. The pastor's attorney filed a motion to dismiss the case, arguing that the First Amendment guaranty of religious freedom prevents the civil courts from resolving such disputes. The trial court agreed, and dismissed the lawsuit. The disgruntled members appealed. The state supreme court began its ruling by noting that "civil courts are precluded by the First Amendment from deciding doctrinal issues," including "membership in a church organization or church discipline," and that "the courts have no jurisdiction over, and no concern with, purely ecclesiastical questions and controversies, including membership in a church organization, but they do have jurisdiction as to civil, contract, and property rights which are involved in or arise from a church controversy."

• A Louisiana court ruled that a trial court had the authority to resolve a dispute regarding the legal validity of a church membership meeting since it could do so by applying provisions of the state nonprofit corporation law involving no interpretation of religious doctrine.[97]

---

[94] Blanton v. Hahn, 763 P.2d 522 (Ariz. App. 1988).

[95] The Word of Life Ministry, Inc. v. Miller, 778 So.2d 360 (Fla. App. 2001).

[96] Holmstrom v. Sir, 590 N.W.2d 538 (Iowa 1999).

[97] Mount Gideon Baptist Church v. Robinson, 812 So.2d 758 (La. App. 2002).

• A Texas court ruled that it could not resolve an internal church dispute on the basis of the church's constitution and bylaws since the critical provisions in these documents could not be applied without the court delving into church doctrine and governance. The case involved the question of "who has the right to select and remove the trustee-directors and the minister." Both sides relied on the church's articles of incorporation in support of their position. The court noted that "ordinarily, we would construe the articles of incorporation of a Texas nonprofit corporation according to the body of neutral legal principles that governs Texas corporations generally. If we could do so without running afoul of constitutional constraints, we would also apply those principles to construe the articles of incorporation of a nonprofit corporation organized for religious or spiritual purposes." However, it concluded that it could not apply neutral legal principles in construing articles of incorporation or bylaws of the church, since both documents used the phrase "custom and practices of the church." Such language, the court concluded, "removed any dispute regarding the selection of its directors from the purview of the judicial system. Interpreting this phrase would require the court to examine the historical, administrative, and ecclesiastical affairs of a religious organization and decide the outcome of the issue based on its determination of what are the customs and practices of the church. . . . Our deciding the central issue here would require us to interpret religious law and usage. Not only is that issue ambiguous, its resolution would require the state, through the judicial system, to determine issues of internal church governance. We may not delve into those issues."[98]

• A church's constitution provided that "the candidate receiving the majority of all votes cast shall, upon unanimous approval, be declared elected." The church convened a congregational meeting to vote on a pastoral candidate, and the candidate received a majority of the votes cast (but not "unanimous approval"). The candidate was subsequently employed, and a group of dissidents filed a lawsuit asking a civil court to enforce the church's constitutional requirement of "unanimous approval." While noting that the First Amendment prohibits a court "from entangling itself in matters of church doctrine or practice," a Washington state court concluded that it could resolve controversies, such as this one, involving the interpretation "of an ambiguous provision in what amounts to a contract between the members of the congregation, dealing with a purely procedural question" and involving "no ecclesiastical or doctrinal issues." The court also noted that it found no "dispute resolution process" within the denomination to which it could defer.[99]

3. Resolutions

Corporate resolutions are not bylaws. A resolution is an informal and temporary enactment for disposing of a particular item of business, whereas bylaws are rules of general applicability. For example, a minister's "housing allowance" generally is designated by his or her church board in a resolution. A church's business expense reimbursement policy or medical insurance reimbursement plan ordinarily appear in resolutions of the church board.

---

[98] Cherry Valley Church of Christ v. Foster, 2002 WL 10545 (Tex. App. 2002).

[99] Organization for Preserving the Constitution of Zion Lutheran Church v. Mason, 743 P.2d 848 (Wash. App. 1987). A dissenting judge, quoting several passages of scripture (Numbers 11:16-17; Matthew 9:35-38; 28:18-20; John 20:19-23; Acts 6:2-7; 2 Corinthians 3:6; Ephesians 4:7-12; Hebrews 5:1-10) characterized the selection of clergy as an ecclesiastical process in which the civil courts may never interfere.

Table 6-1 Provisions Commonly Found in Governing Documents

charter	constitution	bylaws	resolutions
• name • address • duration • purposes • names and addresses of initial board members • dissolution clause	[many churches only use bylaws, and not bylaws plus a constitution; this column assumes that a church has both documents] • doctrinal tenets (and any other matter whose amendment is subject to a greater voting requirement)	• qualifications, selection, and discipline of members • time and place of annual business meetings • calling of special business meetings • notice for annual and special meetings • quorum • voting rights • selection, tenure, and removal of officers and directors • filling of vacancies • responsibilities of directors and officers • method of amending bylaws • purchase and conveyance of property • adoption of a specific body of parliamentary procedure • a clause requiring disputes between church members, or between a member and the church itself, to be resolved through mediation or arbitration • a clause specifying how contracts and other legal documents are to be approved and signed • signature authority on checks • "bonding" of officers and employees who handle church funds • an annual audit by independent certified public accountants • an indemnification clause • specification of the church's fiscal year • "staggered voting" of directors (a portion of the board is elected each year—to ensure year-to-year continuity of leadership)	• housing allowances for clergy • accountable business expense re-imbursement arrangement • clergy com-pensation package

4. Reconciling Conflicting Language

Occasionally, conflicts develop among provisions in a corporation's charter, constitution, bylaws, and resolutions. The general rule is that provisions in a corporate charter take precedence over conflicting provisions in a corporation's constitution, bylaws, or resolutions.

Case Studies

• *A federal appeals court ruled that a local church's articles of incorporation took priority over a conflicting provision in a denominational "Book of Discipline" which the court viewed as the "functional equivalent" of the local church's bylaws. In 1991 the African Union Methodist Protestant Church (the "national church") adopted a "church property" resolution specifying that "the title to all property, now owned or hereafter acquired by an incorporated local church . . . shall be held by or conveyed to the corporate body in its corporate name, in trust for the use and benefit of such local church and of the African Union Methodist Protestant Church." The property resolution was incorporated into the national church's governing Book of Discipline. At the same 1991 meeting of the national church, another resolution was adopted authorizing pastors "to sign official documents pertaining to the individual local church." On the basis of these resolutions, the national church directed a number of pastors to sign a quitclaim deed transferring title to their church's property to the national church. One church, whose property was deeded to the national church by its pastor pursuant to such a directive, voted unanimously to secede from the national church and then challenged the legality of the transfer in court. A federal appeals court ruled that the pastor's attempt to deed his church's property to the national church had to be invalidated. It based this conclusion on a provision in the local church's articles of incorporation that permitted conveyances of church property only upon a vote of at least two-thirds of the church's members. The court noted that this provision conflicted with the national church's "property resolutions" that were incorporated into its Book of Discipline. However, the court concluded that the Book of Discipline "functioned" as the local church's bylaws, and it concluded that whenever there is a conflict between a church's articles of incorporation and its bylaws, the articles of incorporation prevail. As a result, the pastor was bound by the requirement in the articles of incorporation rather than the Book of Discipline since "provisions of a corporation's charter or articles of incorporation enjoy priority over contradictory or inconsistent bylaws."[100]*

• *A church charter provided for seven trustees and the church's bylaws called for nine. A California court ruled that the charter provision took priority over the provision in the church bylaws.[101]*

• *A Florida court ruled that a church board properly removed a pastor without a congregational vote, since this was the procedure specified in the church's articles of incorporation.[102] A church's board of deacons voted to terminate their pastor's employment pursuant to the following provision in the church's articles of*

---

[100] Scotts African Union Methodist Protestant Church v. Conference of African Union First Colored Methodist Protestant Church, 98 F.3d 78 (3rd Cir. 1996).

[101] Morris v. Richard Clark Missionary Baptist Church, 177 P.2d 811 (Cal. 1947).

[102] New Mount Moriah Missionary Baptist Church, Inc. v. Dinkins, 708 So.2d 972 (Fla. App. 1998).

incorporation: "With respect to the hiring of a . . . pastor . . . the sole responsibility for both hiring and firing said individuals shall rest with the deacons, as more fully set out in the bylaws of this not for profit corporation." The bylaws contained a similar provision. However, when several members of the congregation objected to the board's decision, the board decided to submit the question of the pastor's removal to the church membership at a specially called business meeting. The membership voted to retain the pastor. The board ignored this vote, and attempted to enforce its previous decision to remove the pastor by seeking a court order. The pastor, on the other hand, argued that the board had "amended" the bylaws when it permitted the membership vote, and therefore the vote was valid and the pastor was retained. A state appeals court agreed with the board that the pastor had been properly removed. It noted that the state nonprofit corporation law requires that any new bylaws must be consistent with the articles of incorporation. As a result, the pastor's argument that the board "amended" the bylaws by calling a meeting of the membership to vote on the pastor's retention had to be rejected, since such an "amendment" would be in direct violation of the articles of incorporation which allow a pastor to be removed only by the board.

• An Indiana court ruled that a provision in a church's bylaws requiring the church to make retirement payments to two former pastors took precedence over conflicting provisions in individual contracts the church and pastors had executed. The court concluded: "The articles of incorporation and bylaws of a nonprofit corporation constitute a contract between the state and the corporation, the corporation and its members, and the members among themselves." It concluded that this contract superseded the individual pension agreements.[103]

• A New Jersey court ruled that "religious and quasi-religious societies may adopt a constitution and bylaws for the regulation of their affairs, if conformable and subordinate to the charter and not repugnant to the law of the land . . . ."[104]

If the constitution is separate and distinct from the bylaws and is of superior force and effect either by expressly so providing or by reason of a more difficult amendment procedure, then provisions in a corporation's constitution take precedence over conflicting provisions in the bylaws.[105] To illustrate, where a church constitution specified that a pastor was to be elected by a majority vote of the church membership and the bylaws called for a two-thirds vote, the constitution was held to control.[106] Resolutions of course are inferior to, and thus may not contradict, provisions in a corporation's charter, constitution, and bylaws.

Case Study

• The Georgia Supreme Court ruled that a provision in the state nonprofit corporation law mandating annual membership meetings did not take priority over a provision in a church's bylaws calling for membership meetings once every four years. The members

---

[103] Calvary Temple Church v. Paino, 827 N.E.2d 125 (Ind. App. 2005).

[104] Leeds v. Harrison, 87 A.2d 713, 720 (N.J. 1952).

[105] FLETCHER CYC. CORP. § 4195 (perm. ed. 2008).

[106] Pelzer v. Lewis, 269 A.2d 902 (Pa. 1970).

of a church filed a lawsuit in civil court seeking to compel their church to conduct an annual membership meeting. The members relied upon a provision in the state nonprofit corporation law specifying that a nonprofit corporation "shall hold a meeting of members annually at a time stated in or fixed in accordance with the bylaws." The church's bylaws called for a membership meeting once every four years. The state supreme court ruled that state nonprofit corporation law did not override the church's own bylaws and therefore the church was required to conduct meetings only once every four years. The court observed that the state nonprofit corporation law itself specifies that if any of its provisions is inconsistent with religious doctrine governing a nonprofit corporation's affairs on the same subject, "the religious doctrine shall control to the extent required by the Constitution of the United States or the Constitution of this state or both." As a result, the issue "is whether the frequency with which the church's membership meets is a matter of religious doctrine having constitutional precedence over inconsistent statutory provisions of [the nonprofit corporation law]." The court noted that the church in this case was "hierarchical" in nature, and that the members had very limited authority to direct church affairs. It concluded: "An annual meeting as contemplated by [the nonprofit corporation law] would be totally inconsistent with the church's fundamental religious freedom, as a hierarchical religious body, to determine its own governmental rules and regulations. Members have no legal right to wrest the governing of the church from [church officials] by obtaining court-ordered annual meetings conducted in accordance with [nonprofit corporation law]."[107]

▶ Incorporated churches are free to adopt bylaws addressing issues of internal administration, and these bylaws generally take precedence over conflicting provisions in state nonprofit corporation law. In other words, state nonprofit corporation law may be viewed in most cases as a "gap filler"—filling gaps in a church's bylaws. For example, if an incorporated church's bylaws do not address how vacancies on the board are to be filled, or do not define a quorum, the nonprofit corporation law will "fill the gaps."

Table 6-2	
Priority Among Governing Documents in Congregational Churches	
Note: When attempting to resolve any question of church administration in a "congregational" church, relevant provisions in the following sources of authority generally are applied in the following order of priority.	
document	**order of priority**
charter	• the highest order of priority • its provisions take priority over any other source of authority • start with the charter when attempting to resolve a question of administration; if it doesn't address the matter, then proceed on to the next order of priority until an answer is found

---

[107] First Born Church of the Living God, Inc. v. Hill, 481 S.E.2d 221 (Ga. 1997).

Table 6-2
Priority Among Governing Documents in Congregational Churches

Note: When attempting to resolve any question of church administration in a "congregational" church, relevant provisions in the following sources of authority generally are applied in the following order of priority.

document	order of priority
constitution	• the second highest order of priority • takes priority over all other sources of authority except the charter, assuming that it is made superior to the bylaws either by express provision or by a greater voting requirement to amend
bylaws	• the third highest order of priority • takes priority over all other sources of authority except the charter and constitution (assuming the constitution is made superior to the bylaws)
parliamentary law	• the fourth highest order of priority (assuming that a specific body of parliamentary law has been adopted) • takes priority over all other sources of authority if specifically adopted in the church bylaws, except the charter, constitution, and bylaws
state nonprofit corporation law	• the fifth highest order of priority • its provisions generally apply only if the church has not provided otherwise in its charter, constitution, or bylaws (including rules of parliamentary law adopted by the bylaws) • state nonprofit corporation laws ordinarily make a few provisions mandatory despite a bylaw or charter provision to the contrary
resolutions	• the sixth highest order of priority • resolutions can provide guidance in the event that the charter, constitution, bylaws, parliamentary law, and applicable state nonprofit corporation law do not address an issue
established custom	• the seventh highest order of priority • only applies if the custom is established by long and consistent use • it can provide guidance on questions for which an established custom exists, and no higher source of authority applies
majority rule	• the last order of priority; the only basis for resolving issues not addressed in any other manner

Church Records

Key point 6-03. *State nonprofit corporation laws generally require incorporated churches to maintain certain kinds of records. The federal tax code also requires churches to maintain specified records.*

State nonprofit corporation laws generally require incorporated churches to maintain the following records:

(1) correct and complete books and records of account;

(2) minutes of the proceedings of its members;

(3) minutes of the proceedings of its board of directors;

(4) resolutions of its board of directors;

(5) minutes of the proceedings of committees; and

(6) a current list of voting members.

These documents, in addition to the corporate charter, constitution, bylaws, certificate of incorporation, correspondence, insurance policies, employment files, contracts, and tax forms and documentation constitute the records of a church corporation. The Model Nonprofit Corporation Act, under which many churches are incorporated, states:

> Each corporation shall keep correct and complete books and records of account and shall keep minutes of the proceedings of its members, board of directors and committees having any of the authority of the board of directors; and shall keep at its registered office or principal office in this State a record giving the names and addresses of its members entitled to vote. All books and records of a corporation may be inspected by any member, or his agent or attorney, for any proper purpose at any reasonable time.[108]

The Revised Model Nonprofit Corporation Act, which has been adopted in some states, specifies:

> (a) A corporation shall keep as permanent records minutes of all meetings of its members and board of directors, a record of all actions taken by the members or directors without a meeting, and a record of all actions taken by committees of the board of directors . . . .

> (b) A corporation shall maintain appropriate accounting records.

---

[108] MODEL NONPROFIT CORPORATION ACT § 25.

(c) A corporation or its agent shall maintain a record of its members in a form that permits preparation of a list of the name and address of all members, in alphabetical order by class, showing the number of votes each member is entitled to cast.

(d) A corporation shall maintain its records in written form or in another form capable of conversion into written form within a reasonable time.

(e) A corporation shall keep a copy of the following records at its principal office:

   (1) its articles or restated articles of incorporation and all amendments to them currently in effect;

   (2) its bylaws or restated bylaws and all amendments to them currently in effect;

   (3) resolutions adopted by its board of directors relating to the characteristics, qualifications, rights, limitations and obligations of members or any class or category of members;

   (4) the minutes of all meetings of members and records of all actions approved by the members for the past three years;

   (5) all written communications to members generally furnished within the past three years, including the financial statements furnished for the past three years under section 16.20;

   (6) a list of the names and business or home addresses of its current directors and officers; and

   (7) its most recent annual report delivered to the secretary of state . . . .[109]

Churches incorporated under statutes other than the Model Nonprofit Corporation Act (or the revised Act) and unincorporated churches often are under no legal obligation to maintain records.

All records should be as complete as possible, which means that each record should be dated and indicate the action taken, the persons present, and the voting results if any. It is often helpful to include a brief statement of the purpose for each action if it would not otherwise be clear. The secretary of the board of directors usually is the custodian of the corporate records, while accounting records customarily are maintained by the treasurer.

The income tax regulations state that "any person subject to tax . . . shall keep such permanent books of account or records, including inventories, as are sufficient to establish the amount of gross income, deductions, credits, or other matters required to be shown by such person in any return of such tax . . . ."[110]

---

[109] Revised Model Nonprofit Corporation Act § 16.01.

[110] Treas. Reg. § 1.6001-1(a).

Inspection

Key point 6-03.1. *Church members generally have no right to inspect church records unless such a right is conferred by state nonprofit corporation law, a church's charter or bylaws, state securities law (if the church has issued securities), or a subpoena. Church records enjoy no privilege against disclosure, with the exception of documents that are protected by the clergy-penitent privilege under state law.*

Can church members inspect church records? If so, which records can be inspected and under what circumstances? What about nonmembers? Generally, there is no inherent right to inspect church records. Such a right must be granted in some legal document such as a church's bylaws or state nonprofit corporation law. Some of the possible justifications for a right of inspection are reviewed in this section.

1. Nonprofit Corporation Law

Section 25 of the Model Nonprofit Corporation Act, previously quoted, gives members of an incorporated church the right to inspect corporate records for any proper purpose at any reasonable time. The Revised Model Nonprofit Corporation Act gives members broad authority to inspect corporate records, but specifies that "the articles or bylaws of a religious corporation may limit or abolish the right of a member . . . to inspect and copy any corporate records."[111]

Can a church incorporated under the Model Nonprofit Corporation Act refuse a member's request to inspect church records on the ground that such a right conflicts with the church's constitutional guaranty of religious freedom? The courts have reached conflicting answers to this question.

Case Study

• *The Arkansas Supreme Court ruled that members of a church incorporated under the Model Nonprofit Corporation Act do not have a right to inspect church records if doing so would "impinge upon the doctrine of the church." When church elders rejected members' requests to inspect church records, the members incorporated the church under a state nonprofit corporation law making the "books and records" of a corporation subject to inspection "by any member for any proper purpose at any reasonable time." When church elders continued to reject the members' request for*

---

[111] Revised Model Business Corporations Act § 16.02. Some of the special provisions under the revised Act include: (1) ordinarily, a member must give the corporation written notice at least five business days before the date of inspection; (2) the right to inspect includes the right to make copies; (3) the corporation may charge a reasonable fee for the duplicating expenses; (4) for certain types of records, a member's request for inspection must be "in good faith and for a proper purpose," and the member must describe with "reasonable particularity the purpose of the records the member desires to inspect," and the records must be directly related to such purpose; and (5) a member's agent or attorney has the same inspection and copying rights as the member. In addition, the revised Act empowers the civil courts to order a corporation to grant a member's request for inspection.

inspection, the members asked a state court to recognize their legal right to inspection under state law. The elders countered by arguing that application of state corporation law would impermissibly interfere with the religious doctrine and practice of the church, contrary to the constitutional guaranty of religious freedom. Specifically, the elders argued that according to the church's "established doctrine," the New Testament "places within the hands of a select group of elders the sole responsibility for overseeing the affairs of the church," and that this authority is "evidenced by biblical admonitions to the flock to obey and submit to them that have rule over the flock." The state supreme court agreed that "application of our state corporation law would almost certainly impinge upon the doctrine of the church" as described by the elders, and accordingly would violate the constitutional guaranty of religious freedom. The court concluded that if the application of a state law would conflict with the "doctrine, polity, or practice" of a church, then the law cannot be applied to the church without a showing of a "compelling state interest." No such showing was made in this case, the court concluded, and therefore the state law giving members of nonprofit corporations the legal right to inspect corporate records could not be applied to the church.[112]

Other courts have rejected the claim that the First Amendment insulates church records from inspection by members. To illustrate, members of one church sought a court order authorizing them to examine the church's financial records. The church was incorporated under the state's general nonprofit corporation law, which gave members the right to inspect corporate records at any reasonable time. The church and its pastor objected to the inspection on the ground that the First Amendment prohibits the courts from involving themselves in church affairs. The court disagreed with this contention, concluding that "First Amendment values are plainly not jeopardized by a civil court's enforcement of a voting member's right to examine these records."[113]

It is doubtful that most courts would permit churches incorporated under the model Act to refuse members' requests to inspect church records on the basis of the First Amendment guaranty of religious freedom. The statutory right of inspection is a "neutral law of general applicability" that is presumably constitutional without the need for demonstrating a compelling state interest.[114] As a result, church leaders should not assume that the First Amendment permits them to deny inspection rights given to members under state corporation law.

A right of inspection, however, generally applies only to *members*. Persons who are not members of a church generally have no right to demand inspection of church records under nonprofit corporation law.

---

[112] Gipson v. Brown, 749 S.W.2d 297 (Ark. 1988). A "compelling state interest" no longer is required with respect to "neutral laws of general applicability," according to the United States Supreme Court's decision in Employment Division v. Smith, 494 U.S. 872 (1990).

[113] Bourgeois v. Landrum, 396 So.2d 1275, 1277-78 (La. 1981).

[114] Employment Division v. Smith, 110 S. Ct. 1595 (1990).

Case Studies

• *The Alabama Supreme Court ruled that a dismissed church member no longer had a legal right to inspect church records.*[115]

• *A Colorado court ruled that a church member's legal authority to inspect church records pursuant to state nonprofit corporation law ended when his membership was revoked by the church board. The court concluded: "To obtain records . . . such as those at issue here, the member's request [must be based on] good faith and a proper purpose. 'Proper purpose' means a purpose reasonably related to the demanding member's interest as a member. Thus, to obtain records, a person must be a member with a present ability to promote the welfare of the association. . . . [When the plaintiff lost his membership] he could not, by definition, have any interest as a member sufficient to afford him a proper purpose to inspect records. Specifically, as a nonmember, [he] no longer had a member's stake in what had been done with church resources, nor any member's interest in determining church economies, nor any member's voice with which to persuade voting church members to adopt his policies. . . . Thus, [his] good intentions aside, he is now an outsider to the church, and any attempts to use the information contained in the church's records for his stated purposes would be futile. Accordingly, the provisions of the [nonprofit corporation statute] upon which his claim is based give him no right to judicial relief."*[116]

• *A Georgia court ruled that a member of a nonprofit corporation failed to prove that he had a proper purpose for his request to inspect several categories of corporate records, and therefore he had no legal right under the state nonprofit corporation law to inspect the records. A member of a nonprofit corporation sued the corporation on the basis of mismanagement and a violation of the corporate bylaws. The member asked for permission to inspect "all accounting and corporate records . . . for the purpose of determining the performance of management and the condition of the corporation." The member claimed that he wanted the documents "for the purpose of determining the performance of management and the condition of the corporation." The court concluded, however, that the member "has not sufficiently demonstrated that the documents sought are being sought for a proper purpose." Therefore, it denied the member's request to inspect the corporate records.*[117]

• *Some of the members of a charitable organization incorporated under the state nonprofit corporation law demanded to see various corporate records. Their request was denied by corporate officers, and the members sued. An Illinois state appeals court ruled that the members had a broad right to inspect the corporation's records. The court noted that the state nonprofit corporation law specified that "all books and records of a corporation may be inspected by any member . . . for any proper purpose at any reasonable time." The court continued, "The [member] has the burden to establish he has a proper purpose to inspect the corporation's records. A proper purpose is shown when a shareholder has an honest motive, is acting in good faith, and is not proceeding for vexatious or speculative reasons; however, the purpose must*

---

[115] Lott v. Eastern Shore Christian Center, 908 So.2d 922 (Ala. 2005). *Accord* Ex parte Board of Trustees, 2007 WL 1519867 (Ala. 2007) .

[116] Levitt v. Calvary Temple, 2001 WL 423040 (Colo. App. 2001).

[117] Parker v. Clary Lakes Recreation Association, Inc., 2000 WL 426454 (Ga. App. 2000).

be lawful in character and not contrary to the interests of the corporation. A proper purpose is one that seeks to protect the interests of the corporation and the [member] seeking the information. . . . [A member's] right to inspect a corporation's books and records must be balanced against the needs of the corporation depending on the facts of the case. Proof of actual mismanagement is not required; a good faith fear of mismanagement is sufficient to show proper purpose. The [member] is not required to establish a proper purpose for each record he requests. Once that purpose has been established, the [member's] right to inspect extends to all books and records necessary to make an intelligent and searching investigation and from which he can derive any information that will enable him to better protect his interests."[118]

• *A Louisiana court ruled that an incorporated church had to allow members to inspect church records. Four members asked for permission to inspect the following records of their church: (1) bank statements; (2) the check register and cancelled checks for all the church's bank accounts; (3) the cash receipts journal; and (4) monthly financial reports. The pastor denied the members' request. The members then sought a court order compelling the church to permit them to inspect the records. The pastor insisted that such an order would interfere with "internal church governance" in violation of the First Amendment. A state appeals court ruled that allowing the members to inspect records, pursuant to state nonprofit corporation law, would not violate the First Amendment. The court quoted from an earlier Louisiana Supreme Court ruling: "A voting member of a nonprofit corporation has a right to examine the records of the corporation without stating reasons for his inspection. Since the judicial enforcement of this right does not entangle civil courts in questions of religious doctrine, polity, or practice, the First Amendment does not bar a suit to implement the statutory right. First Amendment values are plainly not jeopardized by a civil court's enforcement of a voting member's right to examine these records. No dispute arising in the course of this litigation requires the court to resolve an underlying controversy over religious doctrine."*[119]

• *A New York court ruled that a church member had the legal authority to inspect church records despite the pastor's refusal to allow him to do so. The court acknowledged that only members had a legal right to inspect records, but it concluded that the member had not lost his status as a member of the church. It concluded: "The member is simply trying to enforce his secular rights as a member, using the church's own criteria of membership and the pastor's own admission that he has not been expelled as a member. Nor are the church's First Amendment rights violated by the inspection of the records, as the questions involved here are not concerned with internal ecclesiastical or religious issues, but purely secular ones."*[120]

• *A New York court ruled that members of a nonprofit corporation had a proper purpose in asking to see various records of the corporation, and therefore they had a legal right under the state nonprofit corporation law to see those records. The corporation insisted that the members' purpose was not proper because it was purely personal in nature. The members claimed that the "bad faith" and acts of alleged misconduct on the*

---

[118] Meyer v. Board of Managers, 583 N.E.2d 14 (Ill. App. 1 Dist. 1991).

[119] Jefferson v. Franklin, 692 So.2d 602 (La. App. 1997). The court quoted from the Louisiana Supreme Court's decision in Burgeois v. Landrum, 396 So.2d 1275 (La. 1981), referred to in the text.

[120] Watson v. The Manhattan Holy Bible Tabernacle, 732 N.Y.S.2d 405 (2001). *Accord* Smith v. Calvary Baptist Church, (N.Y.A.D. 2006).

part of the organization's officers and directors justified their demand for inspection. The court noted that the fact that the members' interest "has a personal aspect to it does not preclude there being a legitimate corporate interest involved." It point out that members of nonprofit corporations "often have something personal to gain in their effort to call corporate policies into question," but concluded that this did not make their purpose any less legitimate. The court provided the following additional clarification: "A proper purpose is one that is germane to the members' status in the corporation. This includes members' right to communicate with fellow members regarding amended bylaws, and the right to investigate management conduct." The court concluded that this test was met.[121]

• An Ohio court ruled that a member of a nonprofit corporation did not have a legal right to inspect corporate records. A nonprofit organization was incorporated under an Ohio statute that gives members a legal right to inspect "all corporate records . . . for any reasonable and proper purpose and at any reasonable time." A member of a nonprofit corporation asked to inspect (1) minutes of the board; (2) financial records; and (3) membership records. His stated purpose was to determine whether or not he had been secretly "excommunicated" from the organization. The member sued the corporation when it refused to respond to his request. A court ruled that the member was not entitled to inspect any of the records in question. It noted that Ohio nonprofit corporation law "requires that two elements be met before the books and records of a nonprofit corporation can be examined: (1) the person requesting the records must be a member of the organization; and (2) the member must have a reasonable and proper purpose for wanting to see the corporate books." The court concluded that the member had no legal right to inspect the corporation's records. On the one hand, if he in fact were not a member, then he would fail the first requirement (only members have a legal right to inspect corporate records). On the other hand, if he in fact was still a member, then he failed the second requirement since there would be no "reasonable and proper purpose" in inspecting corporate records to ascertain this fact.[122]

• A Texas court ruled that the First Amendment does not bar the civil courts from enforcing the rights of church members to inspect church records if such a right is granted by the state nonprofit corporation law under which the church is incorporated.[123]

• The Texas Supreme Court ruled that a state nonprofit corporation law that granted a limited right to inspect corporate records did not mandate the disclosure of donor records.[124] The Texas Nonprofit Corporation Act specifies that nonprofit corporation "shall maintain current true and accurate financial records with full and correct entries made with respect to all financial transactions of the corporation." It further specifies that "all records, books, and annual reports of the financial activity of the corporation shall be kept at the registered office or principal office of the corporation . . . and shall be available to the public for inspection and copying there during normal business hours." Based on these provisions, a group of persons demanded that a charity turn over documents revealing the identities of all donors and the amounts of donors' annual

---

[121] Wells v. League of American Theatres, 706 N.Y.S.2d 599 (Sup. Ct. 2000).

[122] Nozik v. Mentor Lagoons Yacht Club, 678 N.E.2d 948 (Ohio App. 1996).

[123] Lacy v. Bassett, 132 S.W.3d 119 (Tex. App. 14th Dist. 2004).

[124] In re Bacala, 982 S.W.2d 371 (Tex. 1998).

contributions. The charity resisted this request, claiming that the inspection right provided under the nonprofit corporation law did not refer to inspection or disclosure of donor lists, and that even if it did, such a provision would violate the First Amendment freedom of association. The state supreme court ruled that the right of inspection did not extend to donor lists. It noted that "the statute does not expressly require that contributors' identities be made available to the public." And, it found that the intent of the legislature in enacting the inspection right "was not to force nonprofit corporations to identify the exact sources of their income; rather, it was to expose the nature of the expenditures of that money once received from the public and to make nonprofit organizations accountable to their contributors for those expenditures." As a result, the statute "can be upheld as constitutional when interpreted as not requiring disclosure of contributors' names."

▶ *The Privacy Act and Freedom of Information Act have no application to religious organizations. They do not provide church members with any legal basis for inspecting church records.*

Inspection of Church Records

Do church members have a legal right to inspect church records as a result of state nonprofit corporation law? Consider the following:

• Most state nonprofit corporation laws give members a limited right to inspect corporate records.

• The right of inspection is not absolute. It only exists if a church is incorporated under a state nonprofit corporation law that gives members such a right.

• The right of inspection only extends to members.

• The right of inspection only extends to those records specified in the statute creating the right.

• Most such laws provide that the member may inspect documents only "for a proper purpose" at a "reasonable time."

• Some courts have ruled that the right of inspection is limited by considerations of privacy, privilege and confidentiality. That is, some documents may be protected from disclosure by legitimate considerations of privacy (such as an employee's health records); privilege (such as communications protected by the clergy-penitent privilege); or confidentiality (such as reference letters submitted by persons who were given an assurance of confidentiality). [125]

• Any decision to withhold documents from a member should be made with the advice of an attorney.

---

[125] *See, e.g.,* Lewis v. Pennsylvania Bar Association, 701 A.2d 551 (Pa. 1997).

2. Church Charter or Bylaws

A right of inspection may be given by the bylaws or charter of a church corporation or association.

3. State Securities Law

Churches that raise funds by issuing securities (*i.e.*, bonds or promissory notes) may be required by state securities laws to allow investors—whether members or not—to inspect the financial statements of the church.

4. Subpoena

Members and nonmembers alike may compel the production (*i.e.*, disclosure) or inspection of church records as part of a lawsuit against a church if the materials to be produced or inspected are relevant and not privileged. For example, Rule 34 of the Federal Rules of Civil Procedure, adopted by several states and used in all federal courts, specifies that any party to a lawsuit

> may serve on any other party a request (1) to produce and permit the party making the request, or someone acting on his behalf, to inspect and copy, any designated documents . . . which are in the possession, custody or control of the party upon whom the request is served; or (2) to permit entry upon designated land or other property in the possession or control of the party upon whom the request is served for the purpose of inspection . . . .

Similarly, Rule 45(b) of the Federal Rules of Civil Procedure states that a subpoena may command the person to whom it is directed "to produce the books, papers, documents, or tangible things designated therein . . . ." Rule 45 also stipulates that a subpoena may be quashed or modified if it is "unreasonable and oppressive." Federal, state, and local government agencies are also invested with extensive investigative powers, including the right to subpoena and inspect documents. However, this authority generally may not extend to privileged or irrelevant matters.

Since church records are not inherently privileged, they are not immune from production or inspection. Although most states consider confidential communications to be privileged when they are made to clergy acting in their professional capacity as a spiritual adviser, several courts have held that the privilege does not apply to church records.

Case Studies

• *In upholding an IRS subpoena of the records of a religious corporation over its objection that its records were privileged, a federal court observed that the "contention of violation of a penitent-clergyman privilege is without merit. A clergyman must be a natural person."*[126]

---

[126] United States v. Luther, 481 F.2d 429, 432 (9th Cir. 1973) (the court did state that its holding would not prevent "a later determination at a time when the issue is properly raised and supported by a proper showing"). *See also* Abrams v. Temple of the Lost Sheep, Inc., 562 N.Y.S.2d 322 (Sup. Ct. 1990); Abrams v. New York Foundation for the Homeless, Inc., 562 N.Y.S.2d 325 (Sup. Ct. 1990).

• The Ohio Supreme Court, in upholding the admissibility of a church membership registration card over an objection that it was privileged, noted that "this information by any flight of the judicial imagination cannot conceivably be considered as a confession made to [a clergyman] in his professional character in the course of discipline . . . and, of course, is not privileged."[127]

• A New York court ruled that a church's books and records were subject to government inspection as part of an investigation into alleged wrongdoing in soliciting contributions.[128] The state attorney general received reports that the church forced residents of its homeless shelter to "panhandle" contributions on the streets in exchange for room, board, and 25 percent of the moneys collected. There also were allegations that most of the contributions were appropriated for the personal benefit of the church's founder. Accordingly, the attorney general issued a subpoena to the church, directing it to make available for inspection its (1) books and records, (2) leases and deeds, (3) minutes of its governing body and the names and addresses of all directors, officers, and trustees, and (4) copies of all materials used to solicit contributions. The church refused to respond to this subpoena on the ground that it violated its "religious rights." In rejecting the church's claim, the court observed: "There is no doubt that the attorney general has a right to conduct investigations to determine if charitable solicitations are free from fraud and whether charitable assets are being properly used for the benefit of intended beneficiaries." It makes no difference whether or not the organization soliciting the donations is a church or other religious organization, since "religious corporations . . . are still within the attorney general's subpoena power, and investigations by the attorney general of alleged fraudulent behavior may proceed based upon law and the public interest against fraudulent solicitations by so-called religious groups." The court emphasized that the attorney general's investigation did not prevent the church or its members "from practicing their religious activity, nor is it disruptive to such activity."[129]

• A Pennsylvania court ruled that a church cannot avoid inspection of its records in a civil lawsuit by placing them in a location that it designates as a "secret archive." A plaintiff filed a lawsuit against a priest and diocese on account of damages suffered as a result of the priest's acts of child molestation. The plaintiff issued a subpoena to the diocese seeking disclosure of various church documents concerning alleged sexual misconduct with minor male children by priests assigned to the diocese; the complete personnel files of specified priests; and documents kept by the diocese in its secret archives. The diocese refused to produce any documents contained in its secret archives. A state appeals ordered the diocese to turn over the requested information. The court concluded that the requested information was clearly relevant to the lawsuit, and not privileged. It acknowledged that Pennsylvania law contains a "priest-penitent privilege," which protects clergy from disclosing in court any confidential communications made to them while acting in their role as a confessor or counselor. However, the court insisted that "this privilege protects priest-penitent communications; it does not protect information regarding the manner in which a religious institution conducts its affairs or information acquired by a church as a result of independent investigations not involving confidential communications between priest

---

[127] In re Estate of Soeder, 220 N.E.2d 547, 572 (Ohio 1966).

[128] Abrams v. New York Foundation for the Homeless, Inc., 562 N.Y.S.2d 325 (Sup. Ct. 1990); Abrams v. Temple of the Lost Sheep, Inc., 562 N.Y.S.2d 322 (Sup. Ct. 1990).

[129] Id. at 328.

and penitent." The court concluded: "We hold . . . that where the only action required of a religious institution is the disclosure of relevant, non-privileged documents to an adversary in civil litigation, such action, without more, poses no threat of governmental interference with the free exercise of religion. . . . The relevant inquiry is not whether the church gives a file a particular name, but whether disclosure of the information requested from that file interferes with the exercise of religious freedom."[130]

• The Pennsylvania Supreme Court ruled that the clergy-penitent privilege did not excuse a Roman Catholic diocese from turning over internal documents pertaining to a priest in response to a subpoena. An individual (the "defendant") was charged with the murder of a Roman Catholic priest. The defendant admitted that he shot the priest, but he insisted that he did so in self-defense. In attempting to prove that he acted in self-defense, the defendant subpoenaed documents from the local Catholic Diocese. Specifically, the defendant requested the priest's personnel records and the Diocese's records concerning the priest's alleged alcohol and drug abuse and sexual misconduct. The defendant insisted that these documents could help prove that he acted in self-defense because of the priest's past violent conduct. The Diocese turned over some documents but refused to turn over any records kept in its "secret archives." It insisted that documents in its secret archives were protected from disclosure by the clergy-penitent privilege since they had been obtained in confidence by the bishop or other clergy in the course of their duties. The court disagreed, noting that there was no proof that the secret records reflected communications between members of the clergy in confidence and for confessional or spiritual purposes.[131]

"Accountings" of Church Funds

§ 6-03.2

Key point 6-03.2. *Most courts have viewed requests by church members for an "accounting" of church funds to be an internal church matter over which the civil courts have no jurisdiction.*

Do church members, or a government agency or officer, have the right to demand an accounting of church funds? The courts have reached conflicting answers to this question.

Case Studies

• A group of church members who had contributed funds to their church demanded that the church give an "accounting" of the use of the contributed funds. When the church refused, the members turned to the courts for relief. A trial judge ordered an immediate accounting, as well as annual audits "forever," and required the church to

---

[130] Hutchison v. Luddy, 606 A.2d 905 (Pa. Super. 1992). *Accord* Niemann v. Cooley, 637 N.E.2d 943 (Ohio App. 1 Dist. 1994). *But see* State v. Burns, 830 P.2d 1318 (Mont. 1992) (Montana Supreme Court ruled that a priest's personnel file maintained by a diocese did not have to be disclosed in response to a subpoena).

[131] Commonwealth v. Stewart, 690 A.2d 195 (Pa. 1997).

disclose the contents of a church safety deposit box to the complaining members. The church appealed, arguing that the civil courts had no jurisdiction over a church, and even if they did, they had no authority to order accountings or annual audits. A Florida court, in upholding the trial judge's ruling regarding an accounting and inspection of the church's safety deposit box, observed that "we are of the opinion that this is not an improper interference by the government into a church, or ecclesiastical, matter. When the members of the church decided to incorporate their body under the laws of the state of Florida, they submitted themselves to the jurisdiction of the state courts in all matters of a corporate nature, such as accounting for funds." However, the court reversed the trial judge's order requiring annual audits forever, since "we cannot agree it is proper to order annual, ad infinitum, audits of the books" of a church.[132]

• The Supreme Judicial Court of Maine ruled that a state has the authority to demand an accounting of church trust funds. In 1939, a wealthy individual made a gift of a substantial amount of stock to a church, subject to the following two conditions: (1) the church was to use the trust fund for "charitable uses and purposes," and (2) the church was not to sell or transfer the stock for a period of fifty years. In 1983, after faithfully observing the terms of the trust for forty-four years, the church sought court permission to sell the stock. It noted that the value of the stock had fallen sharply and the rate of return was substantially less than could be achieved with other investments. The court permitted the church to sell the stock (then valued at $733,000) in order to protect the trust fund. In 1987, the state attorney general received information suggesting that the church was not carrying out the terms of the trust. The attorney general asked the church for an accounting of the trust fund. When the church refused to comply, the attorney general sought a court order compelling the church to provide an accounting. The church argued that the First Amendment guaranty of religious freedom protected the church from complying with the demand for an accounting. The court rejected the church's position. It noted that the attorney general had the legal authority to ensure that the church was complying with the trust purpose, and this authority included the right to demand an accounting of trust funds. In rejecting the church's First Amendment argument, the court observed: "The attorney general is not attempting to inquire into the financial affairs of the church, or impose a regulatory scheme, but only to obtain the information necessary for him to fulfill his statutory obligation to the public. Because we find that the trust is a public trust, separate and distinct from the church, the court ordered accounting can be accomplished by application of neutral principles of law and therefore, does not impinge upon the church's First Amendment freedoms."[133]

• The Oklahoma Supreme Court refused to permit a number of dismissed church members to inspect church records or demand an accounting of church funds. Five members of a local church became concerned over the way their pastor and church board were conducting church business. The members filed a lawsuit asking a civil court to issue an order giving them access to the church's financial records. The members were immediately dismissed by a unanimous vote of the church at a hastily called business meeting. The Supreme Court refused to permit them to inspect the church's financial records. The former members insisted that they needed access to these records to prove that church leaders diverted church funds to uses that were not

---

[132] Matthews v. Adams, 520 So.2d 334 (Fl. App. 1988).

[133] Attorney General v. First United Baptist Church, 601 A.2d 96 (Me. 1992).

authorized by the church. The court observed: "Some of their claims alleging diversion of church property to non-church uses may have been capable of invoking civil judicial relief, and some may not have been. . . . We need not, however, address the extent to which their claims were cognizable when they filed suit, because their expulsion mooted any claims they had as to the diversion of church property to non-church uses." In other words, non-members no longer have "standing" to use the courts to protect their former church from an alleged diversion of funds to unauthorized uses. Only members can sue to protect church assets.[134]

• *An Illinois court ruled that it lacked jurisdiction to resolve a lawsuit brought by church members who demanded an accounting of church funds. Six members of a church filed a lawsuit asking the court to order an accounting of church funds as a result of what they perceived to be financial irregularities involving their minister. A state appeals court declined the members' request. It observed, "It is eminently clear that the basis of this lawsuit is to have the courts examine the way the church is managing its financial affairs; to substitute the prudence of a court's judgment for that of the [minister] who is entrusted by church doctrine to exercise such judgment; to impose court supervision over all financial matters of an entire religious faith; and to have a court interfere with the proper succession in the hierarchy of a religious faith. These matters, however, are beyond the realm of judicial jurisdiction."*[135]

• *A court in the District of Columbia ruled that the First Amendment guaranty of religious freedom prevents the civil courts from resolving internal church disputes over accounting and reporting practices, except in limited circumstances. The court acknowledged that the First Amendment guaranty of religious freedom greatly restricts the authority of the civil courts to resolve internal church disputes, including those involving alleged accounting or reporting irregularities. However, the court concluded that the First Amendment would not bar the civil courts from resolving such disputes if they could do so on the basis of clear, objective accounting and reporting criteria requiring no inquiry into religious doctrine—assuming that a church in fact had adopted them. A civil court could enforce such rules since it "would not have a role in deciding what principles apply to the church; the court merely would be asked to apply, without ecclesiastical judgment or intrusion, a previously prescribed, authoritative, nondiscretionary, and clear, policy." The court gave eight examples of accounting and reporting irregularities that the civil courts cannot resolve: (1) What should be the collection, tithing, or offering practices of the church? (2) Should the church pursue pledges from—or take any other particular type of action affecting—members who neglect to remit their obligations? (3) What cash management and investment decisions should be made? (4) Who in the church establishes its spending priorities? (5) Should the pastor have one or more discretionary funds? (6) Should there be an audit committee, and if so, should its membership be internal, external, or both, and how many members of each type should there be? (7) Should the church maintain any of its funds as imprest accounts useable only for specified purposes, or should church finances be operated as a general account? (8) For each of the above questions, who makes the decision? The civil courts cannot resolve these questions since they cannot do so without delving into church doctrine and polity.*[136]

---

[134] Fowler v. Bailey, 844 P.2d 141 (Okla. 1992).

[135] Rizzuto v. Rematt, 653 N.E.2d 34 (Ill. App. 1995).

[136] Bible Way Church v. Beards, 680 A.2d 419 (D.C. App. 1996)

Public Inspection of
Tax-Exemption Applications   § 6-03.3

Key point 6-03.3. *Federal law requires tax-exempt organizations to provide a copy of their application for exemption (and supporting materials) upon request. There is no exemption for churches, although many churches have not applied for recognition of tax-exempt status and therefore will have no documents to provide in response to such a request. Many churches are covered by a denominational agency's "group exemption" ruling. Such churches must provide a copy of the group ruling in response to a request for a copy of their tax exemption application.*

Any organization that is exempt from federal income taxation (including churches and religious denominations) must make available a copy of the following materials in response to a request from a member of the public:

- the exemption application form (Form 1023) submitted to the IRS;

- any supporting documents submitted with the exemption application, including legal briefs or a response to questions from the IRS; and

- any letter or document issued by the IRS with respect to the exemption application (such as a favorable determination letter or a list of questions from the IRS about the application).[137]

The exemption application must be made available for inspection, without charge, at the organization's principal office during regular business hours. The organization may have an employee present during inspection, but must allow the individual to take notes freely and to photocopy at no charge if the individual provides the photocopying equipment.

An exempt organization also must provide a copy of its exemption application to anyone who requests a copy either in person or in writing at its principal office during regular business hours. If the individual made the request in person, the copy must be provided on the same business day the request is made unless there are unusual circumstances. The organization must honor a written request for a copy of documents or specific parts or schedules of documents that are required to be disclosed. However, this rule only applies if the request (1) is addressed to the exempt organization's principal office; (2) is sent to that address by mail, electronic mail (e-mail), facsimile (fax), or a private delivery service approved by the IRS; and (3) gives the address to where the copy of the document should be sent. The organization must mail the copy within 30 days from the date it receives the request. The organization may request payment in advance and must then provide the copies within 30 days from the date it receives payment.

The organization may charge a reasonable fee for providing copies. It can charge no more for the copies than the per page rate the IRS charges for providing copies. The IRS may not charge more for copies than the fees listed in the Freedom of Information Act (FOIA) fee schedule. Although the IRS charges

---

[137] IRS Notice 88-120, 1988-2 C.B. 4541.

no fee for the first 100 pages, the organization can charge a fee for all copies. For non-commercial requesters, the FOIA schedule currently provides a rate of $.20 per page. The organization can also charge the actual postage costs it pays to provide the copies.

Many churches never filed an exemption application with the IRS because they are covered by a "group exemption" obtained by their denomination. If such a church receives a request for inspection of its exemption application, it must make available for public inspection, or provide copies of: (1) The application submitted to the IRS by the central or parent organization to obtain the group exemption letter, and (2) those documents which were submitted by the central or parent organization to include the local or subordinate organization in the group exemption letter. However, if the central or parent organization submits to the IRS a list or directory of local or subordinate organizations covered by the group exemption letter, the local or subordinate organization is required to provide only the application for the group exemption ruling and the pages of the list or directory that specifically refer to it.

In lieu of allowing an inspection, the local or subordinate organization may mail a copy of the applicable documents to the person requesting inspection within the same time period. In this case, the organization can charge the requester for copying and actual postage costs only if the requester consents to the charge. If the local or subordinate organization receives a written request for a copy of its annual information return, it must fulfill the request by providing a copy of the group return in the time and manner specified earlier. The requester has the option of requesting from the central or parent organization, at its principal office, inspection or copies of group returns filed by the central or parent organization. The central or parent organization must fulfill such requests in the time and manner specified earlier.

If an exempt organization maintains one or more "regional or district offices," the exemption application (and related materials) "shall be made available at each such district or regional office as well as at the principal office." This rule will be relevant to many religious denominations. Churches and religious denominations should be aware of these new requirements, since some undoubtedly will receive requests for inspection.

The penalty for failure to allow public inspection of exemption applications is $20 for each day the failure continues. The penalty for willful failure to allow public inspection of a an exemption application is $5,000 for each return or application. The penalty also applies to a willful failure to provide copies.

Government Inspection of Donor and Membership Lists §6-03.4

Key point 6-03.4. *Church donor and membership lists are subject to government inspection, so long as the government has a compelling interest in obtaining this information.*

Whether the government has the right to compel religious organizations to release the *names of members and contributors* is a hotly contested issue. In 1958, the United States Supreme Court ruled that the freedom to associate with others for the advancement of beliefs and ideas is a right protected by the First Amendment against governmental infringement, whether the beliefs sought to be advanced are political, economic, religious, or cultural.[138] The Court acknowledged that the right of association is nowhere mentioned in the First Amendment, but it reasoned that such a right must be inferred in order to make the express First Amendment rights of speech and assembly more secure. The court concluded that an order by the State of Alabama seeking to compel disclosure of the name of every member of the National Association for the Advancement of Colored People in Alabama constituted an impermissible restraint upon members' freedom of association, since on past occasions "revelation of the identity of its rank-and-file members has exposed these members to economic reprisal, loss of employment, threat of physical coercion, and other manifestations of public hostility. Under these circumstances, we think it apparent that compelled disclosure of [the NAACP's] Alabama membership is likely to affect adversely the ability of [the NAACP] and its members to pursue their collective effort to foster beliefs which they admittedly have the right to advocate, in that it may induce members to withdraw from the Association and dissuade others from joining it . . . ."[139]

It is clear that governmental actions that may have the effect of curtailing the freedom of association are subject to the closest scrutiny. Yet the courts have made it clear that the right to associate is not absolute; a "significant interference" with the right may be tolerated if the government (1) avoids unnecessary interference, (2) demonstrates a sufficiently important interest, and (3) employs the least intrusive means of achieving its interests.[140]

The Supreme Court has observed that "decisions . . . must finally turn, therefore, on whether [the government] has demonstrated so cogent an interest in obtaining and making public the membership lists . . . as to justify the substantial abridgement of associational freedom which such disclosures will effect. Where there is a significant encroachment upon personal liberty, the state may prevail only upon showing a subordinating interest which is compelling."[141]

Government demands for the production and inspection of membership and contributor lists frequently are approved on the ground that a compelling governmental interest exists.

Case Studies

• *A federal appeals court upheld the enforcement of an IRS summons seeking the name of every individual who had contributed property other than securities to Brigham Young*

---

[138] National Association for the Advancement of Colored People v. Alabama, 357 U.S. 449 (1958).

[139] *Id.* at 462-63.

[140] Cousins v. Wigoda, 419 U.S. 477, 488 (1975).

[141] Bates v. Little Rock, 361 U.S. 516, 524 (1960).

University (BYU) during a three-year period.[142] Before issuing the summons, the IRS had audited the returns of 162 taxpayers who had contributed property to the university during the years in question. In each instance the amount of the contribution claimed by the taxpayer was overvalued, and in many cases grossly overvalued. As a result, the IRS surmised that many other contributors had overvalued their contributions as well. The university challenged the summons on the ground that the IRS was without a reasonable basis for believing that the remaining contributors had overvalued their contributions. The university further asserted that the information sought was readily available to the IRS through its own files, and that enforcement of the summons would infringe upon the contributors' freedom of association under the First Amendment. The court, in upholding the summons, observed that "having previously examined the returns of some 162 donors of gifts in kind to BYU and having found that all were overvalued, the IRS has established a reasonable basis for believing that some of the remaining donors of in kind gifts may have also overvalued their gifts."[143]

• The Federal Communications Commission (FCC) received complaints that a religious broadcaster was not expending contributed funds as indicated in over-the-air solicitations. As part of its investigation, the FCC ordered the broadcaster to divulge the names of all contributors and the amount of each contribution. The broadcaster refused to comply on the ground that such information was protected by the First Amendment freedoms of religion and association. An FCC administrative tribunal ruled that under the circumstances the agency had a compelling interest in obtaining disclosure of the names of contributors and the amounts of contributions, and that this interest outweighed the freedoms of religion and association. A federal appeals court affirmed this determination on the grounds that (1) the government has a compelling interest in preventing the diversion of funds contributed for specific, identified purposes, especially when such funds are obtained through the use of the public airwaves, which, by congressional mandate, must be operated in the public interest; (2) the allegations of diversion of funds were made by a former employee and therefore they were entitled to a greater inference of reliability; (3) the government's investigation was narrow and avoided unnecessary interference with the free exercise of religion; and (4) the government's request for records was necessary to serve its compelling interest in investigating the alleged diversion of funds.[144]

• A federal court in the District of Columbia ruled that a church could not be forced to disclose the names of its members in a lawsuit. The court observed: "There is . . . implicit in the First Amendment's guarantee of religious freedom, the right to choose whether or not to disclose one's religious affiliation lest forced disclosure inhibit the free exercise of one's faith. I have to believe that, when a person provides her name and address to a church that has asked her to become a member, she reasonably expects that her name and address will be disclosed to other church members, used by the church to invite her to other church functions, and used to solicit her contribution to the church's financial welfare. There is nothing I know of in the American experience that suggests to me that by giving one's name and address to a church one thereby agrees to the publication of one's religious affiliation to the whole world."[145]

---

[142] United States v. Brigham Young University, 679 F.2d 1345 (10th Cir. 1982).

[143] Id. at 1349.

[144] Scott v. Rosenberg, 702 F.2d 1263 (9th Cir. 1983).

[145] Johnson v. The Washington Times Corporation, 208 F.R.D. 16 (D.D.C. 2002).

• *A California court ruled that the right to associational privacy extends to private lawsuits as well as governmental investigations, and thus a litigant has no right to compel disclosure of the membership list of a church unless he can establish a compelling state interest justifying disclosure.[146]*

• *A New York court ruled that the constitutional guaranty of religious freedom did not excuse a church from producing its records in response to a grand jury subpoena. During a tax investigation, the state attorney general subpoenaed several records and documents from a church. The church challenged the validity of the subpoena on the ground that disclosure of the documents would violate the constitutional rights of the church and its members. Church representatives argued that disclosure of the records would reveal the identities of contributors to the church in violation of the church's belief (based on Matthew 6:1-4) that "charity should be given in secrecy." The court rejected the church's claim. It noted that "it is hard to conceive that release of charge or credit account records, or records of employees' travel expense accounts, would have any likelihood whatsoever" of violating any religious beliefs or tenets of the church. The court agreed that the disclosure of some records would violate contributor's constitutional guaranty of religious freedom. It cited cash receipts records and bank statements. The court further agreed that disclosure of records revealing the charitable recipients of church funds (e.g., canceled checks and bank statements) also might violate the church's rights. However, the church would be required to disclose these records if the state could prove that the alleged violation of the church's rights was outweighed by a "compelling state interest to which the information sought is substantially related" and that the "state's ends may not be achieved by less restrictive means." The court concluded that such was the case here, since the church's records were sought in connection with an investigation into tax-related offenses including underreporting of compensation paid to officers and employees and diversion of church funds to nonreligious purposes, and "it is by now well settled that enforcement of a state's revenue laws constitutes a compelling governmental interest."[147]*

It is not clear whether the government needs to prove a "compelling interest" to inspect church membership or donor records following the Supreme Court's 1990 decision in the *Smith* case.[148] In *Smith*, the Court ruled that "neutral laws of general applicability" are presumably valid without the need for demonstrating a "compelling state interest." Statutes that give government agencies a broad authority to collect information (including church membership or donor information) may well be deemed "neutral laws of general applicability" by the courts. But this does not necessarily mean that such agencies can inspect church records without proof of a compelling state interest.

In the *Smith* case the Supreme Court observed that the compelling government interest test applies if a neutral and generally applicable law burdens not only the exercise of religion, but also some other First Amendment right (such as the right of association, described above). The Court observed: "The only decisions

---

[146] Church of Hakeem, Inc. v. Superior Court, 168 Cal. Rptr. 13 (1980).

[147] Full Gospel Tabernacle, Inc. v. Attorney General, 536 N.Y.S.2d 201 (1988). *See also* Abrams v. Temple of the Lost Sheep, Inc., 562 N.Y.S.2d 322 (Sup. Ct. 1990); Abrams v. New York Foundation for the Homeless, Inc., 562 N.Y.S.2d 325 (Sup. Ct. 1990).

[148] Employment Division v. Smith, 110 S. Ct. 1595 (1990).

in which we have held that the First Amendment bars application of a neutral, generally applicable law to religiously motivated action have involved not the free exercise clause alone, but the free exercise clause in conjunction with other constitutional protections, such as freedom of speech and of the press . . . ." In other words, if a neutral and generally applicable law or governmental practice burdens the exercise of religion, then the compelling governmental interest standard can be triggered if the religious institution or adherent can point to some other First Amendment interest that is being violated. In many cases, this will not be hard to do.

If the identities of all members or contributors are not reasonably relevant to a particular governmental investigation, the government's interest in disclosure will not be sufficiently compelling to outweigh the constitutionally protected interests of members and contributors.[149]

▶ Neither the Privacy Act of 1974 nor the Freedom of Information Act applies to church records.

The Church Audit Procedures Act

§ 6-03.5

Key point 6-03.5. *The Church Audit Procedures Act provides churches with a number of important protections in the event of an IRS inquiry or examination. However, there are some exceptions.*

Section 7602 of the tax code gives the IRS broad authority to examine or subpoena the books and records of any person or organization for the purposes of (1) ascertaining the correctness of any federal tax return, (2) making a return where none has been filed, (3) determining the liability of any person or organization for any federal tax, or (4) collecting any federal tax. This authority has been held to apply to churches.[150] However, in 1984 Congress enacted the Church Audit Procedures Act to provide churches with important protections when faced with an IRS audit. The Act's protections are contained in section 7611 of the tax code. They are summarized below.

1. Church Tax Inquiries

Section 7611 refers to church tax inquiries and church tax examinations. A church tax inquiry is defined as any IRS inquiry to a church (with exceptions noted below) for the purpose of determining whether the organization qualifies for tax exemption as a church or whether it is carrying on an unrelated trade

---

[149] *See, e.g.,* Savola v. Webster, 644 F.2d 743 (8th Cir. 1981); Familias Unidas v. Briscoe, 619 F.2d 391 (5th Cir. 1980).

[150] *See, e.g.,* United States v. Coates, 692 F.2d 629 (9th Cir. 1982); United States v. Dykema, 666 F.2d 1096 (7th Cir. 1981); United States v. Freedom Church, 613 F.2d 316 (1st Cir. 1979).

or business or is otherwise engaged in activities subject to tax. An inquiry is considered to commence when the IRS requests information or materials from a church of a type contained in church records. The IRS may begin a church tax inquiry only if:

• an appropriate high-level Treasury official (defined as "the Secretary of the Treasury or any delegate of the Secretary whose rank is no lower than that of a principal Internal Revenue officer for an internal revenue region") reasonably believes on the basis of written evidence that the church is not exempt (by reason of its status as a church), may be carrying on an unrelated trade or business, or is otherwise engaged in activities subject to taxation; and

• the IRS sends the church written inquiry notice containing an explanation of the following: (1) the specific concerns which gave rise to the inquiry, (2) the general subject matter of the inquiry, and (3) the provisions of the tax code that authorize the inquiry and the applicable administrative and constitutional provisions, including the right to an informal conference with the IRS before any examination of church records, and the First Amendment principle of separation of church and state.

2. Church Tax Examinations

The IRS may begin a church tax examination of the church records or religious activities of a church only under the following conditions: (1) the requirements of a church tax inquiry have been met; and (2) an examination notice is sent by the IRS to the church at least 15 days after the day on which the inquiry notice was sent, and at least 15 days before the beginning of such an examination, containing the following information: (a) a copy of the inquiry notice, (b) a specific description of the church records and religious activities which the IRS seeks to examine, (c) an offer to conduct an informal conference with the church to discuss and possibly resolve the concerns giving rise to the examination, and (d) a copy of all documents collected or prepared by the IRS for use in the examination, and the disclosure of which is required by the Freedom of Information Act.

3. Church Records

Church records (defined as all corporate and financial records regularly kept by a church, including corporate minute books and lists of members and contributors) may be examined only to the extent necessary to determine the liability for and amount of any income, employment, or excise tax.

4. Religious Activities

Religious activities may be examined only to the extent necessary to determine whether an organization claiming to be a church is, in fact, a church.

5. Deadline for completing church tax inquiries

Church tax inquiries not followed by an examination notice must be completed not later than 90 days after the inquiry notice date. Church tax inquiries and church tax examinations must be completed not later than 2 years after the examination notice date. The 2-year limitation can be suspended (1) if the church brings a judicial proceeding against the IRS; (2) if the IRS brings a judicial proceeding to compel compliance by the church with any reasonable request for examination of church records or religious activities; (3) for any period in excess of 20 days (but not more than 6 months) in which the church fails to comply with any reasonable request by the IRS for church records; or (4) if the IRS and church mutually agree.

Key point. *A federal appeals court ruled that the revocation of a church's tax-exempt status by the IRS could not be challenged on the ground that the IRS's examination of the church exceeded the two-year limit imposed by the Church Audit Procedures Act. The court noted that the Act specifies that "no suit may be maintained, and no defense may be raised in any proceeding . . . by reason of any noncompliance by the [IRS] with the requirements of this section."[151]*

6. Written Opinion of IRS Legal Counsel

The IRS can make a determination, based on a church tax inquiry or church tax examination, that an organization is not a church that is exempt from federal income taxation, or that is qualified to receive tax-deductible contributions, or that otherwise owes any income, employment, or excise tax (including the unrelated business income tax), only if the appropriate regional legal counsel of the IRS determines in writing that there has been substantial compliance with the limitations imposed under section 7611 and approves in writing of such revocation of exemption or assessment of tax.

7. Statute of Limitations

Church tax examinations involving tax-exempt status or the liability for any tax other than the unrelated business income tax may be begun only for any one or more of the three most recent taxable years ending before the examination notice date. For examinations involving unrelated business taxable income, or if a church is proven not to be exempt for any of the preceding three years, the IRS may examine relevant records and assess tax as part of the same audit for a total of six years preceding the examination notice date. For examinations involving issues other than revocation of exempt status or unrelated business taxable income (such as examinations pertaining to employment taxes), no limitation period applies if no return has been filed.

8. Limitation on Repeat Inquiries and Examinations

If any church tax inquiry or church tax examination is completed and does not result in a revocation of exemption or assessment of taxes, then no other church tax inquiry or church tax examination may begin with respect to such church during the five-year period beginning on the examination notice date (or the inquiry notice date if no examination notice was sent) unless such inquiry or examination is (1) approved in writing by the Assistant Commissioner of Employee Plans and Exempt Organizations of the IRS, or (2) does not involve the same or similar issues involved in the prior inquiry or examination. The

---

[151] Music Square Church v. United States, 2000-2 USTC ¶50,578 (Fed. Cir. 2000).

five-year period is suspended if the two-year limitation on the completion of an examination is suspended.

9. Exceptions

The limitations on church tax inquiries and church tax examinations do not apply to:

- Inquiries or examinations pertaining to organizations other than churches (the term "church" is defined by section 7611 as any organization claiming to be a church, and any convention or association of churches; the term does not include separately incorporated church-affiliated schools or other separately incorporated church-affiliated organizations).

- Any case involving a knowing failure to file a tax return or a willful attempt to defeat or evade taxes.

- Criminal investigations.

- The tax liability of a contributor to a church, or inquiries regarding assignment of income to a church or a vow of poverty by an individual followed by a transfer of property.[152]

- Routine IRS inquiries, including (1) the filing or failure to file any tax return or information return by the church; (2) compliance with income tax or FICA tax withholding; (3) supplemental information needed to complete the mechanical processing of any incomplete or incorrect return filed by a church; (4) information necessary to process applications for exempt status, letter ruling requests, or employment tax exempt requests; or (5) confirmation that a specific business is or is not owned by a church.

10. Application to Excess Benefit Transactions

The tax regulations specify that the procedures of section 7611 will be used in initiating and conducting any inquiry or examination into whether an excess benefit transaction has occurred between a church and a disqualified person. For purposes of this rule, the reasonable belief required to initiate a church tax inquiry is satisfied if there is a reasonable belief that a section 4958 tax is due from a disqualified person with respect to a transaction involving a church.[153]

11. Remedy for IRS Violations

If the IRS has not complied substantially with (1) the notice requirements, (2) the requirement that an appropriate high-level Treasury official approve the commencement of a church tax inquiry, or (3) the requirement of informing the

---

[152] *See, e.g.,* St. German of Alaska Eastern Orthodox Catholic Church v. Commissioner, 840 F.2d 1087 (2nd Cir. 1988); United States v. Coates, 692 F.2d 629 (9th Cir. 1982); United States v. Life Science Church of America, 636 F.2d 221 (8th Cir. 1980); United States v. Holmes, 614 F.2d 895 (5th Cir. 1980); United States v. Freedom Church, 613 F.2d 316 (1st Cir. 1979).

[153] Treas. Reg. 53.4958-8(b). The subject of excess benefit transactions is addressed fully in chapter 4 of Richard Hammar's annual *Church and Clergy Tax Guide.*

church of its right to an informal conference, the church's exclusive remedy is a stay of the inquiry or examination until such requirements are satisfied.

12. Legal Requirements for an IRS Subpoena

The fact that the IRS has authority to examine church records and the religious activities of a church or religious denomination does not necessarily establish its right to do so. The courts have held that an IRS summons or subpoena directed at church records must satisfy the following conditions to be enforceable.

Issued in good faith

Good faith in this context means that (1) the investigation will be conducted pursuant to a legitimate purpose; (2) the inquiry is necessary to that purpose; (3) the information sought is not already within the IRS's possession; and (4) the proper administrative steps have been followed. In the *Powell* case,[154] the United States Supreme Court held that in order to obtain judicial enforcement of a summons or subpoena, the IRS must prove "that the investigation will be conducted pursuant to a legitimate purpose, that the inquiry may be relevant to the purpose, that the information sought is not already in the Commissioner's possession, and that the administrative steps required by the tax code have been followed."

The *Powell* case did not involve an IRS examination of church records. In the *Holmes* case,[155] a federal appeals court held that section 7605(c) narrowed the scope of the second part of the *Powell* test from mere relevancy to necessity in the context of church records, since it required that an examination of church records be limited "to the extent necessary." The "necessity test" should apply to church inquiries or examinations conducted under section 7611, since the same language is employed.[156]

No violation of the church's First Amendment right to freely exercise its religion

An IRS subpoena will not violate a church's First Amendment rights unless it substantially burdens a legitimate and sincerely held religious belief and is not supported by a compelling governmental interest that cannot be accomplished by less restrictive means. This is a difficult test to satisfy, not only because few churches can successfully demonstrate that enforcement of an IRS summons or subpoena substantially burdens an actual religious tenet, but also because the courts have ruled that maintenance of the integrity of the government's fiscal policies constitutes a compelling governmental interest that overrides religious beliefs to the contrary.[157]

---

[154] United States v. Powell, 379 U.S. 48 (1964).

[155] United States v. Holmes, 614 F.2d 985 (5th Cir. 1980).

[156] United States v. Church of Scientology, 90-2 U.S.T.C. ¶ 50,349 (D. Mass. 1990).

[157] *See, e.g.,* St. German of Alaska Eastern Orthodox Catholic Church v. Commissioner, 840 F.2d 1087 (2nd Cir. 1988); United States v. Coates, 692 F.2d 629 (9th Cir. 1982); United States v. Life Science Church of America, 636 F.2d 221 (8th Cir. 1980); United States v. Holmes, 614 F.2d 895 (5th Cir. 1980); United States v. Freedom Church, 613 F.2d 316 (1st Cir. 1979).

No impermissible entanglement of church and state

The IRS subpoena must not create an excessive entanglement between church and state.[158] Federal law provides that if the IRS wants to retroactively revoke the tax-exempt status of a church, it must show either that the church "omitted or misstated a material fact" in its original exemption application or that the church has been "operated in a manner materially different from that originally represented."[159]

Although IRS authority to examine and subpoena church records is broad, it has limits. To illustrate, one subpoena was issued against all documents relating to the organizational structure of a church since its inception; all correspondence files for a three-year period; the minutes of the officers, directors, trustees, and ministers for the same three-year period; and a sample of every piece of literature pertaining to the church.[160] A court concluded that this subpoena was "too far reaching" and declared it invalid. It noted, however, that a "properly narrowed" subpoena would not violate the First Amendment.

Another federal court that refused to enforce an IRS subpoena directed at a church emphasized that "the unique status afforded churches by Congress requires that the IRS strictly adhere to its own procedures when delving into church activities."[161] The court also stressed that the safeguards afforded churches under federal law prevent the IRS from "going on a fishing expedition into church books and records."

13. Examples

The limitations of section 7611 are illustrated by the following examples.

Example. *First Church receives substantial rental income each year from several residential properties it owns in the vicinity of the church. The IRS has learned of the rental properties and would like to determine whether the church is engaged in an unrelated trade or business. It sends the church an inquiry notice in which the only explanation of the concerns giving rise to the inquiry is a statement that "you may be engaged in an unrelated trade or business." This inquiry notice is defective, since it does not specify the activities which may result in unrelated business taxable income.*

Example. *The IRS receives a telephone tip that First Church may be engaged in an unrelated trade or business. A telephone tip cannot serve as the basis for a church tax inquiry, since such an inquiry may commence only if an appropriate high-level Treasury official reasonably believes, on the basis of written evidence, that a church is not tax-exempt, is carrying on an unrelated trade or business, or otherwise is engaged in activities subject to taxation.*

---

[158] *See generally* United States v. Coates, 692 F.2d 629 (9th Cir. 1982); United States v. Grayson County State Bank, 656 F.2d 1070 (5th Cir. 1981); EEOC v. Southwestern Baptist Theological Seminary, 651 F.2d 277 (5th Cir. 1981) (application of 1964 Civil Rights Act's reporting requirements to seminary did not violate First Amendment).

[159] Treas. Reg. 601.201(n)(6)(i).

[160] United States v. Holmes, 614 F.2d 985 (5th Cir. 1980). *See also* United States v. Trader's State Bank, 695 F.2d 1132 (9th Cir. 1983) (IRS summons seeking production of all of a church's bank statements, correspondence, and records relating to bank accounts, safe deposit boxes, and loans held to be overly broad).

[161] United States v. Church of Scientology of Boston, 739 F.Supp. 46 (D. Mass. 1990).

Example. *The IRS sends First Church written notice of a church tax inquiry on March 1. On March 10 of the same year it sends written notice that it will examine designated church records on April 15. The examination notice is defective. While it was sent at least 15 days before the beginning of the examination, it was sent less than 15 days after the date the inquiry notice was sent. The church's only remedy is a stay of the examination until the IRS sends a valid examination notice.*

Example. *An IRS inquiry notice does not mention the possible application of the First Amendment principle of separation of church and state to church audits. Such a notice is defective. A church's only remedy is a stay of the inquiry until the IRS sends a valid inquiry notice.*

Example. *An IRS examination notice specifies that the religious activities of First Church will be examined as part of an investigation into a possible unrelated business income tax liability. Such an examination is inappropriate, since the religious activities of a church may be examined by the IRS under section 7611 only to the extent necessary to determine if a church is, in fact, a bona fide church entitled to tax-exempt status.*

Example. *The IRS sends First Church written notice of a church tax inquiry on August 1. As of October 20 of the same year, no examination notice had been sent. The church tax inquiry must be concluded by November 1.*

Example. *In 2008 the IRS conducted an examination of the tax-exempt status of First Church. It concluded that the church was properly exempt from federal income taxation. In 2011 the IRS commences an examination of First Church to determine if it is engaged in an unrelated trade or business and if it has been withholding taxes from nonminister employees. Such an examination is not barred by the prohibition against repeated examinations within a five-year period, since it does not involve the same or similar issues.*

Example. *First Church knowingly fails to withhold federal income taxes from wages paid to its nonminister employees despite its knowledge that it is legally required to do so. The limitations imposed upon the IRS by section 7611 do not apply.*

Example. *The IRS commences an examination of a separately incorporated private school that is controlled by First Church. The limitations of section 7611 do not apply.*

Who Owns a Church's Accounting Records? § 6-03.6

Who owns a church's accounting records, and who has the right to maintain possession of them? Consider the following points:

1. The nonprofit corporation laws under which most churches are incorporated require that corporations maintain various kinds of records, including financial books of account. To illustrate, the Model Nonprofit

Corporation Act, which has been adopted by most states, provides that "a corporation shall maintain appropriate accounting records." While this language does not directly address ownership, the fact is that how can a church maintain appropriate accounting records if they are possessed and "owned" by the treasurer? As a result, it should be assumed that the church is the owner of its financial records, and not a volunteer treasurer who takes them home. The takeaway point is that location, and even possession, does not determine ownership.

2. Allowing a volunteer treasurer to take the church's accounting records home is not recommended, for several reasons, including the following: (1) Such a procedure violates two of the core principles of internal control—segregation of duties and oversight over operations. Imagine the financial improprieties that could go undetected under such an arrangement. (2) Irreplaceable financial records may be lost, stolen, or destroyed while in the home of the church treasurer, and confidential information may be accessed by family members. (3) Church staff will be frustrated in the performance of their duties because of the inaccessibility of the church's financial records. (4) Such an arrangement can provide a treasurer with "leverage" that can be exerted to achieve ulterior objectives. (5) Such an arrangement may result in the permanent inaccessibility of church records in the event of a dispute with the treasurer, or at such time as the treasurer leaves office voluntarily or involuntarily.

3. Church leaders should check the church's bylaws or other governing document to determine what, if any, authority the treasurer may have over the church's financial records. Some church bylaws state that the treasurer shall have "custody" of the church's financial records, or "be responsible" for them. But custody and responsibility are not the same as ownership, although such terminology suggests that the treasurer is authorized to remove the church's financial records to his or her home. For the reasons stated, this generally is not advisable, and so church leaders should review their governing document in order to identify and amend such a provision should one exist.

4. The same logic applies to paid employees. A church's bookkeeper, business administrator, or other paid employee should not keep financial records at home. An additional consideration applies to employees—the federal Fair Labor Standards Act. The FLSA guarantees overtime pay for hours worked in excess of 40 during the same week. States have their own requirements. The point is that churches have no way to monitor hours worked by an employee in his or her residence, and so compliance with the FLSA is virtually impossible. Some churches allow employees to take church records home to work on them as unpaid "volunteers." But this is not permissible, according to Department of Labor interpretations of the FLSA. The bottom line is that allowing church employees to take

church records home in order to work with them may expose a church to significant liability under the FLSA or a state counterpart.

5. Some church leaders allow financial records to be kept in the private residence of a treasurer or other church officer or employee to preserve them from theft or a natural disaster affecting the church office. This risk can be managed by storing the records in a locked and immovable fireproof cabinet. After data on financial records is integrated into the church's computer software, backup copies can be stored off-site.

6. AICPA Statement on Auditing Standards (SAS) number 96 ("Audit Documentation") requires CPAs to maintain specified kinds of documentation when performing an audit. Most states have enacted laws specifying that CPAs own the working papers and other documentation they prepare in performing their duties. As a result, a church ordinarily cannot assert ownership in the working papers of CPAs who are retained to perform an audit of the church.

Reporting Requirements § 6-04

Churches may be subject to a number of reporting requirements under state and federal law. The more common requirements are summarized in this section.

State Law § 6-04.1

Key point 6-04.1. *Churches may have a number of reporting requirements under state law. One of the most important is the filing of an annual corporate report with the office of secretary of state. This requirement applies to incorporated churches in many states. Failure to comply with this requirement can cause the church's corporate status to lapse.*

1. Annual Corporate Report

Many state nonprofit corporation laws require the filing of an annual report with the office of secretary of state. Generally, this report calls for the name of the corporation, the address of its registered office in the state of incorporation and the name of its registered agent at such address, a brief statement of the nature of the affairs that the corporation is actually conducting, and the names and addresses of the current directors and officers. A nominal fee usually must accompany the report.

Annual reports are prepared on forms provided by the secretary of state's office. Failure to file the annual reports may result in a small monetary fine, or in some states to loss of corporate status.

The corporate status of many churches has been terminated through inadvertent disregard of the annual reporting requirements, though such churches and their members typically are unaware of their unincorporated status. This obviously can lead to unfortunate consequences, including the potential personal legal liability of members for the obligations of the church—the very risk that most churches seek to avoid through incorporation.[162] Churches should periodically check with the secretary of state's office to ensure that they are "in good standing." Most states issue certificates of good standing to corporations for a nominal fee.

Case Studies

• *The Supreme Judicial Court of Massachusetts upheld an action by the secretary of state revoking the corporate status of 11,000 nonprofit corporations that failed to file their annual corporate reports as required by state law. Massachusetts nonprofit corporation law specifies: "If the corporation fails to submit its [annual report] for two successive years, the state secretary shall give notice thereof by mail, postage prepaid, to such corporation in default. Failure of such corporation to submit the required [report] within ninety days after the notice of default has been given shall be sufficient cause for the revocation of its charter by the state secretary." Pursuant to this statute, the secretary of state revoked the corporate status of 11,000 nonprofit corporations in Massachusetts that failed to file their annual reports for two consecutive years. These revocations were all preceded by the required notice to the lapsed corporations. The president of a nonprofit corporation whose charter had been revoked filed a lawsuit challenging the actions of the secretary of state. The court ruled in favor of the secretary of state, noting that "it is undisputed that there was sufficient cause to revoke the charters of the corporations since they did not file acceptable annual reports for two consecutive years."[163]*

• *The Montana Supreme Court ruled that a church corporation that was reinstated after having been dissolved for failure to submit an annual corporate report to the secretary of state should be treated as a corporation back to the time of its dissolution. A church's corporate status was dissolved by the secretary of state for failure to file its annual reports. A couple donated property to the church three years later. Following this donation, the church discovered that its corporate status had lapsed, and it applied for reinstatement as a corporation. The couple later attempted to revoke their donation on the ground that the church was not a corporation at the time the donation was made. The court ruled that the lapse of the church's corporate status did not affect donations. It relied on the following provision in the state nonprofit corporation law: "Any restoration of corporate rights pursuant to this chapter relates back to the date the corporation was involuntarily dissolved, and the corporation shall be considered to have been an existing legal entity from the date of its original incorporation."[164]*

• *A New Mexico appeals court ruled that a charitable organization's corporate status lapsed when it failed to submit an annual corporate report to the secretary of state, and that the organization's property automatically passed to the organization described in its dissolution clause. A charitable organization was incorporated as a nonprofit corporation in 1957. In 1969, the state corporation commission issued an order dissolving the corporation because of its failure to file annual corporate reports for three years. The dissolved corporation later attempted to "re-incorporate," using the same directors, place of business, and federal tax identification number. The*

---

[162] Shakra v. Benedictine Sisters of Bedford, 553 A.2d 1327 (N.H. 1989).

[163] Brattman v. Secretary of the Commonwealth, 658 N.E.2d 159 (Mass. 1995).

[164] Valley Victory Church v. Sandon, 109 P.3d 273 (Mont. 2005).

directors assumed that the property of the old corporation automatically vested in the new corporation upon its creation. A state appeals court disagreed. The court concluded that "dissolution of a corporation is tantamount to corporate death and effectively terminates the existence of the corporation," and that "after dissolution, a corporation is without power to dispose of its property, except as specifically authorized by law or judicial order." The court noted that under state law (as it existed at the time of the corporation's dissolution in 1969) a nonprofit corporation's corporate existence "dissolved" or lapsed upon its failure to file an annual corporate report with the secretary of state within one year of the due date. Since the corporation's corporate status lapsed as a matter of law in 1969, it was without power to dispose of its property following its dissolution. The court noted that "in the absence of a statute specifying the method of distribution of the assets of a dissolved corporation, the articles of incorporation of the corporation control and are its fundamental and organic law." As a result, the court concluded that the corporation's assets (at the time of its dissolution) passed to the organization described in the "dissolution clause" contained in its corporate charter. In conclusion, the court ruled that the assets of the dissolved corporation did not pass to the successor corporation, but rather went to the organization described in the dissolved corporation's "dissolution clause."[165]

2. New Hire Reporting

Churches are required to report information about "new hires" to a designated state agency pursuant to the Personal Responsibility and Work Opportunity Reconciliation Act, which was enacted by Congress in 1996. These requirements are addressed in section 8-2.

3. Other State Reports

Many states have attempted to regulate charitable solicitations by requiring charitable organizations to register with a state agency prior to soliciting donations. Many states require, in addition to the initial registration, the filing of annual reports. Churches and other religious organizations are exempted from the registration and reporting requirements of most charitable solicitation laws. This subject is addressed in chapter 9.

Some states impose additional reporting requirements on churches. For example, New York requires some churches to seek court approval before selling, mortgaging, or leasing property, and to notify the state attorney general prior to any such transaction.

Case Study

• A New York court upheld the validity of a state law imposing requirements on the sale, mortgage, or lease of church property. New York law specifies that "a religious corporation shall not sell, mortgage or lease for a term exceeding five years any of its real property without applying for and obtaining leave of the court . . . ." New York law also requires several "congregational" (and some hierarchical) churches to notify the state attorney general prior to the sale, mortgage, or lease of their property. A church that violated these requirements argued that they not only violated the First Amendment's ban on the establishment of religion but also violated the

---

[165] Matter of the Will of Coe, 826 P.2d 576 (N.M. App. 1992).

First Amendment's guaranty of religious freedom by involving the government in the internal decisions of churches. The court acknowledged that the New York law discriminated among religions by only requiring "congregational" churches, and some hierarchical churches, to notify the attorney general while exempting most hierarchical churches. However, it concluded that this discriminatory treatment did not violate the establishment clause since it was based on a compelling government interest ("protecting members of religious corporations by safeguarding the potentially substantial proceeds from sales of property, and ensuring that the proceeds are properly disbursed"). The court noted that the hierarchical churches that are exempted from the notice requirement are required to obtain the consent of their top executive officer before seeking court approval. It concluded that the notice requirement applied to those churches, whether congregational or hierarchical, whose structure "does not assure that its members have an opportunity to review the sale of real property." The court also rejected the church's claim that the law in question violated the First Amendment's guaranty of religious freedom, noting that "any inquiry by the attorney general involves only the terms of a real estate transaction; it involves no inquiry into religious beliefs nor does it involve the regulation or prohibition of conduct undertaken for religious reasons."[166]

Federal Law

§ 6-04.2

Key point 6-04.2. *A church may have a number of reporting obligations under federal law, including annual information returns to employees and self-employed workers (W-2 and 1099 forms), the quarterly employer's tax return (Form 941), the unrelated business income tax return (Form 990-T), and the annual certification of racial nondiscrimination (Form 5578).*

Federal law imposes several reporting requirements on charitable organizations. Among them are the following:

1. Application for Recognition of Tax-Exempt Status

Most organizations seeking recognition of exemption from federal income tax must file an application with the IRS. This is done either on IRS Form 1023 or 1024, depending on the nature of the applicant. Churches, their integrated auxiliaries, and conventions or associations of churches are exempted by law from payment of federal income tax and therefore they are not required to file an application with the IRS.[167] Such organizations nevertheless may find it advantageous to obtain IRS recognition of exempt status since this would avoid the need of substantiating their tax-exempt status each time the IRS questions the deductibility of contributions made by a member or adherent. A church may obtain recognition of exemption in either of two ways: (1) by filing a Form 1023

---

[166] Greek Orthodox Archdiocese v. Abrams, 618 N.Y.S.2d 504 (Sup. 1994). The court's conclusion is questionable, since it was attempting (without a shred of supporting evidence) to distinguish between churches on the basis of whether their membership has an opportunity to review property transactions.

[167] I.R.C. § 508(c)(1)(A).

with the IRS, or (2) by being a member of a convention or association of churches that has obtained a "group-exemption ruling" from the IRS.

If a church independently applies for and receives IRS recognition of exemption, it must notify the IRS of any material changes in its sources of support, purposes, character, or methods of operation. Churches that are included in the group exemption ruling of a convention or association of churches must annually notify their convention or association of any changes in their purposes, character, or methods of operation.[168]

2. Annual Information Returns

Section 6033 of the Internal Revenue Code requires most tax-exempt organizations to file an annual information return with the IRS. The annual information return is IRS Form 990. This form sets forth an exempt organization's gross income, expenses, disbursements for exempt purposes, assets and liabilities, net worth, contributions received (including the names and addresses of substantial contributors), and compensation paid to certain employees. Section 6033 provides a "mandatory exemption" for (1) "churches, their integrated auxiliaries, and conventions and associations of churches"; (2) certain religious and charitable organizations whose annual gross receipts normally do not exceed $5,000; and (3) the "exclusively religious activities of any religious order."

Form 990 itself specifies that the following organizations are exempt from the annual information return requirement:

- "a church, an interchurch organization of local units of a church, a convention or association of churches, an integrated auxiliary of a church (such as a men's or women's organization, religious school, mission society, or youth group)";

- "a school below college level affiliated with a church or operated by a religious order";

- "a mission society sponsored by or affiliated with one or more churches or church denominations, if more than one-half of the society's activities are conducted in, or directed at, persons in foreign countries";

- "an exclusively religious activity of any religious order";

- "an organization whose annual gross receipts are normally $25,000 or less."

3. Tax on Unrelated Business Income

Even though a church is recognized as tax-exempt by the IRS, it still may be liable for tax on its *unrelated business income*, that is, income from a regularly carried on trade or business that is not substantially related to the purposes constituting the basis for the church's exemption. A church that has $1,000 or more in gross income from an unrelated trade or business must file an IRS Form 990-T. In computing unrelated business taxable income, churches are entitled

---

[168] The procedures for obtaining an exemption from federal income taxes are discussed in R. HAMMAR, CHURCH AND CLERGY TAX GUIDE (published annually by the publisher of this text).

to deduct all reasonable and necessary expenses directly associated with the unrelated business.[169]

4. Employment Taxes

Every employer, including organizations exempt from federal income tax, that pays taxable wages to employees is responsible for withholding, depositing, paying, and reporting federal income tax, and Medicare tax, and federal unemployment tax unless specifically exempted by law. Churches are exempted from paying federal and state unemployment taxes on their employees.[170]

A church's obligation to withhold federal income tax and (and Medicare) tax from employees' wages, and to deposit such withheld taxes and periodically report the amounts withheld to the IRS, generally are referred to as a church's "payroll tax obligations."

Compliance with the various payroll tax obligations represents the most significant reporting obligation for most churches. This is so for two very important reasons. First, the payroll reporting obligations apply to most churches. Second, there are substantial penalties for failing to comply with these requirements. For example, the church, and possibly some church board members individually, may be responsible for the payment of these taxes if they are not withheld from employee wages. As a result, it is essential for church board members to familiarize themselves with their church's payroll tax reporting obligations, and to be certain that these obligations are being properly discharged. This is not as easy as it sounds, for several reasons.

First, churches often use volunteer treasurers or bookkeepers who serve for limited terms and are unable to devote their full time and attention to such matters. This has a tendency of making church accounting practices sloppy.

Second, a surprisingly large number of church leaders continue to assume that they are immune from legal obligations that apply to everyone else because they represent the church.

Third, the payroll tax reporting procedures are complex. In fact, one private organization presented its annual "most incomprehensible government regulation" award to tax code provisions dealing with payroll tax reporting requirements. These rules are complex, and they are even more complex in the context of church reporting—since special rules apply.

All of a church's payroll tax reporting obligations are addressed in a companion text.[171]

5. Information Returns

Churches must issue annual "information returns" to (1) all employees who were paid wages, and (2) any self-employed person to whom the church paid annual compensation of at least $600. These information returns are referred to

---

[169] The tax on unrelated business income is addressed in R. HAMMAR, CHURCH AND CLERGY TAX GUIDE (published annually by the publisher of this text).

[170] I.R.C. § 3306(c)(6). The application of unemployment taxes to churches and other religious organizations is addressed in R. HAMMAR, CHURCH AND CLERGY TAX GUIDE (published annually by the publisher of this text).

[171] R. HAMMAR, CHURCH AND CLERGY TAX GUIDE (published annually by the publisher of this text).

as the W-2 and 1099-MISC forms, respectively. In addition, churches are required to issue a 1099-INT form to each person who was paid $600 or more in interest income during any one year (a $10 rule applies to certain forms of interest payments). These rules are considered fully in a companion text.[172]

6. Annual Certification of Racial Nondiscrimination

No doubt one of the most widely disregarded federal reporting obligations applicable to churches is the annual certification of racial nondiscrimination (IRS Form 5578). Any church that operates, supervises, or controls a "private school" must submit a Form 5578 each year to the IRS certifying that it operates its school in a racially nondiscriminatory manner.

The term *private school* is defined in the instructions to Form 5578 to include "an educational organization which normally maintains a regular faculty and curriculum and normally has a regularly enrolled body of pupils or students in attendance at the place where its educational activities are regularly carried on. The term includes primary, secondary, preparatory, or high schools, and colleges and universities, whether operated as a separate legal entity or as an activity of a church . . . . The term also includes preschools . . . ." This important reporting obligation is discussed fully in a companion text.[173]

7. Returns Regarding Dissolution or Termination

Section 6043 of the Internal Revenue Code requires a corporation to file a return (Form 966) within 30 days after the adoption of any resolution or plan concerning the dissolution of the corporation. Churches, their integrated auxiliaries, and conventions and associations of churches, however, are exempted by section 6043 from this reporting requirement.

8. EEOC Reports

Title VII of the Civil Rights Act of 1964 prohibits employers from discriminating in any employment decision—including hiring, discharge, compensation, and the terms, conditions, or privileges of employment—on the basis of race, color, religion, sex, or national origin.[174] Title VII applies to every employer, including churches, having 15 or more employees for at least 20 weeks in a year. Part-time employees are to be included in making the calculation. The Act does exempt religious organizations, including churches, from the prohibition against discrimination based on religion, and the United States Supreme Court upheld the constitutionality of this provision in 1987.[175]

The Equal Employment Opportunity Commission (EEOC), an agency created by Congress to enforce Title VII of the Civil Rights Act of 1964, requires all employers, including religious organizations, having 100 or more employees

---

[172] *Id.*

[173] *Id.*

[174] 42 U.S.C. § 2000e-2(a). *See generally* chapter 8, *infra.*

[175] Corporation of Presiding Bishop of the Church of Jesus Christ of Latter Day Saints v. Amos, 483 U.S. 327 (1987).

to submit annually an Employer Information Report. This report is prepared on Standard Form 100, which is also known as Employer Information Report EEO-1. Among other things, this report provides the EEOC with the racial composition of the employer's work force.

Church Names

Key point 6-05. *A church name is a valuable property right that is protected by the legal principle of unfair competition. Protection also is available under federal trademark law.*

Occasionally, a new church will acquire a name that is so similar to the name of another church in the same community that public confusion is likely to result. For example, a new congregation calling itself Calvary Presbyterian Church establishes a church in a community already having a Presbyterian church called "Calvary Church." A confusion of names may occur in other ways, such as a new sect or religious denomination acquiring a name similar to that of an existing one, or a local church withdrawing from a denominational organization but continuing to employ a name associating itself with the denomination. In any of these situations, does the preexisting church body have any legal basis for stopping further use of the similar name by the other church or religious organization?

The courts protect the names of existing commercial enterprises against unauthorized use of confusingly similar names by other commercial organizations.[176] In many instances, the courts are simply enforcing state corporation laws that, in most states, prohibit new corporations from using names that are identical or confusingly similar to those of existing organizations.[177] Other courts have emphasized that such name protection statutes are merely embodiments of the underlying common law of unfair competition, which protects existing corporate names independently of any provisions in state corporate laws.[178]

The courts also will protect the names of nonprofit corporations on the basis of one or more of the following theories:

---

[176] *See, e.g.,* Standard Oil Company of New Mexico v. Standard Oil Company of California, 56 F.2d 973 (10th Cir. 1932); Association of Contracting Plumbers v. Contracting Plumbers Association, 302 N.Y. 495 (N.Y. 1951).

[177] *See, e.g.,* Ariz. Rev. Stats. § 10-401. ("A corporate name shall be distinguishable from . . . the corporate name of a nonprofit corporation incorporated under this title or a foreign nonprofit or not for profit corporation authorized to conduct affairs in this state."); Fla. Stats. § 607.041 ("A corporate name . . . must be distinguishable from the names of all other entities or filings, except fictitious name registrations . . . ."); N.J. Stats. § 14A:2-2 ("The corporate name of a domestic corporation or of a foreign corporation authorized to transact business in this State. . . shall be such as to distinguish it upon the records in the office of the Secretary of State from the names of other for profit and nonprofit domestic corporations and for profit and nonprofit foreign corporations qualified to do business in this State . . . .").

[178] Massachusetts Mutual Life Ins. Co. v. Massachusetts Life Ins. Co., 218 N.E.2d 564, 570 (Mass. 1966) ("It is our view, however, that the corporate name protection statute is a statutory declaration and clarification of a portion of the extant common law of unfair competition . . . ."); Virginia Manor Land Co., v. Virginia Manor Apartments, Inc., 282 A.2d 684, 687 (Pa. 1971) ("[t]he right of the corporation to the exclusive use of its own name exists at common law, and includes the right to prohibit another from using a name so similar to the corporate name as to be calculated to deceive the public").

• the applicable nonprofit corporation statute contains a provision protecting the preexisting names of nonprofit corporations in much the same way as business corporation statutes protect the names of business corporations;[179]

• extension of the name protection provided by business corporation statutes to nonprofit corporations when the state nonprofit law does not specifically provide such protection;[180]

• the common law of unfair competition;[181] and

• trademark protection.

In states having a name protection statute protecting the names of religious corporations, a church's name generally will be protected against later use of the same or a confusingly similar name in either of two ways:

(1) the state official charged with the duty of reviewing applications for incorporation can reject the application of an organization whose name is either identical or deceptively similar to the name of an existing corporation; or

(2) if the state official chooses to recognize the corporate status of an organization whose name is either identical or deceptively similar to that of an existing corporation, the offended corporation may sue to stop further use of the name.

unfair competition

A church may seek legal protection of its name through the law of unfair competition. *Unfair competition* is a civil wrong created to protect existing organizations from the deceptive or unfair practices of competitors. It is entirely separate and distinct from trademark law. Among other things, unfair competition means the use of a name that is either identical with or confusingly similar to that of a preexisting organization. As one court has observed:

In the law of unfair competition, a corporate or trade name used in connection with the business to which it relates may become an asset of great value. When it does, it partakes of the nature of a property right, and equity will enjoin the appropriation and use of such name if confusion of identity is likely to result.[182]

---

[179] *See, e.g.,* 805 ILL. COMP. STATS. § 105/104.05. ch. 32, § 163a(6); MODEL NONPROFIT CORPORATION ACT § 7(b).

[180] First Congressional District Democratic Party Organization v. First Congressional District Democratic Organization, Inc., 177 N.W.2d 224 (Mich. 1970).

[181] Oklahoma District Council of the Assemblies of God v. New Hope Assembly of God, 597 P.2d 1211 (Okla. 1979).

[182] *Id.* at 1214.

Courts have consistently protected charitable as well as business organizations from unfair competition. In a leading case one court observed:

> We hold that the common law principles of unfair competition protecting business corporations against another's use of the same or similar name are applicable to charitable or religious associations and corporations. . . . The right to this protection rests generally upon the fact that the use of identical or similar terms or names is likely to result in confusion or deception.[183]

To successfully establish that the name chosen by another organization constitutes unfair competition, a church must demonstrate:

1. Prior use of the name.

2. Subsequent use of the same or a confusingly similar name by another religious organization.

3. The church with prior use of the name will be adversely affected by continued use of the same or a confusingly similar name by the other religious organization. An adverse impact generally will be established by the unauthorized use of a name identical or confusingly similar to that of a preexisting corporation.

4. The church with prior use of the name did not delay for an unreasonable time in seeking to enjoin further use of the same or a confusingly similar name by the other religious organization.[184]

Generic or highly generalized names are not protected from misappropriation under the doctrine of unfair competition unless a secondary meaning has been established. A generic name acquires a secondary meaning through such continued use that it is commonly associated with a particular church or religious organization in the public mind. Proof of a secondary meaning is a question of fact to be established on a case-by-case basis.

To illustrate, the General Conference of the Seventh-Day Adventists sued the "Seventh-Day Adventist Congregational Church" (located in Kealakekua, Hawaii) and its pastor for trademark infringement and unfair competition. A trial court ruled in favor of the denomination, and ordered the local church to discontinue using a name including the term *Seventh-Day Adventist* or *SDA*, or representing to others that it was connected in any way with the Seventh-Day Adventist denomination.

The local church refused to comply with this order on the ground that the denomination's trademark was invalid since it was "generic." The court found the church to be in contempt of court for ignoring its order, and set a fine of $500 per day until the church and its pastor agreed to comply.

---

[183] *Id.* at 1215. *See also* National Board of YWCA v. YWCA of Charleston, 335 F. Supp. 615 (D.S.C. 1971).

[184] *See generally* Annot., 37 A.L.R.3d 277 (1971).

The church and pastor appealed this decision, and a federal appeals court agreed that the trial court's ruling in favor of the denomination was improper.[185] The court reasoned that the church and its pastor had raised a significant issue (the validity of the denomination's trademark) that should have been heard by a jury. The appeals court noted that "a trademark's function is to identify and distinguish the goods and services of one seller from another." A trademark, however, is always "subject to the defense that it is generic." A "generic" trademark is "one that tells the buyer what the product is, rather than from where, or whom, it came." Generic marks are not eligible for trademark protection since they do "not indicate the product of service's origin, but is the term for the product or service itself."

The church and pastor claimed that the name "Seventh-Day Adventist" is generic since it refers to a religion rather than to a particular church organization. They asserted, "The phrase Seventh-Day Adventist is not theirs alone, as they would like to claim, for it describes a system or set of Bible based Christian beliefs, doctrines, and standards. One therefore is not necessarily Seventh-Day Adventist because of what organization he may be affiliated with, but rather he is a Seventh-Day Adventist because of what he believes."

The appeals court concluded that the denomination's claim of trademark infringement would fail if the local church and its pastor could prove that the name "Seventh-Day Adventist" is generic. On the other hand, if the denomination could establish that its name was not generic, then it would win its trademark infringement suit if it could prove a "likelihood of confusion" caused by the church's continued use of a name similar to that of the denomination. In deciding whether or not there is a likelihood of confusion, a court should consider the following factors: (1) the strength of the denomination's name; (2) the similarity of the parties' goods or services; (3) similarity of the two names; (4) evidence that persons actually have been confused by the similarity of names; (5) marketing methods used; (6) the likely degree of care the public would take in differentiating between the names; (7) the intent of the local church in using the similar name; and (8) likelihood of "expansion of product lines" (i.e., will the local church benefit at the expense of the denomination). The local church claimed that it had "never in any way sought to deceive or confuse anyone in regard to our name," and that its use of the word "Congregational" in its name effectively distinguished it from the Seventh-Day Adventists. The case was sent back to the trial court to determine whether or not the denomination's name is generic, and if not, whether the local church's use of its present name created a "likelihood of confusion."

A local church congregation that votes to disaffiliate from a parent denomination may lose the right to use the denominational name. One court has observed:

> The local name of a church is of great value, not only because business
> is carried on and property held in that name, but also because millions

---

[185] General Conference Corporation of Seventh-Day Adventists v. Seventh-Day Adventist Congregational Church, 887 F.2d 228 (9th Cir. 1989).

of members associate with the name the most sacred of their personal relationships and the holiest of their family traditions. And, since the right to use the name inheres in the institution, not in its members . . . when they cease to be members of the institution, use by them of the name is misleading and, if injurious to the institution, should be enjoined.[186]

Some states have enacted statutes that bar churches from using a name of a parent denomination following their disaffiliation from that denomination. For example, a Nebraska statute provides:

[When a church] withdraws or terminates its affiliation with a statewide denominational cooperative agency, such religious association shall be deemed to have ceased to exist or maintain its organization . . . and shall not be thereafter entitled to use in the name of such religious association the characteristic denominational designation or other words calculated to induce the belief that it is in any way belonging to or affiliated with the denomination maintaining such a statewide cooperative agency.[187]

trademarks

In some cases the name of a church or religious organization can be protected under federal trademark law. *Trademark* is defined by the federal Trademark Act as "any word, symbol, or device, or any combination thereof adopted and used by a manufacturer or merchant to identify his goods and distinguish them from those manufactured and sold by others."[188] Trademark protection is available to any church or religious organization that uses a particular name to identify goods or services it offers to the public. For example, if a religious denomination publishes religious literature for its churches, and affixes its name to such literature, the name identifies the goods and therefore is eligible for trademark registration. Similarly, if a church establishes a counseling center, correspondence school, private elementary or secondary school, nursing home, radio or television station, or magazine that is identified by the church's name, the name may be entitled to trademark protection.

Of course, trademark protection is not available for a name or mark that so resembles a mark already registered with the Patent and Trademark Office, or previously used by another organization and not abandoned, as to be likely to cause confusion or to deceive. There are two ways of determining whether a proposed name conflicts with a preexisting name that is entitled to protection. First, a commercial search service can be retained which, for a fee, will render an opinion on the availability of a specified name. Second, an application for registration can be filed with the Patent and Trademark Office in Washington, D.C. Although the Patent and Trademark Office takes several months to evaluate an application, it eventually will notify the applicant whether its proposed name or mark conflicts with a preexisting mark.

---

[186] Carnes v. Smith, 222 S.E.2d 322, 329 (Ga. 1976) (citations omitted).

[187] NEB. STATS. § 21-2803. *See* Estate of Schwartz v. Methodist Church, 1999 WL 111353 (Neb. App. 1999).

[188] 15 U.S.C. § 1127.

"Descriptive" and highly generalized names and marks are not eligible for registration unless a secondary meaning can be established. A secondary meaning is established by proof of public association of a generic name or mark with a particular church or religious organization. So-called "generic" marks may not be capable of trademark protection even if a secondary meaning is present. The distinction between descriptive and generic marks is a close one that has caused the courts considerable difficulty.

Generic, Descriptive, Suggestive, and Arbitrary Names

Terms that may be registered as trademarks fall into four categories of strength: (1) generic; (2) descriptive; (3) suggestive; or (4) arbitrary. Generic terms are those which name "the class of which an individual article or service is but a member." Descriptive terms "identify a characteristic or quality of an article of service." Suggestive terms suggest characteristics of the goods and services and "require an effort of the imagination by the consumer in order to be understood as descriptive." Arbitrary or fanciful terms are words or phrases that bear no direct relationship to the product.

Generic terms represent the weaker end of the spectrum and arbitrary terms represent the stronger. Generic terms may never be registered as trademarks, and descriptive terms may not be registered as trademarks unless the holder shows that the mark has acquired "secondary meaning" (the mark has become distinctive of the trademark holder's product or services).

A federal court in Florida ruled that a local church's unauthorized use of the name "Seventh-Day Adventist" (and the acronym "SDA") could be prohibited on the ground that they violated the national Seventh-Day Adventist Church's trademark.[189] In 1980 the Seventh-Day Adventist Church (the "national church") obtained a trademark registration for the name "Seventh-Day Adventist" with the United States Patent and Trademark Office. The trademark application indicated that the mark would be used in connection with several goods and services including religious publications, employee health care and benefit programs, medical insurance programs, educational services, film production, health care services, and church services. Several members of a Seventh-Day Adventist church in Florida left the church to form their own congregation (the "new church"). Its name included "Seventh-Day Adventist," and the name was used on its church sign, in newspaper advertisements, fliers, billboards, bulletins, audio tape recordings, and on radio broadcasts. The new church was listed in the section of "Seventh-day Adventist Churches" in the local telephone directory.

The national church sought a court order prohibiting the new church from using the name "Seventh-Day Adventist" or any confusingly similar name, or the acronym "SDA." A federal court issued the order, concluding that the new church had infringed upon the national church's trademark.

---

[189] General Conference Corporation of Seventh-Day Adventists v. Perez, 97 F.Supp.2d 1154 (S.D. Fla. 2000).

The court noted that names that may be registered as trademarks fall into four categories of strength: (1) generic; (2) descriptive; (3) suggestive; or (4) arbitrary. Generic names are the weakest, and normally are not eligible for trademark protection, while arbitrary names are the strongest. The court noted that a suggestive mark is one that "suggests" characteristics of the corresponding goods and services and "requires an effort of the imagination by the consumer in order to be understood as descriptive." Suggestive marks require no proof of secondary meaning to be entitled to protection. The court concluded that the trademark Seventh-Day Adventist was at least suggestive and "at a minimum is descriptive":

The words seventh-day alone define Saturday as the seventh day of the week, but alone do not suggest keeping the seventh day holy within the total doctrines and tenets of [the national church]. Similarly, the word Adventist alone defines the coming of Christ, but alone does not suggest the specificity of Christ's coming within the total doctrines and tenets of the Seventh-day Adventist Church. Finally, in combination the words "seventh-day" and "Adventist" suggest the two concepts (Sabbatarism and Adventism) noted herein, but though suggesting these two concepts, none describe other requisite statements of belief which distinguish the Seventh-day Adventist Church, through the use of the suggestive name Seventh-Day Adventist, from other "Sabbatarians" and "Adventists." The mark Seventh-Day Adventist and the acronym SDA are clearly suggestive (but at a minimum are eminently descriptive (not generic)). Persons who are members of the relevant public recognize the mark Seventh-Day Adventist and the legally equivalent acronym SDA as an indication of source or origin, namely, a name identifying the services and products of the Seventh-day Adventist Church, and the marks should be protected without proof of secondary meaning.

The court defined a descriptive trademark as one that "identifies a characteristic or quality of an article of service." Such marks may not be registered as trademarks unless the holder shows that the mark has acquired secondary meaning (the mark has become distinctive of the trademark holder's product or services). The court concluded that even if the mark "Seventh-Day Adventist" was descriptive, it was still entitled to protection since the mark had acquired a secondary meaning through "the continuous and uninterrupted use" of the mark "for over 139 years." It further observed:

[The mark] is used in [the national church's] denominational, corporate and trade name (Seventh-day Adventist Church) and in all of its Union Conference names, its local conferences, and virtually all of its Seventh-day Adventist Churches throughout the United States. [Its] mark has become distinctive as a result of the large number of people who have been ministered to and served through its churches and publications, its schools, colleges and universities, its hospitals and its national outreach under the mark [and] acronym SDA. Through members, workers, ministers and pastors and associated health and education programs, media centers, publishing houses and the publications thereof, the mark . . . and acronym SDA have become famous and synonymous with the good will and quality of the Seventh-day Adventist Church. Plaintiff has expended considerable effort and expense over the last 139 years in promoting its mark . . . and the products and services associated therewith, and consequently the mark is entitled to broad protection.

The court noted that consumer surveys are "recognized as the most direct and persuasive evidence of secondary meaning," and that a survey conducted by the national church proved that its use of the mark "has resulted in the general public in the United States identifying the words 'Seventh-Day Adventist' with the [national church]."

The court rejected the new church's claim that its use of the national church's mark was permitted by the First Amendment guaranty of religious freedom. It concluded: "It is well established that religious institutions are entitled to the protection of the trademark and unfair competition laws to the same extent as commercial enterprises and enforcement of the trademark statute does not abridge the religious freedom rights of a religious group that is infringing on a church's trademark or service mark."

An application for trademark registration is a relatively simple procedure consisting of the following elements:

1. Preparation of a written application stating the applicant's name, address, state of incorporation or organization; the goods or services in connection with which the name or mark is used; the class of goods or services according to the official international classification system; the date of the first use of the name or mark on or in connection with the goods or services; the date of the first use of the name or mark as a trademark "in commerce"; the mode or manner in which the mark is used on or in connection with the goods.

2. A drawing of the mark, unless the mark consists solely of a name—in which case the name may be typed in capital letters on a piece of paper.

3. Five specimens of the goods bearing the name or mark. No specimens are required for names or marks associated with services.

4. The required filing fee.

If a church name is not used in connection with any specific goods or services, trademark protection is unavailable.

Case Studies

• *A federal appeals court ruled that a website that used a national church's registered trademarks without permission violated federal trademark law. Founded by Mary Baker Eddy in 1872, The First Church of Christ, Scientist (the "Church"), is a Boston-based religious organization with branches located throughout the world. The Church is governed by its Board of Directors (the "Board"), whose functions include supervision and control over the church's publishing enterprise, The Christian Science Publishing Society. In furtherance of its religious mission, the Church provides a variety of products and publications, many of which bear federally registered and common law trademarks owned by the Board. In 1999, a resident of Arizona (the defendant) founded the University of Christian Science ("UCS") as an "electronic campus" on the Internet which would allow present and potential Christian Scientists to "study the teachings of Mary Baker Eddy and to exchange ideas about Christian Science." The Church filed a trademark infringement suit in a federal court, claiming that the defendant and UCS without permission used certain marks belonging to the Church, or marks "confusingly similar thereto," in printed materials and on the UCS website. The Church also alleged that the defendant and UCS "have held themselves out as being affiliated with or sponsored by" the Church. A federal district court ruled that the defendant was guilty of trademark infringement, and this ruling was affirmed on appeal by a federal appeals court.*[190]

• *A federal appeals court ruled that the registered trademark "Church of the Creator" was a descriptive rather than a generic mark that was entitled to legal protection against infringing uses by other organizations using the same or a similar name. The appeals court conceded that generic marks are incapable of trademark protection even if the Patent and Trademark Office registers such a mark. It defined a generic mark as one that "has become the name of a product" such as "sandwich for meat between slices of bread." While the word "church" is generic, the court concluded that the term "Church of the Creator" was descriptive rather than generic:*

> *Church of the Creator is descriptive, like "lite beer." It does not name the class of monotheistic religions. In the contemporary United States, variations on "Church of [Deity]" are used to differentiate individual denominations, not to denote the class of all religions. The list is considerable: Church of God; Church of God (Anderson, Indiana); First Church of God; Worldwide Church of God; Church of God in Christ; Assembly of God; Korean Assembly of God; Church of the Nazarene; Church of Christ; United Church of Christ; Disciples of Christ; Church of Christ, Scientist; Church of Jesus Christ of Latter Day Saints. There is room for extension with Church of Our Savior, Church of the Holy Spirit, Church of the Holy Trinity, Church of Jehovah, and so on. Yet all of these are recognizable as denominational names, not as the designation of the religion to which the denominations belong. No Jewish, Islamic, Baha'i, or Unitarian group would say that it belongs to a "Church of the Creator"; and a Christian congregation would classify itself first into its denomination (e.g., Baptist, Lutheran, Russian Orthodox, Society of Friends), then into one of the major groupings (Roman Catholic, Orthodox, and Protestant), and finally into Christianity, but never into a*

---

[190] Christian Science Board of Directors of the First Church of Christ, Scientist v. Nolan, 259 F.3d 209 (4th Cir. 2001).

"Church of the Creator." No one called or emailed a Baptist church to complain about its complicity in the hate-mongering of the World Church of the Creator; people recognized the name as denominational, and that's why protests ended up in the Church of the Creator's in box. What is more, as these lists show, using "Church of the Creator" as a denominational name leaves ample options for other sects to distinguish themselves and achieve separate identities. . . . Because there are so many ways to describe religious denominations, there is no risk that exclusive use of "Church of the Creator" will appropriate a theology or exclude essential means of differentiating one set of beliefs from another.

The court rejected the defendant's argument that recognizing the trademark status of Church of the Creator violated the First Amendment because it restricts the free exercise of religion. It noted that the Constitution itself authorizes Congress to create rights of this kind.[191]

Officers, Directors, and Trustees—In General § 6-06

Churches and religious organizations conduct their temporal and spiritual affairs through individuals. State laws generally require that church corporations appoint an initial board of directors which in turn elects the corporation's first president, secretary, and treasurer. The initial board of directors adopts a set of bylaws that specifies the term of office of both officers and directors and sets forth the procedure for electing successors.

Directors of church corporations occasionally are called trustees. This terminology is perfectly appropriate if it is intended to suggest that the business and spiritual oversight of the church is delegated "in trust" to such individuals, or if it is required by law.[192] However, in many cases such terminology is a holdover from a church's pre-incorporation status when title to church property was held in the name of church trustees since unincorporated churches were incapable of holding title in their own name. If this is the case, the continued use of the title *trustee* can be misleading. Incorporated churches that retain the use of the term *trustee* ordinarily do not use the names of the trustees as either the transferor or transferee on a deed. Church bylaws, and an attorney, should be consulted to be sure.

Unincorporated churches generally elect officers, consisting of a president, secretary, and treasurer. This is especially true of unincorporated churches that are permitted by law to hold title to property in their own name. Those churches

---

[191] Te-Ta-Ma Truth Foundation v. The World Church of the Creator, 297 F.3d 662 (7th Cir. 2002). This case is important because it recognizes that the names of local churches and religious denominations are entitled to trademark protection even if they include generic terms (such as "church" or "God"). Such names can be descriptive rather than generic, and descriptive names are entitled to protection so long as they have acquired a secondary meaning. This means that through long and uninterrupted use a descriptive name has come to be associated by the public with a particular organization, as is common with the names of religious denominations.

[192] Osnes v. Morris, 298 S.E.2d 803 (W. Va. 1982).

that are still required by law to hold title in the names of trustees should add the words "or their successors" following the names of the church trustees in deeds, mortgages, and other legal documents. This will avoid problems in the event that the named trustees are deceased or otherwise unavailable at some future date when the church wants to sell its property.

Directors of church corporations occasionally are called *deacons*, although it is common for churches to have both directors and deacons—directors having oversight of the temporal affairs of the church and deacons having oversight of the spiritual.[193]

The Model Nonprofit Corporation Act, which has been enacted in many states, specifies that a corporation shall have a president, one or more vice-presidents, a secretary, a treasurer, and such other officers or assistant officers as the corporation deems necessary. The Act permits the same person to hold two or more offices except the offices of president and secretary. The term *officer* occasionally is interpreted broadly to include directors. Normally, however, a church president, secretary, treasurer, and vice-president (if any) are the only officers of the church.

There are no legal requirements regarding the number of trustees an unincorporated association must appoint or elect. Some states require that church corporations have a minimum number of directors.[194]

Election or Appointment §6-06.1

Key point 6-06.1. Churches select their officers and directors in various ways. For example, it is common for members of a church board to be elected by the church's membership, while officers are elected by the board. The civil courts generally refrain from resolving disputes involving the selection of church officers and directors on the ground that the First Amendment guaranty of religious freedom prevents them from becoming involved in ecclesiastical disputes.

It is customary for directors and trustees to be elected by the church membership and for officers to be elected by the board of directors or trustees. However, this is not always the case. For example, it is common for directors to nominate officers who are then elected by the voting membership.

Unless stated otherwise in either the bylaws or state law, officers, directors, and trustees are elected by a majority vote of the congregation's membership. To illustrate, one court ruled that the congregation, and not the board of deacons, had the exclusive authority to elect a treasurer when the church constitution or bylaws did not grant this authority to the board of deacons.[195]

Many churches have adopted a "staggered system" of electing directors whereby a minority (often a third) of the directors are elected at each annual meeting. This normally is accomplished by classifying directors in the bylaws

---

[193] Hayes v. Board of Trustees, 225 N.Y.S.2d 316 (1962).

[194] MODEL NONPROFIT CORPORATION ACT § 18.

[195] Gervin v. Reddick, 268 S.E.2d 657 (Ga. 1980).

according to tenure: the first class holding office for one year, the second class for two years, and the third class for three years. Thereafter successors for each class of directors are elected for three-year terms. This system helps to ensure that a majority of the board at all times will be experienced. Unless forbidden by charter, bylaw, or statute, directors or officers may succeed themselves in office.

Vacancies occurring in any office or on the board of directors or board of trustees are filled according to applicable provisions in state law or in the church's charter or bylaws. Church bylaws often permit vacancies in the board of directors to be filled by the board itself except for vacancies created by an increase in the number of directors. Vacancies typically are filled only for the unexpired term of the predecessor in office.

If the filling of vacancies is not provided for by state law or a church's charter or bylaws, there is no alternative but to await the next annual meeting of the congregation or to call a special meeting of the congregation expressly for the purpose of filling the vacancy for the unexpired term.

A minister it not entitled to serve as president of a church or even as a director or trustee unless specifically authorized in the church's charter or bylaws.[196]

Incorporated and unincorporated churches must follow the procedures in their charter or bylaws and in applicable state laws regarding the election or appointment of church officers, directors, and trustees. The courts have differed, however, as to the legal remedies available in the event that such internal procedures are not followed.

the general rule of judicial nonintervention

Some courts have refused to intervene in such disputes even if the selection of church officers or directors allegedly violated a church's charter or bylaws. These courts have relied primarily on the following language from a 1976 decision by the United States Supreme Court:

The conclusion of the Illinois Supreme Court that the decisions of the [Diocese] were "arbitrary" was grounded upon an inquiry that persuaded the Illinois Supreme Court that the [Diocese] had not followed its own laws and procedures in arriving at those decisions. We have concluded that *whether or not there is room for "marginal civil court review" under the narrow rubrics of "fraud" or "collusion" when church tribunals act in bad faith for secular purposes, no "arbitrariness" exception—in the sense of an inquiry whether the decisions of the highest ecclesiastical tribunal of a hierarchical church complied with church laws and regulations—is consistent with the constitutional mandate that civil courts are bound to accept the decisions of the highest judicatories of a religious organization of hierarchical polity on matters of discipline, faith, internal organization, or ecclesiastical rule, custom or law.* For civil courts to analyze whether the ecclesiastical actions of a church judicatory are in that sense "arbitrary" must inherently entail inquiry into the procedures that canon or ecclesiastical law supposedly require the church adjudicatory to follow,

---

[196] Allen v. North Des Moines Methodist Episcopal Church, 102 N.W. 808 (Iowa 1905).

or else into the substantive criteria by which they are supposedly to decide the ecclesiastical question. But this is exactly the inquiry that the First Amendment prohibits . . . .[197]

This rule of judicial non-intervention in disputes concerning internal church government has been applied by some courts, since 1976, to disputes involving the selection of church officers and directors. To illustrate, a Pennsylvania court declined to rule on which of two warring factions of church trustees rightfully held office.[198] A minister in a local church had ousted several trustees from office, replacing them with new trustees more loyal to himself. The ousted trustees alleged that the minister lacked the authority to replace them, and that they accordingly were still the lawful church board. The court, noting that civil courts must "defer" to churches and their own ecclesiastical organizations regarding any question of "discipline, faith, ecclesiastical rule, custom, or law," held that the question of a minister's authority to replace church trustees involves ecclesiastical law and therefore must be resolved by the church itself. It ordered the trial court to identify the highest body within the church empowered to decide the issue.

Case Studies

• *Maryland's highest court ruled that an arbitration award addressing the composition of a church's board of trustees was not reviewable by the civil courts since any review would require an interpretation of religious doctrine. The court concluded that "in many instances, issues of church polity will be inextricably intertwined with secular issues in contested church elections," and that the civil courts may not "wander into the theological thicket in order to render a decision."[199]*

• *A New Jersey court ruled that a trial court acted improperly in overseeing a church business meeting and the election of a pastor and church officers and trustees. Several ousted church leaders appealed the court's ruling. The ousted leaders claimed that the church elections were void because they were contrary to the church's bylaws that vested ecclesiastical authority to determine the eligibility of nominees for church office exclusively in internal church governing bodies. The court concluded that "in the absence of clear and unambiguous direction in church law, an intrachurch dispute over eligibility for nomination to church office, implicating as it does the more fundamental question of church governance and congregational structure, does not present a proper issue for judicial consideration." It concluded: "Although courts may intervene to determine whether established procedures of a religious organization, as proven, have been followed, courts should not intervene where such procedures are . . . less than clearly defined, or ambiguous. Because of such uncertainty, resolution of intrachurch disputes cannot be made without extensive, and therefore impermissible, inquiry into religious law and polity. . . . In this case, inquiring whether the nominating committee has exclusive ecclesiastical authority to determine eligibility necessitates interpretation*

---

[197] Serbian Eastern Orthodox Diocese v. Milivojevich, 426 U.S. 696, 712-13 (1976) (emphasis added).

[198] Atterberry v. Smith, 522 A.2d 683 (Pa. App. 1987).

[199] American Union of Baptists v. Trustees of the Particular Primitive Baptist Church, 644 A.2d 1063 (Md. 1994).]

of ambiguous religious law, the resolution of which would require a deeper probe into the congregational structure and allocation of power within the church. . . . Simply stated, neutral principles of civil law do not include standards for judging appropriate qualities for church leadership."[200]

• A New York court ruled that it had no authority to interfere with a Baptist church's appointment of "lifetime" deacons, though it could prohibit the appointment of lifetime trustees by the same church. An incorporated Baptist church adopted bylaws that made certain individuals "lifetime deacons." These deacons were invested with virtually absolute authority over the church's affairs. The bylaws also called for the election of trustees, and while trustees were given authority over the "legal and financial matters" of the church, they were subject to the control of the deacons. A dispute arose within the church over the seemingly unlimited authority of the deacons. A group of dissident members filed a lawsuit asking a court to rule that lifetime appointments of deacons are not permissible under state law. The court refused. It began its opinion by observing that the civil courts have no authority to resolve issues relating to a church's "spiritual" affairs, but that they can "with great reluctance" resolve church disputes relating to "temporal" affairs such as property. The court concluded that the selection and tenure of deacons is a spiritual rather than a temporal matter, and accordingly the courts were without authority to resolve disputes involving such issues. It observed, "The office of deacon has primarily a ministerial function and, in large measure, deals with the spiritual well being of the church and its members. In this function, the court will not interfere with the constitution and bylaws of this church. While this may be outside the mainstream of current Baptist practice, it is not impermissible. The life tenure of certain named deacons is clear in the bylaws and as to them cannot be disputed." On the other hand, the court concluded that trustees occupy a "temporal" rather than a spiritual position, and accordingly it would be appropriate for the civil courts to resolve internal church disputes pertaining to the selection or tenure of trustees.[201]

• A Texas court ruled that it could not resolve an internal church dispute involving the selection of church trustees since the critical provisions in the church's governing documents could not be applied without the court delving into church doctrine and governance. The court noted that the "central dispute" between the parties involved "who has the right to select and remove the trustee-directors and the minister." Both sides relied on the church's articles of incorporation in support of their position. The court noted that "ordinarily, we would construe the articles of incorporation of a Texas nonprofit corporation according to the body of neutral legal principles that governs Texas corporations generally. If we could do so without running afoul of constitutional constraints, we would also apply those principles to construe the articles of incorporation of a nonprofit corporation organized for religious or spiritual purposes." However, it concluded that it could not apply neutral legal principles in construing articles of incorporation or bylaws of the church, since both documents used the phrase "custom and practices of the church." Such language "removed any dispute regarding the selection of its directors from the purview of the judicial system. Interpreting this phrase would require the court to examine the historical, administrative, and ecclesiastical affairs of a religious organization and decide the

[200] Solid Rock Baptist Church v. Carlton, 789 A.2d 149 (N.J. Super. 2002).

[201] Ward v. Jones, 587 N.Y.S.2d 94 (Sup. 1992).

outcome of the issue based on its determination of what are the customs and practices of the church."[202]

marginal civil court review if doctrine not implicated

Some courts have been willing to intervene in internal church controversies regarding the selection of officers and directors. To illustrate, members of a church were allowed to challenge in court the legality of a congregational election of directors that allegedly did not conform to the procedural requirements in the church bylaws.[203] And, when a board of directors sought to perpetuate itself in office by refusing to call an election, church members were allowed to obtain legal redress because the state law under which the church was incorporated required annual elections of directors.[204]

Case Studies

• *An Illinois court intervened in a dispute involving the dismissal of local church trustees by the regional diocese of the American-Bulgarian Eastern Orthodox Church. The diocese selected other church members to govern the church, and ordered the discharged trustees to deliver the church's assets and records over to the newly appointed trustees. When the discharged trustees refused to comply with these mandates, the newly appointed trustees filed suit. A state appeals court ruled in favor of the former trustees. The court began its opinion by observing that "the state has a cognizable interest in the peaceful resolution of internal church disputes which are concerned with control or ownership of church property, and the civil courts have general authority to resolve such controversies." However, "when doctrinal or polity issues arise in the determination of a property dispute, the courts must defer to the resolution reached by the church's highest ecclesiastical authority." If doctrinal issues are not involved, "the First Amendment does not require that the state adopt a rule of compulsory deference to religious authorities in resolving property disputes. Instead, the state courts may choose from a variety of approaches." One of these, the neutral principles approach, allows a court to determine who owns or controls church property by applying objective legal principles to church documents and records. The Illinois court applied the "neutral principles" approach and concluded that it was not compelled to rule in favor of the diocese. Only when a church property dispute (or any other internal church dispute) involves doctrine or polity is a civil court compelled to defer to determinations of religious hierarchies. This was not such a case, concluded the court. The appeals court remanded the case to the trial court with instructions to resolve the dispute on the basis of "neutral principles of law."[205]*

• *A Louisiana court ruled that provisions in a church charter listing the requirements of church membership did not apply to members of the church board. A pastor attempted to disqualify three deacons from voting on an important issue because*

---

[202] Cherry Valley Church of Christ v. Foster, 2002 WL 10545 (Tex. App. 2002).

[203] Wilkerson v. Battiste, 393 So.2d 195 (La. 1980); Trinity Pentecostal Church v. Terry, 660 S.W.2d 449 (Mo. App. 1983). *See also* In re Uranian 1st Gnostic Lyceum Temple, 547 N.Y.S.2d 63 (N.Y. App. 1989).

[204] Burnett v. Banks, 279 P.2d 579 (Cal. 1955); Smith v. Riley, 424 So.2d 1166 (La. App. 1982).

[205] Aglikin v. Kovacheff, 516 N.E.2d 704 (Ill. App. 1987).

they no longer qualified as church members under a provision in the church charter requiring members to tithe. A state appeals court rejected the pastor's argument that the three deacons had forfeited their right to vote by virtue of the fact that they failed to tithe. The court pointed out that the tithing requirement applied only to church members—and not to members of the board of deacons. It observed that the church charter "sets forth requirements for corporate membership exclusively; thus, individual directors need not comply with [the charter's] assessment requirements to maintain their status as voting members of the deacon board." Instead, the court concluded that the church's board members were governed by another provision in the church's charter stipulating that "the persons elected deacons of the church shall automatically become members of the board of directors."[206]

• A Missouri court ruled that it could determine whether two board members of a religious organization were qualified to serve, since it could do so without considering religious doctrine. A synagogue created a subsidiary corporation and transferred all of its property to the subsidiary in an attempt to protect its assets from liability. The subsidiary was incorporated as a nonprofit corporation under state law. Its bylaws specified that board members had to be members of the synagogue. A dispute arose among members of the subsidiary's board, and two board members filed a lawsuit against other board members, and attempted to oust other board members and install new ones. In response to these actions, the board voted to expel the two dissident members. The two dissidents refused to honor this vote, but they did nothing to challenge it. The board then asked a court to determine that the dissidents were not qualified to serve as directors since they were no longer members of the congregation as required by the bylaws, and to remove them from office. A state appeals court acknowledged that it had no authority to resolve ecclesiastical matters, and that "the removal or expulsion from a congregation is a matter for an ecclesiastical tribunal to decide and its decision thereon is binding and not reviewable by the civil courts." However, in this case the two dissidents had already been removed, and their removal was not the issue. Rather, the court was asked to determine whether or not the dismissed board members were eligible to continue serving on the board. The court concluded that "to resolve the matter does not require the court to become entangled in religious doctrine or unconstitutionally interfere with a religious body's affairs."[207]

• The Virginia Supreme Court intervened in an internal church dispute concerning the term of office of church trustees. For nearly 70 years, the trustees of an Episcopal church's endowment fund served life terms. A dispute then arose, and the church's vestry sought a court ruling on the trustees' term of office. The court concluded that the trustees' term of office was one year on the basis of a provision in the Virginia nonprofit corporation law specifying that "in the absence of a provision in the articles of incorporation fixing a term of office, the term of office for a director shall be one year." Since the court found no provision in the articles of incorporation "fixing a term of office," it concluded that state law mandated a one-year term. In support of its conclusion, the court observed that "had the organizers intended to take the unusual step of providing life terms for trustees, they surely would have done so in unmistakable fashion." It further noted that the articles of incorporation required "not less than three" trustees to be "vestrymen of the church." And, since the terms

---

[206] Chimney Ville Missionary Baptist Church v. Johnson, 665 So.2d 730 (La. App. 1995).

[207] Beth Hamedrosh Hagodol Cemetery v. Levy, 923 S.W.2d 439 (Mo. App. 1996).

of the church's vestrymen were limited to three years, there were at least three trustees (at any given time) who could not serve life terms. The court found this to be "unmistakable evidence of the organizers' intention not to fix the trustees' terms of office at life." Since no provision in the articles of incorporation specified a life term (or any other term), the nonprofit corporation law fixed the trustees' term at one year.[208]

Authority

§ 6-06.2

Key point 6-06.2. *Officers and directors must be legally authorized to act on behalf of their church. Legal authority can be express, implied, inherent, or apparent. In addition, a church can ratify the unauthorized actions of its officers or directors, but this is not required.*

1. Officers

It is often said that church officers may perform only those acts for which they have authority, and that the authority of church officers is similar to that exercised by officers of private corporations.[209]

The legal authority of a corporate officer may derive from four sources:

- express authority

- implied authority

- inherent authority

- apparent authority

The most basic kind of authority possessed by a church officer consists of *express authority* deriving from those powers and prerogatives conferred by statute, charter, bylaw, or resolution. Some nonprofit corporation laws confer certain powers upon the officers of church corporations, but by far the greatest sources of express authority are a church's charter, bylaws, and resolutions. Article V of the Model Nonprofit Corporation Bylaws lists the powers of corporate officers as follows:

President. The President shall be the principal executive officer of the corporation and shall in general supervise and control all of the business affairs of the corporation. He shall preside at all meetings of the Board of Directors. He may sign, with the Secretary or any other proper officer of the corporation authorized by the Board of Directors, any deeds, mortgages, bonds, contracts, or other instruments which the Board has authorized to

[208] St. John's Protestant Episcopal Church Endowment Fund, Inc. v. Vestry of St. John's Protestant Episcopal Church, 377 S.E.2d 375 (Va. 1989). This case illustrates the important principle that questions of church administration may be resolved by state nonprofit corporation law if the church is incorporated under the general nonprofit corporation law and the church's articles of incorporation do not address a particular matter.

[209] Lewis v. Wolfe, 413 S.W.2d 314 (Mo. 1967).

be executed, except in cases where the signing and execution thereof shall be expressly delegated by the Board of Directors or by these bylaws or by statute to some other officer or agent of the corporation; and in general shall perform all duties incident to the office of President and such other duties as may be prescribed by the Board of Directors from time to time.

Vice President. In the absence of the President or in the event of his inability or refusal to act, the Vice President (or, in the event that there be more than one Vice President, the Vice Presidents in the order of their election) shall perform the duties of the President, and when so acting, shall have all powers of and be subject to all the restrictions upon the President. Any Vice President shall perform such other duties as from time to time may be assigned to him by the President or by the Board of Directors.

Treasurer. If required by the Board of Directors, the Treasurer shall give a bond for the faithful discharge of his duties in such sum and with such surety or sureties as the Board of Directors shall determine. He shall have charge and custody of and be responsible for all funds and securities of the corporation; receive and give receipts for moneys due and payable to the corporation from any source whatsoever, and deposit all such moneys in the name of the corporation in such banks, trust companies or other depositories as shall be selected in accordance with the provisions of . . . these bylaws; and in general perform all the duties incident to the office of Treasurer and such other duties as from time to time may be assigned to him by the President or by the Board of Directors.

Secretary. The Secretary shall keep the minutes of the meetings of the Board of Directors in one or more books provided for that purpose; see that all notices are duly given in accordance with the provisions of these bylaws or as required by law; be custodian of the corporate records and of the seal of the corporation and see that the seal of the corporation is affixed to all documents, the execution of which on behalf of the corporation under its seal is duly authorized in accordance with the provisions of these bylaws . . . and in general perform all duties incident to the office of Secretary and such other duties as from time to time may be assigned to him by the President or by the Board of Directors.

Officers also possess *implied authority* to perform all those acts that are necessary in performing an express power. The law essentially implies the existence of such authority, without which the express powers would be frustrated. To illustrate, the courts have held that express authority to manage a business includes the power to enter into contracts and to make purchases on behalf of the company. Authority to sell property has been held to include the power to execute a mortgage necessary for the sale of the property. And, authority to borrow money has been held to include the power to execute a guaranty.

Certain powers often are said to be *inherent* in a particular office, whether or not expressly granted in an organization's charter, bylaws, or resolutions. For example, it commonly is said that the president has inherent authority to preside at meetings of the corporation, that the vice-president has inherent authority to act as president if the president is absent or incapacitated, that the secretary has inherent authority to maintain the corporate seal and records and to serve as secretary in all corporate meetings, and that the treasurer has inherent authority to receive money for the corporation.[210]

Officers occasionally possess *apparent authority*, that is, authority that has not actually been granted by the corporation but which the corporation through its actions and representations leads others to believe has been granted.[211] The doctrine of apparent authority rests on the principle of estoppel, which forbids persons or organizations to give an officer or agent an appearance of authority that does not in fact exist and to benefit from such misleading conduct to the detriment of one who has relied on it.

Transactions entered into by church officers acting without authority are invalid. To illustrate, one court concluded that a land sales contract executed by a church secretary and treasurer was not legally enforceable.[212] The court observed that the officers of a corporation "have only those powers conferred on them by the bylaws of the corporation or by the resolution of the directors." Neither the bylaws of the church nor any resolution by the board vested the secretary and treasurer with authority to enter into contracts on behalf of the church. Another court rejected the validity of a land sales contract executed by an officer of an unincorporated religious organization.[213] The court emphasized that the officer had no actual or implied authority to sign contracts, and it concluded that "trustees or similar officers of unincorporated religious organizations must have the consent of their organization in order to convey its property. . . . [We] see no evidence that [the officer] had obtained any authorization or consent for the proposed land sale from any membership group."

Corporations can "ratify" the unauthorized acts of their officers and directors by consenting to them. Ratification generally is held to consist of three elements: acceptance by the corporation of the benefits of the officer's action, full knowledge of the facts, and circumstances or affirmative conduct indicating an intention to adopt and approve the unauthorized action. Ratification may not occur before an unauthorized action, and must take place within a reasonable time after such action. Ratifications generally are considered to be irrevocable. Only that body possessing the power to perform or authorize an officer's unauthorized action has the power to ratify it. This generally is the board of directors.

---

[210] Fletcher Cyc. Corp. § 441 (perm. ed. 2008); Note, *Inherent Powers of Corporate Officers: Need for a Statutory Definition*, 61 Harv. L. Rev. 867 (1948).

[211] Continental-Wirt Electronics Corp. v. Sprague Electric Co., 329 F. Supp. 959 (E.D. Pa. 1971).

[212] Daniel Webster Council v. St. James Association, 533 A.2d 329 (N.H. 1987).

[213] Shakra v. Benedictine Sisters of Bedford, 553 A.2d 1327 (N.H. 1989). *Accord* Biscegelia v. Bernadine Sisters, 560 N.E.2d 567 (Mass. App. 1990).

Ratification can be express, such as by formal, recorded action of the board of directors, or it can be implied from the acts and representations of the board. Implied ratification often occurs when a corporation knows or should have known of an unauthorized act and does nothing to repudiate it. Thus, when a church's parish committee should have known of various mortgages executed by the church's minister on behalf of the church but did nothing to disavow them, it was held to have ratified them by implication.[214]

Case Studies

• A New York court ruled that a church could be liable on a contract for a construction project signed by its pastor, without board authorization, because the church had ratified similar transactions in the past.[215]

Section 8.45 of the Revised Model Nonprofit Corporation Act specifies:

> *Any contract or other instrument in writing executed or entered into between a corporation and any other person is not invalidated as to the corporation by any lack of authority of the signing officers in the absence of actual knowledge on the part of the other person that the signing officers had no authority to execute the contract or other instrument if it is signed by any two officers in category 1 [i.e., the presiding officer of the board and the president] or by one officer in category 1 [see above] and one officer in category 2 [i.e., a vice president, the secretary, treasurer and executive director].*

• The Mississippi Supreme Court ruled that a church was legally bound by the misrepresentation of its financial secretary. The church signed a contract with a local contractor for the construction of a building at a cost of $1.2 million. From the start, payments under the contract were late. The contractor eventually informed the church that construction would be stopped until payments were brought up to date and the church placed in escrow sufficient monies to pay the balance of the contract. The church brought payments up to date, and then the church's financial secretary provided the contractor with a letter stating that the church had placed monies in escrow sufficient to pay the balance of the contract. On the basis of this representation, the contractor resumed construction and continued to work until it was informed that no further funds were available. The contractor sued the church for the balance due on the contract (nearly $500,000), claiming that the financial secretary's letter was false and fraudulent, that the financial secretary was an agent of the church, and that the church was responsible for its agent's acts. The state supreme court ruled in favor of the contractor. The church insisted that it had not been aware of its financial secretary's letter, that it did not condone fraud, and that it was an "innocent party." While it acknowledged that the financial secretary was an agent of the church, it claimed that the church could not be responsible for an act of its agent that was unauthorized and contrary to the church's teachings against fraud. The court did not agree. It noted that a church can be responsible for the unauthorized acts of an agent

---

[214] Perkins v. Rich, 429 N.E.2d 1135 (Mass. 1982).

[215] Butler v. Sacred Heart of Jesus English Rite Catholic Church, 680 N.Y.S.2d 909 (N.Y. 1998).

under the theory of "apparent agency" if the following three conditions are satisfied: (1) actions by the church indicating that the agent has authority, (2) reasonable reliance on those actions, and (3) a detrimental change in position as a result of that reliance. The court concluded that all three of these conditions were satisfied in this case, and accordingly that the church was liable for the misrepresentations of its financial secretary.[216]

2. Directors and Trustees

Like officers, the authority of directors and trustees is to be found primarily in a church's charter or bylaws, or in some cases the state nonprofit corporation statute under which a church is incorporated. In addition, directors and trustees have implied authority to do those things that are necessary to fulfill their express powers, and they will be clothed with apparent authority when a church through its actions or representations leads others to believe that authority to perform a particular act has been granted.[217]

There is one significant difference between officers and directors with respect to authority—while one or two corporate officers often have authority to act on behalf of the corporation in certain matters, directors *never* have authority, acting individually or in small groups, to bind the corporation. Directors can only act as a board, not as individuals. Accordingly, a director has no authority, acting alone, to purchase equipment or land, hire employees, or otherwise make legally binding commitments on behalf of the corporation. One or two officers, however, may be vested with this authority.

The United States Supreme Court has stated that "the first place one must look to determine the powers of corporate directors is in the relevant state's corporation law. Corporations are creatures of state law . . . and it is state law which is the font of corporate directors' powers."[218] The Model Nonprofit Corporation Act states that "the affairs of a corporation shall be managed by a board of directors."[219] Most states that have not adopted the Act have similar provisions in their religious or nonprofit corporation laws. As a result, most state nonprofit corporation laws confer general managerial authority upon the directors or trustees of incorporated churches. This authority often is very broad, even to the point of empowering the board to act on behalf of the church in the ordinary business of the corporation without the necessity of obtaining the consent or approval of the membership. This means that the board of a church corporation ordinarily has the authority to enter into contracts; elect officers; hire employees; authorize notes, deeds, and mortgages; and institute and settle lawsuits. The powers of the board, however, may be limited by church charter, bylaw, or resolution. The boards of unincorporated churches generally derive little if any authority from state law.

The courts often have held that a church board occupies a position similar to the managing directors of a business corporation, at least with respect to

---

[216] Christian Methodist Episcopal Church v. S & S Construction Company, Inc., 615 So.2d 568 (Miss. 1993).

[217] Straughter v. Holy Temple of Church of God in Christ, 150 So.2d 124 (La. App. 1963).

[218] Burks v. Lasker, 441 U.S. 471, 478 (1979).

[219] Model Nonprofit Corporation Act § 16.

the temporal affairs of a church, and that the board has authority to act only at regularly assembled meetings.[220] Accordingly, when four out of seven directors met informally and agreed to change the location of an annual church meeting, the election of directors at such a meeting was invalid.[221] Another court observed that "only when acting as a board may trustees of a religious corporation perform or authorize acts binding on the corporation," and therefore the attempt by an individual trustee of a church to employ an attorney on behalf of the church was invalidated.[222] The Revised Model Nonprofit Corporation Act confers upon the board of directors limited "emergency powers" (pertaining to the amendment of bylaws, selection of successors to incapacitated officers, relocation of the corporation's principal office, and notice and quorum requirements).[223]

Directors and trustees may not perform acts not authorized either by state law or the church's charter or bylaws. To illustrate, one court ruled that if a church charter gives the board of trustees authority to institute lawsuits in the corporation's name only after being directed to do so by a majority vote of the church membership, then a lawsuit instituted by the board itself without congregational approval is unauthorized.[224] Another court ruled that the trustees of a church corporation do not possess the authority to adopt bylaws for the church unless the charter or constitution of the church specifically gives them such authority.[225] The Washington Supreme Court ruled that a church's board of elders was powerless to amend the church's articles of incorporation without the pastor's approval.[226] The church's articles of incorporation specified that neither the articles nor the bylaws could be amended without the pastor's approval. The church board members met without the pastor and voted to amend the articles by removing the provision requiring the pastor to approve all amendments to the articles. The pastor immediately filed a lawsuit asking a civil court to determine whether or not the elders had the authority to amend the articles without his approval. A trial court ruled in favor of the elders, and the pastor appealed.

The state Supreme Court ruled in favor of the pastor. It reasoned that the articles clearly specified that they could not be amended without the pastor's approval, and that as a result the elders' attempt to amend the articles without the pastor's approval was null and void. The court observed: "Neither of the parties has called to our attention any case holding that any corporation law in the country, profit or nonprofit, prohibits a provision in the articles of incorporation requiring the concurrence of a special individual to amend the articles." The court agreed that the church's articles "might well, in retrospect, be viewed by some as an improvident provision," but it concluded that "it is not the function of this court . . . to protect those who freely chose to enter into this kind of relationship."

---

[220] Coates v. Parchman, 334 S.W.2d 417 (Mo. 1960).

[221] Id.

[222] Krehel v. Eastern Orthodox Catholic Church, 195 N.Y.S.2d 334, 336 (1959), aff'd, 221 N.Y.S.2d 724 (1961).

[223] REVISED MODEL NONPROFIT CORPORATION ACT §§ 2.07 and 3.03.

[224] Honey Creek Regular Baptist Church v. Wilson, 92 N.E.2d 419 (Ohio 1950).

[225] Lewis v. Wolfe, 413 S.W.2d 314 (Mo. 1967).

[226] Barnett v. Hicks, 792 P.2d 150 (Wash. 1990).

Case Studies

• *An Indiana court ruled that a majority of a congregational church's members, rather than the church's board of trustees, had the legal authority to determine whether or not to retain their pastor. The court noted that for churches of congregational polity, "the religious organization is represented by a majority of its members," and therefore "when presented with a dispute within a church of congregational polity, our courts will uphold the majority's decision, whether that is to purchase property or even remove the minister, unless the church has established its own decision-making body with the power to override the will of the majority."[227]*

• *A New York court ruled that an unincorporated nonprofit organization was not bound by three promissory notes executed by its treasurer without authorization. The treasurer executed three promissory notes totaling $260,000 to a creditor who later sued the organization and its treasurer for nonpayment. A state appeals court ruled that the nonprofit organization could not be liable for payment of the notes since it had not authorized the treasurer to issue them. It observed: "Since a voluntary, unincorporated association has no existence separate and apart from its members, an association is not liable on the contracts of its officers, agents, or individual members in the absence of prior authorization or ratification with full knowledge of the facts by its members. The authority of a member or officer of an unincorporated association to bind the association will not be presumed or implied from the existence of a general power to attend to or transact the business, or promote the objects for which the association was formed, except where the debt contracted is necessary for its preservation. Once the authority of an agent is put in issue, it must be shown that the purported agent of the association had authority to incur any obligation on the association's behalf." The court acknowledged that the creditor served as chairman of the organization's executive committee, and in that capacity directed the treasurer to execute the promissory notes. However, this did not make the organization liable on the notes since the creditor "failed to show that [the treasurer] was authorized to execute the promissory notes, and that the debt was necessary for the [organization's] preservation."[228]*

• *A Pennsylvania court ruled that a church board lacked the authority to remove a pastor because the church was hierarchical in nature and the board's action was in violation of the national church's constitution.[229]*

• *A South Carolina court ruled that a former trustee of a Baptist church who resigned his membership lacked the legal authority to act on behalf of the church. In 1952 a couple deeded property to a new Baptist church in the name of three trustees. One of the trustees (the "trustee") attended this church for three or four years but then stopped attending. Some 40 years later, this former trustee learned that the church was for sale, and he demanded the keys from the current pastor. The former trustee pointed out that he was the only surviving trustee, and that his name still appeared on the deed and accordingly he had the legal authority to determine whether or not the church could be sold. The pastor claimed that the former trustee's authority*

---

[227] Cole v. Holt, 725 N.E.2d 145 (Ind. App. 2000).

[228] Barrett v. Republican State Committee, 625 N.Y.S.2d 769 (A.D. 4 Dept. 1995).

[229] The American Carpatho-Russian Orthodox Greek Catholic Diocese of the U.S.A. v. Church Board, 749 A.2d 1003 (Common. Pa. 2000).

ended when he left the church nearly 40 years before, and also when the church was incorporated in 1965 (following its incorporation the church could hold legal title to its property in the name of the corporation, and no longer needed to hold title in the name of trustees). A state appeals court ruled in favor of the pastor. It observed that the former trustee had abandoned his membership in the church when he quit attending services some 40 years before and began attending other churches. The court then addressed the issue of the legal authority of a church trustee: "Although [the former trustee] was named as a trustee for the church, the deed to him and the other trustees does not purport to create a property interest in him, except to the extent he, as trustee, held legal title for the church and would benefit as a member of the church. . . . The trustees of a church hold the property solely for the congregation whose officers they are at the time of the conveyance. While legal title to the property may be in the trustees, the use of the property is controlled by the discipline of the church in general. Moreover, the duly elected trustees of a church hold office only for the term for which they are elected and until their successors are elected." Finally, the court pointed out that "generally, congregational forms of church government provide that one may not be a trustee without being a member of the church," and that because the former trustee "abandoned his membership in [the church] he likewise forfeited his right to remain a trustee of the church."[230]

Meetings

§ 6-06.3

Key point 6-06.3. *Church boards generally can act only in a meeting that is duly called pursuant to the church's governing documents. Many state nonprofit corporation laws permit church boards to act by written consent, or by conference telephone call.*

The general authority to manage church affairs generally is vested in the directors or trustees, and their acts are binding on the corporation only when done as a board at a legal meeting. Neither a minority nor a majority of the board has the authority to meet privately and take action binding upon the corporation. The reason for this rule has been stated as follows: "The law believes that the greatest wisdom results from conference and exchange of individual views, and it is for this reason that the law requires the united wisdom of a majority of the several members of the board in determining the business of the corporation."[231]

This rule has exceptions. For example, some state nonprofit corporation laws permit directors to take action without a meeting if they all submit written consents to a proposed action.[232] And some states permit directors to conduct meetings by conference telephone call. The entire board of directors of course can take action at a duly convened meeting to ratify an action taken by a minority or majority of the board acting separately and not in a legal meeting.

Corporate bylaws ordinarily specify that regular meetings of the directors or

---

[230] Brock v. Bennett, 443 S.E.2d 409 (S.C. App. 1994).

[231] Trethewey v. Green River Gorge, 136 P.2d 999, 1012 (Wash. 1943).

[232] Section 8.22 of the Revised Model Nonprofit Corporation Act permits such action unless the articles or bylaws provide otherwise.

trustees shall occur at specified times and at a specified location. The designation in the bylaws of the time and place for regular meetings of the board generally will be considered sufficient notice of such meetings. In addition, special meetings may be convened by those officers or directors who are authorized by the bylaws to do so. The bylaws ordinarily require that notice of a special meeting be communicated to all directors at a prescribed interval before the meeting. The notice also must be in the form prescribed by the bylaws.

Can a Church Board Meet in Secret Without the Pastor?

Can a church board meet without informing the senior pastor and transact business on behalf of the church that is not an emergency? Assume that the pastor is available, and that the church bylaws specify that the pastor is the president of the corporation and chairperson of the board.

The answer to this question will depend on the wording of a church's governing documents (i.e., constitution, bylaws). If the governing documents do not address this issue, then refer to the state nonprofit corporation law under which the church is incorporated. To illustrate, the nonprofit corporation law of one state specifies: "Notice of the place, if any, and time of each meeting of the directors shall be given to each director either by personal delivery or by mail, by overnight delivery service, or by means of authorized communications equipment at least two days before the meeting. That notice need not specify the purposes of the meeting."

This is a fairly common provision in state nonprofit corporation laws. According to this language, a group of board members could not hold a secret meeting without giving notice to the pastor. This assumes that (1) the church is incorporated under a state nonprofit corporation law containing such a provision, and (2) the pastor is a member of the board. Any action taken at such a meeting would be nullity.

A meeting of the directors or trustees will not be legal unless a *quorum* is present. A quorum refers to that number or percentage of the total authorized number of directors that must be present in order for the board to transact business. The bylaws typically state the quorum requirements. In the absence of a bylaw provision, the number of directors constituting a quorum ordinarily will be determined by state nonprofit corporation law (for incorporated churches). In many states, a majority of the board will constitute a quorum in the absence of a bylaw or statutory provision to the contrary. Some nonprofit corporation laws specify that a quorum may not consist of less than a certain number. If vacancies in the board reduce the number of directors to less than a quorum, some statutes permit the board to meet for the purpose of filling vacancies.[233]

Board meetings are often informal. The president of the corporation generally presides at such meetings, and the secretary keeps minutes. Actions of the board may be in the form of a resolution, although this is not necessary since it has

---

[233] MODEL NONPROFIT CORPORATION ACT § 19.

been held that actions taken by the board and recorded in the minutes constitute corporate actions as effectively as a formal resolution.[234]

If a board meeting does not comply with the requirements in the corporation's bylaws or in state law, it will be invalid, and its actions will have no legal effect. Thus, meetings will be invalid and ineffective if notice requirements are not satisfied, unless all of the directors waive the defect in notice either verbally or implicitly by their attendance without objection at the meeting. Meetings will also be invalid if quorum requirements are not satisfied, and an action taken by the board even at a duly called meeting will be invalid if it was adopted by less than the required number of votes.

Removal

§ 6-06.4

Key point 6-06.4. *Church officers and directors can be removed from office in the manner authorized by the church's governing documents. It is common for church bylaws to give the membership the authority to remove officers and directors who engage in specified misconduct or change their doctrinal position.*

A corporation possesses the inherent power to remove an officer, director, or trustee for *good cause*.[235] To illustrate, one court ruled that the members of a nonprofit corporation may remove directors from office at a meeting called for this purpose, at any time.[236] Another court held that a church congregation has the inherent authority to remove a director for good cause even though the church bylaws did not address the issue.[237] In the context of church corporations, good cause ordinarily will consist of material doctrinal deviation, conduct deemed unacceptable behavior by established church custom and practice, incompetency, or incapacity. The church membership itself, and not the board, generally has the authority to remove directors or trustees for cause. Officers elected by the board ordinarily may be removed by the board.[238] Officers or directors removed for cause generally have no right to compensation (if any) for the unexpired term of office.

A church has no authority to remove an officer or director without cause prior to the expiration of a stated term of office unless a bylaw or statute specifically grants such authority. But officers or directors elected for an unspecified term generally may be removed at any time with or without cause by the body that elected them. And, when the term of an officer or director expires, a church congregation can fill the vacancy without proving that good cause exists for not reelecting the individual.[239]

---

[234] FLETCHER CYC. CORP. § 419 (perm. ed. 2008).

[235] Rodyk v. Ukrainian Autocephalic Orthodox Church, 296 N.Y.S.2d 496 (1968), aff'd, 328 N.Y.S.2d 685 (1972).

[236] First Union Baptist Church v. Banks, 533 So.2d 1305 (La. App. 1988).

[237] Mangum v. Swearingen, 565 S.W.2d 957 (Tex. 1978).

[238] Beth Hamedrosh Hagodol Cemetery v. Levy, 923 S.W.2d 439 (Mo. App. 1996) ("the body which appoints a director may also remove a director").

[239] Morris v. Richard Clark Missionary Baptist Church, 177 P.2d 811 (Cal. 1947).

State nonprofit corporation laws usually provide for removal of officers and directors. For example, section 18 of the Model Nonprofit Corporation Act states that a director may be removed by any procedure set forth in the corporation's articles of incorporation, and section 24 specifies that an officer may be removed by the persons authorized to elect or appoint such officer whenever in their judgment it serves the best interests of the corporation.

Relevant provisions in state law or a church's bylaws for removal of officers and directors must be followed. To illustrate, if a statute specifies that any ten members of a church can call for a congregational meeting for the purpose of removing directors from office, any action taken at a meeting called by only eight members will be invalid.[240] And, if a church votes to remove certain officers at a meeting conducted in violation of church bylaws, the removal of the officers will be invalid.[241]

Provisions in statutes, charters, or bylaws calling for an officer or director to serve for a prescribed term and until his or her successor is chosen do not prevent an officer or director from resigning. A resignation is complete upon its receipt by the corporation even though the corporate charter states that the office is to be held until a successor is elected and qualified.[242] Furthermore, the resignation of an officer or director will be effective even if not accepted at a formal meeting of the board of directors, at least if the board knew of the resignation and acquiesced in it.[243]

Case Studies

• *The Alabama Supreme Court ruled that the dismissal of two church elders by a minister and his supporters was not legally effective since the church's established procedures were not followed. The minister convened a meeting of 27 church members (out of a total of 162) at which a vote was taken to "disfellowship" the elders. The elders were not notified of this meeting. An announcement was made after the next Sunday morning service that the elders had been removed "because of their willful and persistent violation of scripture in taking [the minister] to court." The elders challenged their dismissal in court. The state supreme court concluded that the dismissal of the elders violated this established procedure in a number of respects and accordingly was invalid. As a result, the court reinstated the elders and directed the minister to vacate the parsonage and discontinue conducting services on behalf of the church. The court concluded: "Clearly, the civil court will not review acts of church discipline or membership expulsion where there is no question as to the invasion of civil or property rights. However, the court has jurisdiction to review an expulsion from a religious society to determine whether the expelling organization acted in accordance with its own regulations, or to determine whether it acted in accordance with the principles of natural justice."[244]*

• *A Georgia court ruled that a church's entire board had properly been dismissed by the church members at a duly called special business meeting, because the meeting was*

---

[240] Miles v. Wilson, 181 N.Y.S.2d 585 (1958).

[241] Tybor v. Ukrainian Autocephalic Orthodox Church, 151 N.Y.S.2d 711 (1956).

[242] Koven v. Saberdyne Systems, Inc., 625 P.2d 907 (Ariz. 1980).

[243] Anderson v. K.G. Moore, Inc., 376 N.E.2d 1238 (Mass. 1978), *cert. denied,* 439 U.S. 1116 (1979).

[244] Shearry v. Sanders, 621 So.2d 1307 (Ala. 1993).

conducted in accordance with applicable provisions of the state nonprofit corporation law.[245]

• *An Illinois court concluded that it had no authority to resolve an internal church dispute regarding the membership of a church's board of deacons. A local congregation adopted bylaws that conflicted with the provisions of the hierarchical denomination with which it was affiliated. The church elected deacons under its bylaws, and these individuals later were deposed by the denomination. A lawsuit was brought to determine the legal authority of the deposed deacons. The deposed deacons argued that the court should resolve this dispute since it did not involve "doctrinal matters" and could be resolved on the basis of non-doctrinal "neutral principles of law." The court disagreed. It observed, "In our opinion, resolution of the questions of who the true members of the board of deacons . . . are and which bylaws govern it would require this court to delve, impermissibly, into matters of church doctrine and polity." It rejected the dismissed deacons' claim that this case involved secular issues that could be resolved using neutral principles of law. In rejecting this contention the court observed: "The real questions presented here are: Who governs? And by what rules? Stated otherwise, which of the factions should be recognized as the true members of the board of deacons?"[246]*

• *The Supreme Judicial Court of Massachusetts ruled that the First Amendment prevented it from resolving an internal church dispute regarding the authority of a denominational official to dismiss members of a local church board.[247] The court conceded that the civil courts can resolve church property disputes on the basis of "neutral principles of law" involving no inquiry into doctrine or policy. However, this was not a property case: "Here the dispute is not one of property as such . . . . The conflict here began when a majority of the parish corporation passed a vote of no confidence in the [pastor], hardly a question of property. The dispute blossomed to encompass wider questions of church governance, including the method of selection of members of the [board]. . . . What is at stake here is the power to exert religious authority."*

• *A Missouri court ruled that it was prevented by the First Amendment guaranty of religious freedom from resolving a lawsuit brought by ousted church officers challenging the legal validity of their removal.[248] The court concluded that this dispute was far more than a disagreement over the meaning and application of corporate bylaws. The "ultimate issue" was whether or not the ouster of church officers was proper. The court noted that "there is no way that can be a non-ecclesiastical issue."*

• *A New York court ruled that a pastor's attempt to remove an entire board of deacons, and several church members, contrary to the procedures set forth in the church constitution were unlawful and of no effect. Since the removal of the deacons, and excommunication of members, were not done in compliance with the church constitution, such actions were "contrary to law." The same was true "of the action taken to effectively abolish the board of deacons by removing all of its members, whose offices for an indefinite term are established by the constitution and bylaws of the church." While the members of a church corporation "have the authority to amend*

---

[245] Members of Calvary Missionary Baptist Church v. Jackson, 603 S.E.2d 711 (Ga. App. 2004).

[246] St. Mark Coptic Orthodox Church v. Tanios, 572 N.E.2d 283 (Ill. App. 1991).

[247] Parish of the Advent v. Protestant Episcopal Diocese, 688 N.E.2d 923 (Mass. 1997).

[248] Rolfe v. Parker, 968 S.W.2d 178 (Mo. App. 1998).

their constitution and bylaws, such action must be preceded by appropriate notice. Since no notice was given before the meeting, the action taken then is null and void. Thus, the former deacons remain members of the board of deacons."[249]

• *An Ohio court ruled that an attempt by church members to remove all of the members of the church board at a specially called membership meeting was invalid because the notice requirements prescribed by state nonprofit corporation law were not followed. The court noted that the members who called the special meeting were required to state the purpose of the meeting and provide at least ten days' notice of the special meeting. Because this notice requirement was not followed, the meeting at which the board was ousted was void. Further, the other actions taken at that meeting (appointment of a new board, and reinstatement of the pastor) also were void.[250]*

• *An Ohio court ruled that a church's board of trustees had been properly ousted and replaced with a new board in a specially-called business meeting that was called in accordance with state nonprofit corporation law.[251]*

• *A South Carolina court ruled that church trustees had been properly removed at a membership meeting. The court concluded that the church was congregational in polity, meaning that it was "an independent organization, self-governing in its religious functions . . . [with] the congregation as the highest religious judicatory." The court rejected the ousted trustees' claim that they created the church to be governed exclusively by trustees.[252]*

Officers, Directors, and Trustees— Personal Liability

§ 6-07

Traditionally, the officers and directors of nonprofit corporations performed their duties with little if any risk of personal legal liability. In recent years, a number of lawsuits have attempted to impose personal liability on such officers and directors. In some cases, directors are sued because of statutes that provide limited legal immunity to churches (discussed in section 6-08).

As a general rule, directors are not responsible for actions taken by the board prior to their election to the board (unless they vote to ratify a previous action). Similarly, directors ordinarily are not liable for actions taken by the board after their resignation. Again, they will continue to be liable for actions that they took prior to their resignation.

A number of state laws permit nonprofit corporations to amend their bylaws to indemnify directors for any costs incurred in connection with the defense of any lawsuit arising out of their status as directors.

The more common theories of liability are summarized below.

---

[249] Briggs v. Noble, 2004 WL 829439, (N.Y. App. 2004).

[250] Calvary Congregational Church v. Eppinger, 2000 WL 193216 (Ohio App. 2000).

[251] North Dayton First Church of God v. Berger, 2000 WL 1597963 (Ohio App. 2000).

[252] Williams v. Wilson, 533 S.E.2d 593 (S.C. App. 2000).

Tort Liability

§ 6-07.01

Key point 6-07.01. *Church board members may be personally liable for their own torts (conduct causing personal injury to another). This is so whether or not the church is incorporated.*

Perhaps the most common basis of legal liability relates to the commission of torts. A "tort" is a civil wrong, other than a breach of contract, for which the law provides a remedy. Common examples include negligence (e.g., careless operation of a church-owned vehicle), defamation, fraud, copyright infringement, and wrongful termination of employees.

Generally, the directors and officers of a nonprofit corporation do not incur personal liability for the corporation's torts merely by reason of their official position. Rather, they will be liable only for those torts that they commit, direct, or participate in, even though the corporation itself may also be liable. To illustrate, directors in some cases may be personally liable if they

- knowingly permit an unsafe condition to exist on church property that results in death or injury;

- cause injury as a result of the negligent operation of a vehicle in the course of church business;

- negligently fail to adequately supervise church activities resulting in death or injury;

- terminate an employee for an impermissible or insufficient reason;

- utter a defamatory remark about another individual;

- authorize an act that infringes upon the exclusive rights of a copyright owner;

- engage in fraudulent acts;

- knowingly draw checks against insufficient funds; or

- knowingly make false representations as to the financial condition of the church to third parties who, in reliance on such representations, extend credit to the church and suffer a loss.

In all such cases, the director must personally commit, direct, or participate in the tort. Therefore, a director ordinarily will not be liable for the torts committed by other board members without his or her knowledge or consent. Obviously, board members having any question regarding the propriety of a particular action being discussed at a board meeting should be sure to have their dissent to the proposed action registered in the minutes of the meeting.

Contract Liability § 6-07.02

Key point 6-07.02. *Church board members may be personally liable for contracts they sign if they do so without authorization, or if they fail to indicate that they are signing as a representative of the church.*

Church board members may be personally liable on contracts that they sign in either of two ways. First, a board member may be personally liable on a contract that he signs without authority. Second, a board member may be personally liable on a contract that he is authorized to sign but which he signs in his own name without any reference to the church or to his representational capacity. To prevent this inadvertent assumption of liability, board members who are authorized to sign contracts (as well as any other legal document) should be careful to indicate the church's name on the document and clearly indicate their own representational capacity (agent, director, trustee, officer, etc.).

Breach of the Fiduciary Duty of Care § 6-07.03

Key point 6-07.03. *Church board members have a fiduciary duty to use reasonable care in the discharge of their duties, and they may be personally liable for damages resulting from their failure to do so.*

1. In General

The board members of business corporations are under a duty to perform their duties "in good faith, in a manner they reasonably believe to be in the best interests of the corporation, and with such care as an ordinarily prudent person in a like position would use under similar circumstances." This duty commonly is referred to as the "prudent person rule" or the "duty of due care." In recent years, some courts have extended this duty to the board members of nonprofit corporations. To illustrate, a federal district court ruled that the directors of a nonprofit corporation breached their fiduciary duty of care in managing the corporation's funds.[253] For nearly 20 years, management of the corporation had been dominated almost exclusively by two officers, whose decisions and recommendations were routinely adopted by the board. The corporation's finance committee had not convened in more than 11 years. Under these facts, the court concluded:

> Total abdication of [a director's] supervisory role, however, is improper . . . .
> A director who fails to acquire the information necessary to supervise . . . or
> consistently fails even to attend the meetings . . . has violated his fiduciary
> duty to the corporation . . . . A director whose failure to supervise permits

---

[253] Stern v. Lucy Webb Hayes National Training School for Deaconesses & Missionaries, 381 F. Supp. 1003 (D.D.C. 1974).

negligent mismanagement by others to go unchecked has committed an independent wrong against the corporation.[254]

A ruling of the bankruptcy court in the PTL ministry bankruptcy case addressed the liability of directors and officers.[255] The court agreed with the bankruptcy trustee that televangelist Jim Bakker (as both an officer and director) had breached his legal duty of care to PTL. It quoted a South Carolina statute (PTL was located in South Carolina) that specifies the duty of care that a director or officer owes to his or her corporation:

A director or officer shall perform his duties as a director or officer, including his duties as a member of any committee of the board of directors upon which he may serve, in good faith, in the manner he reasonably believes to be in the best interest of the corporation and of its shareholders, and with such care as an ordinary prudent person in a like position would use under similar circumstances.[256]

The court, in commenting upon this provision, observed:

Good faith requires the undivided loyalty of a corporate director or officer to the corporation and such a duty of loyalty prohibits the director or an officer, as a fiduciary, from using this position of trust for his own personal gain to the detriment of the corporation. In this instance, there are no shareholders of the corporation; however, even though there are no shareholders, the officers and directors still hold a fiduciary obligation to manage the corporation in its best interest and not to the detriment of the corporation itself.[257]

The court concluded that "the duty of care and loyalty required by [Bakker] was breached inasmuch as he (1) failed to inform the members of the board of the true financial position of the corporation and to act accordingly; (2) failed to supervise other officers and directors; (3) failed to prevent the depletion of corporate assets; and (4) violated the prohibition against self-dealing."

With respect to Bakker's defense that his actions had been "approved" by the board, the court observed that Bakker "exercised a great deal of control over his board" and that "a director who exercises a controlling influence over co-directors cannot defend acts committed by him on the grounds that his actions were approved by the board." The court acknowledged that officers and directors cannot be "held accountable for mere mistakes in judgment." However, it found that "the acts of [Bakker] did not constitute mere mistakes in judgment, but constituted gross mismanagement and a neglect of the affairs of the corporation.

---

[254] *Id.* at 1014.

[255] Heritage Village Church and Missionary Fellowship, Inc., 92 B.R. 1000 (D.S.C. 1988).

[256] *Id.* at 1014-1015, quoting S.C. Stats. Ann. § 33-13-150(a).

[257] *Id.* at 1015.

Clearly the salaries, the awards of bonuses and the carte blanche exercised over PTL checking accounts and credit cards were excessive and without justification and there was lack of proper care, attention and circumspection to the affairs of the corporation. [Bakker] breached [his] duty to manage and supervise . . . ."

In support of its conclusions, the court cited numerous findings, including the following: (a) Bakker failed to require firm bids on construction projects though this caused PTL substantial losses; (b) capital expenditures often greatly exceeded estimates, though Bakker was warned of the problem; (c) Bakker rejected warniAs one court has observed, "the law has no place for dummy directors." ers about the dangers of debt financing; (d) many of the bonuses granted to Bakker were granted "during periods of extreme financial hardship for PTL"; (e) Bakker "let it be known that he did not want to hear any bad news, so people were reluctant to give him bad financial information"; (f) "it was a common practice for PTL to write checks for more money than it showed in its checkbook; the books would often show a negative balance, but the money would eventually be transferred or raised to cover the checks written—this 'float' often would be three to four million dollars"; (g) most of the events and programs at PTL that were made available to the public were operated at a loss; since 1984, "energy was placed into raising lifetime partner funds rather than raising general contributions"; (h) Bakker "during the entire period in question, failed to give attention to financial matters and the problems of raising money and cutting expense."

Though at the time of Bakker's resignation in 1987 PTL had outstanding liens of $35 million, and general contributions were in a state of decline, "millions of dollars were being siphoned off by excessive spending." Such spending, noted the court, "is shocking to the conscience to the extent that it is unbelievable that a religious ministry would be operated in such a manner." The court concluded that "Mr. Bakker, as an officer and director of PTL . . . approached the management of the corporation with reckless indifference to the financial consequences of [his] acts. While on the one hand [he was] experiencing inordinate personal gain from the revenues of PTL, on the other hand [he was] intentionally ignoring the extreme financial difficulties of PTL and, ironically, [was], in fact, adding to them." To illustrate, Bakker accepted huge bonuses at times of serious financial crisis at PTL. "Such conduct," noted the court, "demonstrates a total lack of fiduciary responsibility to PTL."[258] The court emphasized that "*trustees and corporate directors for not-for-profit organizations are liable for losses occasioned by their negligent mismanagement.*"[259]

Lawsuits against nonprofit directors for breach of their "duty of care" are still rare. Directors of churches and religious organizations can reduce the risk of liability even further by (a) attending all of the meetings of the board and of any committees on which they serve; (b) thoroughly reviewing all interim and annual financial statements and reports, and seeking clarification of any irregularities or inconsistencies; (c) affirmatively investigating and rectifying any other problems or improprieties; (d) thoroughly reviewing the corporate charter, constitution, and

---

[258] *Id.* at 1013.
[259] *Id.* at 1015.

bylaws; (e) dissenting from any board action with which they have any misgivings, and insisting that their objection be recorded in the minutes of the meeting; and (f) resigning from the board if and when they are unable to fulfill these duties. As one court has observed, "the law has no place for dummy directors."

Discharging the Fiduciary Duty of Due Care

There are a number of ways that church board members can reduce the risk of liability for breaching the fiduciary duty of due care, including the following:

- attending all of the meetings of the board and of any committees on which they serve

- thoroughly reviewing all interim and annual financial statements and reports, and seeking clarification of any irregularities or inconsistencies

- affirmatively investigating and rectifying any other problems or improprieties

- thoroughly reviewing the corporate charter, constitution, and bylaws

- dissenting from any board action with which they have any misgivings, and insisting that their objection be recorded in the minutes of the meeting

- resigning from the board if and when they are unable to fulfill these duties.

As one court has observed, "the law has no place for dummy directors."

2. Investing Church Funds

Those who serve on a board of directors, whether for a church or any other organization, have a legal duty to perform their duties in good faith, in a manner they reasonably believe to be in the best interests of the corporation, and with such care as an ordinarily prudent person in a like position would use under similar circumstances. This duty commonly is referred to as the "prudent person rule" or the "duty of due care."

The fiduciary duty of due care often is set forth in a state's nonprofit corporation law. To illustrate, the Revised Model Nonprofit Corporation Act, which has been enacted in a small but growing number of states, contains the following language:

A director shall discharge his or her duties as a director . . . (1) in good faith; (2) with the care an ordinarily prudent person in a like position would exercise under similar circumstances; and (3) in a manner the director reasonably believes to be in the best interests of the corporation.

In discharging his or her duties, a director is entitled to rely on information, opinions, reports, or statements, including financial statements and other financial data, if prepared or presented by: (1) one or more officers or employees of the corporation whom the director reasonably believes to be reliable and competent in the matters presented; (2) legal counsel, public accountants or other persons as to matters the director reasonably believes are within the person's professional or expert competence . . . .[260]

This duty of due care applies to the investment of corporate funds. However, directors are not accountable for every bad investment they authorize. They are not held to a standard of perfection. Rather, they are accountable only if an investment decision was not based on "the care an ordinarily prudent person in a like position would exercise under similar circumstances." The courts have been reluctant to impose liability on directors for an exercise of poor judgment. One state Supreme Court, in language that has been quoted by several other courts, observed:

[There is] a presumption that in making a business decision the directors of a corporation acted on an informed basis, in good faith and in the honest belief that the action taken was in the best interests of the company. Absent an abuse of discretion, that judgment will be respected by the courts. The burden is on the party challenging the decision to establish facts rebutting the presumption.

What steps can church officers and directors take to reduce the risk of violating the fiduciary duty of due care? Consider the following:

- **Check state law.** If your church is incorporated under state law, be sure to check your state nonprofit corporation law for any provisions that address the duties of officers and directors. This information should be made available to all of the church's officers and directors.

- **Check the church's governing documents and minutes.** The governing documents (i.e., articles of incorporation or bylaws) of some churches contain restrictions on investments. Such restrictions may also appear in the minutes of congregational or board meetings. It is essential for board members to be familiar with these restrictions and to enforce them.

- **Use an investment committee.** Many nonprofit organizations use an investment committee to make recommendations regarding the investment of funds. This can be an excellent way to reduce the liability of board members for poor investment decisions. Rather than make decisions themselves, the board appoints an investment committee that includes individuals with proven investment or financial expertise. Committee members may include stock brokers, CPAs, attorneys, bankers, financial planners, and business leaders. Of course, the committee's recommendations ordinarily must be approved by the governing board, but by relying on the advice of experts the board is greatly

[260] REVISED MODEL NONPROFIT CORPORATION ACT § 8.30.

reducing the risk of being liable for poor investment decisions. After all, they were relying on the advice of experts.

Key point. *The Model Revised Nonprofit Corporation Act (quoted above) specifies that "in discharging his or her duties, a director is entitled to rely on information, opinions, reports, or statements, including financial statements and other financial data, if prepared or presented by . . . persons as to matters the director reasonably believes are within the person's professional or expert competence . . . ." This language provides directors with considerable protection when relying on the advice of experts on an investment committee.*

- **Investment policy.** A church congregation or board can create an investment policy to govern investment decisions. A policy can prohibit investments in specified instruments or programs.

- **Avoid speculative or risky investments.** If a proposal sounds "too good to be true," it probably is. Any scheme that promises to "double your money" in a short period of time should be viewed with extreme skepticism. It is absolutely essential that such schemes not be pursued without the thorough evaluation and recommendation of persons with financial and investment expertise.

Key point. *Do not rely on the "expert opinion" of persons representing the promoter of an investment scheme. Investment schemes must be reviewed by independent and objective persons having financial and investment expertise. Ideally, these persons will be members of your church, or persons within your community who have a reputation of unquestioned integrity.*

The United States Securities and Exchange Commission (SEC) lists four common investment scams that are perpetrated on religious organizations— pyramid schemes, Ponzi schemes, Nigerian investment scams, and prime bank scams. The SEC has provided the following warning signs of fraudulent bank-related investment schemes:

Excessive guaranteed returns. These schemes typically offer or guarantee spectacular returns of 20 to 200 percent *monthly,* absolutely risk free! Promises of unrealistic returns at no risk "are hallmarks of prime bank fraud."

Fictitious financial instrument. Despite having credible-sounding names, the supposed "financial instruments" at the heart of any prime bank scheme simply do not exist. Exercise caution if you've been asked to invest in a debt obligation of the "top 100 world banks," Medium Term Bank Notes or Debentures, Standby Letters of Credit, Bank Guarantees, an offshore trading program, a roll program, bank-issued debentures, a high yield investment program, or some variation on these descriptions. Promoters frequently claim that the offered financial instrument is issued, traded, guaranteed, or endorsed by the World Bank or an international central bank.

Extreme secrecy. Promoters claim that transactions must be kept strictly confidential by all parties, making client references unavailable. They may characterize the transactions as the best-kept secret in the banking industry, and assert that, if asked, bank and regulatory officials would deny knowledge of such instruments. Investors may be asked to sign nondisclosure agreements.

Exclusive opportunity. Promoters frequently claim that investment opportunities of this type are by invitation only, available to only a handful of special customers, and historically reserved for the wealthy elite.

Claims of inordinate complexity. Investment pitches frequently are vague about who is involved in the transaction or where the money is going. Promoters may try to explain away this lack of specificity by stating that the financial instruments are too technical or complex for "non-experts" to understand.

You should be especially watchful for prime-bank related schemes promoted over the Internet.

It is also best to avoid investing all or a significant portion of available funds in the stock of one company, since the lack of "diversification" creates added risk. Investing in stock generally should be avoided unless investments are sufficiently diversified (for example, through conservative mutual funds) and recommended by a knowledgeable investment committee.

Key point. *Remember, you are investing donated funds. This is no time to be taking risks. Not only do officers and directors have a legal duty to exercise due care in the investment of church funds. Just as importantly, they have a moral duty to be prudent in their investment decisions. No officer or director wants to explain to church members at an annual business meeting how some of their contributions were lost due to poor investments.*

- **Avoid investing in companies or programs in which a board member has a personal interest.** The third case summarized above demonstrates the need to avoid investing in companies or programs with direct ties to a member of your board. Such investments are not always inappropriate. But they demand a higher degree of scrutiny.

Key point. *A church's investments should be reviewed at every board meeting. This ensures that all investments will be continuously monitored, and that necessary adjustments can be made.*

- **Trustees have a higher duty.** Sometimes church board members are designated as the trustees of a charitable trust. For example, a member dies leaving a large sum to the church for a specific purpose and designates the church board as the trustee of the fund. Trustees are held to an even higher degree of care in the investment of trust funds than officers or directors of a corporation. However, the Revised Model Nonprofit Corporation Act specifies that "a director shall not be deemed to be a trustee with respect to the corporation or with respect to any property held or administered by the corporation, including without limit, property that may be subject to restrictions imposed by the donor or transferor of such property." In other words, a church officer or director is not automatically deemed to be a "trustee" of church funds. Officers and directors generally are held to the higher legal standard applicable to trustees only if they are designated as trustees in a legal instrument that creates a trust fund.

- **Conclusion.** Church officers and directors must take steps to inform themselves about any investment decision involving church funds. They can rely on a number of safeguards, including their own research, the recommendations of an investment committee, and common sense.

Case Studies

• *A District of Columbia appeals court ruled that it was prohibited by the First Amendment from resolving a lawsuit brought by members of a church claiming that the board of trustees breached its fiduciary duties by authorizing an interest-free loan to the pastor and by failing to provide the congregation with adequate information regarding the church's finances. The court concluded: "A church's financial regime, including any required reports to members, necessarily reflects an array of decisions about a member's obligation to pledge funds, and about the leaders' corresponding responsibility to account for those funds, that a civil court cannot arbitrate without entangling itself in doctrinal interpretations. . . . Accounting is an area riddled with major subjective decisions. When the entity in question is a religious society, those subjective decisions raise questions of internal church governance which are often themselves based on the application of church doctrine."*[261]

• *A federal court in Indiana ruled that the directors of a church subsidiary could be sued individually for financial losses incurred by investors in a securities scam on the basis of their breach of their fiduciary duty of care.*[262]

• *A Minnesota court ruled that a church officer violated his fiduciary duties to his church as a result of his secret efforts to remove the pastor and have the church property transferred to a new church that he had formed. The court noted that "an officer of a nonprofit corporation owes a fiduciary duty to that corporation to act in good faith, with honesty in fact, with loyalty, in the best interests of the corporation, and with the care of an ordinary, prudent person under similar circumstances." The officer conceded that he owed a fiduciary duty to the church, but he insisted that the evidence did not support a finding that he breached his fiduciary duty because his actions were consistent with the wishes of the church members who supported him. The court disagreed: "As the bearer of a fiduciary duty, the law imposed on him the highest standard of integrity in his dealings with the other officers of [the church] and*

---

[261] Kelsey v. Ray, 719 A.2d 1248 (D.C. App. 1998).
[262] Marwil v. Grubbs, 2004 WL 2278751 (S.D. Ind. 2004).

the entire [church] congregation, not just those who [supported him]. Therefore . . . as an officer of [the church] his fiduciary duty prevented him from assuming positions, and taking actions, that conflicted with the interests of [the church] and the congregation as a whole. . . . There is sufficient evidence in the record to establish that the officer breached his fiduciary duty to [the church]. He admitted that while he was vice president of the church he organized a faction for the purpose of forming another church to directly compete with [the original church]. Further, the formation of a new church was intended to be a method of circumventing the national church's termination provisions governing the pastor's services. To achieve his goals, he held secret meetings and continuously encouraged secrecy among [his supporters]. He did not inform other church officials and members of . . . his plans to form [a new church], separate from [the original church], and transfer the church property from [the original church to the new church] without compensation."[263]

• A Minnesota court dismissed a lawsuit brought by Lutheran pastors against a denominational pension board for allegedly breaching their fiduciary duty to participants by not investing in companies that did business in South Africa. The Evangelical Lutheran Church in America (ELCA) established a board of pensions in 1988 to manage and operate a pension fund for Lutheran pastors and lay employees "exclusively for the benefit of and to assist in carrying out the purposes of the ELCA." The ELCA adopted the position that the system of apartheid in South Africa was so contrary to Lutheran theology that it had to be rejected as a matter of faith. The ELCA passed a resolution to "see that none of our ELCA pension funds will be invested in companies doing business in South Africa." A dissenting group of Lutherans opposed the ELCA's decision to use its assets as a political weapon and asked to withdraw their pension funds. When their request was denied they sued the board of pensions and the ELCA, claiming that both groups had violated their fiduciary duties to participants in the pension program by elevating social concerns over sound investment strategy. A state appeals court dismissed the lawsuit on the ground that a resolution of the lawsuit would require the court to interpret religious doctrine in violation of the First Amendment's nonestablishment of religion clause. The court concluded that the "ELCA enacted the [apartheid] policy in an effort to further its social and doctrinal goals . . . . Accordingly, any review of the Board of Pensions' [investment policy] would entangle the court in reviewing church doctrine and policy."[264]

• A New York court ruled that the officers of a nonprofit organization violated their fiduciary duties and could be removed from office by the attorney general and ordered to pay damages. The state attorney general of New York sued the officers of a charity seeking to hold them personally liable and financially accountable for amounts totaling more than $120,000 which they allegedly received in violation of their fiduciary duties. The attorney general also sought to remove two of the officers and permanently bar them from ever serving as board members of a public charity. One of the officers freely admitted that he charged several personal expenses to the charity, but defended himself by stating, "I erroneously believed that it would be permissible for me to charge certain personal expenses to [the charity] and have them reclassified as personal expenses to be paid back to [the charity]." The court called this allegation

---

[263] Shepherd of the Valley Lutheran Church v. Hope Lutheran Church, 626 N.W.2d 436 (Minn. App. 2001).

[264] Basich v. Board of Pensions, 540 N.W.2d 82 (Minn. App. 1995).

"startling," and further observed, "This court is at a loss as to why anyone would think they could charge something to a not-for-profit corporation as long as they paid it back later. After all, [the charity] is a not-for-profit corporation and not a revolving credit line."[265]

• *A New York appeals court ruled that directors of a charitable trust could be sued for breaching their fiduciary duties. A child of the founder of the trust filed a lawsuit seeking to remove 8 of the trust's 11 directors. He asserted that the 8 directors breached their fiduciary duties, mismanaged the trust's investments, and negligently selected the trust's investment advisor. The court ruled that the 8 directors could be sued. It noted that "it is well established that, as fiduciaries, board members bear a duty of loyalty to the corporation and may not profit improperly at the expense of their corporation." In this case, the lawsuit alleged that the 8 directors breached their fiduciary duties by investing a substantial portion of the trust's assets in speculative securities and in the stock of a company with direct ties to the directors. The court concluded that the "business judgment rule" (which protects directors from any liability for their reasonable and good faith decisions) did not apply in this case, since it was not available "when the good faith or oppressive conduct of the officers and directors is in issue."*[266]

• *The North Carolina Supreme Court ruled that it was barred by the First Amendment from resolving a complaint by church members that their pastor and two other church officials had breached their fiduciary duties by improperly using church funds. The court noted that the plaintiffs alleged that the pastor and other defendants usurped the governmental authority of the church's internal governing body, and breached their fiduciary duties by improperly using church funds, which constitutes conversion. The court concluded: "Determining whether actions, including expenditures, by a church's pastor, secretary, and chairman of the board of trustees were proper requires an examination of the church's view of the role of the pastor, staff, and church leaders, their authority and compensation, and church management. Because a church's religious doctrine and practice affect its understanding of each of these concepts, seeking a court's review of the matters presented here is no different than asking a court to determine whether a particular church's grounds for membership are spiritually or doctrinally correct or whether a church's charitable pursuits accord with the congregation's beliefs. None of these issues can be addressed using neutral principles of law. Here, for example, in order to address plaintiffs' claims, the trial court would be required to interpose its judgment as to both the proper role of these church officials and whether each expenditure was proper in light of the church's religious doctrine and practice, to the exclusion of the judgment of the church's duly constituted leadership. This is precisely the type of ecclesiastical inquiry courts are forbidden to make."*[267]

---

[265] Spitzer v. Lev, 2003 WL 21649444 (N.Y. Sup. 2003).

[266] Scheuer Family Foundation, Inc. v. 61 Associates, 582 N.Y.S.2d 662 (A.D. 1 Dept. 1992).

[267] Harris v. Matthews, 643 S.E.2d 566 (N.C. 2007). The court rejected the plaintiffs' claim that since the church was incorporated the state nonprofit corporation law could be used to resolve the dispute. It simply noted that "a church that incorporates under the North Carolina Nonprofit Corporation Act does not forfeit its fundamental First Amendment rights. Regardless of a church's corporate structure, the Constitution requires courts to defer to the church's internal governing body with regard to ecclesiastical decisions concerning church management and use of funds."

• An Ohio court refused to allow church members to sue board members personally for breaching their fiduciary duties by failing to oust a pastor who allegedly had engaged in financial improprieties. It observed: "Inquiry into the relationship between the trustees and the congregation in matters concerning the pastorship would require the courts to consider each party's view of who should preach from the pulpit. Review of such matters would further require the court to determine the issue of whether the trustees' performance of their duties met the standards of the congregation and would therefore involve an inquiry into ecclesiastical concerns. Therefore . . . civil courts lack . . . jurisdiction to entertain such matters. . . . [We] hold that the lower court has no jurisdiction over the claims brought by the individual members of the congregation seeking to . . . hold the board liable for breach of fiduciary duty to the congregation."[268]

Breach of the Fiduciary Duty of Loyalty

§ 6-07.04

Key point 6-07.04. *Church board members have a fiduciary duty of loyalty to their church, and they may be personally liable for breaching this duty by participating in board decisions that place the interests of one or more board members above the interests of the church itself.*

Directors of nonprofit corporations have a fiduciary duty of loyalty to the corporation. This duty generally requires that any transaction between the board and one of its directors be (a) fully disclosed, (b) approved by the board without the vote of the interested director, and (c) fair and reasonable to the corporation. A board member does not have to offer the church the lowest price for a product or service to discharge the duty of loyalty. All that is required is that the price be fair and reasonable to the corporation.

There are sound reasons why a church might want to do business with a member of the board at a cost that is higher than what another business may charge. To illustrate, a church board may conclude that the church will receive better quality, and customer support, by doing business with a fellow board member. Of course, this does not mean that cost is irrelevant. At some point, the price for a product or service offered by a board member may be so much higher than what is offered by competitors that it ceases to be fair and reasonable to the church. In such a case, the duty of loyalty may be violated.

The duty of loyalty also means that a board member will not usurp a corporate opportunity. This means that board members may not enter into personal transactions in which the church would have an interest. To illustrate, assume that a church is needing to expand its facilities, and a 5-acre tract of undeveloped land lies adjacent to the church's property. The senior pastor of the church (who is president of the church corporation) purchases the land for himself at a cost of $100,000, and later offers to sell it to the church for $250,000. Under these circumstances the pastor likely has violated the fiduciary duty of loyalty by usurping a corporate opportunity.

---

[268] State v. Meagher, 1997 WL 180266 (Ohio App. 1997).

Violation of Trust Terms   § 6-07.05

Key point 6-07.05. *Church board members may be personally liable for diverting designated funds or trust funds to some other purpose.*

1. In General

Church officers and directors may be legally accountable for violating the terms or restrictions of properties and funds held in trust by the church. To illustrate, the trustees of one church were sued by church members when they attempted to sell church assets contrary to the restrictions specified in the church charter.[269] The original charter of the church stated that it was formed "for the purpose of religious worship . . . at the corner of Fifth Street and E Street, Southeast, in the City of Washington."

In 1982, after the safety of the historic church building became an issue, the pastor and board of trustees decided to close the church and move to a new location. For at least ten years prior to the sale of the church property, relations between the board of trustees and a segment of the congregation became increasingly hostile. After the sale of the church building, a group of the dissidents filed a lawsuit alleging that the trustees and pastor had violated their fiduciary duty as trustees to hold church properties for the purposes specified in the corporate charter (i.e., to conduct religious worship "at the church building on the southeast corner of Fifth Street and E Street"). The dissidents claimed they were attempting to "salvage the historic old Mount Jezreel church building." The dissidents pointed out that title to the church's properties was in the name of the trustees who held church properties "in trust" for the members of the congregation, and that church members were "trust beneficiaries" who could sue the trustees for improper or unauthorized transactions with respect to those properties.

A trial court dismissed the lawsuit, but an appeals court ruled in favor of the dissidents. The appeals court observed:

> Although title to the church property is vested in the trustees or directors, the property itself is held in trust for the uses and purposes named and no other. Because the church was incorporated for the purpose of religious worship, and because the property was held in trust for that purpose, the members of the congregation are indeed the beneficiaries of the trust. As such, they have standing to sue the trustees in the event that the trust property is used or disposed of in a manner contrary to the stated purposes of the trust. . . . We therefore hold that, as a general principle, bona fide members of a church have standing to bring suit as trust beneficiaries when there is a dispute over the use or disposition of church property.[270]

---

[269] Mt. Jezreel Christians Without a Home v. Board of Trustees of Mount Jezreel Baptist Church, 582 A.2d 237 (D.C. App. 1990).

[270] *Id.* at 239 (citations omitted).

The same principle may apply to board members who authorize the diversion of designated funds from their intended purposes or projects. For example, assume that a member donates $10,000 to a church's new building fund, and that the church later decides not to build a new facility. Can the church board divert the $10,000 to another use, or must it return the funds to the donor? Or, assume that the church raises several contributions totaling $250,000 for a new building fund and later decides to abandon the project. Does the board have an obligation to track down all of the donors and offer to return their contributions?

Church board members may be liable for diverting designated gifts to other purposes only if someone has the legal right to enforce the original designation. The question of whether donors have a legal right to enforce their designations is addressed fully in a companion text.[271]

2. Enforcement of Designated Contributions

Few courts have addressed this important question, so authoritative legal guidance is sparse. The leading cases and key conclusions are summarized below.

Understanding the legal authority of a donor to enforce the terms of a completed gift to charity requires an understanding of two important concepts: (1) the definition of "gift" and (2) the legal requirement of standing.

definition of "gift"

Section 170 of the tax code allows a deduction, subject to certain limitations, for charitable contributions made during the taxable year. Section 170(c) defines a charitable contribution as a contribution or gift "to or for the use of " a corporation organized and operated exclusively for religious, educational or other charitable purposes, no part of the net earnings of which inures to the benefit of any private individual.

The courts have ruled that a charitable contribution and a gift are synonymous, and so a contribution is not deductible unless it is a valid gift. In one of the most often quoted definitions of "gift," the Ohio Supreme court noted:

> The weight of authority . . . may be summarized in the statement that to support a gift there must be clear and convincing proof, first, of an intention on the part of the donor to transfer the title and right of possession of the particular property to the done then and there, and, second, in pursuance of such intention, a delivery by the donor to the donee of the subject-matter of the gift to the extent practicable or possible considering its nature, with relinquishment of ownership, dominion, and control over it [emphasis added].[272]

Since no gift occurs unless a donor absolutely and irrevocably transfers title, dominion, and control over the gift to the donee, it follows that no charitable

---

[271] See R. Hammar, Church and Clergy Tax Guide chapter 11 (published annually by the publisher of this text).

[272] Bolles v. Toledo Trust Company, 4 N.E.2d 917 (Ohio 1936).

contribution deduction is available unless the contribution is unconditional. Similarly, no charitable contribution deduction is permitted if the donor receives a direct and material benefit for the contribution, since a gift by definition is a gratuitous transfer of property without consideration or benefit to the donor other than the feeling of satisfaction it evokes.

the requirement of standing

A fundamental requirement in any lawsuit is that the plaintiff have "standing." Standing means that the plaintiff has suffered an injury to a legally protected interest that can be redressed by a civil court. Since no gift occurs unless a donor absolutely and irrevocably transfers title, dominion, and control over the gift to the donee, it follows that donors have no legal interest to protect when their designated gifts to charity are not honored.

To illustrate, in a frequently cited case, the Supreme Court of Connecticut observed: "At common law, a donor who has made a completed charitable contribution, whether as an absolute gift or in trust, had no standing to bring an action to enforce the terms of his or her gift or trust unless he or she had expressly reserved the right to do so."[273]

How can a donor who has made a designated contribution to a church sue to enforce the designation when a charitable contribution, by definition, is a transfer of *all* of the donor's interest in the donated funds or property to the church? Standing poses a significant legal barrier to any donor who is considering litigation as a means of enforcing the terms of a designated gift. One judge aptly observed: "In considering the subject of standing, I begin with the observation that, when a charitable gift is made, without any provision for a reversion of the gift to the donor or his heirs, the interest of the donor and his heirs is permanently excluded."[274] This judge quoted from a leading treatise on trust law:

There is no property interest left in the [donor] or his heirs, devises, next of kin, or legatees. The donor or his successors may have a sentimental interest in seeing that his wishes are respected, but no financial [interest] which the law recognizes . . .and hence neither he nor they are as a general rule permitted to sue the trustees to compel them to carry out the trust. . . . The better reasoned cases refuse to permit the donor during his lifetime, or his successors after his death, to sue merely as donor or successors to compel the execution of the charitable trust.[275]

3. The Traditional View: No Donor Enforcement

Section 391 of the *Restatement (Second) of Trusts*, a respected legal treatise that has been adopted in many states, specifies that donors or their heirs may not enforce the terms of a charitable gift: "A suit can be maintained for the enforcement of a charitable trust by the attorney general or other public officer,

---

[273] Carl J. Herzog Foundation, Inc. v. University of Bridgeport, 699 A.2d 995 (Conn. 1997).

[274] Smithers v. St. Luke's-Roosevelt Hospital Center, 723 N.Y.S.2d 426 (2001) (Judge Friedman, dissenting).

[275] Bogert, Trusts and Trustees § 415.

or by a co-trustee, or by a person who has a special interest in the enforcement of the charitable trust, but not by persons who have no special interest or by the [donor] or his heirs, personal representatives or next of kin."

Several courts have concluded that donors lack the legal authority to enforce a designated gift to charity, usually on the basis of one or both of the two principles described above (the definition of a "gift," or a lack of standing). The leading cases are summarized below.

Carl J. Herzog Foundation, Inc. v. University of Bridgeport, 699 A.2d 995 (Conn. 1997).

A charitable foundation (the "donor") made a gift of $250,000 to a university "to provide need-based merit scholarship aid to disadvantaged students for medical related education." A few years later, the university informed the donor that it no longer was using the funds for the specified purpose. The donor sued the university to enforce the terms of the gift. The Connecticut Supreme Court conducted a thorough analysis of the laws and judicial precedent of all 50 states, concluding that donors do not have standing to enforce their completed gifts. The donor insisted that it had standing because the university's decision to discontinue using the donated funds pursuant to the terms of the gift constituted an injury that a court could redress. The donor also claimed that the Uniform Management of Institutional Funds Act (UMIFA) conferred standing on donors to enforce the terms of completed gifts even if no such right was reserved in a gift instrument.

UMIFA, which has been adopted by most states, provides the boards and trustees of charitable organizations with guidance in handling perpetual endowment funds. UMIFA provides that "with the written consent of the donor, the governing board may release, in whole or in part, a restriction imposed by the applicable gift instrument on the use or investment of an institutional fund." The donor insisted that it would be illogical for UMIFA to provide for written consent by a donor to change a restriction and then deny that donor access to the courts to complain of a change without such consent. In other words, UMIFA implicitly confers standing on donors. The Connecticut Supreme Court disagreed, noting that the drafters of UMIFA, in an official comment, stated that "the donor has no right to enforce the restriction, no interest in the fund and no power to change the beneficiary of the fund. He may only acquiesce in a lessening of a restriction already in effect."[276] The court noted that this comment regarding the power of a donor to enforce restrictions on a charitable gift

> arose in the context of debate concerning the creation of potential adverse tax consequences for donors, if UMIFA was interpreted to provide donors with control over their gift property after the completion of the gift. Pursuant to section 170 of the [federal tax code, quoted above] an income tax deduction for a charitable contribution is disallowed unless the taxpayer has permanently surrendered dominion and control over the property or funds in question. Where there is a possibility not so remote

---

[276] UMIFA § 7, comment.

as to be negligible that the charitable gift subject to a condition might fail, the tax deduction is disallowed. The drafters of UMIFA worked closely with an impressive group of professionals, including tax advisers, who were concerned with the federal tax implications of the proposed Act. The drafters' principal concern in this regard was that the matter of donor restrictions not affect the donor's charitable contribution deduction for the purposes of federal income taxation. In other words, the concern was that the donor not be so tethered to the charitable gift through the control of restrictions in the gift that the donor would not be entitled to claim a federal charitable contribution exemption for the gift.[277] In resolving these concerns, the drafters of UMIFA clearly stated their position in the commentary. "No federal tax problems for the donor are anticipated by permitting release of a restriction. The donor has no right to enforce the restriction, no interest in the fund and no power to change the eleemosynary beneficiary of the fund. He may only acquiesce in a lessening of a restriction already in effect." . . . Indeed, it would have been anomalous for the drafters of UMIFA to strive to assist charitable institutions by creating smoother procedural avenues for the release of restrictions while simultaneously establishing standing for a new class of litigants, donors, who would defeat this very purpose by virtue of the potential of lengthy and complicated litigation.

This ruling directly acknowledges that the deductibility of a charitable contribution would be jeopardized if donors were legally capable of suing to enforce the terms of their completed gifts.

Russell v. Yale University, 737 A.2d 941 (Conn. App. 1999).

A graduate of Yale University died in 1918, leaving a substantial sum of money in trust for the erection of a building that would constitute a fitting memorial reflecting his gratitude and affection for his alma mater. The trustees were given broad discretion in the disposition of these funds. In 1930 the trustees voted to contribute money for the erection of the divinity school quadrangle. The divinity school is one of Yale's graduate professional schools, which educates men and women for the ministry and provides theological education for persons engaged in other professions. In 1996, as a result of a comprehensive study, the university decided to demolish large portions of the divinity school quadrangle.

The trustees took exception to this proposal and asked a court to block it on the grounds that it violated the terms of the trust. Relying on the *Herzog* case (summarized above) a Connecticut appellate court concluded that the trustees lacked standing to enforce the terms of the trust: "Although the plaintiffs are sincere in their efforts to maintain the divinity school as a leader in theological education and preparation for the Christian ministry and they acted in good faith based on motives that are beyond question, the plaintiffs, as a matter of law, lack standing to adjudicate the equitable remedies they seek."

---

[277] IRC § 170(a), Treas. Reg. § 1.170A-1(c).

Amundson v. Kletzing-McLaughlin Memorial Foundation College, 73N.W.2d 114 (Iowa 1955).

The Iowa Supreme Court ruled that "where the donor has effectually passed out of himself all interest in the fund devoted to a charity, neither he, nor those claiming under him, have any standing in a court of equity as to its disposition and control."

4. Enforcement by State Attorneys General

While a donor may not have standing to enforce a designated gift to a church, this does not mean the church can ignore it. Most states have enacted laws empowering the attorney general to enforce the terms of such gifts. An official comment to section 348 of the *Restatement (Second) of Trusts,* a respected legal treatise that has been adopted in many states, specifies:

Where property is given to a charitable corporation, particularly where restrictions are imposed by the donor, it is sometimes said by the courts that a charitable trust is created and that the corporation is a trustee. It is sometimes said, however, that a charitable trust is not created. This is a mere matter of terminology. The important question is whether and to what extent the principles and rules applicable to charitable trusts are applicable to charitable corporations. Ordinarily the principles and rules applicable to charitable trusts are applicable to charitable corporations. Where property is given to a charitable corporation without restrictions as to the disposition of the property, the corporation is under a duty, enforceable at the suit of the attorney general, not to divert the property to other purposes but to apply it to one or more of the charitable purposes for which it is organized. Where property is given to a charitable corporation and it is directed by the terms of the gift to devote the property to a particular one of its purposes, it is under a duty, enforceable at the suit of the [state] attorney general, to devote the property to that purpose.[278]

Another leading legal treatise states: "The public benefits arising from the charitable trust justify the selection of some public official for its enforcement. Since the attorney general is the governmental officer whose duties include the protection of the rights of the people of the state in general, it is natural that he has been chosen as the prosecutor, supervisor, and enforcer of charitable trusts, both in England and in the several states."[279] Several courts have recognized the exclusive authority of the state attorney general to enforce the terms of completed gifts.

Carl J. Herzog Foundation, Inc. v. University of Bridgeport, 699 A.2d 995 (Conn. 1997).

The Connecticut Supreme Court, after ruling that donors have no legal right to enforce their gifts to charity, concluded that the attorney general could do so:

---

[278] Section 348, comment f.

[279] BOGERT, TRUSTS AND TRUSTEES § 411.

The general rule is that charitable trusts or gifts to charitable corporations for stated purposes are [enforceable] at the instance of the attorney general. . . . Although gifts to a charitable organization do not create a trust in the technical sense, where a purpose is stated a trust will be implied, and the disposition enforced by the attorney general, pursuant to his duty to effectuate the donor's wishes. . . . Connecticut is among the majority of jurisdictions which have . . . entrusted the attorney general with the responsibility and duty to represent the public interest in the protection of any gifts, legacies or devises intended for public or charitable purposes. . . . The theory underlying the power of the attorney general to enforce gifts for a stated purpose is that a donor who attaches conditions to his gift has a right to have is intention enforced. The donor's right, however, is enforceable only at the instance of the attorney general.

Wier v. Howard Hughes Medical Institute, 407 A.2d 1051 (Del. Ch. 1979).

A Delaware court ruled that the state attorney general "has the exclusive power to bring actions to enforce charitable trusts."

Lopez v. Medford Community Center, Inc., 424 N.E.2d 229 (Mass. 1981).

A Massachusetts court ruled that "it is the exclusive function of the attorney general to correct abuses in the administration of a public charity by the institution of proper proceedings" and that donors have no standing to enforce the terms of their gifts when they have not retained a specific right to do so, such as a right of reverter, after relinquishing physical possession of it.

Marin Hospital District v. State Dept. of Health, 154 Cal. Rptr. 838 (Cal. 1979).

A California court concluded that the fact that a charity is bound to use contributions for purposes for which they were given does not confer upon the donor standing to enforce the terms of the gift.

Smith v. Thompson, 266 Ill. App. 165, 169 (Ill. 1932) (quoting Perry, Trusts and Trustees § 732a).

An Illinois court observed, "As a matter of common law, when a . . . donor of property to a charity fails specifically to provide for a reservation of rights in the trust or gift instrument, neither the donor nor his heirs have any standing in court in a proceeding to compel the proper execution of the trust." The court also noted that "where the donor has effectually passed out of himself all interest in the fund devoted to a charity, neither he nor those claiming under him have any standing in a court of equity as to its disposition and control."

Lefkowitz v. Lebensfeld, 417 N.Y.S.2d 715 (1979).

A New York court observed: "The general rule is that gifts to charitable corporations for stated purposes are [enforceable] at the instance of the attorney general. . . . It matters not whether the gift is absolute or in trust or whether a technical condition is attached to the gift."

169

Brown v. Concerned Citizens for Sickle Cell, 382 N.E.2d 1155 (Ohio. App. 1978).
An Ohio court concluded:

> One of the recognized powers held by the attorney general at common law was to inquire into any abuses of charitable donations. Clearly, the attorney general's traditional power to protect public donations to charity goes beyond the mere enforcement of express trusts where the formal elements of such a trust manifestation of intent to create a trust, the existence of trust property, and a fiduciary relationship are essential to its creation. The attorney general, in seeking to protect the public interest, may also bring suit to impose a constructive trust on funds collected for charitable purposes but subsequently diverted to other purposes. A constructive trust, although not a formal trust at all, serves as a means to prevent the unjust enrichment of those who would abuse their voluntary roles as public solicitors for charity. For this court to hold that the attorney general can only enforce express charitable trusts would greatly hamper his ability to carry out his statutory and common law duties.

Several other courts have concluded that the attorney general alone may enforce designated gifts to charity.[280] The authority of a state attorney general to enforce donors' designated gifts to charity is largely meaningless, since state attorneys general rarely exercise this power. When they do, it is in cases involving large gifts to prominent charities. Attorneys general rarely, if ever, have enforced designated gifts to a church.[281]

5. Enforcement by Persons Having a "Special Interest"

Section 391 of the *Restatement (Second) of Trusts* specifies that others, in addition to the attorney general, may enforce the terms of a charitable trust: "A suit can be maintained for the enforcement of a charitable trust by the attorney general or other public officer, *or by a co-trustee, or by a person who has a special interest in the enforcement of the charitable trust*, but not by persons who have no special interest or by the [donor] or his heirs, personal representatives or next of kin." One court concluded "fiduciaries, such as trustees, have historically been deemed to have a special interest so as to possess standing."[282] However, the court cautioned that the attorney general must be joined as a party to protect the public interest.

Those with no special interest have no standing to bring an action to enforce the conditions of a gift. These include beneficiaries of the charitable gift.[283] The California Supreme Court ruled that "the prevailing view of other jurisdictions is

---

[280] *See, e.g.,* Denver Foundation v. Wells Fargo Bank, 163 P.3d 1116 (Cal. App. 2007); American Center for Education, Inc. v. Cavnar, 145 Cal. Rptr. 736 (Cal. App. 1978); Greenway v. Irvine's Trustee, 131 S.W.2d 705 (Ky. 1930); Weaver v. Wood, 680 N.E.2d 918 (Mass. 1997); In re James' Estate, 123 N.Y.S.2d 520 (N.Y. Sur. 1953).

[281] Attorney General v. First United Baptist Church, 601 A.2d 96 (Maine 1992).

[282] Hartford v. Larrabee Fund Association, 288 A.2d 71 (1971).

[283] Steeneck v. University of Bridgeport, 668 A.2d 688 (Conn. 1995).

that the attorney general does not have exclusive power to enforce a charitable trust and that a trustee or other person having a sufficient special interest may also bring an action for this purpose. This position is adopted by [section 391 of] the Restatement (Second) of Trusts and is supported by many legal scholars."[284]

6. Enforcement by Donors Who Reserved a Property Interest

By expressly reserving a property interest, such as a right of reverter in a gift instrument, donors may bring themselves and their heirs within the special-interest exception to the general rule that donors and beneficiaries of a charitable trust may not bring an action to enforce the trust but rather are represented exclusively by the attorney general. A right of reverter is created when a property owner transfers title to another with the express stipulation that title will revert back to the prior owner upon the occurrence of a specified condition.

To illustrate, a landowner could convey a home or other property to a church "so long as the property is used for church purposes." If the property ceases to be used for church purposes, then the title reverts back to the former owner by operation of law. Such deeds vest only a "determinable" or "conditional" title in the church, since the title will immediately revert back to the previous owner (or such person's heirs or successors) by operation of law upon a violation of the condition.

Reversionary clauses represent one way for donors to ensure that they will be able to enforce a donation of land or a building to a church for specified purposes. However, note that if a reversionary clause is inserted in a deed as part of a donation of property to a church, the donor may be denied a charitable contribution deduction unless the IRS determines that the possibility of a reversion of title from the church back to the former owner is so remote as to be negligible. As the drafters of UMIFA stated:

> Pursuant to section 170 of the [federal tax code] an income tax deduction for a charitable contribution is disallowed unless the taxpayer has permanently surrendered dominion and control over the property or funds in question. Where there is a possibility not so remote as to be negligible that the charitable gift subject to a condition might fail, the tax deduction is disallowed. The drafters of UMIFA worked closely with an impressive group of professionals, including tax advisers, who were concerned with the federal tax implications of the proposed Act. The drafters' principal concern in this regard was that the matter of donor restrictions not affect the donor's charitable contribution deduction for the purposes of federal income taxation. In other words, the concern was that the donor not be so tethered to the charitable gift through the control of restrictions in the gift that the donor would not be entitled to claim a federal charitable contribution exemption for the gift.[285]

---

[284] Holt v. College of Osteopathic Physicians and Surgeons, 40 Cal. Rptr. 244 (1964).

[285] IRC § 170(a), Treas. Reg. § 1.170A-1 (c).

The income tax regulations specify that a charitable contribution deduction "shall not be disallowed . . . merely because the interest which passes to, or is vested in, the charity may be defeated by the performance of some act or the happening of some event, if on the date of the gift it appears that the possibility that such act or event will occur is so remote as to be negligible."

The language "so remote as to be negligible" has been defined as "a chance which persons generally would disregard as so highly improbable that it might be ignored with reasonable safety in undertaking a serious business transaction. It is likewise a chance which every dictate of reason would justify an intelligent person in disregarding as so highly improbable and remote as to be lacking in reason and substance."

The IRS applies the following factors in deciding if a charitable contribution deduction should be allowed or denied: (1) whether the donor and donee intend at the time of the donation to cause the event's occurrence; (2) the incidence of the event's occurring in the past; (3) the extent to which the occurrence of the event would defeat the donation; and (4) whether the taxpayer has control over the event's occurrence.[286]

7. Court-Allowed Donor Enforcement

In recent years a few courts have rejected the traditional rule that donors cannot enforce their completed gifts and have allowed donors (or their heirs) to sue a charity in order to enforce the terms of a completed gift. The leading cases are summarized below.

L.B. Research and Education Foundation v. UCLA Foundation, 29 Cal.Rptr.3d 710 (Cal. App. 2005).

A donor contributed $1 million to establish an endowed chair at a university medical school, which the school accepted along with the conditions imposed by the donor. Several years later, the donor sued the school for specific performance of the agreement and breach of contract, alleging that the school had failed to honor the conditions specified in the original gift. The court concluded that the gift was a "conditional gift" rather than a charitable trust. It defined a conditional gift as a gift in which "it is expressly provided in the instrument that the donee shall forfeit it or that the donor or his heirs may [sue] for breach of the condition." The court noted that standing is presumed in cases of a conditional gift. It acknowledged that donors have no legal authority to enforce a charitable trust unless they have standing, but it concluded that even if the gift in this case were construed to be a charitable trust rather than a conditional gift, the donor would have standing. The court noted:

> The attorney general's power to enforce charitable trusts does not . . . deprive the donor of standing to enforce the terms of the trust it created. . . . The prevailing view of other jurisdictions is that the attorney general does not have exclusive power to enforce a charitable trust and that a trustee or other

---

[286] IRS Letter Ruling 200610017(2005).

person having a sufficient special interest may also bring an action for this purpose. In addition to the general public interest, however, there is the interest of donors who have directed that their contributions be used for certain charitable purposes.

Glenn v. University of Southern California, 2002 WL 31022068 (Cal. App. 2003).

A school asked a wealthy individual to donate $1.5 million to endow a professorial chair to support young, untenured researchers in the field of gerontology. The donor agreed to do so and agreed to give $1.5 million within 10 years. The school added that if the donor promised to increase his pledge to keep pace with inflation until he fully funded the endowment, it would immediately establish the professorship and select and fund the chair's holder without waiting for the donation. The donor agreed to these terms, and over the next 10 years transferred $1.6 million to the school. The donor later learned that the school had not used the donated funds for the specified purpose, and he sued the school for promissory fraud and breach of contract.

The court concluded that a breach of contract claim requires proof of (1) a contract, (2) the donor's performance of his contractual obligation ns, (3) the school's breach of its commitments, and (4) damages. The donor alleged that he had a partly oral, partly written contract with the school to endow a professorial chair, which the school promised to fund while it waited for him to honor his pledge. He claimed that he performed his commitment under the contract when he transferred $1.6 million to the school and that the school breached the contract by not funding the professorship as promised. Finally, he alleged that the school's breach damaged him because he could have put his money to other uses.

The court agreed that the donor had established a claim for breach of contract. The court also agreed that the donor had established a claim for promissory fraud, which it defined as (1) a knowing misrepresentation, (2) made with the intent to induce another's reliance, (3) the other's justifiable reliance, and (4) damages. The donor claimed that the school promised to fund the professorship immediately without intending to do so. He alleged that the school made the promise to encourage him to endow the position, and in giving $1.6 million he justifiably relied on that promise. Surprisingly, the court did not address the question of whether the donor has standing to enforce the terms of his gift.

Maffei v. Roman Catholic Archbishop, 867 N.E.2d 300 (Mass. 2007).

A church launched a capital fund-raising campaign. A retiree in her eighties (Eileen) contributed $35,000 to the campaign. She later testified, "If I had known that the archdiocese . . . was giving any consideration to closing the church, I would not have made the gift of $35,000." A few years later, the archbishop ordered the closure of the church as part of a reorganization. During one of the last worship services before the church closed, Eileen asked the pastor, "Why didn't you tell us the church was closing?" He replied, "I didn't know." Eileen sued the archbishop, claiming negligent misrepresentation and breach of a fiduciary duty. The Massachusetts Supreme Judicial Court ruled that Eileen had standing to pursue her claim:

It is clear that Eileen has alleged an individual stake in this dispute that makes her, and not the state attorney general, the party to bring suit . . . . A gift to a church generally creates a public charity. It is the exclusive function of the attorney general to correct abuses in the administration of a public charity by the institution of proper proceedings. It is his duty to see that the public interests are protected . . . or to decline so to proceed as those interests may require. However, a plaintiff who asserts an individual interest in the charitable organization distinct from that of the general public has standing to pursue her individual claims. In this case, Eileen's claims are readily distinguishable from those of the general class of parishioner beneficiaries. . . . She claims that she lost substantial personal funds as the result of the archbishop's negligent misrepresentation to her. This claim is personal, specific, and exists apart from any broader community interest in keeping the church open. She has alleged a personal right that would, in the ordinary course, entitle her to standing.

As noted below, while the court concluded that Eileen had standing to sue, it rejected her theory of liability.

Smithers v. St. Luke's-Roosevelt Hospital Center, 723 N.Y.S.2d 426 (2001).

A recovered alcoholic devoted the last 40 years of his life to the treatment of alcoholism. In 1971 he announced his intention to make a gift to a hospital of $10 million for the establishment of an alcoholism treatment center. With $1 million from the first installment of the gift the hospital purchased a building for the rehabilitation program. According to the donor's widow, the hospital sought to avoid its obligations under the terms of the gift, and its relationship with the donor was an uneasy one. A year after the donor's death in 1994, the hospital informed his widow that it planned to move the treatment center into a hospital ward and sell the building.

The hospital's plans aroused the suspicions of the donor's widow, and she demanded an accounting of the treatment center's finances. The hospital at first resisted disclosing its financial records, but the widow persisted, and in 1995 the hospital disclosed that it had been misappropriating monies from the endowment fund (funded by the donor's original gift) and transferring them to its general fund, where they were used for purposes unrelated to the treatment center. The widow notified the state attorney general, who investigated the hospital's finances and confirmed that it had transferred restricted assets from the endowment fund to its general fund in what it called "loans." The attorney general demanded the return of these assets, and the hospital returned nearly $5 million to the endowment fund, although it did not restore the income lost on those funds during the intervening years.

The widow was still convinced that the hospital was not fully honoring her husband's gift, so she filed a lawsuit in which she asked a court to compel the hospital to honor the terms of the gift. The state attorney general asked the court to dismiss the widow's lawsuit on the ground that donors lack standing (judicial authority) to enforce the terms of their gifts. The attorney general insisted that standing to enforce the terms of a charitable gift is limited to the attorney general. The court concluded that a donor (or, in this case, a donor's widow acting on his behalf) has the legal authority to enforce the terms of a charitable contribution.

The Episcopal seminary case. The court referred to an earlier decision of the New York Court of Appeals (the highest state court in New York) in a case addressing the question of whether alumni of a seminary, who had donated funds for the endowment of a professorship with specified conditions, could sue to enforce those conditions when they were violated.[287] The court concluded that the donors (alumni) could enforce the conditions of their contributions but could not obtain a return of their contributions. The court described the general rule as follows: "If the trustees of a charity abuse the trust, misemploy the charity fund, or commit a breach of the trust, the property does not revert to the heir or legal representative of the donor unless there is an express condition of the gift that it shall revert to the donor or his heirs, in case the trust is abused, but the redress is by . . . the attorney-general *or other person having the right to sue.*"

The court in the Episcopal seminary case concluded that while the donors were not entitled to a return of their contributions, they "had sufficient standing to maintain an action to enforce the trust."

Conclusion. The court concluded that the Episcopal seminary case "forecloses the conclusion that the attorney general's standing in these actions is exclusive." In other words, the attorney general is not the only person who is legally authorized to enforce the terms of a charitable gift. In some cases, donors can as well. Further, the court concluded that donors may have the right to enforce the terms of charitable gifts even though they do not specifically reserve the right to do so. The court then defended its conclusion that donors can enforce the terms of their gifts to charity:

> The donor of a charitable gift is in a better position than the attorney general to be vigilant and, if he or she is so inclined, to enforce his or her own intent. . . . To hold that, in her capacity as her late husband's representative [the donor's widow] has no standing to institute an action to enforce the terms of the gift is to contravene the well-settled principle that a donor's expressed intent is entitled to protection and the longstanding recognition under New York law of standing for a donor. We have seen no New York case in which a donor attempting to enforce the terms of his charitable gift was denied standing to do so. . . .

> Moreover, the circumstances of this case demonstrate the need for co-existent standing for the attorney general and the donor. The attorney general's office was notified of the hospital's misappropriation of funds by [the donor's widow]. Indeed, there is no substitute for a donor, who has a

---

[287] Associate Alumni of the General Theological Seminary of the Protestant Episcopal Church v. The General Theological Seminary of the Protestant Episcopal Church, 163 N.Y. 417 (1900).

"special, personal interest in the enforcement of the gift restriction" . . . We conclude that the distinct but related interests of the donor and the attorney general are best served by continuing to accord standing to donors to enforce the terms of their own gifts concurrent with the attorney general's standing to enforce such gifts on behalf of the beneficiaries thereof.

Church leaders should be familiar with this case and understand its implications. It is common for churches to receive contributions from donors that are designated for a specific purpose. For example, donors contribute money to the church's building fund or a scholarship fund or missions fund. Can these donors legally enforce their designations if the church decides to divert these contributions to other purposes? This court concluded that they can, even if they retained no right to do so in a written agreement. The attorney general also is authorized to enforce the conditions of a designated gift, but the attorney general's authority is not exclusive. It is "concurrent" with the authority of the donors themselves. As noted above, many courts have rejected this reasoning and have ruled that the authority of the attorney general to enforce charitable gifts is exclusive.

8. Constitutional Considerations

A few courts have concluded that the First Amendment guaranties of nonestablishment and free exercise of religion bar the civil courts from resolving donors' disputes with churches regarding the handling of designated contributions if doing so would implicate religious doctrine.

McDonald v. Macedonia Missionary Baptist Church, 2003 WL 1689618 (Mich. App. 2003).

A Michigan appeals court concluded that the civil courts are barred by the First Amendment guaranty of religious freedom from intervening in such internal church disputes:

It is well settled that courts, both federal and state, are severely circumscribed by the First Amendment [and the Michigan constitution] in resolution of disputes between a church and its members. Jurisdiction is limited to property rights which can be resolved by application of civil law. Whenever the trial court must stray into questions of ecclesiastical polity or religious doctrine the court loses jurisdiction. . . . We hold that this dispute involves a policy of the church for which our civil courts should not interfere. Because the decision of when and where to build a new church building is exclusively within the province of the church members and its officials, the trial court erred in not dismissing the couple's lawsuit.

Hawthorne v. Couch, 911 So.2d 907 (La. App. 2005).

A Louisiana court concluded:

Not all church disputes necessarily involve purely ecclesiastical matters. . . . However, where the dispute is rooted in an ecclesial tenet of the church, the court will not have jurisdiction of the matter. In this case, the testimony focused almost exclusively on the pastor's teachings regarding tithing. Without question, any legal analysis that would require the court to analyze and pass judgment upon such teachings would violate the [First Amendment]. The issue of tithing is at its core a purely ecclesiastical matter.

Maffei v. Roman Catholic Archbishop, 867 N.E.2d 300 (Mass. 2007).

An Italian immigrant (James) established a successful gravel business and owned several tracts of land. Upon the death of James and his wife, most of their property passed to their six children. The pastor of a Catholic church was interested in acquiring an eight-acre tract from the family as the site of a new sanctuary. Two of the siblings agreed to donate their interest in the land to the church, but the other four siblings were reluctant to transfer their interests until the pastor assured them that the new church would be named "St. James," in honor of their father, and that the church would remain a tribute to James "forever." During the negotiations for the property, the pastor did not inform any members of the family that canon law permitted the closure of the church in the future.

A church was constructed on the land in 1958. By the 1990s, however, question arose concerning the continuing viability of the church. A local newspaper story listed the church among those the archdiocese planned to close. The current pastor of the church assured the congregation that the story was false. The church launched a capital fund-raising campaign. A retiree in her eighties (Eileen) contributed $35,000 to the campaign. She later testified, "If I had known that the archdiocese . . . was giving any consideration to closing St. James, I would not have made the gift of $35,000." In 2004 the archdiocese ordered the closure of St. James. During one of the last worship services before the church closed, Eileen asked the pastor, "Why didn't you tell us the church was closing?" He replied, "I didn't know it."

Eileen, as well as the sole surviving sibling to have transferred the land to the church, sued the archbishop. The lawsuit claimed that the oral assurance by church officials that the church would be named "St. James" forever was a binding and enforceable commitment that was breached by the church's closure. The lawsuit also alleged negligent misrepresentation and breach of a fiduciary duty and asked the court to order a reversion of the property to the surviving sibling.

The Supreme Judicial Court noted that the First Amendment guaranty of religious freedom "places beyond our jurisdiction disputes involving church doctrine, canon law, polity, discipline, and ministerial relationships" and that "among the religious controversies off limits to our courts are promises by members of the clergy to keep a church open."

The court concluded that it had jurisdiction over church property disputes "if and to the extent, and only to the extent, that they are capable of resolution under neutral principles of law" involving no inquiry into church doctrine or polity. The court concluded that the sole surviving sibling who conveyed property to the church had standing, since she gave up her rights in the property in reliance on the pastor's assurance that the property would always be used as a church in memory of James. In other words, her rights were different from members of the congregation generally. Similarly, the court concluded that Eileen had standing to sue:

> It is clear that Eileen has alleged an individual stake in this dispute that makes her, and not the state attorney general, the party to bring suit . . . . A gift to a church generally creates a public charity. It is the exclusive function of the attorney general to correct abuses in the administration of a public charity by the institution of proper proceedings. It is his duty to see that the public interests are protected . . . or to decline so to proceed as those interests may require. However, a plaintiff who asserts an individual interest in the charitable organization distinct from that of the general public has standing to pursue her individual claims. In this case, Eileen's claims are readily distinguishable from those of the general class of parishioner-beneficiaries. . . . She claims that she lost substantial personal funds as the result of the archbishop's negligent misrepresentation to her. This claim is personal, specific, and exists apart from any broader community interest in keeping the church open. She has alleged a personal right that would, in the ordinary course, entitle her to standing.

However, the court ruled that the First Amendment prevented it from resolving the sibling's claims. For example, the sibling claimed that the pastor breached a fiduciary duty to her by not informing her at the time she conveyed her interests in the property to the archbishop that the church could be closed according to canon law. In rejecting this argument, the court observed:

> A ruling that a Roman Catholic priest, or a member of the clergy of any (or indeed every) religion, owes a fiduciary-confidential relationship to a parishioner that inheres in their shared faith and nothing more is impossible as a matter of law. Such a conclusion would require a civil court to affirm questions of purely spiritual and doctrinal obligation. The ecclesiastical authority of the archbishop and [the pastor] over the parishioners, the ecclesiastical authority of the archbishop over the pastor, the state of canon law at the date of the property transfer . . . the canonical obligation of the pastor, if any, to inform parishioners of canonical law—all of these inquiries bearing on resolution of the fiduciary claims would take us far afield of neutral principles of law. We decline to hold that, as a matter of civil law, the relationship of a member of the clergy to his or her congregants, without more, creates a fiduciary or confidential relationship grounded in their shared religious affiliation for which redress is available in our courts.

The court also rejected Eileen's claim that the archbishop acted negligently in failing to inform the local pastor of the plans to close the church when he knew he would be soliciting funds to sustain the church "now and for the future." The court noted that Eileen's gift was made in 2002, nearly two years before the archbishop decided to close the church. As a result, the pastor's efforts to raise funds for the maintenance of the church, both now and in the future, was not negligent or a misrepresentation.

9. The Uniform Management of Institutional Funds Act (UMIFA)

This Act, which has been adopted in most states, is designed to provide the boards and trustees of charitable organizations (including churches) with guidance in handling *institutional funds*. The Act defines an institutional fund as a fund that is "not wholly expendable by the institution on a current basis under the terms of the applicable gift instrument." An official interpretation of the Act, adopted by its drafters, further clarifies that

> an endowment fund is an institutional fund . . . which is held in perpetuity or for a term and which is not wholly expendable by the institution. Implicit in the definition is the continued maintenance of all or a specified portion of the original gift. . . . If a governing board has the power to spend all of a fund but, in its discretion, decides to invest the fund and spend only the yield or appreciation therefrom, the fund does not become an endowment fund under this definition . . . .

According to these provisions, the Act would not apply to church building funds (or other designated funds) that exist for a specific project requiring the expenditure of the entire fund. However, some churches have established perpetual endowment funds that will meet the Act's definition of an institutional fund.

An introductory note to the Act states:

> It is established law that the donor may place restrictions on his largesse which the donee institution must honor. Too often, the restrictions on use or investment become outmoded or wasteful or unworkable. There is a need for review of obsolete restrictions and a way of modifying or adjusting them. The Act authorizes the governing board to obtain the acquiescence of the donor to a release of restrictions and, in the absence of the donor, to petition the appropriate court for relief in appropriate cases.

The Act contains the following relevant provisions:

> § 7. (a) With the written consent of the donor, the governing board may release, in whole or in part, a restriction imposed by the applicable gift instrument on the use or investment of an institutional fund.

> (b) If written consent of the donor cannot be obtained by reason of his death, disability, unavailability, or impossibility of identification, the governing board may apply in the name of the institution to the [appropriate] court for release of a restriction imposed by the applicable gift instrument on the use or investment of an institutional fund. The [attorney general] shall be notified of the application and shall be given an

opportunity to be heard. If the court finds that the restriction is obsolete, inappropriate, or impracticable, it may by order release the restriction in whole or in part. A release under this subsection may not change an endowment fund to a fund that is not an endowment fund.

(c) A release under this section may not allow a fund to be used for purposes other than the educational, religious, charitable, or other eleemosynary purposes of the institution affected.

(d) This section does not limit the application of the doctrine of *cy pres*.

An official comment to this section of the Act contains the following additional guidance:

One of the difficult problems of fund management involves gifts restricted to uses which cannot be feasibly administered or to investments which are no longer available or productive. There should be an expeditious way to make necessary adjustments when the restrictions no longer serve the original purpose. . . . This section permits a release of limitations that imperil efficient administration of a fund or prevent sound investment management if the governing board can secure the approval of the donor or the appropriate court.

Although the donor has no property interest in a fund after the gift, nonetheless if it is the donor's limitation that controls the governing board and he or she agrees that the restriction need not apply, the board should be free of the burden. . . . If the donor is unable to consent or cannot be identified, the appropriate court may upon application of a governing board release a limitation which is shown to be obsolete, inappropriate or impracticable.

This section of the Act, which remains largely unknown to church leaders and their advisers, provides important guidance in the event that the purpose of a perpetual endowment fund is frustrated and the church would like to expend the gift for another purpose.

Case Study

• *The Connecticut Supreme Court ruled that the Uniform Management of Institutional Funds Act (UMIFA) does not give donors the authority to enforce designated gifts to charity. The court acknowledged that UMIFA permits a charity to avoid an obsolete designation in a gift without resort to the courts by obtaining the donor's consent: "With the written consent of the donor, the governing board may release, in whole or in part, a restriction imposed by the applicable gift instrument on the use or investment of an institutional fund." However, the court pointed out that the drafters of UMIFA made the following official comments: "It is established law that the donor may place restrictions on his largesse which the donee institution must honor. Too often, the restrictions on use or investment become outmoded or wasteful or unworkable. There is a need for review of obsolete restrictions and a way of modifying or adjusting them. The Act authorizes the governing board to obtain the acquiescence of the donor to a release of restrictions and, in the absence of the donor, to petition the appropriate court for relief in appropriate cases. . . . The donor has no right to enforce the restriction, no interest in the fund and no power to change the [charitable] beneficiary. Carl J. Herzog Foundation, Inc. v. University of Bridgeport, 699 A.2d 995 (Conn. 1997).*

Note that Section 7(c) of UMIFA (quoted above) specifies that the Act does not limit the application of the *cy pres* doctrine. This is a potentially significant provision. The "cy pres" doctrine (which has been adopted by most states) generally specifies that if property is given in trust to be applied to a particular charitable purpose, and it is or becomes impossible or impracticable or illegal to carry out the particular purpose, and if the donor manifested a more general intention to devote the property to charitable purposes, the trust will not fail but the court will direct the application of the property to some charitable purpose which falls within the general charitable intention of the donor.

Case Studies

• *An elderly man drafted a will in 1971 that left most of his estate in trust to his sisters, and upon the death of the surviving sister, to a local Congregational church with the stipulation that the funds be used "solely for the building of a new church." The man died in 1981, and his surviving sister died in 1988. Since the Congregational church had no plans to build a new sanctuary, it asked a local court to interpret the will to permit the church to use the trust fund not only for construction of a new facility but also "for the remodeling, improvement, or expansion of the existing church facilities" and for the purchase of real estate that may be needed for future church construction. The church also asked the court for permission to use income from the trust fund for any purposes that the church board wanted. The state attorney general, pursuant to state law, reviewed the church's petition and asked the court to grant the church's requests. However, a number of heirs opposed the church's position, and insisted that the decedent's will was clear, and that the church was attempting to use the trust funds "for purposes other than building a new church." They asked the court to distribute the trust fund to the decedent's lawful heirs. The local court agreed with the church on the ground that "gifts to charitable uses and purposes are highly favored in law and will be most liberally construed to make effectual the intended purpose of the donor." The trial court's ruling was appealed by the heirs, and the state supreme court agreed with the trial court and ruled in favor of the church. The supreme court began its opinion by observing that "it is contrary to the public policy of this state to indulge in strained construction of the provisions of a will in order to seek out and discover a basis for avoiding the primary purpose of the [decedent] to bestow a charitable trust." The court emphasized that the "cy pres" doctrine clearly required it to rule in favor of the church. Applying the cy pres rule, the court concluded: "The will gave the property in trust for a particular charitable purpose, the building of a new church. The evidence clearly indicated that it was impractical to carry out this particular purpose. Furthermore, the [decedent] did not provide that the trust should terminate if the purpose failed. A trust is not forfeited when it becomes impossible to carry out its specific purpose, and there is no forfeiture or reversion clause." The court concluded* that the trial court's decision to permit the church to use the trust fund for the remodeling, improvement, or expansion of the existing church facilities "falls within the [decedent's] general charitable intention." Accordingly, the trial court's decision represented a proper application of the cy pres rule.[288]

• Another court ruled that church funds earmarked by a donor for a specific purpose could be used by the church for other, related purposes. In 1911, a Quaker church established a fund for the care and maintenance of its graveyard, and began soliciting contributions for the fund. By 1988, the fund had increased to nearly $200,000, and had annual income far in excess of expenses. In 1985, the church discussed the possibility of using the excess income for purposes other than graveyard maintenance, and ultimately expressed a desire to use excess income from the fund for general church purposes (including upkeep and maintenance of church properties). A church trustee who administered the fund took an unbending position that the fund could not be used for any purpose other than graveyard maintenance. The church and trustee thereupon sought an opinion ("declaratory judgment") from a local court as to the use of the fund for other purposes. The trial court ruled that the excess income could be used for general church purposes other than graveyard maintenance, and the trustee appealed the case to a state appeals court on the ground that the trial court's decision "conflicts with the express intent of the donors." The appeals court agreed with the trial court on the basis of the "cy pres" doctrine. The court observed that the cy pres doctrine was created "for the preservation of a charitable trust when accomplishment of the particular purpose of the trust becomes impossible, impractical, or illegal." The court concluded that "if income from a charitable trust exceeds that which is necessary to achieve the donor's charitable objective, cy pres may be applied to the surplus income since there is an impossibility of using the income to advance any of the charitable purposes of the [donor]." Therefore, to the extent that the graveyard fund in question "exceeds maintenance and preservation costs, application of cy pres is appropriate since there is an impossibility of using the excess income to advance the particular purpose expressed by the donors." The only remaining question was whether or not the donors manifested an intention to devote excess income to a charitable purpose more general than graveyard maintenance. The court concluded that the donors to the graveyard fund in fact manifested such an intent: "Since the donations were made for the perpetual maintenance of a graveyard, it is logical to assume that the donors expected excess income would be used . . . "to strengthen the very institution to which [they] entrusted their money" to permit it to survive in perpetuity in order to carry out the donors' intent. A contrary result, that the income be held in the trust and accumulate in perpetuity for maintenance of the graveyard, is both illogical and contrary to the probable intent of the donors. The only sensible conclusion to be reached is that the donors did not intend that the trusts would grow while the [church] itself may cease to exist because of lack of funds. We are also convinced that use of the funds for general meeting purposes is sufficiently similar to the particular purpose of the [donors] to apply the cy pres doctrine." The court emphasized that only trust income in excess of graveyard expenses could be applied for general church purposes, and that the church's bylaws required an annual audit of the fund by certified public accountants.[289]

---

[288] Matter of Trust of Rothrock, 452 N.W.2d 403 (Iowa 1990).

[289] Sharpless v. Medford Monthly Meeting of the Religious Society of Friends, 548 A.2d 1157 (N.J. Super. 1988).

10. Conclusions

Since designated gifts generally can be enforced by someone (even if not the donor), church board members may be legally responsible for diverting designated gifts to other purposes. As a result, it is essential for church leaders to consult with an attorney before using a donor's designated funds for some other purpose.

Securities Law
§ 6-07.06

Key point 6-07.06. *Federal and state securities laws make board members personally liable for acts of fraud committed by an organization in connection with the offer or sale of securities. These laws apply to churches, and as a result church board members may be liable for fraudulent practices occurring in connection with the offer or sale of church securities.*

Section 410(b) of the Uniform Securities Act (adopted in most states) imposes civil liability on every officer or director of an organization that (a) offers or sells unregistered, nonexempt securities; (b) uses unlicensed agents in the offer or sale of its securities (unless the agents are specifically exempted from registration under state law); or (c) offers or sells securities by means of any untrue statement of a material fact or any omission of a material fact. In recent years, a number of churches have violated some or all of these requirements. Such violations render each officer and director of the church potentially liable. Section 410(b) does provide that an officer or director of an organization that sells securities in violation of any of the three provisions discussed above is not liable if he "sustains the burden of proof that he did not know, and in the exercise of reasonable care could not have known of the existence of the facts by reason of which the liability is alleged to exist."

Wrongful Discharge of an Employee
§ 6-07.07

Key point 6-07.07. *Church board members may be personally liable if they participate in a decision to terminate an employee in a way that violates the employee's legal rights.*

According to the tradition rule, an employee hired for an indefinite term was considered terminable at the will of either the employer or the employee. No "cause" was necessary. In recent years, the courts generally have permitted discharged "at will" employees to sue their former employer on the basis of one or more legal theories, including:

- wrongful discharge in violation of public policy (e.g., employee terminated for filing a workmen's compensation claim, or for reporting illegal employer activities);

• intentional infliction of emotional distress (e.g., discharge accompanied by extreme and outrageous conduct);

• fraud (e.g., employee accepts job in reliance on employer misrepresentations);

• defamation (e.g., malicious and false statements made by previous employer to prospective employers);

• breach of contract terms (e.g., employer made oral representations, or written representations contained in a contract of employment or employee handbook, that were not kept).

Directors may be personally liable to the extent that they participate in such activities. The subject of wrongful discharge of employees is addressed fully in chapter 8.

Willful Failure to Withhold Taxes

§ 6-07.08

Key point 6-07.08. *Church board members who have authority to sign checks or make financial decisions on behalf of a church may be personally liable for a willful failure by the church to withhold federal payroll taxes, or to deposit or pay over withheld taxes to the IRS.*

The officers and directors of a church or other nonprofit organization can be personally liable for the amount of payroll taxes that are not withheld or paid over to the government. Section 6672 of the tax code specifies that

any person required to collect, truthfully account for, and pay over any [income tax or FICA tax] who willfully fails to collect such tax, or truthfully account for and pay over such tax, or willfully attempts in any manner to evade or defeat any such tax or the payment thereof, shall, in addition to other penalties provided by law, be liable for a penalty equal to the total amount of the tax evaded, or not collected, or not accounted for and paid over.

Stated simply, this section says that any corporate officer, director, or employee who is responsible for withholding taxes and paying them over to the government is liable for a penalty in the amount of 100 percent of such taxes if they are either not withheld or not paid over to the government. This penalty is of special relevance to church leaders, given the high rate of noncompliance by churches with the payroll reporting procedures. Does the penalty imposed by section 6672 apply to churches and other nonprofit organizations? The answer is yes. Consider the following three points.

1. IRS Policy Statement P-5-60

In Policy Statement P-5-60 (part of the *Internal Revenue Manual*), the IRS states:

> The 100% penalty (applicable to withheld income and Social Security taxes) will be used only as a collection device. If a corporation has willfully failed to collect or pay over income and employment taxes, or has willfully failed to pay over collected excise taxes, the 100% penalty may be asserted against responsible officers and employees of the corporation, including volunteer members of boards of trustees of organizations referred to in section 501 of the Internal Revenue Code [e.g., churches], whenever such taxes cannot be immediately collected from the corporation itself. . . . When the person responsible for withholding, collecting and paying over taxes cannot otherwise be determined, the Service will look to the president, secretary, and the treasurer of the corporation as responsible officers.

The IRS has been criticized for attempting to assess the 100 percent penalty against volunteer directors of charitable organizations having little if any control over finances. The IRS responded to this criticism by amending Policy Statement P-5-60 to include the following significant statements:

Determination of Responsible Persons

Responsibility is a matter of status, duty, and authority. Those performing ministerial acts without exercising independent judgment will not be deemed responsible. In general, nonowner employees of the business entity, who act solely under the dominion and control of others, and who are not in a position to make independent decisions on behalf of the business entity, will not be asserted the trust fund recovery penalty. The penalty shall not be imposed on unpaid, volunteer members of any board of trustees or directors of an organization referred to in section 501 of the Internal Revenue Code to the extent such members are solely serving in an honorary capacity, do not participate in the day-to-day or financial operations of the organization, and/or do not have knowledge of the failure on which such penalty is imposed. In order to make accurate determinations all relevant issues should be thoroughly investigated. An individual will not be recommended for assertion if sufficient information is not available to demonstrate he or she was actively involved in the corporation at the time the liability was not being paid. However, this shall not apply if the potentially responsible individual intentionally makes information unavailable to impede the investigation.

This language indicates that the IRS will not assert the 100 percent penalty against uncompensated, volunteer board members of a church who (1) are solely serving in an honorary capacity, (2) do not participate in the day-to-day or financial operations of the organization, and (3) do not have knowledge of the failure to withhold or pay over withheld payroll taxes.

2. Court Cases Involving Churches

The courts have recognized that church officers can be liable for the section 6672 penalty. Consider the following three cases:

Carter v. United States, 717 F. Supp. 188 (S.D.N.Y. 1989).

A church-operated charitable organization in New York failed to pay over to the IRS withheld income taxes and the employer's and employees' share of Social Security and Medicare taxes for a number of quarters. The IRS assessed a penalty in the amount of 100 percent of the unpaid taxes ($230,245) against *each* of the four officers of the organization pursuant to section 6672 of the tax code, although it acknowledged that it could recover no more than the amount of unpaid taxes. A federal court upheld the penalty.

The court concluded that the four officers were responsible persons since (1) they were directors as well as officers; (2) they had the authority to sign checks (including payroll checks); and (3) they were involved in "routine business concerns such as corporate funding, bookkeeping, salaries, and hiring and firing."

The fact that a nonprofit organization was involved and that the officers donated their services without compensation did not relieve them of liability. The court also ruled that the officers acted willfully, as is required for imposition of liability under section 6674. It defined "willful action" as "voluntary, conscious and intentional—as opposed to accidental—decisions not to remit funds properly withheld to the government." There need not be "an evil motive or an intent to defraud." The court specifically held that "the failure to investigate or to correct mismanagement after having notice that withheld taxes have not been remitted to the government is deemed to be willful conduct." Further, the court concluded that payment of employee wages and other debts with the knowledge that the payment of payroll taxes is late constitutes willful conduct.

In re Triplett, 115 B.R. 955 (N.D. Ill. 1990).

A federal bankruptcy court in Illinois ruled that a church treasurer was not personally liable for his church's failure to withhold and pay over to the IRS some $100,000 in payroll taxes but that the pastor and chairman of the board of deacons might be. The court concluded that the church treasurer did not have sufficient control over the finances of the church to be liable for the 100 percent penalty. It noted that the chairman of the board of deacons made all decisions regarding which bills would be paid, and he (and the pastor) alone were responsible for day-to-day church operations. While the treasurer did not satisfy the definition of a responsible person, the court suggested that the pastor and chairman of the deacon board would. It observed that "ample evidence exists to indicate that other church employees, like [the pastor and chairman of the deacon board] may be liable. It is fortuitous that the treasurer's assessment has been litigated before assessments against these other persons."

This case illustrates that the IRS is committed to assessing the 100 percent penalty under section 6674 of the tax code against church leaders in appropriate cases. While the treasurer in this case did not have sufficient control over church finances to be a "responsible person," there is little doubt that many church treasurers would satisfy the court's definition of a responsible person.

Holmes v. United States, 2004-2 USTC 50,301 (S.D. Tex. 2004).

A church operated a private school for primary and secondary students. The school is incorporated, and its board of directors includes parents of students and members of the affiliated church. The board has six directors. The school suffered a substantial drop in enrollment. The loss of tuition made the school insolvent. The directors chose to pay some creditors while negotiating with others. The board's goal was to keep the school open as long as possible. The school's checks required two signatures. The board's chairman, treasurer, and the school administrator, were signatories. The chairman claimed that he rarely signed checks and only did so when the others were not available. Because of its financial problems, the school did not deposit its employees' withheld taxes for three quarters. The treasurer informed the chairman about the tax liability from the beginning. The chairman discussed it with the board and suggested cutbacks to free up cash to pay the taxes. He claimed that the board rejected his ideas. Nearly $120,000 in withheld payroll taxes were not deposited for the quarters in question.

A few years later the IRS assessed the full amount of payroll taxes against the treasurer and chairman of the board pursuant to section 6672 of the tax code. Both of these individuals insisted that they were not liable and that the IRS had abused its discretion by not assessing other board members for the taxes. A federal district initially found the treasurer personally liable for the full amount of the payroll tax liability. In a subsequent proceeding, the personal liability of the board chairman was addressed by the court. The court noted that "under federal law, a company's agent who is responsible for the collection and payment of employment taxes is liable to the government for the amount of the taxes unpaid" and that a responsible person "has some authority over the payment of the taxes, like paying them himself, ordering their payment, or having some control over the company's treasury." The chairman of the board "had enough responsibility to be personally liable for the unpaid taxes. He knew about the tax burden—he signed a return showing that no tax deposits were made for three months. Also, he signed several checks to some of the school's creditors instead of paying the withheld taxes. He could have seen that the taxes were paid but chose not to."

The court rejected the board chairman's argument that his concern over the use of the withheld taxes was ignored or rejected by the board. It observed, "As chairman, he could have protested the use of the funds or refused to follow the directive. Further, that the school required two signatures on its checks is not a defense; it simply shows that at least two people were jointly in control." The court also ruled that the board chairman was not immune from liability because he was a volunteer for the school, since "he had a real position, he was involved in the financial operations of the school, and he knew about the obligation to the government. His titles, positions, and jobs were not honorary." The court concluded that along with the treasurer the government would "recover jointly from the board chairman the balance of the unpaid employment taxes because he actively participated in the diversion of the funds. Others may share in the responsibility."

Key point. *The Taxpayer Bill of Rights 2 established important limitations on the authority of the IRS to assess the 100 percent civil penalty against church leaders who fail to withhold or deposit payroll taxes. These limitations are discussed below.*

3. Taxpayer Bill of Rights 2 (TBOR2)

Congress enacted the Taxpayer Bill of Rights 2 in 1996. This law contains four important limitations on the application of the penalty under section 6672:

1. Notice requirement

The IRS must issue a notice to an individual it has determined to be a responsible person with respect to unpaid payroll taxes at least 60 days prior to issuing a notice and demand for the penalty.

2. Disclosure of information if more than one person subject to penalty

TBOR2 requires the IRS, if requested in writing by a person considered by the IRS to be a responsible person, to disclose in writing to that person the name of any other person the IRS has determined to be a responsible person with respect to the tax liability. The IRS is required to disclose in writing whether it has attempted to collect this penalty from other responsible persons, the general nature of those collection activities, and the amount (if any) collected. Failure by the IRS to follow this provision does not absolve any individual from any liability for this penalty.

3. Contribution from other responsible parties

If more than one person is liable for this penalty, each person who paid the penalty is entitled to recover from other persons who are liable for the penalty an amount equal to the excess of the amount paid by such person over such person's proportionate share of the penalty. This proceeding is a federal cause of action and is separate from any proceeding involving IRS collection of the penalty from any responsible party.

4. Volunteer board members of churches and other charities

TBOR2 clarifies that the responsible person penalty is not to be imposed on volunteer, unpaid members of any board of trustees or directors of a tax-exempt organization to the extent such members are solely serving in an honorary capacity, do not participate in the day-to-day or financial activities of the organization, and do not have actual knowledge of the failure. However, this provision cannot operate in such a way as to eliminate all responsible persons from responsibility. TBOR2 requires the IRS to develop materials to better inform board members of tax-exempt organizations (including voluntary or honorary members) that they may be treated as responsible persons. The IRS is required to make such materials routinely available to tax-exempt organizations. TBOR2 also requires the IRS to clarify its instructions to IRS employees on application of the responsible person penalty with regard to honorary or volunteer members of boards of trustees or directors of tax-exempt organizations.

Case Studies

• *Bill serves as the treasurer of his church. Due to financial difficulties, the pastor decides to use withheld payroll taxes to pay other debts. The IRS later asserts that the church owes $25,000 in unpaid payroll taxes. The church has no means of paying this debt. The IRS insists that Bill and other church board members are personally liable for the debt. It is likely that Bill is a responsible person who may be liable for the 100 percent penalty, since he has authority over the day-today financial activities of the church. TBOR 2 will not protect him. However, it will protect members of the church board who (1) are volunteer, unpaid members; (2) serve solely in an honorary capacity; (3) do not participate in the day-to-day or financial activities of the organization; and (4) do not have actual knowledge of the failure to pay over withheld taxes to the government.*

• *A church board votes to use withheld taxes to pay other debts of the church. Over a three-year period the church fails to deposit $100,000 in withheld taxes. The IRS claims that the board members are personally liable for the 100 percent penalty for failing to deposit withheld taxes. All of the members of the board claim they are protected by the provisions of TBOR2. They are not correct, since TBOR2 specifies that its provisions cannot operate in such a way as to eliminate all responsible persons from responsibility.*

Key point. *The precedents summarized above demonstrate that church officers and directors (and in some cases employees, such as administrators or bookkeepers) can be personally liable for the payment of income taxes and Social Security and Medicare taxes that they fail to withhold, account for, or pay over to the government. It does not matter that they serve without compensation, so long as they satisfy the definition of a "responsible person" and act willfully. Many church officers and directors will satisfy the definition of a responsible person, and such persons can be personally liable for unpaid payroll taxes if they act under the liberal definition of willfully described above. Clearly, church leaders must be knowledgeable regarding a church's payroll tax obligations and ensure that such obligations are satisfied.*

Exceeding the Authority of the Board

§ 6-07.09

Key point 6-07.09. *Church board members may be personally liable for actions they take that exceed the authority vested in them by the church's governing documents.*

Occasionally, it is asserted that the directors of a nonprofit corporation have exceeded their authority or power. Some courts have held that directors of nonprofit corporations have a fiduciary relationship with the members of the corporation that requires them to follow the corporate charter and bylaws. For example, one court held that directors who attempted to amend the bylaws of a nonprofit corporation without the knowledge or approval of the membership violated their fiduciary duty to the corporation: "In seeking to disenfranchise the members of the corporation, some or all of the officers and directors of the corporation failed to meet their fiduciary obligation to the members."

Loans to Directors §6-07.10

Key point 6-07.10. *Church board members may be personally liable, under state nonprofit corporation law, for loans they authorize for any officer or director of the church.*

The Model Nonprofit Corporations Act, as well as various other laws under which some churches are incorporated, prohibit the board from making loans (out of corporate funds) to other directors or officers. Directors who vote in favor of such loans can be liable for them in the event that the loan is unauthorized or otherwise impermissible. Church boards must check the state law under which they are incorporated before considering any loans to a minister. See Table 6-3 for the text of several state laws.

Table 6-3
Selected State Laws Prohibiting Loans to Directors by Nonprofit Corporations

state	statute
Arizona	"A corporation shall not make any loan, directly or indirectly, to any of its officers or directors or to any person, corporation or other form of organization in which such officer or director is a member, director or officer or in which such officer or director has any interest, direct or indirect, financial or otherwise, except when a full and complete disclosure of the relationship is made at a regularly called meeting of the board of directors of the corporation, entered upon the minutes, and voted on by secret ballot with the officer or director making such disclosure refraining from voting on the motion." (Ariz. Rev. Stats. §10-2263(C))
California	"A director shall perform the duties of a director, including duties as a member of any committee of the board upon which the director may serve, in good faith, in a manner such director believes to be in the best interests of the corporation and with such care, including reasonable inquiry, as is appropriate under the circumstances. . . . The provisions of this section . . . shall govern any action or omission of a director in regard to . . . any loan of money or property to or guaranty of the obligation of any director or officer. No obligation, otherwise valid, shall be voidable merely because directors who benefited by a board resolution to . . . make such loan or guaranty participated in making such board resolution." (Cal. Corp. Code § 9241)

Table 6-3
Selected State Laws Prohibiting Loans to Directors by Nonprofit Corporations

state	statute
Florida	"Loans, other than through the purchase of bonds, debentures, or similar obligations of the type customarily sold in public offerings, or through ordinary deposit of funds in a bank, may not be made by a corporation to its directors or officers, or to any other corporation, firm, association, or other entity in which one or more of its directors or officers is a director or officer or holds a substantial financial interest, except a loan by one corporation which is exempt from federal income taxation under section 501(c)(3) of the Internal Revenue Code of 1986, as amended, to another corporation which is exempt from federal income taxation under section 501(c)(3) of the Internal Revenue Code of 1986, as amended. A loan made in violation of this section is a violation of the duty to the corporation of the directors or officers authorizing it or participating in it, but the obligation of the borrower with respect to the loan shall not be affected thereby." (Fla. Stats. § 617.0833)
Michigan	"Unless otherwise prohibited by law, a corporation may lend money to, or guarantee an obligation of, or otherwise assist an officer or employee of the corporation or of its subsidiary, including an officer or employee who is a director of the corporation or its subsidiary, when, in the judgment of the board, the loan, guaranty, or assistance may reasonably be expected to benefit the corporation. The loan, guaranty, or assistance may be with or without interest, and may be unsecured, or secured in such manner as the board approves. Nothing in this section shall be deemed to deny, limit, or restrict the powers of guaranty or warranty of a corporation at common law or under any statute." (Mich. Comp. Laws. § 450.2548)
Minnesota	"A corporation may not lend money to or guarantee the obligation of a director, officer, or employee of the corporation or a related organization, or of the spouse, parents, children and spouses of children, brothers and sisters or spouses of brothers and sisters of the director, officer, or employee, unless the loan or guarantee may reasonably be expected, in the judgment of the board, to benefit the corporation. If a loan or guarantee is made in violation of this subdivision, the borrower's liability on the loan is not affected. The officers and directors who make a loan in violation of this subdivision or assent to it are jointly and severally liable for its repayment. . . . A loan, guaranty, surety contract, or other financial assistance . . . may be with or without interest and may be unsecured or secured. . . . This section does not grant authority to act as a bank or to carry on the business of banking." (Minn. Stats. § 317A.501)

state	statute
Table 6-3 Selected State Laws Prohibiting Loans to Directors by Nonprofit Corporations	
Texas	"A. No loans shall be made by a corporation to its directors. B. The directors of a corporation who vote for or assent to the making of a loan to a director of the corporation, and any officer or officers participating in the making of such loan, shall be jointly and severally liable to the corporation for the amount of such loan until repayment thereof." (TEXAS CIVIL STATS. § 1396-2.25)
Washington	"No loans shall be made by a corporation to its directors or officers. The directors of a corporation who vote for or assent to the making of a loan to a director or officer of the corporation, and any officer or officers participating in the making of such loan, shall be jointly and severally liable to the corporation for the amount of such loan until the repayment thereof." (WASH. REV. CODE § 24.03.140)

Case Study

• A District of Columbia appeals court ruled that it was prohibited by the from resolving a lawsuit brought by members of a church claiming that the board of trustees breached its fiduciary duties by authorizing an interest-free loan to the pastor and by failing to provide the congregation with adequate information regarding the church's finances. A church employed a new pastor, and the church board authorized a loan to enable the pastor to purchase a new home. Though the pastor was a member of the board by virtue of office, he did not participate in the vote. At a specially called business meeting of the church membership, the board recommended approval of the loan. One church member suggested that the loan be interest-free, commenting "the church should not profit from this loan to the pastor." The membership approved a no-interest loan at the meeting and eventually loaned the pastor some $256,000 for the purchase. A few years later, certain members of the church asked for more details from the church board regarding the loan, and other financial transactions involving the pastor. When their request was ignored, they filed a lawsuit in which they asked a court to declare that the board had breached its fiduciary duties by authorizing the interest-free loan, and that the members "have a right to receive, review and inspect information and documents that will inform the members regarding the church's finances, compliance or non-compliance with federal and local laws, and other liabilities." A trial court agreed to resolve the case, but an appeals court intervened and dismissed the members' claims. It concluded: "A church's financial regime . . . necessarily reflects an array of decisions about a member's obligation to pledge funds, and about the leaders' corresponding responsibility to account for those funds, that a civil court cannot arbitrate without entangling itself in doctrinal interpretations. . . . Accounting is an area riddled with major subjective decisions. When the entity in question is a religious society, those subjective decisions raise questions of internal church governance which are often themselves based on the application of church doctrine."[290]

[290] Kelsey v. Ray, 719 A.2d 1248 (D.C. App. 1998).

Immunity Statutes

§ 6-08

Key point 6-08. *State and federal laws provide limited immunity to uncompensated officers and directors of churches and other charities. This means that they cannot be personally liable for their ordinary negligence. However, such laws contain some exceptions. For example, officers and directors may be personally liable for their gross negligence or their willful or wanton misconduct.*

Most states have enacted laws limiting the liability of church officers and directors. In some states, these laws protect all church volunteers. In some cases, the statute may protect only officers and directors of churches that are incorporated under the state's general nonprofit corporation law. The most common type of statute immunizes *uncompensated* directors and officers from legal liability for their ordinary negligence committed within the scope of their official duties. These statutes generally provide no protection for "willful and wanton" conduct or "gross negligence."

"Compensation" ordinarily is defined to exclude reimbursement of travel expenses incurred while serving as a director or officer. Churches that compensate their directors and officers over and above the reimbursement of travel expenses should reconsider such a policy if they are located in a state that grants limited immunity to uncompensated officers and directors. Obviously, these statutes will not protect ministers who receive compensation from their church.

▶ *Churches should consider adopting an appropriate resolution clarifying that a minister's annual compensation package is for ministerial duties rendered to the church, and not for any duties on the church board. Like any other church officer or director, the minister serves without compensation. Such a provision, if adopted, might qualify the minister for protection under the legal immunity law. It is worth serious consideration.*

Statutes immunizing the directors and officers of nonprofit organizations from liability do not prevent the organization itself from being sued on the basis of the negligence of an officer or director. The immunity statutes only protect the officers or directors themselves. Many of the immunity statutes apply only to the directors and officers of organizations exempt from federal income tax under section 501(c) of the Internal Revenue Code. Some of them appear to apply only to *incorporated* organizations.

Why have states enacted such laws? The primary reason is to encourage persons to serve as directors of nonprofit organizations. In the past, many qualified individuals have declined to serve as directors of such organizations out of a fear of legal liability. The immunity statutes respond directly to this concern by providing directors of nonprofit organizations with limited immunity from legal liability.

Gross Negligence

Church leaders should be familiar with the concept of gross negligence, for the following three reasons:

(1) Punitive damages. Courts can award "punitive damages" for conduct that amounts to gross negligence. Punitive damages are damages awarded by a jury "in addition to compensation for a loss sustained, in order to punish, and make an example of, the wrongdoer." They are awarded when a person's conduct is particularly reprehensible and outrageous. This does not necessarily mean intentional misconduct. Punitive damages often are associated with reckless conduct or conduct creating a high risk of harm. To illustrate, in one case a punitive damage award was based on the fact that church officials repeatedly and knowingly placed a priest in situations where he could sexually abuse boys and then failed to supervise him and disclose his sexual problem. Clearly, church officials did not intend for the priest to molest anyone. But, under the circumstances, the jury concluded that the church's actions were sufficiently reckless to justify an award of punitive damages. Church leaders must understand that reckless inattention to risks can lead to punitive damages, and that such damages may not be covered by the church's liability insurance policy. It is critical to note that many church insurance policies exclude punitive damages. This means that a jury award of punitive damages represents a potentially uninsured risk. Accordingly, it is critical for church leaders to understand the basis for punitive damages, and to avoid behavior which might be viewed as grossly negligent.

(2) Loss of limited immunity under state law. State and federal laws provide uncompensated officers and directors of nonprofit corporations (including churches) with immunity from legal liability for their ordinary negligence. This is an important protection. However, such laws do not protect officers and directors from liability for their gross negligence.

(3) Personal liability. Church leaders who are guilty of gross negligence are more likely to be sued personally than if their behavior is merely negligent. Indifference by church leaders to information that clearly demonstrates improper behavior by a staff member or volunteer worker can be viewed by a court as gross negligence, and this will make it more likely that the church leaders will be sued personally.

Case Studies

• *A federal court in Arizona ruled that the federal Volunteers Protection Act (see sidebar) prevented individual board members of a charity from being personally liable for unpaid wages claimed by a former officer. The officer claimed that the charity had violated the federal Fair Labor Standards Act. Since the charity had no assets, it was undisputed that the individual board members would be responsible for any damages. The board members argued that the Volunteer Protection Act protected them from any personal liability, and the court agreed. The court concluded that the Act was intended to protect all volunteers from tort liability, whether state or federal, and that "the broad, plain language of the Act indicates it covers all liability whether rooted in tort or contract."[291]*

• *A Colorado court ruled that a denominational agency could be sued by a woman with whom a minister had sexual contacts, and that a state statute providing limited immunity to uncompensated officers and directors of nonprofit corporations was not a defense.[292] The statute specifies, "No member of the board of directors of a nonprofit corporation or nonprofit organization shall be held liable for actions taken or omissions*

---

[291] Armendarez v. Glendale Youth Center, 265 F.Supp.2d 1136 (D. Ariz. 2003).
[292] Winkler v. Rocky Mouton Conference, 923 P.2d 152 (Colo. App. 1995).

made in the performance of his duties as a board member except for wanton and willful acts or omissions."[293] The court concluded that this provision did not apply in this case, since there was no evidence that the agency "accomplished its work through unpaid volunteers."

• *An Illinois court ruled that board members could be personally liable for the molestation of a child on a school bus, despite a state law conferring limited immunity from liability, because their behavior in failing to adequately protect the victim was willful and wanton. A 12-year-old special education student (the "victim") at a public school had various developmental and mental disabilities. One day, while being transported to school, the victim was sexually assaulted by a male student who had a deviant sexual history and, as a result of having been declared a sexually aggressive child, was under a "protective plan." While the board employed a bus attendant to supervise the children on the trip to and from school, on the day of the sexual assault the bus attendant called in sick. The victim sued the members of the school board, claiming that they were responsible for his injuries. State law grants limited immunity from liability to school board members, meaning they cannot be personally liable for their acts unless they are guilty of "willful or wanton" misconduct. The victim alleged that the board members were guilty of willful and wanton misconduct because they failed to ensure that a school bus attendant was present on the bus while he was a passenger. A state appeals court ruled that the victim alleged sufficient proof of willful and wanton misconduct by the board to let the case go to a jury. It observed: "Plaintiff has properly pled knowledge on the part of the board that the attacker was likely to commit a sexual assault on the passengers and that an attendant was required."[294]*

• *An Illinois court ruled that the directors of a public charity could not be liable for the dismissal of an employee because they were protected by a state law that provided limited immunity to the uncompensated officers and directors of nonprofit corporations. The court summarized the law as follows: "In order for a director to be immune from liability under the Act, he or she must be unpaid, the corporation must be organized under the Not for Profit Corporation Act, the corporation must be tax exempt under federal law, and the director's conduct must not be willful or wanton." The court noted that "willful or wanton conduct" means "a course of action which shows an actual or deliberate intention to cause harm or which, if not intentional, shows an utter indifference to or conscious disregard for the safety of others or their property." The court noted that the directors in this case were not paid for their services on behalf of the charity, that the charity was organized under the Illinois Not for Profit Corporation Act, and that the Association was tax exempt. In addition, Carol failed to produce any evidence that any of the board's actions amounted to "willful or wanton" conduct. As a result, the court concluded that the board members were properly dismissed from the lawsuit.[295]*

---

[293] Colo. Rev. Stats. § 13-21-116.

[294] Doe v. Chicago Board of Education, 791 N.E.2d 1283 (Ill. App. 2003). *Accord* Doe v. DeSoto Parish School Board, 907 So.2d 275 (La. App. 2005).

[295] Spencer v. Illinois Community Action Association, 164 F.Supp.2d 1056 (C.D. Ill. 2001).

• *The Minnesota Supreme Court rejected the argument that a state limited immunity statute only protected board members when acting collectively as a board.[296] It acknowledged that "it is a longstanding tenet of corporation law that a member of the board has no authority to act individually unless specifically authorized by the corporate bylaws or articles of incorporation." However, the court noted that the statute protects more than directors. It also protects officers, trustees, members, and agents, and these individuals (unlike directors) can act individually rather than collectively. The court concluded that "a director acting outside the specific scope of his or her duty as a member of the board will receive the statute's protection so long as the director is acting on behalf of the nonprofit corporation."*

• *A New York court ruled that a "charitable immunity" law granting limited legal immunity to the uncompensated directors of a nonprofit organization did not protect a church's trustees from liability for the sexual misconduct of their minister. An unincorporated church and its trustees were sued as a result of their minister's alleged rape of a number of minor females in the church. Among other things, the lawsuit alleged that the church and trustees were responsible for the victims' suffering as a result of their "negligent supervision" of the minister's actions. In their defense, the trustees relied on a state law granting uncompensated directors of nonprofit organizations limited immunity from liability for their actions. The court rejected this defense for two reasons: "The [trustees] did not present presumptive evidence of uncompensated status in that they did not present an affidavit of a chief financial officer of the [church]. Further, there is a reasonable probability that the specific conduct of such [trustees] constitutes gross negligence. If the [trustees] did act as the [victims] allege, they may be found to have proceeded in reckless disregard of the consequences of their acts."[297]*

• *The Wisconsin Supreme Court ruled that a state law providing limited immunity to the uncompensated officers and directors of nonprofit corporations only provided protection for acts arising from one's status as an officer or director.[298] A church-sponsored relief agency needed some plumbing work done. Its director negotiated and signed a contract with a plumbing company. The name of the relief agency was mentioned prominently in the contract, as was the fact that the director was signing in his capacity as director of the agency. The agency was unable to pay the plumbing bill, and the plumbing company sued the director personally. The director claimed that he was immune from liability on the basis of a state law protecting uncompensated officers and directors of nonprofit corporations for "monetary liabilities arising from a breach of, or failure to perform, any duty resulting solely from his or her status as a director or officer." The court disagreed. It noted that a director "cannot be granted immunity unless his liability related solely to his status as a director." In this case, however, the director's contractual liability to the plumbing company "stems from his position as an agent to a partially disclosed corporate principal and not from his status as a director."*

---

[296] Rehn v. Fischley, 557 N.W.2d 328 (Minn. 1997).

[297] Karen S. v. Streitferdt, 568 N.Y.S.2d 946 (A.D. 1 Dept. 1991).

[298] Benjamin Plumbing, Inc. v. Barnes, 470 N.W.2d 888 (Wis. 1991).

Volunteer Protection Act

In 1997 Congress enacted the Volunteer Protection Act (42 U.S.C. § 14501) based on the following findings: (1) the willingness of volunteers to offer their services is deterred by the potential for liability actions against them; (2) as a result, many nonprofit organizations have been adversely affected by the withdrawal of volunteers from boards of directors and service in other capacities; and (3) due to high liability costs and unwarranted litigation costs, volunteers and nonprofit organizations face higher costs in purchasing insurance, through interstate insurance markets, to cover their activities.

The Act clarifies that it "preempts the laws of any state to the extent that such laws are inconsistent with this [Act] except that this [Act] shall not preempt any state law that provides additional protection from liability relating to volunteers or to any category of volunteers in the performance of services for a nonprofit organization or governmental entity."

Here is a summary of the Act's main provisions:

• No volunteer of a nonprofit organization shall be liable for harm caused by an act or omission of the volunteer on behalf of the organization or entity if—(1) the volunteer was acting within the scope of the volunteer's responsibilities in the nonprofit organization or governmental entity at the time of the act or omission; (2) if appropriate or required, the volunteer was properly licensed, certified, or authorized by the appropriate authorities for the activities or practice in the state in which the harm occurred, where the activities were or practice was undertaken within the scope of the volunteer's responsibilities in the nonprofit organization or governmental entity; (3) the harm was not caused by willful or criminal misconduct, gross negligence, reckless misconduct, or a conscious, flagrant indifference to the rights or safety of the individual harmed by the volunteer; and (4) the harm was not caused by the volunteer operating a motor vehicle, vessel, aircraft, or other vehicle for which the state requires the operator or the owner of the vehicle, craft, or vessel to possess an operator's license or obtain insurance.

• The Act provides no protection to nonprofit organizations themselves.

• Punitive damages may not be awarded against a volunteer unless the victim proves by clear and convincing evidence that the harm was caused by the volunteer's willful or "criminal misconduct, or a conscious, flagrant indifference to the rights or safety of the individual harmed."

Directors and Officers Insurance

§ 6-08.1

Key point 6-08.1. *Directors and officers insurance provides coverage for various acts committed by board members in the course of their official duties. Such insurance may provide coverage for claims that are excluded under a church's general liability policy. It also may cover acts not protected by the federal and state limited immunity laws.*

Should churches obtain "directors and officers" insurance coverage for the members of their board? Does the enactment of the Volunteer Protection Act (and corresponding state laws) make such insurance unnecessary? Not at all. The legal protection provided by these laws is not absolute. They do not apply if a board member receives any form of compensation (other than travel expense reimbursements), and they do not apply if a board member is accused of gross negligence. Directors and officers insurance will provide coverage for such exceptions. Just as importantly, the insurance company is responsible for providing legal representation in the event a director or officer is sued directly.

Case Study

• *An Alabama court ruled that a church's "directors and officers" insurance policy covered a lawsuit brought against a pastor for improperly obtaining money from an elderly member.[299] The daughter of an elderly church member was appointed guardian of her mother's property. The daughter sued the minister of her mother's church, claiming that he improperly obtained funds from her mother by means of conversion, fraud, and undue influence. The minister notified the church's "directors and officers" insurer of the lawsuit and asked the insurer to provide him with a legal defense. The insurer asked a court to determine whether or not the minister's actions were covered under the insurance policy. The court concluded that the insurer had a legal duty to provide the minister with a defense of the lawsuit. It noted that the church's insurance policy provided coverage for officers and directors (including the minister in this case) in any lawsuit brought against them by reason of alleged dishonesty on their part unless a court determined that the officer or director acted with deliberate dishonesty. Since the minister had not yet been found guilty of "deliberate dishonesty," he was covered under the insurance policy. The court acknowledged that if the minister was found to have acted with deliberate dishonesty in the daughter's lawsuit, the insurer would have no duty to pay any portion of the judgment or verdict.*

---

[299] Graham v. Preferred Abstainers Insurance Company, 689 So.2d 188 (Ala. App. 1997).

Table 6-4
Personal Liability of Church Officers, Directors, and Trustees

theory of liability	definition	examples
tort	conduct that injures another's person or property	• negligent operation of a church vehicle • negligent supervision of church workers and activities • copyright infringement • wrongful termination of employees
contract	executing a contract without authorization, or with authorization but without any indication of a representative capacity	• a church board member signs a contract without indicating he is signing in a representative capacity, on behalf of a named church • a church board member signs a contract without authorization
breach of the fiduciary duty of care	every officer or director has a fiduciary duty of due care to the corporation; a breach of this duty can result in liability	• failure to attend board meetings; question irregularities; review the church's financial records; and dissenting from questionable actions
breach of the fiduciary duty of loyalty	every officer or director has a fiduciary duty of loyalty to the corporation; a breach of this duty can result in liability	• a church board votes in favor of a contract with a member of the board (unless the conflict is fully disclosed, the contract is fair to the church, and is approved by a disinterested majority of the board)
violation of trust terms	board members may be liable for violating or disregarding the terms of an express trust	• a donor contributes money to a church's building fund, and the church board approves the use of the fund for other purposes unrelated to a building (cf. cy pres doctrine)

Table 6-4
Personal Liability of Church Officers, Directors, and Trustees

theory of liability	definition	examples
securities law	selling securities without registering as an agent (if required by state law); engaging in fraudulent activities in the offer or sale of church securities	• church board members sell church securities to members of the congregation without registering as an agent under state securities law • church board members make unfounded guarantees in the sale of church securities. • church board members make material misrepresentations of fact, or fail to disclose material facts, in the offer or sale of church securities
wrongful discharge of employees	dismissing without "good cause" an employee hired for a definite term of employment prior to the expiration of the term; dismissing an "at will" employee in violation of public policy	• a church board dismisses an employee prior to the end of a 2-year term, without good cause • a church board dismisses an "at will" employee for refusing to backdate tax records
willful failure to withhold taxes	section 6672 of the Internal Revenue Code imposes a 100 percent penalty upon any "responsible person" who willfully fails to withhold federal payroll taxes, or who withholds them but fails to pay them over to the government	• a church treasurer uses withheld federal taxes to meet a church's payroll obligations
exceeding the authority of the board	church board members may be accountable for taking action they are not authorized to perform	• a church board purchases real estate on behalf of the church (without congregational approval as required by the church charter)

Table 6-4		
Personal Liability of Church Officers, Directors, and Trustees		
theory of liability	definition	examples
loans to directors	many state nonprofit corporation laws specify that church board members may be liable for approving a loan to an officer or director	• a church board approves a $15,000 loan to the senior minister to enable him to make the down payment on a home

Members—In General § 6-09

It is often important to determine which persons comprise the membership of a church since the church's charter and bylaws, and in some cases state nonprofit corporation law, generally vest considerable authority in the members.[300] In congregational churches, the members typically elect and depose directors and ministers, authorize the purchase and sale of property, adopt and amend the charter or bylaws, and approve budgets. Church members in hierarchical churches typically possess some or all of these powers.

Selection and Qualifications §6-09.1

Key point 6-09.1. *The procedure for selecting members generally is defined by a church's governing documents. The civil courts have refrained from resolving disputes over the selection of members on the ground that the First Amendment guaranty of religious freedom prevents them from deciding whether or not individuals satisfy the requirements for church membership.*

The essence of the relationship between members and a church consists of an agreement, a profession of faith, adherence to church doctrine, and submission to church governance.[301] The membership of a church is typically determined by reference to the church charter and bylaws and to any applicable state corporation law. It is well-settled that (1) the right to determine the qualifications for membership belongs to the church, (2) a determination as to who are "members

---

[300] *See generally* W. TORPEY, JUDICIAL DOCTRINES OF RELIGIOUS RIGHTS IN AMERICA (1948) (while this text is obsolete in most respects, it presents a principled analysis that is of continuing utility); Bernard, *Churches, Members and the Role of the Courts: Toward a Contractual Analysis*, 51 NOTRE DAME LAWYER 545 (1976) (provides useful suggestions regarding judicial involvement in church membership determinations); Ellman, *Driven from the Tribunal: Judicial Resolution of Internal Church Disputes*, 69 CALIF. L. REV. 1380 (1981) (contending that churches must engage in limited involvement in internal church disputes, ideally through construction of doctrinally-neutral internal church "contractual" documents).

[301] Freshour v. King, 345 P.2d 689 (Kan. 1959); Henson v. Payne, 302 S.W.2d 44 (Mo. 1956); Second Baptist Church v. Mount Zion Baptist Church, 466 P.2d 212 (Nev. 1970); Western Conference of Original Free Will Baptists v. Creech, 123 S.E.2d 619 (N.C. 1962).

in good standing" is an ecclesiastical question relating to the government and discipline of a church, and (3) a church's decision about either matter is binding on the courts.[302]

To illustrate, when two purported members of a church sought an accounting of church funds and the church defended its noncompliance on the ground that the plaintiffs were not members in good standing, a court deferred to the church's determination that the plaintiffs were not members and dismissed the case.[303] The court observed that membership in a religious society is an ecclesiastical matter to be determined by the church, not the courts. The United States Supreme Court has stated the general rule of judicial nonintervention in the ecclesiastical affairs of churches, including membership determinations, as follows:

> But it is a very different thing where a subject matter of dispute, strictly and purely ecclesiastical in its character—a matter over which the civil courts exercise no jurisdiction—a matter which concerns theological controversy, church discipline, ecclesiastical government, or the conformity of the members of the church to the standard of morals required of them—becomes the subject of its action. It may be said here, also, that no jurisdiction has been conferred on the tribunal to try the particular case before it, or that, in its judgment, it exceeds the powers conferred upon it, or that the laws of the church do not authorize the particular form of proceeding adopted; and, in a sense often used in the courts, all of those may be said to be questions of jurisdiction. But it is easy to see that if the civil courts are to inquire into all these matters, the whole subject of the doctrinal theology, the usages and customs, the written laws, and fundamental organization of every religious denomination may, and must, be examined into with minuteness and care, for they would become, in almost every case, the criteria by which the validity of the ecclesiastical decree would be determined in the civil court.[304]

The Supreme Court has also held that religious freedom encompasses the "power of [religious bodies] to decide for themselves, free from state interference, matters of church government as well as those of faith and doctrine."[305] And, the Court has stated that "religious controversies are not the proper subject of civil court inquiry."[306] This rule is often followed even when it is alleged that

---

[302] Rodyk v. Ukrainian Autocephalic Orthodox Church, 296 N.Y.S.2d 496 (1968), aff'd, 328 N.Y.S.2d 685 (1972). See also Stewart v. Jarriel, 59 S.E.2d 368 (Ga. 1950); Fast v. Smyth, 527 S.W.2d 673, 676 (Mo. 1975) ("the determination of who are qualified members of a church is an ecclesiastical matter"); Eisenberg v. Fauer, 200 N.Y.S.2d 749 (1960); Presbytery of Beaver-Butler v. Middlesex, 489 A.2d 1317 (Pa. 1985) ("the view of a court as to who are heretics among warring sects is worth nothing, and must count as nothing if our cherished diversity of religious views is to prevail").

[303] Taylor v. New York Annual Conference of the African Methodist Episcopal Church, 115 N.Y.S.2d 62 (1952).

[304] Watson v. Jones, 80 U.S. 679, 733-34 (1871).

[305] Kedroff v. St. Nicholas Cathedral, 344 U.S. 94, 116 (1952).

[306] Serbian Eastern Orthodox Diocese v. Milivojevich, 426 U.S. 696, 713 (1976).

a church deviated from its own charter or bylaws in making a membership determination.[307]

A number of courts, however, have been willing to review church determinations involving members as long as no "strictly and purely ecclesiastical" question is presented. For example, some courts have been willing to review such determinations if:

1) the church determination was the product of fraud or collusion;[308]

2) civil, contract, or property rights of members are affected;[309] or

3) a legitimate dispute occurs over the meaning of the criteria for membership.[310]

The issue of judicial intervention in internal church disputes involving membership determinations is covered later in this section.

Case Studies

• A Michigan court ruled that it was barred by the First Amendment from resolving an internal church dispute since it could not do so without delving into church doctrine. A dispute arose in a church, resulting in the church's "disfellowshiping" of several members. Members of the church sought a court order prohibiting the disfellowshiped members from attending the church. The disfellowshiped members countered by arguing that they had been wrongfully disfellowshiped, and that a

---

[307] Evans v. Shiloh Baptist Church, 77 A.2d 160 (Md. 1950); Jenkins v. New Shiloh Baptist Church, 56 A.2d 788 (Md. 1948).

[308] Gonzalez v. Roman Catholic Archbishop, 280 U.S. 1 (1929). The United States Supreme Court has stated that "arbitrariness" is no longer a basis for civil court review of the ecclesiastical determinations of churches. Serbian Eastern Orthodox Diocese v. Milivojevich, 426 U.S. 696 (1976).

[309] *See, e.g.,* Carden v. La Grone, 169 S.E.2d 168, 172 (Ga. 1969) ("a court of equity will not interfere with the internal management of a religious society where property rights are not involved"); Third Missionary Baptist Church v. Garrett, 158 N.W.2d 771, 776 (Iowa 1968) ("[i]t is a general rule recognized here and in foreign jurisdictions that ordinarily the courts have no jurisdiction over, and no concern with, purely ecclesiastical questions and controversies, including membership in a church organization, but they do have jurisdiction as to civil, contract, and property rights which are involved in or arise from a church controversy"); Mitchell v. Albanian Orthodox Diocese, 244 N.E.2d 276, 278-79 (Mass. 1969) ("courts do not interfere in a controversy that is exclusively or primarily of an ecclesiastical nature. Where civil or property rights or the construction of legal instruments are involved, however, the courts have been less reluctant to interfere"); Fast v. Smyth, 527 S.W.2d 673, 676 (Mo. 1975) ("the determination of who are qualified members of a church is an ecclesiastical matter. There is, however, a well recognized exception to this general rule in this state. Civil courts will review ecclesiastical matters where necessary to protect the property, contracts, or civil rights of members").

[310] *See, e.g.,* Smith v. Riley, 424 So.2d 1166 (La. App. 1982) (in the absence of any evidence to the contrary, the term *members* as used in a church charter includes females); Second Baptist Church v. Mount Zion Baptist Church, 466 P.2d 212 (Nev. 1970) (where church bylaws stipulated that failure to attend church or make financial contributions "without a reasonable excuse" resulted in termination of membership, the court resolved church dispute concerning the meaning of "without a reasonable excuse"); Honey Creek Regular Baptist Church v. Wilson, 92 N.E.2d 419 (Ohio 1950) (court agreed to hear church dispute concerning the issue of whether "extending the right hand of fellowship" was a requirement of church membership).

majority of the church's membership supported them. Both sides produced affidavits and "membership lists" in support of their respective positions. The court concluded: "Unfortunately, the articles of incorporation offer no help in establishing who may become a member of the church. Indeed, the articles provide that 'the New Testament shall be the only rule of faith and practice of said church.' Accordingly, it is not possible for a court to determine which of the parties, if either, is actually the 'church' without delving into religious doctrine or ecclesiastical polity. . . . Although a court may determine rights to church property where such can be determined by application of civil law, resolution of the property dispute in this case would require consideration of religious doctrine and ecclesiastical polity. . . . It is undisputed that [the church] is an independent or congregational church. However, both parties claim to represent the numerical majority and both argue that they are the church officers entrusted with the powers of control. Moreover, each party maintains that they are following the rules of the church. After a careful review of the record, we find we cannot determine which party actually represents the numerical majority, is in control, or is following the rules of the church, without improperly delving into matters of religious doctrine and ecclesiastical polity. Accordingly, the trial court did not have subject matter jurisdiction over either parties' property claim and it properly dismissed the case."[311]

• A Pennsylvania court refused to order church officials to explain why they refused to admit a person as a member. A member asked his church to transfer his membership to another church pursuant to an established church procedure. The minister of the second church rejected the transfer of membership without explanation. The member filed a lawsuit asking a court to order church officials to "show cause" why he should not be admitted as a member. A state appeals court ruled that the civil courts are bound by the First Amendment guaranty of religious freedom to accept the decisions of religious organizations on matters of "discipline, faith, internal organization, and ecclesiastical rule, custom, and law." On the other hand, the civil courts can intervene in church disputes that do not implicate such concerns. The court concluded that this case, which involved an individual's right to membership in a church, was the kind of ecclesiastical matter that was beyond the authority of the civil courts to resolve. It observed: "Membership in a congregation is purely an ecclesiastical matter subject to the church rules and controlled by the decisions of the appropriate church tribunals in so far as they do not contravene the civil law. The heart of [the member's] case is that he desires to become a member in [another church]. Accordingly, it is clear that this case involves a purely ecclesiastical matter."[312]

• A Pennsylvania court ruled that it was barred by the First Amendment from resolving a lawsuit by an individual who wanted to be admitted as a member of a church. The court relied upon what it called the "deference rule" which "provides that civil courts are bound to accept the decisions of the highest judicatories of a religious organization of hierarchical polity on matters of discipline, faith, internal organization, or ecclesiastical rule, custom or law."[313]

[311] Church of Christ v. Gill, 2002 WL 737801 (Mich. App. 2002).
[312] Gundlach v. Laister, 625 A.2d 706 (Pa. Cmwlth. 1993).
[313] In re St. Clement's Church, 687 A.2d 11 (Pa. Common. 1996).

Authority

§ 6-09.2

Key point 6-09.2. *Church members have such legal authority as is vested in them by their church's governing documents, and in some cases by state nonprofit corporation law.*

In churches with a congregational form of government, the general rule is that a majority of the members represent the church and have the right to manage its affairs and to control its property for the use and benefit of the church, and that the law will protect such authority at least as it relates to civil, contract, or property rights.[314] One court has stated the rule as follows: "The courts will give effect to the action of the majority of members of a congregational or independent religious organization . . . insofar as regards civil or property rights when they have acted in harmony with church rules, customs and practices at a meeting properly called."[315]

The United States Supreme Court has observed that "majority rule is generally employed in the governance of religious societies."[316] Other courts have held that a majority of a church's membership has the authority to sell a parsonage and acquire a new one;[317] to oust a minority group that had wrongfully and violently seized possession of the church building;[318] to call a meeting of the church;[319] to expel members;[320] to disaffiliate from one denomination and associate with another;[321] to adopt bylaws;[322] to authorize church activity and direct or control disposition of church property;[323] and to select and remove a minister.[324]

The general authority possessed by the members of a congregational church exists whether the church is incorporated or unincorporated. However, state corporate law may grant the members of an incorporated church additional specific powers. For example, the Model Nonprofit Corporation Act, which has been adopted in whole or in part in a majority of states, specifies that "all books

---

[314] Mitchell v. Dickey, 173 S.E.2d 695 (Ga. 1970); Wright v. Smith, 124 N.E.2d 363 (Ill. 1955); McHargue v. Feltner, 325 S.W.2d 349 (Ky. 1959).

[315] Willis v. Davis, 323 S.W.2d 847, 849 (Ky. 1959).

[316] Jones v. Wolf, 443 U.S. 595, 607 (1979).

[317] McHargue v. Feltner, 325 S.W.2d 349 (Ky. 1959).

[318] Mitchell v. Dickey, 173 S.E.2d 695 (Ga. 1970).

[319] Willis v. Davis, 323 S.W.2d 847 (Ky. 1959).

[320] Smith v. Lewis, 578 S.W.2d 169 (Tex. App. 1979); Moorman v. Goodman, 157 A.2d 519 (N.J. 1960).

[321] Foss v. Dykstra, 342 N.W.2d 220 (S.D. 1983); Douglass v. First Baptist Church, 287 P.2d 965 (Colo. 1955).

[322] First Baptist Church v. State of Ohio, 591 F. Supp. 676 (S.D. Ohio 1983); Lewis v. Wolfe, 413 S.W.2d 314 (Mo. 1967).

[323] Mt. Jezreel Christians Without a Home v. Board of Trustees of Mount Jezreel Baptist Church, 582 A.2d 237 (D.C. App. 1990) ("[w]e therefore hold that, as a general principle, bona fide members of a church have standing to bring suit as trust beneficiaries when there is a dispute over the use or disposition of church property"); Pilgrim Evangelical v. Lutheran Church-Missouri Synod Foundation, 661 S.W.2d 833 (Mo. App. 1983); Blair v. Blair, 396 S.E.2d 374 (S.C. App. 1990).

[324] LeBlanc v. Davis, 432 So.2d 239 (La. 1983).

and records of a corporation may be inspected by any member, or his agent or attorney, for any proper purpose at any reasonable time."[325]

The authority of a majority of members in a church with a congregational form of government is limited. Church members only have the authority vested in them by the church's charter or bylaws or by state corporation law. In a leading case, a court rejected a demand by several church members that their church conduct a meeting at which the pastor and trustees would give a complete accounting of the affairs of the church, since neither the church's charter nor bylaws conferred such authority upon the membership. The court concluded that the members "have only such powers, if any, in the management of the affairs of the corporation as may be conferred upon them by the charter and bylaws."[326]

On the other hand, while no court has reached this conclusion, it would seem reasonable to regard a church's bylaws, like the United States Constitution, as a "delegated powers" instrument. The tenth amendment to the Constitution states that "powers not delegated to the United States by the Constitution, nor prohibited by it to the States, are reserved to the States, respectively, or to the people." In essence, the citizens have delegated certain powers to the federal government in the Constitution, reserving unto themselves all powers not specifically delegated. Similarly, it could be said that the members who organize a church delegate various powers to the church and its officers, directors, and committees, and that any powers not specifically delegated are reserved unto the membership.

The charter and bylaws of many congregational churches limit the authority of a simple majority of members. For example, some require that sales or purchases of property, elections of ministers, and amendments to the charter or bylaws be by a two-thirds or three-fourths vote of the church membership.

The courts generally will disregard the authority of a church's members when property rights or civil liberties protected under state or federal law are violated. As one court has observed, the rights that exist by virtue of state or federal law "cannot be overridden by a majority rule of any organization—church or otherwise."[327]

Members are under no compulsion to adhere to the tenets of their church, but they cannot impose their beliefs upon a majority that rejects them.[328] Members of course have the right to withdraw from one church and join another.[329] But members who withdraw or whose membership is terminated by action of the church no longer possess any authority. They have no interest in church property, and they cannot represent members in any legal action against the church.[330]

Several courts have noted that when persons become a member of a church, they do so upon the condition of submission to its ecclesiastical jurisdiction, and

---

[325] MODEL NONPROFIT CORPORATION ACT § 25.

[326] First Baptist Church v. State of Ohio, 591 F. Supp. 676 (S.D. Ohio 1983); Evans v. Shiloh Baptist Church, 77 A.2d 160, 163 (Md. 1950). *See also* Katz v. Singerman, 127 So.2d 515 (La. 1961).

[327] Stansberry v. McCarty, 149 N.E.2d 683, 686 (Ind. 1958). *See also* Serbian Eastern Orthodox Diocese v. Ocokoljich, 219 N.E.2d 343 (Ill. 1966).

[328] Katz v. Singerman, 127 So.2d 515 (La. 1961).

[329] Trett v. Lambeth, 195 S.W.2d 524 (Mo. 1946); Brady v. Reiner, 198 S.E.2d 812 (W. Va. 1973).

[330] Stewart v. Jarriel, 59 S.E.2d 368 (Ga. 1950); Brady v. Reiner, 198 S.E.2d 812 (W. Va. 1973).

however much they may be dissatisfied with the exercise of that jurisdiction, they have no right to invoke the supervisory power of a civil court so long as their property, contract, or civil rights are not affected.[331] Nor may a member deny the existence of a church's bylaws.[332]

Church members generally have no personal interest in church property since title ordinarily is vested in the church. If a church acquires property by a deed naming the church as grantee, the conveyance is to the church and constitutes no benefit or interest to any individual member.[333]

Prior to 1969 the courts commonly ruled that church property was held in trust for the use and benefit of those members adhering to the original tenets of the church, and thus a majority of the members could not abandon the tenets of the church and retain the right to use the church's property so long as a single member adhered to the original doctrines of the church.[334] This rule was abolished by the United States Supreme Court in 1969.[335]

Members of churches affiliated with an ecclesiastical hierarchy generally are subject to the same limitations on their authority discussed above in connection with members of congregational churches, but in addition they are limited by the bylaws and tribunals of the parent denomination.[336]

Case Studies

• A Georgia court ruled that a church's entire board had properly been dismissed by the church members at a duly called special business meeting. The court relied on the Georgia Nonprofit Corporation Code which specifies that a nonprofit corporation shall hold a special meeting "if the holders of at least 5 percent of the voting power of the corporation sign, date, and deliver to any corporate officer one or more written demands . . . for the meeting describing the purpose or purposes for which it is to be held," unless otherwise specified in the corporation's articles or bylaws. The court noted that the church members properly followed the Nonprofit Corporation Code in scheduling the special meeting and voting to remove the church board members. It concluded: "At the meeting, a majority of the members selected a new board of directors of the church, and they chose not to nominate or elect [the original board members]. Accordingly, following their dismissal from the board, the original board members had no authority to control the temporal assets of the church."[337]

• A Georgia court ruled that church members could obtain a court order blocking a church's planned disposition of its assets, and appointing a receiver to oversee the

---

[331] Stewart v. Jarriel, 59 S.E.2d 368 (Ga. 1950).

[332] State ex rel. Morrow v. Hill, 364 N.E.2d 1156 (Ohio 1977).

[333] Presbytery of Cimarron v. Westminster Presbyterian Church, 515 P.2d 211 (Okla. 1973).

[334] Wright v. Smith, 124 N.E.2d 363,365 (Ill. 1955) ("courts will raise and enforce an implied trust so that the majority faction cannot effect a fundamental change of doctrine").

[335] In Presbyterian Church in the United States v. Mary Elizabeth Blue Hull Memorial Presbyterian Church, 393 U.S. 440 (1969), the Supreme Court held that civil courts could no longer construe or apply religious doctrine in resolving church property disputes. *See generally* chapter 7, *infra*.

[336] Presbytery of Cimarron v. Westminster Presbyterian Church, 515 P.2d 211 (Okla. 1973).

[337] Members of Calvary Missionary Baptist Church v. Jackson, 603 S.E.2d 711 (Ga. App. 2004).

church's property. A church board (consisting of the pastor, the pastor's son-in-law, and a third person) decided to sell the church property for $725,000 because of low attendance. The pastor was to receive a lump sum gift of $100,000 out of these proceeds, and title to the parsonage. The remaining sale proceeds, after payment of debts, were to be used for religious activities with the pastor having control of the funds. Some of the church members brought a lawsuit against the pastor and the church in which they sought the appointment of a receiver to take control of the church's assets. The pastor opposed this action, claiming that (1) the court's exercise of jurisdiction over this dispute was prohibited by the First Amendment's guaranty of religious freedom; (2) the members who brought the lawsuit lacked "standing" to do so since they did not represent a majority of the church's members; and (3) the First Amendment prohibits the appointment of a receiver over church assets. The appeals court rejected all of these claims. The court concluded that the trial court's exercise of jurisdiction over this dispute was permissible since "the property dispute here was capable of resolution by reference to neutral principles of law . . . without infringing upon any First Amendment values." Next, the court rejected the pastor's claim that the members who brought the lawsuit lacked "standing" to do so. It noted that the members who brought the lawsuit "had standing in this action alleging a diversion of the church property from the purpose for which the church and its assets had been devoted." In rejecting the pastor's contention that the First Amendment prohibits a civil court from appointing a receiver over church assets, the court observed, "Under [state] law the superior court has full power to liquidate the assets and affairs of a nonprofit corporation when it is established that the acts of the directors or those in control of the corporation are illegal or fraudulent, the assets are being misapplied or wasted, or where the corporation is unable to carry out its purposes."[338]

• An Indiana court ruled that a majority of a congregational church's members, rather than the church's board of trustees, had the legal authority to determine whether or not to retain their pastor. The court noted that for churches of "congregational" polity, "the religious organization is represented by a majority of its members," and therefore "when presented with a dispute within a church of congregational polity, our courts will uphold the majority's decision, whether that is to purchase property or even remove the minister, unless the church has established its own decision-making body with the power to override the will of the majority."[339]

Members—Discipline and Dismissal

§6-10

Do the civil courts have the authority to review internal church determinations regarding the discipline or dismissal of members? Some courts have strictly avoided any intervention in such disputes, while others have been willing to intervene in limited circumstances. This section will review representative decisions of both positions.

---

[338] Crocker v. Stevens, 435 S.E.2d 690 (Ga. App. 1993). But see Hines v. Turley, 615 N.E.2d 1251 (Ill. App. 1993) (persons who did not satisfy the church bylaws' definition of member lacked standing to challenge their church's disposition of assets).

[339] Cole v. Holt, 725 N.E.2d 145 (Ind. App. 2000).

Judicial Nonintervention §6-10.1

Key point 6-10.1. *According to the majority view, the civil courts will not resolve disputes challenging a church's discipline of a member since the First Amendment guaranty of religious freedom prevents them from deciding who are members in good standing of a church.*

In *Watson v. Jones*,[340] the United States Supreme Court developed a framework for the judicial review of ecclesiastical disputes that has persisted essentially unchanged until today, more than a century later. The Court began its landmark opinion by acknowledging that "religious organizations come before us in the same attitude as other voluntary associations for benevolent or charitable purposes, and their rights of property, or of contract, are equally under the protection of the law, and the actions of their members subject to its restraints." Though recognizing in principle the authority of civil courts to address the "rights of property, or of contract" of ecclesiastical organizations or officers, the Court proceeded to severely limit this authority. Most importantly, the Court held that "whenever the *questions of discipline, or of faith, of ecclesiastical rule, custom, or law* have been decided by the highest church judicatory to which the matter has been carried, the legal tribunals must accept such decisions as final, and as binding on them . . . ."

In 1872, one year after the *Watson* decision, the Supreme Court emphasized that it had *"no power to revise or question ordinary acts of church discipline,* or of excision from membership," nor to "decide who ought to be members of the church, nor whether the excommunicated have been regularly or irregularly cut off."[341] Many courts have followed this rule of judicial "non-intervention," concluding that the discipline and dismissal of church members is exclusively a matter of ecclesiastical concern and thus the civil courts are without authority to review such determinations. This position generally is based upon the First Amendment guarantees of religious freedom and the nonestablishment of religion, or upon the fact that by joining the church a member expressly or implicitly consents to the authority of the church to expel members.[342] As noted in the preceding section, the United States Supreme Court has held that all who unite themselves with a religious organization do so with implied consent to its bylaws and procedures.[343] Another court has noted, "A party having voluntarily assented to becoming a member of the local church thereby subjects himself to the existing

---

[340] 80 U.S. 679, 722 (1871).

[341] Bouldin v. Alexander, 82 U.S. (15 Wall.) 131, 139-40 (1872) (emphasis added).

[342] *See generally* Nunn v. Black, 506 F. Supp. 444 (W.D. Va. 1981), *aff'd*, 661 F.2d 925 (4th Cir. 1981), *cert. denied*, 102 S. Ct. 1008 (1982); Simpson v. Wells Lamont Corp., 494 F.2d 490 (5th Cir. 1974); Konkel v. Metropolitan Baptist Church, Inc., 572 P.2d 99 (Ariz. 1977); Macedonia Baptist Foundation v. Singleton, 379 So.2d 269 (La. 1979); St. John's Creek Catholic Hungarian Russian Orthodox Church v. Fedak, 213 A.2d 651 (N.J. 1965), *rev'd on other grounds*, 233 A.2d 663 (N.J. 1967).

[343] Watson v. Jones, 80 U.S. 679, 729 (1871).

rules and procedures of said church and cannot deny their existence."[344] It is therefore held that a church may promulgate rules governing the expulsion or excommunication of its members, and such rules bind the church's members.

1. Hierarchical Churches

There is little doubt that the civil courts are now required to accept the determinations of *hierarchical churches* concerning ecclesiastical discipline. In 1976, the United States Supreme Court ruled that

> the first and fourteenth amendments permit hierarchical religious organizations to establish their own rules and regulations for internal discipline and government, and to create tribunals for adjudicating disputes over these matters. When this choice is exercised and ecclesiastical tribunals are created to decide disputes over the government and direction of subordinate bodies, the Constitution requires that civil courts accept their decisions as binding upon them.[345]

The Supreme Court further noted, in the same decision:

> We have concluded that whether or not there is room for "marginal civil court review" under the narrow rubrics of "fraud" or "collusion" when church tribunals act in bad faith for secular purposes, no "arbitrariness" exception—in the sense of an inquiry whether the decisions of the highest ecclesiastical tribunal of a hierarchical church complied with church laws and regulations—is consistent with the constitutional mandate that civil courts are bound to accept the decisions of the highest judicatories of a religious organization of hierarchical polity on matters of discipline, faith, internal organization, or ecclesiastical rule, custom or law. For civil courts to analyze whether the ecclesiastical actions of a church judicatory are in that sense "arbitrary" must inherently entail inquiry into the procedures that canon or ecclesiastical law supposedly require the church adjudicatory to follow, or else into the substantive criteria by which they are supposedly to decide the ecclesiastical question. But this is exactly the inquiry that the First Amendment prohibits . . . .[346]

Permitting civil courts to review the membership determinations of hierarchical churches would "undermine the general rule that religious controversies are not the proper subject of civil court inquiry."[347] In other words, the fact that a hierarchical church's determination regarding membership status was "arbitrary" (in the sense that it violated the church's own internal rules) is *not* a justification for civil court review. This extraordinary rule demonstrates the Court's commitment to church

---

[344] State ex rel. Morrow v. Hill, 364 N.E.2d 1156, 1159 (Ohio 1977).

[345] Serbian Eastern Orthodox Diocese v. Milivojevich, 426 U.S. 696, 724-25 (1976).

[346] *Id.* at 713.

[347] *Id.* at 713.

autonomy in the context of membership determinations involving hierarchical churches.

Membership determinations based on "fraud or collusion" *may* constitute a basis for marginal civil court review. The Court left this question unanswered. However, it did note that the concepts of *fraud* or *collusion* both involve "church tribunals [acting] in bad faith for secular purposes." It is virtually inconceivable that such a standard could ever be established, particularly in view of the higher evidentiary standard ("clear and convincing evidence") that generally applies to allegations of fraud.

What is a "hierarchical church"? One legal authority defines "hierarchical" and "congregational" churches as follows:

At least three kinds of internal structure, or "polity," may be discerned: congregational, presbyterial, and episcopal. In the congregational form each local congregation is self-governing. The presbyterial polities are representative, authority being exercised by laymen and ministers organized in an ascending succession of judicatories—presbytery over the session of the local church, synod over the presbytery, and general assembly over all. In the episcopal form power reposes in clerical superiors, such as bishops. Roughly, presbyterial and episcopal polities may be considered hierarchical, as opposed to congregational polities, in which the autonomy of the local congregation is the central principle.[348]

2. Congregational Churches

Do the civil courts have authority to review the membership determinations of *congregational churches*? A few courts have done so on the ground that the Supreme Court's 1976 ruling in *Milivojevich*[349] was limited to hierarchical churches. Such cases are reviewed in the next section.

Most courts, however, have been *unwilling* to intervene in the membership determinations of congregational churches on the ground that the principle enunciated by the Supreme Court in its 1976 ruling is broad enough to apply to congregational churches. For example, a federal district court in Virginia ruled that "it is clear that the fact that the local church may have departed arbitrarily from its established expulsion procedures in removing [members] is of no constitutional consequence [citing *Milivojevich*]."[350]

A federal district court in Ohio acknowledged that "it is not altogether clear whether the Supreme Court, if confronted with an internal dispute within a congregational church, would follow the [*Milivojevich*] analysis in all respects."[351] However, the court concluded that "because the 'hands off' policy espoused by the

---

[348] Note, *Judicial Intervention in Disputes Over the Use of Church Property*, 75 Harv. L. Rev. 1142, 1143-44 (1962).

[349] *See* note 306, *supra*, and accompanying text.

[350] Nunn v. Black, 506 F. Supp. 444 (W.D. Va. 1981), aff'd, 661 F.2d 425 (4th Cir. 1981), *cert. denied*, 454 U.S. 1146 (1982). The court noted that the church apparently was part of a "larger religious society," but that the society had "no structured decision-making process."

[351] First Baptist Church v. State of Ohio, 591 F. Supp. 676 (S.D. Ohio 1983).

[Supreme Court in *Milivojevich*] is of constitutional dimension, we find it difficult to justify the application of a different standard where a congregational church is involved." The court concluded that (1) church discipline is an ecclesiastical matter in a congregational church,[352] and (2) "unless the internal disciplinary decisions of [a congregational church] are tainted by fraud or collusion, or constitute an extreme violation of the rights of a disciplined member, civil court inquiry with respect to the underlying reasons for church disciplinary action is constitutionally impermissible."

A federal district court in the District of Columbia, while acknowledging that *Milivojevich* involved a hierarchical church, concluded that "[we] can discern no justification for refusing to apply the First Amendment analysis and reasoning of the Supreme Court and lower federal court case law involving hierarchical churches to [the membership determinations of a congregational church]."[353] The court noted that membership determinations typically involve standards of membership that are intrinsically ecclesiastical. For example, in this case, the congregational church's bylaws specified that "members are expected . . . to be faithful in all duties essential to the Christian life." The court could not contemplate "any criterion for membership that could more directly implicate ecclesiastical considerations protected by the First Amendment . . . ." It concluded that the church's

> *own internal guidelines and procedures must be allowed to dictate what its obligations to its members are without being subject to court intervention.* It is well-settled that religious controversies are not the proper subject of civil court inquiry. *Religious bodies must be free to decide for themselves, free from state interference, matters which pertain to church government, faith and doctrine.*[354]

Some courts have expressed concern that the rule of judicial non-intervention may lead to injustice due to the lack of a judicial remedy. For example, one Supreme Court justice opined that "if the civil courts are to be bound by any sheet of parchment bearing the ecclesiastical seal and purporting to be a decree of a church court, they can easily be converted into handmaidens of arbitrary lawlessness."[355] It also has been noted that "when a faction of the church arrogates authority to itself, disrupts the organization and sets at naught well-defined rules of church order, there is no recourse left for those who desire their rights settled

---

[352] The court noted that the Supreme Court in *Milivojevich* observed that "questions of church discipline . . . are at the core of ecclesiastical concern."

[353] Burgess v. Solid Rock Baptist Church, 734 F. Supp. 30 (D.D.C. 1990).

[354] *Id.* at 34 (emphasis in original), quoting Dowd v. Society of St. Columbans, 861 F.2d 761, 764 (1st Cir. 1988).

[355] Serbian Eastern Orthodox Diocese v. Milivojevich, 426 U.S. 696, 727 (1976) (Justice Rehnquist, dissenting). Justice Rehnquist also observed, in the same opinion, that "[t]o make available the coercive powers of civil courts to rubber-stamp ecclesiastical decisions of hierarchical religious associations, when such deference is not accorded similar acts of secular voluntary associations, would . . . itself create far more serious problems under the Establishment Clause." *Id.* at 734.

through orderly processes but resort to the courts."[356]

Case Studies

• *A federal appeals court held that religious "shunning" behavior is protected by the First Amendment because imposing liability for such behavior would have the same effect as prohibiting it and would directly restrict the free exercise of religion. The court concluded: "Shunning is an actual practice of the church itself, and the burden of tort damages is direct. . . . Imposing tort liability for shunning on the church or its members would in the long run have the same effect as prohibiting the practice and would compel the church to abandon part of its religious teachings. . . . The church and its members would risk substantial damages every time a former church member was shunned. In sum, a . . . prohibition against shunning would directly restrict the free exercise of the Jehovah's Witnesses' religious faith."[357]*

• *The Alaska Supreme Court ruled that a church could not be sued for "shunning" members of another church that it labeled a "cult." The court noted that the act of shunning was clearly religiously based and sincere. The shunning was undertaken "to force [the members of the other church] to renounce and change their religious beliefs." Also, "shunning has its roots in early Christianity and various religious groups in our country engage in the practice."[358]*

• *An Illinois court ruled that it was barred by the First Amendment from resolving a lawsuit by a former church member challenging various actions taken by the church's board of elders in disciplining him. The court conceded that "where no consideration of religious doctrine is involved the 'neutral principles of law' approach may be applied, permitting a court to interpret provisions of religious documents involving property rights and other nondoctrinal matters, to the extent that the analysis can be done in purely secular terms." But, it concluded that it could not resolve the member's claims without "analyzing and applying ecclesiastical doctrine."[359]*

• *An Illinois court ruled that it was barred by the First Amendment from resolving a lawsuit brought by a dismissed member of an orthodox Jewish community claiming that his dismissal lacked due process and amounted to defamation. The court concluded: "The First Amendment to the Constitution of the United States bars any secular court from involving itself in the ecclesiastical controversies that may arise in a religious body or organization. . . . Where resolution of ecclesiastical disputes cannot be made without extensive inquiry by civil courts into religious law and polity, the First Amendment mandates that civil courts shall not disturb the decisions of the highest ecclesiastical tribunal within a church of hierarchical polity, but must accept such*

---

[356] Epperson v. Myers, 58 So.2d 150, 152 (Fla. 1952). *See also* Jones v. Wolf, 443 U.S. 595 (1979) (United States Supreme Court suggests that judicial review is permissible if restricted to an analysis based exclusively on "neutral principles" of law devoid of any interpretation of religious doctrine); I. Ellman, *Driven From the Tribunal: Judicial Resolution of Internal Church Disputes,* 69 CAL. L. REV. 1380 (1981) (arguing that judicial review of internal church disputes should be permitted as long as doctrinal interpretation is not required).

[357] Paul v. Watchtower Bible & Tract Society, 819 F.2d 875 (9th Cir. 1987).

[358] Sands v. Living Word Fellowship, 34 P.3d 955 (Alaska 2001).

[359] Abrams v. Watchtower Bible and Tract Society, 715 N.E.2d 798 (Ill. App. 1999).

decisions as binding on them, in their application to the religious issues of doctrine or polity before them." The court concluded that Aaron's lawsuit against the rabbinic court had to be dismissed since his claims could not be resolved "without extensive inquiry into religious law and polity."[360]

• The Iowa Supreme Court ruled that it lacked the authority to resolve a lawsuit brought by an individual challenging his dismissal from church membership. It concluded that the member's dismissal was an internal church matter over which the civil courts have no jurisdiction. It observed, "The general rule is that civil courts will not interfere in purely ecclesiastical matters, including membership in a church organization or church discipline." The court concluded: "[The church's] decision to excommunicate [the member] was purely ecclesiastical in nature, and therefore we will not interfere with the action. Interfering with the decision would contravene both our history of leaving such matters to ecclesiastical officials and the first and fourteenth amendments of the United States Constitution."[361]

• A Louisiana court ruled that it could not resolve a lawsuit brought by dismissed church members who claimed that their church acted improperly in dismissing them for suing the church. The church's pastor dismissed the members for filing a legal action against the church, and removed their names from the membership rolls. The pastor acted pursuant to an "essential tenet" of his church that prohibits Christians from taking other Christians to court. The dismissed members sued their pastor and church, claiming that they had been unjustly and illegally dismissed as members of the church. A state appeals court dismissed the dismissed members' claims, noting that, "It is evident to us that this dispute is rooted in an ecclesial tenet of the [church] which prohibits members from suing fellow church members. Certainly, in civil law the [members] had a right to pursue their [initial lawsuit demand seeking inspection of church records]. However, we hasten to add that the religious repercussions that were set into motion as a result of the exercise of their civil right is another matter beyond the reach of judicial authority. In that light, anything we might consider in [resolving this appeal] would require us to apply, interpret, and comment upon the [church's] tenet against the institution of suits among church members. Based upon the Constitution of the United States . . . and the Constitution of the State of Louisiana . . . such action would constitute an impermissible interference in the ecclesiastical matters of the [church]. We decline to do so."[362]

• The Michigan Supreme Court ruled that it was barred from resolving a claim by a dismissed church member that his church violated his legal rights when it dismissed him. The court concluded that the member's claims against both the pastor and church were barred by his own consent to the process of discipline. The court noted that upon becoming a member of the church, he "explicitly consented in writing to obey the church's law, and to accept the church's discipline 'with a free, humble, and thankful heart.'" The court concluded: "As the Supreme Court stated over 130 years ago, 'all who unite themselves to such a body do so with an implied consent to this [church]

---

[360] Thomas v. Fuerst, 2004 WL 74292 (Ill. App. 2004).

[361] John v. Estate of Hartgerink, 528 N.W.2d 539 (Iowa 1995).

[362] Glass v. First United Pentecostal Church, 676 So.2d 724 (La. App. 1996).

government, and are bound to submit to it.'"[363]

• *A Minnesota appeals court ruled that church members could not challenge their dismissal in court. The court noted that the First Amendment "precludes judicial review of claims involving core questions of church discipline and internal governance." It concluded that the members' claims all involved core questions of church discipline that it was not able to resolve.*[364]

• *A Missouri court ruled that it was barred by the First Amendment guaranty of religious freedom from resolving a lawsuit brought by a dismissed church member claiming that his church defamed him in a letter it sent to members of the congregation. The court noted that the First Amendment prevents "civil court intervention in matters involving church discipline, including the discipline of a member of the congregation. . . . Here, the claims of libelous remarks are clearly related to [the pastors'] belief that [the member's] conduct within the church required he be disciplined; the comments were made during the time of the controversy concerning his removal from membership; and the remarks were made to people associated with the church as a part of the pastors' report to the 'church family' about the member's impending removal from the church membership. As such, they fall within the scope of First Amendment protection."*[365]

• *A North Carolina court ruled that the civil courts are barred by the First Amendment from resolving cases involving the discipline of church members unless they can do so "without resolving underlying controversies over religious doctrine." Two dismissed church members challenged their dismissals in court on the ground that the termination of their memberships was not conducted pursuant to the state nonprofit corporation law which specifies that "no member of a corporation may be expelled or suspended, and no membership may be terminated or suspended, except in a manner that is fair and reasonable and is carried out in good faith." In rejecting this argument, the court concluded: "The fact that defendant is a corporation does not alter our analysis of whether the courts of this state have jurisdiction in ecclesiastical disputes. Plaintiffs would have the courts direct that churches cannot terminate membership without following certain due process procedures including notice and an opportunity to be heard. This we refuse to do. A church's criteria for membership and the manner in which membership is terminated are core ecclesiastical matters protected by the [First Amendment]."*[366]

• *An Ohio court ruled that it could not resolve a lawsuit brought by several persons challenging their dismissal as members of their church. The members had been dismissed because they sued the church over certain decisions that had been made regarding a construction project. The dismissed members argued that their church membership was a valuable right that was being denied by the church's actions. They also claimed that the church bylaws did not authorize the board to dismiss members for suing the church. The church bylaws did authorize discipline or dismissal on the*

---

[363] Smith v. Calvary Christian Church, 614 N.W.2d 590 (Mich. 2000), quoting Watson v. Jones, 80 U.S. (13 Wall.) 679 (1871).

[364] Schoenhals v. Mains, 504 N.W.2d 233 (Minn. App. 1993).

[365] Brady v. Pace, 2003 WL 1750088 (Mo. App. 2003).

[366] Tubiolo v. Abundant Life Church, (N.C. App. 2004).

basis of "immoral or un-Christian conduct," but the dismissed members argued that this language did not extend to lawsuits brought against the church. They stressed that the right to go to court for the redress of grievances is a fundamental civil right that was not specifically restricted by the church bylaws. The church asserted that members who sue the church are guilty of "un-Christian" behavior since "there is a basis in Scripture for the exclusion from church membership of those who take church disputes outside the church for resolution." The court agreed with the church, relying on a 1976 decision of the United States Supreme Court holding that the civil courts must accept the decisions of hierarchical churches concerning discipline of members and clergy. Serbian Eastern Orthodox Diocese v. Milivojevich, 426 U.S. 696 (1976). The Ohio court acknowledged that the church in this case was "congregational" rather than hierarchical in structure, but it concluded that there should be no distinction between congregational and hierarchical churches regarding the effect of their decisions to discipline members. It concluded that "a secular court should not resolve disputes over who can be a member of a particular church regardless of whether that church is hierarchical or congregational."[367]

• A church convened a disciplinary hearing to determine the membership status of two sisters accused of fornication. Neither sister attended, and neither sister withdrew her membership in the church. Following the hearing, both sisters received letters from the church informing them that their membership had been terminated. The sisters sued the church and its leaders, claiming that the church's actions in delivering the termination letters and disclosing their contents "to the public" constituted defamation, intentional infliction of emotional distress, and invasion of privacy. The Oklahoma Supreme Court rejected the sisters' claims: "[The relationship between a church and its members] may be severed freely by a member's positive act at any time. Until it is so terminated, the church has authority to prescribe and follow disciplinary ordinances without fear of interference by the state. The First Amendment will protect and shield the religious body from liability for the activities carried on pursuant to the exercise of church discipline. Within the context of church discipline, churches enjoy an absolute privilege from scrutiny by the secular authority." However, the court stressed that this constitutional protection does not apply once a person withdraws his or her church membership.[368]

• The Oklahoma Supreme Court refused to resolve the claim of former church members that their dismissal was improper. The court began its opinion by observing that "the courts will not interfere with the internal affairs of a religious organization except for the protection of civil or property rights." The court concluded that "church membership" was not a "civil or property right" that a civil court could enforce: "A civil or property right that justifies the exercise of civil judicial power has long been distinguished from ecclesiastical or spiritual rights that civil courts do not adjudicate. Civil courts in this country recognize that they have no ecclesiastical jurisdiction, and church disciplinary decisions cannot be reviewed for the purpose of reinstating

---

[367] Alexander v. Shiloh Baptist Church, 592 N.E.2d 918 (Ohio Com. Pl. 1991). *Accord* Howard v. Covenant Apostolic Church, Inc., 705 N.E.2d 305 (Ohio App. 1998).

[368] Hadnot v. Shaw, 826 P.2d 978 (Okla. 1992). The court concluded that churches are immune from the civil "discovery" process with regard to their internal disciplinary proceedings. "Discovery" refers to the process of gathering evidence for civil trial, and includes depositions, interrogatories, and motions to produce documents. The court said that churches are immune from these discovery techniques with regard to internal membership disciplinary proceedings (so long as a member is being disciplined prior to withdrawal from membership).

expelled church members." This is true even if a church fails to follow its own constitution or bylaws in dismissing the members. "The issue of whether the church proceeding complied with church rules or custom in expelling members presents no question for our review on a claim for reinstatement," the court observed. The court concluded: "We cannot decide who ought to be members of the church, nor whether the excommunicated have been justly or unjustly, regularly or irregularly, cut off from the body of the church. We must take the fact of expulsion as conclusive proof that the persons expelled are not now members of the repudiating church; for, whether right or wrong, the act of excommunication must, as to the fact of membership, be law to this court."[369]

• A federal court in South Dakota ruled that it had no authority to interfere with a decision by a religious organization to oust some of its members. The court noted that it was "unable to envision any set of facts which would more entangle the court in matters of religious doctrine and practice. The religious communal system present in this case involves more than matters of religious faith, it involves a religious lifestyle. An individual Hutterian colony member's entire life—essentially from cradle to grave— is governed by the church. Any resolution of a property dispute between a colony and its members would require extensive inquiry into religious doctrine and beliefs. It would be a gross violation of the First Amendment and Supreme Court mandates for this court to become involved in this dispute."[370]

• The Texas Supreme Court ruled that the First Amendment guaranty of religious liberty prevented it from resolving a dismissed church member's claim that her pastor committed "professional negligence" by using information she shared with him in confidence as the basis for disciplining her. The former member claimed that her resignation from the church after she revealed confidences to the pastor "precluded any argument that he was performing a pastoral function in disseminating confidential information to the church." The court disagreed. It noted that the church's constitution required the discipline of members to follow the procedure laid down in Matthew 18. According to this procedure, if a member sins and does not heed the counsel of church leaders, then the matter must be "told to the church." The court concluded that the church's decision to proceed with the formal discipline of the member following her resignation "was based on its interpretation of Matthew 18:15-20, an inherently ecclesiastical matter. We hold that court interference with that decision through imposition of liability in this case would impinge upon matters of church governance in violation of the First Amendment."[371]

"Marginal" Civil Court Review §6-10.2

Key point 6-10.2. *According to the minority view, the civil courts may engage in "marginal review" of disputes involving the discipline of a church member, in a few limited circumstances if they can do so without inquiring into religious*

---

[369] Fowler v. Bailey, 844 P.2d 141 (Okla. 1992), quoting Shannon v. Frost, 42 Ky. 253 (1842).

[370] Wollman v. Poinsett Hutterian Brethren Church, 844 F. Supp. 539 (D.S.D. 1994).

[371] Westbrook v. Penley, 231 S.W.3d 389 (Tex. 2007).

doctrine or polity. For example, a few courts have been willing to review membership dismissals in one or more of the following limited circumstances: (1) the church interfered with a member's civil, contract, or property rights; (2) the disciplining body lacked authority to act; (3) the church failed to comply with its governing documents; (4) the church's decision was based on fraud or collusion; or (5) interpretation of contested terminology in the church's governing documents.

Some courts have been willing to intervene, in limited circumstances, in controversies regarding church membership determinations, if they can do so without interpreting church doctrine or polity. This section will review the following grounds for "marginal civil court review" most commonly cited by the courts:

- interference with civil, contract, or property rights

- the authority of the expelling body

- compliance with the church's governing documents

- fraud or collusion

- contested terminology

1. Interference With Civil, Contract, or Property Rights

Although the civil courts generally acknowledge that they have no authority to review purely ecclesiastical matters, some courts have been willing to review the expulsion of a church member if the expulsion affects "civil, contract, or property rights" and does not implicate church doctrine.[372] The precise meaning of *civil, contract, or property rights* is unclear. Some courts interpret these terms broadly. To illustrate, one court concluded that church membership in itself constitutes a "property right" since church members comprise the body of persons entitled to the use and enjoyment of church properties, and therefore the courts have authority to review all expulsions of church members.[373] Another court concluded that civil rights are involved in the expulsion of church members because of "the humiliation and hurt to personality, the injury to character, reputation, feelings and personal rights and human dignity."[374] Similarly, courts have concluded that (1) the expulsion of a member from a church can constitute a serious emotional deprivation which, when compared to some losses of property or contract rights, can be far more damaging to an individual; (2) the loss of the opportunity to worship in familiar surroundings is a valuable right that deserves the protection of the law; and (3) except in cases involving religious doctrine, there is no reason for treating religious organizations differently from other nonprofit organizations,

---

[372] First Baptist Church v. State of Ohio, 591 F. Supp. 676 (S.D. Ohio 1983); Church of God in Christ, Inc. v. Stone, 452 F. Supp. 612 (D. Kan. 1976); Chavis v. Rowe, 459 A.2d 674 (N.J. 1983); African Methodist Episcopal Zion Church v. Union Chapel A.M.E. Zion Church, 308 S.E.2d 73 (N.C. App. 1983). *See generally* Annot., 20 A.L.R.2d 421 (1951).

[373] Randolph v. First Baptist Church, 120 N.E.2d 485 (Ohio 1954).

[374] *Id.* at 489.

whose membership expulsions are routinely reviewed by the courts.[375]

Other courts take a much narrower view of civil, contract, or property rights. To illustrate, some courts have ruled that church membership in itself does not constitute a property right,[376] a contract right,[377] or a civil right.[378]

One thing is clear—if the civil courts are powerless to resolve internal church disputes involving doctrine or polity, then they should not be permitted to resolve church membership determinations that are essentially ecclesiastical in nature solely because an aggrieved member asserts that his or her discipline or dismissal violated a civil, contract, or property right. The Supreme Court has acknowledged this principle in the context of clergy dismissals. To illustrate, in 1928 the Supreme Court observed, in a case involving the authority of an ecclesiastical organization to discipline a minister, that "the decisions of the proper church tribunals on matters purely ecclesiastical, *although affecting civil rights*, are accepted in litigation before the secular courts as conclusive, because the parties . . . made them so by contract or otherwise."[379]

In 1952, the Supreme Court in the *Kedroff* ruling[380] reaffirmed its pronouncement in *Watson* that civil courts have no authority to resolve "*questions of discipline, or of faith, or of ecclesiastical rule, custom, or law.*" The Court also noted that "in those cases when the *property right* follows as an incident from decisions of the church custom or law on ecclesiastical issues, the church rule controls. This under our Constitution necessarily follows in order that there may be free exercise of religion."[381] The *Kedroff* decision is important since it specifically holds that alleged deprivations or interference with "property rights" cannot serve as a basis for civil court review of ecclesiastical determinations where "the property right follows as an incident from decisions of the church . . . on ecclesiastical issues."

These two rulings indicate that dismissed or disciplined church members will not be able to have their dismissals reviewed by the civil courts merely because they claim that their civil or property rights have been violated. It will be a rare case in which a disciplined or dismissed church member can demonstrate that his or her "civil, contract, or property rights" were violated by the church's action in a manner that does implicate ecclesiastical concerns. As a result, this basis for marginal civil court review of church disciplinary decisions generally will fail. Further, it has no application to hierarchical churches due to the Supreme Court's 1976 ruling in the *Milivojevich* case. Many of the court rulings that have recognized this basis for civil court review occurred prior to 1976.

---

[375] Baugh v. Thomas, 265 A.2d 675 (N.J. 1970).

[376] Anderson v. Dowd, 485 S.E.2d 764 (Ga. 1997); Sapp v. Callaway, 69 S.E.2d 734 (Ga. 1952).

[377] Cooper v. Bell, 106 S.W.2d 124 (Ky. 1937).

[378] Stewart v. Jarriel, 59 S.E.2d 368 (Ga. 1950). *Accord* Anderson v. Dowd, 485 S.E.2d 764 (Ga. 1997) (church membership "is not a property right"); Fowler v. Bailey, 844 P.2d 141 (Okla. 1992).

[379] Gonzalez v. Roman Catholic Archbishop, 280 U.S. 1, 16-17 (1928) (Justice Brandeis) (emphasis added).

[380] Kedroff v. St. Nicholas Cathedral, 344 U.S. 94 (1952).

[381] *Id.* (emphasis added).

Case Studies

• *A North Carolina court ruled that the civil courts are barred by the First Amendment from resolving cases involving the discipline of church members unless they can do so "without resolving underlying controversies over religious doctrine." Two dismissed church members challenged their dismissals in court on the ground that the church board did not have the authority to terminate their memberships. They acknowledged that the church bylaws authorized the church board to administer discipline, but claimed that the bylaws had never been adopted by the congregation. The court noted that the First Amendment does not prohibit the courts from resolving "property disputes" provided that this can be done "without resolving underlying controversies over religious doctrine." The court concluded that the plaintiffs' church membership was a property interest, and that the courts "do have jurisdiction over the very narrow issue of whether the bylaws were properly adopted by the church" since "this inquiry can be made without resolving any ecclesiastical or doctrinal matters."[382]*

• *A North Carolina court ruled that church membership is not a property right that will justify civil court intervention into internal church disputes over the status of members. The court agreed that the First Amendment does not prohibit the civil courts from resolving church property disputes not involving questions of doctrine. But, it disagreed that this case could properly be characterized as a property dispute. It concluded: "The claims of plaintiffs in this case only tangentially affect property rights. The courts of this state should not intervene in a question of whether [a church should be] organized as an unincorporated association or a nonprofit corporation. Plaintiffs have failed to assert a substantial property right which has been affected by the incorporation of the church."[383]*

2. AUTHORITY OF EXPELLING BODY

Some courts have reviewed membership expulsions for the purpose of determining whether members were expelled by the body authorized to do so by the church charter or bylaws. Thus, when certain members of a church were expelled and sought judicial review of their expulsion, a court ruled, over the protests of the church, that it did have jurisdiction to determine whether the expulsions were the act of an authorized and duly constituted body.[384] Another court, in agreeing to review a church's expulsion of certain members, commented:

> If a decision is reached by some body not having ecclesiastical jurisdiction over the matter, then the civil court would not be bound by that decision. . . . Once a determination is made that the proper ecclesiastical authority has acted in its duly constituted manner, no civil review of the substantive ecclesiastical matter may take place as this would be prohibited by Amendments I and XIV of the Federal Constitution . . . .[385]

---

[382] Tubiolo v. Abundant Life Church, (N.C. App. 2004).

[383] Emory v. Jackson Chapel First Missionary Baptist Church, 598 S.E.2d 667 (N.C. App. 2004).

[384] Brown v. Mt. Olive Baptist Church, 124 N.W.2d 445 (Iowa 1963).

[385] Bowen v. Green, 272 S.E.2d 433, 435 (S.C. 1980).

A federal district court that generally agreed with the rule of judicial non-intervention in church membership determinations nevertheless concluded that "it is not beyond the scope of inquiry for a civil court to determine, in a proper proceeding, whether disciplinary action undertaken by [a church] was approved or executed by that body within the church required to take such action under the church covenant, constitution, or bylaws."[386]

Case Studies

• The Alabama Supreme Court ruled that a trial court acted properly in vacating a church election that was conducted in violation of the church's governing document. The court noted that it had on several occasions "exercised jurisdiction to determine whether an election meeting of a church, or a similar meeting, was conducted so improperly as to render its results void." Further, it noted that while the civil courts "will not assume jurisdiction to resolve disputes regarding their spiritual or ecclesiastical affairs . . . there is jurisdiction to resolve questions of civil or property rights." The court concluded that it could "properly exercise jurisdiction, given the financial and property rights of the church that were involved . . . and that the election violated the Book of Discipline in several material respects and also violated basic standards of due process." It emphasized that the parties in this case "argue no issues of differences in religious faith or creed, and argue no spiritual conflicts, or ecclesiastical doctrine. Rather, the underlying dispute revolves around the property of the church—control over its financial assets and affairs—and not God." The court concluded: "The record indeed supports a finding that . . . the procedures for elections, as enumerated in the Book of Discipline, were not followed. Thus, we hold today that the trial court did not err in setting aside the election."[387]

• An Ohio court ruled that the First Amendment guaranty of religious freedom prevented it from resolving a dispute between a dismissed church member and his former church.[388] However, the court concluded that the civil courts retain jurisdiction "to determine whether the proper authority made the decision about church discipline or policy. . . . So long as the appropriate church authority has made the decision, the issue of whether the church followed its internal procedures is a matter of church governance and discipline into which a secular court is prohibited from inquiring."

3. Compliance With Church Charter and Bylaws

In 1872, the Supreme Court commented that "[church trustees] cannot be removed from their trusteeship by a minority of the church society or meeting, without warning, and acting without charges, without citation or trial, and in direct contravention of the church rules."[389] In the years that followed, a number of civil courts intervened in church membership determinations to ensure that they were in compliance with a church's charter or bylaws. However, this basis for

---

[386] First Baptist Church v. State of Ohio, 591 F. Supp. 676, 683 (S.D. Ohio 1983).

[387] Yates v. El Bethel Primitive Baptist Church, 847 So.2d 331 (Ala. 2002).

[388] Howard v. Covenant Apostolic Church, Inc., 705 N.E.2d 305 (Ohio App. 1998). *Accord* Tubiolo v. Abundant Life Church, (N.C. App. 2004).

[389] Bouldin v. Alexander, 82 U.S. (15 Wall.) 131 (1872).

intervening in such disputes came to an abrupt halt in 1976, at least with respect to *hierarchical churches*, when the Supreme Court announced:

> We have concluded that whether or not there is room for "marginal civil court review" under the narrow rubrics of "fraud" or "collusion" when church tribunals act in bad faith for secular purposes, no "arbitrariness" exception—in the sense of an inquiry whether the decisions of the highest ecclesiastical tribunal of a hierarchical church complied with church laws and regulations—is consistent with the constitutional mandate that civil courts are bound to accept the decisions of the highest judicatories of a religious organization of hierarchical polity on matters of discipline, faith, internal organization, or ecclesiastical rule, custom or law. For civil courts to analyze whether the ecclesiastical actions of a church judicatory are in that sense "arbitrary" must inherently entail inquiry into the procedures that canon or ecclesiastical law supposedly require the church adjudicatory to follow, or else into the substantive criteria by which they are supposedly to decide the ecclesiastical question. But this is exactly the inquiry that the First Amendment prohibits . . . .[390]

The Court added that "recognition of . . . an arbitrariness exception would undermine the general rule that religious controversies are not the proper subject of civil court inquiry."[391]

Since 1976, a few courts have intervened in the membership determinations of *congregational churches* to determine whether church rules were followed. For example, where former church members complained that they had been removed improperly from the membership roll at a church meeting convened off of church premises without notice to them of either the location of the meeting or the fact that their dismissal would be discussed, a court concluded that it did have jurisdiction to determine whether the members were expelled in accordance with the charter and bylaws of the church.[392] The court cautioned, however, that if the church had complied with its charter and bylaws, the court would have no jurisdiction to proceed in its review.

Expelled church members' allegations that their expulsions deviated from established church procedures have also been reviewed by the courts in the following contexts: (1) members who allegedly were ineligible to vote according to church bylaws were permitted to vote for the expulsion of certain members;[393] (2) a pastor conducted a church meeting without prior notice, and, without a hearing of any kind, members present voted to expel an opposing faction from

---

[390] Serbian Eastern Orthodox Diocese v. Milivojevich, 426 U.S. 696, 713 (1976).

[391] *Id.*

[392] Konkel v. Metropolitan Baptist Church, Inc., 572 P.2d 99 (Ariz. 1977); LeBlanc v. Davis, 432 So.2d 239 (La. 1983); Wilkerson v. Battiste, 393 So.2d 195 (La. App. 1980).

[393] Anderson v. Sills, 265 A.2d 678 (N.J. 1970).

membership;[394] and (3) members present at a special meeting for which no prior notice had been given voted to summarily expel all members of the church who identified themselves, through attendance or support, with any other church.[395]

Most of the court rulings recognizing noncompliance by a church with its own internal rules as a basis for civil court review either predate the Supreme Court's 1976 ruling in the *Milivojevich* case, or involve congregational churches. Clearly, the civil courts no longer have the authority, since 1976, to review the membership determinations of hierarchical churches on the basis of alleged noncompliance with internal church rules. And, some courts view the constitutional analysis set forth in the *Milivojevich* ruling to be applicable to congregational as well as hierarchical churches.[396]

Case Study

• *The Kansas Supreme Court ruled that the civil courts have limited authority to review decisions by congregational churches to discipline or dismiss members. Twelve persons claiming to be members of a local church attempted to gain information regarding the church's financial affairs and the use of church assets. When their efforts were ignored by church leaders, they filed a class action lawsuit against the pastor, the chairman of the deacon board, the chairman of the trustee board, persons with signature authority over church funds, and other church members who controlled or held title to church assets. The twelve members were expelled some six months after they filed their lawsuit, following a Sunday morning service in which the pastor accused the members of being "anti-Bible" for suing their church. The dismissed members challenged the legality of their dismissal in court. The court concluded: "A congregational church member has a right under common law principles to a fairly conducted meeting on the question of expulsion, and that includes reasonable notice, the right to attend and speak against the proposed action, and the right to an honest count of the vote. In the absence of church law or usage, a majority vote of the members present at a regular Sunday service prevails on expulsion. It does not require formal evidence, the right to counsel, or the right to present witnesses (unless church rules so require)." Since the dismissed members claimed that their expulsions violated their property interests (they had made substantial contributions to the church over many years), and since the church allegedly did not provide them with adequate notice or the right to defend themselves, the civil courts were justified in intervening. This intervention, however, would be limited to a determination of whether or not their allegations were true. If their expulsions violated "fundamental notions of due process," then they were not legally valid, meaning that they were still members who could not summarily be denied the legal right to demand an accounting of church funds.[397]*

---

[394] Abyssinia Missionary Baptist Church v. Nixon, 340 So.2d 746 (Ala. 1976); Longmeyer v. Payne, 205 S.W.2d 263 (Mo. 1947); Randolph v. First Baptist Church, 120 N.E.2d 485 (Ohio 1954); First Baptist Church v. Giles, 219 S.W.2d 498 (Tex. 1949).

[395] David v. Carter, 222 S.W.2d 900 (Tex. 1949).

[396] *See, e.g.,* Burgess v. Rock Creek Baptist Church, 734 F. Supp. 30 (D.D.C. 1990); First Baptist Church v. State of Ohio, 591 F. Supp. 676 (S.D. Ohio 1983).

[397] Kennedy v. Gray, 807 P.2d 670 (Kan. 1991).

4. Expulsion Based on Fraud or Collusion

In 1928, the United States Supreme Court ruled that "in the absence of fraud, collusion, or arbitrariness, the decisions of the proper church tribunals on matters purely ecclesiastical . . . are accepted in litigation before secular courts as conclusive . . . ."[398] However, in 1976 the Court held that ecclesiastical determinations could not be reviewed on account of "arbitrariness," and refused to decide whether or not "fraud" or "collusion" remained permissible grounds for civil court review.[399] The Court observed: "We have concluded that whether or not there is room for 'marginal civil court review' under the narrow rubrics of 'fraud' or 'collusion' when church tribunals act in bad faith for secular purposes, no 'arbitrariness' exception exists." Accordingly, "fraud" and "collusion" *may* constitute grounds for civil court review of internal church determinations regarding membership. That is all that can be said until the Supreme Court provides more guidance.

Some courts have intervened in internal church controversies regarding membership determinations on the basis of fraud or collusion.[400] There are three points to emphasize, however. First, the Supreme Court has expressly refrained from ruling on the viability of civil court review based on fraud or collusion. Second, the higher burden of proof normally required to establish fraud (i.e., clear and convincing evidence) may apply.[401] And third, in 1976 the Supreme Court interpreted "fraud" or "collusion" to imply church actions that are committed "in bad faith for secular purposes." Certainly, it is highly unlikely that any aggrieved member could prove facts satisfying this definition, particularly if the "clear and convincing evidence" standard applies.

5. Interpretation of Contested Terminology

Occasionally a court will agree to review an expulsion based on an ambiguous condition of membership. For example, when a church's bylaws stipulated that failure to attend church or make financial contributions "without a reasonable excuse" would result in termination of membership, a court agreed to resolve the disputed phrase "without a reasonable excuse."[402] Another court agreed to determine whether a church's charter or bylaws made "extending the right hand of fellowship" a condition of membership where this was a disputed question.[403]

Most courts have concluded that churches must interpret their own internal rules regarding membership qualifications and expulsions. In the landmark *Watson* case,[404] the Supreme Court observed that "the right to organize voluntary

---

[398] Gonzalez v. Roman Catholic Archbishop, 280 U.S. 1, 16 (1928).

[399] Serbian Eastern Orthodox Diocese v. Milivojevich, 426 U.S. 696 (1976). The Court did not pass upon the constitutionality of marginal civil court review of ecclesiastical determinations in cases of fraud or collusion. This remains an open question.

[400] First Baptist Church v. State of Ohio, 591 F. Supp. 676 (S.D. Ohio 1983) (noting that the "higher burden of proof typically applied to cases of fraud" is applicable); Hatcher v. South Carolina District Council of the Assemblies of God, Inc., 226 S.E.2d 253 (S.C. 1976); Presbytery of the Covenant v. First Presbyterian Church, 552 S.W.2d 865 (Tex. 1977).

[401] First Baptist Church v. State of Ohio, 591 F. Supp. 676 (S.D. Ohio 1983).

[402] Second Baptist Church v. Mount Zion Baptist Church, 466 P.2d 212 (Nev. 1970).

[403] Honey Creek Regular Baptist Church v. Wilson, 92 N.E.2d 419 (Ohio 1950).

[404] Watson v. Jones, 80 U.S. 679 (1871).

religious associations to assist in the expression and dissemination of any religious doctrine, and to create tribunals for the decision of controverted questions of faith within the association, and for the ecclesiastical government of all the individual members . . . is unquestioned." The Court also observed in *Watson* that:

> Each [religious organization] . . . has a body of constitutional and ecclesiastical law of its own, to be found in their written organic laws, their books of discipline, in their collections of precedents, in their usage and customs, which to each constitute a system of ecclesiastical law and religious faith that tasks the ablest minds to become familiar with. It is not to be supposed that the judges of the civil courts can be as competent in the ecclesiastical law and religious faith of all these bodies as the ablest men in each are in reference to their own. It would therefore be an appeal from the more learned tribunal in the law which should decide the case, to one which is less so.[405]

Similarly, the Court observed:

> The decisions of ecclesiastical courts, like every other judicial tribunal, are final, as *they are the best judges of what constitutes an offense against the word of God and the discipline of the church.* Any other than those courts must be incompetent judges of matters of faith, discipline, and doctrine; and civil courts, if they should be so unwise as to attempt to supervise their judgments on matters which come within their jurisdiction would only involve themselves in a sea of uncertainty and doubt which would do anything but improve either religion or good morals.[406]

In 1952, the Supreme Court ruled that the First Amendment guaranty of religious freedom gives religious organizations "independence from secular control or manipulation, in short, power to decide for themselves, free from state interference, matters of church government as well as those of faith and doctrine."[407] Further, the Supreme Court's prohibition of civil court interpretation of church doctrine will serve as an additional bar to civil court interpretation of many contested terms contained in church bylaws.[408]

Preconditions to Civil Court Review

§6-10.3

Key point 6-10.3. *The civil courts will not resolve a dispute contesting the discipline of a church member if the member failed to "exhaust" remedies available under the church's own governing documents.*

---

[405] *Id.* at 729.

[406] *Id.* at 732.

[407] Kedroff v. St. Nicholas Cathedral, 344 U.S. 94 (1952).

[408] Presbyterian Church v. Mary Elizabeth Blue Hull Memorial Presbyterian Church, 393 U.S. 440 (1969).

The courts will not review church membership expulsions unless the expelled members have exhausted all available procedures within their church for obtaining review of their expulsion. To illustrate, one court refused to resolve a lawsuit brought by a dismissed church member challenging his dismissal since he had not pursued all of the remedies provided by his local church and a parent denomination for the review of such actions.[409]

Case Study

• The Alabama Supreme Court ruled that it could not review a dismissed church member's claim that his membership had been improperly terminated since the member had failed to exhaust remedies provided to him in the church's bylaws. The court concluded: "A church member attacking a church decision may not obtain civil court review of that decision without first exhausting the church's internal appeal procedures. It is undisputed that the church bylaws provide an internal review procedure, which [the member] has not yet exhausted. Thus, he could have no right to an order reinstating his membership pending the church's review of his expulsion."[410]

Remedies for Improper Discipline or Dismissal §6-10.4

Key point 6-10.4. *Courts willing to intervene in disputes challenging the discipline of a church member have granted a variety of remedies to an improperly disciplined member, including reinstatement or monetary damages for defamation or emotional distress.*

1. Decisions Refusing to Recognize a Legal Remedy

Obviously, courts that follow the rule of non-intervention in internal church membership determinations will not provide disciplined or dismissed members with any legal remedy since no cognizable legal harm has occurred.[411] To illustrate, a federal court in New York ruled that it had no authority to stop a religious organization from excommunicating one of its members.[412] The member had been threatened with excommunication because of a lawsuit he had filed against the religious organization. The court observed:

A long line of Supreme Court cases holds that, where a religious body adjudicates relations among its members, courts will not interfere with the

---

[409] First Baptist Church v. State of Ohio, 591 F. Supp. 676 (S.D. Ohio 1983); State ex rel. Nelson v. Ellis, 140 So.2d 194 (La. 1962) aff'd, 151 So.2d 544 (La. 1963); Rodyk v. Ukrainian Autocephalic Orthodox Church, 296 N.Y.S.2d 496 (1968), aff'd, 328 N.Y.S.2d 685 (1972).

[410] Lott v. Eastern Shore Christian Center, 908 So.2d 922 (Ala. 2005).

[411] *See, e.g.,* John v. Estate of Hartgerink, 528 N.W.2d 539 (Iowa 1995) (defamation, intentional infliction of emotional distress); Glass v. First United Pentecostal Church, 676 So.2d 724 (La. App. 1996) (defamation, intentional infliction of emotional distress); Schoenhalls v. Main, 504 N.W.2d 233 (Minn. App. 1993) (defamation, fraud); Hadnot v. Shaw, 826 P.2d 978 (Okla. 1992) (defamation and intentional infliction of emotional distress).

[412] Grunwald v. Bornfreund, 696 F. Supp. 838 (E.D.N.Y. 1988).

decisions of those bodies made in accordance with those bodies' rules. This line of cases is based on the Court's observation that voluntary religious organizations are much like any other voluntary organization and are in the best position to interpret their own rules. As the Court stated in [a previous decision]: "It is not to be supposed that the judges of the civil courts can be as competent in ecclesiastical law and religious faith . . . as the ablest men in each [faith] are in reference to their own. . . ." Thus, federal courts will not interfere with the decisions of a religious body adjudicating the relationships of members in that body; as a matter of jurisprudence federal courts will defer to the decision of the religious body.[413]

The court also noted that "in other cases, the Supreme Court has held that it is contrary to the First Amendment for a court, either federal or state, to engage in an examination of ecclesiastical doctrine, and unless such examination cannot be avoided, a court must defer to the decisions of a religious body." The court noted that in this case, the member had asked the court "to do something it is not able to do either as a matter of federal jurisprudence or under the First Amendment: decide whether [he] should be excommunicated from his religious community for prosecuting this suit . . . ." The court acknowledged that if the member were in fact threatened with imminent physical harm, then "he could come to this court for a remedy." However, "the mere expulsion from a religious society, with the exclusion from a religious community, is not a harm for which courts can grant a remedy." In conclusion, the court permitted the member to pursue a judicial resolution of his dispute with the religious organization, and ruled that the member's threatened excommunication was "beyond the powers of this court to stop, so long as the excommunication results in nothing more than [the member] being excluded from his religious community."

Case Studies

• *A federal appeals court refused to permit a "disfellowshiped" Jehovah's Witness to sue her former church for defamation, invasion of privacy, fraud, and outrageous conduct. The disfellowshiped member claimed that she had been aggrieved by the Jehovah's Witness practice of "shunning," which requires members to avoid all social contacts with disfellowshiped members. The court, acknowledging that the harm suffered by disfellowshiped members is "real and not insubstantial," nevertheless concluded that permitting disfellowshiped members to sue their church for emotional injuries "would unconstitutionally restrict the Jehovah's Witness free exercise of religion." The constitutional guaranty of freedom of religion, observed the court, "requires that society tolerate the type of harm suffered by [disfellowshiped members] as a price well worth paying to safeguard the right of religious difference that all citizens enjoy."[414]*

• *A Michigan court ruled that it lacked jurisdiction to resolve the claims of parishioners that they had suffered intentional infliction of emotional distress as a result of their*

---

[413] *Id.* at 840.

[414] Paul v. Watchtower Bible and Tract Society of New York, 819 F. 2d 875 (9th Cir. 1987).

priest's actions. Several parishioners withheld their financial support from the church because of their opposition to certain changes that a new priest had initiated. In response to this action, the priest refused to give communion to certain dissident members in the presence of the entire congregation, and verbally criticized others during services. The court observed that "it is well settled that courts, both federal and state, are severely circumscribed by [the state and federal constitutions] in the resolution of disputes between a church and its members. Such jurisdiction is limited to property rights which can be resolved by application of civil law." In rejecting the members' claim that the church had intentionally caused them emotional distress, the court remarked, "This is quite a modern tort not yet recognized by the highest court in this state. Hopefully, it never will be. The awesome flood of litigation has already risen to the gunnels. If the courts were to offer to extract money from everyone who intentionally makes someone else mad, we would surely go under."[415]

• *A Michigan court ruled that the First Amendment guaranty of religious freedom provides churches with substantial protection when disciplining members.*[416] *This protection extends to statements made by a minister to the church during worship services or in church publications. But when a member resigns from the church prior to being disciplined, a more difficult question is presented. The court drew a distinction between the discipline of members and nonmembers. It concluded that churches have limited constitutional protection when disciplining nonmembers, meaning that such individuals are more likely to succeed in pursuing legal action against their former church.*

• *The Montana Supreme Court ruled that a husband and wife who had been "disfellowshiped" from a Jehovah's Witness congregation could not sue the church for defamation. The couple had been disfellowshiped for marrying contrary to church doctrine. In announcing the decision to the congregation, the overseer remarked that the couple had been living in adultery according to church teachings and had been disfellowshiped for "conduct unbecoming Christians." The overseer added that "we got the filth cleaned out of the congregation, now we have God's spirit." The court concluded that such comments were not defamatory since they were privileged and protected by the constitutional guaranty of religious freedom. As to the defense of privilege, the court remarked that "it is firmly established that statements of church members made in the course of disciplinary or expulsion proceedings, in the absence of malice, are protected by a qualified privilege." The remarks of the overseer were privileged, concluded the court, and did not involve malice since "malice is defined as reckless disregard for the truth [and] does not include hatred, personal spite, ill-will, or a desire to injure." The court added that it "would be violating the [church's] right to free exercise of religion if [it] were to find [the church's] statements actionable under state defamation law."*[417]

2. Decisions Recognizing a Legal Remedy: The Guinn Case

Those courts that have followed the rule of "marginal civil court review" of internal church membership determinations occasionally will recognize that improperly disciplined or dismissed members have a legal remedy against their church. The best illustration of this is a 1989 ruling of the Oklahoma Supreme

---

[415] Maciejewski v. Breitenbeck, 413 N.W.2d 65 (Mich. App. 1987).

[416] Smith v. Calvary Christian Church, 592 N.W.2d 713 (Mich. App. 1998).

[417] Rasmussen v. Bennett, 741 P.2d 755 (Mont. 1987).

Court.[418] Because of the significance of this ruling, it will be considered in detail.

In 1974, a single woman (the "parishioner") moved with her minor children to Collinsville, Oklahoma, and soon became a member of a local Church of Christ congregation. The first few years of the parishioner's association with the church were without incident. In 1980, however, three "elders" of the church confronted the parishioner with a rumor that she was having sexual relations with a local resident who was not a member of the congregation. According to the elders, they investigated the rumor because of the church's teaching that church leaders are responsible to monitor the actions of church members and confront and discuss problems with anyone who is "having trouble." The Church of Christ follows a literal interpretation of the Bible, which it considers to be the sole source of moral and religious guidance.

When confronted with the rumor, the parishioner admitted violating the Church of Christ prohibition against fornication. As a transgressor of the church's code of ethics, the parishioner became subject to the disciplinary procedure set forth in Matthew 18:13-17. This procedure provides, "If thy brother shall trespass against thee, go and tell him his fault between thee and him alone; if he shall hear thee, thou has gained thy brother. But if he will not hear thee, then take with thee one or two more, that in the mouth of two or three witnesses every word may be established. And if he shall neglect to hear them, tell it unto the church; but if he neglect to hear the church, let him be unto thee as a heathen man and a publican." Pursuant to this procedure, the church elders confronted the parishioner on three occasions over the course of a year. On each occasion, the elders requested that the parishioner repent of her fornication and discontinue seeing her companion. On September 21, 1981, a few days following the third encounter, the elders sent the parishioner a letter warning her that if she did not repent, the "withdrawal of fellowship" process would begin.

Withdrawal of fellowship is a disciplinary procedure that is based on Matthew 18 and carried out by the entire membership in a Church of Christ congregation. When a member violates the church's code of ethics and refuses to repent, the elders read aloud to the congregation those Scripture passages which were violated. The congregation then withdraws its fellowship from the wayward member by refusing to acknowledge his or her presence. According to the elders, this process serves the dual purpose of encouraging transgressors to repent and return to fellowship with other members, and it maintains the purity and holiness of the church and its members. The parishioner had seen one incident of fellowship withdrawal, and was fully aware that such a process would result in the publication of her unscriptural conduct to the entire congregation. Accordingly, she contacted a lawyer who sent the elders a letter signed by the parishioner, and dated September 24, 1981, in which the parishioner clearly stated that she withdrew her membership. The attorney asked the elders not to expose the parishioner's private life to the congregation (which comprised about five percent of the town's population).

---

[418] Guinn v. Church of Christ, 775 P.2d 766 (Okla. 1989). *But see* Hadnot v. Shaw, 826 P.2d 978 (Okla. 1992)(civil courts cannot review a church's discipline of persons who have not withdrawn from church membership).

On September 25, the parishioner wrote the elders another letter imploring them not to mention her name in church except to tell the congregation that she had withdrawn from membership. The elders ignored these requests, and on September 27 (during a scheduled service) they advised the congregation to encourage the parishioner to repent and return to the church. They also informed the congregation that unless the parishioner repented, the verses of Scripture that she had violated would be read aloud to the congregation at the next service and that the withdrawal of fellowship procedure would begin. The parishioner met with one of the elders during the following week, and she was informed that her attempt to withdraw from membership was not only doctrinally impossible, but could not halt the disciplinary process that would be carried out against her. The parishioner was publicly branded a fornicator when the scriptural standards she had violated were recited to the congregation at a service conducted on October 4. As part of the disciplinary process the same information regarding the parishioner's transgressions was sent to four other area Church of Christ congregations to be read aloud during services.

The parishioner sued the three elders and local church, asserting that their actions both before and after her withdrawal from church membership on September 25, 1981 (the date of her letter to the church), invaded her privacy and caused her emotional distress. The invasion of privacy claim alleged that the elders and church had "intruded upon her seclusion," and in addition, had "unreasonably publicized private facts about her life by communicating her transgressions to the [home church] and four other area Church of Christ congregations." A jury ruled in favor of the parishioner, and awarded her $205,000 in actual damages, $185,000 in punitive damages, and $45,000 in interest. The decision was appealed to the Oklahoma Supreme Court.

The elders and church argued that the First Amendment guaranty of religious freedom prevented them from being sued as a result of their exercise of ecclesiastical discipline. The court acknowledged that the United States Supreme Court has banned civil court review of "purely ecclesiastical" matters, but it concluded that the discipline of church members is not always immune from civil court review. It ruled that the First Amendment prevented the church and its elders from being sued for their actions *prior* to the parishioner's withdrawal (which, according to the court, occurred on September 24 when the parishioner sent her letter of withdrawal to the church), but that the church and elders *could* be sued for actions occurring *after* the parishioner's withdrawal. With regard to the parishioner's claim for "pre-withdrawal" damages, the court noted that "under the First Amendment people may freely consent to being spiritually governed by an established set of ecclesiastical tenets defined and carried out by those chosen to interpret and impose them." The court continued, "Under the First Amendment's free exercise of religion clause, parishioner had the right to consent as a participant in the practices and beliefs of the Church of Christ without fear of governmental interference . . . . Her willing submission to the Church of Christ's dogma, and the elders' reliance on that submission, collectively shielded the church's pre-withdrawal, religiously-motivated discipline from scrutiny through secular [courts]."

As authority for this proposition, the court quoted from a decision of the United States Supreme Court:

The right to organize voluntary religious associations to assist in the expression and dissemination of any religious doctrine, and to create tribunals for the decision of controverted questions of faith within the association, and for the ecclesiastical government of all individual members, congregations, and officers within the general association, is unquestioned. *All who unite themselves to such a body do so with an implied consent to this government, and are bound to submit to it.*[419]

The court concluded that "insofar as [the parishioner] seeks vindication for the actions taken by the elders *before* her membership withdrawal, her claims are to be dismissed."

Could the parishioner sue the elders and church for actions occurring *after* her withdrawal? The elders said no, pointing out that the Church of Christ contains no doctrinal provision for withdrawal from membership. Rather, a member remains a part of a congregation for life. Like those born into a family, they may leave but they can never really sever the familial bond. Accordingly, a court determination that the parishioner effectively withdrew from membership and thereby terminated the church's authority to discipline her would amount to "a constitutionally impermissible state usurpation of religious discipline." The elders also emphasized that the disciplinary procedure mandated by Matthew 18:13-17 already had begun at the time of the parishioner's alleged withdrawal (the elders had confronted her on three occasions), and therefore the parishioner could not preempt the disciplinary process by an attempted withdrawal. The parishioner asserted that she had the authority to withdraw from membership in the church, and that her withdrawal terminated the church's authority to discipline her.

The court concluded that the parishioner's September 24, 1981 letter was an effective withdrawal from church membership, and it agreed with the parishioner that the elders and church *could* be sued for their actions following her withdrawal. It observed:

The First Amendment of the United States Constitution was designed to preserve freedom of worship by prohibiting the establishment or endorsement of any official religion. One of the fundamental purposes of the First Amendment is to protect the people's right to worship as they choose. Implicit in the right to choose freely one's own form of worship is the right of unhindered and unimpeded withdrawal from the chosen form of worship. . . . [The local church], by denying the parishioner's right to disassociate herself from a particular form of religious belief is threatening to curtail her freedom of worship according to her choice. Unless the parishioner waived the constitutional right to withdraw her initial consent to be bound by the Church of Christ discipline and its governing elders, her resignation was a constitutionally protected right.[420]

---

[419] Watson v. Jones, 80 U.S. (13 Wall.) 679 (1872) (emphasis added).

[420] 775 P.2d at 776-777.

The court concluded that the parishioner had not "waived" her constitutional right to withdraw from church membership. A waiver, observed the court, is a "voluntary and intentional relinquishment of a known right." The parishioner testified that she had never been informed by the church of its teaching that membership constitutes an insoluble bond of lifetime commitment, and accordingly she was incapable of knowingly and intentionally "waiving" such a right.

The court summarized its thinking as follows:

Disciplinary practices involving members of an ecclesiastical association . . . are among those hallowed First Amendment rights with which the government cannot interfere. . . . [Nevertheless] First Amendment protection does not extend to all religiously-motivated disciplinary practices in which ecclesiastical organizations might engage. By its very nature, ecclesiastical discipline involves both church and member. It is a means of religious expression as well as a means of ecclesiastically judging one who transgresses a church law which one has consented to obey. The right to express dissatisfaction with the disobedience of those who have promised to adhere to doctrinal precepts and to take ecclesiastically-mandated measures to bring wayward members back within the bounds of accepted behavior, are forms of religious expression and association which the First Amendment's free exercise clause was designed to protect and preserve.

And yet the constitutionally protected freedom to impose even the most deeply felt, spiritually-inspired disciplinary measure is forfeited when the object of "benevolent" concern is one who has terminated voluntary submission to another's supervision and command. While the First Amendment requires that citizens be tolerant of religious views different from and offensive to their own, it surely does not require that those like parishioner, who choose not to submit to the authority of a religious association, be tolerant of that group's attempts to govern them. Only those who "unite themselves" in a religious association impliedly consent to its authority over them and are bound "to submit to it."

Parishioner voluntarily joined the Church of Christ and by so doing consented to submit to its tenets. When she later removed herself from membership, petitioner withdrew her consent, depriving the church of the power actively to monitor her spiritual life through overt disciplinary acts. No real freedom to choose religion would exist in this land if under the shield of the First Amendment religious institutions could impose their will on the unwilling and claim immunity from secular [courts] for their tortious acts.[421]

The court distinguished a federal appeals court decision cited by the elders which held that a dismissed member of the Jehovah's Witness church could not

---

[421] 775 P.2d at 779.

sue her former church for the emotional distress, defamation, and invasion of privacy that it allegedly caused by its practice of "shunning" her.[422] Unlike the conduct of the Church of Christ elders, the practice of shunning the former Jehovah's Witness was "passive." The member abandoned her membership in the church, and the church simply instructed its members to avoid any contact with her. The court observed:

> For purposes of First Amendment protection, religiously-motivated disciplinary measures that merely *exclude* a person from communion are vastly different from those which are designed to *control* and *involve*. A church is constitutionally free to exclude people without first obtaining their consent. But the First Amendment will not shield a church from civil liability for imposing its will, as manifested through a disciplinary scheme, upon an individual who has not consented to undergo ecclesiastical discipline.[423]

The court rejected the elders' claim that their statements to the congregations were protected by a "conditional privilege." The court acknowledged that a statement is conditionally privileged if "the circumstances under which the information is published lead any one of several persons having a *common interest* in a particular subject matter correctly or reasonably to believe that there is information that another sharing the common interest is entitled to know." The court concluded that the elders' statements were *not* protected by a conditional privilege since the "parishioner was neither a present nor a prospective church member" at the time of the elders' public statements, and accordingly that the "congregation did not share the sort of 'common interest' in parishioner's behavior" that would render the elders' statements privileged.

The court acknowledged that "communicating unproven allegations of *a present or prospective member's misconduct to the other members of a religious association is a privileged occasion because the members have a valid interest in and concern for the behavior of their fellow members and officers.*" However, it concluded that the elders' claim to a conditional privilege "as it pertains to their actions occurring *after* parishioner's withdrawal from membership, is without merit."

The court acknowledged that churches have a greater interest in receiving information concerning disciplined or dismissed clergy, and accordingly the "common interest privilege" is broader than in the context of lay member discipline. The court concluded that a congregation has "a common interest in being informed about the questionable conduct of one among them who expressed the desire to continue ministering to them or to one of the neighboring [Church of Christ] assemblies. Here, parishioners expressed no interest in continuing her association with [her former church] or with any other Church of Christ [congregation]." Accordingly, the church simply had no "common interest" in her post-withdrawal discipline that would make the elders' statements conditionally privileged.

---

[422] Paul v. Watchtower Bible & Tract Society, 819 F.2d 875 (9th Cir. 1987).

[423] 775 P.2d at 781.

What is the relevance of the Oklahoma Supreme Court's decision to local churches? Obviously, the court's decision is binding only upon churches in the state of Oklahoma. Nevertheless, the case represents one of the most extensive discussions of church discipline by any court, and accordingly it probably will be given special consideration (and no doubt be followed) by the courts of many other states. For this reason, the case merits serious study by church leaders in every state. With these factors in mind, consider the following:

1. Discipline of church members is constitutionally protected

The discipline of *church members* (i.e., persons who have *not* withdrawn from membership) is a constitutionally protected right of churches. If discipline of church members is a possibility in your church, then you should adopt a disciplinary procedure that is based upon and refers to scriptural references. The procedure should specify the grounds for discipline, and describe the process that will be conducted. Avoid references to loaded phrases such as "due process," which have no legal relevance in the context of church law and only create confusion. The Oklahoma court acknowledged that there might be some pre-withdrawal disciplinary actions which would be so extreme as to lose their constitutional protection. However, it concluded that the elders' conduct did not constitute such a case. Recall that the elders' pre-withdrawal actions were limited to three meetings with the parishioner and involved no public dissemination of her alleged misconduct.

2. No constitutional protection after a member resigns

Discipline of persons who have effectively withdrawn their church membership is not a constitutionally protected activity, and churches that engage in such conduct can be sued under existing theories of tort law. In the Oklahoma case, the parishioner sued the church (and its elders) for both invasion of privacy and intentional infliction of emotional distress. The parishioner asserted that the church invaded her privacy in two ways. First, the actions of the elders "intruded upon her seclusion." Second, the elders' notification of their own congregation (as well as four other local congregations) of the parishioner's misconduct amounted to an unreasonable public disclosure of private facts. Both of these assertions constitute well-recognized variations of the tort of invasion of privacy. The parishioner also claimed that the elders' conduct amounted to an intentional infliction of emotional distress (another well-recognized tort), since their actions were extreme and outrageous and of an intentional and reckless nature which caused her severe emotional distress and shock (particularly since the parishioner's minor children were present at the church service during which the elders publicized her misconduct).

3. Church members have a constitutional right to resign

The court concluded that the constitutional right of a church member to withdraw from church membership is protected by the First Amendment guaranty of religious freedom *unless a member has waived that right.* An effective waiver requires the voluntary relinquishment of a known right. In other words, a member can waive the right to resign by a voluntary and intentional act, but not through inadvertence or ignorance. A church wishing to restrict the right of disciplined members to withdraw must obtain a voluntary and knowing waiver by present and prospective members of their constitutional right to withdraw. How can this be done? One approach would be for a church to adopt a provision in its bylaws preventing members from withdrawing if they are currently being disciplined by the church. Obviously, the disciplinary procedure must be carefully specified in the church bylaws so there is no doubt whether the disciplinary process has been initiated with respect to a member. Most courts have held that members are "on notice" of all of the provisions in the church bylaws, and consent to be bound by them when they become members. As a result, the act of becoming a member of a church with such a provision in its bylaws may well constitute an effective waiver of a member's right to withdraw (if the disciplinary process has begun). Such a conclusion is not free from doubt, however. To be as safe as possible, a church could explain to present and prospective members the provision in the bylaws limiting their right to withdraw, and explaining to them that by becoming members they will be waiving their right to withdraw from membership if they are under discipline by the church. The problem in the Oklahoma case was that the church attempted to discipline the parishioner following her withdrawal. According to the court's ruling, the church could have avoided liability by obtaining an effective waiver. Unfortunately, the court did not discuss what forms of waiver it would find acceptable.

> "If discipline of church members is a possibility in your church, then you should adopt a disciplinary procedure that is based upon and refers to scriptural references."

4. Passive discipline

The Oklahoma court concluded that a church retains the right to engage in "passive" discipline of former members. It approved a federal appeals court decision rejecting the claim of a former Jehovah's Witness that her former church had defamed her, invaded her privacy, and caused her emotional distress by its practice of "shunning" former members. The court observed that the decision of the Jehovah's Witness church "to turn away from her was protected under the First Amendment as a passive exercise of religious freedom, the legitimacy of which was not grounded in her prior acquiescence."

5. Communications of matters of "common interest" to members

The court acknowledged that church members have a right to know about matters in which they have a "common interest," and that this right permits some disclosures to church members concerning the discipline or misconduct of current members. Statements by church leaders to church members concerning the discipline of current members are conditionally privileged—meaning that the disciplined member cannot successfully sue the church for making such disclosures unless the church acted maliciously (i.e., it either knew that the disclosures were false or made them with a reckless disregard as to their truthfulness). It must be emphasized that this privilege only protects disclosures made to *church members* about *church members*. Disclosures made to a congregation during a worship service in which *non-members* are present would not be protected. And, statements about former members are not protected (presumably, non-members would need to be removed from the sanctuary before statements regarding church discipline could be made). The court observed: "Communicating unproven allegations of a present or prospective member's misconduct to the other members of a religious association is a privileged occasion because the members have a valid interest in and concern for the behavior of their fellow members and officers."

Obviously, the safest course of action for a church board that has disciplined a member is to refrain from disclosing any information to the congregation. If the board decides that the congregation should be informed, then a general statement that the individual is "no longer a member" is the safest approach. If the board would like to share more details with the church, then it should do so at a congregational meeting or service only after all non-members have been removed. Members present should be instructed to retain the information presented in the strictest confidence. Churches following the disciplinary procedure outlined in Matthew 18 ultimately may wish to let the church membership make the final determination regarding the guilt or innocence of an accused member (and any penalty to be imposed). If so, the church must be careful to remove all non-members from such a meeting, and to apprise the membership of the confidentiality of the information that is disclosed. It would be appropriate for the congregation to adopt a resolution at such a meeting committing itself to maintaining all confidences shared during the meeting.

6. Discipline of clergy

Churches have greater protection in making statements about current or former *clergy*, since the congregation continues to have "a common interest in being informed about the questionable conduct of one among them who expresses the desire to continue ministering to them or to one of the neighboring assemblies." Accordingly, disciplined clergy may find it more difficult to sue their church or denomination.

DID YOU KNOW?
Arbitration

Churches wishing to reduce the risk of litigation by disciplined members (or any other members) should consider, in addition to the observations made in this chapter, the adoption of a binding arbitration policy. Such a policy, if adopted by the church membership at a congregational meeting as an amendment to the church's bylaws, can force church members to resolve their disputes (with the church, pastor, board, or other members) within the church consistently with the pattern suggested in 1 Corinthians 6:1-8.

While a discussion of arbitration policies is beyond the scope of this text, churches should recognize that arbitration is an increasingly popular means of resolving disputes in the secular world since it often avoids the excessive costs and delays associated with civil litigation and the uncertainty of jury verdicts. Of course, any arbitration policy should be reviewed by an attorney and the church's liability insurer before being implemented. A legally effective and properly adopted arbitration policy can force disgruntled members to take their complaints to a panel of church representatives rather than create a costly and protracted spectacle in the secular courts. Such an approach, at a minimum, merits serious consideration by any church.

Arbitration clauses are addressed fully in chapter 10.

On the whole, churches benefit from the Oklahoma Supreme Court's ruling, since the court recognized that:

- churches have a constitutional right to discipline members;

- statements made to church members about disciplined members are "conditionally privileged";

- churches have broad authority to discipline clergy; and

- churches have a constitutionally protected right to discipline a former member who has withdrawn from membership if the former member has effectively waived his or her right to withdraw from membership.

The court's ruling does not go as far as some other court decisions in recognizing a broad authority on the part of churches to discipline persons who have withdrawn from church membership. And, the court failed to adequately refute the elders' claim that the parishioner's right to withdraw was suspended when the elders commenced the church's disciplinary process (a year before the parishioner's withdrawal). Finally, the court acknowledged (on the basis of United States Supreme Court rulings) that "all who unite themselves to [a church] do so with an implied consent to [its] government, and are bound to submit to it." Yet, it greatly limited the effect of this language by permitting the parishioner to completely avoid the church's well-defined disciplinary process (with which she had been familiar) merely because she did not technically "waive" her right to withdraw. This aspect of the court's ruling is unfortunate—particularly since the court provided no guidance whatever to churches regarding the form and contents of an effective waiver.

3. Decisions Recognizing a Legal Remedy: Other Cases

Persons who believe that they have been improperly expelled from membership in a church have a number of potential remedies available to them.

First, they may be able to obtain judicial review of the expulsion if they reside in a jurisdiction that permits marginal civil court review of church membership determinations. If a court agrees to review the expulsion and finds that it was deficient on the basis of one of the grounds discussed in this section, it may declare the expulsion void and reinstate the expelled member.[424]

Second, wrongfully expelled members may be able to recover monetary damages.[425]

Third, they may petition a court for an injunction prohibiting a church from interfering with their rights or privileges as members.[426]

Fourth, they may seek a declaratory judgment setting forth their rights.[427]

Fifth, in some cases they may sue their church or certain of its members for defamation.

Defamation generally is defined to include the following elements: (1) a public statement, whether oral or in writing; (2) reference to another; (3) that is false; and (4) which injures the reputation of the other. Truth is generally held to be an absolute defense to a defamation action. Thus if the allegedly defamatory statements were true, an expelled member will not be able to sue for defamation even if his reputation has been injured.

Defamation actions are limited in another important way. Most jurisdictions recognize that statements made by a person in a reasonable manner and for a proper purpose to others having a common interest with him in the communication are "qualifiedly privileged" and immune from attack unless they are made with malice.[428] Malice in this context refers to either a knowledge that the communication was false or a reckless disregard concerning its truth or falsity.

The common interest among church members about church matters is likely sufficient to create a qualified privilege for communications between members on subjects relating to the church's interests. To illustrate, where expelled church members had been publicly referred to by other members as "totally unworthy of the continued confidence, respect and fellowship of a great church," as willing to lie in order to harm their church, and as possessed of a vile spirit, a court concluded that the remarks were entitled to a qualified privilege. The court nevertheless considered the remarks defamatory because they had been made either recklessly or with a knowledge of their falsity.[429]

---

[424] Ragsdall v. Church of Christ, 55 N.W.2d 539 (Iowa 1952).

[425] Louison v. Fischman, 168 N.E.2d 340 (Mass. 1960).

[426] David v. Carter, 222 S.W.2d 900 (Tex. 1949).

[427] Epperson v. Myers, 58 So.2d 150 (Fla. 1952).

[428] The qualified privilege is addressed more fully in section 4-02.03.

[429] Brewer v. Second Baptist Church, 197 P.2d 713 (Cal. 1948).

In another case, an expelled member alleged that at various times in meetings of his religious group other members had stated that he was a disgrace to his religion, that his conduct was scandalous, that he was guilty of evil conduct and was a man of low character, and that his conduct was so bad that it could not be described publicly. A court, in finding such statements malicious, stated the general rule as follows:

> Members of such bodies may report on the qualifications of applicants, prefer charges against fellow members, offer testimony in support of the charges, and make proper publications of any disciplinary action that may be taken, without liability for any resultant defamation, *so long as they act without malice.* The rule relative to qualified privilege is always subject to the limitation, as stated, that in connection with such activities the parties must act without malice. When a matter which otherwise would be a qualifiedly privileged communication is published falsely, fraudulently, and with express malice and intent to injure the persons against whom it is directed, the communication loses its qualifiedly privileged character and the parties lay themselves liable to a suit for damages in an action for libel or slander.[430]

Members—Personal Liability §6-11

It is a fundamental characteristic of corporations that individual members will not be personally responsible for the misconduct of other members, so long as they do not participate directly in the misconduct or ratify or affirm it. Members of course are personally responsible for their own misconduct, and the corporation itself may be derivatively responsible for a member's misconduct. But other members of the corporation who were not involved in and did not affirm the wrongful act of another member ordinarily will not be personally responsible for it.

Members who are expelled from a church ordinarily are no longer responsible for the church's debts and liabilities.[431]

Meetings of Members § 6-12

Church charters and bylaws typically confer significant authority in the members. Church members may exercise this authority only when acting at a meeting convened according to procedural requirements in the church's charter

---

[430] Loeb v. Geronemus, 66 So.2d 241, 244 (Fla. 1953) (citations omitted). *See also* Joiner v. Weeks, 383 So.2d 101 (La. 1980), *cert. denied,* 385 So.2d 257 (La. 1980); Moyle v. Franz 46 N.Y.S.2d 667 (1944), *aff'd,* 47 N.Y.S.2d 484 (1944).

[431] Smith v. Lewis, 578 S.W.2d 169 (Tex. App. 1979).

and bylaws or in applicable state law. Actions taken at irregularly called meetings generally are considered invalid unless subsequently ratified at a duly convened meeting.

Church bylaws typically call for annual general meetings of the church membership, and for such special meetings as the congregation or board of directors deems necessary.

The pastor of the church, or the senior pastor of a church having more than one pastor on its staff, is legally authorized to preside at membership meetings if authorized by (1) the church charter or bylaws, (2) established church custom, (3) applicable state nonprofit corporation law, or (4) the doctrine of inherent authority.

Although a church is free to determine the order of business to be followed at general or special meetings, the following order is commonly followed:

1. reading and approval of minutes

2. reports of officers, boards, and standing committees

3. reports of special committees

4. special orders

5. unfinished business and general orders

6. new business[432]

Members generally have a right to express their views at church meetings since the very purpose of such meetings is to arrive at decisions through a free and open exchange of ideas. One court ruled that the leaders of two opposing factions within a church had no authority to agree that a church membership meeting would be conducted without discussion.[433]

Case Study

• The Georgia Supreme Court ruled that a provision in the state nonprofit corporation law mandating annual membership meetings did not take priority over a provision in a church's bylaws calling for membership meetings once every four years. The court observed that the state nonprofit corporation law itself specifies that if any of its provisions is inconsistent with religious doctrine governing a nonprofit corporation's affairs on the same subject, "the religious doctrine shall control to the extent required by the Constitution of the United States or the Constitution of this state or both." As a result, the issue "is whether the frequency with which the church's membership meets is a matter of religious doctrine having constitutional precedence over inconsistent statutory provisions of [the nonprofit corporation law]." The court noted that the church in this case was "hierarchical" in nature, and that the members had very limited

---

[432] *See, e.g.,* Robert's Rules of Order Newly Revised § 3 (10th ed. 2000).
[433] Randolph v. Mount Zion Baptist Church, 53 A.2d 206 (N.J. 1947).

authority to direct church affairs. It concluded: "An annual meeting as contemplated by [the nonprofit corporation law] would be totally inconsistent with the church's fundamental religious freedom, as a hierarchical religious body, to determine its own governmental rules and regulations. Members have no legal right to wrest the governing of the church from [church officials] by obtaining court-ordered annual meetings conducted in accordance with [nonprofit corporation law]."[434]

Procedural Requirements   § 6-12.1

Key point 6-12.1. Church membership meetings must be conducted in accordance with the procedural requirements ordinarily specified in the church's governing documents. The most common requirements pertain to notice, quorum, and voting.

A church's charter or bylaws typically specifies procedures for the convening and conduct of church membership meetings. State nonprofit corporation law may impose additional procedural requirements on incorporated churches, although in most cases state corporation law will apply only if the church's charter or bylaws are silent. If there is no specific charter, bylaw, or statutory provision governing church meetings, the established custom of the church generally will control.[435] For example, where it was the established custom of a church to give notice of the annual church membership meeting by public announcement during Sunday morning services on the two Sundays before the date set for the proposed meeting, a court ruled that the election of officers at a purported annual meeting was invalid since this custom was not followed.[436]

The procedural requirements causing the greatest amount of controversy and confusion are notice, quorum, and voting requirements. These subjects will be considered individually.

1. Notice

The church membership ordinarily must be notified of the date, time, and place of both annual and special membership meetings. This "notice" requirement usually is found in the church's bylaws, but it also may appear in the corporate charter or in the body of parliamentary procedure adopted by the church. For example, *Robert's Rules of Order Newly Revised*, which has been adopted by many churches, specifies:

> With the possible exception of motions that related to procedure without direct reference to a particular substantive item of business, only business mentioned in the call of a special meeting can be transacted at such a meeting. If, at a special meeting, it becomes urgent in an emergency to take action for which no notice was given, that action, to become legal, must be

---

[434] First Born Church of the Living God, Inc. v. Hill, 481 S.E.2d 221 (Ga. 1997).

[435] McDaniel v. Quakenbush, 105 S.E.2d 94 (N.C. 1958).

[436] Coates v. Parchman, 334 S.W.2d 417 (Mo. 1960).

ratified by the organization at a regular meeting (or, if the ratification cannot wait, at another special meeting properly called for that purpose).[437]

If a church is incorporated and its bylaws do not contain notice requirements, the state nonprofit corporation law ordinarily will contain the applicable requirements. To illustrate, section 14 of the Model Nonprofit Corporation Act, which has been adopted by many states, specifies:

> Unless otherwise provided in the articles of incorporation or the bylaws, written notice stating the place, day and hour of the meeting and, in the case of a special meeting, the purpose or purposes for which the meeting is called, should be delivered not less than ten nor more than fifty days before the date of the meeting, either personally or by mail . . . to each member entitled to vote at such meeting.

Section 7.05 of the Revised Model Nonprofit Corporation Act, which has been adopted by a few states, specifies that "a corporation shall give notice consistent with its bylaws of meetings of members in a fair and reasonable manner." The Act goes on to specify that notice is "fair and reasonable" if (1) the corporation notifies its members of the place, date, and time of each annual, regular, and special meeting of members no fewer than 10 (or if notice is mailed by other than first class or registered mail, 30) nor more than 60 days before the meeting date; (2) notice of an *annual or regular meeting* must include a statement of purpose only with respect to any of the following matters—director conflict of interest, indemnification of officers or agents, amendment of the articles of incorporation, amendment of the bylaws, mergers, some sales of corporate assets, dissolution by directors or members; and (3) notice of a *special business meeting* must include "a description of the matters for which the meeting is called."

Unincorporated churches that have no bylaws or written regulations are bound by their established customs regarding notice of church membership meetings. However, some courts have held that notice requirements established by custom can be disregarded if the notice actually given is more likely to provide notice to all church members than the form of notice prescribed by custom.[438]

A church must comply with the manner and method of giving notice prescribed in its charter or bylaws, in applicable state nonprofit corporation law, or by established church custom. Failure to follow applicable notice requirements may render any action taken at the improperly called meeting invalid.

---

[437] Robert's Rules of Order Newly Revised § 9 (10th ed. 2000).
[438] State Bank v. Wilbur Mission Church, 265 P.2d 821 (Wash. 1954).

Case Study

• A church convened a special meeting of the congregation. Notice of the meeting consisted of announcements from the pulpit on the three consecutive Sundays prior to the meeting. These announcements did not indicate that a vote would be taken on the minister's continued employment. At the meeting, a motion was made from the floor to terminate the minister's services. The minister, acting as chairman of the meeting, ruled the motion out of order since there had been no prior notice that such a vote would be taken. A deacon then proceeded to conduct a vote over the minister's objection, and the members present voted to terminate the minister's services. The ousted minister attempted to return to the pulpit on the following Sunday, but was prevented from doing so. The church later obtained a court order prohibiting the minister from attempting to occupy his former position. The minister appealed this decision, arguing that the church had improperly fired him since it had not given proper notice of the business to be transacted at the congregational meeting. A state appeals court agreed. It noted that neither the church's charter nor bylaws specified the type of notice needed for special meetings. And, since the charter and bylaws were silent, the state nonprofit corporation law under which the church was incorporated had to be consulted. A provision in this law specified that "unless otherwise provided in the [charter] or bylaws . . . the authorized person calling a members' meeting shall cause written notice of the time, place and purpose of the meeting to be given to all members entitled to vote at such meeting, at least ten days and not more than sixty days prior to the day fixed for the meeting." Notice of the church's special congregational meeting was defective since it was not in writing (it had been announced from the pulpit), and it failed to specify the purposes of the meeting. "The notice of the meeting was clearly deficient," concluded the court, "and the meeting was therefore invalid."[439]

Actions taken at church membership meetings have been declared void under the following circumstances: (1) notice of a special meeting was read publicly by a church secretary instead of by a church trustee as required by the applicable state nonprofit corporation law;[440] (2) a pastor publicly notified his congregation during a worship service that a special meeting would be convened immediately following the service, though the church's bylaws stipulated that notice of special meetings had to be mailed to members at a prescribed time in advance of a meeting;[441] (3) a pastor convened a special meeting following a Sunday morning service without any notice other than an oral announcement during the service, despite an applicable provision in state nonprofit corporation law requiring written notice to be posted in a conspicuous place near the main entrance of

---

[439] Bethlehem Missionary Baptist Church v. Henderson, 522 So.2d 1339 (La. App. 1988). This case is significant for two reasons. First, it emphasizes the significance of giving proper notice of church business meetings. Second, the case illustrates the principle (which is followed in many states) that an incorporated church may be governed by state nonprofit corporation law in the event that it fails to address certain matters of administration and operation in its charter or bylaws. Of course, churches in such states are free to adopt provisions contrary to the nonprofit corporation law in their own charter or bylaws, and such provisions will be controlling. But in the event that they fail (for whatever reason) to address certain issues of church administration in their organizational documents, state law may step in to "fill the void."

[440] Hayes v. Brantley, 280 N.Y.S.2d 291 (1967).

[441] Mount Zion Baptist Church v. Second Baptist Church, 432 P.2d 328 (Nev. 1967).

the church for at least seven days before the meeting;[442] (4) a small number of members present at a Wednesday evening church service publicly called a special meeting of the church membership for the following Saturday, in violation of an established church custom requiring notice to be read publicly during at least two Sunday morning services prior to such a meeting;[443] and (5) a church's attempted removal of its trustees at a special business meeting was "null and void" since the church had not fulfilled the legal notice requirements imposed by state law for calling a special business meeting.[444]

One state supreme court has observed that "it is proper for the courts to inquire whether a congregational meeting, at which church business is to be transacted, was preceded by adequate notice to the full membership, and whether, once called, the meeting was conducted in an orderly manner . . . ." However, "once the court is presented with sufficient evidence regarding the regularity of the meeting, it will then generally refuse to inquire further as to the fruits of the meeting."[445]

The courts have held that action taken at an improperly called meeting will be invalid no matter how many members are present, and that even a majority of church members present at an improperly called meeting cannot "validate" the meeting by waiving the notice requirements.[446] However, action taken at an improperly called meeting can be ratified or affirmed by the church membership at a properly called meeting.[447]

If notice has been given according to a church's bylaws, a meeting may not be challenged by a disgruntled minority. Thus, when oral notice of a special church membership meeting was announced from the church pulpit in accordance with the church's bylaws, a minority of members who had ceased attending the church and therefore did not receive actual notice of the meeting were not permitted to overturn the actions taken at the meeting on the basis of inadequate notice.[448]

Case Studies

• *A California court ruled that it was not barred by the First Amendment guaranty of religious freedom from resolving a lawsuit brought by dismissed members challenging the legal validity of their dismissals, since the church was congregational rather than hierarchical in polity and a "civil or property" right was involved. The court concluded that this dispute did implicate the members' civil and property rights, namely, "the right under the church constitution to petition the board to call a special*

---

[442] Bangor Spiritualist Church, Inc. v. Littlefield, 330 A.2d 793 (Me. 1975).

[443] In re Galilee Baptist Church, 186 So.2d 102 (Ala. 1966).

[444] First Union Baptist Church v. Banks, 533 So.2d 1305 (La. App. 1988).

[445] McKinney v. Twenty-fifth Avenue Baptist Church, Inc., 514 So.2d 837 (Ala. 1987).

[446] Hollins v. Edmonds, 616 S.W.2d 801 (Ky. 1981); Bangor Spiritualist Church, Inc. v. Littlefield, 330 A.2d 793 (Me. 1975); Brooks v. January, 321 N.W.2d 823 (Mich. App. 1982); Old Folks Mission Center v. McTizic, 631 S.W.2d 433 (Tenn. 1981).

[447] Hill v. Sargent, 615 S.W.2d 300 (Tex. 1981).

[448] Gelder v. Loomis, 605 P.2d 1330 (Okla. 1980). *See also* Zimbler v. Felber, 445 N.Y.S.2d 366 (1981).

congregational meeting, and the right not to be expelled from the church except as provided in the constitution." The court concluded: "This case does not require the court to decide whether the members' actions violated the biblical principles upon which the church is founded, but whether the church may discipline members for exercising rights guaranteed them by the civil law under which the church is organized." The court stressed that it was only dealing with a "congregational" church that was not subject to the rules of a church hierarchy. It conceded that "there is a constitutionally significant difference between a situation where a higher judicatory tribunal within a hierarchical church has resolved an internal dispute in a local church."[449]

• *A Michigan court ruled that it was barred by the First Amendment guaranty of religious freedom from resolving a dismissed pastor's claim that his dismissal was legally void because of noncompliance with procedural requirements. Twenty-two members at a church business meeting voted sixteen to six in favor of the pastor's dismissal. The pastor claimed that the vote was invalid because it did not comply with a bylaw notice provision requiring that special meetings be held only if notice is given on the two preceding worship services. The court disagreed: "The pastor fails to note that the vote was not taken at a special meeting, but rather at a regular business meeting of the church. Under the church's bylaws, regular church business meetings are conducted on the Saturday before the first Sunday of each month, and there are no special notice requirements for the regular meetings. The meeting in question was held on . . . the Saturday immediately preceding the first Sunday in October. Thus, it was a regular business meeting, not a special one, and no special notice was required."*[450]

• *A Missouri court ruled that a church's board of directors was not properly elected in accordance with the state nonprofit corporation law at a specially called business meeting, and therefore had to be removed. The court noted that the notice for the meeting said nothing about the meeting's purpose, and in particular made no mention of elections of board members. As a result, the meeting was not a "special meeting" because it was not called according to the procedures set out in the nonprofit corporation law, and therefore the election of the board members was invalid.*[451]

• *A New York court ruled that a church business meeting in which the board of deacons was deposed was invalid because the church failed to comply with the notice requirements contained in the church's bylaws. The court concluded that while the members of a church corporation "have the authority to amend their constitution and bylaws, such action must be preceded by appropriate notice. Since no notice was given before the meeting, the action taken then is null and void. Thus, the former deacons remain members of the board of deacons."*[452]

• *An Ohio court ruled that an attempt by church members to remove all of the members of the church board at a specially called membership meeting was invalid because the notice requirements prescribed by state nonprofit corporation law were not followed. The church's bylaws did not address how notice was to be provided for*

---

[449] The Cross Church Men's Society v. Executive Committee, 2005 WL 555270 (Cal. App. 2005).

[450] White v. First United Baptist Church, 2002 WL 1575243 (Mich. App. 2002).

[451] First Missionary Baptist Church v. Rollins, 151 S.W.3d 846 (Mo. App. 2004).

[452] Briggs v. Noble, 2004 WL 829439, (N.Y. App. 2004).

membership meetings, and so the nonprofit corporation law applied. According to this provision the members who called the "special meeting" were required to state the purpose of the meeting and provide at least ten days' notice of the special meeting. Because this notice requirement was not followed, the meeting at which the board was ousted was void. Further, the other actions taken at that meeting (appointment of a new board, and reinstatement of the pastor) also were void.[453]

• A Pennsylvania court ruled that a financial transaction approved by the church board in a special meeting was null and void because the board did not comply with the applicable notice requirements. The court noted that the special board meeting in which the transaction was approved was "held on two days notice [which] means that the meeting was held in violation of [the state nonprofit corporation law] that requires written notice of a special meeting of the board of a nonprofit corporation be given to each director or member of that board at least five days before the day named for the meeting. Any action taken at that meeting was, therefore, void."[454]

• A Rhode Island court ruled that a church's removal of its board of directors, and election of a new board, in violation of the notice requirement in its bylaws could not be challenged because the membership "acquiesced" in these actions. The court acknowledged that the notice provisions were not followed in convening a church membership meeting, but it concluded that this did not invalidate the actions taken at the meeting since the church often disregarded the notice provisions in its bylaws in convening membership meetings and this long-established custom amounted to a waiver by the membership of the notice requirements.[455]

• A Washington court ruled that a church's election of new board members was legally invalid because the church failed to comply with state nonprofit corporation law in providing the members with notice of the meeting. The state nonprofit corporation law requires that notice of an annual or special meeting be delivered "not less than 10 or more than 50 days" before the date of the meeting. Since the notice of the church meeting had been given 7 days before the meeting, the election was invalid and the newly elected board members were not the duly elected board of directors of the church. The court ordered a court-supervised election of board members, consistent with state nonprofit corporation law. It concluded that this order did not violate the First Amendment guaranty of religious freedom since "the issues in this case are not ecclesiastical but rather concern property rights and nonprofit corporate law."[456]

2. Quorum

Churches should and often do prescribe in their charter or bylaws the number of members that must be present at general or special membership meetings in order for business to be transacted. This minimum number is generally called a *quorum*. State nonprofit corporation law specifies a quorum for incorporated churches that have not defined this term in their charter or bylaws. To illustrate,

---

[453] Calvary Congregational Church v. Eppinger, 2000 WL 193216 (Ohio App. 2000).

[454] In re the Lord's New Church, 817 A.2d 559 (Pa. Common. 2003).

[455] Church of God in Christ Jesus, Inc. v. Griffin, 1998 WL 895898 (R.I. Super. 1998).

[456] Kidisti Sellassie Orthodox Tewehado Eritrean Church v. Medlin, 2003 WL 22000635 (Wash. App. 2003).

section 16 of the Model Nonprofit Corporation Act provides:

> The bylaws may provide the number or percentage of members entitled to vote represented in person or by proxy, or the number or percentage of votes represented in person or by proxy, which shall constitute a quorum at a meeting of members. In the absence of any such provision, members holding one-tenth of the votes entitled to be cast on the matter to be voted upon represented in person or by proxy shall constitute a quorum.

Established church custom will control in the case of unincorporated churches having no bylaws or written regulations.

Ordinarily, so long as a quorum is present, a majority of members has the authority to act on behalf of the entire membership provided the meeting was properly called and a greater number or percentage of votes is not mandated by church charter or bylaws. This of course means that in some cases a minority of members can bind a church.[457] For example, if a church's bylaws fix the quorum at 50 percent of the voting members, then as few as 26 percent of the total membership can act on behalf of the church. On the other hand, efforts to avoid minority rule by boosting the quorum requirement may result in too few members being present to conduct business.

If a church has no bylaw provision or established custom concerning quorums, it is unnecessary to demonstrate that a majority or any other percentage of the total membership attended a particular meeting in order to validate the action taken at the meeting.[458]

3. Voting

In general

Unless otherwise restricted by charter, bylaw, statute, or custom, every member of a church congregation is entitled to vote at a membership meeting, and a majority of those members present at a duly called meeting at which a quorum is present can take action on behalf of the church. Section 15 of the Model Nonprofit Corporation Act defines the voting rights of members as follows:

> The right of the members . . . to vote may be limited, enlarged or denied to the extent specified in the articles of incorporation or the bylaws. Unless so limited, enlarged or denied, each member . . . shall be entitled to one vote on each matter submitted to a vote of the members.

Church charters, bylaws, customs, and applicable state nonprofit corporation laws occasionally impose limitations on the right to vote. To illustrate, some nonprofit corporation laws restrict the right to vote in church membership meetings to members who have contributed financially to the support of the

---

[457] Padgett v. Verner, 366 S.W.2d 545 (Tenn. 1963).

[458] State Bank v. Wilbur Mission Church, 265 P.2d 821 (Wash. 1954).

church.[459] Churches themselves sometimes enact similar resolutions or bylaws. For example, a church can adopt a resolution restricting the right to vote to members who are "paid up" and who do not neglect their offerings for three consecutive months. Such a resolution will prohibit any member from voting who has neglected to pay offerings for three consecutive months even if the failure to pay was a matter of conscience.[460]

If the right to vote is not restricted by charter, bylaw, custom, or statute, then some courts have ruled that all members of a church may vote in a church membership meeting regardless of age[461] or sex.[462] And, where the signing of a church's bylaws was a condition of church membership, a person who joined the church but failed to sign the bylaws was ineligible to vote.[463] Churches occasionally restrict the right to vote to members who have attended the church for a prescribed period, and of course such limitations must be satisfied in order for a member to be eligible to vote.

A member's right to vote may be lost by voluntary withdrawal from a church. Certainly, members who quit attending a church and publicly state that they will never be back have abandoned their membership and no longer are eligible to vote in membership meetings.[464] But in many cases determining with certainty whether a member has voluntarily withdrawn from a church is difficult, since withdrawal often is a process that sometimes is temporarily or permanently reversed. Churches can reduce confusion in this area by defining voting membership in terms of prescribed attendance or financial support.

Members wishing to contest some irregularity in a particular election or vote must object to the irregularity at the meeting. One court has ruled that objections to voting procedures must start when a vote is being taken, not months later when the events have passed from peoples' minds and the matters that were voted on have been accomplished.[465]

proxy voting

Section 15 of the Model Nonprofit Corporation Act recognizes proxy voting:

A member entitled to vote may vote in person or, unless the articles of incorporation or the bylaws otherwise provide, may vote by proxy executed

---

[459] First Slovak Church of Christ v. Kacsur, 65 A.2d 93 (N.J. 1949) (members held not qualified to vote because they did not satisfy the statutory requirement that they "contribute regularly" to the support of their church); Anthony v. Cardin, 398 N.Y.S.2d 215 (1977) (holding that contributions of ten cents per week were inadequate to satisfy the statutory requirement that voting members contribute to the support of the church).

[460] Sixth Baptist Church v. Cincore, 91 So.2d 922 (La. 1957).

[461] Hopewell Baptist Church v. Gary, 266 A.2d 593, 597 (N.J. 1970) (rejected contention that only members who had attained the age of 21 years be permitted to vote despite fact that almost two-thirds of a church's 900 members were under 21, since "[s]ound policy dictates that this court refrain from establishing such a limitation by judicial fiat"). See also In re Galilee Baptist Church, 186 So.2d 102 (Ala. 1966); Randolph v. Mount Zion Baptist Church, 53 A.2d 206 (N.J. 1947).

[462] Smith v. Riley, 424 So.2d 1166 (La. App. 1982).

[463] Kubilius v. Hawes Unitarian Congregational Church, 79 N.E.2d 5 (Mass. 1948).

[464] Lewis v. Wolfe, 413 S.W.2d 314 (Mo. 1967).

[465] Cosfol v. Varvoutis, 213 A.2d 331 (Pa. 1965).

in writing by the member or by his duly authorized attorney-in-fact. No proxy shall be valid after eleven months from the date of its execution, unless otherwise provided in the proxy . . . .

Proxy voting refers to voting by means of a substitute. For example, a church member designates another member to vote on his behalf at a membership meeting. Churches rarely intend to permit proxy voting. *Robert's Rules of Order Newly Revised* specifically discourages it:

Ordinarily, it should neither be allowed nor required, because proxy voting is incompatible with the essential characteristics of a deliberative assembly in which membership is individual, personal, and non-transferable. . . . Voting by proxy should not be permitted unless the state's corporation law . . . absolutely requires it.[466]

Few if any state nonprofit corporation laws require proxy voting. Rather, they recognize proxy voting only in the event that a corporation has not eliminated this type of voting by a provision in its charter or bylaws. This can lead to unexpected consequences when an incorporated church's charter and bylaws do not prohibit proxy voting.

Case Studies

• *During a regular church business meeting, a member moved to terminate the services of the church's minister. Of the members present, 42 voted to retain the minister, and 32 voted to remove him. In addition, one of the 32 dissidents produced a list of 57 proxy (absentee) votes to remove the minister from office. The moderator of the business meeting refused to recognize the proxy votes, and the attempt to remove the minister failed. The dissident members thereafter filed a lawsuit seeking a court order upholding the validity of proxy votes in church business meetings. A state trial court ruled against the dissidents, and the case was appealed directly to the Alaska Supreme Court. In an important decision, the court reversed the trial court and held that the proxy votes should have been counted. It based its decision on the provisions of the Alaska Nonprofit Corporations Act (under which the church had incorporated) which authorized proxy voting by members of nonprofit corporations absent a contrary provision in an organization's charter or bylaws. The court rejected the church's claim that requiring it to recognize proxy votes violated the constitutional guaranty of religious freedom. Finally, the court observed that a church could easily avoid the recognition of proxy votes by simply amending its charter or bylaws to so state. [467]*

• *A Jewish congregation called a special business meeting to determine whether or not to retain its rabbi. The congregation, by a vote of 23 to 21, voted to submit the dispute to a panel of three orthodox rabbis for a final decision. The minority challenged this vote*

---

[466] Robert's Rules of Order Newly Revised § 45 (10th ed. 2000).

[467] Herning v. Eason, 739 P.2d 167 (Alaska 1987). *But see* First Union Baptist Church v. Banks, 533 So.2d 1305 (La. App. 1988).

on the ground that four proxy votes (which were not counted at the business meeting and which agreed with the minority) were improperly disregarded at the meeting. Had they been counted, the vote would have been 25 to 23 against submitting the dispute to an arbitration panel. The court observed that the state nonprofit corporation law (under which the synagogue had been incorporated) permits proxy voting unless prohibited by the corporation's charter or bylaws. The court noted that the bylaws adopted "Robert's Rules or Order," which rejects proxy voting. The court concluded that this case perfectly illustrated the reason why proxy voting is discouraged: "It is obvious from the tenor of the membership meeting . . . that the congregation was split almost evenly among those members who 'loved' [the rabbi] or 'disliked' him vociferously. Such a meeting, by its nature, would call for extensive deliberation. Who can tell how many congregants were swayed to vote one way or the other based upon the arguments presented at the meeting?"[468]

• *A New York court refused to recognize proxy voting in a congregational meeting conducted by a synagogue. The court concluded that proxy voting was not permissible since it was not authorized by the synagogue's charter (articles of incorporation) or bylaws—even if the membership voted at a meeting to permit it. The court observed that unless specifically authorized by state nonprofit corporation law, or a church's articles of incorporation or bylaws, "proxy voting by members of a religious corporation is not authorized." As a result, proxy votes should not have been counted at the synagogue's membership meetings.*[469]

• *An Ohio court ruled that the members of a nonprofit corporation could not vote by proxy at a special business meeting since proxy voting was not authorized in the corporation's articles of incorporation or bylaws.*[470] *It noted that Ohio's Nonprofit Corporation Law specifies that "unless the articles of incorporation or the regulations otherwise provide, no member who is a natural person shall vote or act by proxy." While the corporation's bylaws allowed amendments by proxy voting, the articles of incorporation did not. Since the proposed amendment involved the definition of "members" in the articles of incorporation, proxy voting was not authorized and was invalid.*

Incorporated churches not wanting to recognize proxy voting should review their charter and bylaws to determine if either contains a provision prohibiting it. If not, an amendment would be in order. It should not be assumed that a church's formal adoption of *Robert's Rules of Order Newly Revised* will result in the prohibition of proxy voting.

how many votes are required?

After determining the qualified voting members of a church who are present at a church membership meeting, a church must ensure that all other voting requirements imposed by charter, bylaw, custom, or statute are satisfied. Often there is confusion over the number of votes required to adopt a particular action. For example, if the church bylaws require a particular vote to be by "a majority of members," does this mean a majority of the total church membership or a majority

[468] Frankel v. Kissena Jewish Center, 544 N.Y.S.2d 955 (1989).

[469] Holler v. Goldberg, 623 N.Y.S.2d 512 (Sup. 1995).

[470] Hecker v. White, 688 N.E.2d 289 (Ohio App. 1996).

of those members present at a duly convened membership meeting? If only a majority of those present at a membership meeting is required, then it is possible for an action to be adopted by a minority of the total church membership. To illustrate, if 60 percent of the total church membership attends a duly convened meeting, and 55 percent of those present vote to take a particular action, then the church has taken an official action even though only 33 percent (*i.e.*, 55 percent of 60 percent) of the total church membership assented to it. Can this be said to constitute a vote by a majority of members?

Of course, a church can and should define the term *majority of members* to avoid this confusion. For example, a provision in a church's bylaws requiring that a particular kind of vote be by majority vote of the church's total membership would preclude action by a majority of members present at a duly called meeting unless they comprised a majority of the church's entire membership. But if a church nowhere defines *majority of members*, or any other term relating to the required number of votes needed to adopt an action, the fraction or percentage of votes needed to adopt an action generally has reference to the members present at a duly called meeting and not to the entire church membership.[471] To illustrate, section 16 of the Model Nonprofit Corporation Act specifies that "a majority of the votes entitled to be cast on a matter to be voted upon by the members present or represented by proxy at a meeting at which a quorum is present shall be necessary for the adoption thereof unless a greater proportion is required by . . . the articles of incorporation of the bylaws."

One court was asked to define the term *three-fourths of the voting members present* in a controversy involving the dismissal of a pastor.[472] Certain members of the congregation became dissatisfied with a new pastor, and a special church business meeting was called to determine whether or not he should be discharged. Of the 26 members who attended the meeting, 18 voted to discharge the pastor and 8 did not vote. The church bylaws specified that "a pastor may be terminated by the church congregation . . . but only if . . . the vote equals or exceeds *three-fourths of the voting members present.*" The pastor refused to acknowledge that the vote resulted in his dismissal, since less than "three-fourths of the voting members present" had voted to dismiss him (18 is only 70 percent of 26). Several disgruntled members of the congregation disagreed with this interpretation, and petitioned a court for a ruling recognizing that the congregational vote had resulted in the dismissal of the pastor. The members argued that the phrase "three-fourths of the voting members present" should be interpreted to mean three-fourths of the individuals who actually cast votes at the business meeting rather than three-fourths of all members actually present and eligible to vote. Since all 18 of the persons who actually voted at the meeting voted to dismiss the pastor, 100 percent of the votes were cast in favor of dismissal.

A state appeals court ruled that the pastor had not been lawfully dismissed in the meeting in question. The court relied on *Robert's Rules of Order*, which had

---

[471] Mack v. Huston, 256 N.E.2d 271 (Ohio 1970). *See generally* FLETCHER CYC. CORP. § 2020 (perm. ed. 2008).

[472] Blanton v. Hahn, 763 P.2d 522 (Ariz. App. 1988).

been adopted by the church (in its bylaws) as the governing body of parliamentary procedure. The following excerpt from *Robert's Rules of Order* was quoted by the appeals court in support of its decision in favor of the pastor:

> Assume, for example, that at a meeting of a society with a total membership of 150 and a quorum of 10, there are 30 members present, of whom 25 participate in a given counted vote. Then, with respect to that vote: a two-thirds vote is 17; a vote of two-thirds of the members present is 20; a vote of two-thirds of the entire membership is 100 . . . . Regarding these bases for determining a voting result, the following points should be noted—voting requirements based on the number of members present, while possible, are generally undesirable. *Since an abstention in such cases has the same effect as a negative vote, these bases deny members the right to maintain a neutral position by abstaining. For the same reason, members present who fail to vote through indifference rather than through deliberate neutrality may affect the result negatively.*[473]

According to this language, concluded the court, the phrase "three-fourths of the voting members present" meant three-fourths "of the individuals present and eligible to vote." Accordingly, the pastor had not been dismissed by the congregational vote since less than three-fourths of the members present and eligible to vote had voted to dismiss him.

If a church's charter, constitution, or bylaws do not designate the required percentage of votes for an affirmative action, then there is a presumption of majority rule. The United States Supreme Court has observed that "majority rule is generally employed in the governance of religious societies."[474] Other courts similarly have concluded that majority representation is presumed to apply to church determinations unless such a presumption is overcome by express provision in the church's organizational documents, or by a provision in the constitution or bylaws of a parent denomination.[475]

Occasionally, a church's charter, bylaws, and, in some cases, its constitution contain conflicting provisions regarding the required number of votes necessary for adoption of a particular action. As has been noted elsewhere, provisions in the charter prevail over provisions in the constitution, bylaws, or resolutions; provisions in the constitution prevail over provisions in the bylaws, or resolutions; and provisions in the bylaws prevail over provisions in resolutions.[476] In most cases, an incorporated church is bound by the provisions of state nonprofit corporation law only where it has not expressly provided otherwise in its own charter, constitution, or bylaws.

---

[473] *Id.* at 524 (emphasis in original).

[474] Jones v. Wolf, 443 U.S. 595, 607 (1979).

[475] Foss v. Dykstra, 342 N.W.2d 220 (S.D. 1983).

[476] *See* § 6-02.2, *supra.*

Case Study

• *The South Carolina Supreme Court ruled that it lacked the authority to resolve an internal church dispute regarding the percentage vote required to retain the pastor in a vote of confidence. The group supporting the pastor argued that the church bylaws required a three-fourths vote of the congregation for a "no-confidence" vote, while the group opposing the pastor argued that only a simple majority vote was needed. The court ruled that it was without legal authority to "dictate procedures for the church to follow in terminating its pastor."[477]*

other methods of voting (by hand, secret ballot, absentee voting)

Votes can be cast orally, by show of hands, or by secret ballot. The method used is governed by the church's charter or bylaws. If the charter and bylaws are silent, established church custom will control. The members present at a meeting can also approve of a particular manner of voting if the church charter or bylaws do not speak to the subject. It has been held that a vote will be upheld even if it was not conducted by secret ballot as required by the corporate bylaws if no one objected to the vote during the meeting.[478] *Robert's Rules of Order Newly Revised*, which has been adopted by many churches, specifies:

The bylaws of the organization may prescribe that the vote be by ballot in certain cases, as in the election of officers and in admission to membership. Any vote related to charges or proposed charges before or after a trial of a member or an officer should always be by ballot. Except as may be otherwise provided by the bylaws, a vote by ballot can be ordered by a majority vote—which may be desirable in any case where it is believed that members may thereby be more likely to vote their true sentiments.[479]

Absentee voting is not ordinarily permitted unless expressly sanctioned by charter, bylaw, custom, or statute. Again, *Robert's Rules of Order Newly Revised*, specifies:

It is a fundamental principle of parliamentary law that the right to vote is limited to the members of an organization who are actually present at the time the vote is taken in a legal meeting. Exceptions to this rule must be expressly stated in the bylaws. . . . An organization should never adopt a bylaw permitting a question to be decided by a voting procedure in which the votes of persons who attend a meeting are counted together with ballots mailed in by absentees, since in practice such a procedure is likely to be unfair.[480]

---

[477] Knotts v. Williams, 462 S.E.2d 288 (S.C. 1995).

[478] FLETCHER CYC. CORP. § 2017 (perm. ed. 2008).

[479] ROBERT'S RULES OF ORDER NEWLY REVISED § 45 (10th ed. 2000).

[480] *Id.*

Case Study

• *A Utah court ruled that an action taken by members of a nonprofit association by mail-in ballot was invalid since it was not authorized by nonprofit corporation law or the association's own bylaws.*[481]

Minutes

§ 6-12.2

Key point 6-12.2. *Written minutes should be maintained for every church membership meeting. Minutes should reference (1) the date of the meeting, (2) the number of members present, (3) the progression of every action from motion to final action, (4) some statement that each adopted action was approved by the necessary number of votes, and (5) a verbatim transcript of each approved action.*

The church secretary should prepare written minutes of every church membership meeting, being careful to note (1) the date of the meeting, (2) the number of members present, (3) the progression of every action from motion to final action, (4) some statement that each adopted action was approved by the necessary number of votes (a tally of the votes for and against a particular action should be inserted in the minutes if the vote is close or the action is of an extraordinary nature), and (5) a verbatim transcript of each approved action. Minutes should be signed by the church secretary, but this is not a legal requirement.[482]

The purpose of the minutes is to memorialize in a permanent and official form the actions taken by a church's membership. It has been said that the minutes are the "voice" of the corporation, and that a corporation will be bound by representations contained in its minutes that are relied upon by outsiders, even if the minutes were irregular.[483]

Parliamentary Procedure

§ 6-12.3

Key point 6-12.3. *Every church should adopt a system of parliamentary procedure to govern membership meetings. While Robert's Rules of Order Newly Revised, is a commonly used system, it is not the only available system and will not apply unless a church has adopted it in its governing documents.*

An organization may adopt any procedure that it desires for the conduct of membership meetings. *Robert's Rules of Order Newly Revised*, or any other body of parliamentary procedure is not applicable unless specifically adopted.[484]

---

[481] Levanger v. Vincent, 3 P.3d 187 (Utah App. 2000).

[482] *Id.*

[483] Fletcher Cyc. Corp. § 2190 (perm. ed. 2008).

[484] Abbey Properties Co. v. Presidential Insurance Co., 119 So.2d 74 (Fla. 1960). *See also* Blanton v. Hahn, 763 P.2d 522 (Ariz. App. 1988); Frankel v. Kissena Jewish Center, 544 N.Y.S.2d 955 (1989).

Churches can and should select a specific body of parliamentary procedure by an appropriate clause in the church charter or bylaws. If a particular system of parliamentary procedure has been used by common consent long enough to constitute a church practice or custom, then it probably would be considered as binding as if specifically adopted by a provision in the church's charter or bylaws. If no body of parliamentary procedure has been adopted, either expressly or by custom, it has been held that the ordinary rules of parliamentary law should be observed in the conduct of a meeting.[485] It also has been held that the courts may review an action taken at a church membership meeting to ensure compliance with applicable parliamentary procedure.[486]

There are three important considerations for churches to note regarding parliamentary procedure:

First, churches should not assume that *Robert's Rules of Order Newly Revised*, is the only system of parliamentary procedure. It is not. On the contrary, there are dozens of alternative systems of parliamentary procedure, some of which are excellent (some would say superior) alternatives.

Second, many churches adopted the original *Robert's Rules of Order*, or one of the early revisions. The original text was published in 1876, and it has been revised on seven occasions. The current revision was released in 1981. Obviously, churches that select "Robert's Rules" should be sure to identify this system of parliamentary procedure as "the most recent revision of *Robert's Rules of Order*." Otherwise, they may have to resort to obsolete rules to resolve parliamentary questions.

Third, no system of parliamentary procedure should serve as a substitute for specific provisions in a church's bylaws. In other words, the fact that a church wanting to prohibit absentee voting has adopted *Robert's Rules of Order Newly Revised*, should not serve as substitute for a bylaw provision prohibiting absentee voting. There is no assurance that a civil court would regard the adoption of "Robert's Rules" as an exception to the general rule that state nonprofit corporation law will control when a church's bylaws are silent.

Once it is determined that a particular body of parliamentary procedure has been adopted by a church, the civil courts have expressed willingness to apply and enforce that procedure on the ground that no doctrine or substantive ecclesiastical question is involved.[487] Similarly, a federal appeals court ruled that the United States Constitution bars the civil courts from resolving disputes over parliamentary rulings.[488] Noting that the contested parliamentary action (made at the 1985 Southern Baptist Convention) had been reviewed and upheld by the highest Southern Baptist tribunal, the court concluded that "where religious organizations establish rules for their internal discipline and governance, and tribunals for adjudicating disputes over these matters, the Constitution requires that civil courts accept their decisions as binding upon them."

---

[485] Randolph v. Mount Zion Baptist Church, 53 A.2d 206 (N.J. 1947).

[486] Umberger v. Johns, 363 So.2d 63 (Fla. 1978).

[487] Umberger v. Johns, 363 So.2d 63 (Fla. App. 1978).

[488] Crowder v. Southern Baptist Convention, 828 F.2d 718 (11th Cir. 1987).

Effect of Procedural Irregularities §6-12.4

Key point 6-12.4. *Most courts refuse to intervene in church disputes concerning the validity of a membership meeting that was not conducted in accordance with the procedural requirements specified in the church's governing documents. However, some courts are willing to intervene in such disputes if they can do so without inquiring into religious doctrine or polity.*

As noted in the previous section, many courts have been willing to resolve challenges to the legality of actions taken by a church during a membership meeting that was conducted in violation of procedural requirements (i.e., notice, quorum, or voting) specified in the church's governing documents, so long as no interpretation of church doctrine is required.[489] But other courts have refused to intervene in the internal affairs of churches, and will not review decisions made in church membership meetings even if the church disregarded procedural requirements specified in its governing documents.[490] This view generally is based on the assumption that the First Amendment prohibits courts from interfering with the purely internal affairs of churches. Such an interpretation of the First Amendment may be too broad under the prevailing interpretation of that Amendment by the United States Supreme Court.

It is true that there is no room for civil court review of any internal church decision based on the interpretation of religious doctrine. On this point all courts would agree. But, many internal church disputes involve the interpretation of purely secular language in church charters, bylaws, deeds, and trusts. The Supreme Court has suggested that there is room for marginal civil court review of the internal decisions of churches and church tribunals where the reviewing court can resolve the dispute solely on the basis of "neutral principles" of law.[491] The Court specifically held that "neutral principles" of law include nondoctrinal language in charters, deeds, and bylaws. One court in upholding the majority view observed that "we have no hesitancy in holding that this controversy is properly before us, our decisions being controlled entirely by neutral principles of law."[492]

Procedural requirements pertaining to notice, quorums, and voting generally involve no references to religious doctrine and so actions adopted at a church membership meeting conducted in violation of a church's procedural requirements

---

[489] Third Missionary Baptist Church v. Garrett, 158 N.W.2d 771 (Iowa 1968); Hollins v. Edmonds, 616 S.W.2d 801 (Ky. 1981); Bangor Spiritualist Church, Inc. v. Littlefield, 330 A.2d 793 (Me. 1975); Fast v. Smyth, 527 S.W.2d 673 (Mo. 1975); Atkins v. Walker, 200 S.E.2d 641 (N.C. 1973); Old Folk Mission Center v. McTizic, 631 S.W.2d 433 (Tenn. 1981).

[490] *See, e.g.,* White v. First United Baptist Church, 2002 WL 1575243 (Mich. App. 2002); Rodyk v. Ukrainian Autocephalic Orthodox Church, 296 N.Y.S.2d 496 (1968), *aff'd,* 328 N.Y.S.2d 685 (1972); Hill v. Sargent, 615 S.W.2d 300 (Tex. 1981).

[491] Jones v. Wolf, 443 U.S. 595 (1979). The Court in *Jones* expressly repudiated the apparent holding in Serbian Eastern Orthodox Diocese v. Milivojevich, 426 U.S. 696 (1976), that the courts *must defer* to the determinations of religious tribunals within hierarchical churches by noting that the first amendment did not require such a rule where no issue of religious doctrine is involved.

[492] Bangor Spiritualist Church, Inc. v. Littlefield, 330 A.2d 793 (Me. 1975).

occasionally are invalidated by a civil court.[493] In the case of incorporated churches, this rule has been justified on the ground that a religious corporation is an artificial entity created by law and capable of acting only in the manner prescribed by state law or its own internal regulations, and therefore compliance with such procedural requirements is a prerequisite to a valid meeting.[494]

The subject of civil court intervention in internal church disputes is addressed more fully in chapter 9.

Case Studies

• *The Alabama Supreme Court ruled that a trial court acted properly in vacating a church election that was conducted in violation of the church's governing document. The court began its opinion by noting that it had on a number of occasions "exercised jurisdiction to determine whether an election meeting of a church, or a similar meeting, was conducted so improperly as to render its results void." Further, it noted that while the civil courts "will not assume jurisdiction to resolve disputes regarding their spiritual or ecclesiastical affairs . . . there is jurisdiction to resolve questions of civil or property rights." The court concluded that it could "properly exercise jurisdiction, given the financial and property rights of the church that were involved . . . and that the election violated the book of discipline in several material respects and also violated basic standards of due process." It emphasized that the parties in this case "argue no issues of differences in religious faith or creed, and argue no spiritual conflicts, or ecclesiastical doctrine. Rather, the underlying dispute revolves around the property of the church—control over its financial assets and affairs—and not God." The court concluded: "The record indeed supports a finding that . . . the procedures for elections, as enumerated in the book of discipline, were not followed. Thus, we hold today that the trial court did not err in setting aside the election."*[495]

• *A Florida court ruled that a church board's attempts to amend the articles of incorporation were invalid because procedural requirements were not followed. The court concluded that the First Amendment religion clauses did not prevent it from resolving this dispute since the case "implicates neutral legal principles only" and "precedent supports judicial resolution of the parties' dispute over corporate assets, the corporation's religious purposes notwithstanding." It further observed: "The doctrine of either side is . . . of no moment here. The courts are not concerned with the articles of faith of either, nor with the question as to whether or not the articles of faith or the religious doctrines of either are respected and observed. The only question which is sought to be presented here which may be addressed to the courts is in regard to the right to control the church property. The parties have asked neither us nor the trial court to become entangled in essentially religious controversies or intervene on behalf of groups espousing particular doctrinal beliefs."*[496]

• *A Louisiana court ruled that a trial court had the authority to resolve a dispute regarding the legal validity of a church membership meeting since it could do so by applying provisions of the state nonprofit corporation law involving no interpretation*

---

[493] *Id.*

[494] *Id.*

[495] Yates v. El Bethel Primitive Baptist Church, 847 So.2d 331 (Ala. 2002).

[496] The Word of Life Ministry, Inc. v. Miller, 778 So.2d 360 (Fla. App. 2001).

*of religious doctrine. The court concluded: "The procedural niceties attending the
election of a board of directors for a nonprofit religious corporation have nothing to
do with religious law, custom or policy and are not ecclesiastical matters within the
exclusive domain of a particular religious group."*[497]

• *A New Jersey court held that procedural irregularities in a congregational meeting did
not affect the congregation's vote to affiliate with a denomination. A local congregation
was duly informed that a vote would be taken at its annual business meeting on whether
or not to affiliate with the Catholic Church. The pastor of the church adjourned the
business meeting and rescheduled it for a week later to allow representatives of the
Catholic Church to speak. At the rescheduled meeting the congregation voted to affiliate
with the Catholic Church. Members who voted against the affiliation sought a court
order invalidating the vote on the ground that it was conducted at an improperly called
meeting. The dissenters pointed out that the church's bylaws specified that only the
board of trustees had the authority to adjourn and reschedule congregational meetings.
The court concluded it would not invalidate the vote of the congregation despite the fact
that the meeting was conducted in violation of the church's bylaws. It based this result
on two factors. First, the civil courts have the authority to resolve property disputes
within local congregations so long as they can do so without interpreting religious
doctrine. There were two property interests involved in this case, the court observed—
"the right to worship in a familiar surrounding," and a lease agreement entered into
between the congregation and Catholic Church following the vote to affiliate. Second,
the court concluded that the subject of the congregational meeting (whether or not to
affiliate with the Catholic Church) was religious in nature and therefore the civil courts
had no authority to interfere with what was done even though the bylaws had been
violated. The court observed: "This court can discern a no more spiritual matter than a
determination by the congregation of who should shepherd its flock. The majority of the
congregation . . . chose to invite the priests of [the Catholic Church] to be its spiritual
leaders. . . . To invalidate [the meeting and vote] would subjugate the will of the
majority on the basis of a minor procedural infraction."*[498]

• *A New York court ruled that a congregational meeting called by members of a synagogue
to vote on the rehiring of a dismissed rabbi was not valid since it was not called according
to the synagogue's bylaws. The synagogue's membership was bitterly divided over the
continued retention of their rabbi. The dispute was submitted to an arbitration panel
which ruled that the synagogue's board of trustees was authorized to discontinue the
rabbi's employment. In response to this ruling, a group of ten members called for a
special meeting "concerning the tenure of our rabbi." At this meeting, the membership
voted to rehire the rabbi. Members of the congregation asked a civil court to determine
the legality of this special meeting, and the vote that was taken. A court ruled that the
meeting was legally invalid because it was not called in accordance with the synagogue's
bylaws. The bylaws permit any ten members to call for a special meeting, provided that at
least five days notice of the meeting is given to members by the recording secretary. The
court concluded that "since it is clear that the notice was not sent by the secretary of the
synagogue, as required by the bylaws, to the members in good standing as of the date of
mailing, I declare that the [special business meeting] was not validly held."*[499]

---

[497] Mount Gideon Baptist Church v. Robinson, 812 So.2d 758 (La. App. 2002).

[498] Ardito v. Board of Trustees, 658 A.2d 327 (N.J. Super. Ch. 1995).

[499] Holler v. Goldberg, 623 N.Y.S.2d 512 (Sup. 1995).

• *A North Carolina court ruled that it was barred by the First Amendment from resolving a lawsuit brought by church members claiming that the decision by a church congregation to incorporate as a nonprofit corporation was invalid because it was made at a meeting that failed to comply with the procedure specified in the church bylaws. The court observed that a court's exercise of jurisdiction is improper where "purely ecclesiastical questions and controversies" are involved. An ecclesiastical matter is one which concerns doctrine, creed, or form of worship of the church, or the adoption and enforcement within a religious association of needful laws and regulations for the government of membership, and the power of excluding from such associations those deemed unworthy of membership by the legally constituted authorities of the church; and all such matters are within the province of church courts and their decisions will be respected by civil tribunals." The court pointed out that "numerous ambiguities exist in the bylaws, conflicts remain between both parties' interpretations of the bylaws, and long-established church customs exist that may alter the interpretation of the notice requirements listed in the bylaws," and that both sides disagreed about the type of meeting actually held. As a result, to resolve this lawsuit a court "would be required to delve into ecclesiastical matters regarding how the church interprets the bylaws' notice requirements and types of meetings," and therefore the case had to be dismissed.[500]*

Judicial Supervision of Church Elections
§6-12.5

Key point 6-12.5. *Some courts will supervise church elections to ensure compliance with the procedural requirements specified in the church's governing documents, if they can do so without inquiring into religious doctrine or polity.*

Some courts have been willing to supervise a church election to ensure compliance with applicable procedural requirements if the church requests such supervision or if certain members allege that the church has disregarded procedural requirements in the past.[501] To illustrate, in one case, former members who had been expelled by their church asserted that the meeting at which the congregation voted to expel them had not been called with adequate notice. The trial court held that the meeting at which the dissidents had been expelled was invalid due to inadequate notice. It also scheduled an election at which the congregation would determine, by majority vote, the proper membership of the church; prescribed the notice to be given; provided for the counting of ballots by a court officer; and ordered an accounting of all church funds. The Alabama Supreme Court upheld the decision of the trial court, noting that "it is proper for the courts to inquire whether a congregational meeting, at which church business

---

[500] Emory v. Jackson Chapel First Missionary Baptist Church, 598 S.E.2d 667 (N.C. App. 2004).

[501] First Union Baptist Church v. Banks, 533 So.2d 1305 (La. App. 1988); LeBlanc v. Davis, 432 So.2d 239 (La. 1983); Fast v. Smyth, 527 S.W.2d 673 (Mo. 1975); Second Baptist Church v. Mount Zion Baptist Church, 466 P.2d 212 (Nev. 1970); Rector, Church Wardens and Vestrymen of St. Bartholomew's Church v. Committee to Preserve St. Bartholomew's Church, 56 N.Y.2d 71 (1982).

is to be transacted, was preceded by adequate notice to the full membership, and whether, once called, the meeting was conducted in an orderly manner and the expulsion was the act of the authority within the church having the power to order it."[502] However, "once the court is presented with sufficient evidence regarding the regularity of the meeting, it will then generally refuse to inquire further as to the fruits of the meeting."

On the other hand, the same court ruled that it had no authority to determine which members in a Baptist church are qualified to vote in a church election. A dispute arose in a local Baptist church, and certain members petitioned a state trial court to order a church election to resolve the matter. At the election the votes of 35 individuals were challenged and not counted. The result of the ballots counted was a 74 to 74 tie. One group of members petitioned the court to have the challenged votes counted. The trial court refused to grant this request, noting that "if this court ordered the challenged ballots to be counted, it would be determining that they were members who were eligible to vote. This it cannot do . . . ."

The court acknowledged that its refusal to order the challenged ballots to be counted "leaves the [church] without redress in the courts for even arbitrary acts of a preacher in either falsely challenging voters or intentionally bringing in non-members to vote." However, the trial court concluded that "there is nothing this court can do about it" since prior rulings of the state supreme court prohibited courts from resolving church membership issues. The trial court's ruling was appealed to the Alabama Supreme Court, which agreed that its previous rulings "do not authorize courts to determine the eligibility of church members to vote," and that "to order that certain votes be counted, which theretofore were not counted, would have been tantamount to doing that very thing, i.e., determining eligibility." The supreme court concluded: "In each Baptist church the majority of the members of the church control the business of the church. Also, all the members of a Baptist church are entitled to vote at a congregational meeting, regardless of age. However, *the issue as to which members are eligible to vote is a matter within the discretion of the members of the church.* . . . Because each Baptist church is a democratic institution whose membership possesses the right to vote, perforce it is the church itself under its rules that must examine the eligibility of its individual members to participate in that democracy."[503]

Another court ruled that it had the authority to order a church election since the church board refused to call one.[504]

Case Studies

*   *The Alabama Supreme Court ruled that it was proper for a trial court to resolve an internal church dispute over a church election since both sides to the dispute agreed to civil court involvement. The court began its opinion by observing that "civil courts*

---

[502] McKinney v. Twenty-fifth Avenue Baptist Church, Inc., 514 So.2d 837 (Ala. 1987).

[503] Mount Olive Baptist Church v. Williams, 529 So.2d 972 (Ala. 1988).

[504] Willis v. Davis, 323 S.W.2d 847 (Ky. 1959).

cannot adjudicate religious disputes concerning spiritual or ecclesiastical matters, but the courts can resolve disputes concerning civil or property rights." However, the court noted that "certainly, in this case, where both sides agreed to let the court determine the eligibility of the voters, this court has the authority to hear the case."[505]

• *A Georgia court ruled that a trial court did not violate the First Amendment guaranty of religious freedom when it intervened in a local church dispute and called a supervised membership meeting to determine the identity of lawful voting members. The court concluded: "The trial court did not exceed its authority, as it limited the election procedures to resolving the issue of which faction represented the majority, the only proper question before the court. Moreover, the election called for majority rule, which was in compliance with church practice and the law governing congregational churches."*[506]

• *A Missouri court ordered the trial court to call a meeting of a church's members to elect a board in compliance with state law.*[507]

• *A Texas state appeals court concluded that a trial court had the authority to call a new church election. The court defended the trial court's action by noting that "an election was held which resulted in [the pastor's discharge], that he has refused to accept the termination, that he has since interfered with church services and will continue to do so . . . and will dissipate funds and property owned by the church unless he is restrained from doing so." The court rejected the pastor's claim that the trial court's intervention violated the constitutional guaranty of religious freedom. It noted that "the vote of a majority of the members of a Baptist church is generally binding in any matter touching the church government or affairs," and that "rules and regulations, including election procedures, made by church functionaries or by long usage will be enforced by the civil courts if not in conflict with some civil law bearing upon the subject of such rules and regulations." It concluded that the trial court had "sought to act in accord with church rules and regulations as dictated by long established custom and usage" and accordingly did "not usurp church authority."*[508]

• *A Washington court ruled that a church's election of new board members was legally invalid because the church failed to comply with state nonprofit corporation law in providing the members with notice of the meeting. The court ordered a court-supervised election of board members, consistent with state nonprofit corporation law. It concluded that this order did not violate the First Amendment guaranty of religious freedom since "the issues in this case are not ecclesiastical but rather concern property rights and nonprofit corporate law."*[509]

---

[505] Bacher v. Metcalf, 611 So.2d 1030 (Ala. 1992).

[506] Howard v. Johnson, 592 S.E.2d 93 (Ga. App. 2003).

[507] First Missionary Baptist Church v. Rollins, 151 S.W.3d 846 (Mo. App. 2004).

[508] Ex parte McClain, 762 S.W.2d 238 (Tex. App. 1988).

[509] Kidisti Sellassie Orthodox Tewehado Eritrean Church v. Medlin, 2003 WL 22000635 (Wash. App. 2003).

Who May Attend

§ 6-12.6

Key point 6-12.6. *Whether or not a church can prevent an individual from attending a membership meeting will depend on the provisions of the church's governing documents as well as the system of parliamentary procedure adopted by the church.*

Who is entitled to be present at a church meeting? Who may lawfully be excluded? These questions often cause confusion, particularly in the context of schismatic churches in which one or more factions desire to prevent attorneys, news media personnel, or members of the public from attending. The following considerations will determine to what extent a church can exclude nonmembers from attending church membership meetings:

First, the charter, constitution, and bylaws of the church should be consulted to determine if they address the question. Ordinarily, they do not.

Second, determine what body of parliamentary procedure the church has adopted. Many systems of parliamentary procedure permit nonmembers to be excluded from a membership meeting. One authority states the rule as follows:

Nonmembers, on the other hand—or a particular nonmember or group of nonmembers—can be excluded any time from part or all of a meeting of a society, or from all of its meetings. Such exclusion can be effected by a ruling of the chair in cases of disorder, or by the adoption of a rule on the subject, or by an appropriate motion as the need arises—a motion of the latter nature being a question of privilege.[510]

Third, many states and the federal government have enacted public meeting laws which generally provide that meetings of specified governmental agencies, commissions, and boards, at which official acts are taken, must be open to the public. Such laws, often called sunshine acts, ordinarily do not apply to private, nonprofit organizations,[511] and they certainly do not apply to entities, such as churches, receiving no tax revenues and having no regulatory authority or relationship with any governmental body. The fact that a church is incorporated will not subject it to the provisions of public meeting laws.[512]

Powers of a Local Church

§6-13

It often is necessary to determine the nature and extent of a church's powers, for a church's actions may be subject to challenge if they exceed the church's

---

[510] ROBERT'S RULES OF ORDER NEWLY REVISED § 61 (10th ed. 2000).

[511] *See, e.g.,* Marston v. Wood, 425 So.2d 582 (Fla. App. 1982) (public meeting law did not apply to a law school committee organized to select a new dean); Perlongo v. Iron River Co-op TV Antenna Corp., 332 N.W.2d 502 (Mich. App. 1983) (state public meeting law did not apply to a nonprofit, nonstock corporation).

[512] Perlongo v. Iron River Co-op TV Antenna Corp., 332 N.W.2d 502 (Mich. App. 1983).

authority. As has been noted elsewhere,[513] unincorporated churches possess only such authority as is granted to them by state law. Many states have enacted legislation enabling unincorporated churches to sue and be sued and to hold property in the name of trustees. But without any specific delegation of authority from the state, an unincorporated church has no legal powers and must act in the name of its members.[514]

In many states a church may incorporate under either a general nonprofit corporation law or a religious corporation law. State nonprofit corporation law ordinarily confers several specific powers upon organizations that incorporate. To illustrate, section 5 of the Model Nonprofit Corporation Act states that a corporation has the authority:

1. to exist perpetually;

2. to sue and be sued;

3. to acquire or dispose of property;

4. to lend money to its employees other than its officers and directors;

5. to make contracts, incur liabilities, borrow money, and issue notes and bonds;

6. to lend money;

7. to elect or appoint officers and directors; (8) to adopt bylaws not inconsistent with the articles of incorporation;

8. to indemnify directors or officers against expenses incurred in connection with lawsuits arising because of the performance of their duties (but there is no indemnification if the director or officer is found to have been guilty of negligence or other misconduct);

9. to establish pension plans;

10. to cease its corporate activities; and

11. to have and exercise all powers necessary or convenient to accomplish any of the purposes for which the corporation is organized.

Some courts have recognized that statutes governing religious corporations reflect a public policy of granting religious organizations wide latitude in the conduct of their affairs, both spiritual and temporal.[515]

It is important to recognize that corporations derive their existence and powers from the state. It follows that corporations are without authority to do

---

[513] *See* § 6-01, *supra*.

[514] Jacobs v. St. Mark's Baptist Church, 415 So.2d 253 (La. App. 1982).

[515] Hopewell Baptist Church v. Gary, 266 A.2d 593 (N.J. 1970), *aff'd*, 270 A.2d 409 (N.J. 1970).

any act not expressly authorized by statute or implied from a power specifically granted.[516]

Some states place restrictions on the power of religious corporations to own property. These restrictions include limitations on the number of acres a religious corporation may own, limitations on the total dollar value of the property a religious corporation may own, limiting the property a religious corporation may own to only such property as is reasonably necessary for the corporation's purposes, and limiting the kinds of property that a religious corporation may own.

Some states limit the power of religious corporations to sell or encumber property. For example, some states limit the power of churches to sell property without court approval,[517] or without a specified percentage of voter approval.[518] A number of states limit the power of religious corporations to receive testamentary gifts. These restrictions generally fall into two categories: statutes limiting the amount of property that a religious organization may receive under a will, and statutes invalidating any testamentary gift to a religious organization if the will was executed within a prescribed time before the grantor's death. For example, some states prohibit certain testamentary gifts to a church if the will is executed within 90 days before the grantor's death.[519] A few states invalidate certain testamentary gifts that exceed a specified portion of the total value of the grantor's estate.[520] The subject of state limitations on testamentary gifts to charity is discussed in detail elsewhere.[521]

The powers of churches affiliated with religious hierarchies often are restricted or regulated by the parent ecclesiastical body. For example, the local churches of some denominations possess either limited authority or no authority to purchase or sell property, incur obligations, elect officers, or adopt bylaws.[522]

In addition to conferring specific, express powers upon charitable corporations, state nonprofit corporation laws typically contain a provision granting to incorporated charities the power to have and exercise all powers necessary or convenient to effect any or all of the purposes for which the organization is organized. Such a provision enables a church corporation to list in its charter various powers not specifically delegated by state corporation law. Therefore, in determining whether a church is empowered to take a particular action, the church charter must be reviewed in addition to the statute under which the church was incorporated. It is important to note, however, that a church may

---

[516] Succession of Fisher, 103 So.2d 276 (La. 1958); Babcock Memorial Presbyterian Church v. Presbytery of Baltimore, 464 A.2d 1008 (Md. App. 1983); Old Folks Mission Center v. McTizic, 631 S.W.2d 433 (Tenn. 1981).

[517] Application of Church of St. Francis De Sales, 442 N.Y.S.2d 741 (1981) (applying section 12 of the New York Religious Corporations Law).

[518] MODEL NONPROFIT CORPORATION ACT § 44 (requiring approval of a two-thirds majority for a sale of all or substantially all of the property of a corporation).

[519] GA. CODE § 53-2-10; MISS. CODE ANN. § 91-5-31.

[520] OHIO REV. CODE § 2107.06.

[521] *See* § 9-03, *infra*.

[522] Babcock Memorial Presbyterian Church v. Presbytery of Baltimore, 464 A.2d 1008 (Md. App. 1983).

not include a power in its charter that would contravene law or public policy.[523] It is a well-settled rule of law that religious corporations, like business corporations, also possess *implied authority* to take all actions that are reasonably necessary in order to accomplish those powers expressly granted by charter or statute.[524]

In summary, in determining whether a church corporation possesses the authority to take a particular action, the following analysis should be employed:

1. Review the statute under which the church was incorporated to determine if the power was expressly granted.

2. Review the church's charter to see if the power was expressly granted.

3. If the proposed church action is not expressly authorized by either statute or the church's charter, determine whether the church possesses implied authority to perform the act. Generally, a church possesses implied authority to take any action reasonably necessary to carry out the powers expressly granted by charter or state corporation law.

4. A corporation is never authorized to perform an act that is prohibited by law or public policy.

ultra vires = an act performed by a church corporation in excess of its express and implied powers

The courts generally have held that a corporation's bylaws cannot confer powers upon the corporation that are not granted by statute or charter, although the bylaws may regulate the manner in which a corporation's powers are exercised.[525] It is often said that corporations lack the authority to perform any act that is illegal, contrary to public policy, or that would constitute a public nuisance. Thus, it has been held that a church has no authority to exercise powers, even those expressly granted, in such a way as to cause a disturbance of the peace.[526]

Since most church corporations are incorporated under statutes expressly limiting them to nonprofit or religious purposes, churches generally have no authority to engage in substantial commercial enterprises for profit. An act performed by a church corporation in excess of its express and implied powers is referred to as *ultra vires*. Considerable confusion surrounds the

---

[523] *See generally* FLETCHER CYC. CORP. § 2477 (perm. ed. 2008). Molasky Enterprises, Inc. v. Carps, Inc., 615 S.W.2d 83, 86-87 (Mo. 1981) ("The powers and existence of a corporation are derived from the state creating it. It functions under its charter which is a contract between it and the state in which it is organized. The statutory laws of the state applicable to it enter into and become a part of its articles of incorporation.").

[524] Synod of Chesapeake, Inc. v. City of Newark, 254 A.2d 611, 613-614 (Del. 1969) ("Any contemporary church group, to be worth its salt, must necessarily perform nonreligious functions . . . . Accordingly, such activities may not be banned as unrelated to church ritual."); Sales v. Southern Trust Co., 185 S.W.2d 623 (Tenn. 1945).

[525] FLETCHER CYC. CORP. § 2494 (perm. ed. 2008).

[526] *See* § 7-09, *infra*.

legal status of *ultra vires* actions. A majority of states permit *ultra vires* acts of a corporation to be challenged in only the following three situations:

1. A proceeding by a member or director against the corporation seeking an injunction prohibiting the corporation from doing an unauthorized act.

2. A proceeding by the corporation against the officers or directors of the corporation for exceeding their authority.

3. A proceeding by the state to dissolve the corporation or to enjoin the corporation from performing unauthorized acts.

If the *ultra vires* act was a contract that has already been executed, it is generally held that the parties to the contract are entitled to compensation for the loss or damages sustained by them as a result of a judicial determination setting aside or prohibiting the performance of the contract.[527]

Merger and Consolidation §6-14

Key point 6-14. *Two or more religious congregations can merge or consolidate. In a merger, one corporation absorbs the other and remains in existence while the other is dissolved, whereas in a consolidation a new corporation is created and the consolidating corporations are extinguished. The procedure for merging and consolidating incorporated churches is specified by state nonprofit corporation law.*

Although the terms *merger* and *consolidation* frequently are used interchangeably, they have separate legal meanings. In a merger, one corporation absorbs the other and remains in existence while the other is dissolved, whereas in a consolidation a new corporation is created and the consolidating corporations are extinguished.

One court has observed that a church's decision to either merge or consolidate is a religious question that should be of concern to no one other than the congregations involved, that the choice is one to be made by the respective members in the exercise of their religious beliefs, and that their freedom to make this choice is guaranteed by the First Amendment against federal or state interference.[528]

Although the state may not interfere with a church's decision to merge or consolidate, a church must follow those procedures in its own governing documents or in applicable state nonprofit corporation law for a valid merger or consolidation to occur. State nonprofit corporation laws governing mergers and consolidations often are separate and distinct. As a result, a church seeking to merge with another church may not employ a state law governing consolidations, and two churches desiring to consolidate may not use a state law governing mergers. State nonprofit

[527] *See generally* Fletcher Cyc. Corp. ch. 40 (perm. ed. 2008); Free For All Missionary Baptist Church, Inc. v. Southeastern Beverage & Ice Equipment Co., Inc., 218 S.E.2d 169 (Ga. 1975).

[528] Mount Zion Baptist Church v. Second Baptist Church, 432 P.2d 328 (Nev. 1967).

corporation law may contain a single procedure governing both mergers and consolidations, but this must not be assumed. The Model Nonprofit Corporation Act contains separate procedures, and this is the practice in most states.

Unincorporated congregational churches generally are not restricted by state corporation law, and may merge or consolidate whenever the respective congregations of the merging or consolidating churches so desire, provided that applicable provisions in each church's bylaws are followed. However, an unincorporated church and an incorporated church will not be permitted to merge under a state nonprofit law requiring that both of the merging churches be incorporated.[529]

Incorporated churches, like any other form of corporation, derive their corporate existence and powers from the state. It follows that an incorporated church has the power to merge or consolidate only if such power is expressly delegated by state corporation law. Most religious and nonprofit corporation laws grant churches the power to merge or consolidate. Such laws typically prescribe the following procedure:

1. **Board resolutions.** The board of directors of each church desiring to merge or consolidate adopts a resolution approving of the proposed plan and submits it to a vote of members having voting rights at a general or special meeting.

2. **Notice.** Written notice of the proposed plan is given to each member eligible to vote.

3. **Approval.** The proposed plan is adopted if at least two-thirds of the votes cast approve of the plan.

4. **Articles of merger or consolidation.** Upon approval of the plan by the voting members, each corporation executes either *articles of merger* or *articles of consolidation* on a form prescribed by the secretary of state. This document sets forth the plan of merger or consolidation, the date of the meeting at which the plan was approved, and a statement that a quorum was present and that the plan received at least two-thirds voter approval. The articles of merger or articles of consolidation are filed with the secretary of state.[530]

Church charters or bylaws may impose further requirements that must be followed.[531] And, if a proposed merger or consolidation would alter the doctrines of a church, it is essential to the validity of such a merger or consolidation that the church congregation possess the authority to change its doctrine and that the required number of members assent to the change.[532] Church corporations

---

[529] Trinity Pentecostal Church v. Terry, 660 S.W.2d 449 (Mo. App. 1983).

[530] MODEL NONPROFIT CORPORATION ACT §§ 38-43.

[531] In re Estate of Trimmer, 330 N.E.2d 241 (Ill. 1975); In re First Methodist Church, 306 N.Y.S.2d 969 (1970).

[532] *See generally* FLETCHER CYC. CORP. ch. 61 (perm. ed. 2008).

affiliated with religious hierarchies must of course comply with applicable procedures in the constitution or bylaws of the parent ecclesiastical body.

The legal effect of a merger or consolidation generally is determined by state corporation law and the terms of the merger or consolidation agreement. State corporation law typically stipulates that all the properties of a church corporation that merges with another congregation belong to the surviving corporation. Similarly, the properties of two consolidating churches belong to the new corporation resulting from the consolidation. The surviving corporation in the case of a merger or the new corporation in the case of a consolidation is responsible for all the liabilities and obligations of each of the corporations so merged or consolidated. Thus, neither the rights of creditors nor any liens upon the property of such corporations is affected by a merger or consolidation.

Dissolution

§ 6-15

Key point 6-15. *The procedure for dissolving an incorporated church is specified by state nonprofit corporation law.*

The dissolution of incorporated churches generally is regulated by state corporation law since the state alone has the authority to dissolve those organizations it has created.[533] Corporate dissolutions may be either voluntary or involuntary. A voluntary corporate dissolution is accomplished by the corporation itself. Most state religious and nonprofit corporation laws contain a specific procedure for voluntary dissolution, which generally consists of the following elements:

1. **Board resolution.** The board of directors adopts a resolution recommending that the corporation be dissolved and directing that the question of dissolution be submitted to the church membership.

2. **Notice to members.** All voting members are notified in writing that the question of dissolution will be discussed at a special or general meeting of the members.

3. **Approval.** A resolution to dissolve the corporation is adopted if it receives at least two-thirds voter approval.

4. **Notice to creditors.** Notice of the dissolution is mailed to all creditors of the former corporation.

5. **Payment of debts.** All corporate liabilities are paid. Any assets remaining after payment of liabilities are transferred to the organization or organizations, if any, prescribed in the dissolved corporation's charter or in the controlling rules of a church hierarchy, if any, with which the church is affiliated. If neither the charter nor controlling rules of a religious hierarchy specifies how corporate assets are to be distributed following dissolution, the assets are conveyed to one or more

---

[533] FLETCHER CYC. CORP. § 7971 (perm. ed. 2008).

organizations engaged in activities substantially similar to those of the dissolving corporation.

6. **Articles of dissolution prepared.** The articles of dissolution are executed. The articles set forth the name of the corporation, the date of the meeting of members at which the resolution to dissolve was adopted, and an acknowledgment that a quorum was present, that the resolution was adopted by at least two-thirds of the members present at such meeting, that all debts of the corporation have been paid, and that all remaining assets of the corporation have been transferred to the organization specified in the corporation's charter, or, if no organization is specified, to an organization engaged in activities substantially similar to those of the dissolving corporation.

7. **Articles of dissolution filed.** The articles of dissolution are filed with the secretary of state. If the articles of dissolution conform to all legal requirements, the secretary of state issues to a representative of the dissolved corporation a certificate of dissolution, which is recorded with the office of the recorder of deeds of the county in which the church had been located.[534]

It is important to recognize that the IRS maintains that every incorporated church must contain a provision in its charter ensuring that in the event of a dissolution the assets of the church will pass to a tax-exempt organization. The IRS has stated that the following provision will suffice:

Upon the dissolution of the corporation, assets shall be distributed for one or more exempt purposes within the meaning of section 501(c)(3) of the Internal Revenue Code, or the corresponding section of any future federal tax code, or shall be distributed to the federal government, or to a state or local government, for a public purpose. Any such assets not so disposed of shall be disposed of by a Court of Competent Jurisdiction of the county in which the principal office of the corporation is then located, exclusively for such purposes or to such organization or organizations, as said Court shall determine, which are organized and operated exclusively for such purposes.[535]

A church, of course, may specify in its charter the tax-exempt organization to which its assets will pass upon dissolution. A dissolution clause is necessary in order to ensure the tax-exempt status of a church, since a church will not be considered entitled to tax-exempt status if any part of its net earnings or assets is payable to or for the benefit of any private individual.[536]

---

[534] MODEL NONPROFIT CORPORATION ACT §§ 45-51.

[535] IRS Publication 557. An abbreviated version of this language, which also is acceptable to the IRS, appears in Rev. Proc. 82-2, 1982-1 C.B. 367.

[536] I.R.C. § 501(c)(3). The income tax regulations also specify that an organization is not organized exclusively for exempt purposes if its assets are payable to individuals or nonexempt organizations upon dissolution.

It is important to emphasize that the property of a dissolved church will be conveyed to a charitable organization having purposes and activities substantially similar to those of the dissolved church if neither the church charter nor controlling rules of an ecclesiastical hierarchy provide otherwise. To illustrate, one court ruled that the members of a dissolving church had no authority to distribute church assets to a theological seminary or a servicemen's center, since neither organization was substantially related in purpose or activity to the dissolving church.[537] And, if a dissolving church is affiliated with a religious hierarchy whose internal rules require that the assets of a dissolving local church revert to the parent organization, the members of a dissolving church have no authority to distribute the church's assets to another organization.[538] In addition to the procedures specified by state corporation law, church corporations also are bound by the procedural requirements of their own charters and bylaws, or the controlling rules of a parent ecclesiastical body, in a dissolution proceeding.[539]

The corporation law of many states provides that church corporations may be dissolved involuntarily by the attorney general upon the occurrence of one or more of several grounds, including failure to pay fees prescribed by law, failure to file an annual report, fraudulent solicitation of funds, and exceeding the authority conferred by state corporation law.[540] Such laws typically permit church corporations to be dissolved involuntarily by a director or member if the directors are so deadlocked in the management of the corporation that irreparable injury to the corporation is being suffered; the acts of the directors are illegal, oppressive, or fraudulent; the corporation's assets are being wasted; or the corporation is unable to carry out its purposes.[541]

To illustrate, one court found that an involuntary dissolution of a church was warranted since dissension over the dismissal of one minister and the hiring of another was so bitter that the church could no longer conduct its operations.[542] However, one court held that riots and violence within a church that lasted for only two weeks was not a frustration of the church's purposes and did not constitute an adequate basis for involuntary dissolution.[543]

Case Study

• *An Illinois appeals court dismissed a lawsuit brought by members of a church seeking to dissolve their church and have a receiver appointed to liquidate church assets. A schism occurred in a Baptist church over the retention of the pastor. Problems worsened due to disagreements over the pastor's plan to use church funds*

---

[537] Metropolitan Baptist Church v. Younger, 121 Cal. Rptr. 899 (1975).

[538] Polen v. Cox, 267 A.2d 201 (Md. 1970); German Evangelical Lutheran St. Johannes Church v. Metropolitan New York Synod of the Lutheran Church in America, 366 N.Y.S.2d 214 (1975), *appeal denied*, 378 N.Y.S.2d 1025 (1975).

[539] Presbytery of the Covenant v. First Presbyterian Church, 552 S.W.2d 865 (Tex. App. 1977).

[540] MODEL NONPROFIT CORPORATION ACT § 51.

[541] *Id.* at § 54(a).

[542] Fuimaono v. Samoan Congregational Christian Church, 135 Cal. Rptr. 799 (1977).

[543] Hill v. Abyssinia Missionary Baptist Church, 370 So.2d 1389 (Ala. 1979).

to build a school. Some members opposed placing a mortgage on the debt-free church building to raise construction funds. When efforts to remove the pastor and those deacons who supported him failed, some of the disgruntled members filed a lawsuit in civil court seeking an order dissolving the church and transferring its assets to a receiver for distribution to another nonprofit organization. Illinois law permits a voting member or director to "involuntarily dissolve" a nonprofit corporation that is unable to carry out its purposes. The disgruntled members claimed that this procedure was available since the church was unable to carry out its purpose of conducting religious worship because of the controversy. A trial court agreed to dissolve the church and turn over its assets to a receiver for distribution to another nonprofit organization, but a state appeals court reversed this ruling on the ground that the persons who brought the lawsuit did not qualify as members of the church and therefore lacked "standing" to sue. The court noted that even if the former members had standing to sue, they could not prevail since the civil courts lack jurisdiction to determine whether or not the church "could carry out its purposes since the court's decision of that issue [would violate] the First Amendment's prohibition against civil courts' involvement in religious matters. . . . The underlying dispute, who will be the pastor at [the church], is an ecclesiastical matter which is not within the court's purview."[544]

If a church, in the regular course of its affairs, is unable to pay its debts and obligations as they come due, the nonprofit corporation laws of many states permit an incorporated church to be involuntarily dissolved by a creditor whose claims are unsatisfied.[545]

Unincorporated churches having no affiliation with a religious hierarchy are mere voluntary associations of persons and may dissolve on their own initiative by a vote of the membership, by abandonment of the church, or by withdrawal of all members from the church, assuming that all applicable provisions in the church's bylaws or other internal rules are followed. The property of unincorporated churches generally is in the name of trustees.

The IRS maintains that an unincorporated church is not eligible for exemption from federal income taxes unless its organizational document stipulates that all assets held in trust for the use and benefit of the church will pass to another charitable, tax-exempt organization upon dissolution of the church. Obviously, neither the trustees nor former members have any personal claim to trust assets following the dissolution of a church. This requirement is based on the fact that the Internal Revenue Code prohibits tax-exempt status to any organization whose net earnings or assets are payable to or for the benefit of any private individual.[546]

If an unincorporated church has failed to include a provision in its organizational document providing for disposition of trust assets following dissolution of the church, a court may nonetheless direct that all trust assets pass to another charitable organization having similar purposes to those of the dissolved church. This power of the courts to determine the status of the trust assets of a dissolved church is known as the *cy pres* doctrine.

---

[544] Hines v. Turley, 615 N.E.2d 1251 (Ill. App. 1993).

[545] MODEL NONPROFIT CORPORATION ACT § 54(b).

[546] I.R.C. § 501(c)(3).

Instructional Aids to Chapter 6

Key Terms

apparent authority

articles of incorporation

books of account

bylaws

certificate of incorporation

charter

Church Audit Procedures Act

church tax examination

church tax inquiry

civil, contract, or property rights

common interest privilege

congregational

consolidation

constitution

corporation sole

cy pres doctrine

de facto corporation

defamation

directors

dissolution

employment taxes

express authority

good faith

hierarchical

implied authority

incorporation

inherent authority

IRS audits

maturity of members

margin of civil court review

meetings

members

membership corporation

merger

minutes

Model Nonprofit Corporation Act

neutral principles of law

nonprofit

notice

officers

proxy voting

quorum

religious activities

resolution

Revised Model Nonprofit Corporation Act

subpoena

tax-exempt

trademark

trustee corporation

trustees

unfair competition

unincorporated association

Uniform Management of Institutional Funds Act

Volunteer Protection Act

Learning Objectives

• Understand the legal differences between an unincorporated and an incorporated church, and explain the advantages of the corporate form of organization.

• Define the terms *charter, constitution, bylaws,* and *resolution,* and explain the legal priorities among these terms.

• Describe the legal authority of church members to inspect church records.

• Explain the purpose and application of the Church Audit Procedures Act.

• Summarize several state and federal reporting requirements that apply to many churches.

• Identify several potential theories of personal legal liability for church officers and directors.

• Explain the application of charitable immunity laws to church officers and directors.

• Describe the two approaches to civil court intervention in church membership determinations.

• Explain the legal effect of church meetings that are conducted in violation of a church's bylaws.

Short-Answer Questions

1. A church is not incorporated. G, a member, is driving a church van during a church-sponsored activity, and he negligently causes an accident injuring 2 other members in the van and the driver of another vehicle. Answer the following questions, and explain your reasoning:

    a. Can the 2 injured members sue G?

    b. Can the 2 injured members sue the church?

    c. Can the 2 injured members sue other members of church?

    d. Can the injured driver of the other vehicle sue G?

    e. Can the injured driver of the other vehicle sue church?

    f. Can the injured driver of the other vehicle sue the members of church?

2. Same facts as question 1, except that church is incorporated.

    a. Can the 2 injured members sue G?

    b. Can the 2 injured members sue church?

    c. Can the 2 injured members sue other members of church?

    d. Can the injured driver of the other vehicle sue G?

    e. Can the injured driver of the other vehicle sue church?

f. Can the injured driver of the other vehicle sue the members of church?

3. Some pastors believe that a church will be immune from government regulation so long as the church remains unincorporated. Assess this claim.

4. A pastor insists that his church is not required to withhold payroll taxes from its lay employees because the church is not incorporated. Assess the validity of this claim.

5. Are unincorporated churches required to hold title to church property in the name of trustees?

6. What are three features of the Uniform Unincorporated Nonprofit Association Act?

7. A volunteer youth worker sexually molests three children at a church. The parents retain an attorney who believes that a jury will award damages well in excess of the church's insurance. The attorney learns that the church is not incorporated. Can the attorney sue the members of the church in order to recover adequate damages for her clients? Explain.

8. Same facts as question 7. Would it matter if the state in which the church is located has enacted the Uniform Unincorporated Nonprofit Association Act? Why or why not?

9. Same facts as question 7. Would it matter if the church is a corporation rather than an unincorporated entity?

10. List 3 advantages and 3 disadvantages of the corporate form of organization.

11. What steps can a church take to confirm that it is a corporation in good standing under state law?

12. Do churches incorporate under state or federal law?

13. Some attorneys say that they would be guilty of "legal malpractice" if they advised a church not to incorporate. What is the basis for this position?

14. How does a church become an unincorporated entity?

15. Summarize the process for incorporating a church under a state law based on the Model Nonprofit Corporation Act.
16. It is sometimes said that in most states a church has more than one option for incorporating. Explain.

17. A church incorporates under a state law based on the Model Nonprofit Corporation Act. Its bylaws do not specify a quorum. What percentage of members will constitute a quorum at a church business meeting?

18. A church is incorporated under a state law based on the Model Nonprofit Corporation Act. It has not sent in its annual report to the Secretary of State's office for the past three years. What is the legal effect of this omission?

19. A religious organization (not a church) incorporates under a state nonprofit corporation law. Does this render it exempt from federal income taxes? Explain.

20. Explain the difference between tax-exempt and nonprofit.

21. Why do some churches prefer not to incorporate under the Model Nonprofit Corporation Act?

22. What is a corporate charter? Is it the same as the church constitution?

23. Some churches have a constitution and bylaws, while others have only a constitution or set of bylaws. Explain the advantages and disadvantages of both positions..

24. A church charter specifies that "all church property shall be sold in the event the church ceases to function and the proceeds distributed equally among the former members." Is this clause legally permissible? Explain.

25. Some church charters specify the church's period of duration as perpetual. Some specify a fixed number of years. Which is the better practice, and why?

26. What body of parliamentary law governs church business meetings?

27. A church charter recites the church's purpose as "religion, that is, the proclamation of the Gospel through all available means." Why might this purpose clause be inadequate?

28. What is the difference between a resolution and a bylaw?

29. This question addresses corporations sole.

   a. What is a corporation sole?

   b. Can churches incorporate as a corporation sole? Why or why not?

   c. Are corporations sole immune from all government regulation?

d. Are corporations sole immune from civil liability?

30. A church constitution specifies that a quorum consists of one-half of the active membership. The church bylaws specify that a quorum consists of "60 members." The church board, recognizing the disparity, enacts a resolution stipulating that "the bylaws control in matters of quorums." How many members constitute a quorum?

31. A church charter specifies that the church shall have four board members. The church constitution provides for six. The church bylaws are amended to provide for one board member for each 100 church members. The church has 300 members. How many board members does the church have as a matter of law?

32. The IRS has drafted paragraphs that churches can insert in their charter. What do these paragraphs address? Can they be modified, or must the IRS version be used?

33. Where would one most likely find a church's designation of a housing allowance for its pastor: the church constitution, the church bylaws, the church charter, or a board resolution? Explain.

34. Which ordinarily has the higher priority—a church's bylaws, or the state nonprofit corporation law under which the church is incorporated? Explain.

35. A member demands to see a church's financial records. The member claims that he has a right to see the church's records, and he cites the following legal grounds for his position. Which, if any, of these grounds would support the member's claim:

a. The church is incorporated under the Model Nonprofit Corporation Act.

b. The federal Privacy Act.

c. The federal Freedom of Information Act.

d. The church has issued $500,000 of church securities (promissory notes) to members, and the securities were registered under state securities law.

e. The church bylaws give members the right to inspect church records at reasonable times for reasonable purposes.

36. Same facts as question 35. What (if any) defenses are available to the church in the event it does not want to disclose the records to the member?

37. A church receives a subpoena demanding production in court of various church records. Under what circumstances, if any, may the church disregard this

subpoena?

38. A church owns a large parking lot and two homes. It rents the parking lot to employees and patrons of neighboring businesses during the week, and rents the two homes on an annual lease basis. The IRS learns of the rental properties and would like to determine whether the church is engaged in an unrelated trade or business. It sends the church an inquiry notice in which the only explanation of the concerns giving rise to the inquiry is a statement that "you may be engaged in an unrelated trade or business." Is this inquiry notice legally sufficient under the Church Audit Procedures Act? Explain.

39. A church receives an IRS inquiry notice that does not mention the possible application of the First Amendment principle of separation of church and state to church audits. Is this inquiry notice legally sufficient under the Church Audit Procedures Act? Explain.

40. Assume that the IRS receives a telephone tip that a church may be engaged in an unrelated trade or business. Can a telephone tip serve as the basis for a church tax inquiry? Explain.

41. The IRS sends a church written notice of a church tax inquiry on July 1. As of September 15 of the same year, no examination notice had been sent. The church tax inquiry must be concluded by what date? Why?

42. The IRS sends a church written notice of a church tax inquiry on June 10. On June 20 of the same year it sends written notice that it will examine designated church records on July 15. Is the examination notice legally sufficient under the Church Audit Procedures Act? Explain.

43. If the examination notice in question 42 is not legally sufficient, what is the church's remedy?

44. An IRS examination notice specifies that the "religious activities" of a church will be examined as part of an investigation into a possible unrelated business income tax liability. Is the examination notice legally sufficient under the Church Audit Procedures Act? Explain.

45. The IRS sends an examination notice to a church on March 20 of the current year. On June 1 of the same year, as part of its examination, the IRS requests several documents that it reasonably believes are necessary. The church refuses to disclose the documents, and the IRS seeks a court order compelling disclosure. This order is issued two years later, on July 1. Must the IRS examination be terminated on the ground that it was not completed within the 2-year statute of limitations? Explain.

46. Three years ago the IRS conducted an examination of the tax-exempt status of a local church. It concluded that the church was properly exempt from

federal income taxation. During the current year the IRS initiates an examination of the same church to determine if it is engaged in an unrelated trade or business, and if it has been withholding taxes from nonminister employees. Is such an examination barred by the prohibition against repeated examinations within a five-year period? Explain.

47. The IRS initiates an audit against K, a member of a church. The audit focuses on the issue of whether or not K in fact made the substantial contributions to the church that she claimed on her tax return. The IRS contacts church officials, and asks to review contribution records. Is this inquiry subject to the Church Audit Procedures Act? Explain.

48. A church operates a separately-incorporated private elementary school. The IRS contacts the school concerning the basis for its tax-exempt status. Is this inquiry subject to the Church Audit Procedures Act? Why or why not?

49. A state attorney general suspects that a church has engaged in fraud in soliciting donations. Can the attorney general subpoena the church's donor list?

50. Name two reporting requirements under state law that apply to churches.

51. What federal reporting requirement applies to most churches?

52. What is IRS Form 5578? Are churches required to file this form? Explain.

53. Define the legal principle of "unfair competition."

54. A church votes to disaffiliate from a denomination. May it continue to use the denomination's name in its title? Explain.

55. Calvary Church is an independent church that was organized in 1940. This year, another independent church calling itself "Calvary Church" opens in the same community. What, if any, legal right does the original church have to prevent the new church from using the same name?

56. Should an incorporated church hold title to property through trustees? Why or why not?

57. Briefly describe the four categories of authority of church officers, directors, and trustees.

58. Many churches use "staggered elections" of board members. What does this mean?
59. Explain the legal difference between an officer and a director of a church corporation.

60. T is a board member (not an officer) of a church. T, without express authority, signs a contract on behalf of the church to purchase a new duplicating machine for the church. Answer the following questions:

a. Did T have apparent authority to execute the contract?

b. Assume that the machine is delivered to the church, and that the church accepts the machine and uses it for a month. It then finds another machine it likes better. Can it now seek to avoid T's contract on the ground that T had no legal authority to sign the contract?

61. Five years ago Bob donated $5,000 to his church with the stipulation that the money be used exclusively for the building program. This year the church board decides to cancel the building program. Bob demands a full refund of his contribution. If the church refuses to comply, what are Bob's legal rights? Can he ask a court to compel the church to return his designated contribution? Explain.

62. A church asked its members to contribute toward a missions project with a budget of $10,000. Barb donated $1,000 to the project, but learned later that the budget had been reached before she made her contribution. She asks the church to return her contribution. If the church refuses to comply, what are Barb's legal rights? Can she ask a court to compel the church to return her designated contribution? Explain.

63. A church plans to build a home for a low-income family. While much of the work is done by volunteer labor, and some of the materials are donated, the church still must raise $25,000 to complete the project. Bill does not attend the church, but he learns of the project and donates $1,000 to it. Several weeks after making his contribution Bill learns that the budget had been reached before he made his contribution. He asks the church to return his contribution. If the church refuses to comply, what are Bill's legal rights? Can he ask a court to compel the church to return his designated contribution? Explain.

64. A mother informs a member of the church board that her minor child was molested by a volunteer youth worker at a church activity. The board member does nothing about the allegation. The same volunteer later molests another child. Is the board member legally responsible for the injuries suffered by the second victim? Explain.

65. Can a church board take action by a conference telephone call?

66. Do the civil courts ordinarily resolve internal church disputes concerning the selection or removal of board members? Explain.

67. This question addresses fiduciary duties.

a. Define "fiduciary duty."

b. Do church members have fiduciary duties?

c. Do church officers and directors have fiduciary duties?

d. What are two fiduciary duties?

68. What are three ways for a church board to discharge its fiduciary duties in the investment of church funds?

69. Tim owns a carpet business. He also serves on a church board. His church would like to recarpet several large areas, and they enter into a contract with Tim for the carpet and installation. Which fiduciary duty may be violated by such an arrangement?

70. Same facts as question 69. What, if any, steps could the church board take to avoid breaching their fiduciary duties?

71. A church's senior pastor and treasurer agree to defer payment of withheld payroll taxes during the summer due to a slump in giving. Can either of them be personally liable for payment of these payroll taxes? Explain.

72. A church would like to make a loan to its new youth pastor to assist with a down payment on a new home. What, if any, legal issue is raised by this transaction?

73. M, a member of the board of her church, engages in conduct in violation of the church's moral teachings. The remaining board members vote to dismiss M from the board. M has served only 1 year of a 3-year term of office. She had been elected by the church membership. Do the other board members have the legal authority to remove M from the board? Explain.

74. Same facts as previous question. Does the church membership have the legal authority to remove M from the board? Explain.

75. B is a church board member. While driving a church vehicle on church business he negligently causes an accident that injures C, an occupant of another vehicle. Can C sue B personally? Explain.

76. A child drowns during a church youth activity. The board is sued on the basis of "negligent supervision." Do board members have personal liability?

77. A church board member is not able to attend most meetings of the board, is not familiar with the church's financial statements or with its charter and

bylaws, and does not ask questions about apparent irregularities. Has the board member violated any legal duty owed to the church?

78. A church decides to raise funds for a new building by selling church bonds that it issues. The pastor and board actively sell the bonds to church members during and after church services. Do they incur any potential legal liability for doing so?

79. Same facts as the previous question. The board members represent to potential investors that the bonds are "as safe as if your money were invested in a bank, because they are invested in God's economy." Do the board members incur any potential legal liability for making such statements? Explain.

80. Several members ask the church board to institute a program for screening volunteers who work with minors. The board discusses these proposals, but decides that such a program is not necessary. It bases its conclusion on the fact that no incident of child molestation has ever occurred at the church. A few months later, three minors are molested by a volunteer worker. Answer the following questions:

    a. Why might the parents be motivated to sue the board members personally, in addition to the church?

    b. If the board members are sued personally, what is the likely outcome?

    c. The board members insist that they are protected against any liability by a "limited immunity" statute in their state. Are they correct?

81. Many states have enacted laws providing church board members with limited immunity from personal liability. Describe the requirements and exceptions that ordinarily are associated with these laws.

82. Summarize the two approaches the civil courts have taken when asked to intervene in internal church disputes involving discipline and dismissal of members.

83. A church member is accused of engaging in conduct that violates the church's moral teachings. The church board investigates the matter, determines the member is guilty, and dismisses him from membership in the church. The former member sues the church on the basis of a number of alleged wrongs. Evaluate whether any of the following allegations would support civil court review of the dismissal:

    a. "I have attended this church for many years and have made substantial contributions. My church membership is a valuable right that has been denied by the church's actions."

b. "The church did not follow the procedure outlined in the church bylaws in dismissing me."

c. "The church board did not have the authority to dismiss me. The church bylaws give this authority to the church membership."

d. "The church bylaws do not clearly specify that what I did violated the church's moral teachings."

84. A church votes to expel a member, and its vote is upheld by an ecclesiastical commission of the denomination with which the church is affiliated. The member wants to challenge his expulsion in court. Under what circumstances will the civil courts review the membership determinations of ecclesiastical tribunals within hierarchical denominations?

85. A church's bylaws specify that notice of special business meetings must be given at the two Sunday morning services preceding the meeting. A special business meeting is called for September 1. Notice is given on only the immediately preceding Sunday morning. At the meeting, the senior pastor is voted out of office. He contests the vote. Result?

86. A church's bylaws specify that "a pastor shall be considered elected if elected by a majority of members." At a church election at which a quorum of 52 out of 100 members is present, a pastor receives 28 votes. Is the pastor re-elected? Explain.

87. Church services and functions have been disrupted by a disgruntled member. What legal authority, if any, does the church have to exclude this individual from participating in church services and activities?

88. Explain the difference between merger and consolidation.

89. Define the term *dissolution*. What is a *dissolution clause* in a church charter?

Discussion Questions

1. Do you think it would be advisable to incorporate a church under a state nonprofit corporation law that regulated most areas of church procedure and administration in the absence of provisions to the contrary in the church's own charter, constitution, or bylaws? Or, would you prefer to incorporate a church under a nonprofit corporation law that left churches free to govern their own procedure and administration, and that did not "fill in the gaps" in a church's organizational documents. Explain.

2. The civil courts have struggled with the question of whether or not to intervene in internal church disputes involving membership determinations. Do you believe that the courts should have the authority to review church membership determinations in these areas? Explain. How might such disputes be avoided?

Church Property

Legal Briefs

There are many legal issues associated with church property. This chapter addresses several of them. For example, assume that a schism occurs in a local church and a dispute arises over ownership of the church's property. How do the civil courts resolve such a case? Which group will be awarded ownership of the property?

Another important issue is the application of local zoning laws to religious congregations. Zoning laws specify the permitted uses of property within a community, and these laws sometimes conflict with a church's desire to use property for church purposes. Similarly, most communities have enacted building codes. To what extent do they apply to church buildings? Many communities have enacted "landmarking" ordinances that prohibit historic properties from being demolished or modified without approval. Do such laws apply to historic church buildings? For example, assume that a city designates a church as an historic landmark, and rejects the church's request to expand its building to accommodate a growing membership. Does the city have this authority? What about the church's constitutional right to freely exercise its religion?

> "Zoning laws specify the permitted uses of property within a community, and these laws sometimes conflict with a church's desire to use property for church purposes.

Other issues addressed in this chapter include title to church property; conveyances of church property; embezzlement of church funds; reversionary and dissolution clauses; restrictive covenants; materialmen's liens; liability for injuries occurring on church property; criminal liability for defacing church property; discrimination in the sale or rental of church property; eminent domain; and the removal of disruptive persons from church services. Most churches will face at least some of these issues, and so a familiarity with this chapter is important.

Church Property Disputes— In General

§ 7-01

Church property disputes can arise in a variety of ways. In some cases, a church congregation splits over a doctrinal issue or the retention of a minister, with both groups claiming ownership of the church property. In other cases, a congregation votes to disaffiliate from a parent denomination, and the denomination asserts that it now owns the church's property. There are many other ways in which such disputes may occur. The courts have developed a number of rules for resolving such disputes, and these rules are described in the following sections.

Church Property Disputes— Supreme Court Rulings

§ 7-02

1. Watson v. Jones (1871)

A study of the law of church property disputes must begin with the United States Supreme Court's decision in *Watson v. Jones*,[1] for the methodology outlined in *Watson* served as the principal means of resolving such disputes for nearly a century and continues to exert considerable influence. In *Watson*, the Court was faced with the problem of determining which of two factions in the Third or Walnut Street Presbyterian Church of Louisville, Kentucky, which had split in 1863 over the slavery controversy, was entitled to ownership of the church property. The Court began its analysis by observing: "The questions which have come before the civil courts concerning the rights of property held by ecclesiastical bodies, may, so far as we have been able to examine them, be profitably classified under three general heads . . . ."[2]

1. The first of these is when the property which is the subject of controversy has been, by the deed or will of the donor, or other instrument by which the property is held, by the express terms of the instrument devoted to the teaching, support, or spread of some specific form of religious doctrine or belief.

2. The second is when the property is held by a religious congregation which, by the nature of its organization, is strictly independent of other ecclesiastical associations, and so far as church government is concerned, owes no fealty or obligation to any higher authority.

---

[1] 80 U.S. 679 (1871) [hereinafter cited as *Watson*].

[2] *Id.* at 722.

3. The third is where the religious congregation or ecclesiastical body holding the property is but a subordinate member of some general church organization in which there are superior ecclesiastical tribunals with a general and ultimate power of control more or less complete, in some supreme judicatory over the whole membership of that general organization.[3]

As to the first type of case, the Court concluded that "it would seem . . . to be the obvious duty of the Court . . . to see that the property so dedicated is not diverted from the trust which is thus attached to its use,"[4] and

[t]hough the task may be a delicate one and a difficult one, it will be the duty of the court in such cases, when the doctrine to be taught or the form of worship to be used is definitely and clearly laid down, to inquire whether the party accused of violating the trust is holding or teaching a different doctrine, or using a form of worship which is so far variant as to defeat the declared objects of the trust.[5]

As to the second type of case, the Court concluded:

In such cases where there is a schism which leads to a separation into distinct and conflicting bodies, the rights of such bodies to the use of the property must be determined by the ordinary principles which govern voluntary associations. If the principle of government in such cases is that the majority rules, then the numerical majority of members must control the right to the use of the property.[6]

The Court went on to observe:

This ruling admits of no inquiry into the existing religious opinions of those who comprise the legal or regular organization; for, if such were permitted, a very small minority, without any officers of the church among them, might be found to be the only faithful supporters of the religious dogmas of the founders of the church. There being no such trust imposed upon the property when purchased or given, the Court will not imply one for the purpose of expelling from its use those who by regular succession and order constitute the church, because they may have changed in some respect their views of religious truth.[7]

---

[3]   *Id.* at 722-23.

[4]   *Id.* at 723.

[5]   *Id.* at 724.

[6]   *Id.* at 725.

[7]   *Id.*

In summary, *Watson* held that property disputes in a purely "congregational" church (i.e., "a religious congregation which, by the nature of its organization, is strictly independent of other ecclesiastical associations") are to be decided by majority rule, and that this rule would apply even if the majority had defected from the faith of the church's founders.

As to the third type of case, the Court concluded:

> In this class of cases we think the rule of action which should govern civil courts . . . is, that, whenever the questions of discipline, or of faith, or ecclesiastical rule, custom, or law have been decided by the highest of these church judicatories to which the matter has been carried, the legal tribunals must accept such decisions as final, and as binding on them, in their application to the case before them. . . . All who unite themselves to such a body do so with an implied consent to this government, and are bound to submit to it. But it would be a vain consent and would lead to the total subversion of such religious bodies, if anyone aggrieved by one of their decisions could appeal to the secular courts and have them reversed. It is of the essence of these religious unions, and of their right to establish tribunals for the decision of questions arising among themselves, that those decisions should be binding in all cases of ecclesiastical cognizance, subject only to such appeals as the organism itself provides for.[8]

This third holding of *Watson* became known as the *compulsory deference rule*—courts must defer to the determinations of church tribunals with respect to "questions of discipline or of faith, or ecclesiastical rule, custom, or law," and, by implication, to any decision of a church tribunal. This holding applies generally to *hierarchical* churches, which the Court defined as churches that are "subordinate members of some general church organization in which there are superior ecclesiastical tribunals with a general and ultimate power of control more or less complete, in some supreme judicatory over the whole membership of that general organization." Some churches are independent of denominational control for some purposes, but not for others. In other words, they may be "hierarchical" only for some purposes. The analysis for hierarchical churches articulated in *Watson* would apply to such churches only if they are hierarchical with respect to the ownership or control of church property.

Civil courts generally have followed the Supreme Court's classification of churches into two categories—congregational and hierarchical. A few courts and legal commentators have divided churches into three categories. To illustrate, one commentator has observed:

> At least three kinds of internal structure, or "polity," may be discerned: congregational, presbyterial, and episcopal. In the congregational form each local congregation is self-governing. The presbyterial polities are

---

[8] *Id.* at 727, 729.

representative, authority being exercised by laymen and ministers organized in an ascending succession of judicatories—presbytery over the session of the local church, synod over the presbytery, and general assembly over all. In the episcopal form power reposes in clerical superiors, such as bishops. Roughly, presbyterial and episcopal polities may be considered hierarchical, as opposed to congregational polities, in which the autonomy of the local congregation is the central principle.[9]

In the years following *Watson*, nearly every court that decided a church property dispute cited *Watson* and claimed to be following its methodology. In cases involving express trusts and hierarchical churches (the first and third "general heads"), the professed adherence to *Watson* was largely real.

But soon after *Watson* was decided, cases involving the ownership of property in divided congregational churches (the second "general head") began to deviate from the rule enunciated in *Watson*—that the majority in such congregations should dictate the ownership of church property whether or not that majority remained faithful to the doctrine of the church's founders. The seeming inequity of this rule prompted many courts to disregard *Watson*. Many courts adopted the *implied trust doctrine*, under which church properties were deemed to be held in trust for the benefit of those members adhering to the original doctrines of the church.[10] Under this doctrine, the property of congregational churches following a church split went to the faction adhering to the original doctrines of the church, whether it represented a majority or a minority of the church membership. This obviously was contrary to the spirit if not the letter of *Watson*, wherein the Court had observed: "There being no such trust imposed upon the property when purchased or given, the Court will not imply one for the purpose of expelling from its use those who by regular succession and order constitute the church, because they may have changed in some respect their views of religious truth."[11]

Several other courts held that if a majority of the members of a congregational church voted to change the denominational ties of the congregation, church property would be vested in the minority desiring to remain faithful to the original denomination.[12] Some courts applied the law of corporations to vest ownership of

---

9   Note, *Judicial Intervention in Disputes Over the Use of Church Property*, 75 HARV. L. REV. 1142, 1143-44 (1962).

10   *See, e.g.,* Davis v. Ross, 53 So.2d 544 (Ala. 1951); Holiman v. Dovers, 366 S.W.2d 197 (Ark. 1963); Chatfield v. Dennington, 58 S.E.2d 842 (Ga. 1950); Sorrenson v. Logan, 177 N.E.2d 713 (Ill. 1961); Pentecostal Tabernacle of Muncie v. Pentecostal Tabernacle of Muncie, 146 N.E.2d 573 (Ind. 1957); Ragsdall v. Church of Christ, 55 N.W.2d 539 (Iowa 1952); Huber v. Thorn, 371 P.2d 143 (Kan. 1962); Philpot v. Minton, 370 S.W.2d 402 (Ky. 1963); Davis v. Scher, 97 N.W.2d 137 (Mich. 1959); Protestant Reformed Church v. Tempelman, 81 N.W.2d 839 (Minn. 1957); Mills v. Yount, 393 S.W.2d 96 (Mo. 1965); Reid v. Johnston, 85 S.E.2d 114 (N.C. 1954); Beard v. Francis, 309 S.W.2d 788 (Tenn. 1957); Baber v. Caldwell, 152 S.E.2d 23 (Va. 1967); Anderson v. Byers, 69 N.W.2d 227 (Wis. 1955).

11   80 U.S. 679 at 725.

12   *See, e.g.,* Holt v. Scott, 42 So.2d 258 (Ala. 1949); Ables v. Garner, 246 S.W.2d 732 (Ark. 1952); Wright v. Smith, 124 N.E.2d 363 (Ill. 1955); Hughes v. Grossman, 201 P.2d 670 (Kan. 1949); Scott v. Turner, 275 S.W.2d 421 (Ky. 1954); Blauert v. Schupmann, 63 N.W.2d 578 (Minn. 1954); Montgomery v. Snyder, 320 S.W.2d 283 (Mo. 1958); Reid v. Johnston, 85 S.E.2d 114 (N.C. 1954); Beard v. Francis, 309 S.W.2d 788 (Tenn. 1957).

property in a minority faction of a congregational church where the majority had voted to deviate from the original doctrines. To illustrate, one court observed:

> It is the law of all corporations that a mere majority of its members cannot divert the corporate property to uses foreign to the purposes for which the corporation was formed. There is no difference between the church and other corporations in this regard. Where a church corporation is formed for the purpose of promoting certain defined doctrines of religious faith, which are set forth in its articles of incorporation, any church property which it acquires is impressed with a trust to carry out such purpose, and a majority of the congregation cannot divert the property to other inconsistent religious uses against the protest of a minority, however small. The matter of use of the property of the church corporation, within the range of its corporate powers, may be determined by the majority of the congregation, but no majority, even though it embrace all members but one, can use the corporate property for the advancement of a faith antagonistic to that for which the church was established and the corporation formed.[13]

A few courts remained true to the ruling in *Watson* and awarded title to congregational church property to the majority faction without any consideration of church doctrine.[14]

2. Presbyterian Church in the United States v. Mary Elizabeth Blue Hull Memorial Presbyterian Church (1969)

The wholesale disregard of *Watson's* holding with respect to congregational churches was reformed by the United States Supreme Court nearly a century after Watson in the landmark decision of *Presbyterian Church in the United States v. Mary Elizabeth Blue Hull Memorial Presbyterian Church.*[15] The question presented in *Hull* was whether a local Presbyterian church could retain title to its property after disassociating itself from the Presbyterian Church in the United States. In 1966, the membership of the Hull Memorial Presbyterian Church of Savannah, Georgia, voted to withdraw from the parent body on the grounds that it had so departed from the original tenets of the Presbyterian faith that it could no longer be considered the true Presbyterian Church. Specifically, the Hull church majority contended that the parent body had departed from Presbyterianism in "making pronouncements and recommendations concerning civil, economic, social and political matters, giving support to the removal of Bible reading and prayer by children in the public schools, . . . causing all members to remain in the National Council of Churches of Christ and willingly accepting its leadership which advocated . . . the subverting of all parental authority, civil disobedience and intermeddling in civil affairs," and also in "disseminating publications denying the

---

[13] Lindstrom v. Tell, 154 N.W. 969 (Minn. 1915).

[14] *See, e.g.,* Booker v. Smith, 214 S.W.2d 513 (Ark. 1948); Ennix v. Owens, 271 S.W. 1091 (Ky. 1925); Holt v. Trone, 67 N.W.2d 125 (Mich. 1954).

[15] 393 U.S. 440 (1969) [hereinafter cited as *Hull*].

Holy Trinity and violating the moral and ethical standards of faith." Accordingly, the local church argued that it had not disaffiliated itself from Presbyterianism, but rather that the Presbyterian Church in the United States had disassociated itself from Presbyterianism, and hence the parent denomination had no right to claim an interest in the property of the local church.

A state trial court ruled that the parent body had indeed abandoned Presbyterianism, and thus the Hull church was entitled to retain title to its property. The Supreme Court of Georgia affirmed. However, the United States Supreme Court reversed both rulings, concluding that

> the First Amendment severely circumscribes the role that civil courts may play in resolving church property disputes. It is obvious, however, that not every civil court decision as to property claimed by a religious organization jeopardizes values protected by the First Amendment. Civil courts do not inhibit free exercise of religion merely by opening their doors to disputes involving church property. And there are neutral principles of law, developed for use in all property disputes, which can be applied without "establishing" churches to which property is awarded. But First Amendment values are plainly jeopardized when church property litigation is made to turn on the resolution by civil courts of controversies over religious doctrine and practice. If civil courts undertake to resolve such controversies in order to adjudicate the property dispute, the hazards are ever present of inhibiting the free development of religious doctrine and of implicating secular interests in matters of purely ecclesiastical concern. Because of these hazards, the First Amendment enjoins the employment of organs of government for essentially religious purposes . . . ; the amendment therefore commands civil courts to decide church property disputes without resolving underlying controversies over religious doctrine. Hence, States, religious organizations, and individuals must structure relationships involving church property so as not to require the civil courts to resolve ecclesiastical questions.[16]

Hull thus may be reduced to the following two principles:

1. Civil courts *are forbidden* by the First Amendment to decide church property disputes if the resolution of such disputes is dependent upon the interpretation of religious doctrine.

2. Civil courts *can* decide church property disputes consistently with the First Amendment if they do so on the basis of principles involving no analysis of religious doctrine. Illustratively, the Court observed that there are "neutral principles of law developed for use in all property disputes, which can be applied without 'establishing' churches to which property is awarded." Unfortunately, the Court neither described what it meant by

---

[16] *Id.* at 449.

"neutral principles of law," nor mentioned other doctrinally neutral and hence acceptable grounds for resolving church property disputes.

In effect, *Hull* wiped away much of the gloss that had been judicially applied to circumvent the second holding of *Watson*: that the majority faction in a congregational church has the right to all church property whether or not it supports or deviates from the original doctrines of the church. No longer could civil courts award congregational church property to a minority faction as a result of a judicial interpretation of religious doctrine. The first ruling in *Watson*—that property received by a church in an instrument expressly limiting the use of such property to the adherents of a particular religious doctrine or belief—was invalidated by *Hull* to the extent that civil courts are called upon to interpret religious doctrine. In many cases, of course, the civil courts could determine the ownership of property conveyed to a church subject to an express trust, for no interpretation of religious doctrine would be involved. Thus, Justice Harlan, concurring in *Hull*, noted:

> I do not . . . read the Court's opinion to . . . hold that the Fourteenth Amendment forbids civilian courts from enforcing a deed or will which expressly and clearly lays down conditions limiting a religious organization's use of the property which is granted. If, for example, the donor expressly gives his church some money on the condition that the church never ordain a woman as a minister or elder . . . or never amend certain specified articles of the Confession of Faith, he is entitled to his money back if the condition is not fulfilled. In such a case, the church should not be permitted to keep the property simply because church authorities have determined that the doctrinal innovation is justified by the faith's basic principles.[17]

The Supreme Court failed to discuss the effect of its decision on the third ruling of *Watson*—that the decision of an ecclesiastical judicatory is binding upon a local church in a hierarchical denomination. This omission was unfortunate and gave rise to much confusion.

In summary, the Supreme Court's decision in *Hull* was deficient in three respects: (1) it sanctioned a "neutral principles of law" approach to resolving church property disputes, but failed to describe what it meant by this new term; (2) it implied that the neutral principles of law approach was one of many acceptable methods of resolving church property disputes, but it failed to describe any other methods; and (3) it failed to explain the relationship between a neutral principles of law approach and the compulsory deference approach (*i.e.*, civil courts are compelled to defer to the rulings of church tribunals) of *Watson*.

---

[17] *Id.* at 452.

3. Maryland and Virginia Eldership of the Churches of God v. Church of God (1970)

Subsequent cases have provided further clarification. In *Maryland and Virginia Eldership of the Churches of God v. Church of God*,[18] the United States Supreme Court was asked to review the constitutionality of the methodology employed by the courts of Maryland in resolving church property disputes. The Maryland approach involved the inspection by the courts of nondoctrinal provisions in (1) state statutes governing the holding of property by religious corporations; (2) language in the deeds conveying the properties in question to the local church corporations; (3) the terms of the charters of the corporations; and (4) provisions in the constitution of a parent denomination relating to the ownership and control of church property. Maryland courts awarded title to disputed church property according to the wording and effect of such documents, provided that this could be done without any inquiries into religious doctrine. The Supreme Court, in a *per curiam* opinion, summarily approved of the Maryland approach to the resolution of church property disputes.

Per curiam = by the court as a whole rather than by a single justice.

In a concurring opinion, Justice Brennan, who had written the Court's opinion in *Hull*, attempted to resolve some of the questions raised by the *Hull* decision. First, Justice Brennan attempted to define the term *neutral principles of law*:

> [C]ivil courts can determine ownership by studying deeds, reverter clauses and general state corporation laws. Again, however, general principles of property law may not be relied upon if their application requires civil courts to resolve doctrinal issues. For example, provisions in deeds or in a denomination's constitution for the reversion of local church property to the general church, if conditioned upon a finding of departure from doctrine, could not be civilly enforced.[19]

Next, Justice Brennan suggested two other acceptable means of resolving church property disputes:

> [T]he States may adopt the approach of *Watson v. Jones* and enforce the property decisions made within a church of congregational polity "by a majority of its members or by such other local organism as it may have instituted for the purpose of ecclesiastical government," and within a church of hierarchical polity by the highest authority that has ruled on the dispute at issue, unless express terms in the instrument by which the property is held condition the property's use or control in a specified manner. . . . [Another] approach is the passage of special statutes governing church property arrangements in a manner that precludes state interference in doctrine. Such statutes must be carefully drawn to leave control of

---

[18] 396 U.S. 367 (1970) [hereinafter cited as *Maryland & Virginia Eldership*].

[19] *Id.* at 370.

ecclesiastical polity, as well as doctrine, to church governing bodies.[20]

Finally, Justice Brennan emphasized that "a state may adopt *any* one of various approaches for settling church property disputes so long as it involves no consideration of doctrinal matters, whether the ritual and liturgy of worship or the tenets of faith."[21]

Thus, a court can properly resolve a church property dispute if it can do so solely on the basis of nondoctrinal language in deeds, state corporation laws, constitutions and bylaws of local churches or of parent ecclesiastical bodies, or state statutes pertaining to church property arrangements. Accordingly, a court could not intervene in a church property dispute involving a deed containing a reverter clause specifying that title to church property reverts to the parent ecclesiastical body if the local church deviates from the doctrine of the parent body, since the court would necessarily become involved in an interpretation of religious doctrine. But a reverter clause conditioned on a disaffiliation of a local church could be enforced by the courts, since enforcement would involve the nondoctrinal determination of whether or not a disaffiliation had occurred.

Further, a minority faction in a congregational church remaining faithful to the original doctrines of the church can no longer contend that the state law of corporations is violated when a majority votes to divert corporate property to uses foreign to the purposes for which the corporation was formed, since this obviously will necessitate interpretation of religious doctrine. If the constitution and bylaws of a parent ecclesiastical body provide for the reversion of local church property to the parent body itself in the event of a disaffiliation by a local church, the civil courts will intervene and enforce such a provision since it would not involve a question of religious doctrine. However, if the reverter clause conditioned reversion upon a departure or deviation from the doctrines of the parent body, an interpretation of religious doctrine would become necessary and accordingly such a clause would not be judicially enforceable.

The Court in *Maryland & Virginia Eldership* commented that civil courts can examine the ecclesiastical rulings of church judicatories in church property disputes to ensure that such rulings are not the product of "fraud, collusion, or arbitrariness."[22]

---

[20] *Id.* at 369, 370. Note that the concurring opinion emphasized that the civil courts "do not inquire whether the relevant church governing body has power under religious law to control the property in question. Such a determination, unlike the identification of the governing body, frequently necessitates the interpretation of ambiguous law and usage." *Id.* at 369. The concurring opinion concluded that "the use of the *Watson* approach is consonant with the prohibitions of the First Amendment only if the appropriate church governing body can be determined without the resolution of doctrinal questions and without extensive inquiry into religious polity." *Id.* at 370.

[21] *Id.* at 368.

[22] In 1976, the Court ruled that the determinations of ecclesiastical judicatories in hierarchical churches involving questions of clergy discipline may not be disturbed by the civil courts on the basis of *arbitrariness*. Arbitrariness was defined as a failure by a judicatory to follow its own ecclesiastical procedure. The Court left unanswered the question of whether *fraud* or *collusion* remain legitimate grounds for civil court review of the disciplinary determinations of hierarchical judicatories. Presumably, arbitrariness is no longer a basis for civil court review of ecclesiastical determinations regarding property ownership, meaning that the civil courts cannot review such determinations even if it is alleged that a judicatory failed to follow its own stated procedures in reaching its result. Serbian Eastern Orthodox Diocese v. Milivojevich, 423 U.S. 696 (1976).

4. Serbian Eastern Orthodox Diocese v. Milivojevich (1976)

In *Serbian Eastern Orthodox Diocese v. Milivojevich*,[23] the Supreme Court strongly affirmed *Watson's* compulsory deference approach to resolving church property disputes:

> In short, the first and Fourteenth Amendments permit hierarchical religious organizations to establish their own rules and regulations for internal discipline and government, and to create tribunals for adjudicating disputes over these matters. When this choice is exercised and ecclesiastical tribunals are created to decide disputes over the government and direction of subordinate bodies, the Constitution requires that civil courts accept their decisions as binding upon them.[24]

The Court also held that civil courts could not review the rulings of church tribunals for arbitrariness, although it did imply that courts could review such rulings for fraud or collusion.

The Court's emphatic endorsement of the compulsory deference rule in *Serbian* caused considerable confusion about the continuing validity of the neutral principles of law approach. What, for example, would be the effect of a church tribunal's ruling in a church property dispute in a jurisdiction that followed the neutral principles of law approach? Would neutral principles supersede the church tribunal's ruling? Once again, the need for clarification was evident.

5. Jones v. Wolf (1979)

In *Jones v. Wolf*,[25] which was decided in 1979, the Supreme Court again turned its attention to church property disputes. Before analyzing *Jones*, it would be helpful to summarize the law of church property disputes as it existed prior to that decision:

1. **Express trusts.** When property is conveyed to a local church by an instrument that contains an express provision restricting the use of such property, such a restriction will be recognized by the civil courts if this can be done without any consideration of religious doctrine. If a consideration of religious doctrine would be necessary, then the courts will not be able to resolve the question of ownership on the basis of the restrictive provision.[26]

2. **Congregational churches.** When a split occurs in a local congregational church, and a dispute arises as to the ownership of such property, courts may resolve the dispute in any of the following four ways:

---

[23] 426 U.S. 696 (1976) [hereinafter referred to as *Serbian*].

[24] *Id.* at 724-25.

[25] 443 U.S. 595 (1979) [hereinafter referred to as *Jones*].

[26] Maryland & Virginia Eldership, 396 U.S. 367, 369 (1970) (Brennan, J., concurring).

Method 1. Civil courts may resolve the dispute on the basis of neutral principles of law, provided that this can be done without inquiries into religious doctrine. Neutral principles of law include nondoctrinal language in the following types of documents:

    a. deeds[27]

    b. local church charters[28]

    c. constitution and bylaws of local church, and of parent ecclesiastical body[29]

Method 2. Civil courts may resolve the dispute on the basis of state statutes governing the holding of property by religious corporations, provided that application of such statutes involves no inquiries into religious doctrine.[30]

Method 3. Civil courts may resolve the dispute on the basis of the *Watson* rule of deference to the will of a majority of the members of a congregational church.[31] Ordinarily, this method is used only if method 1 and method 2 do not resolve the question of property ownership.

Method 4. Civil courts may resolve the dispute on the basis of any other methodology that they may devise "so long as it involves no consideration of doctrinal matters, whether the ritual and liturgy of worship or the tenets of faith."[32]

3. **Hierarchical churches.** When a split occurs in a local hierarchical church, and a dispute arises as to the ownership of church property, courts may resolve the dispute in any of the following three ways:

Method 1. Civil courts may resolve the dispute on the basis of neutral principles of law, provided that this can be done without inquiries into religious doctrine. Neutral principles of law include nondoctrinal language in the following types of documents:

---

[27] Maryland & Virginia Eldership, 396 U.S. 367, 370 (1970) (Brennan, J., concurring).

[28] *Id.*

[29] *Id.*

[30] See note 21, *supra*, and accompanying text.

[31] See note 6, *supra*, and accompanying text.

[32] Maryland & Virginia Eldership, 396 U.S. 367, 368 (1970) (Brennan, J., concurring).

a. deeds[33]

b. local church charter[34]

c. constitution and bylaws of local church, and of parent ecclesiastical body[35]

Method 2. Civil courts may resolve the dispute on the basis of state statutes governing the holding of property by religious corporations, provided that application of such statutes involves no inquiries into religious doctrine.

Method 3. Civil courts may resolve the dispute on the basis of the *Watson* compulsory deference rule, under which courts defer to the rulings of church tribunals in *all* church property disputes, whether or not questions of religious doctrine and polity are involved.[36]

Method 4. Civil courts may resolve the dispute on the basis of any other methodology that they may devise "so long as it involves no consideration of doctrinal matters, whether, the ritual and liturgy of worship or the tenets of faith."[37]

In *Jones*,[38] the United State Supreme Court was confronted with a dispute over the ownership of property following a schism in a local church affiliated with the Presbyterian Church in the United States (PCUS). The church had been organized in 1904, and had always been affiliated with the PCUS (a hierarchical denomination). In 1973, the church membership voted (164 to 94) to separate from the PCUS. The majority informed the PCUS of its decision, and then united with another denomination, the Presbyterian Church in America. The PCUS appointed a commission to investigate the dispute. The commission ultimately issued a ruling declaring the minority faction to be the "true congregation" and withdrawing from the majority faction "all authority" to continue to hold services at the church. The majority took no part in the commission's inquiry, and did not appeal the ruling to a higher PCUS tribunal.

The minority faction brought suit against the majority, after it became obvious that the majority was not going to honor the commission's ruling. The Georgia courts held that there was no neutral principle of law vesting any interest in the church property in the PCUS, and that as a result the local congregation itself had to determine the disposition of the property. On the ground that religious associations are generally governed by majority rule, the Georgia Supreme Court ultimately awarded the property to the majority faction that wanted to disaffiliate. The minority appealed the matter directly to the United States Supreme Court.

---

[33] See note 30, *supra*, and accompanying text.

[34] See note 31, *supra*, and accompanying text.

[35] See note 32, *supra*, and accompanying text.

[36] See note 8, *supra*, and accompanying text.

[37] See note 22, *supra*.

[38] 443 U.S. 595 (1979).

The Court accordingly was confronted with a situation in which a church tribunal's decision in a property dispute conflicted with the decision reached by the courts. The Court characterized the issue as "whether civil courts . . . may resolve the dispute on the basis of 'neutral principles of law,' or whether they must defer to the resolution of an authoritative tribunal of the hierarchical church."

The Supreme Court began its opinion by reiterating the principles enunciated in *Hull* and *Watson* that "the First Amendment prohibits civil courts from resolving church property disputes on the basis of religious doctrine and practice,"[39] and that civil courts must "defer to the resolution of issues of *religious doctrine* or *polity* by the highest court of a hierarchical church organization."[40]

The Court also prefaced its decision by observing that a hierarchical church was involved, that the controversy was intimately connected with Georgia law, and that "a State may adopt *any* one of various approaches for settling church property disputes so long as it involves no consideration of doctrinal matters . . . ."

Having established these general guidelines, the Court proceeded with an analysis of the methodology applied by the Georgia courts in resolving church property disputes. In essence, the Georgia methodology involved a two-step process. First, the courts determined whether neutral principles of law imposed a trust upon local church property in favor of a parent denomination. If such a trust existed, and its validity was not dependent upon any analysis of religious doctrine or polity, then the courts would give the property in dispute to the parent denomination. If neutral principles of law did not impose such a trust, then the property was subject to control by the local congregation, at least if title to the church property was vested in the local church or church trustees. The second step of the Georgia methodology, employed when neutral principles of law did not impose a trust and the local congregation was divided, permitted courts to award disputed church property to the majority of the church members provided that this presumptive rule of majority representation was not overcome by a showing that neutral principles of law dictated another result.

The Supreme Court approved of this methodology, provided the Georgia courts could demonstrate that Georgia in fact had adopted "a presumptive rule of majority representation, defeasible upon a showing that the identity of the local church is to be determined by some other means." The Court sent the case back to the Georgia courts for proof that Georgia in fact had adopted such a rule.

The Court's decision clarified the scope of the compulsory deference rule, and the rule's relationship to the neutral principles of law approach. The Court ultimately concluded that civil courts are compelled to defer to the rulings of church tribunals only with respect to "issues of religious doctrine or polity." It observed: "We cannot agree . . . that the First Amendment requires the States to adopt a rule of compulsory deference to religious authority in resolving church property disputes . . . ."[41] The compulsory deference rule was accordingly limited to matters of religious doctrine and polity.

---

[39] See note 16, *supra*, at 449.

[40] See note 1, *supra*, at 733-34 (emphasis added).

[41] 443 U.S. 595, 605 (1979).

The four dissenting Justices were distressed by the Court's limitation of the compulsory deference rule to matters of religious doctrine and polity. The dissenters argued that "in each case involving an intrachurch dispute—including disputes over church property—the civil court must focus directly on ascertaining, and then following the decision made within the structure of church governance." By doing so, the dissenters concluded,

the court avoids two equally unacceptable departures from the genuine neutrality mandated by the First Amendment. First, it refrains from direct review and revision of decisions of the church on matters of religious doctrine and practice that underlie the church's determination of intrachurch controversies, including those that relate to control of church property. Equally important, by recognizing the authoritative resolution reached within the religious association, the civil court avoids interfering directly with the religious governance of those who have formed the association and submitted themselves to its authority.[42]

> "The four dissenting Justices were distressed by the Court's limitation of the compulsory deference rule to matters of religious doctrine and polity."

The Court, while emphasizing that the question before it involved a hierarchical church, also stated that the Georgia "neutral principles" methodology was "flexible enough to accommodate all forms of religious organization and polity." The Court also noted that church property disputes, even in Georgia, need not necessarily be resolved by the courts, for

the parties can ensure, if they so desire, that the faction loyal to the hierarchical church will retain the church property. They can modify the deeds or the corporate charter to include a right of reversion or trust in favor of the general church. Alternatively, the constitution of the general church can be made to recite and express trust in favor of the denominational church. The burden involved in taking such steps will be minimal. And the civil courts will be bound to give effect to the result indicated by the parties, provided it is embodied in some legally cognizable form. . . . Through appropriate reversionary clauses and trust provisions, religious societies can specify what is to happen to church property in the event of a particular contingency, or what religious body will determine the ownership in the event of a schism or doctrinal controversy. In this manner, a religious organization can ensure that a dispute over the ownership of church property will be resolved in accord with the desires of the members.[43]

---

[42] *Id.* at 618.

[43] *Id.* at 606, 604.

The Supreme Court in *Jones* clarified the law of church property disputes. It affirmed that church property disputes not involving questions of religious doctrine or polity can be resolved on the basis of any doctrinally neutral method, including neutral principles of law or a rule of compulsory deference to the determinations of church tribunals. The Court emphatically declared that no one method is constitutionally required, at least where no question of religious doctrine or polity is involved. Where, as in *Jones*, no question of doctrine is involved and the compulsory deference and neutral principles of law approaches would yield conflicting results, a court or legislature is free to choose either method (or some other doctrinally neutral method). If it chooses the neutral principles of law approach, as did the Georgia courts in the *Jones* case, it is entitled to reach a decision contrary to the decision of a church tribunal, provided that no question of religious doctrine or polity is involved.

The Supreme Court, in *Jones*, expressed a clear preference for the neutral principles approach over the compulsory deference rule, even while recognizing that a state could adopt the compulsory deference rule without violating the federal constitution:

> The primary advantage of the neutral principles approach is that it is completely secular in operation, and yet flexible enough to accommodate all forms of religious organization and polity. The method relies exclusively on objective, well-established concepts of trust and property law familiar to lawyers and judges. It thereby promises to free civil courts completely from entanglement in questions of religious doctrine, polity, and practice. . . . Under the neutral principles approach, the outcome of a church property dispute is not foreordained. At any time before the dispute erupts, the parties can ensure, if they so desire, that the faction loyal to the hierarchical church will retain the church property . . . .The burden involved in taking such steps will be minimal. And the civil courts will be bound to give effect to the result indicated by the parties, provided it is embodied in some legally cognizable form.[44]

Jones did not alter the methodology for resolving church property disputes that had existed previously. It merely clarified the relationship between the available methods of resolution.

State and Lower Federal Court Rulings

§ 7-03

How have state and lower federal courts resolved church property disputes since *Jones*? A few courts have repudiated the neutral principles approach

---

[44] *Id.* at 603-04.

approved by the United States Supreme Court in *Jones*, and have adopted a rule of compulsory deference by the courts to the determinations of ecclesiastical commissions or judicatories in church property disputes, whether or not religious doctrine is implicated.[45] However, a majority of courts have either adopted the principle of *Jones* that the compulsory deference rule is limited to issues of "religious doctrine or polity,"[46] or have applied a neutral principles approach to the resolution of church property disputes involving hierarchical churches.[47] A few courts continue to adhere to the "implied trust" doctrine that was repudiated by the Supreme Court in *Hull*.[48] Such cases illustrate that diversity will characterize states' solutions to these intractable problems. Representative state court rulings are summarized below.[49]

Congregational Churches §7-03.1

Key point 7-03.1. *The civil courts resolve disputes over the ownership and control of property in a "congregational" church on the basis of one of the following principles: (1) the provisions of an express trust, if any; (2) the application of neutral principles of law involving no inquiry into church doctrine; (3) state laws governing the disposition of church property; or (4) a majority vote of the church membership.*

The courts have uniformly resolved property disputes in "congregational" churches by resorting to (1) the express trust rule, (2) the neutral principles of law rule, (3) state laws governing the disposition of church property, or (4) majority

---

[45] Townsend v. Teagle, 467 So.2d 772 (Fla. App. 1985); Fonken v. Community Church, 339 N.W.2d 810 (Iowa 1983) (rejecting the claim that "the compulsory deference approach is applicable only to purely ecclesiastical matters"); Calvary Presbyterian Church v. Presbytery of Lake Huron, 384 N.W.2d 92 (Mich. App. 1986); *but cf.* Bennison v. Sharp, 329 N.W.2d 466 (Mich. App. 1982); Tea v. Protestant Episcopal Church, 610 P.2d 181 (Nev. 1980); Protestant Episcopal Church v. Graves, 417 A.2d 19 (N.J. 1980), *cert. denied,* 449 U.S. 1131 (1981); Southside Tabernacle v. Pentecostal Church of God, Pacific Northwest District, Inc., 650 P.2d 231 (Wash. 1982); Original Glorious Church of God in Christ v. Myers, 367 S.E.2d 30 (W. Va. App. 1988); Church of God v. Noel, 318 S.E.2d 920 (W. Va. 1984) (dissenting justice urged adherence to *Jones*). *But see* Antioch Temple, Inc. v. Parekh, 422 N.E.2d 1337 (Mass. 1981).

[46] *See, e.g.,* Graffam v. Wray, 437 A.2d 627 (Me. 1981); Beaver-Butler Presbytery v. Middlesex Presbyterian Church, 489 A.2d 1317 (Pa. 1985).

[47] *See, e.g.,* Harris v. Apostolic Overcoming Holy Church of God, Inc., 457 So.2d 385 (Ala. 1984); Bishop and Diocese of Colorado v. Mote, 716 P.2d 85 (Colo. 1986); New York Annual Conference of the United Methodist Church v. Fisher, 438 A.2d 62 (Conn. 1980); Aglikin v. Kovacheff, 516 N.E.2d 704 (Ill. App. 1987); York v. First Presbyterian Church, 474 N.E.2d 716 (Ill. App. 1984); Grutka v. Clifford, 445 N.E.2d 1015 (Ind. App. 1983); First Presbyterian Church v. United Presbyterian Church in U.S., 476 N.Y.S.2d 86 (N.Y. 1984); Orthodox Church of America v. Pavuk, 538 A.2d 632 (Pa. Common. 1988); Foss v. Dykstra, 319 N.W.2d 499 (S.D. 1982); Templo Ebenezer, Inc. v. Evangelical Assemblies, Inc., 752 S.W.2d 197 (Tex. App. 1988).

[48] For example, a New York court ruled in 1985 that the "implied trust" doctrine may be used to the extent that it "involves no interpretation of religious doctrine." It observed that "if the original precepts of a church were known, uncontested and unambiguous, then those precepts could form the basis of a doctrinal trust to which claimants to that church's property must be faithful." Park Slope Jewish Center v. Stern, 491 N.Y.S.2d 958 (N.Y. App. 1985).

[49] *See also* Pentecostal Church of God v. Pentecostal Church of God International Movement, 2001 WL 1669383 (unpublished decision, Conn. Super. 2002) (court ordered a national church to return control of a local church to the congregation);

rule. The express trust and neutral principles rules are similar in their application, since both determine title on the basis of nondoctrinal provisions contained in a local church's deed, or the charters or bylaws of the church or a denomination with which it is affiliated. The express trust rule focuses on language creating a trust either in favor of the local church or a denomination. The neutral principles approach looks to nondoctrinal language in deeds, charters, and bylaws to determine who holds legal title. A few states have statutes that attempt to resolve church property disputes. In some cases, these rules do not clearly identify the owner of church property. In such cases, the courts have consistently (since *Jones*) resorted to majority rule, meaning that a majority of members within the church determines the question of property ownership.

Hierarchical Churches—the Compulsory Deference Rule   § 7-03.2

Key point 7-03.2. *Some courts apply the "compulsory deference" rule in resolving disputes over the ownership and control of property in "hierarchical" churches. Under this rule, the civil courts defer to the determinations of denominational agencies in resolving such disputes.*

A few states have adopted the *compulsory deference rule* in resolving church property disputes involving hierarchical churches, and have awarded title to local church property to a denominational agency.[50] The Supreme Court has recognized this as one of many possible options available to the civil courts in resolving church property disputes.

Case Studies

• *A California appeals court ruled that a national church held title to the property of a local church that had voted to disaffiliate. A local Episcopal church voted to disaffiliate from the national church in 2004 and take the local church property with it. The church amended its articles of incorporation to delete all references to the national church. A majority of the congregation voted to support the decision, but a minority of 12 members voted against it. The national church, along with other plaintiffs, filed a lawsuit in which they asked a court to rule that the local church property was held in trust for the local diocese. A state appeals court, in one of the most lengthy discussions of church property disputes, ruled that the local church property was held in trust for the diocese. It based this conclusion on the following considerations: (1) Six rulings by the California Supreme Court, spanning the years from 1889 to 1952, "consistently used a 'highest church judicatory' approach to resolve disputes over church property,*

---

[50] *See, e.g.,* Cumberland Presbytery v. Branstetter, 824 S.W.2d 417 (Ky. 1992) (Cumberland Presbyterian Church retained title to the property of a local church that voted to disaffiliate, because of a trust provision in the national church's constitution); Dixon v. Edwards, 172 F. Supp.2d 702 (D. Md. 2001), *aff'd*, 290 F.3d 699 (4th Cir. 2002); The American Carpatho-Russian Orthodox Greek Catholic Diocese of the U.S.A. v. Church Board, 749 A.2d 1003 (Common. Pa. 2000).

an approach it applied to hierarchically organized churches and non-hierarchically organized churches alike." (2) Section 9142 of the California Corporations Code specifies that "no assets of a religious corporation are or shall be deemed to be impressed with any trust, express or implied, statutory or at common law unless one of the following applies . . . (ii) the articles or bylaws of the corporation, or the governing instruments of a superior religious body or general church of which the corporation is a member, so expressly provide . . . ." The court concluded that this language permitted national churches to adopt a provision in their governing instrument imposing a trust on all local church property in favor of the national church. And this is exactly what the national Episcopal Church did in 1979 when it enacted a canon imposing a trust on all affiliated church property in favor of the diocese.[51]

• The Iowa Supreme Court ruled that the property of a local Presbyterian church that attempted to disaffiliate from the United Presbyterian Church in the United States of America (UPCUSA) belonged to the denomination. It based its decision on the compulsory deference rule (a church judicatory determined that the denomination owned the property), but it also noted that the same result would occur under an application of the neutral principles of law approach. The court observed: "When its provisions are construed together, the Book of Order gives UPCUSA exclusive ultimate control of the uses and disposition of local property. Local church property decisions are subject to general church approval, and the general church may take over local church government, as it did in this case, when it disagrees with the local church handling of church affairs."[52]

• A Massachusetts court applied the compulsory deference rule in resolving a property dispute between a church and a hierarchical denomination, and enforced the denomination's resolution of the dispute. The court concluded: "It is one thing to defer to the determination of religious matters by ecclesiastical authorities, or even to decline jurisdiction over a request by dissident church members to reexamine or to set aside that determination. It is quite another to refuse jurisdiction over a request by the ecclesiastical authorities themselves for civil enforcement of their resolution of matters subjected, by church structure, to their control. Other courts have exercised jurisdiction within that limited scope where necessary to enforce ecclesiastical determinations within a hierarchical church."[53]

• A Michigan state appeals court applied the compulsory deference rule to a church property dispute involving an hierarchical denomination (the Protestant Episcopal Church in the United States of America, or simply the "PECUSA"). The court observed: "In the freedom of conscience and the right to worship allowed in this country, the defendants and members of this church undoubtedly possessed the right to withdraw from it, with or without reason. But they could not take with them, for their own purposes, or transfer to any other religious body, the property dedicated to and conveyed for the worship of God under the discipline of this religious association; nor could they prevent its use by those who choose to remain in the church, and who represent the regular church organization. If complainants maintain the allegations of

---

[51]   In re Episcopal Church Cases, 61 Cal.Rptr.3d 845 (Cal. App. 2007).

[52]   Fonken v. Community Church, 339 N.W.2d 810 (Iowa 1983).

[53]   Episcopal Diocese of Massachusetts v. Devine, 797 N.E.2d 916 (Mass. App. 2003). The court also ruled that the local church held its property in trust for a parent denomination as a result of a canon adopted by the denomination in 1979.

their bill—that they represent the regularly organized body of the church, and are its regular appointees—they are entitled to the relief prayed."[54]

• A Texas court awarded title to a local church's property to a denomination following the church's attempt to disaffiliate. The court observed: "[Texas] courts have consistently followed the deference rule in deciding hierarchical church property disputes since the Texas Supreme Court adopted the rule . . . . The deference rule imputes to members 'implied consent' to the governing bylaws of their church. Persons who unite themselves to a hierarchical church organization do so with 'implied consent' that church bylaws will govern . . . ." The court concluded: "Where a congregation of a hierarchical church has split, those members who renounce their allegiance to the church lose any rights in the property involved and remain loyal to the church. It is a simple question of identity."[55]

• A West Virginia appeals court awarded the assets of a local church to a national denomination. The congregation voted to secede from a parent denomination and establish a new church. The church's trustees attempted to convey the church's assets to the new organization. This conveyance was challenged by the denomination, which asserted that the church's assets belonged to it. It cited a provision in its constitution dictating that "no church group desiring to leave this body shall have any legal claim on church property if the property in question was purchased and paid for with general funds or if general funds were in any way used in the purchase thereof." Since the denomination produced a copy of a check in the amount of $300 that it had issued to the local church in 1964 to assist with church construction, the court concluded that the church's assets belonged to the denomination and that the attempted conveyance by the local trustees was void. The court further noted that with respect to hierarchical churches the civil courts "should respect, and where appropriate enforce, the final adjudications of the highest church tribunals, provided that such adjudications are not procured by fraud or collusion. If a church has a hierarchical structure and its leaders have addressed a doctrinal or administrative dispute, the civil courts do not intervene, absent fraud or collusion." Since the denomination had addressed the issue of property disputes in its constitution, the civil courts were bound to defer to that document and award the local congregation's assets to the denomination.[56]

---

[54] Bennison v. Sharp, 329 N.W.2d 466 (Mich. App. 1982). *See also* Calvary Presbyterian Church v. Presbytery, 384 N.W.2d 92 (Mich. App. 1986). A Michigan appeals court ruled that "it would be inappropriate to apply the neutral principles test to determine disputes between people who have agreed, as a part of the establishment of their church, to resolve disputes between themselves within their internal power structure." In Board of Trustees v. Michigan District Missionary Church, 2003 WL 21854519 (unpublished decision, Mich. App. 2003), a Michigan appeals court ruled that a regional church had the legal authority to control the property of a local church that attempted to disaffiliate. The court noted that the United States Supreme Court has approved the resolution of church property disputes on the basis of "neutral principles of law," but concluded that this approach is not required. The court applied a "theory of hierarchy" as the "preferred approach" in Michigan. Under this approach, if "a religious organization is but a subordinate part of a general church in which there are superior ecclesiastical tribunals with a more or less complete power of control," then the higher authorities within the church are entitled to control the property.

[55] Green v. Westgate Apostolic Church, 808 S.W.2d 547 (Tex. App. 1991).

[56] Original Glorious Church of God in Christ v. Myers, 367 S.E.2d 30 (W. Va. App. 1988).

Hierarchical Churches— Neutral Principle of Law

§ 7-03.3

Key point 7-03.3. *Most courts apply the "neutral principles of law" rule in resolving disputes over the ownership and control of property in "hierarchical" churches. Under this rule, the civil courts apply neutral principles of law, involving no inquiry into church doctrine, in resolving church property disputes. Generally, this means applying neutral legal principles to nondoctrinal language in any one or more of the following documents: (1) deeds to church property; (2) a church's corporate charter; (3) a state law addressing the resolution of church property disputes; (4) church bylaws; or (5) a parent denomination's bylaws.*

Most state courts have adopted the neutral principles of law approach in resolving church property disputes involving hierarchical churches. The cases validate the Supreme Court's pronouncement in *Jones* that "under the neutral principles approach, the outcome of a church property dispute is not foreordained."[57] Both local churches and denominations have been awarded title to contested church property by courts applying the neutral principles approach. Representative cases are summarized below.

1. Title Awarded to Local Churches

A number of courts, applying the neutral principles of law approach, have awarded property to local churches that have disaffiliated from a denomination.

Case Studies

• *The Arkansas Supreme Court ruled that a local church maintained ownership of its property following its disaffiliation from the Cumberland Presbyterian Church since it had acquired title prior to the effective date of an amendment in the national church's governing document imposing a trust in its favor over the property of all affiliated churches. The court rejected the national church's argument that a 1984 constitutional amendment imposed a trust in its favor on the property of all local churches. It pointed out that all of the church's property had been acquired prior to the 1984 amendment, and noted that the national church cited no cases "that allow a grantor to impose a trust upon property previously conveyed without the retention of a trust. . . . We have long held that parties to a conveyance have a right to rely upon the law as it was at that time."[58]*

• *An Illinois state appeals court awarded ownership of church property to a local church that had disaffiliated from the American-Bulgarian Eastern Orthodox Church. The appeals court chose to apply the "neutral principles" approach and accordingly concluded that it was not compelled to rule in favor of the national church.[59]*

---

[57] *Id.* at 603-04.

[58] Arkansas Presbytery of the Cumberland Presbyterian Church v. Hudson, 40 S.W.3d 301 (Ark. 2001).

[59] Aglikin v. Kovacheff, 516 N.E.2d 704 (Ill. App. 1987).

• The Kentucky Supreme Court rejected the claim of the Protestant Episcopal Church in the United States of America (PECUSA) to the property of a local church that voted unanimously to disaffiliate from the parent body. The church voted to disaffiliate from the PECUSA because of disagreement with certain denominational policies, and a dispute arose between the church and PECUSA regarding ownership of the church's property. The court emphasized that (a) the congregation's withdrawal from the PECUSA "was unequivocal, and there was no dissenting faction," (b) the "church property was acquired exclusively by the efforts of the local congregation," (c) through the years title to the property was held by the church trustees and later by the church when it incorporated, and (d) the church "freely engaged in transactions such as purchase, encumbrance, and sale of its real property without any involvement by PECUSA." Such evidence, observed the court, created an "appearance of absolute ownership" in the local church. However, the PECUSA maintained that certain denominational documents imposed a trust on the local church's property in favor the national church, and that in any event the civil courts were required to defer to the conclusions of a hierarchical denomination such as the PECUSA (under the so-called "compulsory deference rule"). Both of these contentions were rejected by the court. It refused to adopt the "compulsory deference rule," choosing instead the "neutral principles of law" approach to resolving church property disputes. Under this approach, the court concluded that the local church and not the PECUSA was the rightful owner of the property in question since nondoctrinal language in the church's charter and deed clearly vested title in the local church.[60]

• Maryland's highest court ruled that the property of a local church that disaffiliated from a national church belonged to the local church, based on the application of neutral principles of law. A local church was organized as an affiliate of the African Methodist Episcopal Zion Church ("national church"). The court conceded that (1) the national church is hierarchical in polity; (2) the Book of Discipline requires local churches to insert clauses in deeds to their property recognizing a trust in favor of the national church; and (3) the Book of Discipline imposes the trust requirement even if local churches fail to include a trust provision in their deed. However, it cited the following evidence suggesting the absence of a trust in favor of the national church: (1) the church acquired all of its properties in its own name, without any reference to the national church; (2) none of the church's deeds contained any language indicating that the property was being held in trust for the national church; (3) the church's articles of incorporation do not mention the national church; (4) the church's bylaws contain no reference to the national church. The court stressed that to resolve church property disputes solely on the basis of provisions in a national church's governing documents with no consideration of other evidence "comes quite close to . . . violating the First Amendment's prohibition against resolving rights to the use and control of church property on the basis of a judicial determination that one group of claimants has adhered faithfully to the fundamental faiths, doctrines and practices of the church prior to the schism, while the other group of claimants has departed substantially therefrom. Pressed to its logical conclusion, such a judicial inquiry becomes a heresy

---

[60] Bjorkman v. Protestant Episcopal Church in the United States of America, 759 S.W.2d 583 (Ky. 1988). The court concluded: "It should be remembered that [the church] acquired the property with no assistance from PECUSA; that the property was managed and maintained exclusively by the church; that the church improved and added to its property; and that PECUSA deliberately avoided acquisition of title or entanglement with the property to ensure that it would not be subject to civil liability. The record is clear that PECUSA's relationship with the church was exclusively ecclesiastical and the church was at all times in control of its temporal affairs."

trial." The court conceded that there is no need to consider other evidence "when there is clear trust or reverter language in the deed to the property." But, this was not such a case.[61]

• *A Massachusetts court ruled that a local church could retain its property after disaffiliating from a parent denomination. The members of a local church voted to amend the church's bylaws to remove all reference to a parent denomination. The executive board of the denomination asked a court to declare the congregational meeting illegal and to rule that all of the church's properties were subject to the control of the denomination. A state appeals court conceded that denominational documents "provide considerable force" to the denomination's claim that it is hierarchical in terms of the control of local church property. But the court also noted that there had been "considerable movement in and out of the [denomination] by individual parishes who took with them their own property without claim by the [denomination]." Based on this evidence, the court concluded that the local church was congregational as far as the control and use of its property was concerned, and owned its own property.[62]*

• *The Missouri Supreme Court adopted the neutral principles approach and awarded church property to a schismatic church that disaffiliated from an hierarchical denomination (the United Presbyterian Church in the United States of America, or "UPCUSA"). The court observed that title to the church property was in the name of the local church, and nothing in the church or denominational bylaws or discipline provided any express trust in favor of the denomination. [63]*

• *A federal appeals court, applying Missouri law, ruled that a Church of God in Christ congregation that voted to secede from the national church retained control of its property. The court noted that Missouri courts had adopted the "neutral principles of law" approach to resolving church property disputes, and concluded that the local congregation retained title to its properties under the neutral principles of law approach on the basis of the following considerations: (1) The national Church contributed nothing to the acquisition of the congregation's property. (2) The local congregation exercised complete control over the property without any interference from the Church. Indeed, the court pointed out that never in the congregation's history, until the events leading to this lawsuit, had the Church attempted to exercise any control over the congregation. (3) The congregation's articles of incorporation explicitly declare its independence from the national Church. (4) The deeds to the congregation's properties vest title and control in the hands of the local congregation. The court rejected the Church's claim that the congregation held its properties "in trust" for the national Church. It noted that "[t]he Church did not automatically provide local pastors with a copy of its manual, nor was it distributed generally to [the congregation's] members. To require the . . . congregation to hold its property in trust for another without proper notice as to that requirement would too severely distort the application of*

---

[61]   From the Heart Church Ministries v. African Methodist Episcopal Zion Church, 803 A.2d 548 (Md. 2002). The court stressed that the national church's Book of Discipline did not contain a provision "dealing with the disposition of church property when a local church disaffiliates from the denomination" and that "consent to holding property in trust during the course of affiliation does not automatically constitute consent to relinquishing that property once the affiliation terminates."

[62]   Primate Synod v. Russian Orthodox Church Outside Russia, 617 N.E.2d 1031 (Mass. App. 1993), *aff'd*, 636 N.E.2d 211 (Mass. 1994).

[63]   Presbytery of Elijah Parish Lovejoy v. Jaeggi, 682 S.W.2d 465 (Mo. 1984).

neutral principles of Missouri law. With only its charter and constitution to point to, no evidence that [the congregation] actually acquiesced in that constitution, and all the other considerations pointing in favor of [the congregation] we conclude that the national Church cannot wrest ownership from the . . . congregation under neutral principles of Missouri law."[64]

• A federal appeals court, applying New Jersey law, refused to recognize a national church body's attempt to gain control over local church properties through amendments in its Book of Discipline. A church was incorporated in 1915 and affiliated with the African Union Methodist Protestant Church (the "national church"). In 1991 the national church held a meeting at which a "church property" resolution was adopted. This resolution specified that "the title to all property, now owned or hereafter acquired by an incorporated local church . . . shall be held by or conveyed to the corporate body in its corporate name, in trust for the use and benefit of such local church and of the African Union Methodist Protestant Church." Another provision in the property resolution directed churches to include a similar "trust clause" in their deeds. The property resolution, as adopted, was incorporated into the national church's governing Book of Discipline. At the same 1991 meeting of the national church, another resolution was adopted authorizing pastors "to sign official documents pertaining to the individual local church." On the basis of these resolutions, the national church directed a number of pastors to sign a quitclaim deed transferring title to their church's property to the national church. One church, whose property was deeded to the national church by its pastor pursuant to such a directive, voted unanimously to secede from the national church. The court concluded that the pastor's attempt to deed his church's property to the national church had to be invalidated on the basis of neutral principles of law. It noted that the church's articles of incorporation allowed conveyances of church property only upon a vote of at least two-thirds of the church's members. It conceded that this provision conflicted with the "property resolutions" in the national church's Book of Discipline, but it concluded that the Book of Discipline "functioned" as the local church's bylaws, and that whenever there is a conflict between a church's articles of incorporation and its bylaws, the articles of incorporation prevail.[65]

• The New York Court of Appeals adopted the neutral principles approach in a dispute involving ownership of property owned by a church that disaffiliated from the United Presbyterian Church in the United States of America (UPCUSA), and awarded the church's property to the local church. The court reasoned that there was no neutral principle of law vesting title in the denomination. The court rejected the denomination's argument that "it is presumed that the local church intended to dedicate the property to the purposes of the larger body by voluntarily merging itself with it." The court criticized the "compulsory deference" rule, since this rule "assumes that the local church has relinquished control to the hierarchical body in all cases, thereby frustrating the actual intent of the local church in some cases. Such a practice, it is said, discourages local churches from associating with a hierarchical church for purposes of religious worship out of fear of losing their property and the indirect result of discouraging such an association may constitute a violation of the free

---

[64] Church of God in Christ v. Graham, 54 F.3d 522 (8th Cir. 1995).

[65] Scotts African Union Methodist Protestant Church v. Conference of African Union First Colored Methodist Protestant Church, 98 F.3d 78 (3rd Cir. 1996).

exercise clause. Additionally, by supporting the hierarchical polity over other forms and permitting local churches to lose control over their property, the deference rule may indeed constitute a judicial establishment of religion . . . ."[66]

• A New York court ruled that a local church that disaffiliated from the Episcopal Church in 1976 retained control of its property. The church was organized in 1859 for the purpose of establishing a church "in communion with the Protestant Episcopal Church in the Diocese of New York, and in the United States of America, and in accordance with its doctrine, discipline, and worship." In 1976 the church disaffiliated from the Episcopal Church in the United States and its New York Diocese on the basis of changes in doctrine and practice approved by the national church at a General Convention held earlier that year. The church then associated with the Anglican Church. The New York Diocese filed a lawsuit asserting ownership and control of the congregation's property. The court ruled that the local congregation retained ownership and control of its property following its disaffiliation from the Episcopal Church. The court observed: "[E]ven though members of a local group belonged to a hierarchical church, they may withdraw from the church and claim title to either personal or real property provided that they have not previously ceded the property to the denominational church. In other words, the facts that this [church] was originally part of a hierarchical body does not necessarily bind a court if it is possible to decide the controversy through the application of "neutral principles of law." The court acknowledged that there can be an implied trust in church property for the denominational church. However, to establish such a trust there must be a sufficient manifestation of the intention to do so. The court concluded that there was insufficient evidence in this case of an implied trust in favor of the diocese or national church. It observed: "[I]t is clear that [the congregation] acquired the property in question on its own and there is no specific evidence either in the deeds which form a part of the record nor by any other evidence . . . that [the congregation] intended to hold the property in trust. When [it] disassociated itself and revised its corporate charter, the [national church's] ecclesiastical law was not in place to govern the disposition of [the congregation's] property." The court pointed out that the "deeds to this [church] contain no forfeiture or significant reversionary clauses. Further, the "in communion with" language was ecclesiastical and accordingly was of no legal significance.[67]

• A North Carolina court ruled that title to a local Church of God congregation that disaffiliated from the denomination belonged to the local church rather than to denominational officials. In 1955, the congregation voted to affiliate with the Church of God denomination "for purposes of fellowship." In 1988, the church voted to disaffiliate from the denomination. In response to this action, the "state overseer" of the Church of God dismissed the local church's board of trustees and appointed a successor board consisting of denominational trustees. The successor trustees executed a deed conveying to themselves title to the church's property. When local church members opposed this denominational control of their property, the

---

[66] First Presbyterian Church v. United Presbyterian Church in the United States of America, 476 N.Y.S.2d 86 (Ct. App. 1984). *Accord* Park Slope Jewish Center v. Congregation B'Nai Jacob, 664 N.Y.S.2d 236 (Ct. App. 1997).

[67] Diocesan Missionary and Church Extension Society v. Church of the Holy Comforter, 628 N.Y.S.2d 471 (Sup. 1994). *Accord* Presbytery v. Trustees of First Presbyterian Church, 821 N.Y.S.2d 834 (N.Y. App. 2006). The court concluded that amendments to the Book of Order of the Presbyterian Church (U.S.A.) did not impose a trust upon the property of affiliated churches in favor of the national church.

denominational trustees asked a court to determine the lawful owner of the church property. The denominational bylaws specify that a local board of trustees shall hold title to local church property and that "all such property shall be used, managed, and controlled for the sole and exclusive use and benefit of the Church of God." The court noted that as a general rule the parent body of a "connectional church" has the right to control the property of local affiliated churches. However, a local church "may have retained sufficient independence from the general church so that it reserved its right to withdraw at any time, and, presumably, take along with it whatever property it independently owned prior to and retained during its limited affiliation with the general church." The court concluded that such was the case here. It based its ruling on the fact that "when the local church affiliated with the denominational church, the property was deeded to trustees of . . . the local church, not to the denominational church."[68]

• A Pennsylvania state appeals court ruled that a dissident church was entitled to retain its property following its disaffiliation from the Russian Orthodox Church because of a proposed revision by the Orthodox Church in its calendar. The court held that an award of a local church's assets to a parent denomination is possible only if the denomination can demonstrate "(1) an actual transfer of property from the congregation to the hierarchical church body, or (2) clear and unambiguous documentary evidence or conduct on the part of the congregation evincing an intent to create a trust in favor of the hierarchical church body." The court observed that the denomination could not satisfy the first test, since the local congregation "never relinquished its right to possession or legal title to the church property." On the contrary, the church's original affiliation with the Orthodox Church was accompanied by a letter expressing its intent to retain ownership and control of its property. As to the second requirement, the court observed, after reviewing the church's charter, constitution, bylaws, and the bylaws of the Orthodox Church, that none of these documents contained any "clear and unambiguous" language creating a trust in favor of the Orthodox Church. The court also rejected the denomination's claim that its "hierarchical structure" compelled an award in its favor, since "regardless of the form of government of the church in question, we must examine the relevant deeds, contracts, or other evidence to determine ownership of the disputed property."[69]

• A Tennessee court ruled that a local church retained control of its property following its withdrawal from a parent denomination, based on the wording of the deed to the property. The court concluded that the language of the deed demonstrated an intent by the grantor that the locally appointed trustees "are to retain governing power over the property in case of a division or misunderstanding of any kind in the parent church." It concluded: "Although [the grantor] was not a literate man, he was careful to . . . make sure that the local trustees would always have the power to decide what to do with the property in case of a controversy."[70]

---

[68] Looney v. Community Bible Holiness Church, 405 S.E.2d 811 (N.C. App. 1991).

[69] Orthodox Church of America v. Pavuk, 538 A.2d 632 (Pa. Common. 1988). *See also* Board of Bishops of the Church of the Living God v. Milner, 513 A.2d 1131 (Pa. Common. 1986) (court awarded property to local church that disaffiliated from hierarchical denomination—on basis of neutral principles).

[70] Emmanuel Churches of Christ v. Foster, 2001 WL 327910 (unpublished decision, Tenn. App. 2001).

2. Title Awarded to Denominations

A number of courts that have awarded the property of a dissident church to a parent denomination based on provisions in the denomination's governing documents.[71] This conclusion is based on either or both of the following grounds:

> **(1) Neutral principles of law.** The denomination's governing documents contain a provision directing that the property of a church that votes to terminate its affiliation reverts or otherwise belongs to the denomination, and, to the extent that such a provision can be applied without recourse to church doctrine, it constitutes a neutral principle of law that can be used to resolve a dispute over ownership of church property.

> **(2) Trust.** The denomination's governing documents impose a trust, either express or implied, on the property of affiliated churches in favor of the parent denomination.

It may be more accurate to say that those courts that resolve church property disputes on the basis of a trust created by a denomination's governing documents are following the Supreme Court's admonition in Watson that "it would seem . . . to be the obvious duty of the court . . . to see that the property so dedicated is not diverted from the trust which is thus attached to its use,"[72] rather than using a neutral principle of law analysis. The result, however, generally is the same, and so this section will include both kinds of cases.

Case Studies

• *The Alabama Supreme Court ruled that a national denomination owned the property of a local church that voted to disaffiliate from the denomination, since the deed to the local church property vested title in the denomination, and denominational rules specified that "[i]f any members of the [denomination] leave or cease to be members of the [denomination], irrespective of the amount or number thereof, the fact that they leave or cease to be a member of the [denomination] shall not, in any manner, affect the property of the said church, and said party or parties or persons leaving the congregation or membership of the [denomination], in any manner, cannot and shall not take any property of the [denomination], in any manner, and all church property, irrespective, whether acquired by the local congregation, local church or otherwise, is the property of the [denomination]."[73]*

• *The Alabama Supreme Court was asked to decide whether a local church or a parent denomination owned the church's property following its disaffiliation from the*

---

[71] *See, e.g.,* Fry v. Emmanuel Churches of Christ, Inc., 839 S.W.2d 406 (Tenn. App. 1992) (Assembly of the Emmanuel Churches of Christ).

[72] See notes 1 and 4, *supra.*

[73] Harris v. Apostolic Overcoming Holy Church of God, Inc., 457 So.2d 385 (Ala. 1984). *Contra* Haney's Chapel Methodist Church v. United Methodist Church, 716 So.2d 1156 (Ala. 1998).

denomination. A local church had been affiliated with the African Methodist Episcopal Zion Church in America since 1908. In 1985, a majority of the church's membership voted to disaffiliate with the parent denomination. The denomination wrote the church a letter acknowledging the disaffiliation, and requesting all dissident members to vacate the premises. Dissident members refused to vacate the property, and the denomination filed a lawsuit seeking to have itself declared the owner of the church's property. In support of its claim, the denomination quoted a provision contained (since 1884) in its Book of Discipline that pertained to local church property: "In trust, that said premises shall be used, kept, maintained, and disposed of as a place of divine worship for the use of the ministry and membership of the African Methodist Episcopal Zion Church in America, subject to the discipline, usage and ministerial appointments of said church as from time to time authorized and declared by the General Conference of said church." The court ruled in favor of the denomination. It surveyed the close ties that had existed between the local church and parent denomination in the 77 years of affiliation, and noted that since 1884 every prospective member of a church affiliated with the denomination had agreed to be "cheerfully governed" by the denomination's Book of Discipline. In light of such evidence, the supreme court concluded: "[The church] has been a member of [the denomination] for three-quarters of a century, by an association that both the national denomination and the local church acknowledge. For the entire time, the [Book of Discipline] provided that the [church's] property be held for the [denomination] by the local church. Individuals who have been members of the [church] the longest acknowledge that, for as long as they can remember, everyone who became a member of [the church] promised to abide by the rules and regulations of the . . . denomination. [The church] cannot now sever the relationship between [the denomination] and itself and unilaterally declare that obligations incumbent upon itself because of three-quarters of a century of association do not exist. [The church's] choice to join [the denomination] means it is obligated to obey all the rules and regulations its members promised to uphold, not just the rules and regulations they prefer; at least in regard to property disputes, the [denomination's Book of Discipline] binds [the local church]." [74]

• A California court ruled that title to the properties of a local church that voted to disaffiliate from a parent denomination belonged to the denomination rather than to the church. The local church was the oldest Korean immigrant congregation in the Presbyterian Church (U.S.A.) ("PCUSA"). It had participated actively in the Presbyterian Church for more than 80 years. PCUSA had assisted the church in acquiring its first properties, and in obtaining financing for various projects. A schism developed within the church. Attempts by the PCUSA to resolve the problems failed. As a result of the schism, a group (numbering up to 30 percent of the church's membership) left the church and formed a "church in exile." The pastor thereafter had the remaining congregation vote to disaffiliate from the PCUSA. Acting in accordance with the Presbyterian Book of Order, the PCUSA designated the exiled congregation as the "true church," and as the rightful owner of the church properties. A lawsuit was filed to determine the ownership of the church properties. A state appeals court awarded the church properties to the "exiled" congregation designated by the PCUSA as the true church. The court based its decision on the following 3 considerations: (1) "[I]t has long been the law in California that the identification of a religious body as the

---

[74] African Methodist Episcopal Zion Church in America, Inc. v. Zion Hill Methodist Church, Inc., 534 So.2d 224 (Ala. 1988).

true church is an ecclesiastical issue," and accordingly the civil courts must accept the decisions of hierarchical denominations that identify a particular faction as the true representative of a local church. (2) When the church voted to disaffiliate from the PCUSA its members in effect renounced any further obligation to be subject to the doctrines or discipline of the PCUSA. This action also resulted in the loss of their church membership since the church's articles of incorporation required adherence to the doctrines and disciplines of PCUSA as a condition of membership. Having abandoned their membership in the local church, they "lost all power and ability to determine its future status." (3) Express trust provisions in the church's deed, as well as the Book of Order of the PCUSA vested title in the exiled group.[75]

• A California court ruled that the governing documents of the Open Bible Church ("national church") prevented a local church from disaffiliating from it and retaining control of church property. The national church's bylaws specify that affiliated churches may be placed under "regional supervision" under specified conditions. Under regional supervision, the regional board of directors becomes the governing board of the affiliated church, with power to manage the local church's property and to remove the pastor. A church was placed under regional supervision, and later attempted to disaffiliate from the national church. A state appeals court noted that the United States Supreme Court "has adopted a two-pronged analysis in intra-church disputes involving property. Civil courts may employ neutral principles of law as the basis for resolving such disputes, unless this determination depends on the resolution of an ecclesiastical controversy over religious doctrine, practice or polity." As a result, "where the matter at issue in a church dispute involves questions of ownership of property and assets, civil courts applying neutral principles of law must defer to the authoritative decisions of hierarchical ecclesiastical bodies on any matters of internal church polity necessarily involved in resolving the issue." The court concluded that the issues in this case (including the imposition of regional supervision) were "precisely the kinds of issues to which both the United States Supreme Court and the courts of this state have traditionally applied the ecclesiastical rule of judicial deference. . . . Thus, we conclude the trial court correctly determined that Open Bible was a hierarchical church as to which a civil court must defer with respect to its ecclesiastical decisions."[76]

• The Colorado Supreme Court ruled that a national denomination owned the property of a local church that voted to disaffiliate from the Protestant Episcopal Church in the United States of America (PECUSA) when the denomination approved the ordination of women. The court acknowledged that title to the church property was vested in the local congregation; that the deeds contained no reference to PECUSA and no language suggesting that the property was held by the local church in trust for the national denomination; and that PECUSA did not provide any financial assistance to the local church in purchasing the property. Nevertheless, the court concluded that "an intent on the part of the local church corporation to dedicate its property irrevocably to the purposes of PECUSA was expressed unambiguously in the combination of the [church's] articles of incorporation, the local church bylaws, and the canons of the general church . . . ." The court noted that the local church's articles of incorporation stated that the church was organized "to administer the temporalities of the Protestant Episcopal Church in the parish," and that the church "does hereby expressly accede

---

[75] Korean United Presbyterian Church v. Presbytery of the Pacific, 281 Cal. Rptr. 396 (Cal. App. 2 Dist. 1991).

[76] Concord Christian Center v. Open Bible Standard Churches, 34 Cal.Rptr.3d 412 (Cal. App. 2005).

to all the provisions of the constitution and canons adopted by the General Convention of the Protestant Episcopal Church in the United States of America, and to all of the provisions of the constitution and canons of the Diocese of Colorado." These provisions, observed the court, "strongly indicate that the local church property was to be held for the benefit of the general church . . . . There are no provisions in the articles implicitly or explicitly expressing an intent to the contrary." This and other evidence convinced the court that there was a "unity of purpose on the part of the parish and of the general church reflecting the intent that property held by the parish would be dedicated to and utilized for the advancement of the work of PECUSA. These provisions foreclose the possibility of the withdrawal of property from the parish simply because a majority of the members of the parish decide to end their association with PECUSA. We hold that the facts . . . establish that a trust has been imposed upon the real and personal property of the [local church] for the use of the general church."[77]

• The Connecticut Supreme Court ruled that title to a local Episcopalian church reverted to the Episcopal Diocese of Connecticut following its vote to disaffiliate from the Diocese. The church had been affiliated with the Diocese for more than a century, but voted to disaffiliate and join the Anglican Church in 1986. Both the church and Diocese claimed ownership of the church property. The court noted that the national Episcopal Church adopted the following provision at a national conference in 1979 creating an express trust over local church properties in favor of the national church: "All real and personal property held by or for the benefit of any parish, mission or congregation is held in trust for this church and the diocese thereof in which such parish, mission or congregation is located." Because this provision was not adopted until 1979, the court concluded that it did not apply in this case since the church's properties were acquired long before 1979. However, the court concluded that the polity of the Episcopal denomination and the historical relationship of local churches with the denomination clearly demonstrated an "implied trust" in favor of the Diocese over the property of local churches. The court based this conclusion on the following factors: (1) Local churches accepted the doctrine of the denomination. (2) The Diocesan canons permit the establishment of a church only with the permission of the bishop. (3) The Diocesan canons permit the disaffiliation of a local church from the diocese only with the permission of the bishop. (4) The Diocesan canons prohibit the transfer of local church property without the permission of the bishop. (5) The local church in this case submitted annual reports to the Diocese, as required by Diocesan canons. (6) The local church in this case sent delegates (both clergy and laypersons) to the annual conventions of the Diocese. (7) The local church in this case paid its annual assessments to the Diocese as required by Diocesan canons. The court concluded that these factors "strongly reflect the polity of the church as one in which the parish is the local manifestation of [the denomination] to be used for its ministry and mission."[78]

• The Delaware Supreme Court ruled that a Methodist church had no legal authority to block a decision by the United Methodist Church to close the church because of dwindling membership. The court, applying neutral principles of law, concluded

---

[77] Bishop and Diocese of Colorado v. Mote, 716 P.2d 85 (Colo. 1986).

[78] Rector, Wardens and Vestrymen of Trinity-St. Michael's Parish, Inc. v. Episcopal Church in the Diocese of Connecticut, 620 A.2d 1280 (Conn. 1993). *But see* Annual Conference v. St. Luke Unison Free Will Baptist Church, 2004 WL 425176 (unpublished decision, Conn. Super. 2004). A Connecticut court ruled that a denominational agency had no authority to retain the property of a church that voted to withdraw since there was no evidence that the church's property was ever "dedicated to the use of the regional church or to a particular organization."

that the local church property was subject to an "implied trust" in favor of the United Methodist Church, and therefore the local church leaders acted unlawfully in withholding ownership and possession.[79]

• A Florida court ruled that the property of a local church that attempted to secede from an hierarchical denomination remained with the denomination. An African Methodist Episcopal church disaffiliated from the parent denomination, and claimed ownership of its property following the disaffiliation. A state appeals court ruled that in Florida the property of such a church reverts to the denomination following the church's disaffiliation. It concluded that a prior ruling of the state supreme court "requires that church property remain with the parent church where, as here, the church is hierarchical in structure. Given the trial court's finding that the AME Church is hierarchical, judgment should have been entered in favor of [the national church] as representative of the original church."[80]

• The Georgia Supreme Court ruled that a national church controlled the property of a local church that desired to separate from the national church, as a result of a provision in the governing documents of the national church. The court concluded: "It is undisputed that the [national church] remains a hierarchy, that the local church has been a member of the national church for over thirty years, and that the church is subject to the national church's discipline. Such discipline unquestionably provides that the national church 'shall hold all church property,' thereby implying a trust for the benefit of the national church. And this is irrespective of the church's continuing membership in the national church."[81]

• A Kansas court ruled that a national church owned the property of a local church that attempted to disaffiliate. From its inception in 1979, a local church was affiliated with the Church of God in Christ (the "national church"). The court observed: "The applicable civil law respecting religious societies governed by trustees is clear in this state and does not differ significantly from the law in jurisdictions across the country. When a local religious organization has acquired property through the contributions and sacrifices of many members, past and present, all of whom have adhered to certain doctrines regarded as fundamental to a particular national denomination, no faction may be permitted to divert the church property to another denomination or to the support of doctrines, usages, and practices basically opposed to those characteristic of the particular denomination." The court stressed that "the [local church] maintained a longstanding, formal affiliation with the national church. There was continual, substantial participation of the [church] and its members in the national, state, and district meetings, activities, and functions. Pastors of the [church] were appointed by the Jurisdictional Bishop of the Kansas Southwest Jurisdiction and given a certificate of appointment as pastor of the local church. The [church] made state and national reports, which were financial contributions to help carry on the business of the national church. The national church issued a certificate of membership to the local church."[82]

---

[79] East Lake Methodist Episcopal Church, Inc. v. Trustees of the Peninsula-Delaware Annual Conference, 731 A.2d 798 (Dela. 1999).

[80] Bethel AME Church v. Domingo, 654 So.2d 233 (Fla. App. 1 Dist. 1995).

[81] Holiness Baptist Association v. Barber, 552 S.E.2d 90 (Ga. 2001). *Accord* Pritchett v. Wesleyan Pentecostal Church, (Ga. App. 2004).

[82] Church of God in Christ v. Board of Trustees of New Jerusalem Church of God in Christ, 992 P.2d 812 (Kan. App. 1999).

• *The Louisiana Supreme Court adopted the neutral principles of law approach, but ruled that the property of a local church that disaffiliated from the African Methodist Episcopal Church belonged to the denomination (A.M.E. Church). The court relied on provisions in the denomination's discipline requiring (a) denominational approval of transfers of local church property, and (b) reversion of title in "abandoned" or "disbanded" churches to the denomination. The court observed: "Applying the neutral principles which are evoked by our examination of the documents in purely secular terms, we concluded that it was the intention of the parties . . . that [the church property] not be alienated without A.M.E.'s consent, and will be considered abandoned to A.M.E. upon [the church's] disbanding as an A.M.E. society. Accordingly, because of [the local church's] disaffiliation without a prior valid transfer of [its property], A.M.E. has become vested with the exclusive right to control its use and to compel the transfer of title if necessary.*[83]

• *A Maryland court ruled that a parent denomination retained control of the property of a local congregation that voted to disaffiliate. The congregation of a church affiliated with the African Methodist Episcopal (A.M.E.) Church voted in 1993 to disaffiliate from the parent body as a result of what it perceived to be burdensome financial demands and a decline in moral conditions within the denomination. Both the dissident congregation and the A.M.E. Church claimed the church's property. A state appeals court awarded the church's property to the national church. The court acknowledged that the deed and the A.M.E. Church Discipline did not contain any trust provision or reverter clause. However, the court insisted that these omissions did not mean that the seceding church retained its property. Quite to the contrary, "the absence of an explicit reverter upon withdrawal clause does not necessarily mean that the local church is entitled to retain control of its property." Rather, a court must consider all relevant documents. The court noted that the church's articles of incorporation specified that the "powers and authority of the trustees shall be in subjection to" the national church. It concluded: "Based exclusively on the language in the [articles of incorporation] requiring that the trustees hold the property 'in trust' for the A.M.E. Church, we hold that [the local church] was not entitled to retain control of the land after their departure from the A.M.E. Church."*[84]

• *The Mississippi Supreme Court ruled that a local church held its property "in trust" for the benefit of the Christian Methodist Episcopal Church (CME), and therefore the church's property remained with the CME when the local church voted to disaffiliate. The court noted that for the CME to prevail, it had to demonstrate (1) an actual transfer of property from the church to the CME; (2) an express trust in favor of the CME; or (3) clear and convincing evidence showing an intent by the church to create a trust in favor of the CME. The court found no evidence of an actual transfer of property to the CME, and therefore the CME had to prove that an express or implied trust was established in its favor in order to win. The court concluded that this test was met: "An analysis of the portions of the CME Book of Discipline governing the holding of church property reveals that the property in question has been held in trust for the CME by the trustees appointed by the Annual Conference. . . . The Book of Discipline states that titles to all property held by local churches are held in trust for CME and are subject*

---

[83]   Fluker Community Church v. Hitchens, 419 So.2d 445 (La. 1982).

[84]   Board of Incorporators v. Mt. Olive African Methodist Episcopal Church, 672 A.2d 679 (Md. App. 1996).

to the provisions of the discipline. The property in question was conveyed by deed to the trustees of [the local church] and their successors and assigns. The trustees, although members of the local congregation, are appointed by the CME organization at its Annual Conference. Because the trustees are appointed by CME, it follows that the trustees are holding the property in trust for CME."[85]

• A Missouri court ruled that the property of a dissident church belonged to a national church body with which it was affiliated. The local church opposed a 1984 resolution of the national church which permitted the ordination of women into the priesthood. After efforts to work out their differences failed, the national church attempted in install a new minister. When the congregation overwhelmingly voted to retain their original minister, the national church had the locks to the church property changed, barricades erected, and notices posted to keep people off the property. The congregation proceeded to have keys made to the new locks, removed the barricades, and held services on the premises. The national church then sought and obtained a court order banning the minister "and those acting in concert with him" from entering onto church property and from in any way disrupting the worship services conducted on the property. The congregation appealed this order, and a Missouri appeals court ruled in favor of the national church. With regard to the ownership of the church property, the court applied the neutral principles of law approach, observing that the national church owned the property since the deed to the property created an express trust in favor of the national church, as did relevant documents of the national church. Further, such provisions did not require any inquiries into religious doctrine. [86]

• A New York court ruled that the property of a church that voted to disaffiliate from the Protestant Episcopal Church (national church) belonged to the national church rather than the local church. The court analyzed various documents to determine if the dispute could be resolved on the basis of neutral principles of law: (1) The court found no language in the deeds to the church property indicating that title was to be held in trust for the national church. Further, none of the deeds contained a forfeiture or reverter clause in favor of the national church. (2) The court noted that while the church's certificate of incorporation "expressly acknowledged [the church's] affiliation with the national church . . . nothing in its certificate of incorporation indicates how church property is to be owned." (3) The court noted that the New York Religious Corporations Law was silent as to the ownership of property. (4) The court referred to the following canon that had been adopted by the national church in 1979: "All real and personal property held by or for the benefit of any Parish, Mission or Congregation is held in trust for this Church and the Diocese thereof in which Parish, Mission or Congregation is located. Existence of this trust, however, shall in no way limit the power and authority of the Parish, Mission or Congregation otherwise existing over such property so long as the particular Parish, Mission or Congregation remains a part of, and subject to, this Church and its Constitution and Canons." The court concluded that this canon could be applied to the church property in this case even though the church had acquired its property prior to the adoption of the canon.[87]

---

[85] Bouldes v. Christian Methodist Episcopal Church, 748 So.2d 672 (Miss. 1999).

[86] Reorganized Church of Jesus Christ of Latter Day Saints v. Thomas, 758 S.W.2d 726 (Mo. App. 1988).

[87] Trustees of the Diocese of Albany v. Trinity Episcopal Church, 684 N.Y.S.2d 76 (Sup. Ct. 1999). *Accord* North Central New York Annual Conference v. Felker, 816 N.Y.S.2d 775 (N.Y.A.D. 2006).

• A North Carolina court ruled that the property of a local church that voted to withdraw from the Protestant Episcopal Church in the United States of America ("PECUSA") automatically vested in the PECUSA because of the following trust provisions in its canons.

"All real or personal property held by or for the benefit of any Parish, Mission or Congregation is held in trust for this Church and the Diocese thereof in which such Parish, Mission or Congregation is located. The existence of this trust, however, shall in no way limit the power and authority of the Parish, Mission or Congregation otherwise existing over such property so long as the particular Parish, Mission or Congregation remains a part of, and subject to, this Church and its Constitution and Canons." PECUSA Canon I.7.4.

"In the event of the dissolution of any Parish or Mission by the Convention, the real and personal property of the Parish or Mission shall immediately vest in the Trustees of the Diocese, in trust for the dissolved Parish or Mission." Diocese Canon II.6.2.[88]

• A Pennsylvania court ruled that a national denomination retained ownership of the property of a local church that seceded from the denomination. A local congregation affiliated with the Conference of African Union First Colored Methodist Protestant Church in 1977. The church's articles of incorporation stated its purposes to include "Christian worship and fellowship subject to the law and usage of the Holy Bible and the Book of Discipline of the African Union First Colored Methodist Protestant Church." The Conference's book of discipline contains the following clause: "All church property and other property belonging to the [Conference] shall be deeded to the members and [Conference], and should the members disband or secede the property shall remain in the possession of the [Conference], and that each local church should be so incorporated that if the members should disband or secede, the said church and property shall remain in the [Conference]." In 1989 the congregation voted to disaffiliate from the Conference. The Conference asked a court to declare that it was the owner of the church's property. A state appeals court ruled in favor of the Conference. The court noted: "A hierarchical denomination claiming a trust in its favor from a local congregation must demonstrate the trust through clear and unambiguous language or conduct evidencing an intent to create the trust. . . . The record fully demonstrates that the Conference met its burden of proof. [The church] accepted and agreed to be bound by the book of discipline, which governs matters related to the use and disposition of property held by a member church and represents a contractual agreement that may be enforced by the courts."[89]

• The Supreme Court of South Carolina suggested that when a majority of the membership in a local church votes to disaffiliate the church from a parent denomination, a minority desiring to remain faithful to the parent church will receive title to church property. The court observed: "Counsel . . . argues the lower court should be reversed because neutral principles of law require that the property in

---

[88]   Daniel v. Wray, 580 S.E.2d 711 (N.C. App. 2003).

[89]   Conference of African Union First Colored Methodist Protestant Church v. Shell, 659 A.2d 77 (Pa. Common. 1995). Accord In re Church of St. James the Less, 888 A.2d 795 (Pa. 2005). The Pennsylvania Supreme Court upheld the validity of a canon adopted by the Protestant Episcopal Church (PECUS) in 1979 imposing a trust upon the properties of affiliated churches in favor of the national church.

question should be in the possession and control of the appellants as representing the majority of the members of the First Presbyterian Church of Rock Hill . . . . For this proposition appellants rely largely on the case of Presbyterian Church in the United States v. Mary Elizabeth Blue Hull Memorial Presbyterian Church . . . . A review of that case convinces us that it is of no comfort to the appellants here . . . . By a determination of this case, this Court exercises no role in determining ecclesiastical questions. We merely settle a dispute on the question of identity, which in turn necessarily settles a dispute involving the control of property. . . . The appellants voluntarily associated themselves with the First Presbyterian Church of Rock Hill and became subject to the discipline and government of the Presbyterian Church in the United States. They voluntarily severed their connection, and when they did they forfeited any right to the use and possession of the property of that church under the long established law of the church and of South Carolina. . . . By joining the First Presbyterian Church of Rock Hill the members did not acquire such an interest in the property that they are entitled to take with them upon seceding. The property belonged to the First Presbyterian Church of Rock Hill before the members joined the church, and it belongs to the same after they have withdrawn. They simply are not now a part of that church. There is nothing in the ruling of the lower court, nor in our ruling today, which establishes, sponsors, advances, or supports either the religious belief of the majority or the minority in this case. This Court has traditionally avoided any intrusion upon religious matters and has confined its rulings in such cases to identifying the faction which represents the church after the schism occurred. . . . In so doing, we applied neutral principles of law referred to in Hull." Identifying the church, when a majority faction votes to disaffiliate, involves no interpretation of religious doctrine. It is a doctrinally neutral act, and therefore is consistent with Hull. [90]

• A South Carolina appeals court ruled that a national church organization was entitled to the property of a local church that withdrew from the organization. The court observed that the local church was bound by the provision in the national church's "decree book" specifying that all local church properties belonged to the national church. The court further explained: "The main issue of this case is whether when the congregation of an hierarchical church withdraws from the church, the congregation is entitled to the church property. The well-settled answer to this question is that the title and right of possession of the church property remains in the hierarchical church . . . . The South Carolina appellate courts have yet to face a situation in which the congregation as a whole withdrew and contended that the church property belonged to it. The law on this question is settled. . . . [W]hen a church splits, the courts will not undertake to inquire into the ecclesiastical acts of the several parties, but will determine the property rights in favor of the party or division maintaining the church organization as it previously existed. We accordingly hold that when the entire congregation withdraws from the hierarchical church, the title to the church property remains in the church and does not follow the congregation. [91]

• A Texas state appeals court resolved a church property dispute in which a denomination and a local church both claimed title to the church's property. The church was established in 1970, and in the same year was affiliated with the

[90] Adickes v. Adkins 215 S.E.2d 442 (S.C. 1975), *cert. denied*, 423 U.S. 913 (1975).

[91] Dillard v. Jackson, 403 S.E.2d 136 (S.C. App. 1991). *Accord* Fire Baptized Holiness Church of God of the Americas v. Greater Fuller Tabernacle of Fire Baptized Holiness Church, 475 S.E.2d 767 (S.C. App. 1996).

Evangelical Assemblies denomination. Pursuant to the Evangelical Assemblies' constitution, the church paid for its property but title was vested in the name of the denomination. In 1983, a majority of the church's members voted to disassociate the church from the denomination, whereupon a lawsuit was commenced to determine legal ownership of church property. The court concluded that the Evangelical Assemblies was "in every respect" a hierarchical church organization, and accordingly, "as the parent church, Evangelical Assemblies owns and is entitled to possession of the property under the mutually binding constitution." [92]

Church Property Disputes— Dispute Resolution Procedures § 7-04

Key point 7-04. *Churches and denominational agencies can avoid church property disputes by adopting appropriate nondoctrinal language in deeds, trusts, local church bylaws, or denominational bylaws.*

How may a denomination ensure that it will retain the property of an affiliated church that votes to disaffiliate? How may an independent church congregation ensure that its property will remain with a particular group in the event of a church split? When can a local church seeking to disaffiliate from a particular denomination safely assume that it will retain the church property? And, how will a faction (a majority or a minority of church members) in an independent church know what its rights are, if any, in church property following a schism? The Supreme Court responded to these concerns in *Jones*:

> [T]he neutral principles analysis shares the peculiar genius of private-law systems in general—flexibility in ordering private rights and obligations to reflect the intentions of the parties. Through appropriate reversionary clauses and trust provisions, religious societies can specify what is to happen to church property in the event of a particular contingency, or what religious body will determine the ownership in the event of a schism or doctrinal controversy. In this manner, a religious organization can insure that a dispute over the ownership of church property will be resolved in accord with the desires of the members. [93]

Private resolution of church property disputes may be facilitated in a number of ways, including the following:

- deeds

- trusts

---

[92] Templo Ebenezer, Inc. v. Evangelical Assemblies, Inc., 752 S.W.2d 197 (Tex. App. 1988).

[93] 443 U.S. 595, 603 (1979).

- governing documents of local churches

- governing documents of denominational agencies

- state statutes

- resulting trusts

- constructive trusts

- arbitration

- buy-sell agreements

- characterization of denominational financing as a loan

Each of these options is summarized in the following paragraphs.

1. Deeds

Deeds to church property can provide for private resolution of church property disputes in a variety of ways.

a. **Denomination holds title to local church property.** Some denominations have title to local church property deeded to themselves, because of a mandate in the denomination's governing documents, or because the denomination contributed significantly toward the acquisition of the property or for some other reason has an equitable interest in the property. In such a case, neutral principles of law ordinarily would confirm the denomination's ownership of the property.

b. **A trust provision.** A deed can specify that a local church holds title in trust for a parent denomination.[94] The civil courts will enforce such a trust as long as no interpretation of church doctrine is required.

c. **Reverter clauses.** A deed could vest title in the local church, subject to a reversion clause or a possibility of reverter stipulating that in the event a stated condition occurs title will vest in a parent denomination or in a particular faction of the church. The condition must be worded in such a way that a court could enforce it without interpreting religious doctrine or polity. Neutral conditions might include disaffiliation or a

---

[94] To illustrate, a Georgia state appeals court awarded contested church property to a parent denomination on the basis of the following provision contained in the deed to a local church's property: "The aforesaid property is conveyed to the trustees above-named as trustees of First Evangelical Methodist Church, Lafayette, Georgia, affiliated with the Evangelical Methodist Church of Abilene, Texas, and other places, it is understood that this conveyance is made to the trustees hereinbefore named as trustees in connection with the affiliations aforesaid and that said connection is to be maintained in the use of the property herein conveyed." First Evangelical Methodist Church v. Clinton, 360 S.E.2d 584 (Ga. 1987).

disagreement about who owns church property. In either case, a court would be called upon to determine whether a disaffiliation or a property dispute had in fact occurred. Such a determination would not necessarily involve religious doctrine.

Alternatively, a reverter clause could specify that a church's property immediately reverts to a parent religious body upon an attempted conveyance of property by the church. Such a provision would prevent a church from deleting a reverter clause in its deed by reconveying property to itself, either outright or through an intermediary, by a deed not containing the reverter clause. However, any reverter clause conditioned on an attempted conveyance of church property would automatically vest title in a parent denomination upon any attempted conveyance, even those unrelated to a disaffiliation.

Most conveyances of church property are not associated with a disaffiliation. Rather, they are prompted by a desire for a new location or a larger facility. But unless the church obtains a written release or renunciation of the reverter clause from the parent denomination and has it recorded in the office of the recorder of deeds for the county in which the property is located, the property may automatically revert to the denomination whenever a church conveys its property. In many states the parent denomination could execute a quitclaim deed in favor of the local church. The parent denomination of course could condition the execution of a release or quitclaim deed upon the inclusion of a reverter clause in the deed by which the local church acquires title to its new property.

A church deed could include a reverter clause conditioned on either an attempted conveyance of church property or disaffiliation. Such a clause presumably would be effective if its enforcement would not require an interpretation of church doctrine.

Subordination Agreements

A church whose property is held subject to a reversion in favor of a parent religious body, whether through a provision in a deed, charter, bylaw, or constitution, ordinarily is not permitted to borrow money from a commercial lending institution unless the parent body signs a "subordination agreement" agreeing to subordinate its interests under the reversionary clause to the mortgage securing the lender's loan. Such agreements have three objectives.

First, they insure that the lender will have priority over the parent religious body in the event of a default.

Second, they insure that the lender will be able to recover some or all of its losses by selling the church's property in a foreclosure sale.

Subordination Agreements

Third, they insure that the church's execution of a mortgage agreement in favor of the lender will not inadvertently trigger the reverter clause in favor of the parent religious body. A mortgage constitutes a conveyance of a church's legal or equitable interest in its property to the lending institution (or, in the case of a deed of trust, to a trustee) until such time as the loan is repaid.

Many commercial lending institutions remain unaware of the danger of failing to secure a subordination agreement from the beneficiary of a reverter clause.

d. Title held jointly. Title to local church property is sometimes held jointly by both the church and a denominational agency as joint tenants or tenants in common. However, note that depending on how the property is titled, a majority faction in the church may be able to have the property partitioned (the denomination and the local church would each be declared absolute owner of a fraction of the whole).

Case Studies

• *A California court ruled that a provision in a church's deed that required church property to revert to a denominational agency (the "regional church") in the event that it determined that the church no longer was in fellowship with it, was legally enforceable by the civil courts. The court stressed that it was not required to determine if the church remained in fellowship or doctrinal unity with the regional church: "If in the opinion of [the regional church] the church is no longer in fellowship and doctrinal unity with [it] this property shall go to, vest in and become the property, in fee simple, of the [regional church]." As a result, the trial court "had no reason to determine whether the parties were in fellowship and doctrinal unity. It made no such finding, which would have been legally improper and irrelevant in any event. The terms of the deed did not call for the court to determine that issue; it was the regional church's opinion that mattered."[95]*

• *A North Carolina court ruled that a local church, rather than a national denomination, was the legal owner of its property. A local church disaffiliated from a parent denomination (the "national church"). The national church asked a court to determine which entity was the legal owner of the local church's property. The court ruled*

---

[95] New Hope Community Church of God v. Association of Church of God Southern California, 2007 WL 1493806 (unpublished decision, Cal. App. 2007).

that the property belonged to the local church, noting that while the denomination was "connectional" in nature, it was not connectional with respect to the local churches' property. The national church appealed, citing the following provision in the denomination's "Discipline": "It shall be specified in each deed to church property that it shall be for the use and benefit of the ministry and membership who are worshipping according to the customs and usages of the [denomination]." The deeds by which the local church in this case acquired its property did not make these required specifications. They contain no reference to the customs and usages of the denomination. The court concluded, "Under the language of the Discipline, it seems clear that local church property that is recorded as specified in the Discipline belongs to the denomination, and that a local church seeking to secede from the denomination could not keep such property. Here, though, the deeds were not recorded as set out in the Discipline."[96]

• A Kansas court concluded: "Our cases have consistently held that property conveyed to a local church which is a part of a connectional church does not remain the property of the local church even when there is no trust language in the deed. Therefore, when a local church acquires real property by deed, it is held in trust for the parent church even in the absence of express trust language. . . . According to these cases the law would appear to be established in Tennessee. A local church that is a part of a connectional church holds property in trust for the benefit of the superior organization."[97]

2. Trusts

Some denominations have amended their governing documents to declare that all affiliated churches hold property "in trust" for the denomination. The objective is to insure that the denomination will control the property of any affiliated church that votes to disaffiliate. As an example, the Supreme Court in the Jones case cited paragraph 1537 of the Methodist Book of Discipline:

Title to all real property now owned or hereafter acquired by an unincorporated local church . . . shall be held by and/or conveyed to its duly elected trustees . . . and their successors in office . . . in trust, nevertheless, for the use and benefit of such local church *and of The United Methodist Church*. Every instrument of conveyance of real estate shall contain the appropriate trust clause as set forth in the Discipline . . . .

The Court noted that Section 2503 of the Book of Discipline requires that the following "trust clause" be incorporated in any deed transferring real estate to a church:

In trust, that said premises shall be used, kept, and maintained as a place of divine worship of the United Methodist ministry and members of the

---

[96] Fire Baptized Holiness Church of God in the Americas v. McSwain, 518 S.E.2d 558 (N.C. App. 1999).

[97] Church of God v. Middle City Church of God, 774 S.W.2d 950 (Tenn. App.1989).

United Methodist Church; subject to the Discipline, usage, and ministerial appointments of said church as from time to time authorized and declared by the General Conference and by the Annual Conference within whose bounds the said premises are situated. This provision is solely for the benefit of the grantee, and the grantor reserves no right or interest in said premises.

The Book of Discipline also stipulates that in the absence of a trust clause, a trust in favor of The United Methodist Church would be implied if:

• the conveyance is to the trustees of a local church associated with any predecessor to The United Methodist Church;

• the local church uses the name of any predecessor to The United Methodist Church and is known to the community as a part of The United Methodist Church; or

• the local church accepts ministers appointed by any predecessor to The United Methodist Church.

The Supreme Court inferred that such "implied trusts" would be legally enforceable since they necessitate no interpretation of religious doctrine.

Churches that receive title to property subject to an express trust ordinarily must release the trust when the property is sold. For example, if a deed to church property specifies that the property is held by the church in trust for the use and benefit of a particular denomination, this trust attaches to the property and must be released upon a sale of the property in order to relieve the transferee of the terms of the trust.

In 1979, the Protestant Episcopal Church in the United States of America (PECUSA) adopted Canon 1.7.4, which provides:

All real and personal property held by or for the benefit of any parish, mission or parish, mission or congregation is located. The existence of this trust, however, shall in no way limit the power and authority of the parish, mission or congregation otherwise existing over such property so long as the particular parish, mission or congregation remains a part of, and subject to this Church and its constitution and canons.

PECUSA Canon II.6.2, further provides:

In the event of the dissolution of any Parish or Mission by the Convention, the real and personal property of the Parish or Mission shall immediately vest in the Trustees of the Diocese, in trust for the dissolved Parish or Mission.

The Book of Order of the Presbyterian Church (U.S.A.) ("PCUSA") contains several paragraphs subjecting local church properties to an express trust in favor of the PCUSA. These include the following:

> All property held by or for a particular church . . . whether legal title is lodged in a corporation, a trustee or trustees, or an unincorporated association . . . is held in trust nevertheless for the use and benefit of the Presbyterian Church (U.S.A.).[98]
>
> Whenever property of, or held for, a particular church of the Presbyterian Church (U.S.A.) ceases to be used by that church as a particular church of the Presbyterian Church (U.S.A.) in accordance with this constitution, such property shall be held, used, applied, transferred, or sold as provided by the presbytery.[99]
>
> The relationship to the Presbyterian Church (U.S.A.) of a particular church can be severed only by constitutional action on the part of the presbytery. . . . If there is a schism within the membership of a particular church and the presbytery is unable to effect a reconciliation or a division into separate churches within the Presbyterian Church (U.S.A.), the presbytery shall determine if one of the factions is entitled to the property because it is identified by the presbytery as the true church within the Presbyterian Church (U.S.A.). This determination does not depend upon which faction received the majority vote within the particular church at the time of the schism.[100]

The Cumberland Presbyterian Church denomination amended its constitution in 1984 to include a provision subjecting all local church property to a trust in favor of the denomination. The amendment provides, in relevant part:

> 3.32 The Cumberland Presbyterian Church is a connectional church and all lower judicatories of the church to-wit: synod, presbytery, and the particular churches are parts of that body and therefore all property held by or for a particular church, a presbytery, a synod, the General Assembly, or the Cumberland Presbyterian Church, whether legal title is lodged in a corporation, a trustee or trustees, or an unincorporated association, and whether the property is used in programs of the particular church or of a more inclusive judicatory or retained for the production of income, and whether or not the deed to the property so states, is held in trust nevertheless for the use and benefit of the Cumberland Presbyterian Church.
>
> 3.33 Whenever property of, or held for, a particular church of the Cumberland Presbyterian Church, ceases to be used by the church, as a

---

[98] BOOK OF ORDER ¶ G-8.0200.

[99] BOOK OF ORDER ¶ G-8.0300.

[100] BOOK OF ORDER ¶ G-8.0600.

particular church of the Cumberland Presbyterian Church in accordance with this Constitution, such property shall be held, used, applied, transferred or sold as provided by the presbytery in which that particular church is located.

3.34 Whenever a particular church is formally dissolved by the presbytery, or has become extinct by reason of dispersal of its members, the abandonment of its work, or other cause, such property as it may have shall be held, used, and applied for such uses, purposes, and trusts as the presbytery in which said particular church is located may direct, limit, and appoint, or such property may be sold or disposed of as the presbytery may direct, in conformity with the Constitution of the Cumberland Presbyterian Church. . . .

3.35 A particular church shall not sell, nor lease its real property used for purposes of worship, nurture or ministry, without the written permission of the presbytery in which the particular church is located, transmitted through the session of the particular church.

Trust provisions should be drafted in such a way as to avoid any interpretation of religious doctrine. To illustrate, an Arizona state appeals court refused to enforce an express trust on the basis of a deed conveying title to the "trustees of The Word Chapel, a religious body," since this

would require an examination into religious doctrine of [the church], and a determination of who the real [beneficiary] is according to their current beliefs. . . . [S]uch an approach was . . . expressly declared unconstitutional by the United States Supreme Court in [*Hull*]. . . . [W]e hold that any express trust, sought to be enforced in favor of some specific doctrine or belief, must be written so that the court can enforce it on purely secular terms.[101]

Case Studies

• *A New York court ruled that a local church retained ownership of its property following its disaffiliation from the Presbyterian Church (U.S.A.), despite an attempt by the PCUSA to impose a trust on all church property through an amendment to its Book of Order. The court concluded that this provision was not enforceable in this case: "Only the owner of real property can convey an interest in the property; B can not create a future interest in A's property without A's consent . . . . In the absence of any language in the deed to [the church] indicating that title is held subject to the laws or discipline of the national church a change in the laws of the national church does not affect title to the property held by the local church. Moreover, when [the church] acquired the real property [the amendments to the Book of Order] did not exist. . . . Mere silence and continuing its membership in the denominational church, absent*

---

[101] Skelton v. Word Chapel, Inc., 637 P.2d 753, 756 (Ariz. App. 1981).

more, is an insufficient expression of an intent to create a trust."[102]

• A North Carolina court ruled that the property of a local church that voted to withdraw from the Protestant Episcopal Church (PECUSA) automatically vested in the PECUSA because of a trust provision in the denomination's canons. The court referred to Canon I.7.4 (quoted above), and concluded: "Prior to its withdrawal, the entire congregation had adhered to the Constitutions and Canons of PECUSA and the Diocese for nearly fifty years. During that time, [the church] elected delegates to participate in various conventions at which new and revised canons were adopted, and did not contest the adoption of those canons thereafter. Under the language of these canons, it is clear that the [church's] property was to be held in trust for the Diocese. Its withdrawal essentially resulted in a dissolution of the parish whereby the property immediately vested in the Diocesan trustees until the Executive Council of the Diocese passed a resolution recognizing those members of the original congregation that remained loyal to PECUSA and the Diocese as the new [church]. Thus, the canons clearly established a form of governance impliedly assented to by the defendants that precluded the seceding vestry from taking control of the property."[103]

3. Local Church Charter or Bylaws

In the event of a church dispute, the local church charter or bylaws may provide for the disposition of property. Again, to be enforceable, such a provision must not require an interpretation of church doctrine.[104] This method of private resolution of church property disputes is of limited value, since the governing documents of many local churches can be amended by a vote of the church membership.[105]

4. Constitution or Bylaws of a Parent Denomination

The governing documents of a parent denomination may contain a provision vesting title to church property in the denomination in the event of a dispute or disaffiliation. Again, such a provision must be made dependent upon doctrinally neutral conditions. To illustrate, a provision mandating reversion of church property to the denomination in the event that a local church "departs" or "deviates" from the doctrine of the denomination would not be recognized by the courts, since enforcement would necessitate an interpretation of religious doctrine. As noted above, a number of denominations have adopted provisions attempting to control the disposition of local church property in the event of a disaffiliation through the imposition of a trust. Clauses adopted by the United Methodist Church and the Protestant Episcopal Church are quoted in the preceding paragraphs.

---

[102] Presbytery v. Trustees of First Presbyterian Church, 821 N.Y.S.2d 834 (N.Y. App. 2006).

[103] Daniel v. Wray, 580 S.E.2d 711 (N.C. App. 2003). The court rejected the dissident's arguments that Canon I.7.4 was unenforceable because it had never been recorded with the local recorder's office, and that the dissidents owned the property as a result of adverse possession. The court noted that recordation was not required, and that the church's possession of the property had not been adverse. *Accord* In re Church of St. James the Less, 833 A.2d 319 (Pa. Common. 2003).

[104] Clay v. Illinois District Council of the Assemblies of God, 657 N.E.2d 688 (Ill. App. 1995).

[105] York v. First Presbyterian Church, 474 N.E.2d 716 (Ill. App. 1984).

Case Studies

• *A Kansas court ruled that the Church of God in Christ (the "national church") owned the property of a local church that attempted to disaffiliate. The court noted that the Official Manual of the national church specifies: "A local church, which has been accepted by the Church of God in Christ and issued a Certificate of Membership, shall not have the legal right or privilege to withdraw or sever its relations with the General Church, except by and with the permission of the General Assembly."*[106]

• *A South Carolina court ruled that the property of a church that voted to disaffiliate from a parent denomination belonged to the denomination as a result of provisions in the denomination's bylaws.*[107]

5. State Statutes

State legislatures can enact statutes that provide for the disposition of property in the event of a church dispute. Illustratively, the Georgia legislature has enacted a law which provides that "the majority of those who adhere to its organization and doctrines represent the church. The withdrawal by one part of a congregation from the original body, or uniting with another church or denomination, is a relinquishment of all rights in the church abandoned."[108] Pennsylvania adopted a statute several years ago referred to as the "Lay Control of Church Property Act," which provides:

Whensoever any property, real or personal, has heretofore been or shall hereafter be bequeathed, devised, or conveyed to any ecclesiastical corporation, bishop, ecclesiastic, or other person, for the use of any church, congregation, or religious society, for or in trust for religious worship or sepulture, or for use by said church, congregation, or religious society, for a school, educational institution, convent, rectory, parsonage, hall, auditorium, or the maintenance of any of these, the same shall be taken and held subject to the control and disposition of such officers or authorities of such church, congregation, or religious society, having a controlling power according to the rules, regulations, usages, or corporate requirements of such church, congregation, or religious society, which control and disposition shall be exercised in accordance with and subject to the rules and regulations, usages, canons, discipline and requirements of the religious body, denomination or organization to which such church, congregation, or religious society shall belong, but nothing herein contained shall authorize the diversion of any property from the purposes, uses, and trusts to which it may have been heretofore lawfully dedicated, or to which it may hereafter,

---

[106] Church of God in Christ v. Board of Trustees of New Jerusalem Church of God in Christ, 992 P.2d 812 (Kan. App. 1999).

[107] South Carolina District Council of Assemblies of God v. River of Life International Worship Center, 643 S.E.2d 104 (S.C. App. 2007).

[108] Ga. Code § 22-5504.

consistently herewith, be lawfully dedicated . . . .[109]

A Pennsylvania court, in commenting on this statute, noted that it "requires that properties attached to seceding local churches formerly in union with hierarchically governed denominations remain with the denomination." The court concluded that the statute was consistent with and anticipated the neutral principles approach—and required that title to a seceding Presbyterian church revert to the denomination.[110]

Such statutes must not involve any interpretation of religious doctrine or polity. The Georgia statute involves no doctrinal interpretations. A court only has to determine whether a faction in a church has withdrawn from the original body or united with another church or denomination. Such determinations normally would involve no interpretation of religious doctrine or polity, and as a result would constitute an appropriate means of resolving church property disputes.

6. Resulting Trusts

In many states, a "resulting trust" arises by operation of law in favor of the person who purchases property in the name of another. The law presumes that it ordinarily is not the intention of a person paying for property to make a gift to the one receiving title. This presumption is rebuttable, however. Similarly, if a person contributes only a part of the purchase price of a piece of property placed in the name of another, a resulting trust will arise in favor of the payor on a prorata basis. In such cases, however, the courts often require the payor to demonstrate the precise percentage contributed toward the entire purchase price.

A local church that acquires property because of the contributions of a parent denomination may hold title subject to a resulting trust in favor of the denomination in proportion to its contribution. For example, a denominational agency contributing all or substantially all of the funds used to purchase a local church property should be entitled to the benefit of a resulting trust interest in the entire property.[111]

Case Study

• An Ohio court ruled that a home purchased by a church for its pastor was subject to a "purchase money resulting trust" in favor of the church and therefore the home could not be considered in a property settlement following the pastor's divorce. A pastor and his wife filed for a divorce. While the couple was engaged in dividing their assets, the pastor's church intervened in the divorce action and asserted a legal interest in the couple's home. The court ruled that when property is purchased by one person, but

---

[109] PA. STAT. title 10, §81.

[110] Beaver-Butler Presbytery v. Middlesex Presbyterian Church, 471 A.2d 1271 (Pa. Common. 1984). This case was reversed on appeal by the state Supreme Court, which ruled in favor of a local church—but with no mention of the state law cited by the lower court. Beaver-Butler Presbytery v. Middlesex Presbyterian Church, 489 A.2d 1317 (Pa. 1985). *See also* New York Annual Conference of the Methodist Church v. Nam Un Cho, 548 N.Y.S.2d 577 (1989).

[111] Grace Evangelical Lutheran Church v. Lutheran Church—Missouri Synod, 454 N.E.2d 1038 (Ill. App. 1983).

title is vested in another, the person holding title does so subject to a "purchase money resulting trust" in favor of the person who paid for the property—at least if the parties intended that the purchaser have some equitable interest in the property. The court pointed out that the church purchased the home and adjoining property as a site for a new church building. As a result, the pastor and his wife held title to the home in trust for the church, and the home was not marital property that could be divided between the pastor and his wife.[112]

7. Constructive Trusts

A constructive trust may be imposed if one person holds title to property that in equity and good conscience should be held by another. A constructive trust may arise as a result of several factors, including misrepresentation, failure to use property or funds for stated purposes, refusal to carry out the terms of an express trust, frustration of the terms of a will, or wrongful conveyance of another's property. It is possible for the law of constructive trusts to apply to church property so long as no inquiries into church doctrine or polity are involved.[113]

8. Arbitration

A church could insert a provision in its charter, constitution, or bylaws specifying that any dispute concerning title to any of its properties will be resolved through binding arbitration. Such provisions occasionally are contained in the organizational documents of nonprofit corporations, and they ordinarily are upheld as binding agreements on the part of the membership.

9. Buy-sell Agreements

A buy-sell (or "preemption") agreement requires a property owner to offer the property to a designated person at a stipulated price before selling it to another. Religious denominations wanting to maintain control over the property of dissident churches could require churches to execute such an agreement, giving the parent denomination a preemptive right to purchase the church's property at a specified price at or below market value. Such an agreement obviously would be of no value unless a dissident church wanted to sell its property. Alternatively, a denomination could enter into a purchase agreement with a local church giving the denomination the right to purchase the church's property in the event of a disaffiliation. Such agreements, if supported by adequate consideration, ordinarily will be enforceable.[114]

10. Characterization of Denominational Financing as a "Loan"

A denomination that invests funds in a local, affiliated church could have the church execute a promissory note in favor of the denomination, secured by an appropriate mortgage instrument (with a "future advances clause" securing

---

[112] Cayten v. Cayten, 659 N.E.2d 805 (Ohio App. 1995).

[113] *Id.*

[114] *Id. See also* Grace Evangelical Lutheran Church v. Lutheran Church-Missouri Synod, 454 N.E.2d 1038 (Ill. App. 1983), *cert. denied*, 469 U.S. 820 (1984).

the repayment of any additional advances by the denomination), specifying that payment shall be due in full within a specified number of days (e.g., 30 days) after the church votes to disaffiliate from the denomination. This arrangement could protect the investment of the denomination in the local church. Some rate of interest should be specified to adequately compensate the denomination for the lost opportunity costs associated with the loss of its capital from the time of the "loan" to the time the church votes to disaffiliate.

11. Conclusion

If none of these neutral principles of law disposes of church property in the event of a dispute, then the courts will be compelled to apply the methodology of resolution that they have adopted.

In the sixth chapter of the apostle Paul's first letter to the church at Corinth, he wrote:

> If any of you has a dispute with another, dare he take it before the ungodly for judgment instead of before the saints? . . . [I]f you have disputes about such matters, appoint as judges even men of little account in the church! I say this to shame you. Is it possible that there is nobody among you wise enough to judge a dispute between believers? But instead one brother goes to law against another—and this in front of unbelievers! The very fact that you have lawsuits among you means you have been completely defeated already. Why not rather be wronged. Why not rather be cheated?[115]

Paul's denunciation of lawsuits involving Christians is clearly based in part upon the fear that such suits will give unbelievers a negative impression of Christianity. This fear is still warranted. In the *Watson* decision, the United States Supreme Court itself remarked:

> [W]e have held [the case] under advisement for a year; not uninfluenced by the hope, that . . . charity, which is so large an element in the faith of both parties, and which, by one of the apostles of that religion, is said to be the greatest of all the Christian virtues, would have brought about a reconciliation. But we have been disappointed. It is not for us to determine or apportion the moral responsibility which attaches to the parties for this result.[116]

Similarly, a state court observed:

> Any church dispute has a deep effect upon all involved. If we all followed the teachings of Jesus as to turning the other cheek, there would be no need for courts. Likewise, if the teachings of Paul were followed, a religious dispute would never reach the civil courts. However, these disputes

---

[115] 1 Corinthians 6:1, 4-7 (NIV).

[116] See note 1, *supra*, at 735.

have plagued churches from time immemorial. Paul's First Epistle to the Corinthians was written over such a dispute. As long as we are humans, such disputes will arise. In any religious dispute there is no winner; only losers. All sides lose and the cause for which the church was organized must lose.[117]

The decision to take other Christians to court, like most ethical determinations, is not a private decision. It is a decision that also affects outsiders' perceptions of the Christian faith. And, it is a decision that, in many cases, will directly contradict Paul's command in First Corinthians 6. Such considerations, at the least, should encourage utilization of the various methods of private resolution promoted by the Supreme Court in *Jones v. Wolf*. In most cases such methods would avoid litigation. Their effect, however, would be cosmetic, covering over real and festering disputes among believers for whom Jesus prayed "that they may be one." Only grace—not courts or neutral principles—can resolve these disputes.

Transferring Church Property   § 7-05

Key point 7-05. *An incorporated church generally can transfer title to church property, following authorization of the transaction pursuant to the church's governing document, by means of a deed that identifies the church by its corporate name and that is signed by one or more authorized officers. In most states, an unincorporated church can transfer title in the same manner as an incorporated church. In some states unincorporated churches must select trustees to hold and transfer title to church property.*

Since one of the attributes of a corporation is the ability to hold title in the corporate name, it is a good practice for an incorporated church to identify itself as a corporation in deeds, mortgages, contracts, promissory notes, and other legal documents. For example, identifying a church as "First Church, a nonprofit religious corporation duly organized under the laws of the state of Illinois," ordinarily will suffice. Such a practice will indicate that the church is incorporated and therefore capable of executing legal documents in its name by its officers or other authorized persons.

In some states, an unincorporated church must execute such documents in the name of church trustees since the church itself lacks authority to execute legal documents. It is a common practice for unincorporated churches to execute such documents in the name of the church with the signatures of only the minister and church secretary. Such documents may be invalid in some states absent ratification by the church membership. Deeds to property present the greatest problem, and many title examiners will object to a deed executed by an unincorporated church in such a manner even if it is later ratified.

---

[117] Board of Trustees v. Richards, 130 N.E.2d 736, 743 (Ohio App. 1954).

In most states, a business corporation is required to include terminology in its name identifying itself as a corporation. Such terminology may include such words and abbreviations as *corporation, corp., incorporated,* or *inc.* This practice ordinarily does not apply to religious corporations. The absence of such a requirement, of course, makes it imperative for a church corporation to identify itself as a corporation following reference to its name in legal documents to avoid any suggestion that it might be an unincorporated association and thereby incapable of conveying title to property in its own name.

A few states have statutes restricting the transfer of property by religious organizations. To illustrate, a New York law specifies that "a religious corporation shall not sell, mortgage or lease for a term exceeding five years any of its real property without applying for and obtaining leave of the court . . . ."[118] A New York court upheld the constitutionality of this statute. A church had argued that this requirement not only violated the First Amendment's ban on the establishment of religion but also violated the First Amendment's guaranty of religious freedom by involving the government in the internal decisions of churches. In rejecting the church's "establishment clause" argument, the court applied the United States Supreme Court's three-part "*Lemon* test" for determining whether or not the New York law constituted an impermissible establishment of religion. Under this test, first announced in a 1971 decision,[119] a law or government practice challenged as an establishment of religion will be valid only if it satisfies the following three conditions—a secular purpose, a primary effect that neither advances nor inhibits religion, and no excessive entanglement between church and state.

The New York court concluded that all of these tests were met. First, the New York law had a secular purpose—"to insure that such [sales are] in the best interest of the corporation and its members and that the proceeds are properly disbursed." The court noted that the New York law was prompted by "several instances of questionable practices resulting in lawsuits to enjoin and set aside transfers of religious property within congregational-type religious churches." Second, the notice requirement did "nothing to convey any message whatsoever that could be construed to advance or inhibit any religion or religious belief." Third, the notice requirement did not result in an excessive entanglement between church and state since it was a mere "routine regulatory interaction" involving "no inquiries into religious doctrine . . . no detailed monitoring and close administrative contact between secular and religious bodies."

The court also concluded that the notice requirement did not violate the First Amendment guaranty of religious freedom. It noted that a violation of this guaranty requires proof that a law or government practice "burdens the adherent's practice of his or her religion by pressuring him or her to commit an act forbidden by the religion or by preventing him or her from engaging in conduct or having a religious experience which faith mandates." Such was not the case here, the court concluded. It further noted that "any inquiry by the attorney general involves only the terms of a real estate transaction; it involves no inquiry into religious

---

[118] N.Y. Religious Corporations § 12.

[119] Lemon v. Kurtzman, 403 U.S. 602 (1971).

beliefs nor does it involve the regulation or prohibition of conduct undertaken for religious reasons."[120]

Zoning Law

§ 7-06

Key point. *The definition of the term "church" and the subject of accessory uses are addressed in chapter 5.*

Most municipalities in the United States have enacted zoning laws. The purpose of a municipal zoning law

is to regulate the growth and development of the city in an orderly manner. Among the objectives to be served is to avoid mixing together of industrial, commercial, business and residential uses; the prevention of undue concentrations of people in certain areas under undesirable conditions; making provisions for safe and efficient transportation; for recreational needs; and for the enhancement of aesthetic values, all in order to best serve the purpose of promoting the health, safety, morals and general welfare of the city and its inhabitants.[121]

Municipalities have no inherent authority to enact zoning laws. Zoning laws constitute an exercise of the police power—that is, the authority inherent in state governments to enact laws in furtherance of the public health, safety, morals, and general welfare. Unless a state specifically delegates such authority to a municipality, the municipality will have no authority to enact a zoning ordinance. Most states, however, have adopted "enabling acts" which delegate such authority to designated municipalities.

"...zoning ordinances that restrict the location of churches in certain areas must not run afoul of the constitutional guarantees of assembly and the free exercise of religion."

The authority of a municipality to enact a zoning ordinance is limited by the terms of the enabling statute. It is also limited by constitutional considerations, for many courts have ruled that the United States Constitution prohibits the enactment of zoning ordinances that are unreasonable, discriminatory, or arbitrary. And, since a state's delegation of zoning power to a municipality constitutes a delegation of state "police power," a municipal zoning ordinance to be valid must in fact further the public health, safety, morals, or general welfare. Further, zoning ordinances that restrict the location of churches in certain areas must not run afoul of the constitutional

---

[120] Greek Orthodox Archdiocese v. Abrams, 618 N.Y.S.2d 504 (Sup. 1994).

[121] Naylor v. Salt Lake City Corporation, 410 P.2d 764, 765 (Utah 1966).

guarantees of assembly and the free exercise of religion.

The typical zoning ordinance divides a municipality into zones or districts in which only certain activities or uses are permitted. For example, it is common for a municipal zoning ordinance to divide a municipality into residential, commercial, and industrial districts, with the activities and uses permitted in each district described in the ordinance. Nonconforming uses and activities may be authorized in some cases through variances, special use permits, or by the fact that the nonconforming use preceded the enactment of the zoning ordinance.

Historically, churches presented few problems for municipal planners. Churches were allowed in residential districts so that they would be within walking distance of parishioners' residences. It was unthinkable to locate churches anywhere else. The vast majority of municipalities still permit churches in residential zones. With the advent of the automobile, churches became more incompatible with residential districts for two reasons. First, most parishioners drive their automobiles to church, making it less essential for churches to locate within walking distance of their membership. Second, on at least one day each week the church is the biggest source of traffic congestion, noise, and pollution in many residential neighborhoods. For a growing number of churches, this is becoming true on several days of the week due to additional church services, youth activities, weddings, funerals, child care, rehearsals, civic events, and programs for the poor and elderly. Understandably, many municipalities have reconsidered the traditional view of allowing churches in residential zones without restriction.

This process of reconsidering the proper location of churches within a modern-day community has resulted in a number of views. Most municipalities continue to allow churches in residential zones, but many require churches to obtain a permit prior to obtaining and using property in a residential zone. The permit procedure gives municipal planners greater control over the location of churches within residential zones. Some municipal zoning ordinances prohibit churches in any residential zone, and a few municipalities have attempted to bar churches altogether.

Communications Towers on Church Property

Many churches have allowed telecommunications companies to construct antennae on church property in exchange for a monthly rental fee. Such arrangements raise a number of legal and tax issues, including those listed below. It is essential for church leaders to discuss these issues with a local attorney before entering into an agreement with a telecommunications company to erect an antenna on church property.

- **Terms and conditions.** Be sure to have an attorney review the rental agreement before you sign it. Usually, these agreements are very one-sided in favor of the communications company. There should be a definite term, with renegotiation of rental payments on a periodic basis. Also, the church should have the right to terminate the contract at specified intervals for any reason. Many churches have signed rental agreements that they soon regret.

Communications Towers on Church Property

• **Zoning law.** Is the construction of a telecommunications antenna on church property consistent with the classification of the property under local zoning law? The few courts that have addressed this question have suggested that zoning laws would not be violated by such a use of church property. [122]

• **Property tax exemption.** It is possible that the use of church property for a telecommunications antenna would jeopardize the exemption of the property from local property taxes. In many states, an exemption from property taxes is conditioned on the fact that the property is not used for the generation of income. Loss of exempt status ordinarily will be limited to the portion of a church's property that is actually being used for the production of income rather than to the entire premises. However, in some states a church may lose an exemption for all of its property though only a small amount is used for an antenna.

• **Unrelated business income.** Federal law imposes a tax (equal to the corporate income tax) on the net income generated by a tax-exempt organization from any unrelated trade or business that is "regularly carried on." This tax is called the unrelated business income tax (or UBIT for short). There are a number of exemptions, including rental income. However, in order to be exempt from UBIT, the rental income must be from the rental of a debt-free facility. In 1998, the IRS ruled that rental fees received by charities for the erection of telecommunications towers on their property were exempt from UBIT. However, the IRS revoked this ruling in 2001 and concluded that rents received by charities for the use of communications towers or antennae constructed on their property are subject to the unrelated business income tax. The IRS limited its ruling to "receipts attributable solely to the rental of the broadcasting tower." This suggests that the rental of a specified area of *church property* on which a communications tower is erected *may* be partially or wholly exempt from the unrelated business income tax. The IRS did not specifically address this issue in its 2001 ruling. [123]

The Majority View: Churches May Build in Residential Zones   § 7-06.1

Key point 7-06.1. *Most courts have ruled that churches have a legal right to locate in residential districts.*

---

[122] *See, e.g.,* AT&T Wireless PCS, Inc. v. City Council, 979 F. Supp. 416 (E.D. Va. 1997).

[123] IRS Letter Ruling 200104031.

1. In General

It is the view of "the long line of cases"[124] or "the wide majority of courts"[125] that churches may not be excluded from residential districts. This conclusion generally rests upon one of two grounds: First, the exclusion of churches from residential districts infringes upon the freedom of religion guaranteed by the First Amendment; and second, a total exclusion of churches is an invalid and impermissible exercise of the police power since it cannot be said to further the public health, safety, morals, or general welfare.[126]

A few courts have ruled that churches may not be regulated regarding their purchase or use of property within residential zones.[127] However, most courts have concluded that while churches may not be excluded from residential zones, their location within a residential zone can be regulated through a permit application procedure.

To illustrate, a New York court observed:

> With respect to zoning restrictions, New York adheres to the majority view that religious institutions are beneficial to the public welfare by their very nature. Consequently, a proposed religious use should be accommodated, even when it would be inconvenient for the community. A religious use may not be prohibited merely because of potential traffic congestion, an adverse effect upon property values, the loss of potential tax revenues, or failure to demonstrate that a more suitable location could not be found. In order to deny a special use permit for a religious use as "detrimental to the public health, safety and welfare," it must be "convincingly shown that the [proposed use] will have a direct and immediate adverse effect upon the health, safety or welfare of the community." A distinction must be drawn between danger to the public and mere public inconvenience. Every effort must be made to accommodate the religious use subject to conditions reasonably related to land use.[128]

---

[124] 5. E. YOKLEY, ZONING LAW AND PRACTICE § 35-14 (4th ed. 1980 and Supp.).

[125] State v. Maxwell, 617 P.2d 816, 820 (Hawaii 1980).

[126] See generally A. RATHKOPF, THE LAW OF ZONING AND PLANNING ch. 29 (2008) [hereinafter cited as RATHKOPF]; E. YOKLEY, ZONING LAW AND PRACTICE § 35-14 (4th ed. 1978 and Supp.) [hereinafter cited as YOKLEY]; N. WILLIAMS, AMERICAN LAND PLANNING LAW ch. 77 (2003 and Supp. 2008) [hereinafter cited as WILLIAMS]; Note, Churches and Zoning, 70 HARV. L. REV. 1428 (1957); Note, Land Use Regulation and the Free Exercise Clause, 84 COLUM. L. REV. 1562 (1984); Comment, Zoning Ordinances Affecting Churches: A Proposal for Expanded Free Exercise Protection, 132 UNIV. PA. L. REV. 1131 (1984); Pearlman, Zoning and the Location of Religious Establishments, 31 CATH. U. L. REV. 314 (1988); Reynolds, Zoning the Church: The Police Power versus the First Amendment, 64 B.U.L. REV. 767 (1988); Clowney, An Empircal Look at Churches in the Zoning Process, 116 YALE L.J. 859 (2007).

[127] See, e.g., Community Synagogue v. Bates, 1 N.Y.S.2d 445 (1956).

[128] Holy Spirit Association for Unification of World Christianity v. Rosenfeld, 458 N.Y.S.2d 920 (N.Y.A.D. 1983). See also Genesis Assembly of God v. Davies, 617 N.Y.S.2d 202 (A.D. 2 Dept. 1994) (the court observed that "it is well settled that while religious institutions are not exempt from local zoning laws, greater flexibility is required in evaluating an application for a religious use than an application for another use and every effort to accommodate the religious use must be made").

Another New York court similarly observed:

We have not said that considerations of the surrounding area and potential traffic hazards are unrelated to the public health, safety or welfare when religious structures are involved. We have simply said that they are outweighed by the constitutional prohibition against the abridgement of the free exercise of religion and by the public benefit and welfare which is itself an attribute of religious worship in a community.[129]

This position often is referred to as the *New York rule*, since the courts of New York have been the most consistent and forceful in upholding the right of churches to locate without restriction in residential zones. The application of this rule can be demonstrated by reviewing a few representative court rulings.

Case Studies

• *A New York court ruled that a city acted improperly in denying a synagogue's application for a special use permit without making any attempt to accommodate the proposed religious use. The synagogue applied for a special use permit that would have allowed it to operate in a residential property. The city council rejected the permit application, and the synagogue appealed. An appeals court concluded that the city's denial of the permit was "arbitrary, capricious, and an abuse of discretion." The court acknowledged that "there is no exemption from zoning rules for religious uses, nor is there any conclusive presumption that any religious use automatically outweighs its ill effects." However, "where the applicant is a religious institution, more flexibility is required and efforts must be made to accommodate the religious use, if possible." In fact, "every effort must be made to accommodate the religious use subject to conditions reasonably related to land use." The court noted that the city council rejected the synagogue's permit application "without making any attempt to accommodate the proposed religious use." Such an act, concluded the court, was improper. The city had "an affirmative duty to suggest measures to accommodate the proposed religious use." The court found that the synagogue's proposed religious use could have been accommodated by the city: "For example, we observe that the accommodation of the religious use and maintenance of the public's safety, health, and welfare could have been achieved by limiting the number of persons who could attend services or meetings at any given time, and by posting 'no parking' signs along the street to prevent hazardous road conditions, and by limiting the hours during which meetings or instruction could be held . . . ." The court ordered the city council "to issue the permit upon such reasonable conditions as will allow the [synagogue] to establish its house of worship, while mitigating any detrimental or adverse effects on the surrounding community."[130]*

• *A New York court struck down as unreasonable a city's refusal to grant a church's request for a special use permit authorizing it to build a new sanctuary. Noting that churches "enjoy a presumptively favored status with respect to the police powers*

---

[129] Application of Covenant Community Church, 444 N.Y.S.2d 415 (N.Y. Sup. 1981).

[130] Harrison Orthodox Minyan v. Town Board, 552 N.Y.S.2d 434 (N.Y. App. 1990).

sought to be protected by zoning laws," the court concluded that "our examination of the reasons enumerated by the [city] for denying [the church] a special use permit discloses that the rejection was unreasonable. No expert evidence was proffered concerning any detrimental effect on traffic or drainage."[131]

• *In another New York case, a municipality denied a congregation permission to construct a church on a two-acre tract of undeveloped property in a residential district on the grounds that the presence of a church and its associated traffic would devalue the adjoining properties, create a fire hazard, and adversely affect the health, safety, and welfare of neighborhood residents. A New York appellate court, in overruling the action of the municipality, held that the potential traffic and safety hazards and property devaluation were outweighed by "the constitutional prohibition against the abridgement of the free exercise of religion and by the public benefit and welfare which is itself an attribute of religious worship in a community."*[132]

The courts of several other states have reached similar conclusions.[133] Several illustrative cases are summarized below.

• *A federal district court in Alabama ruled that a county's practice of prohibiting churches from building new facilities if neighboring residents object violated the churches' constitutional right of religious freedom. A county adopted a new zoning ordinance that limited churches to "institutional districts." The ordinance purposely failed to recognize any land as an institutional district, so that churches would be forced to seek a zoning variance before purchasing property for church use. This procedure was designed to give the county "better site development controls over institutional construction." A Mormon congregation that had outgrown its existing facility attempted to purchase land on which it proposed to construct a new sanctuary. It filed an application to have the property rezoned as an "institutional district," but its application was denied by the county following a hearing in which several neighboring residents expressed "vociferous opposition." The residents lived in an affluent residential district adjacent to the church's proposed building site, and they were horrified by the impact the church would have on the "aesthetics" of the community and the value of existing homes. The county commission based its denial of the church's application on the basis of the "will of the people." The court noted that the church had outgrown its present facility, and that the church had "as a central tenet of its faith the need to assemble together and strengthen the faith of each other and to partake of communion." The court concluded that the church's constitutional right to exercise its religion was violated by the county's procedure: "The court's primary conclusion is that the burden here on religion is that the ability of a church to locate or not is dependent on the acceptability of that church, or any church, to the surrounding community, without there having been any predetermination that churches are allowed*

---

[131] North Syracuse First Baptist Church v. Village of North Syracuse, 524 N.Y.S.2d 894 (1988). *Accord* Church of Jesus Christ of Latter-Day Saints v. Planning Board, 687 N.Y.S.2d 794 (Sup. Ct. 1999). *But see* Western New York Dist., Inc. of Wesleyan Church v. Village of Lancaster, 841 N.Y.S.2d 740 (N.Y. Sup. 2007), in which a New York court affirmed a city's decision to deny a church's application for a special use permit that would have allowed it to relocate to an area of the city that was zoned exclusively for industrial use.

[132] American Friends of the Society of St. Pius, Inc. v. Schwab, 417 N.Y.S.2d 991, 993 (1979), *appeal denied*, 425 N.Y.S.2d 1027 (1980).

[133] *See, e.g.,* RATHKOPF, *supra* note 126 at § 20.04(1)(b).

to go in any area.[134]

• *A Connecticut court ruled that a local zoning commission acted improperly in denying a church a special permit to construct a sanctuary in a residential zone. The court observed: "[E]ven though churches may not be completely excluded from residential zones they can be subject to reasonable regulation as to their location without violation of the constitutional guarantee of freedom of religion. . . . Cases from other states have held that it is illegal for a municipality to exclude churches in all zones, from all residential zones, to allow them in the municipality only with a special permit, or have held that there was no compelling reason to deny a special permit. . . . These cases are based on the concept that such zoning restrictions must yield to the right of freedom of religion protected by the . . . United States constitution and comparable provisions in state constitutions where the zoning regulations unreasonably hinder or restrict religious activities. Constitutional provisions do not prevent all governmental regulation of churches and religious organizations, and they may be subject to religiously neutral regulation for a secular governmental purpose under the police power, such as, fire inspection and building and zoning regulations." The court concluded that "some increased traffic from construction of a church . . . is not a sufficiently significant factor to warrant limitation of freedom of religion by denial of a special permit."*[135]

• *A Florida court ruled that a county commission acted unlawfully in limiting a church school to grades K-6 and 150 students. The court noted that the church only had to demonstrate that its proposal was "consistent with the county's land use plan; that the uses are specifically authorized as special exceptions and unusual uses in the applicable zoning district; and that the requests meet with the applicable zoning code standards of review. If this is accomplished, then the application must be granted unless the opposition carries its burden, which is to demonstrate that the applicant's requests do not meet the standards and are in fact adverse to the public interest." The court noted that the commission based its decision on county zoning maps, staff recommendations, aerial photographs, and testimony of neighboring property owners who expressed concern about increased traffic and a loss of "green space." Such evidence, however, was not sufficient to limit the school to 150 students and grades K-6.*[136]

• *An Illinois court ruled that a city's refusal to grant a church's application for a "conditional use permit" violated the church's First Amendment guaranty of religious freedom. A Lutheran church in a Chicago suburb experienced explosive growth, but was left with inadequate parking space. To help solve its parking problem, the church sought permission from the city to convert two private residences that it owned on adjoining property into 57 additional parking spaces. The city denied this request on the grounds that the proposed parking lots would adversely affect the value of neighboring properties (the church was located at the entrance to a residential subdivision), and would "injure the use and enjoyment" of the neighborhood. It rejected the church's claim that a limitation on the number of its parking spaces*

---

[134] Church of Jesus Christ of Latter-Day Saints v. Jefferson County, 741 F. Supp. 1522 (N.D. Ala. 1990).

[135] Grace Church v. Planning and Zoning Commission, 615 A.2d 1092 (Conn. Super. 1992). *Accord* Christian Fellowship, Inc. v. Planning and Zoning Commission, 807 A.2d 1089 (Ct. App. 2002).

[136] Jesus Fellowship v. Miami-Dade County, 752 So.2d 708 (Fla. App. 2000).

would interfere with the free exercise of its religion. The court concluded that the city had not given due weight to the church's constitutional right to freely exercise its religion. While conceding that city zoning ordinances are presumed to be valid, the court observed that this presumption "diminishes" when an ordinance "limits the free exercise of religion." Significantly, the court concluded: "The location of a church can be regulated by zoning ordinances in proper cases; however, in determining whether this is a proper case for such a restriction, we must take into account that the freedom of religion, and other First Amendment freedoms, rise above mere property rights. In addition, First Amendment rights and freedoms outweigh considerations of public convenience, annoyance, or unrest." The court concluded that the city had erred in denying the church's request for a permit to convert the two residential properties into additional parking spaces. It rejected the city's claim that the "parking needs of a church should be considered on different legal principles than those applied to the church building itself." This decision represents one of the strongest statements by a court of the right of a church to develop its property despite the complaints of neighboring landowners. [137]

• An Indiana court, in striking down a municipal ordinance that prohibited churches in residential areas, held that the ordinance constituted "a violation of the fundamental right of freedom to worship protected by the first and Fourteenth Amendments to the United States Constitution . . . ." The court observed that "[e]arly and modern case law alike has not countenanced the exclusion of churches from residential districts, even though inconveniences may be caused by the influx into a neighborhood of vehicular or pedestrian traffic." The court also acknowledged that churches are subject to such reasonable regulations as may be necessary to promote the public health, safety, and general welfare, but insisted that "[r]easonable restrictions . . . are not tantamount to exclusion." [138]

• A federal appeals court (with jurisdiction over Louisiana, Mississippi, and Texas) decision strongly supports the right of churches to locate in residential districts. The court ruled that a city's refusal to permit an Islamic center to operate within city limits near a university campus violated the constitutional guaranty of religious freedom. A city zoning ordinance prohibited the use of any building as a church in all areas of the city near a university campus unless a special permit was obtained from the city council. Twenty-five churches were granted permits to operate in restricted areas. However, the Islamic center's request for a permit was denied. No reason was given for the denial, though a neighborhood spokesman expressed concern over "congestion, parking, and traffic problems." The center sued the city, arguing that the city's action in banishing it from the restricted area near the university campus, while allowing 25 churches to meet in the same area, violated the right of Muslims to the free exercise of their religion. The city denied that the Muslims' rights were violated, since "they can establish a mosque . . . outside the city limits or buy cars and ride to more distant places within the city." The federal appeals court observed that the city's suggestion was "reminiscent of Anatole France's comment on the majestic equality of the law that forbids all men, the rich as well as the poor, to sleep under bridges, to beg in the

---

[137] Our Saviour's Evangelical Lutheran Church of Naperville v. City of Naperville, 542 N.E.2d 1158 (Ill. App. 2nd Cir. 1989). *See also* Hope Deliverance Center, Inc. v. Zoning Board, 452 N.E.2d 630 (Ill. App. 1983) (church could build, despite allegations of increased traffic, and other adverse effects).

[138] Church of Christ v. Metropolitan Board of Zoning, 371 N.E.2d 1331, 1333-34 (Ind. 1978).

streets, and to steal bread." The court further observed that "laws that make churches accessible only to those affluent enough to travel by private automobile obviously burden the free exercise of religion by the poor." And, while "the constitution does not forbid all governmental regulation that imposes an incidental burden on worship by making the free exercise of religion more difficult or more expensive," once it is established that a governmental action burdens religious exercise, "the government must offer evidence of an overriding interest" to justify its action. In this case, however, the city "advanced no rational basis other than the neighborhood opposition to show why the [permit] granted all other religious centers was denied the Islamic center . . . . Neighbors' negative attitudes or fears, unsubstantiated by factors properly cognizable in a zoning proceeding, are not a permissible basis" for denying a permit. Further, the court concluded that the city had acted improperly in "applying different standards" to the Islamic center than to the "worship facilities of other faiths." [139]

• A New Jersey court ruled that a city cannot totally exclude churches from residential districts. A Jehovah's Witness congregation applied to city officials for approval to build a church in an area zoned for manufacturing use. The city then rezoned much of the community, changed the area where the church was to be built from a manufacturing to a residential district, and then prohibited the building of churches in all residential districts. The congregation challenged the city's action as a violation of the constitutional guaranty of religious freedom. The court agreed: "Municipalities have the power to zone their districts, but to exclude churches and other places of worship from the very areas (residential communities) that they draw their members from and relocate them to a less desirable zone of the township . . . offends the very essence of . . . the New Jersey Constitution." [140]

A number of courts have concluded that a city cannot exclude churches from residential districts if other non-residential facilities are permitted to locate there. This result generally is based on the federal constitution's guaranty of the "equal protection of the laws."[141] To illustrate a federal district court in Illinois ruled that a city ordinance requiring churches to obtain a special use permit from the city prior to acquiring property in any location violated the constitutional guaranty of the equal protection of the laws since the permit requirement did not apply to certain other organizations (e.g., theaters, funeral homes, hotels, community centers). As a result, the ordinance treated churches differently and less favorably without any apparent basis.

The court agreed that the city's permit procedure violated the church's constitutional right to the "equal protection of the laws," and it awarded the church nearly $18,000 in damages under title 42, section 1983 of the United States Code. This law allows persons and organizations whose constitutional

---

[139] Islamic Center of Mississippi, Inc. v. Starkville, 840 F.2d 293 (5th Cir. 1988).

[140] Jehovah's Witnesses v. Woolrich Township, 532 A.2d 276, 280 (N.J. Super. 1987). Accord Lakewood Residents Association v. Congregation Zichron Schneur, 570 A.2d 1032 (N.J. Super. 1989); Shim v. Washington Township Planning Board, 689 A.2d 804 (N.J. Super. 1997).

[141] See, e.g., Ellsworth v. Gercke, 156 P.2d 242 (Ariz. App. 1949); North Shore Unitarian Society v. Village of Plandome, 109 N.Y.S.2d 803 (1951); Andrews v. Board of Adjustment, 143 A.2d 262 (N.J. App. 1958); Black v. Town of Montclair, 167 A.2d 388 (N.J. App. 1961); Garden Grove Congregation of Jehovah's Witnesses v. City of Garden Grove, 1 Cal. Rptr. 65 (1959) (dismissed on procedural grounds).

rights are violated to sue the offender for money damages—even if the offender is a city or other government unit. Significantly, the court granted the church a "summary judgment," meaning that it found the church's position so clearly correct that it refused to submit the case to a jury. A federal appeals court later dismissed the case on the technical ground that the church lacked "standing" to challenge the city's permit procedure since the city had never enforced the special permit requirement and accordingly there was no threat of legal consequences if the church disregarded it.[142]

This case is significant (despite the appeals court's decision) since it illustrates the potential relevance of the equal protection guaranty in the context of zoning, and the availability of monetary damages under "section 1983" for a city's violation of a church's constitutional rights. The importance of such rulings cannot be overstated—for they represent a recognition of a potent weapon that is available to churches. To be sure, the federal appeals court dismissed the case, but it did so for technical reasons that in no way diminish the significance of the district court's decision. Further, the appeals court seemed to concede that it would have affirmed the district court's award of monetary damages had the city ever enforced its permit procedure, or had the church presented more evidence of the unwillingness of landlords to rent to the church. In many cases, these factors will be present, and presumably churches in such cases will be entitled to monetary damages.

Obviously, any attempt by a municipality to totally exclude churches from all districts, whether residential, commercial, or industrial, would be unconstitutional.[143]

2. Special Use Permits

Many courts have ruled that while a city cannot exclude churches from residential zones, it can require them to obtain a special use permit in order to use a particular property for church use. To illustrate, an Indiana court ruled that a city ordinance requiring churches to obtain a "special use permit" before using property for religious purposes did not violate the First Amendment guaranty of religious freedom.[144] A city required property owners to obtain a special permit before using their property for any one of 33 different uses, including the operation of a church. A property owner who wanted to use his property as a church obtained a 1-year special use permit. When this permit expired, he filed a lawsuit claiming that the special permit procedure was an unconstitutional interference with the exercise of religion. A state appeals court disagreed. The court provided a useful summary of "special permit" ordinances:

> Special uses are designated because they are necessary to the life and economic health of the community, but have characteristics of operation that do not readily permit classification in the usual residential, commercial,

---

[142] Love Church v. City of Evanston, 896 F.2d 1082 (7th Cir. 1990).

[143] Diocese of Rochester v. Planning Board, 154 N.Y.S.2d 849 (1956).

[144] Area Plan Commission v. Wilson, 701 N.E.2d 856 (Ind. App. 1998).

or industrial districts. A property owner may utilize his property to exercise a special use in a traditional zoning district as long as the property owner secures a special use permit and the special use is permitted in that zoning district. A property owner wishing to utilize his property as a school or church is permitted to do so in any residential, commercial, or industrial zoning district. In order to obtain a special use permit, any property owner intending to utilize his property for any of the special uses must comply with the procedure set forth in the special use ordinance.

The purpose of the special use ordinance . . . is the accommodation of desirable land uses which cannot be subject to rigid and restrictive classification into the traditional residential, commercial, and industrial zoning districts. It is the legislative accommodation of special uses which necessitates an administrative review of the impact of the special use at a particular location within a given zoning district. Accordingly, the requirement for a use permit is set out in the ordinance so that the body entrusted with the task of reviewing the application can make certain that it would not adversely affect the public interest if placed in a particular location within the permitted zone.

The court rejected the claim that applying the special use permit procedure to churches violated the First Amendment. It noted that the United States Supreme Court has ruled that a government regulation which clearly furthers a secular public purpose does not violate the free exercise clause, though the regulation as applied burdens a religious belief or practice, as long as the regulation is "a valued and neutral law of general applicability." *Employment Division v. Smith, 494 U.S. 872 (1990)*. A special permit procedure is such a law, the Indiana court concluded. Regulation of land use "is a secular public purpose, and the special use ordinance carries out this purpose in a manner which is generally applicable to all special uses."

The court also rejected the property owner's claim that the procedure for obtaining a special use permit imposed a substantial and unreasonable burden on the exercise of religion. It concluded that any burden imposed by compliance with the special use procedure was minimal.

Case Studies

• *A federal court in Illinois ruled that the legal rights of churches were not violated by a city zoning ordinance that required churches to obtain a special use permit before locating in certain commercial and manufacturing districts. The court concluded that the zoning ordinance was neutral and of general applicability, and did not single out churches for adverse treatment. As a result, it did not violate the First Amendment. It observed: "The requirement that an individual must go through the processes and meet the standards, is a requirement imposed on all special use applicants, regardless of the character of the proposed use. Therefore, the zoning ordinance and related provisions are valid neutral and generally applicable zoning regulations that impose no substantial burden to the free exercise of religion."[145]*

• *A Missouri court ruled that a church's constitutional rights were not violated by a city ordinance requiring it to obtain a special permit before building a multi-purpose building on its property. The court noted that "numerous decisions have acknowledged that municipalities, in the exercise of their police powers, may regulate churches" in order to promote the "health, safety, morals, or the general welfare of the community." The court concluded that "it is clear from these cases that the fact that a municipality exercises some control over the conduct of churches is not, per se, violative of a church's right to the free exercise of religion; but rather a determination of whether such regulation is tantamount to an infringement of the free exercise of religion depends on the facts and circumstances of each case. Thus, city's mere requirement that the church apply for a special use permit did not infringe on the free exercise of religion."[146]*

• *The Washington State Supreme Court ruled that the First Amendment guaranty of religious freedom did not exempt a church from having to obtain a "conditional use permit" before using property in a rural area for church purposes. It relied on the following language from a United States Supreme Court decision: "It is a reality of the modern regulatory state that numerous state laws, such as the zoning regulations at issue here, impose a substantial burden on a large class of individuals. When the exercise of religion has been burdened in an incidental way by a law of general application, it does not follow that the persons affected have been burdened any more than other citizens, let alone burdened because of their religious beliefs."[147] The court concluded that requiring the church to apply for and obtain a conditional use permit before using property in a rural district for church purposes did not create "anything more than an incidental burden upon the free exercise of religion.[148]*

The Minority View: The Government May Restrict Church Construction in Residential Zones
§ 7-06.2

Key point 7-06.2. *Some courts permit local zoning commissions to restrict the location of churches in residential areas.*

---

[145] C.L.U.B. v. City of Chicago, 157 F.Supp.2d 903 (N.D. Ill. 2001). The court rejected the churches' claim that the zoning ordinance violated the Religious Land Use and Institutionalized Persons Act. It observed: "RLUIPA is inapplicable to the present matter by its own terms. . . . The city amended its zoning ordinance and adjusted its policies concerning special use permits and related districts. By removing any potential substantial burden, the city has avoided the threat of heightened scrutiny under RLUIPA."

[146] Village Lutheran Church v. City of Ladue, 997 S.W.2d 506 (Mo. App. 1999).

[147] City of Boerne v. Flores, 521 U.S. 507 (1997).

[148] Open Door Baptist Church v. Clark County, 995 P.2d 33 (Wash. 2000).

Some courts are willing to exclude churches from residential zones. Generally, this result has been accomplished in two ways: (1) Courts have simply upheld municipal decisions denying a church's application for a permit to acquire property in a residential zone. These courts reason that the interests of neighboring residents and the integrity of the residential community as a whole outweigh any interest the church has in locating in the zone. (2) Some courts have upheld the legal validity of municipal zoning laws prohibiting churches in residential zones.

In one of the first cases to break from the majority rule, a California state appeals court upheld a city's exclusion of churches from single-family residential districts. In defending its conclusion, the court observed:

It is a matter of common knowledge that people in considerable numbers assemble in churches and that parking and traffic problems exist where crowds gather. This would be true particularly in areas limited to single family dwellings. There necessarily is an appreciable amount of noise connected with the conduct of church and youth activities. These and many other factors may well enter into the determination of the legislative body in drawing the lines between districts, a determination primarily the province of the city. A single-family residence may be much more desirable when not in an apartment house neighborhood or adjacent to a public building such as a church. The municipal legislative body may require that church buildings be erected to conform to health and safety regulations as provided in its building code and we see no reason to hold that churches may be erected in a single family residential area when a duplex, triplex, or other multiple dwelling can lawfully be excluded therefrom. The provision in the ordinance for a single-family residential area affords an opportunity and inducement for the acquisition and occupation of private homes where the owners thereof may live in comparative peace, comfort and quiet. Such a zoning regulation bears a substantial relation to the public health, safety, morals and general welfare because it tends to promote and perpetuate the American home and protect its civic and social value.[149]

In other words, since a city can exclude apartment complexes from single-family residential districts to avoid noise and traffic congestion, it can exclude churches for the same reason.

Since California courts pioneered the "minority view," this view is sometimes called the *California rule*.[150] However, even in California there have been court decisions upholding the right of churches to locate in residential districts despite the protests of neighboring residents.[151]

In another early case parting with the majority view, an Oregon state court observed:

---

[149] Corporation of Presiding Bishop v. City of Porterville, 203 P.2d 823, 825 (Cal. App. 1949).

[150] *See also* Matthews v. Board of Supervisors, 21 Cal. Rptr. 914 (Cal. App. 1962).

[151] *See, e.g.,* Gray v. Board of Supervisors, 316 P.2d 678 (Cal. App. 1957); McLain v. Planning Commission, 319 P.2d 24 (Cal. App. 1957).

Traffic congestion is a phrase comprehending many facets. As used in a matter of this kind, it implies all of the nuisances, inconveniences and hazards to which the public generally, and those residing in the same area, may be exposed. Off-street parking would, no doubt, in some places tend to minimize some of the disadvantages of such congestion, but it cannot be expected to avoid all of its resulting annoyances and potential dangers. The incidents of traffic congestion include, among other things, noise, fumes, the intrusion of automobile lights, the blocking of private driveways by parked cars, and delays in normal travel for those using the highways. But most important are the increased dangers of injury to persons and property. We do not mean to infer that the church-going public is less diligent than others in their respect for the traffic laws. However, even the worthy and cautious persons of that class and their children are too often the victims of the careless.

The test of whether or not the building of a church in a given zone will produce traffic congestion or augment existing traffic conditions to a point of hazard cannot be made solely in terms of what a given number of church members might produce with their probable use of a certain number of automobiles. If a church is perchance, in an area where few people live or travel, then it might be relatively easy for a zoning board to determine, in the absence of other circumstances, that the building of a place of worship at such a given site, within the restricted zone, would not create traffic problems. If so, it would be unreasonable to deny such a religious organization an opportunity to erect its building at that point. On the other hand, if traffic congestion is already a real or threatening problem near the site where a congregation desires to build, and the church would bring to that community enough additional vehicles to definitely establish congestion at that point, then the [city] council would be reasonably warranted, if not duty bound, to deny a permit for its erection.[152]

In recent years, many courts have been willing to balance the interests of the church, neighboring residents, and the community as a whole, in deciding whether or not to allow a church to locate on a particular piece of property within a residential zone. In many cases, the courts have concluded that the exclusion of churches from residential districts is justified.

---

[152] Milwaukee Company of Jehovah's Witnesses v. Mullen, 330 P.2d 5, 18-20 (Ore. App. 1958).

Case Studies

• The federal appeals court for the sixth circuit (comprising the states of Kentucky, Michigan, Ohio, and Tennessee) ruled that a zoning ordinance that prohibited churches from all residential zones did not violate a church's constitutional rights. A church in need of a larger facility found a parcel of vacant land in a residential zone, and applied to the city for a permit to construct a church. The city denied the application on the basis of the zoning ordinance that prohibited churches in all "low density" residential zones. The church sued the city on the ground that the ordinance violated its constitutional right to freely exercise its religion. It stressed that only 10 percent of the community was zoned to accommodate churches, and that available building sites were more expensive and less conducive to worship than residential zones. In rejecting the church's claim, the appeals court noted that while the city's action made the practice of the church's religion more costly and less desirable aesthetically, these "burdens" did not amount to a violation of the First Amendment guarantee of religious freedom. The court emphasized that the First Amendment only protects governmental interference with a "fundamental tenet" or "cardinal principle" of a church. It observed: "The effect of the [city] ordinance is not to prohibit the congregation or any other faith from worshiping in the city. . . . The lots available to the congregation may not meet its budget or satisfy its tastes but the First Amendment does not require the city to make all land or even the cheapest or most beautiful land available to churches. . . . [T]he [city] ordinance does not exclude the exercise of a First Amendment right, religious worship, from the city." [153]

---

[153] Lakewood, Ohio Congregation of Jehovah's Witnesses v. City of Lakewood, 699 F.2d 303 (6th Cir. 1983). The court suggested that an ordinance that permitted churches but not secular organizations within residential zones would violate the First Amendment's nonestablishment of religion clause. The court's First Amendment analysis presumably is binding upon the state and federal courts within the sixth circuit, which comprises the states of Kentucky, Michigan, Ohio, and Tennessee.

• *The federal appeals court for the ninth circuit (comprising the states of Alaska, Arizona, California, Hawaii, Idaho, Montana, Nevada, Oregon, and Washington) ruled that a municipal zoning ordinance prohibiting churches in single-family residential areas without a conditional use permit did not violate the constitutional guaranty of religious freedom. The San Francisco City Code prohibits churches in residential districts unless a conditional use permit is granted. Before granting a permit, the city must determine that the proposed use is necessary, and compatible with the neighborhood, and will not be detrimental to the health, safety, convenience, or general welfare of persons residing in the vicinity. A church desiring to establish a church in a single-family residence applied to the city for a permit. A group of 190 neighboring residents signed a petition in opposition to the permit, based on the following considerations: (1) there already are too many churches in the neighborhood; (2) the church would not maintain neighborhood characteristics; (3) there is a housing shortage in the neighborhood; (4) an additional church would create additional traffic that would create safety hazards for neighbors; (5) inadequate parking spaces; and (6) excessive noise. A city zoning commission denied the church's permit request, and the church filed a lawsuit claiming that the city's actions violated its constitutional rights. The court ruled in favor of the city. It concluded that in evaluating whether a city's denial of a church's zoning permit application violates the constitutional guaranty of religious freedom, the following three factors must be considered: (1) the magnitude of the impact on the exercise of religious beliefs; (2) the existence of a compelling governmental interest justifying the burden on the exercise of religious belief; and (3) the extent to which recognition of an exemption from the permit procedure would interfere with the objectives sought to be advanced by the city. The court concluded that the impact of its ruling on the congregation's religious belief was not significant; the city's decision was supported by a compelling interest; and, allowing the church an exemption from the permit procedure would materially interfere with the purpose of that procedure.* [154]

• *The federal appeals court for the 10th circuit (comprising the states of Colorado, Kansas, New Mexico, Oklahoma, Utah, and Wyoming) ruled that a church's constitutional right to religious freedom was not violated by a county's refusal to permit the church to construct a sanctuary on land not specifically zoned for church uses. The church owned an 80-acre tract of vacant land in an area zoned for agricultural uses. Its application for a special permit to construct a sanctuary was rejected by the county planning commission because of a number of concerns, including access problems, erosion hazards, and inadequate fire protection at the site. The appeals court rejected the church's claim that its right to freely exercise its religion had been violated by the county's action. It found that the county's action did "not in any way regulate the religious beliefs of the church," and did not regulate "any religious conduct of the church or its members." The court concluded that "a church has no constitutional right to be free from reasonable zoning regulations nor does a church have a constitutional*

---

[154] Christian Gospel Church, Inc. v. San Francisco, 896 F.2d 1221 (9th Cir. 1990). The court's First Amendment analysis presumably is binding upon the state and federal courts within the ninth circuit, which comprises the states of Alaska, Arizona, California, Hawaii, Idaho, Montana, Nevada, Oregon, and Washington.

right to build its house of worship where it pleases." [155]

• *The federal appeals court for the eleventh circuit (comprising the states of Alabama, Florida, and Georgia) ruled that a city zoning ordinance excluding churches from single-family residential zones did not violate the constitutional guaranty of religious freedom. The zoning ordinance of Miami Beach, Florida, excluded churches from single-family residential zones, but permitted them in other zones comprising 50 percent of the city's territory. An orthodox Jewish rabbi who conducted daily religious services in his residence was ordered by the city to discontinue the services on the ground that his residence was located in a single-family district that did not permit religious services. The rabbi sued the city, arguing that the ordinance violated his constitutional rights to freely exercise his religion. The court rejected the rabbi's claim and upheld the city's ordinance. It concluded that the burden imposed by the zoning ordinance on religious freedom "stands toward the lower end of the spectrum," since the ordinance "does not prohibit religious conduct per se [but rather] prohibits acts in furtherance of this conduct in certain geographical areas." The court stressed that the zoning ordinance permitted churches in over half of the city's territory, and that a permissible zone was located just four blocks from the rabbi's residence. These facts persuaded the court that the balance tipped in favor of the city in this case. The court was quick to add that "all should understand that we have not written today for every situation in which these issues might arise—only that we have done our best . . . in solving this very, very delicate problem."* [156]

• *A federal court in Minnesota ruled that a city's refusal to allow a church to operate in a commercial zone did not violate the church's constitutional rights.*[157] *A city zoning ordinance permitted churches in residential zones, but not in commercial or industrial zones. A new church congregation began meeting in a pastor's home. As the congregation grew, it began meeting in a public school building, and then in a commercial building. Eventually, the city notified the church that use of the commercial building violated city zoning law. The church unsuccessfully sought to amend the zoning ordinance to permit churches in commercial zones, and then*

---

[155] Messiah Baptist Church v. County of Jefferson, 859 F.2d 820 (10th Cir. 1988). The court's First Amendment analysis presumably is binding upon the state and federal courts within the tenth circuit, which comprises the states of Colorado, Kansas, New Mexico, Oklahoma, Utah, and Wyoming. One of the three judges who participated in this case dissented from the court's decision. The dissenter insisted that the court had improperly viewed the church's interest as "merely a secular building activity." On the contrary, "places of worship have in almost all religions been as integral to their religion as have Sunday School, preaching, hymn singing, prayer, and other forms of worship . . . . Churches are the situs for the most sacred, traditional exercise of religion: baptisms, confirmations, marriages, funerals, sacramental services, ordinations, and rites of passage of all kinds." Indeed, "if First Amendment free exercise rights are not triggered by the impingement on places of worship, the right of free exercise of religion is for practical purposes subject to broad infringement in all of its aspects except perhaps belief." The dissenter further noted that when government agencies seek to encumber the use of buildings for religious worship, they are, in fact, impinging on . . . three different interests recognized by the First Amendment itself—speech, assembly, and religious exercise." Because of this significant impact on constitutionally protected rights, the court had erred in too quickly dismissing the church's interest as "merely a secular building activity" that required little judicial deference.

[156] Grosz v. City of Miami Beach, 721 F.2d 729 (11th Cir. 1983). The court's First Amendment analysis presumably is binding upon the state and federal courts within the eleventh circuit, which comprises the states of Alabama, Florida, and Georgia. However, the eleventh circuit ruled in a subsequent case that the First Amendment guaranty of religious freedom outweighed a city's interest in enforcing its zoning law. Shuster v. City of Hollywood, 725 F.2d 693 (11th Cir. 1984).

[157] Cornerstone Bible Church v. City of Hastings, 740 F. Supp. 654 (D. Minn. 1990).

it sought to locate other sites for church services. The church was not able to find suitable accommodations in a residential zone, and continued to meet in the commercial building. When the city ordered the church to vacate the building, the church filed a lawsuit alleging that the city's actions violated the constitutional guaranty of religious freedom. The court rejected the church's position. It noted the constitutional guaranty of religious freedom is not violated unless "something is prohibited because of its religious affiliation or its display of religious belief." This was not the case here, the court concluded, since the city had not barred churches from commercial zones because of their religious character: "The zoning ordinance neither excludes only churches from the commercial and industrial zones nor reveals an anti-religious intent."

A number of state courts have reached similar results.[158] However, this view still represents a minority position among the states.

Legal Remedies Available to Churches § 7-06.3

Key point 7-06.3. Local zoning commissions may violate a church's First Amendment right to the free exercise of religion by imposing unreasonable restrictions on the church's ability to purchase and develop land for church use. Churches whose constitutional rights are violated in this manner may be able to sue for money damages under federal law.

What legal recourse does a church have if its exclusion from a city (or portion of a city) violates its constitutional rights? In the past, churches that have been denied access to certain locations by action of a zoning board generally have been content to seek a reversal of such a determination in the civil courts. In recent years, however, some churches have gone a step further and have sued cities for violating their constitutional rights. The relevant statute is title 42, section 1983, of the United States Code, which specifies:

Every person who, under color of any statute, ordinance, regulation, custom, or usage, of any State or Territory or the District of Columbia, subjects, or causes to be subjected, any citizen of the United States or other person within the jurisdiction thereof to the deprivation of any rights, privileges, or immunities secured by the Constitution and laws, shall be liable to the party injured in an action at law, suit in equity, or other proper proceeding for redress.

To illustrate, a New Jersey state court ruled that a church could sue a city that had improperly denied its request to build two radio antenna towers on

---

[158] *See generally* RATHKOPF, *supra* note 126, at § 20.01; YOKLEY, *supra* note 126, at § 35-14; WILLIAMS, *supra* note 126, at § 77.02.

its property.[159] An Assemblies of God church in New Jersey owned 106 acres of land, on which it operated a church and a school with 300 students and a fleet of 35 buses. The church wanted to establish a radio station on its property for broadcasting religious and educational programs. The station required a zoning variance permitting the construction of two 184-foot radio antenna towers. A local zoning board denied the church's request on the grounds that the proposed towers would create a safety hazard and would interfere with radio, television, and telephone usage in the neighborhood. A state court reversed the zoning board's decision, and ordered it to grant the church's request for a variance to construct the towers. The court's ruling did not end the litigation, however, for the church promptly sued the city and zoning board, alleging that they had violated its constitutional right to freely exercise its religion. The church relied on title 42, section 1983, of the United Stated Code. The court not only ruled that the church was entitled to money damages under "section 1983," but it did so by granting the church's motion for summary judgment. This means that the court found the church's demand for money damages to be so clearly authorized by law that it refused to submit the question to a jury.

The court rejected the city's claim that it was "immune" from being sued, noting that "municipalities have no immunity in a suit for damages under the Civil Rights Act" and that "it is clear" that a city that violates a church's constitutional rights "is liable for damages." The court agreed with the church that the radio antenna towers were needed to advance its religious beliefs, and accordingly they served a religious function that was protected by the First Amendment guaranty of religious liberty. The court emphasized that the courts of New Jersey have "provided broad support for the constitutional guarantees of religious freedom" and that a city "may not exercise its zoning power in violation of the fundamental tenets of the First Amendment." It added: "Churches convey their constitutionally protected religious messages primarily by means of the written and spoken word. In doing so, they are not confined to utterances within a church building but are free to disseminate their beliefs through every avenue of communication. Radio and television facilities are not denied to them."

The court conceded that a zoning board could interfere with a church's constitutional right of religious freedom if an "overriding governmental interest" exists. The court found no compelling interest in this case that outweighed the church's rights under the First Amendment. The only two concerns raised by the city were that the antenna towers would create a safety hazard and would cause radio interference in the immediate neighborhood. The court denied that either of these concerns presented a sufficiently compelling interest. As to the safety claim, the court simply observed that the church planned to build the towers on

---

[159] Burlington Assembly of God Church v. Zoning Board, 570 A.2d 495 (N.J. Super. 1989). *See also* Burlington Assembly of God Church v. Zoning Board, 588 A.2d 1297 (N.J. Super. 1990), in which the same court rejected the church's claim that it was entitled to damages of nearly $800,000, comprised mostly of the projected revenues it lost by not being able to broadcast programs for some four years during the lawsuit. The court concluded that the proper measure of damages was the lost property value resulting from the city's denial of the church's constitutional rights. Since the value of the church's property was in no way diminished by the city's denial of the tower permit, the court refused to award the church any monetary damages.

its 106 acres "a good distance from neighboring properties." Further, the evidence demonstrated that the proposed towers were "too well designed" to "give any weight" to the city's concern that they might fall over. As to the city's concern about radio interference, the court noted that the church had obtained a license from the Federal Communications Commission (FCC) to operate the station, and that the FCC had concluded that the station "could be operated at acceptable interference levels." This case is significant in its recognition that churches may sue governmental agencies that deny them their constitutional rights.

A federal district court in Illinois ruled that a church could sue a city for violating its constitutional rights.[160] The city of Evanston, Illinois, adopted a zoning ordinance permitting churches to locate anywhere in the city provided they first obtain a special use permit from the city. To secure a permit, a church must file a detailed plan for the use of the facilities and pay a fee. The city zoning board then holds a hearing and renders a decision. The entire process takes between four and six months. Churches conducting services without a permit are guilty of a misdemeanor and are subject to fines of $25 to $500 per day. A small fundamentalist church began conducting services in Evanston without a permit. The church met in the pastor's apartment, and then in a rented hotel room. It sought a permanent location, but allegedly could not find one since landlords either were unwilling to rent to the church until it obtained a permit, or increased the rent to an unaffordable level. The church filed a lawsuit against the city in federal court, alleging that its constitutional rights were violated by the city's permit procedure. Specifically, it argued that the procedure violated the constitutional guarantees of religious freedom and the "equal protection of the laws." With regard to the equal protection claim, the church claimed that other organizations (e.g., theaters, funeral homes, hotels, community centers) were not required to obtain permits to operate, and thus the permit procedure treated churches differently and less favorably without any apparent basis.   The federal trial court dismissed the church's religious claim, but it did agree that the city's permit procedure violated the church's constitutional right to the "equal protection of the laws," and it awarded the church nearly $18,000 in damages under title 42, section 1983 of the United States Code. Significantly, the court granted the church a "summary judgment," meaning that it found the church's position so clearly correct that it refused to submit the case to a jury. The city promptly appealed this decision to a federal appeals court, which dismissed the case on the technical ground that the church lacked "standing" to challenge the city's permit procedure since the city had never enforced the special permit requirement and accordingly there was no threat of legal consequences if the church disregarded it.

This case is significant (despite the appeals court's interpretation of the standing requirement) since it represents another example of a court (in this case, the federal district court) awarding a church monetary damages under "section 1983" for a violation of a church's constitutional rights. The importance of such rulings cannot be overstated—for they represent a recognition of an extremely potent weapon that is available to churches. To be sure, the federal appeals court

---

[160] Love Church v. City of Evanston, 896 F.2d 1082 (7th Cir. 1990).

"The importance of such rulings cannot be overstated—for they represent a recognition of an extremely potent weapon that is available to churches."

dismissed the case, but it did so for technical reasons that in no way diminish the significance of the trial court's decision. Further, the appeals court seemed to concede that it would have affirmed the district court's award of monetary damages had the city ever enforced its permit procedure, or had the church presented more evidence of the unwillingness of landlords to rent to the church. In many cases, these factors will be present, and presumably churches in such cases will be entitled to monetary damages.

Case Study

• *The Washington State Supreme Court ruled that a religious organization is entitled to monetary damages if a city violates its constitutional rights. A religious organization applied for a conditional use permit to construct a building on its property. A city official denied this application, and the organization promptly filed a second application. This application also was denied, and this denial was affirmed by the city council. The organization appealed to a local trial court, which declared the city's actions to be in error. The organization then filed a third application for a conditional use permit, and this application was denied by the same city official. When the city council upheld the denial of this application, the organization filed another lawsuit. This time, the organization demanded monetary damages on the ground that the city's actions had violated its constitutional rights. Specifically, the organization alleged that the city's actions violated its constitutional right to due process of law. The court ruled that the organization's constitutional rights had been violated by the city' actions, and that the organization was entitled to monetary damages. It observed: "Along with the vast majority of federal courts, we recognize that denial of a building permit, under certain circumstances, may give rise to a substantive due process claim. . . . Such a violation is made out, however, only if the decision to deny the permit is 'invidious or irrational' or 'arbitrary or capricious.'" The court concluded that the city's actions in denying the building permit satisfied this standard. In particular, it pointed to the fact that the city's decisions were "without consideration and in disregard of the relevant facts and circumstances."*[161]

The Religious Land Use and Institutionalized Persons Act (RLUIPA)

§ 7-06.4

Key point § 7-06.4. *The federal Religious Land Use and Institutionalized Persons Act prohibits state and local governments from imposing a*

---

[161] Lutheran Day Care v. Snohomish County, 829 P.2d 746 (Wash. 1992).

land use regulation in a manner that imposes a substantial burden on the exercise of religion unless the regulation is in furtherance of a compelling governmental interest and is the least restrictive means of furthering that compelling governmental interest.

The federal Religious Land Use and Institutionalized Persons Act ("RLUIPA" or "the Act") was enacted by Congress in 2000. The Act, which had been enacted by unanimous consent of both the Senate and House of Representatives, addressed two areas where religious freedom had been threatened: (1) land use regulation, and (2) persons in prisons, mental hospitals, nursing homes and similar institutions.

The Act will ensure that if a government action substantially burdens the exercise of religion in these two areas, the government must demonstrate that imposing that burden serves a "compelling public interest" and does so by the "least restrictive means." In addition, with respect to land use regulation, the Act specifically prohibits various forms of religious discrimination and exclusion. This section will review the background the Act, explain each of its major provisions, and then provide several practical examples that will illustrate the significance of the Act to religious congregations.

1. Background

(1) prior to 1990 the government needed a compelling interest to restrict the free exercise of religion

The First Amendment to the United States Constitution protects a number of fundamental rights, including the free exercise of religion. The First Amendment specifies that "Congress shall make no law . . . prohibiting the free exercise of religion." For many years, the United States Supreme Court interpreted this language to mean that the government could not impose substantial burdens on the exercise of sincerely held religious beliefs unless its actions were justified by a *compelling state interest* that could not be served through "less restrictive means."[162] In a 1990 ruling (the "*Smith* case"), the Supreme Court revised its understanding of the "free exercise" clause.[163]

(2) the Smith *case (1990)—no compelling interest needed to sustain "neutral laws of general applicability" that impose burdens on religious belief and practice*

The *Smith* case addressed the question of whether the state of Oregon could deny unemployment benefits to employees who had been terminated for using illegal drugs as part of a religious ceremony. Oregon law prohibits the intentional possession of a "controlled substance," including the drug peyote. Two employees of a private drug rehabilitation organization were fired from their jobs because they consumed peyote for "sacramental purposes" at a ceremony of the Native American Church. The two individuals applied for unemployment benefits under Oregon law, but their application was denied on the grounds that benefits are

---

[162] Sherbert v. Verner, 374 U.S. 398 (1963).
[163] Employment Division v. Smith, 494 U.S. 872 (1990).

not payable to employees who are discharged for "misconduct." The two former employees claimed that the denial of benefits violated their constitutional right to freely exercise their religion. The Supreme Court ruled that (1) the constitutional guaranty of religious freedom did not prohibit a state from criminalizing the sacramental use of a narcotic drug, and (2) the state of Oregon could deny unemployment benefits to individuals who were fired from their jobs for consuming peyote.

The Court began its opinion by noting that "we have never held that an individual's religious beliefs excuse him from compliance with an otherwise valid law prohibiting conduct that the state is free to regulate." On the contrary, the constitutional guaranty of religious freedom "does not relieve an individual of the obligation to comply with a valid and neutral law of general applicability on the ground that the law [prohibits] conduct that his religion prescribes."

Key point. *The Court did not throw out the compelling state interest requirement in all cases involving governmental restrictions on religious freedom. Rather, the Court stated that this requirement does not apply to restrictions caused by a "neutral law of general applicability." A law or other government act that targets or singles out religious organizations must be supported by a compelling state interest. Further, as noted below, the compelling state interest requirement applies if a second constitutional right is burdened by a law or other government act.*

The real significance of the Court's ruling was its refusal to apply the compelling state interest test as requested by the discharged employees. As noted above, the Supreme Court previously had interpreted the constitutional guaranty of religious freedom to mean that the government could not impose substantial burdens on the exercise of sincerely-held religious beliefs unless its actions were justified by a compelling state interest that could not be served through less restrictive means. The former employees argued that the Oregon law's denial of unemployment benefits to persons using peyote for sacramental purposes was not supported by a compelling state interest and accordingly could not be applied without violating the constitution.

The Court justified its refusal to apply the compelling state interest test by noting that

• it had not applied the test in a number of its recent decisions

• it had never found a state law limiting religious practices invalid on the ground that it was not supported by a compelling state interest, and

• the compelling state interest test should never be applied "to require exemptions from a generally applicable criminal law"

The Court rejected the former employees' suggestion that the compelling state interest test be applied only in cases involving religiously motivated conduct that is "central" to an individual's religion. This would require the courts to make judgments on the importance of religious practices—and this the civil courts may never do. The only options are to apply the compelling state interest test to all attempts by government to regulate religious practices, or to not apply the test at all. Applying the test in all cases involving governmental attempts to regulate religious practices would lead to "anarchy," since it would render "presumptively invalid" every law that regulates conduct allegedly based on religious belief. This would open the floodgates of claims of religious exemption

> from civic obligations of almost every conceivable kind—ranging from compulsory military service to the payment of taxes, to health and safety regulation such as manslaughter and child neglect laws, compulsory vaccination laws, drug laws; to social welfare legislation such as minimum wage laws, child labor laws, animal cruelty laws, environmental protection laws, and laws providing for equality of opportunity for the races. The First Amendment's protection of religious liberty does not require this.

The Court's ruling represents a clear departure from its previously well-established understanding of the constitutional guaranty of religious freedom. No longer must a state demonstrate that a compelling state interest supports a law that prohibits or restricts religious practices. This is unfortunate since it is now more difficult to prove that a state's interference with religious practices violates the guaranty of religious freedom. Four of the Court's nine justices disagreed with the Court's analysis, and with the virtual elimination of the compelling state interest test. The minority asserted that the Court's ruling diminished the guaranty of religious liberty by making it more difficult for persons to prove a violation of this fundamental constitutional guaranty. One of the dissenting Justices lamented that the Court's decision tilts the scales "in the state's favor," and "effectuates a wholesale overturning of settled law concerning the religion clauses of our Constitution. One hopes that the Court is aware of the consequences . . . ."

(3) Congress responds – the Religious Freedom Restoration Act (1993)

The consequences of the Supreme Court's reinterpretation of the First Amendment guaranty of religious freedom were predictable. Scores of lower federal courts and state courts upheld laws and other government actions that directly restricted religious practices. In many of these cases, the courts based their actions directly on the *Smith* case, suggesting that the result would have been different had it not been for that decision.

Congress responded to the *Smith* case by enacting the Religious Freedom Restoration Act by a unanimous vote of both houses. RFRA was signed into law by President Clinton in 1993. RFRA states its purposes as follows: "(1) to restore the compelling interest test . . . and to guarantee its application in all cases where free exercise of religion is burdened; and (2) to provide a claim or defense to persons whose religious exercise is burdened by government."

The key provision of RFRA is section 3, which specifies:

(a) IN GENERAL. Government shall not substantially burden a person's exercise of religion even if the burden results from a rule of general applicability, except as provided in subsection (b) . . . .

(b) EXCEPTION. Government may substantially burden a person's exercise of religion only if it demonstrates that application of the burden to the person—(1) is in furtherance of a compelling governmental interest; and (2) is the least restrictive means of furthering that compelling governmental interest.

(c) JUDICIAL RELIEF. A person whose religious exercise has been burdened in violation of this section may assert that violation as a claim or defense in a judicial proceeding and obtain appropriate relief against the government. Standing to assert a claim or defense under this section shall be governed by the general rules of standing under article III of the Constitution.

In practical terms, how did the enactment of RFRA affect local churches and other religious organizations? There is little doubt that it provided significant protections to the exercise of religion. Any law or government practice (whether at the local, state, or federal level) that "burdened" the exercise of religion was legally permissible only if the law or practice (1) was in furtherance of a compelling governmental interest, and (2) was the least restrictive means of furthering that compelling governmental interest. These were difficult standards to meet. As the Supreme Court itself observed in 1993, the concept of a "compelling governmental interest" is a very difficult standard for the government to satisfy:

A law burdening religious practice that is not neutral or not of general application must undergo the most rigorous of scrutiny. To satisfy the commands of the First Amendment, a law restrictive of religious practice must advance interests of the highest order and must be narrowly tailored in pursuit of those interests. The compelling interest standard that we apply once a law fails to meet the *Smith* requirements is not "watered . . . down" but "really means what it says." A law that targets religious conduct for distinctive treatment or advances legitimate governmental interests only against conduct with a religious motivation will survive strict scrutiny only in rare cases.[164]

In the years following the enactment of RFRA a number of government attempts to regulate or interfere with religious practices were struck down by the courts on the basis of the Act.

(4) the City of Boerne case (1997)

The city council of Boerne, Texas, passed an ordinance authorizing the city's Historic Landmark Commission to prepare a preservation plan with proposed historic landmarks and districts. Under the ordinance, the commission must

---

[164] Church of the Lukumi Babaluaye, Inc. v. City of Hialeah, 508 U.S. 520 (1993).

pre-approve construction affecting historic landmarks or buildings in a historic district. Soon afterwards the Archbishop of San Antonio applied for a building permit to allow the expansion of St. Peter's Catholic Church in Boerne. The church was so overcrowded that several persons had to be turned away from worship services because the existing facility was not large enough to accommodate them. City authorities, relying on the ordinance and the designation of a historic district (which, they claimed, included the church), denied the application. The Archbishop filed a lawsuit challenging the city's denial of the permit. The lawsuit relied upon RFRA as one basis for relief from the refusal to issue the permit. A federal district court concluded that by enacting RFRA Congress exceeded the scope of its authority. A federal appeals court reversed this decision, and upheld the constitutionality of RFRA. The city appealed to the United States Supreme Court. The appeal addressed the question of the constitutional validity of RFRA.

The Supreme Court ruled that RFRA was unconstitutional since Congress did not have the authority to enact it. The Court began its opinion by noting that the federal government "is one of enumerated powers." That is, each branch (legislative, executive, judicial) can only do those things specifically authorized by the Constitution. The First Amendment specifies that "Congress" cannot enact legislation "prohibiting the free exercise" of religion. Of course, "Congress" refers to the federal legislature, and so the First Amendment guaranty of religious freedom, as originally worded, was not a limitation on the power of state or local governments. In 1868, the Fourteenth Amendment to the Constitution was ratified, which prohibits any state from depriving "any person of life, liberty, or property without due process of law." Then, in 1940, the Supreme Court ruled that the "liberty" protected by the Fourteenth Amendment against state interference included the First Amendment guaranty of religious freedom. For the first time, this limitation upon the power of Congress to prohibit the free exercise of religion now applied to state and local governments as well. The Fourteenth Amendment contained a section (section 5) which gave Congress "power to enforce, by appropriate legislation, the provisions of this [amendment]." Congress pointed to this section as the source of its authority to enact RFRA. Members of Congress insisted that they were only protecting by legislation one of the liberties guaranteed by the Fourteenth Amendment that had been diminished by the Supreme Court's ruling in *Smith*.

The Supreme Court ruled that section 5 of the Fourteenth Amendment did not authorize Congress to enact RFRA. It acknowledged that section 5 authorizes Congress to "enforce" the Fourteenth Amendment, and therefore Congress can enact legislation "enforcing the constitutional right to the free exercise of religion." However, the Court then observed:

> Congress' power under section 5, however, extends only to enforcing the provisions of the Fourteenth Amendment. . . . The design of the amendment and the text of section 5 are inconsistent with the suggestion that Congress has the power to decree the substance of the Fourteenth Amendment's restrictions on the states. Legislation which alters the meaning of the free exercise [of religion] clause cannot be said to be enforcing the

clause. Congress does not enforce a constitutional right by changing what the right is. It has been given the power "to enforce," not the power to determine what constitutes a constitutional violation. Were it not so, what Congress would be enforcing would no longer be, in any meaningful sense, the "provisions of [the Fourteenth Amendment] . . . ."

If Congress could define its own powers by altering the Fourteenth Amendment's meaning, no longer would the Constitution be "superior paramount law, unchangeable by ordinary means." It would be "on a level with ordinary legislative acts, and, like other acts . . . alterable when the legislature shall please to alter it." Under this approach, it is difficult to conceive of a principle that would limit congressional power. Shifting legislative majorities could change the Constitution and effectively circumvent the difficult and detailed amendment process contained [therein].

The Court conceded that it is not always clear whether Congress is "enforcing" the Fourteenth Amendment or making unauthorized substantive changes in the Constitution. However, it insisted that there must be a "proportionality between the injury to be prevented or remedied and the means adopted to that end." The Court concluded that this test was not met in this case, since RFRA was not a "proportional" response to the "injury to be prevented or remedied." Rather, RFRA was an expansive law that was enacted to address minimal threats to religious freedom. The Court noted that

sweeping coverage ensures [RFRA's] intrusion at every level of government, displacing laws and prohibiting official actions of almost every description and regardless of subject matter. RFRA's restrictions apply to every agency and official of the federal, state, and local governments. RFRA applies to all federal and state law, statutory or otherwise, whether adopted before or after its enactment. RFRA has no termination date or termination mechanism. Any law is subject to challenge at any time by any individual who alleges a substantial burden on his or her free exercise of religion.

Further, this massive response was not warranted by any significant threat to religious freedom:

RFRA's legislative record lacks examples of modern instances of generally applicable laws passed because of religious bigotry. The history of persecution in this country detailed in the [congressional] hearings mentions no episodes occurring in the past 40 years. . . . The absence of more recent episodes stems from the fact that, as one witness testified, "deliberate persecution is not the usual problem in this country." Rather, the emphasis of the [congressional] hearings was on laws of general applicability which place incidental burdens on religion. Much of the discussion centered upon anecdotal evidence of autopsies performed on Jewish individuals and Hmong immigrants in violation of their religious beliefs . . . and on zoning regulations and historic preservation laws (like the one at issue here), which as an incident of their normal operation, have adverse effects on churches and synagogues. . . . It is difficult to maintain that they are examples of legislation enacted or enforced due to animus or hostility to the burdened religious practices or that they indicate some widespread pattern of religious discrimination in this country. Congress' concern was with the incidental burdens imposed, not the object or purpose of the legislation.

The stringent test RFRA demands of state laws reflects a lack of proportionality or congruence between the means adopted and the legitimate end to be achieved. If an objector can show a substantial burden on his free exercise, the State must demonstrate a compelling governmental interest and show that the law is the least restrictive means of furthering its interest. Claims that a law substantially burdens someone's exercise of religion will often be difficult to contest. Requiring a state to demonstrate a compelling interest and show that it has adopted the least restrictive means of achieving that interest is the most demanding test known to constitutional law. If "compelling interest" really means what it says . . . many laws will not meet the test. . . . [The test] would open the prospect of constitutionally required religious exemptions from civic obligations of almost every conceivable kind." Laws valid under *Smith* would fall under RFRA without regard to whether they had the object of stifling or punishing free exercise. . . . [RFRA] would require searching judicial scrutiny of state law with the attendant likelihood of invalidation. This is a considerable congressional intrusion into the states' traditional prerogatives and general authority to regulate for the health and welfare of their citizens.

The substantial costs RFRA exacts, both in practical terms of imposing a heavy litigation burden on the states and in terms of curtailing their traditional general regulatory power, far exceed any pattern or practice of unconstitutional conduct under the free exercise clause as interpreted in *Smith*. Simply put, RFRA is not designed to identify and counteract state laws likely to be unconstitutional because of their treatment of religion. In most cases, the state laws to which RFRA applies are not ones which will have been motivated by religious bigotry. . . .

It is a reality of the modern regulatory state that numerous state laws, such as the zoning regulations at issue here, impose a substantial burden on a large class of individuals. When the exercise of religion has been burdened in an incidental way by a law of general application, it does not follow that the persons affected have been burdened any more than other citizens, let alone burdened because of their religious beliefs. (emphasis added)

Key point. *Several courts have ruled that the Supreme Court in the Boerne case only invalidated RFRA as it pertains to local and state governments, and that RFRA remains a viable limitation on attempts by the federal government to restrict the exercise of religion.*

(5) the Religious Liberty Protection Act of 1999

In 1999 the House of Representatives passed overwhelmingly (306-118) the Religious Liberty Protection Act of 1999. The express purpose of this legislation was to "repeal" the Supreme Court's *City of Boerne* decision and reinstate the requirement that any state or local law that imposes a substantial burden on the exercise of religion is invalid unless supported by a compelling governmental interest. However, this legislation was not acted on by the Senate, and so never became law.

(6) the Religious Land Use and Institutionalized Persons Act of 2000

This legislation is analyzed below.

2. The Religious Land Use and Institutionalized Persons Act of 2000

RLUIPA, like RFRA and the Religious Liberty Protection Act of 1999, seeks to protect religious liberty. However, its protections are far more limited. Rather than protecting religious practices from all governmental encroachments, it focuses only on zoning regulations and persons who are institutionalized (in prisons, hospitals, and retirement homes).

substantial burden

RLUIPA specifies that state and local governments cannot subject religious organizations to a zoning or landmarking law that imposes substantial burdens on the free exercise of religion unless the law is supported by a compelling governmental interest:

No government shall impose or implement a land use regulation in a manner that imposes a substantial burden on the religious exercise of a person, including a religious assembly or institution, unless the government demonstrates that imposition of the burden on that person, assembly, or institution—(A) is in furtherance of a compelling governmental interest; and (B) is the least restrictive means of furthering that compelling governmental interest.[165]

A substantial burden to religious exercise involves more than inconvenience; it is "akin to significant pressure which directly coerces a religious adherent to conform his or her behavior accordingly."[166]

---

[165] 42 U.S.C.A. § 2000cc. Some pre-RLUIPA cases concluded that a city's refusal to allow a religious organization to construct a new facility did not constitute a substantial burden of the exercise of religion. *See, e.g.,* Messiah Baptist Church v. Jefferson, 859 F.2d 820 (10th Cir. 1988); Lakewood, Ohio, Congregation of Jehovah's Witnesses v. Lakewood, 699 F.2d 303 (6th Cir. 1983); United States v. Airmont, 839 F.Supp. 1054 (S.D.N.Y. 1993); Love v. Evanston, 671 F.Supp. 508 (N.D. Ill. 1987).

[166] Midrash Sephardi v. Town of Surfside, 366 F.3d 1214 (11th Cir. 2004). The court noted that a substantial burden on religious exercise in violation of RLUIPA can result from a zoning ordinance that "exerts pressure tending to force religious adherents to forego religious precepts, or mandates religious conduct."

RLUIPA clarifies the application of the substantial burden limitation with the following three provisions:

(A) the substantial burden is imposed in a program or activity that receives Federal financial assistance, even if the burden results from a rule of general applicability;

(B) the substantial burden affects, or removal of that substantial burden would affect, commerce with foreign nations, among the several States, or with Indian tribes, even if the burden results from a rule of general applicability; or

(C) the substantial burden is imposed in the implementation of a land use regulation or system of land use regulations, under which a government makes, or has in place formal or informal procedures or practices that permit the government to make, individualized assessments of the proposed uses for the property involved.[167]

prohibition of "discrimination and exclusion"

In addition to restoring the compelling governmental interest requirement in the context of state and local zoning and landmarking laws that impose substantial burdens on the exercise of religion, RLUIPA also prohibits attempts by state and local governments to discriminate against, or exclude, religious organizations when applying zoning and landmarking laws. There are three specific prohibitions:

No government shall impose or implement a land use regulation in a manner that treats a religious assembly or institution on less than equal terms with a nonreligious assembly or institution.[168]

No government shall impose or implement a land use regulation that discriminates against any assembly or institution on the basis of religion or religious denomination.

---

[167] *Id.* An "individualized assessment" occurs when city officials may use their authority to individually evaluate and either approve or disapprove of churches in potentially discriminatory ways. Town of Foxfield v. Archdiocese, 148 P.3d 339 (Or. App. 2006). One court observed that RLUIPA codifies numerous precedents holding that systems of individualized assessments, as opposed to generally applicable laws, are subject to the compelling government interest requirement. Cottonwood Christian Center v. Cypress Redevelopment Agency, 218 F.Supp.2d 1203 (C.D. Cal. 2002).

[168] A religious organization that challenges a land-use regulation under the "equal terms" provision of RLUIPA does not need to present evidence that the regulation imposes a substantial burden on its religious exercise. Rather, "a plaintiff must show (1) it is a religious assembly or institution, (2) subject to a land use regulation, which regulation (3) treats the religious assembly on less than equal terms with (4) a nonreligious assembly or institution (5) that causes no lesser harm to the interests the regulation seeks to advance. Lighthouse Institute for Evangelism v. City of Long Branch, 510 F.3d 253 (3rd Cir. 2007). *See also* Primera Iglesia Bautista Hispana v. Broward County," 450 F.3d 1295 (11th Cir. 2006) (applied a four factor test that deleted the fifth factor in the test).

No government shall impose or implement a land use regulation that—(A) totally excludes religious assemblies from a jurisdiction; or (B) unreasonably limits religious assemblies, institutions, or structures within a jurisdiction.[169]

The third of these three protections is probably the most important for churches since it common for local governments to require churches to obtain special use permits in order to build new facilities in certain areas. RLUIPA requires that local officials cannot "unreasonably limit" church structures within their jurisdiction.

Some courts have recognized that while "an unreasonable limitation on religious uses within a jurisdiction undoubtedly would impose a substantial burden on religious institutions, to interpret the substantial burden provision as being coextensive with the [discrimination and exclusion] provision would be to render one of the provisions superfluous."[170]

A federal appeals court ruled that the equal terms provision of RLUIPA may be violated by a land use regulation in at least three ways: "(1) by facially differentiating between religious and nonreligious assemblies or institutions; (2) by 'gerrymandering' to place a burden solely on religious, as opposed to nonreligious, assemblies or institutions, despite being neutral on its face; or (3) or through selective enforcement against religious, as opposed to nonreligious, assemblies or institutions of a truly neutral regulation."[171]

constitutional validity

Will the courts rule that RLUIPA, like RFRA, represents an unconstitutional attempt by Congress to change the meaning of the First Amendment by requiring that any state or local law that substantially burdens the exercise of religion in the contexts of zoning and institutionalized persons must be supported by a "compelling governmental interest," even if it is a "neutral law of general application" that is presumably valid under the Supreme Court's *Smith* ruling? Possibly not. Congress carefully attempted to avoid such a fate in drafting RLUIPA through a number of precautions.

As noted previously, RLUIPA addresses two areas where religious freedom has been threatened: (1) Section 2 specifies that state and local governments cannot subject religious organizations to a land use regulation that imposes substantial burdens on the free exercise of religion unless the law is supported by a compelling governmental interest; (2) Section 3 seeks to protect the religious practices of

---

[169] *Id.*

[170] Murphy v. Zoning Commission, 402 F.3d 342 (2nd Cir. 2005). *See also* Digrugilliers v. Consolidated City of Indianapolis, 506 F.3d 612 (7th Cir. 2007), in which a federal appeals court observed: "The equal-terms section is violated whenever religious land uses are treated worse than comparable nonreligious ones, whether or not the discrimination imposes a substantial burden on the religious uses. If proof of substantial burden were an ingredient of the equal-terms provision, the provisions would be identical, which could not have been Congress's intent." *See also* Hollywood Community Synagogue v. City of Hollywood, 430 F.Supp.2d 1296 (S.D. Fla. 2006).

[171] Primera Iglesia Bautista Hispana v. Broward County, 450 F.3d 1295 (11th Cir. 2006)

institutionalized persons.

In 2005, the United States Supreme Court affirmed the constitutionality of section 3 (pertaining to institutionalized persons).[172] This case is important because it suggests (although does not specifically hold) that section 2 of RLUIPA (pertaining to land use regulations) does not violate the First Amendment's nonestablishment of religion clause. Several previous state and federal cases have suggested that section 2 of RLUIPA is an impermissible establishment of religion. This conclusion is now far less likely.

Key point. RLUIPA contains the following provision: "A government may avoid the preemptive force of any provision of this Act by changing the policy or practice that results in a substantial burden on religious exercise, by retaining the policy or practice and exempting the substantially burdened religious exercise, by providing exemptions from the policy or practice for applications that substantially burden religious exercise, or by any other means that eliminates the substantial burden."

Key point. RLUIPA specifies that "this Act shall be construed in favor of a broad protection of religious exercise, to the maximum extent permitted by the terms of this Act and the Constitution

Key point. RLUIPA defines "religious exercise" to include "any exercise of religion, whether or not compelled by, or central to, a system of religious belief." It further provides that "the use, building, or conversion of real property for the purpose of religious exercise shall be considered to be religious exercise of the person or entity that uses or intends to use the property for that purpose."

3. Judicial Relief

Persons or religious organizations whose rights under RLUIPA are violated by state or local governmental action are provided with the following remedy: "A person may assert a violation of this Act as a claim or defense in a judicial proceeding and obtain appropriate relief against a government." RLUIPA sets forth the following procedure:

If a plaintiff produces prima facie evidence to support a claim alleging a violation of the free exercise clause or a violation of [this Act], the government shall bear the burden of persuasion on any element of the claim, except that the plaintiff shall bear the burden of persuasion on whether the law (including a regulation) or government practice that is challenged by the claim substantially burdens the plaintiff's exercise of religion.

Key point. RLUIPA provides that a court may award attorneys' fees to any party who prevails in a lawsuit brought to enforce rights granted under the Act.

---

[172] Cutter v. Wilkinson, 125 S.Ct. 2113 (2005).

4. Illustrative Cases

Summarized below are several leading cases illustrating the application of RLUIPA to religious organizations.

Cases in which RLUIPA was violated

• *A federal appeals court ruled that a city violated RLUIPA in denying a private religious school permission to expand its facility, since the denial imposed a substantial burden on religious exercise. The court concluded: "A burden need not be found insuperable to be held substantial. When the school has no ready alternatives, or where the alternatives require substantial delay, uncertainty, and expense, a complete denial of the school's application might be indicative of a substantial burden."[173]*

• *A federal appeals court ruled that a city's zoning ordinance that permitted a range of different uses in the central commercial district (including a restaurant, variety store, college, assembly hall, bowling alley, movie theater, municipal building, new automobile and boat showroom), but barred religious organizations from the same district, violated RLUIPA since it treated religious organizations on less than equal terms with non-religious institutions.[174]*

• *A church submitted an application to rezone its property from residential to institutional so that it could build a church facility. To allay the city's concerns that the property could be used for other purposes if the church failed to raise sufficient construction funds, the church coupled the rezoning proposal with a zoning device that would limit the use of the property to church related uses. The city's planning commission denied the application. A federal appeals court concluded that "having either to sell the [property] and find a suitable alternative parcel or be subjected to unreasonable delay by having to restart the permit process to satisfy the planning commission about a contingency for which the church has already provided complete satisfaction constituted a substantial burden under RLUIPA." In reaching this conclusion, the court suggested that the city had been "playing a delaying game"; and that its concerns were "legal chimeras." Under these circumstances, the church was not required to prove that it had been entirely excluded from the jurisdiction to establish a substantial burden."[175]*

• *A federal appeals court ruled that a county board of supervisors' denial of a religious organization's application for a permit to construct a temple on land zoned for agricultural use violated RLUIPA since it imposed a substantial burden on the organization's religious exercise. The court noted that the board gave such broad reasons for denying the application (increased traffic and noise) that very little property was left in the community upon which the temple could be built.[176]*

---

[173] Westchester Day School v. Village of Mamaroneck, 504 F.3d 338 (2nd Cir. 2007).

[174] Lighthouse Institute for Evangelism v. City of Long Branch, 510 F.3d 253 (3rd Cir. 2007).

[175] Sts. Constantine & Helen Greek Orthodox Church v. New Berlin, 396 F.3d 895 (7th Cir. 2005). Another court interpreted this case to "stand for the proposition that, when the government has acted arbitrarily and capriciously in prohibiting a religious land use, no further demonstration of a substantial burden is required." Cambodian Buddhist Society v. Planning and Zoning Commission, 941 A.2d 868 (Conn. 2008).

[176] Guru Nanak Sikh Society v. County of Sutter, 456 F.3d 978 (9tn Cir. 2006).

- *A federal appeals court ruled that when the government inconsistently applied development concerns, rejected adequate mitigating conditions and significantly reduced the area in which a religious facility could be built, a substantial burden had been established.[177]*

- *A federal appeals court ruled that a city violated RLUIPA's equal terms provision by forbidding a rabbi to conduct religious services in his residence without a permit while allowing other non-religious uses in the same district, including cub scouts and family gatherings.[178]*

- *A federal court in California ruled that a city's attempt to condemn a church's property using the power of eminent domain constituted a land use regulation subject to RLUIPA.[179]*

- *A federal court in California ruled that a city violated RLUIPA in the manner in which it applied its conditional use permit requirement to a church. The court noted that the church received a permit of only half the length it requested, with no reasonable expectation for an extension. This constituted a substantial burden on the church's exercise of religion. The court noted that the church "experienced outright hostility to its application, decision-making that is seemingly arbitrary or pretextual, and ignorance regarding the requirements of federal law regarding the application of land use laws to religious institutions." The court rejected the city's contention that its actions were based on the compelling interest of preserving industrial properties in an industrial park. It noted that the zoning ordinance permitted several non-industrial uses in the area, including churches.[180]*

- *A federal court in Florida ruled that a city's land use code violated the RLUIPA's equal terms provision by prohibiting religious organizations in all business districts, but permitting numerous non-religious uses within business districts, including day care centers, indoor recreational facilities such as movie theaters, centers offering personal improvement services such as aerobic studios, art, music dance and drama schools, and places where people could gather for meetings or business related to trade associations or unions.[181]*

- *A federal court in Massachusetts ruled that application of a zoning ordinance's density, setback and parking restrictions to a church which wanted to construct a parish center, imposed a "substantial burden" under RLUIPA. The court concluded that these restrictions were not the least restrictive means of furthering a compelling government interest.[182]*

---

[177] Guru Nanak Sikh Society v. Sutter, 456 F.3d 978 (9th Cir. 2006).

[178] Konikov v. Orange County, 410 F.3d 1317 (11th Cir. 2005). *Accord* Midrash Sephardi v. Town of Surfside, 366 F.3d 1214 (11th Cir. 2004).

[179] Cottonwood Christian Center v. Cypress Redevelopment Agency, 218 F.Supp.2d 1203 (C.D. Cal. 2002).

[180] Grace Church v. City of San Diego, 555 F.Supp.2d 1126 (S.D. Cal. 2008).

[181] Chabad of Nova, Inc. v. City of Cooper City, 533 F.Supp.2d 1220 (S.D. Fla. 2008).

[182] Mintz v. Roman Catholic Bishop, 424 F.Supp.2d 309 (D. Mass. 2006).

• A Michigan court ruled that a city's denial of a variance to a parochial school for its proposed use of its property as a faith-based primary school violated RLUIPA since it placed a substantial burden on the school's religious exercise. The court noted that no other suitable property was available to the school at a cost it could afford, and the city presented no evidence that it had a compelling governmental interest requiring it to deny the variance.[183]

Cases in which RLUIPA was not violated

• A federal appeals court ruled that a city's denial of a church's application for a special use permit to build a new facility in excess of 25,000 square feet on its property did not violate RLUIPA since it did not amount to a substantial burden on the church's religious exercise. The court stressed that the city's denial did not require the church to violate or forego its religious beliefs or choose between those beliefs and a benefit to which it was entitled.[184]

• A federal appeals court ruled that a city's plan to acquire a church cemetery using the power of eminent domain in order to facilitate expansion of an airport was not a land use regulation subject to RLUIPA.[185] The court observed: "Given the importance of eminent domain as a governmental power affecting land use, we think that if Congress had wanted to include eminent domain within RLUIPA, it would have said something. Indeed, before federal law starts interfering with the fundamental state power of eminent domain, it is likely that we would need a clear statement from Congress."

• A federal appeals court ruled that a city's zoning ordinance did not impose a substantial burden on local religious institutions because it "did not render impracticable the use of real property . . . for religious exercise, much less discourage churches from locating or attempting to locate there."[186]

• A federal appeals court ruled that a city's zoning ordinance that required churches to obtain a special use permit to construct a sanctuary in a residential district did not violate RLUIPA since the requirement of a permit did not amount to a total exclusion of churches. The court noted that the zoning ordinance set forth the factors to be considered by the city in evaluating an application for a special use permit, and the permit requirement was neutral since it applied to schools, utilities, and other secular institutions, and was justified by legitimate, non-discriminatory municipal planning goals of limiting development, traffic, and noise, and preserving open space.[187]
The Connecticut Supreme Court ruled that RLUIPA's substantial burden provision applies in a zoning case only when the government has the discretion to apply a land use regulation in a manner that discriminates against religious institutions in general or

---

[183] Montessori Center v. Ann Arbor Charter Township, 739 N.W.2d 664 (Mich. App. 2007).

[184] Living Water Church of God v. Charter Township, 258 Fed. Appx. 729 (6th Cir. 2007).

[185] St. John's United Church of Christ v. City of Chicago, 502 F.3d 616 (7th Cir. 2007). *Contra* Cottonwood Christian Center v. Cypress Redevelopment Agency, 218 F.Supp.2d 1203 (C.D. Cal. 2002).

[186] Civil Liberties for Urban Believers v. Chicago, 342 F.3d 752 (7th Cir. 2003).

[187] Vision Church v. Village of Long Grove, 468 F.3d 975 (7th Cir. 2006). *Accord* Town of Mount Pleasant v. Legion of Christ, 800 N.Y.S.2d 34 (2005).

against a particular religion or denomination.[188]

• A federal court in Illinois rejected a church's claim that a city violated RLUIPA by forbidding it to construct a new building in an industrial park. The court concluded that the church failed to demonstrate that the city's denial amounted to a substantial burden on religious exercise. Petra Presbyterian Church v. Village of Northbrook, 409 F.Supp.2d 409 (N.D. Ill. 2006).

• A Maryland court ruled that a city's denial of a church's request for a variance to install a sign ten times larger than what was permitted by the applicable zoning ordinance did not violate RLUIPA since it did not impose a substantial burden on religious exercise. The court noted that the church had other means of attracting members, including the rental of existing billboards.[189]

• A federal district court in Michigan rejected a RLUIPA claim on the ground that religious exercise was not substantially burdened by a denial of a special use permit to demolish an existing structure and to build a new one when "there [was] no indication that [the religious institution was] precluded from fulfilling its religious mission through worship as a whole . . . in other locations throughout the city."[190]

• The Supreme Court of Michigan ruled that a city's refusal to rezone property to allow construction of a religious facility was not a substantial burden on religious exercise when other land in jurisdiction was zoned for that use.[191]

• The Oregon Supreme Court ruled that a church's rights under the Religious Land Use and Institutionalized Persons Act were not violated by a city's denial of its application for a conditional use permit to construct a new sanctuary. The court noted that RLUIPA prohibits only "land use regulations" that impose a substantial burden on religious exercise. It concluded that "a government regulation imposes a substantial burden on religious exercise only if it pressures or forces a choice between following religious precepts and forfeiting certain benefits, on the one hand, and abandoning one or more of those precepts in order to obtain the benefits, on the other." It concluded that the city had not imposed a "substantial burden" on the church's religious exercise according to this definition. It conceded that "the denial of the conditional use permit has several adverse consequences for the church's effort to build a meetinghouse. . . . Those hardships, however, do not constitute substantial burdens under RLUIPA." The court noted that there was no evidence that "the crowded conditions at the meetinghouse have forced the church to turn away anyone who wished to attend church or to eliminate or reduce church activities. Nor is there any evidence in the record to suggest

[188] Cambodian Buddhist Society v. Planning and Zoning Commission, 941 A.2d 868 (Conn. 2008). The court concluded: "Because RLUIPA's substantial burden provision applies only when the government has made an 'individualized [assessment] of the proposed [use]' we conclude that the provision applies only when the government has the discretion to apply a land use regulation in a manner that discriminates against religious institutions in general or against a particular religion or denomination."

[189] Trinity Assembly of God v. People's Counsel, 941 A.2d 560 (Md. 2008).

[190] Episcopal Student Foundation v. Ann Arbor, 341 F.Supp.2d 691 (E.D. Mich. 2004).

[191] Greater Bible Way Temple v. Jackson, 733 N.W.2d 734 (Mich. 2007).

that the city's denial was motivated by religious animus."[192]

• *An Oregon court ruled that a county's decision denying special use approval for a weekday parochial school did not impose a substantial burden on a church's religious exercise in violation of RLUIPA. The court noted that the county had granted special use approvals for the church and its daycare facility on the property, but denied approval for proposed school; and, that the church had failed to demonstrate that the county's decision would require it to forgo its religious precepts because it could not reasonably locate and acquire alternative site for its proposed combined uses.*[193]

• *A Pennsylvania court ruled that a city zoning hearing board's denial of a church's application for use of a campground and hiking trails as an accessory use did not amount to a substantial burden on religious exercise in violation of RLUIPA since the church was not required to forego the exercise of its religion, and there were city-owned campsites nearby that were available.*[194]

• *A Pennsylvania court ruled that a church-operated daycare, while assisting in carrying out church's religious mission, was not a fundamental religious activity of the church, and therefore a city did not substantially burden the church's religious exercise by denying it a permit to operate the daycare.*[195]

• *A Washington appeals court ruled that a church failed to show that a city's requirement that it obtain a permit before hosting a homelessness encampment, and the city's refusal to accept a permit application based on a zoning moratorium, substantially burdened church's homeless shelter activities in violation of the church's rights under RLUIPA. The court noted that the church did not show that use of indoor church buildings was an ineffective option for providing shelter to the homeless, and it was unclear whether there were other potential sites outside of zone that were not city-owned that might have been used to host encampment.*[196]

5. Maintaining a RLUIPA Claim

How should a church proceed when its rights under RLUIPA are possibly violated? Consider the following examples.

Example 1. *A city ordinance prohibits churches and all other charitable organizations from locating in residential areas without obtaining a "special use permit" from city officials. A church applies for a permit, and a hearing is conducted at which several neighboring homeowners complain that their property valuations will decline if a church is allowed in their neighborhood. The church's application for a permit is denied. The church sues the city, claiming that its rights under RLUIPA have been violated. Consider the following analysis: (1) RLUIPA specifies that state and local governments cannot impose*

---

[192] Corporation of the Presiding Bishop of the Church of Jesus Christ of Latter-Day Saints v. City of West Linn, 111 P.3d 1123 (Ore. 2005).

[193] Timberline Baptist Church v. Washington County, 154 P.3d 759 (Or. App. 2007).

[194] City of Hope v. Sadsbury Township Zoning Hearing Board, 890 A.2d 1137 (Pa. Common. 2006).

[195] Ridley Park United Methodist Church v. Zoning Hearing Board, 920 A.2d 953 (Pa. Common. 2007).

[196] City of Woodinville v. Northshore United Church of Christ, 162 P.3d 427 (Wash. App. 2007).

"a land use regulation in a manner that imposes a substantial burden on the religious exercise of a person, including a religious assembly or institution, unless the government demonstrates that imposition of the burden on that person, assembly, or institution—(A) is in furtherance of a compelling governmental interest; and (B) is the least restrictive means of furthering that compelling governmental interest." (2) RLUIPA defines "religious exercise" to include "any exercise of religion, whether or not compelled by, or central to, a system of religious belief." It further provides that "the use, building, or conversion of real property for the purpose of religious exercise shall be considered to be religious exercise of the person or entity that uses or intends to use the property for that purpose." (3) Proving a compelling governmental interest is very difficult. The Supreme Court has observed: "A law burdening religious practice that is not neutral or not of general application must undergo the most rigorous of scrutiny. To satisfy the commands of the First Amendment, a law restrictive of religious practice must advance interests of the highest order and must be narrowly tailored in pursuit of those interests. The compelling interest standard that we apply once a law fails to meet the Smith requirements . . . means what it says."[197] (4) The church can sue the city, and allege a violation of its rights under the First Amendment and RLUIPA. If it produces "prima facie evidence" to support a claim alleging a violation of the free exercise clause or a violation of RLUIPA, the city government "shall bear the burden of persuasion on any element of the claim, except that the plaintiff shall bear the burden of persuasion on whether the law or government practice that is challenged by the claim substantially burdens the plaintiff's exercise of religion." (5) If the church prevails, a court may allow it to recover any attorneys' fees it paid. (6) The First Amendment also guarantees the rights of assembly and association, and a strong case can be made that these rights are violated by the zoning ordinance since the right of some members to engage in religious services (assembly and association) is being restricted. By asserting that these First Amendment rights are being violated in addition to the free exercise of religion, the church may be able to force the city to demonstrate a compelling government interest supporting its decision to deny the church permission to expand its facilities. It is doubtful that the city could meet this requirement. (7) RLUIPA specifies that "this Act shall be construed in favor of a broad protection of religious exercise, to the maximum extent permitted by the terms of this Act and the Constitution."

Example 2. Same facts as example 1, except that the city ordinance only required religious organizations to apply for a special use permit in order to use property in residential areas for religious purposes. Several other charitable organizations are not required to obtain such a permit. Such a law is not "neutral" toward religion, and so the city will be required to prove a compelling government interest in support of the ordinance. The Supreme Court observed in the Smith case (summarized above) that laws that are not "neutral" towards religion, or that are not of "general applicability," will violate the First Amendment guaranty of religious freedom unless supported by a compelling government interest. Therefore, the church can bring a lawsuit against the city on the basis of the First Amendment guaranty of religious liberty. The Supreme Court has ruled that "a law that targets religious conduct for distinctive treatment or advances legitimate governmental interests only against conduct with a religious motivation will survive strict scrutiny only in rare cases."[198] The church can also assert a claim under RLUIPA.

---

[197] Church of the Lukumi Babaluaye, Inc. v. City of Hialeah, 508 U.S. 520 (1993).
[198] Id.

Example 3. *A city council receives several complaints from downtown business owners concerning homeless shelters that are operated by churches. In response to these complaints, the city council enacts an ordinance banning any church from operating a homeless shelter. This ordinance is neither neutral nor of general applicability and so the analysis in example 2 would apply. This means that the city will need to demonstrate that the ordinance is supported by a compelling government interest. It is doubtful that it will be able to do so. As the Supreme Court observed in the Hialeah case (discussed above), "a law that targets religious conduct for distinctive treatment or advances legitimate governmental interests only against conduct with a religious motivation will survive strict scrutiny only in rare cases."*

Example 4. *Same facts as the previous example, except that the ordinance bans any homeless shelter in the downtown area, whether or not operated by a church. The church sues the city, claiming that its rights under RLUIPA have been violated. RLUIPA specifies that state and local governments cannot impose "a land use regulation in a manner that imposes a substantial burden on the religious exercise of a person, including a religious assembly or institution, unless the government demonstrates that imposition of the burden on that person, assembly, or institution—(A) is in furtherance of a compelling governmental interest; and (B) is the least restrictive means of furthering that compelling governmental interest." RLUIPA defines "religious exercise" to include "any exercise of religion, whether or not compelled by, or central to, a system of religious belief." The analysis in example 1 would apply to this example as well.*

Example 5. *A city council decides that there are "enough" houses of worship in the city and so it refuses to allow any new or existing congregations to construct a house of worship. This ordinance is neither neutral nor of general applicability. This means that the city will need to demonstrate that the ordinance is supported by a compelling government interest. It is doubtful that it will be able to do so. As the Supreme Court observed in the Hialeah case (discussed above), "a law that targets religious conduct for distinctive treatment or advances legitimate governmental interests only against conduct with a religious motivation will survive strict scrutiny only in rare cases." In addition, churches could challenge the city council's actions by filing a civil lawsuit asserting a violation of their rights under RLUIPA. RLUIPA provides that "no government shall impose or implement a land use regulation that—(A) totally excludes religious assemblies from a jurisdiction; or (B) unreasonably limits religious assemblies, institutions, or structures within a jurisdiction."*

Example 6. *A city enacts an ordinance establishing a "landmark commission." The commission is authorized to designate any building as an historic landmark. Any building so designated cannot be modified or demolished without the commission's approval. A church is designated as an historic landmark. A few years later, the church asks the commission for permission to enlarge is facility in order to accommodate its growing congregation. The commission rejects this request, despite proof that several persons are "turned away" each Sunday because of a lack of room in the current church facility. RLUIPA specifies that state and local governments cannot impose "a land use regulation in a manner that imposes a substantial burden on the religious exercise of a person, including a religious assembly or institution, unless the government demonstrates that imposition of the burden on that person, assembly, or institution—(A) is in furtherance of a compelling governmental interest; and (B) is the least restrictive means of furthering that compelling governmental interest." RLUIPA defines "religious exercise" to include* *"any exercise of religion, whether or not compelled by, or central to, a system of religious belief." The analysis in example 1 would apply to this example as well.*

Example 7. *A church is located on a major highway. It constructs a billboard on its property that contains religious messages. The city enacts an ordinance prohibiting any billboards along the highway, and a city official orders the church to remove its billboard. RLUIPA specifies that state and local governments cannot impose "a land use regulation in a manner that imposes a substantial burden on the religious exercise of a person, including a religious assembly or institution, unless the government demonstrates that imposition of the burden on that person, assembly, or institution—(A) is in furtherance of a compelling governmental interest; and (B) is the least restrictive means of furthering that compelling governmental interest." RLUIPA defines "land use regulation" as "a zoning or landmarking law, or the application of such a law, that limits or restricts a claimant's use or development of land." This definition clearly includes the construction of a sign on church property. In addition, RLUIPA provides that "the use . . . of real property for the purpose of religious exercise shall be considered to be religious exercise of the person or entity that uses or intends to use the property for that purpose." The analysis in example 1 would apply to this example as well.*

Restricting Certain Activities Near Church Property §7-07

Key point 7-07. *Many cities have enacted ordinances banning "adult" bookstores and entertainment facilities, and the sale of alcoholic beverages, within a specified distance of a church. These ordinances have been upheld by the courts so long as such businesses are left with a reasonable opportunity to operate in other locations within the city.*

Several courts have upheld municipal zoning ordinances prohibiting the location of "adult theaters" within a prescribed distance of a church, despite the claim that such ordinances constitute an impermissible establishment of religion.[199] To illustrate, the United States Supreme Court has ruled that cities are free to ban adult bookstores or theaters within 1,000 feet of churches, schools, or residences, provided that such restrictions do not deny such businesses "a reasonable opportunity to open and operate an adult theater [or bookstore] within the city."[200]

However, the United States Supreme Court struck down an ordinance giving churches the authority to "veto" applications for liquor licenses by facilities located within a 500-foot radius of a church.[201] The Court concluded that the ordinance substituted the unilateral and absolute power of a church for the decisions of

---

[199] *See, e.g.,* City of Stanton v. Cox, 255 Cal. Rptr. 682 (4th Dist. 1989); Amico v. New Castle County, 101 F.R.D. 472 (D.C. Del. 1984); City of Whittier v. Walnut Properties, Inc., 197 Cal. Rptr. 127 (1983).

[200] Renton v. Playtime Theaters, Inc., 475 U.S. 41 (1986).

[201] Larkin v. Grendel's Den, Inc., 459 U.S. 116 (1982).

a public legislative body, and thereby "enmeshed" churches in the process of government.

Building Codes

Key point 7-08. Most cities have enacted building codes that prescribe minimum standards in the construction of buildings. The courts have ruled that these laws may be applied to churches so long as they are reasonably related to the promotion of public health and safety.

Many municipalities have enacted building codes prescribing minimum standards in the construction of buildings. Such codes typically regulate building materials, construction methods, building design, fire safety, and sanitation. The validity of such codes has consistently been upheld by the courts.[202]

The courts consistently hold that churches must comply with municipal building codes that are reasonably related to the legitimate governmental purpose of promoting the public health, safety, morals, or general welfare. To illustrate, one court ruled that "the building of churches is subject to such reasonable regulations as may be necessary to promote the public health, safety, or general welfare."[203] In another case, a municipality brought an action against a church in order to prevent the continued use of a church school that did not comply with the building code.[204] The church school was allegedly deficient in several respects, including inadequate floor space, inadequate ventilation, no approved fire alarm system, no fire extinguishers, no fire detectors, no sprinkler system, no fire-retardant walls, no exit signs, uneven stairs, and doors that did not open outward. The Supreme Court of Washington acknowledged that application of the building code to the church school would result in a closing of the school, and that this in turn would impair the church members' constitutional right to guide the education of their children by sending them to a church-operated school. However, the court observed that this constitutional right was not absolute, but could be limited by a showing that the building code was supported by a compelling state interest and that it was the least restrictive means of accomplishing the state's interest.

Similarly, another court upheld the action of a municipality in ordering substantial renovations in a church-operated school to bring it into compliance with the building code.[205] The court rejected the church's claims that the less stringent building code provisions applicable to church buildings should apply

---

[202] See YOKLEY, *supra* note 126, at § 31-2.

[203] Board of Zoning v. Decatur, Ind. Co. of Jehovah's Witnesses, 117 N.E.2d 115, 118 (Ind. 1954). *Accord* City of Solon v. Solon Baptist Temple, Inc., 457 N.E.2d 858 (Ohio App. 1982); City of Sherman v. Simms, 183 S.W.2d 415 (Tex. 1944); Wojtanowski v. Franciscan Fathers Minor Conventuals, 148 N.W.2d 54 (Wis. 1967); Hintz v. Zion Evangelical United Brethren Church, 109 N.W.2d 61 (Wis. 1961).

[204] City of Sumner v. First Baptist Church, 639 P.2d 1358 (Wash. 1982).

[205] Faith Assembly of God v. State Building Code Commission, 416 N.E.2d 228 (Mass. 1981).

to the school, and that application of the more stringent building code provisions applicable to schools would infringe upon the church's right to freely exercise its religion. The court observed:

> This is not a case where application of the Code forces a choice between abandoning one's religious principles and facing criminal charges. . . .
> The Code does not restrict or make unlawful any religious practice of the plaintiff; the Code simply regulates the condition of the physical facility if it functions as a school . . . .

It is also clear that state laws establishing minimum standards for the safety of children in child care facilities and enforcing such standards through inspections and licensing does not violate the religious freedom of a children's home administered by a religious organization.[206]

Sign ordinances regulating the height, size, and number of signs have been applied to churches despite the claim that they violate a church's constitutional right to freely exercise its religion.[207]

Case Studies

• An Alabama court rejected a church's argument that a state law prohibiting it from erecting a sign larger than 8 square feet without a special permit violated its constitutional rights. The Alabama Highway Beautification Act prohibits the erection of signs along a "primary highway" that do not meet certain requirements pertaining to size, location, lighting, and spacing. Among other things, a church sign cannot exceed 8 square feet unless a special permit is issued. A church erected a sign on the property of a private business that was located on a state highway. The sign gave the name of the church, an arrow indicating where motorists should turn to find the church, and three crosses. The state department of transportation ordered the church to remove the sign on the ground that it exceeded 8 square feet. The church protested, claiming that removal of the sign would violate its constitutional right of religious freedom. A state appeals court rejected the church's argument, and upheld the removal of the sign. The court noted that the Highway Beautification Act "makes no reference to the content of the sign. It merely regulates the manner in which churches may display signs . . . by limiting their signs to no more than 8 square feet in area. The [Act] does not attempt to regulate the views of the various churches. It simply regulates the size of the signs."[208]

• A Colorado court ruled that a church had to demolish or "modify" a new addition that it built in violation of a local building code. The court noted that in

---

[206] Roloff Evangelistic Enterprises, Inc. v. State, 556 S.W.2d 856 (Tex. 1977), *appeal denied*, 439 U.S. 803 (1978). *See also* Corpus Christi Peoples' Baptist Church, Inc. v. Texas Department of Human Resources, 481 F. Supp. 1101 (S.D. Tex. 1979), *aff'd*, 621 F.2d 638 (5th Cir. 1980); State Fire Marshall v. Lee, 300 N.W.2d 748 (Mich. 1980); State v. Fayetteville Street Christian School, 258 S.E.2d 459 (N.C. 1979), *vacated*, 261 S.E.2d 908 (N.C. 1980), *appeal dismissed*, 449 U.S. 808 (1980).

[207] Temple Baptist Church v. City of Albuquerque, 646 P.2d 565 (N.M. 1982).

[208] Corinth Baptist Church v. State Department of Transportation, 656 So.2d 868 (Ala. App. 1995). *Accord* Wilson v. City of Louisville, 957 F. Supp. 948 (W.D. Ky. 1997).

determining whether the church had to remove the new addition, three factors had to be considered: (1) good faith reliance on the building permit; (2) the neighbors' injury compared to the builder's investment; and (3) general respect for municipal ordinances. However, the court noted that these three factors are considered only if a builder acted in good faith. The court concluded that the facts in this case did not demonstrate that the church acted in good faith, and therefore the principle of relative hardship could not be applied to protect its new addition from demolition. In support of its conclusion, the court noted that the church started construction without investigating building requirements; it was notified of a thirty-foot height restriction prior to issuance of a building permit; when neighbors learned of this violation, they promptly notified the church; and, the church began construction before obtaining a necessary building permit. Moreover, it continued construction even after the city finally notified it of the thirty-foot height limit.[209]

• A Missouri court ruled that a city did not violate the First Amendment guaranty of religious freedom in refusing to grant a church's request for a permit to construct a sign on its property. A church applied for a sign permit to construct a monument sign near the entrance of its property. A city engineer denied the permit request for the following reasons: (1) the proposed sign exceeded the maximum allowable height of 10 feet; (2) the proposed sign exceeded the maximum sign face area; and (3) the proposed sign included a changeable letter area in excess of that allowed under code, and included moving letters or characters, which the sign code strictly prohibited. A zoning board affirmed the denial of the sign permit, and the church appealed to the courts, claiming that the city's sign regulations were an "unconstitutional infringement on the church's right to freely exercise its religious mission." A state appeals court concluded that "a mere requirement that a church obtain a special use permit before building . . . does not infringe on the free exercise of religion."[210]

• A New York court ruled that a applying a city's sign ordinance to a church did not violate the First Amendment. The court concluded that "it is wholly appropriate to impose limitations on a church property and its accessory uses when reasonably related to the general welfare of the community, including the community's interest in preserving its appearance." The court noted that because the restrictions imposed on the construction of the church's sign were not arbitrary and capricious, and because the city sought to balance the church's request with aesthetic and safety concerns, the city did not act wrongly in regulating the church's sign request.[211]

• A Texas court ruled that a city could compel a church-operated school to close because it failed to comply with various safety provisions in a city building code. A church-operated private school applied to the city for a permit to add a stairwell to its basement so that it could be used for a lunchroom. When reviewing this application, a city building official noticed that the school was not in compliance with the city building code and did not have a certificate of occupancy. The building official inspected the building to determine if it complied with the building code. She concluded that it did not because it did not meet the minimal life-safety requirements. She also concluded that the building posed a substantial danger to its students

[209] Olson v. Hillside Community Church, 42 P.3d 52 (Colo. App. 2001).

[210] St. John's Evangelical Lutheran Church v. City of Ellisville, 122 S.W.3d 635 (Mo. App. 2003).

[211] Lakeshore Assembly of God Church v. Village Board, 508 N.Y.S.2d 819 (N.Y. App. 1986).

from fire and smoke because of the inadequate smoke detection system, the narrow corridors, the hollow doors, and the chipboard and wood construction. The city ordered the school to cease operations until it complied with the building code. A state court affirmed this ruling. The court acknowledged that the building complied with the code as long as it was being used as a church, but concluded that "a building being used for church and Sunday school is classified differently than one being used as a school. In determining that a school must comply with stricter safety requirements, the drafters of the building code may have considered the extended amount of time a child spends at school, the use of various appliances to cook lunch, and the increased use of electrical equipment." The court also rejected the school's argument that the city's order violated the First Amendment guaranty of religious freedom. The court noted that the building code is a "religion-neutral" law that is presumably valid even without proof of a compelling government interest. However, even if a compelling government interest were required, the court noted that "as a matter of law, the state has a compelling interest of the highest order in protecting the health and safety of children."[212]

• A Wisconsin court ruled that a city did not violate the constitutional rights of a church by requiring it to install a sprinkler system in its 35-year-old sanctuary. A state appeals court began its opinion by noting that the church had the burden of proving that (1) it has a sincerely held religious belief, (2) that is burdened by application of the state law at issue. Upon such proof, the burden shifts to the state to prove: (3) that the law is based on a compelling state interest, (4) which cannot be served by a less restrictive alternative. The court concluded that the church failed to meet the threshold requirement of proving that installing a sprinkler system in its sanctuary would violate a sincerely held religious belief. It noted that "at best, the installation of a sprinkler system would prove distracting and aesthetically displeasing."[213]

Lead Paint on Church Property
§ 7-08.1

Key point 7-08.1. *Many children are poisoned each year by eating lead-based paint. In at attempt to address this problem, the federal government has issued regulations imposing strict requirements on the sale or lease of residential property constructed prior to 1978. There are no exceptions for churches or other nonprofit organizations. Church leaders need to be aware of these requirements whenever they sell or lease church-owned residential property. Failure to comply with these requirements can result in substantial liability, including "triple damages."*

Many churches own residential properties, including homes, duplexes, and even small apartment buildings. In many cases, homes are acquired as parsonages. But homes, duplexes, and apartment buildings in the immediate vicinity of the church also may be acquired for future expansion, and in some cases they are donated to the church. Church leaders need to be aware of strict federal regulations

---

[212] Christian Academy of Abilene v. City of Abilene, 62 S.W.3d 217 (Tex. App. 2001).

[213] Peace Lutheran Church v. Village of Sussex, 631 N.W.2d 229 (Wisc. App. 2001).

that regulate the sale or lease of some residential properties. The objective of these regulations is to reduce cases of poisoning among children who consume lead-based paint. This section will describe the background of this problem, summarize the federal regulations, and explain their practical significance to churches.

1. Background

in general

Lead affects virtually every system of the body. While it is harmful to individuals of all ages, lead exposure can be especially damaging to children, the unborn, and women of childbearing age. Recent studies have raised concern over blood-lead levels once thought to be safe. Since 1978, the federal Centers for Disease Control (CDC) has lowered the blood-lead level of concern from 60 to 10 micrograms per deciliter.

Lead poisoning has been called "the silent disease" because its effects may occur gradually and imperceptibly, often showing no obvious symptoms. Blood-lead levels as low as 10 micrograms per deciliter have been associated with learning disabilities, growth impairment, permanent hearing and visual impairment, and other damage to the brain and nervous system. In large doses, lead exposure can cause brain damage, convulsions, and even death. Lead exposure before or during pregnancy can also alter fetal development and cause miscarriages.

In 1991, the Secretary of the United States Department of Health and Human Services characterized lead poisoning as the "number one environmental threat to the health of children in the United States." Although the percentage of children with elevated blood-lead levels has declined in recent years, millions of U.S. children still have blood-lead levels high enough to threaten their health. The Third National Health and Nutrition Examination Survey (NHANES III) indicates that over the past two decades, the average child's blood-lead level has decreased from 12.8 to 2.8 micrograms per deciliter. NHANES III also indicates, however, that in 1991 approximately 1.7 million U.S. children under the age of 6 still had blood-lead levels that exceeded the 10 micrograms per deciliter level of concern.

lead-based paint

Efforts to reduce exposure to lead from sources like gasoline and food cans have played a large role in the past reductions of blood-lead levels in the United States. Despite these successes, a significant human health hazard remains from improperly managed lead-based paint. From the year 1900 through the 1940's, paint manufacturers used lead as a primary ingredient in many oil-based interior and exterior house paints. Usage gradually decreased through the 1950's and 1960's, as largely lead-free latex paints became more popular. Although the federal government banned lead-based paints from residential use in 1978, the federal Environmental Protection Agency (EPA) estimates that 83 percent of the privately owned housing units built in the United States before 1980 contain some lead-based paint. By these estimates, approximately 64 million homes may contain lead-based paint that may pose a hazard to the occupants if not managed properly.

Lead from exterior house paint can flake off or leach into the soil around the outside of a home, contaminating children's playing areas. Dust caused during normal lead-based paint wear (especially around windows and doors) can create a hard-to-see film over surfaces in a house. In some cases, cleaning and renovation activities can increase the threat of lead-based paint exposure by dispersing fine lead dust particles in the air and over accessible household surfaces. If managed improperly, both adults and children can receive hazardous exposures by inhaling the fine dust or by ingesting paint dust during hand-to-mouth activities. Children under age 6 are especially susceptible to lead poisoning.

2. The Residential Lead-Based Paint Hazard Reduction Act

Congress passed the Residential Lead-Based Paint Hazard Reduction Act of 1992 to address the need to control exposure to lead-based paint hazards. The Act established the infrastructure and standards necessary to reduce lead-based paint hazards in housing. Within this law, Congress recognized lead poisoning as a particular threat to children under age 6 and emphasized the needs of this vulnerable population. Section 1018 of the Act requires EPA to promulgate regulations for disclosure of any known lead-based paint or any known lead-based paint hazards in "target housing" offered for sale or lease.

The key provisions of this Act are summarized below.

target housing

The Act only regulates "target housing," which it defines as follows:

Target housing means any housing constructed prior to 1978, except housing for the elderly or persons with disabilities (unless any child who is less than 6 years of age resides or is expected to reside in such housing) or any 0-bedroom dwelling. . . . 0-bedroom dwelling means any residential dwelling in which the living area is not separated from the sleeping area. The term includes efficiencies, studio apartments, dormitory housing, military barracks, and rentals of individual rooms in residential dwellings.

There are no exceptions for housing that is owned by churches or other charitable organizations.

exemptions

The following transactions are exempted from the Act's requirements:

(1) Sales of target housing at foreclosure.

(2) Leases of target housing that have been found to be lead-based paint free by an inspector certified under the Federal certification program or under a federally accredited State or tribal certification program. Until a Federal certification program or federally accredited State certification program is in place within the State, inspectors shall be considered qualified to conduct an inspection for this purpose if they have received certification under any existing State or tribal inspector certification program. The

lessor has the option of using the results of additional test(s) by a certified inspector to confirm or refute a prior finding.

(3) Short-term leases of 100 days or less, where no lease renewal or extension can occur.

(4) Renewals of existing leases in target housing in which the lessor has previously disclosed all information required by the Act and where no new information has come into the possession of the lessor.

requirements for sellers of target housing

Each contract to sell target housing must include an "attachment" that contains specific disclosure and acknowledgment elements. The required elements are described below:

(1) a lead warning statement

Each contract must contain the following lead warning statement:

Every purchaser of any interest in residential real property on which a residential dwelling was built prior to 1978 is notified that such property may present exposure to lead from lead-based paint that may place young children at risk of developing lead poisoning. Lead poisoning in young children may produce permanent neurological damage, including learning disabilities, reduced intelligence quotient, behavioral problems, and impaired memory. Lead poisoning also poses a particular risk to pregnant women. The seller of any interest in residential real property is required to provide the buyer with any information on lead-based paint hazards from risk assessments or inspections in the seller's possession and notify the buyer of any known lead-based paint hazards. A risk assessment or inspection for possible lead-based paint hazards is recommended prior to purchase.

(2) statement disclosing known lead-based paint

The second requirement is a statement disclosing the presence of any known lead-based paint and lead-based paint hazards in the target housing, or indicating no knowledge of the presence of lead-based paint or lead-based paint hazards. The Act defines a lead-based paint hazard as follows:

Lead-based paint hazard means any condition that causes exposure to lead from lead-contaminated dust, lead-contaminated soil, or lead-contaminated paint that is deteriorated or present in accessible surfaces, friction surfaces, or impact surfaces that would result in adverse human health effects as established by the appropriate federal agency.

The seller must also provide any additional information available concerning the known lead-based paint and lead-based paint hazards, such as (1) the basis for the determination that lead-based paint and lead-based paint hazards exist in the housing, (2) the location of the lead-based paint or lead-based paint hazards, and (3) the condition of the painted surfaces. The statement must also list all records and reports pertaining to lead-based paint and lead-based paint hazards that are available to the seller and that have been provided to the purchaser. If no such records or reports are available to the seller, the statement must so indicate.

(3) receipt of required information

The third requirement is a statement by the purchaser affirming that he or she has received (1) the lead warning statement, (2) and seller's statement disclosing the presence of any lead paint or lead-based paint hazards, and (3) a lead hazard information pamphlet required (the pamphlet may be the federal pamphlet entitled "Protect Your Family from Lead in Your Home" or a state-developed pamphlet that has been approved by EPA).

(4) 10-day inspection right

The fourth requirement is a statement that the purchaser has received a 10-day opportunity to conduct a risk assessment or inspection for the presence of lead-based paint and/or lead-based paint hazards (unless the parties have mutually agreed to a different period of time), before becoming obligated under the contract to purchase the housing. Alternatively, a purchaser who chooses to waive the risk assessment or inspection opportunity must so indicate in writing.

(5) real estate agents

The fifth requirement is a statement by any agent involved in the transaction that the agent has informed the seller of the seller's obligations and that the agent is aware of his or her duty to ensure compliance with the requirements of this rule.

(6) signatures of seller

The sixth requirement is the signatures of the seller, real estate agent, and purchaser, certifying the accuracy of their statements on the attachment, along with their dates of signature. These signatures document the acceptance by the parties of the information they have provided on the attachment as a whole and alert the various parties to their respective roles and responsibilities.

requirements for lessors of target housing

Each contract to lease target housing must include an "attachment" that contains specific disclosure and acknowledgment elements. The required elements are described below:

(1) a lead warning statement

Each contract must contain the following lead warning statement:

Housing built before 1978 may contain lead-based paint. Lead from paint, paint chips, and dust can pose health hazards if not managed properly. Lead exposure is especially harmful to young children and pregnant women. Before renting pre-1978 housing, lessors must disclose the presence of known lead-based paint and/or lead-based paint hazards in the dwelling. Lessees must also receive a federally approved pamphlet on lead poisoning prevention.

(2) statement disclosing known lead-based paint

The second requirement is a statement disclosing the presence of any known lead-based paint and lead-based paint hazards in the target housing, or indicating no knowledge of the presence of lead-based paint or lead-based paint hazards. The Act defines a lead-based paint hazard as follows:

Lead-based paint hazard means any condition that causes exposure to lead from lead-contaminated dust, lead-contaminated soil, or lead-contaminated paint that is deteriorated or present in accessible surfaces, friction surfaces, or impact surfaces that would result in adverse human health effects as established by the appropriate federal agency.

The seller must also provide any additional information available concerning the known lead-based paint and lead-based paint hazards, such as (1) the basis for the determination that lead-based paint and lead-based paint hazards exist in the housing, (2) the location of the lead-based paint or lead-based paint hazards, and (3) the condition of the painted surfaces. The statement must also list all records and reports pertaining to lead-based paint and lead-based paint hazards that are available to the lessor and that have been provided to the lessee. If no such records or reports are available to the lessor, the statement must so indicate.

(3) receipt of required information

The third requirement is a statement by the lessee affirming that he or she has received (1) the lead warning statement, (2) and lessor's statement disclosing the presence of any lead paint or lead-based paint hazards, and (3) a lead hazard information pamphlet (the pamphlet may be the federal pamphlet entitled "Protect Your Family from Lead in Your Home" or a state-developed pamphlet that has been approved by EPA).

(4) real estate agents

The fourth requirement is a statement by any agent involved in the transaction that the agent has informed the lessor of the lessor's obligations and that the agent is aware of his or her duty to ensure compliance with the requirements of this rule.

(5) signatures of seller

The sixth requirement is the signatures of the lessor, real estate agent, and lessee, certifying the accuracy of their statements on the attachment, along with their dates of signature. These signatures document the acceptance by the parties of the information they have provided on the attachment as a whole and alert the various parties to their respective roles and responsibilities.

recordkeeping requirements

The Residential Lead-Based Paint Hazard Reduction Act requires sellers and their agents to retain a copy of the completed disclosure and acknowledgment contract attachment (discussed above), for 3 years from the completion date of the sale. Similarly, lessors and their real estate agents are required to retain a copy of the completed lease or attachment for 3 years from the commencement of the lease period.

3. Legal Liability

Churches may be legally liable for injuries caused by persons who purchase or rent church-owned residential property and who are poisoned by lead-based paint. Summarized below are some of the bases of liability.

(1) the Residential Lead-Based Paint Hazard Reduction Act

Violation of the requirements that apply to sellers and lessors of target housing may result in (1) civil and criminal penalties, (2) potential triple damages in a private civil suit, and (3) an obligation to pay the attorney fees and expert witness fees of victims.

(2) state and local law

The Act specifies that it does not "relieve a seller, lessor, or agent from any responsibility for compliance with state or local laws, ordinances, codes, or regulations governing notice or disclosure of known lead-based paint and/or lead-based paint hazards."

(3) negligence

Churches may be sued on the basis of negligence for injuries to children (including lead-based paint poisoning) that occur while the children are participating in a preschool or head start program on church premises, even if the program is operated by another organization that leases church property.

Case Studies

• *A New York court ruled that a church was not legally responsible for the injuries sustained by a 3-year-old child who suffered lead poisoning when she swallowed lead-based paint while residing in a church-owned home. A church owned a two-*

story residence that it leased to a community center that made emergency short-term housing available to families in need. A mother and her three young children moved into the home, and the youngest child sustained injuries from lead poisoning as a result of lead that she swallowed while residing in the home. A public health agency later inspected the home and found lead paint, which it ordered the church to remove. The victim's mother sued the church, arguing that her daughter's injuries had been caused by the church's negligence in maintaining a dangerous condition on the premises. The court noted that for the mother to prevail, she had to prove not only that a dangerous condition existed, but also that the church had notice of the condition for a sufficient length of time to have remedied it. The church claimed that it had no knowledge of any hazardous lead or lead paint condition prior to notification from the public health agency, and therefore it could not be liable on the basis of negligence. It rejected the mother's claim that the existence of stained glass windows and chipped and peeled paint constituted notice of a lead hazard. The mother's lawsuit did not seek damages from the church on the basis of a violation of the Residential Lead-Based Paint Hazard Reduction Act. This was probably due to unfamiliarity with the law. However, this case illustrates that lessors also may be liable on the basis of negligence for injuries to children who consume lead-based paint while living in a church-owned residence.[214]

4. Case Studies

The following examples will illustrate the application of the principles summarized above.

• A church purchased a home in 1960 to use as a parsonage. The church's senior pastor moves out of the parsonage this year and purchases a home. The church decides to retain the parsonage, and later the parsonage is leased to a family with two young children. Church leaders are not familiar with the Residential Lead-Based Paint Hazard Reduction Act, and do not comply with any of its provisions. After living in the parsonage for several months the lessees' children begin to exhibit serious neurological problems. A physician diagnoses the condition as lead poisoning, and it is later determined that the children have been eating lead-based paint in the parsonage. The parents sue the church, alleging that their children's injuries are permanent and severe, and amount to $1 million per child. Since the Residential Lead-Based Paint Hazard Reduction Act permits lessors to be liable for "triple damages," the church faces damages of up to $6 million. In addition, a court can order the church to pay for the parents' attorney fees and expert witness fees.

• Same facts as the previous example, except that the parsonage was constructed in 1980, and acquired by the church in 1983. Since the parsonage was constructed in or after 1978, it is not "target housing" and is not subject to the Residential Lead-Based Paint Hazard Reduction Act. However, the church may be subject to local or state regulations, and it may be liable on the basis of ordinary negligence for the children's lead poisoning.

• A church purchased a home in 1970 to use as a parsonage. This year the senior pastor moves out of the parsonage, and the church allows its youth pastor to move in.

---

[214] Alexander v. Westminster Presbyterian Church, 719 N.Y.S.2d 457 (N.Y. 2000).

The youth pastor has three minor children. Is this transaction subject to the Residential Lead-Based Paint Hazard Reduction Act? Since the home was constructed prior to 1978, it is target housing. However, the question is whether or not the transaction constitutes a "lease." The Act does not define the term "lease," but it does define a "lessor" as "any entity that offers target housing for lease," and it defines a "lessee" as "any entity that enters into an agreement to lease, rent, or sublease target housing, including but not limited to individuals, partnerships, corporations . . . and nonprofit organizations." Is a youth pastor who moves into a church-owned parsonage a "lessee" under this definition? An argument can be made that the youth pastor is not a lessee, since he did not "enter into an agreement to lease" the parsonage. On the other hand, it could be argued that an oral or implied "agreement" did exist by which the youth pastor and his family were allowed to occupy the parsonage, on a rent-free basis, for such time as he served as youth pastor. Since this interpretation of the Act is certainly possible (and probably would be vigorously asserted by a plaintiff's attorney), church leaders may wish to comply with the requirements that the Act imposes on lessors who lease target housing. An attorney should be consulted for a legal opinion. Note that compliance with these requirements is relatively simple, and would impose a minimal burden on a church in return for a significant reduction in risk.

• *A church leases a portion of its premises to another congregation on Sunday afternoons. The other congregation conducts religious services, and education classes for adults and children. While the church is leasing its premises to the other congregation, it is not subject to the provisions of the Residential Lead-Based Paint Hazard Reduction Act because it is not leasing "target housing."*

• *A church has a "studio apartment" located on its premises, that consists of one room. The church leases this apartment to its custodian. While the church is leasing its premises to the custodian, it is not subject to the provisions of the Residential Lead-Based Paint Hazard Reduction Act because a "studio apartment" is a "0-bedroom dwelling" that does not meet the Act's definition of "target housing."*

• *A denominational agency owns a campgrounds which consists of recreational facilities, a chapel, and several dormitories. The campgrounds are leases to several groups during the year. While the denominational agency is leasing the campgrounds, it is not subject to the provisions of the Residential Lead-Based Paint Hazard Reduction Act because "dormitory housing" is a "0-bedroom dwelling" that does not meet the Act's definition of "target housing."*

• *A church purchases three homes next to its parking lot, to accommodate future expansion. The homes were each constructed in the 1950s. The church rents the homes. These rental arrangements are subject to the Residential Lead-Based Paint Hazard Reduction Act, and so the church is required to comply with the requirements summarized above. Failure to do so exposes the church to potentially significant liability, including triple damages.*

• *Bob donates a home to his church this year. The pastor knows a family in the church who are wanting to purchase a home, and he asks if they would be interested in buying Bob's home. The family visits the home, and decides to buy it. The pastor picks up a "legal forms" book at a local bookstore, and prints out a real estate sales contract. If the home was constructed prior to 1978, it s "target housing" and the sales transaction is subject to the Residential Lead-Based Paint Hazard Reduction Act.*

• *A church sells its sanctuary and buys a larger church building. A church sanctuary is not "target housing," and so the church's sale of its sanctuary is not subject to the Residential Lead-Based Paint Hazard Reduction Act.*

5. Risk Management for Churches

Here is a checklist of steps that church leaders can take to reduce the risk of liability based on the Residential Lead-Based Paint Hazard Reduction Act.

1. Buying residential property. Church leaders should be certain that the seller is complying with the Residential Lead-Based Paint Hazard Reduction Act whenever the church is buying residential property constructed prior to 1978. It is important to note that the Act does not require sellers to remove lead-based paint from their property, or inspect their property for the existence of lead-based paint. Rather, they are only required to notify a buyer of any *known* lead-based paint or lead-based paint hazards on the property so that the buyer can make an informed decision regarding acquisition of the property and be alerted to any potential health problems in the future.

The fact that a seller is not aware of the presence of any lead-based paint on his or her property does *not* mean that the property is free of this hazard. The Act gives buyers a 10-day right of inspection to look for the presence of lead-based paint or lead-based paint hazards before becoming obligated under a contract to purchase residential property. A buyer can waive this right. Church leaders should consider the following precautions:

• **Ensure compliance with the Act.** Be sure that the seller is complying with the terms of the Residential Lead-Based Paint Hazard Reduction Act.

• **Review the seller's disclosures.** Did the seller disclose the presence of lead-based paint? If so, church leaders should consider whether or not they want to proceed with the purchase of the property. They may want to condition the purchase of the property on the seller's removal of the paint, or insist on a reduction in the purchase price to cover the cost of eliminating the hazard.

• **Exercise the right of inspection.** If the seller is not aware of the presence of any lead-based paint, then consider exercising your 10-day right of inspection. Do not sign any real estate contract containing a provision waiving this right of inspection. Also, the contract should contain a provision allowing you to cancel the contract in the event that lead-based paint or a lead-based paint hazard is discovered during an inspection.

The EPA regulations contain the following sample "contingency" clause that buyers may want to include in a real estate contract (it is not required, however):

This contract is contingent upon a risk assessment or inspection of the property for the presence of lead-based paint and/or lead-based paint hazards at the Purchaser's expense until 9 p.m. on the tenth calendar-day after ratification [Insert date 10 days after contract ratification or a date mutually agreed upon]. This contingency will terminate at the above predetermined deadline unless the Purchaser (or Purchaser's agent) delivers to the Seller (or Seller's agent) a written contract addendum listing the specific existing deficiencies and corrections needed, together with a copy of the inspection and/or risk assessment report. The Seller may, at the Seller's option, within _____ days after Delivery of the addendum, elect in writing whether to correct the condition(s) prior to settlement. If the Seller will correct the condition, the Seller shall furnish the Purchaser with certification from a risk assessor or inspector demonstrating that the condition has been remedied before the date of the settlement. If the Seller does not elect to make the repairs, or if the Seller makes a counter-offer, the Purchaser shall have _____ days to respond to the counter-offer or remove this contingency and take the property in "as is" condition or this contract shall become void. The Purchaser may remove this contingency at any time without cause.

• **Consult with an attorney.** Be sure to consult with an attorney concerning your rights, and the potential risks the church faces if lead-based paint is found on the property. This is very important if the church will be renting the property, or making it available as a parsonage.

2. **Selling residential property.** Church leaders should be certain that they are complying with the Residential Lead-Based Paint Hazard Reduction Act whenever the church is selling residential property constructed prior to 1978. Note the following:

• **Using a real estate agent.** If the church will use a real estate agent in selling residential property, it is very likely that the agent will be familiar with the requirements of the Act and will help to ensure compliance. However, in some cases churches sell residential property without the assistance of a real estate agent. Under these circumstances it is much more likely that there will not be full compliance with the Act. If you are using an agent, be sure that the agent is familiar with the requirements of the Act and is complying with them.

• **Complying with the Act.** Be sure that a real estate contract is used, and that it contains the information summarized above, including a lead warning statement, a statement disclosing any known lead-based paint or lead-based paint hazard, a 10-day right of inspection, a statement by the buyer affirming that he or she has received the lead warning statement, the seller's statement disclosing the presence of any lead paint or lead-based paint hazards, and a lead hazard information pamphlet (the pamphlet may be the federal pamphlet entitled "Protect Your Family from Lead in Your Home" or a state-developed pamphlet that has been approved by EPA).

• **Consult with an attorney.** Be sure to consult with an attorney concerning your responsibilities under the Act, and the potential risks the church faces if it fails to comply.

3. Renting residential property. Church leaders should be certain that they are complying with the Residential Lead-Based Paint Hazard Reduction Act whenever the church is renting residential property constructed prior to 1978. It is important to note that the Act does not require lessors to remove lead-based paint from their property, or inspect their property for the existence of lead-based paint. Rather, they are only required to notify a lessee of any *known* lead-based paint or lead-based paint hazards on the property so that the lessee can make an informed decision regarding rental of the property and be alerted to any potential health problems in the future. Church leaders should consider the following precautions:

• **Using a real estate agent.** If the church will use a real estate agent in renting church-owned residential property, it is very likely that the agent will be familiar with the requirements of the Act and will help to ensure compliance. However, in most cases churches rent their property without the assistance of a real estate agent. Under these circumstances it is much more likely that there will not be full compliance with the Act.

• **Complying with the Act.** Be sure that a lease agreement is used, and that it contains the information summarized above, including a lead warning statement; a statement disclosing any known lead-based paint or lead-based paint hazard; a statement by the lessee affirming that he or she has received the lead warning statement, the lessor's statement disclosing the presence of any lead paint or lead-based paint hazards, and a lead hazard information pamphlet (the pamphlet may be the federal pamphlet entitled "Protect Your Family from Lead in Your Home" or a state-developed pamphlet that has been approved by EPA).

• **Consult with an attorney.** Be sure to consult with an attorney concerning your responsibilities under the Act, and the potential risks the church faces if it fails to comply.

Key point. *You should consider complying with the Act when allowing a pastor to occupy a church-owned parsonage constructed prior to 1978. It is possible that a court would conclude that an oral or implied "lease agreement" did exist by which the pastor and his or her family were allowed to occupy the parsonage, on a rent-free basis, for such time as he or she served as pastor. Since this interpretation of the Act is certainly possible (and probably would be vigorously asserted by a plaintiff's attorney), church leaders may wish to comply with the requirements that the Act imposes on lessors who lease target housing. An attorney should be consulted for a legal opinion. Note that compliance with these requirements is relatively simple, and would impose a minimal burden on a church in return for a significant reduction in risk.*

4. **Insurance.** Discuss with your insurance agent the availability of insurance coverage in the event that the church is sued as a result of lead paint poisoning, or violating the Residential Lead-Based Paint Hazard Reduction Act.

5. **Rental of church property by outside groups.** Churches may be liable for lead-based paint poisoning when they rent non-residential church property to outside groups, such as a preschool or head start program. Be sure to check with your insurance agent about coverage for such a risk.

Example. *A church leased a portion of its premises to another organization that conducted a Head Start preschool program. A minor child was injured when she ate lead-based paint while participating in the Head Start program. The minor and her mother sued the church, along with the Head Start provider. The church insisted that it could not be liable for the child's poisoning since it had no notice of a lead paint condition on its premises until after the child left the Head Start program. A year after the child left the program, the department of health issued a notice of lead paint violations for certain parts of the building. A court refused to dismiss the church from the lawsuit. It noted that the notice from the department of health listed violations including peeling paint in two classrooms and a kitchen, and dust and dirt accumulating in various areas. The court stressed that "a standard higher than common law negligence applies here. Courts have repeatedly held that schools are subject to a higher standard of care [and] must exert the same [duty] of care and supervision over the pupils under [their] control as a reasonably prudent parent would exercise under the same circumstances. . . . A school owes a special duty to its students because, by taking compulsory custody over them, it temporarily deprives them of the protection of their parents and guardians." The court concluded that the church, as a landlord, must ensure that "no defective conditions exist which harm the safety of the young children participating in the head start program. . . . [T] he existence of lead-based paint in nurseries, kindergartens and day care centers is hazardous to children. Indeed, because buildings containing kindergartens, nurseries and day care centers invariably house children, the landlords of these buildings should know that any lead paint problem are extremely dangerous. Given this, a reasonably prudent parent would abate any lead-based paint problems over which it had control. Because of the pervasiveness of the lead paint problem prior to 1960, if given notice of a peeling paint condition in a building containing his or her child and erected before 1960, a reasonably prudent parent would investigate to determine whether there is a lead paint condition. This is true even though laws were not in place regarding lead paint abatement in kindergartens and day care centers, as the issues surrounding lead paint poisoning had been sufficiently publicized to put the landlords of these establishments on notice. Therefore, this court holds that, in a building constructed prior to 1960 that houses a head start program, notice of peeling paint condition in an area used by the children creates a rebuttable presumption that the landlord had* *notice of a lead paint hazard.*[215]

6. **State and local regulations.** This section has addressed the federal Residential Lead-Based Paint Hazard Reduction Act. Many state and local governments have enacted their own regulations addressing lead-based paint hazards, and it is important for church leaders to consider the application of these additional regulations whenever they buy, sell, or lease property.

Nuisance § 7-09

Key point 7-09. *A nuisance is any use of property that results in significant annoyance or discomfort to neighboring landowners. Some church activities may constitute a nuisance. The courts will weigh the annoyance and discomfort to neighboring landowners with the church's constitutional right to exercise its religion. In some cases the courts may order a church to limit the activity causing the nuisance, or eliminate it entirely.*

In general, the term *nuisance* refers to an activity or use of property that results in material annoyance, inconvenience, discomfort, or harm to others. It is, for example, a nuisance to use one's property in such a way as to cause excessive noise, odor, smoke, vibration, debris, drainage, obstruction, or injury to neighboring landowners. It ordinarily is not a defense that the condition constituting a nuisance existed before the arrival of neighboring residents.

An activity or condition permitted on church property can constitute a nuisance. One court has held:

> A church building is as lawful as any other structure. It is not only lawful, but essential to our Christian civilization . . . . It is not, however, above the law. Like any other edifice or structure, however lawful in purpose and use ordinarily, it may become unlawful. The place of its location, and the time and manner of its use, may be such, under the circumstances, as to constitute that interference with the rights of others as to become in law a nuisance . . . .[216]

To illustrate, a church that conducted lengthy revival services punctuated by shouting and singing that could be heard more than a mile away was found guilty of permitting a nuisance.[217]

Another court refused to prevent the construction of a church in a residential district despite the allegations of neighboring landowners that the church consisted of "holy rollers" who would conduct boisterous services until the late

---

[215] Espinal v. North Presbyterian Head Start Child Development Center, 667 N.Y.S.2d 223 (Sup. Ct. 1997).

[216] Waggoner v. Floral Heights Baptist Church, 288 S.W. 129, 131 (Tex. 1926).

[217] Assembly of God Church v. Bradley, 196 S.W.2d 696 (Tex. 1946).

hours of the evening, making neighboring homes unfit for habitation.[218] The court reasoned that the existence of a church building close to the homes of neighboring landowners, as well as the noise that might result from an "orderly and properly conducted Christian service therein," were not matters that would constitute a nuisance. The court did acknowledge that it was possible for a church to conduct services with sufficient noise to constitute a nuisance. Nevertheless, the court concluded that it could not prevent the construction of a church in a residential neighborhood based on the mere conjecture of neighboring landowners that the church ultimately would constitute a nuisance.

Another court, in a similar case, concluded that "something more than the threatened commission of an offense against the law of the land is necessary to call into exercise the injunctive powers of the court."[219] The court also held that a church building itself is not a nuisance, and therefore its construction cannot be enjoined on the ground that it will be the source of unreasonably loud worship services. The proper remedy for unreasonably loud services, concluded the court, would be to halt or abate the excessive noise, and not to prevent the construction of the church.

The playing of church bells three times a day and four times on Sundays at regular hours for a period of approximately four minutes has been held not to constitute a nuisance despite the contention of neighboring landowners that the volume of the bells adversely affected their health and serenity. The court held that a material interference with physical comfort must occur before a nuisance can exist, and that the ringing of church bells simply did not constitute a material interference:

> Bells in one form or another are a tradition throughout the world. . . . In the Christian world, every church is proud of its bells. The bells are rung for joy, for sadness, for warnings and for worship. There are people who find total beauty in the . . . daily ritual ringing at the Cathedral of Notre Dame in Paris. There is little question that the sound is often deadening when these bells start to ring, but for the general enjoyment of the public, it is considered acceptable.[220]

One court concluded that the use of church property for school purposes does not amount to a nuisance.[221]

Case Study

• A federal court in New York ruled that a city did not violate the rights of neighbors by refusing to enforce a noise ordinance against a church that broadcast amplified music

---

[218] Dorsett v. Nunis, 13 S.E.2d 371 (Ga. 1941).

[219] Murphy v. Cupp, 31 S.W.2d 396, 399 (Ark. 1930).

[220] Impellizerri v. Jamesville Federated Church, 428 N.Y.S.2d 550 (1979).

[221] Mooney v. Village of Orchard Lake, 53 N.W.2d 308 (Mich. 1952).

from its steeple.[222] *For two weeks a Congregational church broadcast amplified sounds and music for lengthy periods of time from speakers located in its steeple. Certain neighbors found the volume and duration of these sounds so distressful that they called the state police to advise them of the noises. The state trooper who responded to the call allegedly told the neighbors that the noises were loud enough to constitute a violation of state law. The neighbors also insisted that the church's actions violated a village ordinance relating to "peace and good order," which prohibits persons or organizations from ringing a bell or making other improper noises that disturb the peace, comfort, or health of the community. The city council and district attorney's office both refused to act on the neighbors' complaints. A court eventually directed the church to limit the amount of sounds and music which were being amplified from its steeple. The neighbors later sued the city, claiming that its refusal to enforce the law demonstrated an improper preference for the church that deprived the neighbors of their civil rights, including their constitutional right to equal protection of the law. They further maintain that the city's actions violated the First Amendment's nonestablishment of religion clause. A state appeals court rejected the neighbors' claims. First, it ruled that the city had not violated the neighbors' constitutional right to the equal protection of the laws. It pointed out that an equal protection claim requires a showing of intentional discrimination, and this requires proof that "similarly situated persons" have been treated differently. The neighbors failed to present such evidence. Further, the court ruled that the city's failure to enforce state and local law did not violate the First Amendment. In particular, it noted that the neighbors failed to explain how a failure to enforce a noise ordinance amounts to state action endorsing religion. It also pointed out that a local court did impose restrictions to reduce the amount of noise coming from the church. The court concluded: "Plaintiffs have alleged that the loudness and duration of the church music was distressful to them, and the town does not deny this accusation. Indeed, although some might consider the church's actions unneighborly or lacking in Christian forbearance, unneighborly behavior is not necessarily unconstitutional behavior. Given the facts and circumstances as plaintiffs have alleged them, there can be no argument that defendants' actions violated plaintiffs' constitutional rights."*

Landmarking   § 7-10

Key point 7-10. *Several cities have enacted ordinances permitting certain buildings to be designated as "landmarks" because of their historical or cultural significance. Buildings designated as landmarks generally may not be demolished or renovated without government approval. The Supreme Court has ruled that such laws do not violate a church's First Amendment right to the free exercise of religion.*

A number of municipalities have enacted ordinances designed to protect and preserve buildings having historic or cultural significance. Such ordinances often are referred to as "landmark" laws. Occasionally, municipalities attempt to block the sale or demolition of church property on the basis of landmark ordinances. Of course, churches respond by claiming that use of a landmark law in such a context violates the First Amendment's guaranty of religious freedom.

---

[222] Diehl v. Village of Antwerp, 964 F. Supp. 646 (N.D.N.Y. 1997).

To illustrate, a federal appeals court ruled that a New York City "landmark" law that prevented a church from developing its property did not violate any of the church's constitutional rights.[223] St. Bartholomew's Church is a Protestant Episcopal Church located in New York City. The church sanctuary was constructed in 1919. Next to the sanctuary is a 7-story community house built by the church in 1928. The community house provides a variety of services, including athletic facilities, a theater, a preschool, meeting rooms, office space, and sleeping quarters for the homeless. In 1967, the church and community house were designated as "landmarks" by the city, meaning that they could not be demolished without city approval. The city may grant approval if it finds that a failure to do so would "seriously interfere" with a charity's ability to carry out its purposes.

In 1983, the church sought permission to tear down the community house and erect in its place a 59-story office tower. This application was denied by the city as inappropriate. In 1984, the church sought permission to tear down the community center and build a 47-story office tower. This application was also denied. The church claimed that the denial of its request to demolish its community center and construct an office building violated its constitutional rights. In particular, it claimed that as a result of the city's actions it could no longer carry out its religious mission and charitable purpose because the existing facility was no longer adequate and the church could not afford the sums necessary to remodel the present building to make it adequate. The court rejected the church's claim that the city's actions violated the First Amendment's guaranty of religious freedom, or the Fifth Amendment prohibition of a "taking" of the church's property without "just compensation." The court acknowledged that applying the landmarks law to the church "has drastically restricted the church's abilities to raise revenues to carry out its various charitable and ministerial programs." However, this burden did not constitute a violation of the First Amendment's guaranty of religious freedom. The court emphasized that decisions of the United States Supreme Court have clarified that "neutral regulations that diminish the income of a religious organization do not implicate the free exercise clause." The First Amendment is violated only if "the claimant has been denied the ability to practice his religion or coerced in the nature of those practices."

The court also rejected the church's claim that the landmark law so severely restricted its ability to use its property that it constituted a confiscation of property without just compensation in violation of the Fifth Amendment to the United States Constitution. The Fifth Amendment specifies "nor shall private property be taken for public use without just compensation." The court observed:

[T]he constitutional question is whether the land-use regulation impairs the continued operation of the property in its originally expected use. We conclude that the landmarks law does not effect an unconstitutional taking because the church can continue its existing charitable and religious activities in its current facilities. Although the regulation may freeze the church's

---

[223] Rector, Wardens, and Members of the Vestry of St. Bartholomew's Church v. City of New York, 914 F.2d 348 (2nd Cir. 1990).

property in its existing use and prevent the church from expanding or altering its activities, [Supreme Court rulings] explicitly permit this. . . . [T]he deprivation of commercial value is palpable, but . . . it does not constitute a taking so long as continued use for present activities is viable.[224]

A number of other courts have addressed the application of landmarking laws to religious congregations. Selected cases are illustrated by the following examples.

Case Studies

• A federal court in Maryland ruled that a church's First Amendment right to the free exercise of religion was violated by a city landmarks ordinance that barred the church from demolishing an old chapel to construct a new facility. The court concluded that the church's decision to demolish the chapel "involves the exercise of the Roman Catholic faith and implicates First Amendment free exercise principles." The court conceded, however, that according to the Supreme Court's 1990 decision in the Smith *case the church's First Amendment rights would not be violated by a "neutral law of general applicability." But the court concluded that the landmarks law was not such a law. It emphasized the fact that the landmarks ordinance "had a series of exemptions" demonstrating a "legislative judgment that the city's interest in historic preservation should, under certain circumstances, give way to other interests." The court then referred to the Supreme Court's conclusion in the* Smith *case that "where the government enacts a system of exemptions, and thereby acknowledges that its interest in enforcement is not paramount, then the government may not refuse to extend that system [of exemptions] to cases of religious hardship without compelling reason." The court concluded that the city failed to demonstrate such an interest, and therefore its refusal to permit the church to demolish its chapel amounted to a violation of the First Amendment.[225]*

• The Massachusetts Supreme Judicial Court ruled that the City of Boston could not declare a church's interior as a "landmark." Faced with an aging, oversized building, the leaders of a Catholic church adopted a plan to renovate the facility into office, counseling, and residential space. When work began, ten citizens asked the city to designate the interior of the church as a landmark. The city approved the citizens' request, and prohibited permanent alteration of "the nave, chancel, vestibule and organ loft on the main floor—the volume, window glazing, architectural detail, finishes, painting, the organ, and organ case." Church leaders filed a lawsuit, claiming that their constitutional right to freely exercise their religion was violated by the city' action. The court agreed, citing the state constitution's guaranty of religious freedom. In rejecting the city's claim that it was merely addressing a "secular question of interior design," the court observed that "the configuration of the church interior is so freighted with religious meaning that it must be considered part and parcel of [Catholic] religious worship." The court concluded that the state constitution "protects the right freely to design interior space for religious worship, thus barring the government from regulating

---

[224] *Id.* at 356-357.
[225] Keeler v. Mayor and City Council, 940 F. Supp. 879 (D. Md. 1996).

changes in such places, provided that no public safety question is presented."[226]

• *The Washington Supreme Court ruled that a municipal landmarking law violated a church's constitutional right to religious freedom. The city of Seattle adopted an ordinance giving the city authority to declare any building to be a landmark. The ordinance was designed to preserve and protect those sites reflecting significant elements of the city's cultural or historic heritage. Buildings designated as a landmark by the city could not be structurally altered without city approval. The city designated a church to be a landmark, and the church sued the city arguing that the landmarks ordinance violated the church's constitutional right to freely exercise its religion. Specifically, the church claimed that its designation as a landmark impaired its religious freedom in the following ways: (1) city approval and bureaucratic "red tape" would be required prior to making any structural alterations in the sanctuary; (2) a secular government had the authority to grant or deny a church's request to develop its worship facility; (3) the value of the church property was decreased significantly by the landmark designation; and (4) the ability of the church to sell its property was diminished. The court agreed with the church's position. It concluded that the city's landmark law placed a substantial burden on the church's religious practices, and that no compelling governmental interest justified the burden: "The practical effect of the [ordinance] is to require a religious organization to seek secular approval of matters potentially affecting the church's practice of its religion." This "creates unjustified governmental interference in religious matters of the church and thereby creates an infringement on the church's constitutional right of free exercise." The court concluded: "We hold that the preservation of historical landmarks is not a compelling state interest. Balancing the right of free exercise [of religion] with the aesthetic and community values associated with landmark preservation, we find that the latter is clearly outweighed by the constitutional protection of free exercise of religion and the public benefits associated with the practice of religious worship within the community."*[227]

---

[226] Society of Jesus v. Boston Landmarks Commission, 564 N.E.2d 571 (Mass. 1991).

[227] First Covenant Church v. City of Seattle, 787 P.2d 1352 (Wash. 1990). This ruling was "vacated" by the United States Supreme Court as a result of its ruling in Employment Division v. Smith, 110 S. Ct. 1595 (1990). But the Washington state supreme court, upon reconsideration, again concluded that the city's landmarking law violated the church's constitutional right to religious freedom. 840 P.2d 174 (Wash. 1992). *See also* First United Methodist Church v. Hearing Examiner, 916 P.2d 374 (Wash. 1996), in which the Washington state supreme court concluded that the mere designation of a church as an historic landmark violated the constitutional rights of churches that were opposed to such a designation.

The City of Boerne Case

In 1997 the United States Supreme Court upheld the validity of the landmark law of Boerne, Texas, though the law prohibited an historic church from expanding to accommodate its growing membership. The church claimed that the law violated its rights under the Religious Freedom Restoration Act. The Court concluded that this Act was an unconstitutional attempt by Congress to amend the Constitution by changing the meaning of the guaranty of religious freedom. [228]

The Supreme Court ruled in 1990 that "neutral laws of general applicability" are presumably valid even though they burden the free exercise of religion.[229] The government need not demonstrate that such laws further a "compelling interest." In most cases, a landmarking law will be a neutral law of general applicability, and as a result is presumably valid without the need to prove a compelling government interest. This makes such laws very difficult to challenge.

However, the Supreme Court observed in its 1990 ruling that the compelling government interest test is triggered if a neutral and generally applicable law burdens not only the exercise of religion, but also some other First Amendment right (such as speech, press, or assembly). The compelling government interest requirement makes it much more difficult for a city to defend a landmarking law that infringes upon the exercise of religion. The Court observed: "The only decisions in which we have held that the First Amendment bars application of a neutral, generally applicable law to religiously motivated action have involved not the free exercise clause alone, but the free exercise clause in conjunction with other constitutional protections, such as freedom of speech and of the press . . . ."

In other words, if a neutral and generally applicable law burdens the exercise of religion, then the compelling governmental interest standard can be triggered if the religious institution can point to some other First Amendment interest that is being violated. In many cases, this will not be hard to do. For example, the First Amendment guaranties of "assembly" and free speech often will be burdened by the designation of a church as a landmark. The Washington state supreme court reached this conclusion, finding that the application of a landmark law to a church (against its will) violated the church's constitutional rights of speech and religion and therefore could be sustained only if it furthered a compelling governmental interest. No such interest existed, the court concluded. [230]

Eminent Domain

§ 7-11

Key point 7-11. *Eminent domain refers to the power of the government to take*

---

[228] City of Boerne v. Flores, 117 S. Ct. 2157 (1997). *See also* section 7-06.4 for a full analysis of this ruling.

[229] Employment Division v. Smith, 110 S. Ct. 1595 (1990).

[230] First United Methodist Church v. Hearing Examiner, 916 P.2d 374 (Wash. 1996).

private property for a public purpose without the owner's consent. A property owner whose property is taken by a governmental exercise of eminent domain is entitled to compensation. Church property is not immune from eminent domain.

1. In General

Eminent domain refers to the power of the government to take private property for a public purpose without the owner's consent. It often is referred to as *condemnation*. A property owner whose property is taken by a governmental exercise of eminent domain is entitled to compensation. Obviously, attempts to take church property by this process have generated controversy. The relatively few courts that have addressed this issue generally have concluded that church property is not immune from a proper exercise of eminent domain.[231] However, they also have concluded that the government's power of eminent domain must be balanced against the interests of the church, and that in some cases the church will prevail. For example, the Colorado Supreme Court rejected an attempt by a municipal urban renewal authority to condemn a church building that served as "the mother church and fountainhead" of a religious sect.[232] The court observed:

The First Amendment protects freedom of religion, which has its roots in the hearts and souls of the congregation, not in inanimate bricks and mortar. Yet, religious faith and tradition can invest certain structures and land sites with significance which deserves First Amendment protection. We recognize that church property is private property which can be taken by eminent domain for paramount public use, just as religious conduct is subject to appropriate regulations for the public good. When regulating religious conduct, however, the state may be challenged to justify its infringement of the totally free exercise of religion. We hold that under these circumstances, the state may be so challenged to justify a use of its power of eminent domain. The [trial court] must weigh the plans and goals of the [city] as they bear on the particular land in question, against the right of the [church] to maintain a brick structure which the church claims is unique and does not conform to the general plan for development of the block or the area. . . .

The only conclusion which we can draw is that we must balance the interests involved in the controversy before us and recognize that the state must show a substantial interest without a reasonable alternate means of accomplishment if the state is to be constitutionally allowed to take the birthplace of the [sect].

---

[231] *See, e.g.,* First English Evangelical Lutheran Church v. Los Angeles County, 482 U.S. 304 (1987); United States v. Two Acres of Land, 144 F.2d 207 (7th Cir. 1944); Redevelopment Agency v. First Christian Church, 189 Cal. Rptr. 749 (Cal. App. 1983); State Highway Department v. Augusta District of North Georgia Conference of the Methodist Church, 154 S.E.2d 29 (Ga. App. 1967); State Highway Department v. Hollywood Baptist Church, 146 S.E.2d 570 (Ga. App. 1965); First Baptist Church v. State Department of Roads, 135 N.W.2d 756 (Nebr. 1965); Gallimore v. State Highway and Public Works Commission, 85 S.E.2d 392 (N.C. 1955); Trustees of Grace and Hope Mission v. Providence Redevelopment Agency, 217 A.2d 476 (R.I. 1966); Assembly of God Church v. Vallone, 150 A.2d 11 (R.I. 1959).

[232] Pillar of Fire v. Denver Urban Renewal Authority, 509 P.2d 1250 (Colo. 1973).

The same court later rejected an attempt by a city to condemn the parking lot of a church that had been declared a historic landmark.[233] The court emphasized that the trial court had

> a duty to weigh and balance the competing interests, public and religious. Only after such a hearing and upon finding that there is a substantial public interest involved which cannot be accomplished through any other reasonable means, can the court proceed with the condemnation of [church] property.

Assuming that the government has the authority, in a particular case, to take church property through the process of eminent domain, the Fifth Amendment to the United States Constitution requires that the church be given "just compensation" for its property. The United States Supreme Court has noted that "the Fifth Amendment provides 'nor shall private property be taken for public use, without just compensation,' and applies to the states through the Fourteenth Amendment."[234] But what is "just compensation"? In many cases, cities and churches come to widely differing interpretations of this critical term. Most courts have rejected "fair market value" as the standard for computing just compensation. The United States Supreme Court has observed that just compensation means "the full and perfect equivalent in money of the property taken," and, that "[w]here, for any reason, property has no market, resort must be had to other data to ascertain its value."[235]

In a leading case, a California state appeals court was asked to determine the value of an old but ornately-decorated, 2,000-seat sanctuary that had been condemned by a city government for urban renewal purposes.[236] The city's appraiser valued the church at $1 million, a figure obtained by reducing the replacement cost of the building by a "depreciation" factor of 75 percent. The appraiser used a 75 percent depreciation factor since the only other comparable church in the community had sold for little more than the value of the land on which it stood. The church's appraiser valued the church at $4.6 million, a figure obtained by reducing the replacement cost by a depreciation factor of 40 percent. The court agreed with the trial court's finding that a fair value of the property was $3 million. It observed:

> The ultimate goal in any eminent domain proceeding is of course to determine constitutionally required "just compensation." That compensation is to be measured by what the owner lost and not what the condemnor has gained. . . . Generally speaking, the most widely used and perhaps most easily applied concept is that of "fair market value." But even that test, which is described as what a willing buyer would pay to a willing seller under

---

[233] Order of Friars Minor v. Denver Urban Renewal Authority, 527 P.2d 804 (Colo. 1974).

[234] First English Evangelical Lutheran Church v. Los Angeles County, 482 U.S. 304, 310 n.4 (1987).

[235] United States v. Miller, 317 U.S. 369, 373-374 (1943).

[236] Redevelopment Agency v. First Christian Church, 189 Cal. Rptr. 749 (Cal. App. 1983).

circumstances totally free from external pressures, may not, in every case achieve a correct result . . . . The economic reality of course is that certain types of buildings such as churches are not, as such, regularly bought and sold in the commercial market and to ordinary buyers of real estate have no greater value than the use which can be made of the land free of the building. The constitutional mandate of just compensation, of course, would not be met if public agencies could thus exercise the power of eminent domain by simply paying for the value of the raw land when it is occupied by some special type of building. . . . Recognized alternatives to the market data approach to valuation are reproduction or replacement costs less depreciation or obsolescence. These methods, in reality, provide a more just and equitable approach in evaluating special use buildings such as churches.[237]

Similarly, another court has observed that

Where there is proof that there is no market value of property with a specialized use, such as a church . . . the general rule is that resort may be had to some other method of fixing the value of property. . . . Depending on the nature of the property, the authorities have supported different methods of determining value in these situations. Expert testimony as to reproduction of replacement cost, less depreciation, has been approved in many cases as competent foundation evidence to support an opinion as to valuation.[238]

A federal appeals court has noted that

In the case of nonprofit, religious or service properties, cost of replacement is regarded as cogent evidence of value although not in itself the only standard of compensation. But people do not go about buying and selling country churches. Such buildings have no established market values. Consideration must be given to the elements actually involved and resort had to any evidence available, to prove value, such as the use made of the property and the right to enjoy it.[239]

---

[237] *Id.* at 753-754. The court added:

We hasten to point out, however, that in our view depreciation and obsolescence should not be used as a "back door" method of nullifying the reproduction and replacement approach to valuation. For example, a large ornate church, as here, because it was used by only a small congregation [average weekly attendance was 200] might be viewed by some as obsolete and having no value beyond that of the land itself. The church, however, does have value to the congregation and the congregation is entitled to compensation therefore. A property owner should not be penalized by application of a concept of locational or functional obsolescence simply because it happens to be in the wrong place at the wrong time when a condemning agency decides to make its move. *Id.* at 754.

[238] State Highway Department v. Hollywood Baptist Church, 146 S.E.2d 570, 759-760 (Ga. App. 1965).

[239] United States v. Two Acres of Land, 144 F.2d 207, 209 (7th Cir. 1944).

Occasionally, a church's property is "taken" by a city or governmental agency through a process known as "inverse condemnation." This refers to some regulatory action, short of a formal condemnation proceeding, that has the effect of making a church's property of little or no value. The United States Supreme Court addressed this issue in an important ruling.[240] In 1957, a Lutheran church in California purchased a 21-acre parcel of land in a canyon along the Mill Creek. The church constructed several buildings on the property, including a dining hall, two bunkhouses, a lodge, and a chapel, and used the improved property as a campgrounds known a "Lutherglen." In 1977, a fire destroyed the forest upstream of the campgrounds, creating a serious flood hazard. A severe storm in 1978 flooded Lutherglen and destroyed its buildings. In response to the dangerous conditions in the area, the County of Los Angeles adopted a temporary ordinance prohibiting anyone from building any structure within a flood zone that included Lutherglen. The church thereafter sued the state of California, arguing that the state's prohibition of any further use of the campgrounds violated the Fifth Amendment to the United States Constitution, which specifies that "private property [shall not] be taken for public use, without just compensation." The Fifth Amendment, argued the church, does not require that the government seize private property by condemnation. It can also be violated by governmental regulations that effectively deny a landowner the use of his land, even on a temporary basis. The California state courts rejected the church's contention, but the United States Supreme Court agreed that the county's ban on further development of the campgrounds amounted to a "regulatory taking" of the church's property without compensation in violation of the Fifth Amendment.

DID YOU KNOW?
Eminent Domain Proceeds and the Unrelated Business Income Tax

Many churches have had their property converted to a public use through eminent domain (sometimes called "condemnation"). For example, a state government acquires property (including church properties) for a new highway. Of course, property holders must be paid a fair amount for their property. Does a charity have to pay the unrelated business income tax on such proceeds? No, said the IRS in a private letter ruling, so long as the charity did not acquire and hold the land for resale.[241]

---

[240] First English Evangelical Lutheran Church v. Los Angeles County, 107 S. Ct. 2378 (1987).

[241] IRS Letter Ruling 9629032.

2. Seizing Private Property to Expand the Tax Base or Promote Economic Development

The Fifth Amendment to the United States Constitution states simply, "Nor shall private property be taken for public use, without just compensation." There are three important principles embodied in this phrase. First, government agencies have the authority to acquire private property, even if the property owner objects. Second, government agencies can only acquire private property for a public use. Third, government agencies must provide "just compensation" to private property owners whose land is seized. The taking of private property by an act of government for a public use is commonly called "eminent domain" or "condemnation."

Just what is a "public use?" The definition of this term is critical, since it describes the purposes for which private property can be seized by an act of government. In the Kelo case, the United States Supreme Court defined the concept of "public use" very broadly.[242]

The Kelo Case

In 2000, the city of New London, Connecticut approved a development plan that was "projected to create in excess of 1,000 jobs, to increase tax and other revenues, and to revitalize an economically distressed city, including its downtown and waterfront areas." In assembling the land needed for this project, the city purchased property from willing sellers, and sought to use the power of eminent domain to acquire the remainder of the property from unwilling owners in exchange for just compensation.

One property owner whose property the city sought to acquire was born in her home in 1918 and had lived there her entire life. Her husband had lived in the house since they married some 60 years ago. This couple, along with other property owners, went to court to block the seizure of their property by the city. They claimed that the concept of "public use" did not include expanding the tax base or the promotion of economic development. The state supreme court ruled that the city was pursuing a public purpose and dismissed the landowners' claims. The case was appealed directly to the United States Supreme Court.

The Court began its opinion by observing, "The disposition of this case therefore turns on the question whether the city's development plan serves a public purpose." It noted that "without exception, our cases have defined that concept broadly, reflecting our longstanding policy of deference to legislative judgments in this field," and that "for more than a century [we] have eschewed rigid formulas and intrusive scrutiny in favor of affording legislatures broad latitude in determining what public needs justify the use of the takings power." The Court continued,

The city has carefully formulated an economic development plan that it believes will provide appreciable benefits to the community, including—but by no means limited to—new jobs and increased tax revenue. As with other

---

[242] Kelo v. City of New London, 545 U.S. 469 (2005).

exercises in urban planning and development, the city is endeavoring to coordinate a variety of commercial, residential, and recreational uses of land, with the hope that they will form a whole greater than the sum of its parts. To effectuate this plan, the city has invoked a state statute that specifically authorizes the use of eminent domain to promote economic development. . . . Because that plan unquestionably serves a public purpose, the takings challenged here satisfy the public use requirement of the Fifth Amendment.

The private property owners who opposed the seizure of their property insisted that economic development and expansion of the tax base never qualify as a public use. The Court disagreed, noting that "clearly, there is no basis for exempting economic development from our traditionally broad understanding of public purpose," and that "the public end may be as well or better served through an agency of private enterprise than through a department of government." Further, "any number of cases illustrate that the achievement of a public good often coincides with the immediate benefiting of private parties." The Court also observed:

It is further argued that without a bright-line rule nothing would stop a city from transferring citizen A's property to citizen B for the sole reason that citizen B will put the property to a more productive use and thus pay more taxes. Such a one-to-one transfer of property, executed outside the confines of an integrated development plan, is not presented in this case. While such an unusual exercise of government power would certainly raise a suspicion that a private purpose was afoot, [such] hypothetical cases can be confronted if and when they arise. They do not warrant the crafting of an artificial restriction on the concept of public use.

The Court insisted that it did not "minimize the hardship that condemnations may entail, notwithstanding the payment of just compensation." And, it stressed that

nothing in our opinion precludes any state from placing further restrictions on its exercise of the takings power. Indeed, many states already impose public use requirements that are stricter than the federal baseline. Some of these requirements have been established as a matter of state constitutional law, while others are expressed in state eminent domain statutes that carefully limit the grounds upon which takings may be exercised. . . . The necessity and wisdom of using eminent domain to promote economic development are certainly matters of legitimate public debate. This Court's authority, however, extends only to determining whether the city's proposed condemnations are for a "public use" within the meaning of the fifth amendment to the federal Constitution. Because over a century of our case law interpreting that provision dictates an affirmative answer to that question, we may not grant petitioners the relief that they seek.

Four of the Court's nine justices dissented from this ruling. One of the dissenting justices' opinions concludes with these remarks:

> The consequences of today's decision are not difficult to predict, and promise to be harmful. So-called "urban renewal" programs provide some compensation for the properties they take, but no compensation is possible for the subjective value of these lands to the individuals displaced and the indignity inflicted by uprooting them from their homes. Allowing the government to take property solely for public purposes is bad enough, but extending the concept of public purpose to encompass any economically beneficial goal guarantees that these losses will fall disproportionately on poor communities. . . . [The Court's decision in this case] encourages those citizens with disproportionate influence and power in the political process, including large corporations and development firms, to victimize the weak.

relevance to churches and other religious organizations

Does this ruling mean that city and state governments can seize church property to promote an economic development plan, or to increase the tax base? To illustrate, could a city "take" a church's property (for just compensation) in order to allow a developer to demolish the church and construct a commercial building that will provide property tax revenue to the city? It is important to remember that churches are different from other private property owners in three important respects.

• The First Amendment guaranty of religious liberty provides churches with some enhanced protection that would not be available to other property owners. While this protection has been diminished by the Supreme Court in recent years, it retains some vitality.

• State constitutions also provide churches with guarantees of religious liberty. These protections vary widely from state to state. They may provide churches with additional protections when a city wants to take their property.

• The federal Religious Land Use and Institutionalized Persons Act states that "no government shall impose or implement a land use regulation in a manner that imposes a burden on the religious exercise of a person, including a religious assembly or institution, unless the government demonstrates that imposition of the burden on that person, assembly, or institution—(A) is in furtherance of a compelling governmental interest; and (B) is the least restrictive means of furthering that compelling governmental interest." This law may provide churches with additional protections when confronted with an attempt by a city government to take their property for economic development or to increase the tax base.[243]

---

[243] See § 7-06.4, *supra.*

the Cottonwood Christian Center case

In the *Cottonwood Christian Center* case, a federal district court in California ruled that a city could not seize a church's property through eminent domain in order to allow a discount warehouse to be constructed that would generate more tax revenues.[244] A church grew rapidly from 50 members to more than 5,000. As a result of this growth, the church outgrew its 700-seat sanctuary and the church was forced to conduct six services each weekend and "bus" parishioners from remote parking areas. But even with the buses and multiple weekend services, the church was unable to accommodate all the people that wanted to attend its services and it was unable to conduct outreach to potential new members. The physical constraints of its facility also limited the church's ability to conduct many of its different programs including youth conferences, women's ministries, daycare facilities, English language classes for native Spanish speakers, and missionary training.

The church eventually purchased 18 acres of property, and developed detailed plans to use the property. Its proposed church center included a 300,000 square foot worship center with more than 4,700 fixed seats, multiple classrooms and a multi-purpose room for youth and other ministries. The proposed center also included a youth activity center, gymnasium, and study rooms for after school youth programs. The facility included a daycare facility for church members and the surrounding community and a religious bookstore. The proposed center had sufficient space for all of the church's current ministries, community service programs, and worship services. The church contacted city officials to obtain a conditional use permit allowing it to build its new facility.

What the church did not know was that city officials had other plans for the church's property. Initially, the city planned a 45-acre development that included the church's property, and that would have three major retail anchor stores and a mix of restaurants, smaller retail stores, and movie theaters. This plan was eventually abandoned, and a modified plan was adopted that only pertained to the church's 18 acres. The city planned on allowing a large discount warehouse (such as Costco) to locate on the property. The city then offered to buy the property from the church at a specified price. When the church rejected this offer, the city instituted eminent domain proceedings to compel the church to sell its property to the city.

The church filed a lawsuit in federal court, claiming that the city's refusal to issue the conditional use permit and the eminent domain proceeding violated the Religious Land Use and Institutionalized Persons Act (RLUIPA) as well as federal and state constitutional protections of religious liberty.

RLUIPA prohibits any government agency from imposing or implementing "a land use regulation in a manner that imposes a substantial burden on the religious exercise of a person, including a religious assembly or institution, unless the government demonstrates that imposition of the burden on that person, assembly, or institution—(A) is in furtherance of a compelling governmental interest; and (B) is the least restrictive means of furthering that compelling governmental interest."

---

[244] Cottonwood Christian Center v. Cypress Redevelopment Agency, 218 F.Supp.2d 1203 (C.D. Cal. 2002).

The court concluded that the city's refusal to grant the church a conditional use permit "involves a land use regulation or system of land use regulations, under which a government makes, or has in place formal or informal procedures or practices that permit the government to make, individualized assessments." The court also concluded that the city's attempt to seize the church's property through eminent domain "falls under RLUIPA's definition of land use regulation which is defined as a zoning or landmarking law, or the application of such a law, that limits or restricts the claimant's use or development of land. The city's authority to exercise eminent domain . . . would unquestionably limit or restrict the church's use or development of land."

The court also ruled that the city's actions violated the First Amendment guaranty of religious freedom. In 1990 the United States Supreme Court ruled that "neutral laws of general applicability" that impose burdens on religious practice do not violate the First Amendment guaranty of religious freedom, and need not be based on a "compelling government interest." However, the federal district court noted that the city's refusal to grant the church's conditional use permit was an "individualized assessment" for which a compelling government interest must be proven. It observed: "The city's land-use decisions here are not generally applicable laws. [Its] refusal to grant the conditional use permit invites individualized assessments of the subject property and the owner's use of such property, and contain mechanisms for individualized exceptions." Even the city's eminent domain proceeding constituted an individualized assessment, the court concluded.

The court ruled that the city's actions were not neutral, but instead specifically aimed at discriminating against the church's religious uses. It observed:

> Why had the city, so complacent before the church purchased the property, suddenly burst into action? Although some innocent explanations are feasible—such as new leadership or robust economic growth—the activity suggests that the city was simply trying to keep the church out of the city, or at least from the use of its own land. This suspicion is heightened by the nature of the projects. The city's plan called for the church's property to be used as business offices. Yet, while the city has been insistent that a church would be inconsistent with this plan, it has proceeded to plan a shopping/ entertainment center and a strip mall anchored by Costco, neither of which are [sic] consistent with a business park. . . . Similarly, the city's claim that it needs the tax revenue of a retail store is dubious. In her state of the city address [the mayor] trumpeted [the city's] good fiscal condition, stating that the city continues to set aside 25 percent in reserves annually while still delivering the highest quality of service to our community.

There can be no violation of RLUIPA or the First Amendment unless government action imposes a substantial burden on core religious beliefs. The court concluded that this requirement was met: "Preventing a church from building a worship site fundamentally inhibits its ability to practice its religion. Churches are central to the religious exercise of most religions. If a congregation could not build a church it could not exist." The court also concluded that no compelling governmental interest supported the city's actions. In rejecting the city's argument that "revenue generation" (having a Costco store on the church's property) was a compelling interest, the court observed, "If revenue generation were a compelling state interest, municipalities could exclude all religious institutions from their cities."

The Cottonwood Christian Center Case

The Cottonwood Christian Center *case is a useful precedent for any church that is encountering resistance from city officials in building a new sanctuary. Here are the main points:*

(1) A city's refusal to grant a conditional use permit is a "land use regulation" that is subject to the protections of RLUIPA.

(2) A city's attempt to seize church property through the exercise of eminent domain is a "land use regulation" that is subject to the protections of RLUIPA.

(3) "Neutral laws of general applicability" can impose burdens on the exercise of religion without offending the First Amendment whether or not they are supported by a compelling government interest. However, the court concluded that a compelling governmental interest was required to sustain the city's actions in this case because (a) the city's actions were not "neutral" but rather were hostile to religion, and (b) the city's actions amounted to "individualized assessments."

(4) The city's desire for additional tax revenue is not a compelling governmental interest that would justify its denial of the church's conditional use permit or its attempt to seize the church's property through eminent domain.

Defacing Church Property §7-12

Key point 7-12. *Federal law makes it a crime to intentionally deface, damage, or destroy religious property because of the religious character of that property. Many states have enacted similar laws.*

Federal law makes it a crime to intentionally deface, damage, or destroy any religious property because of the religious character of that property.[245] The same law makes it a crime to intentionally deface, damage, or destroy any religious property "because of the race, color, or ethnic characteristics of any individual associated with that religious property."[246] Religious property is defined to

---

[245] 18 U.S.C. § 247. The offense must affect interstate commerce.

[246] *Id.*

include "any church, synagogue, mosque, religious cemetery, or other religious real property, including fixtures or religious objects contained within a place of religious worship." A federal appeals court affirmed the constitutionality of this law in a case involving an arsonist who set fire to 11 churches in four states.[247]

Several states have enacted similar laws, and the courts have upheld their validity against the claim that they favor religious property.

Case Study

• *A Florida court upheld a state law imposing harsher penalties upon persons who damage church property than other kinds of property. A defendant was convicted of defacing church properties by spray-painting them with anti-religious symbols and words. His sentence was harsher because state law imposed increased penalties upon those who deface religious property. The defendant appealed his conviction, arguing that the state law unconstitutionally favored religion. A state court rejected this argument and upheld the validity of the law. It concluded that the purpose of the law was not to advance religion but to deter incidents of vandalism occurring in places of worship and cemeteries. Further, the law's primary effect neither advanced nor inhibited religion. Any "benefit" to religion under the law was indirect and insignificant. Finally, the law did not result in an excessive entanglement between church and state since it did not involve "comprehensive, discriminating and continuing state surveillance" or "administration of religious activities." The court also rejected the defendant's claim that the law violated the constitutional guaranty of "equal protection of the laws" by treating vandalism to church property differently from damage to other kinds of property. The court observed that states may treat criminals differently so long as the classifications are reasonable. The court concluded that this test was met, since the state clearly had a legitimate interest in deterring crime, especially when crimes involving defacement of religious properties and cemeteries was on the rise.[248]*

Restrictive Covenants　　　§ 7-13

Key point 7-13. *A restrictive covenant is a restriction on the use of property. Such restrictions often are noted in deeds to property, but they may appear in other documents as well. Such restrictions apply to a church's use of its property.*

A restrictive covenant is a restriction on the use of property. Often, such covenants appear in deeds. Property owners, including churches, are legally bound by such restrictions. As a result, it is important for church leaders to review the deed to their property to be sure they are familiar with any such restrictions. However, as the following examples illustrate, such restrictions are not always legally enforceable.

---

[247] United States v. Ballinger, 395 F.3d 1218 (11th Cir. 2005).

[248] Todd v. State, 643 So.2d 625 (Fla. App. 1 Dist. 1994).

Case Studies

• *A Connecticut court ruled that a church could construct a parsonage in a subdivision despite a "restrictive covenant" prohibiting any use other than a "strictly private residence."* [249] *A group of homeowners asked a court to issue an order barring a church from constructing a parsonage in their subdivision. The homeowners asserted that their deeds, and the other deeds to lots in their subdivision, contained a restrictive covenant stating that the lots could not be used for "any business purpose whatsoever, or for any other purpose, other than a strictly private residence." They further insisted that the construction of a parsonage breached the restrictive covenant because church business would be conducted in the residence, violating the requirement that any residence be "strictly private." The homeowners also noted that a parsonage is exempt from property tax under state law if occupied by a minister. They reasoned that the property was exempt from property tax since it is used for "religious purposes," and this demonstrated that the planned use would not be "residential" and therefore the restriction would be violated. A state appeals court ruled that the parsonage might violate the restrictive covenant, and it sent the case back to the trial court for further proceedings. It noted that the church failed to offer any evidence to support its claim that the parsonage would be used solely for residential purposes. On the other hand, the homeowners did produce evidence to support their claim that the parsonage would not be used solely for residential purposes. One document, created by the church and entitled "A Fact Sheet for the Future," discussed the church's need to provide a residence for the pastor. However, this document indicated that the church may use the residence for "smaller church functions." Another document cited by the homeowners was a pamphlet prepared by the church stating that the parsonage "will accommodate various social events to which the [pastor] or spouse invite parishioners, i.e. gatherings in the living room, seated and buffet dinners, teas, parties and cook outs."*

• *A Missouri court ruled that a restrictive covenant contained in the deed to church property prevented a church from building a parking lot. The church owned and occupied several lots within a subdivision. Church leaders wanted to construct parking lots on three of the lots it owned. A homeowners' association sought a court order permanently enjoining the church from building parking lots on its property. The association claimed that the building of parking lots would violate a 1917 restrictive covenant covering each lot in the subdivision. The covenant specified that "none of said lots shall be improved, used nor occupied for other than private residence purposes." The court found conceded that restrictive covenants are "regarded unfavorably and are strictly construed because the law favors the free and untrammeled use of real property." Nevertheless, restrictive covenants "will be enforced where the intention is clear." The court rejected the church's argument that the restrictive covenant could be ignored as a result of "changed circumstances." To establish changed conditions warranting non-enforcement of a restrictive covenant, "the burden rests on the defendant to prove: (1) the radical change in condition; (2) that as a result enforcement of the restrictions will work undue hardship on him; (3) and will be of no substantial benefit to the plaintiff." The court acknowledged that "no hard and fast rule can be laid down as to when changed conditions have defeated the purpose of restrictions, but it can be safely asserted the changes must be so radical as practically to destroy the essential objects and purposes of the agreement." The court disagreed*

---

[249] Asjes v. Parish of Christ Church, 1997 WL 139450 (unpublished decision, Conn. App. 1997).

that "changed circumstances" warranted non-enforcement of the covenant.[250]

• A Missouri court ruled that a church was free to remove homes on adjacent property that it owned in order to expand its parking lot, despite a restrictive covenant limiting use of the property to residential purposes. A church purchased two homes adjacent to its property in order to expand its parking lot. Title to the properties was conveyed to the church subject to any "restrictions." Neighboring landowners protested the church's plan, and claimed that the church was barred from demolishing the homes and extending its parking lot by a "restrictive covenant" limiting use of the properties to residential purposes. A state appeals court ruled that the church could remove the homes and extend its parking lot without violating the restrictive covenant. It noted that "restrictive covenants are not favorites of the law, and any doubt is resolved in favor of the free use of land." It concluded that the purpose of the restrictive covenant in this case was to maintain the residential character of the neighborhood, and that the expansion of a church parking lot was consistent with this purpose since churches and their "accessory uses" (including parking lots) were permitted uses in residential areas.[251]

• A North Carolina court ruled that a restrictive covenant in a deed to a church's property requiring it to use the property for residential purposes was not legally enforceable because of nonresidential uses by several lots covered by the covenant, and because the restrictions had been waived. The court noted that restrictive covenants may be terminated in several ways: "Covenants may be terminated when they provide for their own termination. Covenants may also be terminated when changes within the covenanted area are so radical as practically to destroy the essential objects and purposes of the agreement." Even if a restrictive covenant has not been terminated, it is possible that it will not be given effect if it has been "waived." The court concluded that the covenant was no longer enforceable because of the "changes within the covenanted area are so radical as practically to destroy the essential objects and purposes of the agreement." It conceded that the residential restriction was put in place for the "protection and general welfare of the community," and that residential restrictions are generally "a property right of distinct worth." However, in this case, "the changes have destroyed the uniformity of the plan and the equal protection of the restriction."[252]

• A Texas court ruled that a church was justified in abandoning a rented building upon learning that a restriction in the owner's deed prohibited him from renting the property to a church. A development company developed a tract of property and imposed various deed restrictions on sites that it sold. Those restrictions specified that the property was for the operation and maintenance of any lawful, commercial retail business or offices. Religious facilities were not approved for the location. An individual purchased a site and constructed a building which he later rented to a church, despite his knowledge of the restrictions in his deed. After signing the lease agreement on behalf of his church, the pastor testified that the owner said to him, "by the way, now, I don't know whether there was any truth to this matter, but I heard about the possibility that [the developer] may not allow a church here." A few months later, having learned that the church was operating on the premises, the developer informed the owner that he was in violation of the deed restriction because a church was on the premises. The owner sent

---

[250] Country Club Homes v. Country Club Christian Church, (Mo. App. 2003).

[251] Fitzwilliam v. Wesley United Methodist Church, 882 S.W.2d 343 (Mo. App. W.D. 1994).

[252] Medearis v. Trustees of Meyers Park Baptist Church, (N.C. App. 2001).

a copy of this letter to the church. The church responded by sending the owner a letter informing him that it was vacating the premises and enclosing a check with the notation "final payment, terminating our lease agreement," written on it. The owner later sued the church for breaching the rental contract. A court ruled in favor of the church, concluding that it justifiably abandoned the property after receiving the letter from the developer informing the owner that the church's lease violated the deed restrictions.[253]

• *A Texas court ruled that a church had to be evicted from its property because its use of the property for religious purposes violated a restrictive covenant in a prior deed. The covenant stated that the property "shall be used for commercial/light industrial purposes only." The court noted that "the issue we must address here is not, of course, whether these sorts of religious activities on property are generally permissible or desirable, but whether the church's use of the property is a distinct or substantial breach of the restrictive covenant's requirement that the property be used solely for commercial/light industrial purposes. . . . We conclude that the church's use of the property for church purposes is a distinct or substantial breach of the terms of the restrictive covenant."*[254]

Restrictive Covenants Checklist

Many churches have purchased property that contains one or more restrictive covenants. Such covenants restrict a church's lawful use of its property. If church leaders are not aware of the existence of a covenant, they may inadvertently violate it. This can trigger an immediate lawsuit by neighboring landowners. Here are three rules to note:

☐ Be careful to inspect the proposed deed to any property you are acquiring by purchase or gift. Does it contain one or more restrictive covenants that could hinder the church's use of the property? If so, this issue should be resolved before title to the property is transferred to the church.

☐ Check out prior deeds in the "chain of title" of property prior to purchase, since restrictive covenants may be imposed in a prior deed. Such covenants "run with the land" because each subsequent deed, like the deed in this case, recites that it is "subject to any and all restrictions, encumbrances, easements, covenants and conditions" on the property.

☐ Check out the deed to your current property to see if it contains one or more restrictive covenants. If it does, has your church (and other neighbors) been violating them for years? If so, you may be able to argue that the restrictions have been "waived" by continual violation without objection, or that they have been "terminated" by substantial changes in the lots covered by the restriction. Do the same with prior deeds in the chain of title. A title company or real estate attorney can perform this task for you.

---

[253] Ruiz v. Hilley, 1996 WL 580940 (unpublished decision, Tex. App. 1996).

[254] Cornerstone Church Corporation v. Pizza Property Partners 160 S.W.3d 657 (Tex. App. 2005). The court rejected the church's argument that enforcing the restrictive covenant violated its right of religious freedom under the state constitution. It noted that the courts have "routinely rejected the notion that a neutral, otherwise valid restrictive covenant violates constitutional religious freedom protections if applied against a church."

Reversion of Church Property to the Prior Owner § 7-14

Key point 7-14. *Some deeds to church property contain a "reversion" clause stating that title will revert back to the previous owner in the event that a specified condition occurs. The courts will enforce such provisions, so long as they can do so without interpreting church doctrine.*

Property owners sometimes sell or give property to a church with a deed specifying that the property will revert to the previous owner if the church violates a specified condition. For example, a deed may convey title to a church "for so long as the property is used for church purposes." Or, a deed may convey title to a church "for so long as the property is used as a Baptist church." Such deeds vest only a "determinable" or "conditional" title in the church, since title will immediately revert back to the previous owner (or such person's heirs or successors) by operation of law upon a violation of the condition. It is essential for church leaders to be aware of any such conditions in the deed to their property. Unfamiliarity can lead to unexpected and harsh consequences.

Case Studies

• *An Arkansas court ruled that title to a church's property reverted to a national church when local church trustees attempted to convey the property without permission of the national church as required by a restriction in the deed to the property. In 1973, a couple transferred real estate to the trustees of a Church of God congregation. The deed stated that the trustees could not "sell, convey or encumber" the real estate without the written consent of the national church. In 1993, the trustees conveyed the property by quitclaim deed to a second group of trustees acting on behalf of the local church, and a month later this group of trustees conveyed the property by quitclaim deed to themselves as trustees for an independent church. This conveyance was made for the sole purpose of separating the congregation from the national church. The national church sued the trustees, claiming that their actions amounted to a breach of the restrictions in the church's original deed. A state appeals court declared the two deeds to be void and ruled that the national church owned legal title to the church property. It observed: "[B]y the plain language of the deed, the [trustees] were not authorized to make any conveyances inasmuch as they never obtained the necessary approval to do so."*[255]

• *The Georgia Supreme Court ruled that the property of a church "reverted" to the previous owner when the church moved to another location. In 1947 a landowner transferred property to a local church with a deed that contained a "reverter clause." This clause specified that the church would own the property "only so long as said lot is used for church purposes, it being expressly provided that if said lot of land*

---

[255] Conway v. Church of God of Prophesy, 1996 WL 617274 (unpublished decision, Ark. App. 1996).

should ever cease to be used for such church purposes, then the title thereto . . . shall immediately revert to the [previous owner]." The church constructed a building on the property and used it continually as its place of worship. In 1979 the majority of the church's membership voted to move to another location. A minority continued to worship at the original site, with the permission of the majority. Shortly after the majority of members vacated the property, the prior owner filed a lawsuit claiming that the majority's relocation triggered the reverter clause—meaning that neither the majority nor minority of church members had any further right to the property. The Supreme Court ruled that the reverter clause had been triggered by the majority's relocation, and that the prior owner was entitled to the property. It observed: "[T]he language of the reverter clause is clear that the property is to be used for the sole use, benefit and enjoyment of [the church] and the members thereof, the same to be used as a place of divine worship by the congregation of said church, and that title reverts when the property is not used for such church purposes. The use of the property by the minority which formed its own congregation . . . is not a permitted use of the property by [the majority] under the plain language of the reverter clause, even though that use is with the permission of the majority . . . . Accordingly, the property reverted to [the prior owner] in 1979 when it was no longer used by the majority for its church purposes."[256]

• *A New York court ruled that a church could transfer its property despite a provision in its deed that required the property to be used forever for religious purposes. In 1891 a family sold a parcel of land to a church. Pursuant to a restriction contained in the deed, the premises were conveyed to the church "and its successors forever for the use of the Protestant Episcopal Church in the Diocese of Long Island but without any power, right, or authority to grant, convey, or mortgage the same or any part thereof in any way or manner whatsoever." A court found that the church was entitled to sell its property despite the deed restrictions. It relied on a state law giving the civil courts the authority to extinguish restrictions on the sale of property by charities. It noted that one of the criteria courts are to consider in deciding whether or not to extinguish such a restriction is "whether the existence of the restriction substantially impedes the owner of the property in the furtherance of the purpose for which the land is held." The court concluded that this test clearly supported the elimination of the deed restriction, since continued ownership of the property by the church "was a burden and a drain on financial resources that could otherwise be used to provide programs and services to the community."[257]*

• *A New York court ruled that a church could transfer its property despite a provision in its deed that required the property to be used forever for religious purposes. In 1885 a family sold a parcel of land to a church. Pursuant to a restriction contained in the deed, the premises were conveyed to the church "and its successors forever for the use of the Protestant Episcopal Church in the Diocese of Long Island but without any power, right, or authority to grant, convey, or mortgage the same or any part thereof in any way or manner whatsoever." In 1993 the church, which was in severe financial distress, filed a voluntary petition in bankruptcy pursuant to Chapter 11 of the bankruptcy code. The bankruptcy court directed that certain properties owned by the church be sold, including the property subject to the deed restrictions. The church*

---

[256] First Rebecca Baptist Church v. Atlantic Cotton Mills, 440 S.E.2d 159 (Ga. 1994).

[257] Cathedral of the Incarnation v. Garden City Company, 697 N.Y.S.2d 56 (1999).

asked a court to extinguish the deed restrictions so that it could sell the property. The court concluded that the original deed in 1885 did not create a right of reversion since it "did not contain any language providing for the automatic termination of the church's interest in the property in the event that the property was no longer used for religious and educational purposes." At best, the deed created a right of reentry, and the court concluded that "any attempt by the heirs of the original grantors to assign a right of reentry to the company would be rendered void, since, under the common law, such a right was not assignable or devisable at the time that the original deeds were executed."[258]

• A Washington court ruled that a church's property did not "revert" to the previous owner because of immaterial violations of a condition in the deed that the property be used "exclusively for church purposes." The church began allowing a public transit company to use two of its parking spaces as handicapped parking for commuters, and allowed the company to place a bus shelter, bike rack, and a "park and ride" sign on the property. The estate of the previous owner sued, claiming that these collateral uses by the church triggered the reversion clause in the deed. The court laid down the following ground rules: (1) Words in a deed restricting the use of property are construed strictly against the grantor and those claiming the benefit of the restriction. (2) A forfeiture clause in a deed must always be strictly enforced against the grantor, and nothing will be held to cause a forfeiture unless it plainly appears to be such. (3) In order to justify a forfeiture for the violation of the condition, the violation must be willful and substantial and not merely technical. The court concluded that the church's collateral uses of its property were insignificant, and so did not result in a reversion to the prior owner's estate.

• The Washington Supreme Court ruled that a clause in a church deed limiting any future conveyance of the property to "Protestant evangelical churches" was not enforceable. The court began its opinion by observing: "This case requires us to consider whether an alleged restrictive covenant in a deed . . . prevents the receiving church from selling [its property] in order to relocate to a larger, nearby property." The court concluded that the doctrine of equitable deviation allowed it to approve a deviation from the deed's original purpose if (1) changed, unanticipated circumstances occurred, and (2) a deviation would further the purposes of the trust. As to the first requirement, the court described "present-day material circumstances not anticipated by the grantor" including significant congregational growth; limitations with the building and property; stricter development and building codes; drastic changes in the community; and changes in the attitudes, expectations, and needs of parishioners. The court also concluded that the second requirement (deviation would further the purposes of the condition) was met. It noted that "growth is an essential and necessary part of a successful evangelical church," that the previous owner "subscribed to growth being one of the obligations placed upon an evangelical Christian church," and that there was numerous problems with the current property making it impracticable for the church to carry out its mission.[259]

[258] In the Matter of Incorporated Village of Garden City, 734 N.Y.S.2d 225 (N.Y.A.D. 2001).
[259] Niemann v. Vaughn Community Church, 113 P.3d 463 (Wash. 2005).

Reversionary Clauses in Deeds: A Checklist

Many churches received title to their property by means of a deed containing a restriction. It is imperative for church leaders to be aware of such conditions. Consider the following points:

☐ Never purchase property without a clear understanding of the existence of any restrictive covenants and how such covenants may limit the church's use of the property. The presence of a restrictive covenant can prevent a church from using property for its intended purpose. In most cases, restrictive covenants will be spelled out, or referenced, in the deeds to church property.

☐ If your church owns property, be sure you are familiar with any restrictive covenants before you plan any changes in the use of the property.

☐ Deeds to property may contain restrictions on the sale of the property. Two common restrictions are "powers of reentry" and "possibilities of reverter." These interests are very similar, but they have very different legal consequences. A possibility of reverter arises when one person transfers property to another by means of a deed containing language clearly providing that title will automatically revert to the prior owner if the current owner violates a restriction in the deed. Language creating a possibility of reverter includes words such as "so long as," "until," or "until such time as." To illustrate, assume that A transfers land to B with a deed specifying that title is transferred "so long as" B uses the property for church purposes. Here, the language is clear that if the land ceases to be used for church purposes, it will automatically revert to A. The significance of this is that the reversion of title to A is automatic, and requires no action by a court. On the other hand, deeds often contain conditions that do not call for an automatic reversion of title to the previous owner upon the occurrence of some condition. In such cases the prior owner has a "right of reentry." Such a right does not vest automatically in the prior owner. Rather, the prior owner must go to court to have his or her interest recognized. As this case illustrates, this is a more uncertain interest in property, since it does not operate automatically.

☐ Churches should check their deeds to see if they contain a condition that may give the prior owner either a possibility of reverter or a right of reentry. In either case, the prior owner may attempt to claim title to the church's property in the event the specified condition is violated. However, if the prior owner retained a possibility of reverter, the transfer of title back to the prior owner occurs immediately. This can cause major problems for a church when it belatedly discovers that it no longer owns the property.

☐ The courts generally have a negative attitude toward restrictions on the sale of property by charities. Some states have enacted laws giving the civil courts some leeway in extinguishing such restrictions. If your church deed contains restrictions on the sale of property, you may want to consult with a local attorney concerning the existence of such a law in your state.

Reversionary Clauses in Deeds: A Checklist

☐ In some cases, restrictive covenants can be modified or ignored because of widespread disregard by property owners, or because of substantial changes in the properties subject to the restrictions. However, as the church in this case learned, establishing such an exception can be a very costly legal battle that may take years. The attorneys fees you incur ordinarily will not be covered by any insurance policy, so they will be an expense the church must bear. Church leaders should never assume that a covenant can be ignored. Check with a real estate attorney for an opinion regarding the current viability of a covenant.

☐ It is possible in some cases to have conditions "released" by the previous owner (if he or she is willing to do so). Often this is done by having the previous owner execute a quitclaim deed. If the previous owner is no longer living (a fairly common circumstance), then the condition can be released only by all of the legal heirs of the deceased owner. This can be a very cumbersome process.

☐ Be sure your church complies with any deed restrictions to the extent you are unsuccessful in getting them removed.

☐ When acquiring property through purchase or gift, discourage the property owner from encumbering the title with any restrictions that could later create substantial inconvenience for the church.

☐ Church leaders also should be aware that restrictive covenants often provide that a property owner who violates the restrictions is required to pay the legal fees incurred by other property owners in enforcing them. In other words, restrictive covenants not only may prevent a church from using property for a purpose that violates the covenant, but they also may force the church to incur an unbudgeted and possibly substantial expense in paying the legal fees of neighbors who successfully sue to enforce the covenant.

Materialmen's Liens

§ 7-15

Key point 7-15. *A company that supplies building materials for a construction project can claim a "materialmen's lien" against the property if it is not paid. This means that the company can sell the property to enforce its lien and recover the cost of the materials. Churches are not exempt from such liens.*

In most states, a company that supplies building materials for a construction project can claim a "materialman's lien" against the property in the event it is not paid. A lien is a security interest in property, much like a mortgage, that gives the supplier the legal right to sell the property to recover the cost of the materials. In many cases, a property owner pays a general contractor for construction materials, but the general contractor fails to pay the supplier. In such a case the owner must pay the supplier in order to avoid the sale of its property to enforce the lien. In other words, the property owner ends up paying twice for the same materials. Of course the owner can sue the general contractor, but in some cases this person cannot be found or is insolvent.

Case Studies

• A company provided materials for a church construction project. Before delivering the materials, the company wrote the church a letter warning it that if the general contractor failed to pay for the materials, the company could claim a lien against the church's property. When the company failed to receive payment from the general contractor, it sued to enforce its lien. The company sought not only payment in full for the materials it had supplied, but also finance charges and attorney fees. A court ruled that a materialman's lien only allows a supplier to collect the full price of materials that were supplied. The supplier is not entitled to an additional amount, whether for finance charges or attorney fees, unless the contract between the parties specifically provides for it.[260]

• A church entered into a contract with a contractor for the purpose of constructing a driveway and parking lot on its property (at a total cost of $12,500, including all labor and materials). The church paid the contractor the full contract price, but the contractor failed to pay the concrete supplier for $6,500 worth of concrete. The concrete supplier sued the church, demanding payment for the concrete. The church in turn sued the contractor (who could not be located). A jury ordered the church to pay the concrete supplier for the concrete, and acknowledged that the church could sue the contractor if he ever was found. An appeals court observed that under North Carolina law the church's full payment of the contract price to the contractor extinguished the concrete supplier's right to a "materialmen's lien" in the church's property, but that the church had failed to raise this defense at either the trial court or on appeal.[261]

Avoiding Double Payment of Construction Materials

It is important for church leaders to be familiar with the concept of materialmen's liens in order to avoid paying twice for construction materials. There are a various ways to avoid such a predicament. Here are some recommendations:

(1) Only deal with reputable contractors who have been in business in your community for several years and who have an excellent reputation. Many churches use a contractor who is a member of their congregation.

---

[260] Sherman v. Greater Mt. Olive Baptist Church, 678 So.2d 156 (Ala. App. 1996).

[261] Concrete Supply Co. v. Ramseur Baptist Church, 383 S.E.2d 222 (N.C. 1989).

Avoiding Double Payment of Construction Materials
(2) Withhold all payments to a general contractor in any construction project until "lien waivers" (signed by all material suppliers) are presented. The same is true for construction laborers.
(3) Insist upon a construction contract.
(4) Incorporate the lien waiver requirement into the contract.
(5) Be sure that the materialmen's lien is restricted to the price of delivered materials, and does not include attorney's fees, finance charges, or other "add ons."
(6) Hold back a portion of the contract price until you are assured that all suppliers and workers have been paid.
(7) Consider asking the contractor to submit bills from suppliers and workers directly to the church, and inform the contractor that the church will pay these bills directly.
(8) Retain a local attorney to draft (or review) the construction contract, and have the attorney review the materialmen's lien procedures under your state law. And, if your church is ever sued by a supplier seeking to enforce a materialmen's lien, remember that the supplier may not be able to recover attorney's fees or finance charges.

Religious Discrimination in the Sale or Rental of Church Property

§ 7-16

Key point 7-16. *Federal law prohibits discrimination in the sale or rental of residential property on the basis of race, color, national origin, religion, or sex. However, religious organizations are permitted to discriminate in the sale or rental of residential property in favor of persons of the same religion.*

The Fair Housing Act (Title VIII of the Civil Rights Act of 1968) prohibits discrimination in the sale or rental of residential property on the basis of race, color, national origin, religion, or sex. However, the Act specifically exempts religious organizations from the ban on religious discrimination. The Act provides:

Nothing in this subchapter shall prohibit a religious organization, association, or society, or any nonprofit institution or organization operated, supervised or controlled by or in conjunction with a religious organization, association, or society, from limiting the sale, rental or occupancy of dwellings which it owns or operates for other than a commercial purpose to persons of the same religion, or from giving preference to such persons, unless membership in such religion is restricted on account of race, color, or national origin.[262]

One court explained the rationale for this exemption as follows:

When Congress considered the FHA, it recognized that the Act might impose an undue burden on various religious organizations, which, without any discriminatory animus, merely sought to provide housing for its members. Thus, Congress made it clear that these organizations could, under certain circumstances, give preference to their members, without any fear of liability under the Act.[263]

However, religious organizations may violate the Act if they discriminate in the sale or rental of residential property on the basis of race, color, national origin, or sex.[264]

Removing Disruptive Individuals
§ 7-17

Key point 7-17. *Churches do not have to tolerate persons who disrupt religious services. Church leaders can ask a court to issue an order barring the disruptive person from the church's premises. If the person violates the order, he or she may be removed from church premises by the police, and may be found to be in contempt of court.*

Q Does a church have the legal authority to remove disruptive individuals from church services?

A This issue has been addressed by a number of courts. Generally, the courts have been sympathetic to attempts by churches to deny access to disruptive individuals. To illustrate, a Connecticut court agreed that a church could bar a disruptive individual from entering onto church premises.[265] It noted that "there was ample evidence that the defendant entered church property, on the three occasions charged, as a knowing trespasser. The record reveals that the defendant had been unequivocally informed and understood that his privilege to attend

---

[262] 42 U.S.C. § 3607(a).

[263] U.S. v. Lorantffy Care Center, 999 F.Supp. 1037 (N.D. Ohio 1998).

[264] *Id.*

[265] State v. Steinmann, 569 A.2d 557 (Conn. App. 1990).

church services had been revoked. . . . The record here is replete with evidence that this defendant knew that he was trespassing upon church property and was unwelcome at services." With regard to the defendant's claim that a church is "public property" and that one cannot be convicted of trespassing for attending services, the court observed that "property does not lose its private character merely because the public is generally invited to use it for designated purposes. . . . The owner or one in lawful possession has the right to determine whom to invite, the scope of the invitation and the circumstances under which the invitation may be revoked." As to the defendant's claim that his constitutional rights were violated by his conviction for attending church services, the court observed that there is "no constitutional right to 'freedom of movement' or 'freedom of worship' on private property where there is no license or privilege to be there."

A Texas appeals court ruled that a trespasser could be ordered off church property.[266] A trespasser entered onto a church's premises just prior to the conclusion of Sunday morning services. He carried a sign and attempted to speak with persons leaving the church services about "taxes" and "civil rights." A security guard asked the trespasser to leave the premises, and when he refused, the police were called in. When the trespasser continued speaking with church members, two security guards physically restrained him and held him in a church building until the police arrived. The trespasser was convicted of criminal trespass and was sentenced to 90 days in jail. The court further ordered the trespasser "not to go onto or within 200 yards of the [church]." He appealed his conviction on the grounds that he had a constitutional right to be on the church's property, and that the requirement that he not go within 200 yards of the church in the future was unreasonable.

A state appeals court rejected both of these arguments. In rejecting the trespasser's claim that his criminal conviction for trespass violated his constitutional right of free speech, the court emphasized that the First Amendment guaranty of free speech "is not protected" on private property, and therefore had no application to a church. In concluding that the church's property was private property, the court observed that (1) the trespasser ignored warnings to stay off the property, (2) the church had signs posted on its premises clearly stating that the premises were for church use only, and (3) church policy prohibited picketing or demonstrating on its property. Finally, the court concluded that the trial court's order prohibiting the trespasser from coming within 200 yards of the church property was reasonable: "It significantly contributes to [his] rehabilitation by removing from him the temptation of trespassing on the church's property. The condition also insures that those persons legally using the property will be protected from any unlawful interference."

---

[266] Gibbons v. State, 775 S.W.2d 790 (Tex. App. 1989).

Case Studies

• *A California court ruled that a disruptive person who engaged in outbursts during church services and harassed members before and after worship services could be legally restrained from the church property. The court concluded that person's right of free speech "does not trump the church's right to prohibit her disruptive conduct on its property." The court observed: "The more an owner, for his advantage, opens up his property for use by the public in general, the more do his rights become circumscribed by the statutory and constitutional rights of those who use it. But, in this case, the church is not an open forum. And if the expression [of speech] is inappropriate for the property or is incompatible with the intended use of the property, then the expression may be totally barred and the property is considered a non-forum. . . . Here, in the absence of a restraining order, the church and the congregation would continue to suffer from [this person's] outbursts and disruptive behavior. This is not a dispute over free speech. The church has expelled a member who was harassing the congregation and disrupting religious services. With each passing day, the church risks losing more members. And the church should not have to conduct services or meetings in secret just to avoid the interference of an expelled congregant. Without a restraining order, the church and its members would suffer irreparable harm. If a restraining order is granted, the affect on [the expelled member] would be negligible. She would no longer be able to annoy the congregation, tear down church bulletins, or frighten children. She has said that she will continue her disruptive behavior until a court directs otherwise. That time has come."[267]*

• *A Louisiana court ruled that a church has a legal right to use reasonable force in removing a potentially disruptive individual from its premises. A former pastor attended a business meeting of his former church, even though (1) he was no longer pastor, (2) he was not a member, (3) he had no legal right to be present, and (4) had been notified not to attend. He was asked to leave the church, but refused to do so. In response, a few members took him by each arm and physically removed him from the church. The former pastor later sued the members who removed him claiming that they had committed battery. A state appeals court disagreed. The court defined a battery as "harmful or offensive contact to another without that person's consent, done with an intent" to cause the contact. The court concluded that the church members did not intend any offensive or harmful contact with the former pastor when they removed him from the building. It added: "They had a legal right to see that [he] left the church meeting so its business would not be impeded and disrupted by his presence. Their contact with him was a reasonable means of accomplishing that intention. When, with no intent to cause offensive or harmful contact, reasonable force is used by persons in authority against one who has provoked an incident, the resulting contact is not a battery."[268]*

• *A Minnesota court upheld the legal validity of a restraining order prohibiting a disruptive individual from entering onto a church's premises. A person (the*

---

[267] Church of Christ v. Superior Court, 121 Cal.Rptr.2d 810 (Cal. App. 2002). *Accord* Church of Christ v. Lady Cage-Barile, 2004 WL 2943265 (unpublished decision, Cal. App. 2004); Christ Lutheran Church v. Stude, 2004 WL 2813584 (unpublished decision, Cal. App. 2004) (a California court ruled that a trial court's order prohibiting an abusive 84-year-old church member from entering church property was reasonable and valid).

[268] Robinson v. Dunn, 683 So.2d 894 (La. App. 1996).

"defendant") disrupted services at a Catholic church. The church's board of directors adopted a resolution authorizing the pastor to send a letter to the defendant banning him from church property, and to enforce the ban through appropriate legal action. This letter was hand-delivered to the defendant. Later, on three separate occasions, the defendant attended services at the church despite being banned from the premises. The church board asked a court to issue a "harassment restraining order." Following a hearing, a court issued a restraining order that provided, "[The defendant] shall not enter upon the premises of the [church] and/or any other church property." The defendant challenged the legality of this order on appeal. A state appeals court ruled that the order was valid and enforceable. The court noted that the First Amendment prohibits civil courts from deciding ecclesiastical or doctrinal disputes, but that "civil courts can hear non-doctrinal disputes that can be determined utilizing neutral principles of law." The court concluded that the church board's resolution banning the defendant from the property was a "secular" document that provided the court "with a familiar and neutral basis to decide the harassment action before it." The court also rejected the defendant's claim that the restraining order was too broad.[269]

• A New York court upheld the convictions of religious protestors who disrupted a church service. As a Catholic church was preparing to conduct a mass in honor of gay pride, a group of protestors began disrupting the service. One protestor grabbed a microphone and shouted at a priest, "You shouldn't be here. You are not fit to be a priest. You should be ashamed of yourself. You're not worthy to sell shoes." Other protestors engaged in similar behavior. The protestors were charged with violating a state law that provides: "A person is guilty of aggravated disorderly conduct, who makes unreasonable noise or disturbance while at a lawfully assembled religious service or within one hundred feet thereof, with intent to cause annoyance or alarm or recklessly creating a risk thereof." The protestors claimed that a mass is "a sacrifice of God to God on behalf of mankind," and that a mass in honor of gay pride "would be in the name of sin and evil, therefore making the mass a sacrilege." They argued that "all Catholics are under an obligation to prevent such a sacrilege from occurring within a church." A court ruled that the protestors could be charged with violating the state law prohibiting disturbance of religious services, and that the law was not unconstitutional. The court concluded that the state may lawfully "protect the rights of those individuals who choose to exercise their fundamental right of freedom of religion." It further observed that "the constitutional guarantees of the free exercise of religious opinion and of the people peaceably to assemble and petition for a redress of grievances, would be worth little if outsiders could disrupt and prevent such a meeting in disregard of the customs and rules applicable to it."[270]

• An Oregon court affirmed the criminal conviction of a man for "stalking" a woman on church property.[271]

---

[269] Naumann v. Zimmer, 1997 WL 10520 (unpublished decision, Minn. App. 1997).

[270] People v. Morrisey. 614 N.Y.S.2d 686 (N.Y. City Crim. Ct. 1994).

[271] State v. Maxwell, 998 P.2d 680 (Ore. App. 2000).

Adverse Possession

§ 7-18

Key point 7-18. *Churches can lose a portion of their property to a neighboring landowner as a result of "adverse possession," if the neighbor openly and adversely occupies church property for the length of time prescribed by state law.*

Churches can lose a portion of their property to a neighboring landowner as a result of "adverse possession," if the neighbor openly and adversely occupies church property for the length of time prescribed by state law.

Case Studies

• *An Arkansas court ruled that a neighboring landowner had a legal right to use a roadway across church property to access a public road because he and his family had used the roadway for a sufficient length of time without objection by the church. A trial court ruled that the neighboring family had a legal right to use the driveway on the basis of an "easement by prescription." Such an easement arises by operation of law after a landowner uses a roadway across another's property for a sufficient length of time. A state appeals court agreed. It conceded that Arkansas does not have a statute specifying the length of time needed to establish an easement by prescription, but it noted that the state Supreme Court has applied the seven-year period for acquiring title to land by adverse possession. The court noted that "where there is usage of a passageway over land, whether it began by permission or otherwise, if that usage continues openly for seven years after the landowner has actual knowledge that the usage is adverse to his interest or where the usage continues for seven years after the facts and circumstances of the prior usage are such that the landowner would be presumed to know the usage was adverse, then such usage ripens into an absolute right."*[272]

• *A neighboring landowner claimed title to 2 portions of a church's property as a result of adverse possession. The first portion of land claimed by the neighbor was land up to a boundary line that was set back several feet onto the church's property. For at least 11 years, the church and neighboring landowner considered this line to be their actual boundary line. The second portion of land claimed by the neighbor was a tract that he maintained for more than 11 years. A New York appellate court concluded that the church had lost its right to both portions of land. With respect to the first portion (land lost by the incorrect boundary line), the court observed, "Testimony shows the practical location of the boundary line and acquiescence thereto by the respective property owners for at least 11 years. Practical location and acquiescence for the statutory period is conclusive as to the location of the boundary line." With respect to the second portion of property (that had been maintained by the neighboring landowner), the court observed that for 14 years the neighboring landowner "cultivated and maintained the subject parcel, mowed it, planted a garden and trees on it, and erected a garage, swimming pool, storage shed and clothes line on it. We find that these facts established that [the neighbor] possessed the parcel hostilely and under claim of right, actually, openly and notoriously, exclusively and continuously for the statutory period."*

---

[272] Johnson v. Jones, 977 S.W.2d 903 (Ark. App. 1998).

This case demonstrates the potential loss of property that may result from erroneous boundary lines and fences, and the maintenance and use of a portion of a church's property by a neighbor.[273]

• *A Tennessee court ruled that a woman who used a path across a church's property had not acquired an easement because her years of use were less than the 20 years prescribed by law for adverse possession.[274]*

Accounting for Depreciation   § 7-19

Key point 7-19. *The Financial Accounting Standards Board (FASB) requires nonprofit organizations to recognize the depreciation of property and assets in their financial statements. As a result, churches that do not report depreciation will not be eligible for an unqualified opinion from a CPA at the conclusion of an audit.*

In 1987, the "Financial Accounting Standards Board" (FASB) issued "Statement of Financial Accounting Standards No. 93," which required all nonprofit organizations (including churches) to recognize depreciation in their financial statements. FASB based the new rule on its conclusion that a nonprofit organization has assets that are used up in providing services, and that this "using up" of assets is a real "cost" that should be recognized (as depreciation) in the organization's financial statements in order to fairly present its financial condition. To illustrate, FASB noted that the value of a cathedral "is used up not only by wear and tear in intended uses but also by the continuous destructive effects of pollutants, vibrations, and so forth. The cultural, aesthetic, or historical value of [such assets] can be preserved, if at all, only by periodic major efforts to protect, clean, and restore them, usually at significant cost. Thus, [it was] concluded that depreciation of those assets needs to be recognized."

Stated another way, a nonprofit organization "produces and distributes goods and services by using resources . . . . Some of its resources (assets) are used up in providing services at the time they are received, others are used up at a later date, and still others are used up gradually over time." In any event, "using up assets in providing services has a cost whether those assets have been acquired in prior periods or in the current period and whether acquired by paying cash, incurring liabilities, or by contribution."

FASB further noted that "even if that organization plans to replace the asset through future contributions from donors, and probably will be able to do so, it has not maintained its net assets during the current period." Not reporting depreciation (the cost of using up assets), on a nonprofit organization's financial statements "produces results that do not reflect all costs of services provided." FASB rejected the argument that depreciation need not be recognized on a nonprofit organization's donated properties since "whether an organization's use of an asset

---

[273] Chavoustie v. Stone Street Baptist Church, 569 N.Y.S.2d 528 (A.D. 4 Dept. 1991).

[274] Thompson v. Hulse, 2000 WL 124787 (unpublished decision, Tenn. App. 2000).

results in an expense does not depend on how the asset was acquired."

FASB did concede that "depreciation need not be recognized on individual works of art or historical treasures whose economic benefit or service potential is used up so slowly that their estimated useful lives are extraordinarily long. A work of art or historical treasure shall be deemed to have that characteristic only if verifiable evidence exists demonstrating that (a) the asset individually has cultural, aesthetic, or historical value that is worth preserving perpetually and (b) the holder has the technological and financial ability to protect and preserve essentially undiminished the service potential of the asset and is doing that."

What is the relevance of this rule to churches and religious organizations? Simply this—if your financial statements are audited by a CPA firm each year, you will not receive an "unqualified opinion" if you do not recognize depreciation on your long-lived assets. An unqualified opinion cannot be given because readers of your financial statements will not receive information about the cost of using up your assets, and accordingly they are not presented with information reflecting your organization's true costs. What difference will this make? None, if your financial statements are not audited by a CPA firm. Even if you have an annual CPA audit, the failure to report depreciation will probably result in a "qualified" opinion by your CPA (i.e., an unqualified opinion except for your failure to report depreciation).

According to FASB, the best reason to record depreciation in your accounting records is to ensure that the readers of your financial statements receive an accurate picture of your financial condition because of the inclusion of all relevant cost information. Whether or not your church or organization will record depreciation is a matter that should be addressed by the church board.

Premises Liability §7-20

Persons can be injured on church premises in a number of ways. Many parishioners have slipped on icy sidewalks or parking lots, fallen down stairs, tripped on wet floors, walked through plate glass windows, or been assaulted on church parking lots. Many churches allow outside groups to use their premises, and it is not uncommon for injuries to occur during such activities. What is a church's liability in such cases?

Liability Based on Status as Invitee, Licensee, or Trespasser

§ 7-20.1

Key point 7-20.1. *In most states, whether a church is liable for injuries occurring on its premises will depend on whether the victim is an invitee, a licensee, or a trespasser. Churches, like any property owner, owe the highest degree of care to invitees, a lesser degree of care to licensees, and a very minimal degree of care to trespassers. As a result, it is more likely that churches will be liable for injuries to persons who meet the definition of an "invitee."*

In most states, the liability of a church for injuries caused on its premises depends upon the status of the victim, since the degree of care which a church must exercise in safeguarding and inspecting its premises depends entirely upon the status of the victim. Most courts hold that a person may be on another's property as an *invitee*, a *licensee*, or a *trespasser*. An *invitee* may be either a public invitee or a business visitor. Section 332 of the Restatement (Second) of Torts, which has been adopted in many states, specifies that:

(a) An invitee is either a public invitee or a business visitor.

(b) A public invitee is a person who is invited to enter or remain on land as a member of the public for a purpose for which the land is held open to the public.

(c) A business visitor is a person who is invited to enter or remain on land for a purpose directly or indirectly connected with business dealings with the possessor of the land.

Landowners owe the greatest duty of care to *invitees*, since invitees by definition are on a landowner's property because of an express or implied invitation. Most courts hold that landowners owe invitees a duty to use reasonable and ordinary care to keep their premises safe, including the responsibility of correcting those concealed hazards of which they know or reasonably should know, or at least warning invitees of such hazards. Even so, a landowner is not a guarantor of the safety of invitees. So long as a landowner exercises reasonable care in making the premises safe for invitees or if adequate warning is given about concealed perils, a landowner will not be responsible for injuries that occur. Many courts have refused to hold landowners responsible for an invitee's injuries caused by an obvious hazard or by a concealed hazard of which the invitee was aware. Some courts have concluded that church members attending church services or activities are invitees because they satisfy the definition of *public invitee*. For example, one court concluded that a church member who was injured when she tripped and fell over a wooden cross that had been used in a skit presented at a church meeting was a public invitee since she had been invited to enter the premises as a member of the public for a purpose for which the property was held open to the public.[275]

A *licensee* generally is defined as one who is privileged to enter or remain on property because of the owner's express or implied consent. It is often said that invitees enter one's property by invitation, either express or implied, and that licensees are not invited but their presence is tolerated or merely permitted. In most states a landowner is responsible for warning licensees of hidden dangers of which the landowner is actually aware and to refrain from willfully or wantonly injuring them or recklessly exposing them to danger. The landowner has no duty to protect a licensee against hidden dangers of which the landowner is unaware. Thus, landowners are under no duty to make their premises safe by inspecting for and correcting hidden conditions that may cause injury.

A *trespasser* is a person who enters another's property without invitation or consent. In general, a landowner owes no duty to an undisclosed trespasser, and thus trespassers have no legal remedy if they are injured by a dangerous condition on another's property.[276] However, landowners who are reasonably apprised of the presence of trespassers ordinarily must refrain from willfully or wantonly injuring them, and, according to some courts, must warn them of concealed hazards of which the owner is actually aware.[277]

In a leading case, the Michigan Supreme Court ruled that nonmembers who visit churches for noncommercial reasons are licensees to whom churches owe a minimal duty of care making it less likely that churches will be liable for injuries occurring to such persons while on church premises.[278] A woman (the "plaintiff") was injured when she tripped over a concrete tire stop in a church's parking lot. She was visiting the church to attend a Bible study. She sued the church, alleging that it negligently placed the tire stops and failed to provide adequate lighting in the parking lot. A jury ruled in favor of the church on the ground that she was a licensee rather than an invitee and therefore the church owed her a minimal duty of care.

The state Supreme Court accepted an appeal of the case "to determine the proper standard of care owed to individuals on church property for noncommercial purposes." The court began its opinion by noting that Michigan, like most states, recognizes three categories for persons who enter upon the land or premises of another: (1) trespasser, (2) licensee, or (3) invitee. Each of these categories corresponds to a different standard of care that is owed to those injured on the owner's premises. As a result, a landowner's duty to a visitor depends on that visitor's status.

The court provided the following summary of the duty owed by a landowner

---

[275] Stevens v. Bow Mills Methodist Church, 283 A.2d 488 (N.H. 1971). *See also* Hedglin v. Church of St. Paul, 158 N.W.2d 269 (Minn. 1968).

[276] Adams v. Atlanta Faith Memorial Church, 381 S.E.2d 397 (Ga. 1989); Richards v. Cincinnati West Baptist Church, 680 N.E.2d 191 (Ohio App. 1996).

[277] *See, e.g.,* Reider v. city of Spring Lake Park, 480 N.E.2d 662 (Minn. App. 1992) (a church has a duty to warn trespassers of danger on its property if trespassers regularly use portions of the property).

[278] Stitt v. Holland Abundant Life Fellowship, 614 N.W.2d 88 (Mich. 2000).

to each category of visitor:

A "trespasser" is a person who enters upon another's land, without the landowner's consent. The landowner owes no duty to the trespasser except to refrain from injuring him by "willful and wanton" misconduct.

A "licensee" is a person who is privileged to enter the land of another by virtue of the possessor's consent. A landowner owes a licensee a duty only to warn the licensee of any hidden dangers the owner knows or has reason to know of, if the licensee does not know or have reason to know of the dangers involved. The landowner owes no duty of inspection or affirmative care to make the premises safe for the licensee's visit. Typically, social guests are licensees who assume the ordinary risks associated with their visit. The final category is invitees.

An "invitee" is "a person who enters upon the land of another upon an invitation which carries with it an implied representation, assurance, or understanding that reasonable care has been used to prepare the premises, and make [it] safe for [the invitee's] reception." The landowner has a duty of care, not only to warn the invitee of any known dangers, but the additional obligation to also make the premises safe, which requires the landowner to inspect the premises and, depending upon the circumstances, make any necessary repairs or warn of any discovered hazards. Thus, an invitee is entitled to the highest level of protection under premises liability law. A possessor of land is subject to liability for physical harm caused to his invitees by a condition on the land if the owner: (a) knows of, or by the exercise of reasonable care would discover, the condition and should realize that the condition involves an unreasonable risk of harm to such invitees; (b) should expect that invitees will not discover or realize the danger, or will fail to protect themselves against it; and (c) fails to exercise reasonable care to protect invitees against the danger.

The court concluded that persons who visit churches for noncommercial purposes should be regarded as licensees to whom a church owes a lower duty of care. It observed:

We conclude that the imposition of additional expense and effort by the landowner, requiring the landowner to inspect the premises and make them safe for visitors, must be directly tied to the owner's commercial business interests. It is the owner's desire to foster a commercial advantage by inviting persons to visit the premises that justifies imposition of a higher duty. In short, we conclude that the prospect of pecuniary gain is a sort of quid pro quo for the higher duty of care owed to invitees. Thus, we hold that the owner's reason for inviting persons onto the premises is the primary consideration when determining the visitor's status: In order to establish invitee status, a plaintiff must show that the premises were held open for a commercial purpose. With regard to church visitors, we [conclude] that such persons are licensees. . . . The solicitation of entirely voluntary donations by a nonprofit organization is plainly not a commercial activity. Accordingly, a church providing an opportunity for voluntary donations during a religious service that are in no way required to attend the service, i.e., passing a collection plate, does not transform one who attends the church service and elects to make a donation from a licensee into an invitee. Indeed, we imagine that many religious individuals would find it offensive to have their voluntary donations to a church regarded as part of a business or commercial transaction, rather than as a gift intended to aid in various religious good works.

In many cases, a church's liability for injuries occurring on its premises will depend on the victim's status. It is far more likely that a church will be found liable if the victim is an invitee, since a church owes a much greater duty of care to invitees than to either licensees or trespassers. This case makes a strong case for treating visitors to churches as licensees rather than invitees. However, the court cautioned that many states have adopted section 332 of the Restatement of Torts (a respected, but nonbonding legal text), that defines "invitee" to include "a person who is invited to enter or remain on land as a member of the public for a purpose for which the land is held open to the public." The court acknowledged that this language "creates an invitee status that does not depend on a commercial purpose." However, the court declined to adopt this definition.

A few states in recent years have abandoned the prevailing view of assessing a landowner's liability for injuries occurring on his premises by focusing on the status of the victim. These states have substituted a simple standard of reasonable care that a landowner owes to all lawful visitors. In determining a landowner's liability, the status of a victim is still relevant but not controlling. For example, the fact that an injured victim was a trespasser will reduce the landowner's duty of care since a reasonable person would not take the same steps to ensure the safety of trespassers that he would for invitees.

The great majority of cases involving accidents on church property have determined the church's liability on the basis of the status of the victim. Often, an accident victim's recovery of monetary damages against the church depends on his or her characterization as an invitee by a court, since this status creates the highest duty of care on the part of the church. If the victim is deemed to be a mere licensee, then often any monetary recovery is precluded. Many courts have concluded that accident victims are invitees of a church.

Slips and Falls Can Be Costly

While in most cases the amount of monetary damages involved in slip and fall cases is modest, there are exceptions, as a recent case in Indiana demonstrates. A surgeon slipped on a puddle of water in a break room in the hospital where he worked, and suffered nerve damage to one of his arms. He sued the hospital, claiming that it was negligent in allowing the puddle to remain on the floor for an unreasonable amount of time. But the real shocker was the jury's verdict—$17 million! A state appeals court upheld this verdict, rejecting the hospital's claim that it was grossly excessive.[279] The court concluded that the accident caused permanent damage to the surgeon's arm (it atrophied and developed a tremor), and the extra burden placed on his "good" arm caused him to develop carpal tunnel syndrome. The end result was that the number of surgeries he performed annually dropped from 250 to just a few. The jury concluded that $17 million was a reasonable figure to compensate the surgeon for the loss of income for the remainder of his life.

What is the significance of this case to church leaders? It illustrates that seemingly simple accidents on church premises may result in astronomical liability, depending on the nature of the resulting injuries, the victim's job, and the impact of the injuries on the victim's ability to work. This case graphically demonstrates the importance of practicing sound risk management to reduce the risk of slips and falls on church premises.

1. Cases Recognizing Invitee Status

A number of courts have ruled that members and certain other persons who are injured on church property are entitled to recover damages because of their status as invitees.

Case Studies

• *An Indiana appeals court concluded that a member who tripped over a plastic runner covering an aisle in a synagogue was an invitee rather than a licensee, and accordingly that the synagogue was legally responsible for his injuries. The court concluded that persons who are invited to enter upon premises for a purpose for which the premises are held open to the public or for business dealings with the owner of the premises are invitees who may recover for such injuries. The court concluded that members who attend activities at a church or synagogue are invitees under this test, since they are invited to enter the premises for the purposes for which they are held open to the public. Accordingly, a church or synagogue has a duty to protect them against negligent conditions on the premises, including improperly maintained aisle runners.[280]*

---

[279] St. Mary's Medical Center v. Loomis, 783 N.E.2d 274 (Ind. App. 2003).

[280] Fleischer v. Hebrew Orthodox Congregation, 504 N.E.2d 320 (Ind. App. 1987).

• The Iowa Supreme Court ruled that the president of a state organization of church women who was injured when she fell down a darkened church stairway was an invitee of the church because she had been invited to appear and preside over a women's meeting, and her presence was of mutual benefit to herself and the church. Since she was an invitee, the court concluded that the church owed her a duty to exercise ordinary care to keep the premises in reasonably safe condition and that this duty had been breached.[281]

• The Mississippi Supreme Court ruled that a church and its board of trustees could be sued by a member who was injured when she slipped and fell on a waxed floor while leaving a Sunday school class. The member argued that she was an invitee and accordingly that the church had a duty "to exercise reasonable care to keep the premises in a reasonably safe condition and, if the [church] knows of, or by the exercise of reasonable care should have known of, a dangerous condition, which is not readily apparent to the invitee, the [church] is under a duty to warn the invitee of such condition." The member claimed that the church breached this duty of care. On the other hand, the church maintained that the member was merely a licensee to whom it owed a minimal duty of refraining from willfully and wantonly injuring her through active negligence. The state supreme court ruled that the member was an invitee at the time of her injury: "Members of religious associations, in general . . . fall within the category of public invitees. Religious bodies do expressly and impliedly invite members to come and attend their services and functions. They hold their doors open to the public. While they do not charge admission fees . . . churches do depend on contributions . . . in order that they may continue to be open to the public. Therefore, a church member who does not exceed the scope of the church's invitation is an invitee while attending a church for church services or related functions." As a result, the member who slipped and fell on the waxed floor was an invitee to whom the church owed a high degree of care, rather than a mere licensee to whom the church owed only a minimal duty of care.[282]

• The Missouri Supreme Court ruled that a woman who was injured when she slipped and fell on a freshly waxed floor inside a church while on a tour at the invitation of her son was an invitee to whom the church was liable because of its failure to remedy the dangerous condition. The church's contention that the victim was not an invitee because the church received no benefit from her presence was rejected by the court: "Not only was she welcome, but her status as a potential member and future contributor provided a benefit to the church in an economic sense. That benefit so derived is not speculative but is comparable to, and no less than, that where the customer shops but does not buy. This was sufficient to give her all the required attributes of an invitee."[283]

• The New Jersey Supreme Court rejected a church's claim that a Sunday school teacher who was injured when she slipped and fell on an icy sidewalk in front of the church was not entitled to recovery as an invitee since she was a mere social guest. The court acknowledged that those who enter another's property as guests, whether for benevolent or social reasons, are licensees to whom the landowner owes a very minimal

[281] Sullivan v. First Presbyterian Church, 152 N.W.2d 628 (Iowa 1967).

[282] Clark v. Moore Memorial United Methodist Church, 538 So.2d 760 (Miss. 1989). *Accord* Heath v. First Baptist Church, 341 So.2d 265 (Fla.App.1977), *cert. denied*, 348 So.2d 946 (Fla.1977).

[283] Claridge v. Watson Terrace Christian Church, 457 S.W.2d 785 (Mo. 1970).

duty of care. The court concluded that the operation of a church is more than a mere social gathering: "To very many people it concerns a business of extreme moment, however unworldly." The court also insisted that the injured teacher's presence on church property was primarily for the benefit of the church, for "despite the voluntary and unrecompensed status of the plaintiff, she entered these premises as a matter of duty to the [church], and for the furtherance of the important interest, albeit a spiritual one, of the church, as distinguished from her own." The court accordingly held that the teacher was a business invitee to whom the church had breached its duty of reasonable care.[284]

• *The Washington State Supreme Court concluded that a church member who was injured in a fall from a negligently assembled scaffolding while donating his labor in the construction of a church building was an invitee of the church since the business or purpose for which he had entered the premises was of economic benefit to the church. Accordingly, the church was found liable for breaching its duty of exercising reasonable care to render its premises safe from, or at least warn of, dangerous conditions of which the church knew or could discover with reasonable diligence.*[285]

2. Cases Recognizing Licensee Status

In other cases, courts have concluded that a particular accident victim was present on church premises as a licensee. In most cases, a finding that an accident victim is a licensee will insulate the church from liability, since the only duty that a church owes to a licensee in most states is the duty to refrain from injuring a licensee willfully or wantonly and to exercise ordinary care to avoid imperiling the licensee by any active conduct. In some states, a church also owes a licensee a duty to correct concealed hazards of which it is actually aware or at least to warn a licensee of such hazards. But a church does not owe a licensee a duty to exercise reasonable care in maintaining church premises in a reasonably safe condition, and it does not have a duty to make inspections for dangerous conditions. This latter duty is owed only to invitees.

To illustrate, courts have found the following persons to be licensees and as a result have denied a legal remedy for injuries suffered on church premises: a member of an industrial basketball league that played its games in a church gymnasium;[286] a five-year-old girl who was visiting a church at which her grandmother was employed;[287] a church member who was injured while walking across a church lawn seeking entrance into a church to light a candle for her daughter;[288] a policeman who was investigating a complaint that a church was being broken into;[289] and a child who was burned by a fire while playing on church property.[290]

---

[284] Atwood v. Board of Trustees, 98 A.2d 348 (N.J. 1953).

[285] Haugen v. Central Lutheran Church, 361 P.2d 637 (Wash. 1961).

[286] Turpin v. Our Lady of Mercy Catholic Church, 202 S.E.2d 351 (N.C. 1974).

[287] Lemon v. Busey, 461 P.2d 145 (Kan. 1969).

[288] Coolbaugh v. St. Peter's Roman Catholic Church, 115 A.2d 662 (Conn. 1955).

[289] Scheurer v. Trustees of Open Bible Church, 192 N.E.2d 38 (Ohio 1963).

[290] Wozniczka v. McKean, 247 N.E.2d 215 (Ind. 1969).

Case Studies

• *The Alabama Supreme Court ruled that a church was not responsible for injuries sustained by a visiting choir member who slipped and fell on church premises. The court based its decision on the status of the choir member while present as a guest on the other church's property. It concluded that a person attending a church service is a licensee while on the church premises, and not an invitee. It noted that a choir member visiting another church to participate in a special service is not an invitee since the person's presence does not provide a "material benefit" to the other church. It further observed that special church services are common, and that guests who participate in such services are "in much the same position as social guests enjoying unrecompensed hospitality in a private home by invitation." As such, they are licensees. The court concluded that the church did not breach any duty it owed to the choir member as a licensee, since it did not willfully or wantonly injure her, and it was not aware of any condition of the floor that would cause an injury.*[291]

• *A Michigan court ruled that a volunteer who was injured by a sliding glass door during a Vacation Bible School class at a church was a licensee to whom the church owed a minimal duty of care. The court noted that invitees are persons who enter the premises of another for the other's material or commercial benefit. It concluded that "we do not discern any basis upon which to conclude that [the victim] volunteered to provide child-care services for a material or commercial purpose rather than one of a spiritual, religious or social nature." The court noted that "a landowner owes a licensee a duty only to warn the licensee of any hidden dangers the owner knows or has reason to know of, if the licensee does not know or have reason to know of the dangers involved. The landowner owes no duty of inspection or affirmative care to make the premises safe for the licensee's visit." However, a landowner "is required to take into consideration that a child's ability to appreciate the full extent of the risk is different from that of an adult."*[292]

• *A Washington court ruled that a man who accompanied a friend to a church-sponsored event at a member's home was a licensee to whom the church owed a minimal duty of care.*[293]

3. Trespassing Children

It is common for neighborhood children to play on church property. This may include skateboarding, bicycling, use of motorized recreational vehicles, basketball, baseball, or several other activities. Some of these activities expose minors to a significant risk of harm. Is the church legally responsible for injuries that may result? The answer depends on whether the victim entered onto church

---

[291] Hambright v. First Baptist Church, 638 So.2d 865 (Ala. 1994). *Accord* Prentiss v. Evergreen Presbyterian Church, 644 So.2d 475 (Ala. 1994); Davidson v. Highlands Church, 673 So.2d 765 (Ala. App. 1995).

[292] Kosmalski ex rel. Kosmalski v. St. John's Lutheran Church, 680 N.W.2d 50 (Mich. App. 2004). The court remanded the case back to the trial court to determine if a glass door used by children presents an unreasonable risk of harm.

[293] Neilson v. Corporation of Presiding Bishop of Church of Jesus Christ of Latter Day Saints, 2002 WL 31188444 (unpublished decision, Wash. App. 2002).

property because of an "artificial condition."

injuries caused by an artificial condition

If a minor is injured because of an artificial condition on church property, then the church's potential liability is described in section 339 of the *Restatement (Second) of Torts*, a respected legal treatise that is recognized in most states:

A possessor of land is subject to liability for physical harm to children trespassing thereon caused by an artificial condition upon the land if:

(a) the place where the condition exists is one upon which the possessor knows or has reason to know that children are likely to trespass, and

(b) the condition is one of which the possessor knows or has reason to know and which he realizes or should realize will involve an unreasonable risk of death or serious bodily harm to such children, and

(c) the children because of their youth do not discover the condition or realize the risk involved in intermeddling with it or in coming within the area made dangerous by it, and

(d) the utility to the possessor of maintaining the condition and the burden of eliminating the danger are slight as compared with the risk to children involved, and

(e) the possessor fails to exercise reasonable care to eliminate the danger or otherwise to protect the children.

An artificial condition is any condition that does not naturally exist. For example, the following conditions would be artificial: a basketball court, swimming pool, parking lot, or playground equipment.

Case Study

• *A New Jersey court ruled that a church may be liable for injuries sustained by a neighborhood child while playing on church premises. A church was located on a large lot without a fence.[294] The lot contained a low point where rain water accumulated. One day it rained quite heavily and a deep pond-like puddle formed in the low area. A three-year-old child who lived across the street often played on the church's property. She looked out the window of her home and noticed her tricycle on the church's property and wanted to bring it out of the rain. Her mother (the "victim") instructed the little girl to stay in the house and told her that she would retrieve the tricycle. The mother crossed the street to get the tricycle and noticed the large pond-like puddle*

---

[294] Blackburn v. Broad Street Church, 702 A.2d 1331 (N.J. Super. 1998).

that had accumulated on the church's property as a result of the rain. The tricycle was on the other side of puddle and the mother began walking around the puddle to retrieve it. Suddenly, she heard her little girl behind her saying that she would get the tricycle. The mother instantly realized that her daughter had walked into the large puddle and was in the middle of it. The mother was fearful that due to the young age of the child and given the depth of the water that the child was in danger. She immediately walked towards the child, but before she could reach her, she slipped in the mud under the water, fracturing her leg. The mother sued the church. A state appeals court concluded that the church could be sued for the mother's injuries. It quoted the general rule from section 339 of the Restatement (Second) of Torts, and concluded that each of these conditions was met. First, the pastor knew that children played on the church's property. Second, the pastor was aware of the accumulation of water on the property after a heavy rain, and the risk this posed to small children. Third, the pastor should have realized that the flooding condition on the property created an unreasonable risk of serious harm to young children. Fourth, the burden of eliminating the danger was slight compared with the risk to children. The pastor testified that the cost of installing a fence to keep children from walking in the area was approximately $2,000. The court pointed out that the church in fact did install a fence following the incident. Fifth, the church failed to exercise reasonable care to eliminate the danger or otherwise to protect the children. At the time of the incident, "the church had taken no steps to remove the condition or to warn children of the danger." The court noted that the Restatement addresses liability of property owners associated with injuries to children caused by artificial conditions on their property. It concluded that the "ponding effect" was an artificial condition: "The church buildings and the parking lot had been constructed on the property. The engineer testified that rain water from portions of the roof and from the stone driveway area contributed to the accumulation of water in the low area. The church building, with the resulting flow of rain water from the roof and the stoned parking lot were not natural conditions of the land, but instead were artificial conditions contributing to the accumulation of rain water on the property." The court concluded that if a church owes a duty of care to a trespassing child under the Restatement analysis summarized above, it also owes a duty of care to an adult rescuer. As a result, the church could be responsible for the mother's injuries incurred while attempting to save her child from the dangerous condition on the property.

injuries not caused by an artificial condition

Churches owe a minimal degree of care to trespassing children who are injured due to a natural condition (such as a tree or naturally occurring pond or lake). In general, the church must refrain from wantonly or willfully injuring such children.

Case Study

• An Ohio court ruled that a church was not responsible for injuries sustained by a minor who was injured while trespassing on church property.[295] A church owned a "water drenching machine" that was used at various church activities. The machine was designed to be connected to a hose, and anyone who hit a lever on the machine

---

[295] Richards v. Cincinnati West Baptist Church, 680 N.E.2d 191 (Ohio App. 1996).

with a ball caused an individual in the machine to be drenched with water. When not in use, the church stored the machine against a wall in the back of the church. A "no trespassing" sign was posted by the church. In addition, neighborhood children were not permitted to play on church premises during the week. The pastor and his wife frequently chased uninvited children off the property. One day a 6-year-old boy entered the church's premises, walked around to the back of the church, and crawled onto the machine. He was injured when it fell on him. The boy's parents sued the church. They claimed that they were not aware that neighbor children were not allowed to play on church property, although they did acknowledge that they were aware of the "no trespassing" sign. A state appeals court ruled in favor of the church. It noted that the boy was a trespasser, and that a property owner's only duty with respect to a trespasser is to "refrain from wantonly or willfully injuring him." The parents admitted that the church had not acted wantonly or willfully, but they insisted that the church was liable for their son's injuries on the basis of the "dangerous instrumentality" rule. Under this rule, a property owner has a higher duty of care to a child trespasser when it operates hazardous equipment "the dangerousness of which is not readily apparent to children, on or immediately adjacent to a public place." The court concluded that this exception did not apply in this case, since the machine was not "on or immediately adjacent to a public place." To the contrary, the machine was "private property, behind the church building and up against a wall. It was not within easy reach of a child in a public area."

4. Conclusion

Ultimately, the liability of a church for injuries suffered on its premises depends upon how narrowly or expansively the courts of a particular state define the term *invitee*. As the cases previously discussed illustrate, there is some difference of opinion regarding the definition of this term. Clearly, however, those states that have adopted the Restatement (Second) of Torts definition of an invitee ordinarily will regard most participants in church activities and services to be invitees. The United States Supreme Court has observed:

> In an effort to do justice in an industrialized urban society, with its complex economic and individual relationships, modern common-law courts have found it necessary to formulate increasingly subtle verbal refinements, to create subclassifications among traditional common-law categories, and to delineate fine gradations in the standards of care which the landowner owes to each. Yet even within a single jurisdiction, the classifications and subclassifications bred by the common law have produced confusion and conflict. . . . Through this semantic morass the common law has moved, unevenly and with hesitation, towards "imposing on owners and occupiers a single duty of reasonable care in all the circumstances."[296]

---

[296] Kermarec v. Compagnie Cenerale, 358 U.S. 625, 630-31 (1959).

Defenses to Premises Liability § 7-20.2

Key point 7-20.2. *A variety of defenses are available to a church that is sued as a result of an injury occurring on its premises.*

Churches have been found innocent of wrongdoing in several cases regardless of the status of the person injured on their property because the condition or activity that caused the injury could not under any circumstances serve as a basis for legal liability. For example, the courts have held that a church is under no duty to illuminate its parking lot when no church activities are in process;[297] to remove oil and grease from its parking lot;[298] to place markings on a sliding glass door;[299] to begin removing snow from church stairways before the end of a snowstorm;[300] to remove every square inch of snow and ice from its parking lot following a storm;[301] to correct hazardous conditions in a church attic that is inaccessible to the congregation;[302]or to prevent crowded stairways.[303]

The parents of an infant whose eye was seriously injured in a church nursery during worship services were denied any recovery since no one witnessed the accident and there was no evidence that it was caused by any negligence on the part of the church.[304] Similarly, a church member doing volunteer work for his church was denied recovery for injuries sustained when a ladder fell on him. The court noted that the member was an invitee, and that the church owed him a legal duty to correct or give notice of concealed, dangerous conditions of which it was or should have been aware. However, the court denied recovery on the ground that the member was aware of the unsecured ladder and the danger it presented, and this knowledge excused the church from its duty of correcting the condition or notifying the member of its existence.[305]

One or more defenses may be available to a church that is sued by a person who is injured on church premises. Many of these are addressed in chapter 10.

---

[297] Huselton v. Underhill, 28 Cal. Rptr. 822 (1963).

[298] Goard v. Branscom, 189 S.E.2d 667 (N.C. 1972), *cert. denied*, 191 S.E.2d 354 (N.C. 1972).

[299] Sullivan v. Birmingham Fire Insurance Co., 185 So.2d 336 (La. 1966), *cert. denied*, 186 So.2d 632 (La. 1966).

[300] Hedglin v. Church of St. Paul, 158 N.W.2d 269 (Minn. 1968).

[301] Byrne v. Catholic Bishop, 266 N.E.2d 708 (Ill. 1971).

[302] Miller v. Catholic Bishop of Spokane, 2004 WL 2074328 (unpublished decision, Wash. App. 2004).

[303] Gamble v. Shiloh Baptist Church, Inc., 2005 WL 3047274 (unpublished decision, Conn. Super. 2005).

[304] Helton v. Forest Park Baptist Church, 589 S.W.2d 217 (Ky. App. 1979).

[305] Fisher v. Northmoor United Methodist Church, 679 S.W.2d 305 (Mo. App. 1984). Contra Coates v. W.W. Babcock Co., 560 N.E.2d 1099 (Ill. App. 1990).

Case Studies

• The Florida Supreme Court held that a church member who was injured when she fell while walking in a dark hallway connecting the sanctuary with a social hall was precluded from suing the church by her own contributory negligence. The court observed that darkness is in itself sufficient warning to signal caution to one entering an unfamiliar situation, and that if one fails to heed the signal, he is guilty of contributory negligence.[306]

• A Georgia court ruled that a church was not responsible for injuries suffered by a woman who slipped and fell on church property. The woman had taken her daughter up a wooden ramp to the entrance of a church school, and was injured when she slipped and fell on the way down. It was raining at the time of the accident, and the ramp was wet. Immediately after she fell the woman told the church's pastor that "it's not your fault . . . it was just raining and I was in a hurry and slipped and fell." The woman had slipped before on the same ramp, and was aware that it was slippery even under dry conditions. She later sued the church as a result of her injuries. A state appeals court, in upholding the trial court's dismissal of the lawsuit, observed: "Everyone knows that any wet surface may be slippery. [The woman] has slipped on the ramp when it was dry. She had knowledge of its danger equal and perhaps superior knowledge to [that of the church], and she fell either because she was hurrying or because she chose to negotiate the ramp despite the danger which was obvious to her. The mere fact that a dangerous condition exists, whether caused by a building code violation or otherwise, does not impose liability on the [property owner]."[307]

• A Michigan court ruled that a church could be sued by the estate of an individual who was killed as a result of a defective ladder while performing work on church property. The decedent was engaged in performing repair and maintenance of a church building when he fell from a church-owned ladder and was killed. His estate sued the church, claiming that its negligence was the cause of the decedent's death. The court concluded that the decedent was an "invitee" on the church's premises. It noted that "an invitor must warn of hidden defects; there is no duty to warn of open and obvious dangers unless the [property owner] anticipates harm to the invitee despite the invitee's knowledge of the defect." The court concluded that "an extension ladder is an essentially uncomplicated instrument which gains a propensity for danger only because it will allow the user to reach great heights. This danger is most obvious to all but children of tender years . . . ." As a result, a church cannot be legally responsible for injuries suffered by workers who are injured when they fall from a ladder. However, the court cautioned that this rule did not necessarily apply in this case, since the estate of the decedent claimed that the decedent's fall was caused not by the general nature of the ladder itself but rather by a missing or malfunctioning safety latch. The court observed, "The real inquiry is whether this defect must be deemed an open and obvious danger. We think not. The danger that an extension ladder might slip and telescope down because of inadequate bracing at its base . . . is a danger readily apparent to persons of ordinary intelligence and experience. However, the fact that a safety latch is missing or malfunctioning creates a different, or at least an additional,

[306] Trinity Episcopal Church v. Hoglund, 222 So.2d 781 (Fla. 1969).

[307] Patterson v. First Assembly of God, 440 S.E.2d 492 (Ga. App. 1994).

danger that is not so obvious absent specific knowledge of the defect."[308]

• *A Michigan court ruled that a church was not liable for injuries a woman sustained when she tripped on an elevated step to exit a pew, since the step was marked with yellow tape and was an open and obvious hazard that should have been recognized. The court noted that the duty to protect an invitee "does not extend to a condition from which an unreasonable risk of harm cannot be anticipated, or from a condition that is so open and obvious that an invitee could be expected to discover it for himself." Deciding if a dangerous condition is open and obvious "depends on whether it is reasonable to expect that an average person with ordinary intelligence would have discovered the danger upon casual inspection."*[309]

• *A Minnesota court concluded that a church member who slipped and fell on an icy stairway while leaving a church service was not entitled to recover damages from the church because her failure to use an available handrail made her contributorily negligent.*[310]

• *A Minnesota court concluded that a church was not responsible for injuries sustained by a member who tripped on a dark stairway. The court noted that "evidence of the church's negligence was minimal. [The member] did not establish that the lights were turned off by a person for whose negligence the church could be held vicariously liable."*[311]

• *A New York court dismissed a lawsuit brought against a church by a woman who was injured during a church-sponsored activity. The woman and her husband attended a "country fair and barbecue" sponsored by her church. Following dinner, the couple took a raft ride on a nearby lake. After the ride, they were directed to walk on a back lawn area to return to the front of the church building. As the woman walked up a sloping lawn around the outside of a large tree, she slipped and fell, injuring her leg. She claimed that she slipped on ice cubes that were on the ground. A state appeals court dismissed the case. The court concluded that "plaintiff was required to demonstrate . . . that the condition was caused by [the church's] agents or existed for a sufficient period of time to require [the church] to have corrected it." Since the woman offered no evidence that an agent of the church caused the ice to be discarded on the lawn, or that the ice had been on the lawn for an unreasonable amount of time without*

---

[308] Eason v. Coggins Memorial Christian Church, 532 N.W.2d 882 (Mich. App. 1995).

[309] Holman v. Church, 2007 WL 292979 (unpublished decision, Mich. App. 2007).

[310] Hedglin v. Church of St. Paul, 158 N.W.2d 269 (Minn. 1968). *But cf.* Davis v. Church of Jesus Christ of Latter Day Saints, 796 P.2d 181 (Mont. 1990). In the *Davis* case, the Montana Supreme Court upheld a jury's award of more than $400,000 to a young woman who was injured when she slipped and fell on an icy church sidewalk. The church argued that it was not responsible for "natural accumulations" of snow and ice and that it had no duty to warn of a danger that was clearly apparent to a reasonable person. The court concluded that "a property owner may be held liable for falls on accumulations of ice and snow where the hazard created by the natural accumulation is increased or a new hazard is created by an affirmative act of the property owner. Even where such a condition is actually known or obvious, a property owner may be held liable if he should have anticipated that injuries would result from the dangerous condition." The court concluded that the church janitor's act of shoveling the sidewalk without applying any salt left the sidewalk covered with a "sheen of ice" that constituted a new hazard different from the natural accumulation of snow and ice that existed previously. It was this hazard, along with the dangerous slope of the sidewalk (without a railing), that constituted negligence on the part of the church.

[311] Thies v. St. Paul's Evangelical Lutheran Church, 489 N.W.2d 277 (Minn. App. 1992).

being corrected, the lawsuit had to be dismissed.[312]

• A New York court ruled that a church was not legally responsible for injuries sustained by a woman who slipped on a patch of ice in the church parking lot. The woman had attended a meeting of a local community group on the church's premises. On her way to her car, she slipped and fell on a patch of snow-covered ice and sustained serious injuries. She sued the church. The court ruled that the church was not responsible for the accident, since it was not aware of the ice and snow accumulation (no church employees were present at the time of the meeting) and the church did not have a reasonable opportunity to remove the snow and ice. The icy condition developed only two hours before the accident, and the snow (that concealed the ice) began falling only 15 minutes prior to the accident. Under these circumstances the court concluded, "[The church] as the owner of the premises, had a duty to exercise reasonable care under the circumstances. In order to impose liability upon [the church] there must be evidence that it knew, or in the exercise of reasonable care should have known, that an icy condition existed in its parking lot. Additionally, a party in possession or control of property is afforded a reasonable time after the cessation of the storm or temperature fluctuation which created the dangerous condition to exercise due care in order to correct the situation." There simply was not sufficient time in this case for the church to have removed the snow or ice prior to the accident, and accordingly the church was not legally responsible for the woman's injuries.[313]

• An Ohio court ruled that a church was not responsible for injuries sustained by a woman who slipped on a wet floor and broke her leg while attending a wedding reception on church property since the wet condition was an obvious risk. A woman (the "victim") was seated with friends and family at a wedding reception in a church. While on her way to the restroom, she stepped in some liquid, slipped and fell. She did not see the liquid on the floor, but three witnesses did see it. The court noted that the victim was a "business invitee" since she was on church premises by the implied invitation of the church, but it concluded that the church was not responsible for her injuries since "an owner is under no duty to protect its customers from dangers known to the customer, or otherwise so obvious and apparent that a customer should reasonably be expected to discover them and protect herself from them." The rationale behind this "open and obvious doctrine" is that "the open and obvious nature of the hazard itself serves as a warning, and allows the owner to expect visitors to discover the danger and take appropriate actions to protect themselves." The presence of wet floors "is a frequently encountered condition that a reasonable person would be expected to recognize and exercise caution to protect herself from. . . . Simply put, the fact that she stepped in an obvious wet spot because she was not looking makes it irrelevant whether the liquid had been on the floor for 45 minutes or 45 seconds, she would have slipped and fallen either way. . . . The open and obvious nature of the liquid obviates a

---

[312] Torani v. First United Methodist Church, 558 N.Y.S.2d 272 (A.D. 3 Dept. 1990).

[313] Byrd v. Church of Christ, 597 N.Y.S.2d 211 (A.D. 3 Dept. 1993). *But see* Graff v. St. Luke's Evangelical Lutheran Church, 625 N.E.2d 851 (Ill. App. 1993), in which the court concluded that "there is generally no duty to remove natural accumulations of ice and snow" and that "[t]he mere removal of snow leaving a natural ice formation underneath does not constitute negligence." However, a church or other property owner can be legally responsible for injuries in at least two situations: (1) snow is removed in a negligent manner, or (2) "an injury occurred as the result of snow or ice produced or accumulated by artificial causes or in an unnatural way, or by the defendant's use of the premises."

duty."[314]

• An Ohio court ruled that a church was no responsible for injuries sustained by a member who fell while stepping off a curb in the church parking lot and broke his hip. The court concluded that the hazard was obvious, and so the church was not responsible for the injury even though the member was an invitee: "An invitee is defined as a person who rightfully enters and remains on the premises of another at the express or implied invitation of the owner and for a purpose beneficial to the owner. The owner or occupier of the premises owes the invitee a duty to exercise ordinary care to maintain its premises in a reasonably safe condition, such that its invitees will not unreasonably or unnecessarily be exposed to danger. A premises owner must warn its invitees of latent or concealed dangers if the owner knows or has reason to know of the hidden dangers. However, a premises owner is not, an insurer of its invitees' safety against all forms of accidents that may happen. Invitees are expected to take reasonable precautions to avoid dangers that are patent or obvious. Therefore, when a danger is open and obvious, a premises owner owes no duty of care to individuals lawfully on the premises. Open and obvious dangers are not concealed and are discoverable by ordinary inspection. . . . The underlying rationale is that the open and obvious nature of the hazard itself serves as a warning. Thus, the owner or occupier may reasonably expect that persons entering the premises will discover those dangers and take appropriate measures to protect themselves."[315]

• A Pennsylvania court ruled that a Catholic church and diocese were not responsible for the injuries sustained by a woman who slipped and fell on an icy church parking lot. The woman, who was attending the church to participate in a bingo game, alleged that the parking lot was covered with a sheet of ice and also 5 inches of new snow. She alleged that the church had been negligent in failing to "implement some remedial measure (placing salt or ashes, warning visitors of the presence of ice, or barricading the icy area)," and accordingly the church was responsible for her injuries. A state appeals court ruled that the church was not responsible for the woman's injuries. It observed, "[A]n owner or occupier of land is not liable for general slippery conditions, for to require that one's walks be always free of ice and snow would be to impose an impossible burden in view of the climatic conditions in this hemisphere. Snow and ice upon a pavement create merely a transient danger, and the only duty upon the property owner or tenant is to act within a reasonable time after notice to remove it when it is in a dangerous condition. . . . [I]n order to recover for a fall on an ice or snow covered sidewalk, a plaintiff must prove (1) that snow and ice had accumulated on the sidewalk in ridges or elevations of such size and character as to unreasonably obstruct travel and constitute a danger to pedestrians traveling thereon; (2) that the property owner had notice, either actual or constructive, of the existence of such condition; (3) that it was the dangerous accumulation of snow and ice which caused the plaintiff to fall." The court concluded that the injured woman had failed to satisfy this test, and accordingly the church was not responsible for her injuries.[316]

---

[314] Andamasaris v. Annunciation Greek Orthodox Church, 2005 WL 313691 (unpublished decision, Ohio App. 2005).

[315] Aycock v. Sandy Valley Church of God, 2008 WL 115829 (unpublished decision, Ohio App. 2008). *Accord* Burdette v. Stevens, 2007 WL 2541774 (unpublished decision, Ohio App. 2007); Eagle v. Owens, 2007 WL 1574616 (unpublished decision, Ohio App. 2007).

[316] Harmotta v. Bender, 601 A.2d 837 (Pa. Super. 1992).

• The Rhode Island Supreme Court ruled that a church was not responsible for the death of a parishioner who was killed when she was struck by a vehicle while crossing a street to enter a parking lot. Three adult members of a Catholic church drove to the church to attend midnight mass on Christmas Eve. As was the practice of many parishioners, they parked their car in a small parking lot across the street from the church. The parking lot was owned by a neighboring commercial establishment, but church members were allowed to use the parking lot during church services by common consent. The parking lot was separated from the church by a public street. After mass ended, the three members left the church and proceeded to cross the street to reach their car in the parking lot. While in a crosswalk they were struck by a vehicle driven by a drunk driver. One of the members was killed, and another received severe and permanent injuries. On prior occasions the church had asked the city police to provide a traffic officer to control traffic after church services. The police occasionally provided officers in response to the church's requests if any were available. At no time did the church have a contract with the police to provide traffic officers. No representative of the church had asked the police to provide a traffic officer on the night of the accident. A lawsuit was brought against the church by the injured member and the estate of the member who was killed (the "plaintiffs"). The state supreme court dismissed the lawsuit on the ground that "the duty to control traffic has traditionally rested squarely with the government." Further, "[t]he fact that a landowner may request public traffic control on a public street does not vest in that landowner the personal right or obligation to control such a public way."[317]

Use of Church Property by Outside Groups

§ 7-20.3

Key point 7-20.3. Churches may be legally responsible for injuries occurring on their premises while being used by an outside group, if they maintain sufficient "control" over their premises during such use.

Churches often let outside groups use their premises. Examples include scout troops, preschools, aerobics classes, substance abuse groups, childbirth classes, and music classes. Some courts have found churches liable for injuries occurring on their premises while being used by such groups so long as they maintained "control" over their premises while the outside group was present.

Case Studies

• An Indiana court ruled that a church was liable for an injury occurring on its premises while being used by an outside group. A church permitted a local community group to use its facilities for an annual one-day celebration. The event was advertised in the church bulletin, and included a religious ceremony. After the ceremony, guests were ushered into another room for a reception where refreshments were served. While refreshments were being served, volunteers disassembled the tables and chairs in the

---

[317] Ferreria v. Strack, 636 A.2d 682 (R.I. 1994).

room where the ceremony occurred. Although the guests were asked to proceed to the reception immediately following the ceremony, a few guests remained behind to socialize. As one of these guests proceeded to the reception area a few minutes later, she tripped and fell over some of the disassembled tables. She later sued the church. The church claimed that it was not responsible for the guest's injuries since it had not retained any control over its facilities while they were being used by the community group for its celebration. The church also pointed out that the group was permitted to use the facilities without charge, that it was responsible for cleaning up the facilities following its activities, and that the church did not retain any control over the facilities during the celebration. A state appeals court noted that "the church is correct in observing that control of the premises is the basis of premises liability." However, the court concluded that there was ample evidence of control by the church. It observed: "[The priest] testified . . . that if he chose to do so, he could have decided not to allow the [community group] to hold their function there; that there was a janitor on the premises to make sure the buildings were locked; that the [organization] was not in charge of securing the premises; that the church placed an announcement in the church bulletin regarding when and where the celebration was to take place; that the church conducted a religious ceremony as a part of the celebration; and that he would not say that the church relinquished control over the property. This testimony was enough to create an issue of fact as to whether the church retained control over the premises."[318]

• Can a charity be legally responsible for an injury occurring on its premises while being used by an outside group? That was the question addressed by a Louisiana court in a recent decision. A charity permitted an outside group to use its facility for a Christmas party. During the party, a woman suffered serious injuries when she fell on a slippery floor. As a result of her injuries the woman underwent surgery for a complete hip replacement. She later sued the charity, claiming that it was responsible for her injuries because it had retained control over the premises during the party. She claimed that the floor was unreasonably slippery, and this dangerous condition caused her to fall. One witness testified, "It was obvious that floor was slippery. It was just waxed or something. I mean it wasn't dirty. It was clean. Probably too clean." The charity asked the court to dismiss the case, but its request was denied. On appeal, a state appeals court suggested that there was sufficient evidence that the charity retained control over its premises during the party to send the case to a jury. The court began its opinion by acknowledging that a property owner may be legally responsible for injuries that occur on its premises when they are under its custody or control. The court suggested that the charity had retained control over its premises during the Christmas party on the basis of the following factors: (1) the charity was responsible for setting up tables for the party; (2) the charity provided a custodian during the entire party; and (3) the charity was responsible for opening the premises at the beginning of the party and locking the premises at the conclusion of the party. The charity's custodian admitted that he had cleaned the floor prior to the party and that he was on duty and responsible for cleaning the floor during the party.[319]

---

[318] St. Casimer Church v. Frankiewics, 563 N.E.2d 1331 (Ind. App. 1990).

[319] Aufrichtig v. Progressive Men's Club, 634 So.2d 947 (La. App. 2 Cir. 1994).

Use of Church Property by Outside Groups: A Checklist

Many churches allow community groups to use their facilities. Before doing so, there are a number of issues that church leaders should consider, including the following:

☐ Have the outside group sign a "facilities use agreement" that (1) provides the group with a mere license to use the property; (2) contains a hold harmless and indemnification clause; (3) states that the church provides no supervision or control over the property when being used by the group. This document should be prepared by an attorney. The agreement should clearly specify that it is a license agreement and not a lease. The church's potential liability for injuries that occur during the use of its property by an outside group will depend to some extent on the nature of the relationship. A license exposes the church to less liability than a lease.

☐ The church should be named as an additional insured under the group's liability policy.

☐ Review the group's liability policy to ensure that it provides adequate coverage, and does no exclude sexual misconduct.

☐ If the outside group's use of the property will involve any participants who are minors (including minor children of participants), then the outside group should warrant that it has exercised a high degree of care in conducting background investigations on all persons who will have access to one or more minors to determine their suitability for working with or being present with minors during the outside group's use of the property. The outside group also should warrant that it will use a high degree of care in supervising all activities involving minors during its use of the property under the terms of the agreement.

☐ Check with the church insurer to determine coverage issues in the event the church is sued as a result of an accident or injury occurring during the group's use of the property.

☐ If you deny use of your property to any group because of its religious affiliation, be sure that you are legally permitted to do so under applicable federal, state, and local laws. Many jurisdictions permit religious organizations to discriminate on the basis of religion when allowing outside groups to use their property. Check with an attorney regarding the application of such laws to your church.

☐ The Americans with Disabilities Act prohibits places of public accommodation from discriminating against persons with a disability. The Act exempts religious organizations from this provision. Be sure to see if state and local law contains a similar exemption.

Use of Church Property by Outside Groups: A Checklist

☐ There are several potential violations of copyright law that may arise when an outside group is using the church, including the following: (1) An outside group that plays copyrighted music or shows copyrighted videos or images may be committing copyright infringement. (2) If the outside group makes audio or video recordings containing copyrighted music, this is another possible example of copyright infringement. (3) If a musical group performs a concert in which copyrighted music is performed, then this may result in copyright infringement. At a minimum, the agreement should include a statement making the outside group solely responsible for compliance with copyright law.

☐ The fees received by the church may be subject to the federal "unrelated business income tax."[320] Generally, this tax will not apply unless the rented facilities are subject to an "acquisition indebtedness" (a mortgage loan).

☐ The agreement should clarify that the outside group will be solely responsible for the collection of any sales taxes on the sale of any product during its use of the facilities, and that it will indemnify the church for any taxes it is assessed as a result of the outside group's sales occurring on (or a result of) its use of the premises.

☐ The outside group should agree to indemnify not only the church but also the church's officers, agents, and employees from any and all claims or damages in connection with the use of the property by the outside group.

☐ The agreement should contain a non-assignability clause.

☐ The agreement should state that the church does not warrant or represent that the property is safe or suitable for the purposes for which it is permitted to be used under the terms of this agreement, and that the outside group (for itself and on behalf of all of its members, guests, or participants who will be using the property) acknowledge that the church is providing the property and all appliances on as "as is" basis.

☐ The agreement should clarify that the church will bear no liability if the agreement is cancelled due to any legal or regulatory compliance issue, such as a zoning ordinance.

---

[320] This tax is addressed fully in chapter 12 of Richard Hammar's annual CHURCH & CLERGY TAX GUIDE, available from the publisher of this text.

Assaults on Church Property § 7-20.4

Key point 7-20.4. *A church may be legally responsible for assaults occurring on its premises if similar assaults occurred on or near the premises in the recent past and the church failed to take reasonable precautions.*

Most churches in America are safe places. While incidents of shootings on church property are shocking, they are rare, averaging one or two per year. But because of the "open access" policy of most churches, they remain easy targets for violent acts. While such acts cannot be prevented, there are steps that church leaders can take to manage the risk.

> "Yet again, we have seen a sanctuary violated by gun violence, taking children brimming with faith and promise and hope before their time. Our nation's support and prayers are with the families of the victims, those still suffering in the hospital, and the entire Fort Worth community. Federal law enforcement officials are now working with state officials and local authorities to find all the answers. But we know we have to redouble our efforts to protect our children. We know we have to act as if it were our own children being targeted by gun violence. We know that there is nothing we can do to assure that this will never happen, but there is a lot more we can do to assure that it will happen more rarely; and I can only hope that the shock of this event will spur that kind of action."
>
> —*President Bill Clinton, following a 1999 shooting rampage in a Texas church that left seven dead and seven more wounded.*

1. Recent Church Shootings

Here is a summary of major church shooting incidents from 1999 through 2007:

(1) December 9, 2007 — New Life Church, Colorado Springs, Colorado

A 24-year-old gunman shot and killed two people at a missions training facility in Arvada, Colorado. Later that day he drove 70 miles to the New Life Church in Colorado Springs. Wearing a black trench coat and armed with a high-powered rifle, the gunman began shooting at people in the church parking lot. He killed two teenage sisters, and wounded their father and two other adults. The gunman entered the church building as a worship service was ending, firing several rounds. He was confronted by Jeanne Assam, a church member who had a permit to carry a concealed weapon. Assam shot the gunman several times before he took his own life with a self-inflicted wound.

It was later learned that the gunman had been expelled by the missions training center in Arvada, and had sent several threatening emails to the facility in the weeks leading up to the shooting. Church leaders had placed the New Life Church on high security alert following the shooting in Arvada.

(2) August 12, 2007 – First Congregational Church, Neosho, Missouri

A 52-year-old man burst into the First Congregational Church in Neosho, Missouri during a worship service conducted by a Micronesian congregation that had been renting space at the church while looking for a permanent church home. The gunman ordered children to leave the church, and then started shooting with a 9mm semiautomatic handgun. He killed an associate pastor and two deacons, and wounded four other worshipers. Following the shootings he held the congregation hostage before surrendering to police.

(3) May 20, 2007 — First Presbyterian Church, Moscow, Idaho

A 36-year-old sniper with an automatic weapon fired over 75 shots at a courthouse shortly before midnight, and then shot and killed a police officer who responded to the scene. He also wounded a second officer who was attempting to assist his fellow officer, and two civilians, before fleeing to the First Presbyterian Church a short distance away. The church was quickly surrounded by several police officers. At 6 AM the following morning, three swat teams entered the church and discovered that the gunman had killed the church custodian before killing himself with a self-inflicted wound. The custodian lived on the church's premises.

(4) July 28, 2006 — Jewish Federation of Greater Seattle, Seattle, Washington

A man shoved his way through a security check at the entrance to a Seattle synagogue, shouted "I am a Muslim-American angry at Israel," and began shooting at the congregation. One member of the congregation was killed, and another five were injured. Police responded quickly to calls for help. In the meantime, the gunman had seized a hostage. Following a brief discussion with a police negotiator, the gunman laid down his guns and walked out of the synagogue with his hands on his head. He was arrested, and charged with one count of first degree murder and five counts of attempted murder.

(5) May 21, 2006 — The Ministry of Jesus Christ Church, Baton Rouge, Louisiana

A gunman opened fire in a church during a worship service, killing four persons and wounding the church's pastor (the mother of the gunman's estranged wife). After the shootings, the gunman fled with his estranged wife and three young children. The police cornered the gunman in a nearby apartment complex, where he surrendered without incident. Following the arrest, police officers discovered the body of the gunman's estranged wife in a parked car. She had been shot.

> "The one thing we want to focus on as Christians is to make sure Christ is lifted up. The torch has been passed to us from Columbine, and we want to carry it well."
>
> —*Pastor Jim Gatliff, following a 1999 shooting rampage in his Texas church that left 7 dead and 7 more wounded.*

(6) February 26, 2006 — Zion Hope Missionary Baptist Church, Detroit, Michigan

A 22-year-old man entered a church just before a scheduled worship service, looking for his former girlfriend. He walked up to the girl's mother and demanded to know the whereabouts of her daughter. When she refused to answer, the man pulled a shotgun from underneath his overcoat and shouted that he was going to "kill your daughter." ·

Church members quickly intervened and attempted to escort the gunman out of the church. He wheeled around and fired his shotgun, killing the mother and wounding a young girl sitting next to her. He then fired at the pulpit, and fled the church. He attempted to carjack a woman's car to make his escape, and shot and killed the woman's husband when he tried to intervene. Police spotted the gunman several hours later walking about a mile from the church. The gunman fled behind a house, where he killed himself with a self-inflicted wound.

(7) October 2005, Chad Weltman Synagogue, Boca Raton, Florida

A 79-year-old man shot a man who was leaving Rosh Hashanah services at the Chad Weltman Synagogue near Boca Raton, Florida. The gunman apparently was angry at the victim for helping a former girlfriend obtain a restraining order against him. The victim died nine months later. The gunman was found guilty of first degree murder and sentenced to life in prison.

(8) August 29, 2005 – Sash Assembly of God Church, Sash, Texas

On a Sunday evening following a church service, a church's pastor and his wife, and another couple, were talking in the church parking lot. A homeowner from across the street, Frederick Leroy Cranshaw, approached the group shouting obscenities and complaining about religious persecution. When the pastor asked him to stop, Cranshaw opened fire with a .38 caliber handgun, killing the pastor and the other male in the group.

Cranshaw drove from the scene in his truck, and later killed two women in another vehicle. He then returned to his home, shooting at buildings along the way. Police quickly surrounded the home, and two attempts by a swat team to break in were repulsed by gunfire from Cranhshaw. After a 9-hour standoff, the police entered the home, and found Cranshaw dead from a self-inflicted wound. Cranshaw had few if any prior dealings with the church, and apparently never attended religious services there. There is no record of any previous threats made by him against the church or its members.

"I don't know of a law—a governmental law—that will put love in people's hearts. It's hard to explain how hatred lurks in somebody's heart to the point where he walks into a church where children and adults were seeking God's guidance and shoots them."

—Texas governor George W. Bush, following a 1999 shooting rampage in a Texas church that left 7 dead and 7 more wounded.

(9) July 30, 2005 – World Changers Church International, College Park, Georgia

An man entered the 7,000-seat World Changers Church International on a Saturday night when it was unoccupied except for security and custodial personnel. He became belligerent when asked to leave, prompting a security guard to call the police. A police officer arrived on the scene, and was forced to strike the intruder with a baton in an effort to subdue him. The officer shot and killed the intruder when he reached for the officer's revolver.

(10) March 12, 2005 – Living Church of God, Brookfield, Wisconsin

The 60 church members of the Living Church of God in Brookfield, Wisconsin, rented a Sheraton Hotel conference room for their religious services. It is doubtful that any members were concerned when 44-year-old Terry Ratzmann showed up for the Sunday morning worship service on March 12, 2005. He often attended worship services at the hotel, and was well-known to several members who considered him quiet and harmless.

But shortly after he entered the room where the congregation was assembled, he opened fire with a 9mm semiautomatic pistol, killing seven members and wounding four others before taking his own life. Members begged him to stop shooting during the rampage, to no avail. He stopped to reload his handgun on one occasion. The rampage lasted no more than a minute.

Among the dead were the church's pastor and the pastor's 16-year-old son. The police speculated that Ratzmann may have been upset over a sermon the pastor preached a few weeks earlier in which he suggested that many of life's problems are caused by our own actions. Church members later stated that Ratzmann got up and left the room in the midst of that sermon "in a huff." Police investigators learned that Ratzmann may have been about to lose his job. They also reported that he had no criminal record, and that he had never made any threats to anyone in the congregation.

(11) October 5, 2003 — Turner Monumental AME Church, Atlanta, Georgia

Shelia Chaney Wilson and her mother were preparing communion at the altar of their church prior to a morning worship service when the senior pastor stopped by to greet them. Wilson pulled out a .44-caliber handgun and shot him in the head, killing him instantly. She then shot and killed her mother, and then took her own life with a single shot to the head. Police were summoned, but Wilson and her two victims were dead when officers arrived at the church shortly after the shootings. Wilson had no criminal history, and had made no known threats to either the pastor or the church.

(12) June 10, 2002 – Conception Abbey, Conception, Missouri

Lloyd Jeffress entered a Benedictine monastery in rural Missouri, removed two rifles from two boxes he was carrying, and began shooting. He killed two monks, and wounded two others, before killing himself with a self-inflicted wound.

(13) March 12, 2002 — Our Lady of Peace Catholic Church, Lynbrook, New York

Peter Troy, a patient in a psychiatric hospital, left the hospital without a doctor's approval. According to family members, his caseworkers lost track of him and eventually closed the case. A year later, he entered a Catholic church during mass, pulled a .22-caliber semi-automatic rifle from under a trench coat, and fired six shots toward the altar where the parish priest was concluding his homily. The priest, and a female parishioner, were killed. A church member was able to wrestle the rifle away from Troy, who fled the scene on foot. Police officers tracked him to his apartment a few blocks away. After a 7-hour standoff, the police broke into the apartment. Troy stabbed one officer before being subdued.

Among other incriminating evidence found in the apartment was a notebook with a smiley face on the cover, with the caption "church death list." The notebook contained 30 names, but did not include the names of either victim.

Troy was later convicted of two counts of murder, and sentenced to two life terms without the possibility of parole. The court rejected his insanity defense.

"He was right by me. He pulled the gun out, and I guess went to cock it, but it jammed and a shell fell out and I hollered, 'Thank you, Jesus!'"

"He started waving the gun and he was trying to shoot it but it would not go off. I just feel like God shut down that gun."

—Eyewitness descriptions of a gunman who shot and killed two persons during a church service in Kentucky.

(14) May 18, 2001 — Greater Oak Missionary Baptist Church, Hopkinsville, Kentucky

A married couple separated, and the wife maintained custody of their 2-year-old son. At the time of the separation, the wife obtained a protective order based on her husband's violent behavior. Two months later, the wife was attending a revival service in her church on a Friday night while her husband watched their son. The wife left the service briefly to speak with her husband, who was waiting outside. When the wife returned to the service, her husband followed, holding their son. The three of them sat on the front row of the church, as the guest evangelist was concluding the service.

A church member noticed that the husband was carrying a handgun. She mentioned this to the pastor's wife and suggested that she call the police. The pastor's wife went to the church office, picked up a cordless phone, and returned to the sanctuary. The husband, seeing the phone, assured her that "there is no problem, we're going to pray at the altar." When his wife asked for the phone, the husband grabbed it, and pulled out his gun. His wife fell backward, and was assisted by a woman sitting nearby. The husband shot his wife and the woman who was assisting her. As his wife begged for mercy, he shot her again, and then wheeled around and attempted to shoot at the congregation. The gun jammed, and he ran out of the church, holding his son. He got into his car and drove away, but was soon stopped by a police officer. A brief standoff ensued when the husband held a gun to his son's head, threatening to shoot him. He eventually surrendered.

> "This is a tragic occurrence. We've discussed things like this over the past few months at the city in light of the tragedies that have occurred in other parts of the country. But, frankly, there's no way the city government, or anyone, for that matter, can prepare for this kind of catastrophe."
>
> —*Forth Worth, Texas Mayor Kenneth Barr, following a 1999 shoot, following a 1999 shooting rampage in his Texas church that left 7 dead and 7 more wounded.*

(15) September 15, 1999 — Wedgewood Baptist Church, Fort Worth, Texas

Some neighbors called him "Crazy Larry." Many described 47-year-old Larry Ashbrook as a "paranoid loner," a "recluse," and "very troubled." He had trouble holding a job, and had received a less than honorable discharge from the Navy for drug use. At 7 PM on September 15, 1999, dressed in black and smoking a cigarette, he walked into a "See You at the Pole" youth rally at the Wedgewood Baptist Church in Forth Worth, Texas, and started shooting at the crowd of 150 teenagers and adult workers, killing 7 and wounding 7 others. One of the wounded was a 200-pound high school football player who was shot in the spine, leaving him paralyzed from the chest down. Ashbrook also attempted to detonate a pipe bomb, but it caused no damage or injury.

The police were called during the rampage, and quickly responded. Ashbrook shot a few rounds at the police before killing himself with a single shot to the head. He still had three full clips of ammunition in his pockets.

> "This has the appearance of being a very troubled man who for whatever reason in his own mind sought to quiet whatever demons were bothering him."
>
> —*FBI agent Bob Garrity, following a 1999 shooting rampage in a Texas church that left 7 dead and 7 more wounded*

Summary of Major Church Shooting Incidents Since 1998

date	place	shooter	victims	weapon
December 2007	**New Life Church, Colorado Springs, Colorado**	24-year-old Matthew Murray	2 dead, 3 wounded	high-powered rifle
August 2007	First Congregational Church of Neosho, Missouri	52-year-old Eiken Elam Saimon	3 dead, 4 wounded	9mm semi-automatic pistol, and a small caliber handgun
May 2007	First Presbyterian Church, Moscow, Idaho	36-year-old Jason Hamilton	1 dead	AK-47 and M1A assault rifles
July 2006	Jewish Federation of Greater Seattle, Seattle, Washington	30-year-old Naveed Afzal Haq	1 dead, 5 wounded	2 handguns
May 2006	The Ministry of Jesus Christ Church, Baton Rouge, Louisiana	25-year-old Anthony Bell	5 dead, 2 wounded	handgun
February 2006	Zion Hope Missionary Baptist Church, Detroit, Michigan	22-year-old Kevin Collins	2 dead	shotgun
October 2005	Chabad Weltman Synagogue, Boca Raton, Florida	79-year-old Marc Benayer	1 dead	handgun
August 2005	Sash Assembly of God church, Sash, Texas	54-year-old Frederick Leroy Cranshaw	2 dead	9 mm semi-automatic pistol and a .38-caliber revolver
July 2005	World Changers Church International, College Park, Georgia	27-year-old John Givens	none	handgun
March 2005	Living Church of God, Brookfield, Wisconsin	44-year-old Terry Ratzmann	7 dead, 4 wounded	9mm semi-automatic pistol
October 2003	Turner Monumental AME Church, Atlanta, Georgia	43-year-old Shelia Chaney Wilson	2 dead,	handgun
June 2002	Benedictine monastery, Conception, Missouri	71-year-old Lloyd Jeffress	2 dead, 2 wounded	AK-47 assault rifle, .22 caliber rifle
March 2002	Our Lady of Peace Catholic Church, Lynbrook, New York	34-year-old Peter Troy	2 dead	.22 caliber semi-automatic rifle
May 2001	Greater Oak Missionary Baptist Church, Hopkinsville, Kentucky	35-year-old Fredrick Radford	2 dead	handgun
September 1999	Wedgewood Baptist Church, Fort Worth, Texas	47-year-old Larry Ashbrook	7 dead, 7 wounded	9mm semi-automatic pistol

Summary of Major Church Shooting Incidents Since 1998

how resolved	possible motive	gunman a church member?	gunman made prior threats?	shooting occured during church services?
gunman committed suicide when confronted by armed church member	revenge (expelled from Arvada missions agency)	no	no	yes
gunman surrendered to police	family argument	no	no	yes
gunman committed suicide when cornered by police	unknown	no	no	no
gunman surrendered to police	hate crime	no	no	yes
arrested in an apartment building away from the church	family dispute (all victims were relatives of the gunman's estranged wife)	no	no	no
gunman died of self-nflicted wound while fleeing police	family dispute	no	no	yes
gunman arrested	revenge (victim helped gunman's ex-girlfriend obtain a restraining order against him(	no	no	no
gunman committed suicide when cornered by police several miles from the church	unknown	no	no	yes
gunman killed by police officer	unknown	no	no	no
gunman died of self-inflicted wound	depression, alcohol use, upset over a sermon, frustration over inability to find a spouse	yes	no	yes
gunman died of self-inflicted wound	loss of job; some church members considered the shooter "mentally unstable"	yes	no	yes
gunman died of self-inflicted wound	unknown	no	no	no
gunman arrested at his home by police	unknown	no	no	yes
gunman arrested at church police	domestic dispute (one victim was his estranged wife)	unknown	yes	yes
gunman died of self-inflicted wound	hate crime (gunman shouted anti-religious curses); friends described gunman as a paranoid loner and "very troubled"	no	no	yes

457

2. Church Liability

Is a church potentially liable to the victims of shootings on its premises? If so, on what grounds? Few churches have been sued as a result of acts of violence, but many other places of public accommodation have been, and here are some of the leading theories of liability:

- premises liability

- failure to hire security guards

- negligent selection of security guard or security service

- liability for negligent acts of security guards

Each of these theories of liability is addressed below.

(1) premises liability

Generally, property owners have no duty to protect others from the criminal acts of third parties who are not subject to their control. But, there are exceptions. For example, property owners have a duty to use ordinary care to protect "invitees" from criminal acts of third parties if the owner knows or has reason to know of an *unreasonable and foreseeable risk of harm* to invitees. Persons who are on church property to attend religious services or other scheduled activities generally are considered to be invitees, whether members of visitors, since they are on the premises by reason of an actual or implicit invitation.

The *Restatement (Second) of Torts*, a respected legal treatise, states the general rule as follows:

[A property owner] is not liable where he neither knows nor should know of the unreasonable risk. . . . He is not required to take precautions against a sudden attack from a third person which he has no reason to anticipate. *Section 314A, comment e.*

Similarly, *Restatement (Second) of Torts* § 344 (comment f), provides:

Since the possessor is not an insurer of the visitor's safety, he is ordinarily under no duty to exercise any care until he knows or has reason to know that the acts of the third person are occurring, or are about to occur. He may, however, know or have reason to know, from past experience, that there is a likelihood of conduct on the part of third persons in general which is likely to endanger the safety of the visitor, even though he has no reason to expect it on the part of any particular individual.

The foreseeability of an unreasonable risk of criminal conduct is a precondition to imposing a duty on a property owner to protect others from that risk. It is important to note that criminal conduct of a specific nature at a particular location is never foreseeable merely because crime is increasingly random and violent and may possibly occur almost anywhere, especially in a large city. If a [property owner] had a duty to protect people on his property from criminal conduct whenever crime *might* occur, the duty would be universal. This is not the law. A duty exists only when the risk of criminal conduct is so great that it is both unreasonable and foreseeable. Whether such risk was foreseeable must not be determined in hindsight but rather in light of what the premises owner knew or should have known before the criminal act occurred. *Lefmark Management Company v. Old, 946 S.W.2d 52 (Tex. 1997).*

In deciding if criminal conduct on a landowner's premises was foreseeable the courts have applied four tests:

- **The specific harm test.** Under this test, a landowner owes no duty unless the owner knew or should have known that the specific harm was occurring or was about to occur. Most courts are unwilling to hold that a criminal act is foreseeable only in these situations.

- **The prior similar incidents (PSI) test.** Under this test, a landowner may owe a duty of reasonable care if evidence of prior similar incidents of crime on or near the landowner's property shows that the crime in question was foreseeable. Although courts differ in the application of this rule, all agree that the important factors to consider are the number of prior incidents, their proximity in time and location to the present crime, and the similarity of the crimes. While this approach establishes a relatively clear test for landowner liability, many courts have rejected this test for public policy reasons. The public policy considerations are that under the PSI test the first victim is never entitled to recover, landowners have no incentive to implement even nominal security measures, the test incorrectly focuses on the specific crime and not the general risk of foreseeable harm, and the lack of prior similar incidents relieves a defendant of liability when the criminal act was, in fact, foreseeable.

- **The totality of the circumstances test.** Under this test, a court considers all of the circumstances surrounding an event, including the nature, condition, and location of the land, as well as prior similar incidents, to determine whether a criminal act was foreseeable. The most frequently cited limitation of this test is that it tends to make the foreseeability question too broad and unpredictable, effectively requiring that landowners anticipate crime.

- **The balancing test.** Under this test, a court balances "the degree of foreseeability of harm against the burden of the duty to be imposed." In other words, as the foreseeability and degree of potential harm increase, so, too, does the duty to prevent against it. This test still relies largely on prior similar incidents in order to ensure that an undue burden is not placed upon landowners.

Most courts apply either the totality of circumstances test or the balancing test, and focus on the following factors:

- whether any criminal conduct previously occurred on or near the property

- how recently and how often similar crimes occurred

- how similar the conduct was to the conduct on the property

- what publicity was given the occurrences to indicate that the landowner knew or should have known about them.

Each of these factors is summarized below.

(i) other crimes have occurred on the property or in its immediate vicinity

Criminal activity occurring far from a landowner's property bears less relevance because crime rates often vary significantly within a large geographic area. This is not to say that evidence of remote criminal activity can never indicate that crime is approaching a landowner's property. But such evidence must show that the risk of criminal conduct on the landowner's property is not merely increasing but has reached a level as to make crime likely. One court explained foreseeability as follows: "It does not necessarily follow that the prior similar criminal activity must have taken place at the premises; it is required only that the criminal act or acts occurring near the premises in question give notice of the risk that crime may travel to the premises of the business owner."

(ii) how recently and often similar crimes occurred on or near the property

Foreseeability also depends on how recently and how often criminal conduct has occurred in the past. The occurrence of a significant number of crimes within a short time period strengthens the claim that a particular crime was foreseeable. On the other hand, the complete absence of previous crimes, or the occurrence of a few crimes over an extended time period, negates the foreseeability element.

To illustrate, the courts have found a criminal act to be foreseeable when similar crimes occurred on or near the property in question (1) ten times within three years; (2) 394 times within two and one-half years; (3) 40 times within one year; (4) 85 times within three or four years; (5) seven times within one year; and (6) 75 to 100 incidents within three years.

On the other hand, the courts have concluded that a criminal act was not foreseeable in several cases, including the following: (1) apartment owner not liable for a criminal assault on a tenant because no violent crimes had occurred at the premises); (2) sexual assault on a female customer of a parking ramp was unforeseeable in light of only 17 previous crimes over a ten-year period; (3) bank could not foresee an assault at one of its ATMs based on two previous crimes within the eight preceding years; (4) an assault in a grocery store was not foreseeable because no robberies or assaults had ever occurred in the store; (5) "because there are no reports of prior similar crimes occurring on the Wal-Mart Supercenter parking lot, the crime was unforeseeable"; (6) a cab company could not foresee an employee's criminal act based upon one prior incident in a twenty year period.

(iii) similarity of previous crimes

The previous crimes must be sufficiently similar to the crime in question to place the property owner on notice of the specific danger. To illustrate, one court found that the stabbing of a guest at an apartment complex was not foreseeable from four prior incidents of vandalism and the theft of a refrigerator.

The prior crimes need not be identical. A string of assaults and robberies in an apartment complex make the risk of other violent crimes, like murder and rape, foreseeable. On the other hand, a spate of domestic violence in the complex does not portend third party sexual assaults or robberies.

To be sure, this factor is often difficult to apply because, as one court observed, "criminal activity is not easily compartmentalized." In addition, property crimes may facilitate personal crimes. For example, a burglar who breaks into a home to steal property may decide to assault a person who is discovered inside. On the other hand, vandalism to automobiles in an apartment complex's parking lot generally does not suggest the likelihood of sexual assault.

(iv) publicity given to prior crimes

The publicity surrounding the previous crimes helps determine whether a property owner knew or should have known of a foreseeable danger. Actual notice of past incidents strengthens the claim that future crime was foreseeable. However, unreported criminal activity on the premises is no evidence of foreseeability. Previous similar incidents cannot make future crime foreseeable if nobody knows or should have known that those incidents occurred. One court noted that "property owners bear no duty to regularly inspect criminal records to determine the risk of crime in the area. On the other hand, when the occurrence of criminal activity is widely publicized, a property owner can be expected to have knowledge of such crimes."

In summary, these factors (proximity and recency, frequency, similarity, and publicity) must be considered together in determining whether criminal conduct is foreseeable. The frequency of previous crimes necessary to show foreseeability lessens as the similarity of the previous crimes to the incident at issue increases. The frequent occurrence of property crimes in the vicinity is not as indicative of foreseeability as the less frequent occurrence of personal crimes on the landowner's property itself. The court must weigh the evidence using all the factors.

▶ *If a church receives a threat of an attack by an armed assailant, this will immediately elevate foreseeability toward certainty, triggering a corresponding duty on the part of the church to implement the most stringent safeguards. Depending on the circumstances, this may require the cancellation of church services. It is imperative that church leaders coordinate the church's response with local enforcement agencies.*

No court has addressed the liability of a church for a shooting incident on church premises. However, a few courts have addressed the liability of churches for other violent assaults. The main cases are summarized below.

Case Studies

• *A Georgia court ruled that a church was not liable for an assault on a woman who was passing by an abandoned property owned by the church. A woman (the "victim") was assaulted and seriously injured on her way home late one evening from a neighborhood convenience store. Her assailant crept up behind her as she walked along the sidewalk near a church. The church building was owned by the church, but no longer used since the church moved to another location a few years before. During the attack, the victim's back was injured and her legs paralyzed. While she lay immobile, a second assailant emerged from a door on the church property. This person raped the victim and left her. The victim sued the church, claiming that it was responsible for her injuries because it should have foreseen that a criminal might use an abandoned building as a hideout when preying on the general public. In rejecting the victim's claims, the court concluded: "[The victim's] unsupported speculation that her assailant may have concealed himself in the bushes near the church building before attacking her on the public sidewalk does not establish a causal relation between the condition of the property and the attack or a duty on the part of the church to protect her from such a criminal assault by a third party. . . . A contrary ruling would, in effect, impose a duty upon all property owners, especially those in high crime areas, to protect the general public from criminal activity committed on the property by third persons. This would include most unimproved lots and well-maintained buildings wherever the criminal could perform his misdeeds out of the public's watchful eye. Public policy, we believe, would not favor such a holding. Although defendants may have owed a duty to plaintiff against harm caused by the dilapidated condition of the building (e.g., injury caused by a falling brick or broken glass), that duty does not extend to the unforeseeable criminal activity of third persons."*[321]

• *A New York court ruled that a church was not responsible on the basis of negligent supervision or negligent retention for a sexual assault committed by a church employee. The court concluded that the church had received no complaints of inappropriate behavior concerning the employee for the five years of his employment, and therefore his assault was not foreseeable. The court acknowledged that the employee "may have used drugs in the past," was an HIV positive homosexual, and may have made "inappropriate expenditures" or hired "ex-convicts" to perform community service at the church, but if found all of these factors "irrelevant to any propensity to commit an act of sexual aggression."*[322]

• *A South Carolina court ruled that a church was not liable for injuries sustained by a person when he was attacked on church property. A church owned an apartment complex that is used as low-income housing. Despite the fact that the apartment building was in a high-crime area, and church leaders were aware of numerous incidents of criminal behavior occurring within the building, the church did not provide*

---

[321] Barnes v. St. Stephen's Missionary Baptist Church, 580 S.E.2d 587 (Ga. App. 2003).

[322] Osvaldo D. v. Rector Church Wardens and Vestrymen, 834 N.Y.S.2d 94 (N.Y.A.D. 2007).

a security guard. A man (the "victim") was injured when he was attacked while visiting a friend in the apartment building. The victim sued the church, claiming that it was responsible for his injuries on the basis of negligence. A state appeals court disagreed. The court observed: "A [property] owner has a duty to take reasonable care to protect invitees. However, this duty does not extend to protection from criminal attacks from third persons unless the owner knew or had reason to know the criminal attack would occur. . . . In this case [the victim and his mother] stated they knew of criminal activity that had occurred at [the apartment building] in the past, including an alleged shooting. In addition [the victim] asserted he knew [his attacker] was a violent person and that he had seen [him] involved in other fights at the complex. However, there is no evidence in the record that [the church] was aware of [the attacker's] previous fights or of any incident that day that would put management on notice the attack [on the victim] might occur. Therefore [the church] had no duty to protect [the victim] from an intentional attack."[323]

"Foresight, not retrospect, is the standard of diligence. It is nearly always easy, after an accident has happened, to see how it could have been avoided. But negligence is not a matter to be judged after the occurrence. It is always a question of what reasonably prudent men under the same circumstances would or should, in the exercise of reasonable care, have anticipated. Reasonable anticipation is that expectation created in the mind of the ordinarily prudent and competent person as the consequence of his reaction to any given set of circumstances. If such expectation carries recognition that the given set of circumstances is suggestive of danger, then failure to take appropriate safety measures constitutes negligence. On the contrary, there is no duty to guard when there is no danger reasonably to be apprehended. Negligence is gauged by the ability to anticipate. Precaution is a duty only so far as there is reason for apprehension. Reasonable apprehension does not include anticipation of every conceivable injury. There is no duty to guard against remote and doubtful dangers."[324]

Summarized below are recent court rulings addressing the liability of property owners for shooting incidents and other violent assaults occurring on their premises:

Case Studies

• *On a clear and sunny day in 1984, a man entered a McDonald's restaurant dressed in camouflage pants and armed with a 9mm semi-automatic rifle, a semi-automatic 9mm*

---

[323] Goode v. St. Stephens United Methodist Church, 494 S.E.2d 827 (S.C. 1998).

[324] Lopez v. McDonald's Corporation, 238 Cal.Rptr. 436 (Cal. App. 1987) (quoting SHEARMAN AND REDFIELD ON NEGLIGENCE).

pistol and a 12 gauge shotgun. He immediately began indiscriminately slaughtering patrons and employees within the glass-enclosed structure. During the hour of terror before he was killed by a police sharpshooter, the assailant showed no intent to rob the restaurant; made no demands for money; made no effort to take hostages; loaded his weapons several times; and killed 21 people in the restaurant and wounded 11 others. His single apparent purpose was to kill as many people as possible before he himself was slain. Several victims and their families sued for damages for wrongful death and personal injuries, claiming that McDonald's failed to provide adequate security personnel to protect customers from dangerous and known risks. In support of their theory of liability, the plaintiffs alleged that McDonald's knew of the area's high-crime rate, increasing gang activity, and nearby incidents of violent crimes. Claiming economic reasons, McDonald's declined to provide a uniformed security officer.

The plaintiffs presented evidence showing that within the three years preceding the shootings, the crimes committed at the restaurant included two robberies, two petty thefts, one unlawful use of a vehicle, vandalism, grand theft and theft by fraud. During the same period, crime statistics revealed that within a one-tenth of a mile radius of the restaurant, six burglaries, five batteries, one assault with a deadly weapon, two drawings of a deadly weapon, numerous grand thefts and various other crimes were committed.

A California appeals court noted that property owners may be responsible for the criminal acts of third parties only if those acts are reasonably foreseeable under the "totality of circumstances." The court concluded that the shooting rampage in this case was not foreseeable:

> The risk of a maniacal, mass murderous assault is not a hazard the likelihood of which makes McDonald's conduct unreasonably dangerous. Rather, the likelihood of this unprecedented murderous assault was so remote and unexpected that, as a matter of law, the general character of McDonald's nonfeasance did not facilitate its happening. [The assailant's] deranged and motiveless attack, apparently the worst mass killing by a single assailant in recent American history, is so unlikely to occur within the setting of modern life that a reasonably prudent business enterprise would not consider its occurrence in attempting to satisfy its general obligation to protect business invitees from reasonably foreseeable criminal conduct. . . .
>
> Plaintiffs' reliance on the evidence of mostly theft-related crimes on and nearby the [restaurant] and the crime rate in the surrounding area, to show the event here was reasonably foreseeable, is misplaced. We recognize foreseeability of third-party criminal conduct does not require prior identical or even similar incidents. However, here the evidence does not portend disasters of this type. As McDonald's argues: "To the extent it can be foreseen at all, such an attack, like a meteor falling from the sky, can occur in any neighborhood regardless of the crime rate." Rather, the predominantly theft-related character of the crimes is simply probative of the foreseeability of such crimes, more precisely defining its duty to provide protective measures designed to deter theft-related and ordinary criminal conduct (i.e., vandalism). In comparison, not only was [the assailant's] crime not theft-related, but the narrow focus on slaughter and [his] obvious suicidal motive are unrelated to the area's general crime rate as a matter of law. . . . A review of the surrounding circumstances emphasized by plaintiffs does not render the occurrence of a mass murderous assault any more foreseeable. . . .
>
> Further, although the policy of preventing future harm is great, the extent of the burden to the defendant and the consequences to the community of imposing

a duty to protect against heavily-armed, suicidal murderers is onerous. As already explained, where the burden of preventing future harm is great, a high degree of foreseeability is required. Absent such a high degree of foreseeability, the courts have declined to declare a duty where its imposition "would place an extremely onerous burden on both the defendant and the community, and where the defendant is not morally culpable, and where the proposed duty and the measures to be applied in discharge of the duty defy exact delineation and suffer from inherent vagueness. . . ."

[W]hat protective measures should be pursued to protect against a mass murderous assault truly defy exact delineation, because how can one know which measures will be effective against a degenerate, a psychopath or a psychotic? The type of unforeseeable criminal conduct involved here would require expensive protective measures of questionable deterrent value when confronted by an assailant bent on committing a mass murder. In other words, the kind of harm involved here cannot be deterred by such measures as security cameras and alarms which help deter ordinary criminal conduct because of the potential of identification and capture.[325]

• *A Georgia court ruled that two building owners were not liable for a shooting spree in their buildings that killed and wounded several persons. A customer entered the offices of two investment companies, pulled out a gun, and started firing. Nine persons were killed, and another twelve injured. Several of the victims and their relatives sued the two-day trading firms and a company that provided security services for the two buildings. A state appeals court ruled that a property owner is liable for shootings that occur on the premises only if the shootings are reasonably foreseeable. The plaintiffs insisted that the shootings were foreseeable, since it is "common knowledge that some people will become violent and seek revenge against a party they hold responsible for their financial losses." The plaintiffs also attempted to prove foreseeability by noting that (1) after the stock market crash of 1929 several brokers committed suicide; and (2) several years prior to the shootings in this case a distraught investor "shot up" a brokerage office in Florida, killing another customer, and another investor made unfulfilled death threats to the managers of an investment company, and twelve years in 1993, a man upset over large real estate losses shot several people in his lawyer's office in California. The court observed that these allegations "illustrate vividly" that "arguably similar acts of violence were so unusual, contrary to ordinary experience, and rare that no reasonable jury could find the trading firms should have guarded against them."[326]*

• *A woman was shot in the parking lot of a shopping center during an armed robbery attempt by an unknown assailant. The victim sought to impose liability on the owner of the shopping center for failing to provide security for the area. The Kansas Supreme Court concluded:*

In determining whether there is a duty owed, we start with two general rules. The owner of a business is not the insurer of the safety of its patrons or customers. The owner ordinarily has no liability for injuries inflicted upon patrons or customers by the criminal acts of third parties in the business' parking lot,

---

[325] Lopez v. McDonald's Corporation, 238 Cal.Rptr. 436 (Cal. App. 1987).

[326] Brown v. All-Tech Inv. Group, 595 S.E.2d 517 (Ga. App. 2003).

as the owner has no duty to provide security. Such a duty may arise, however, where circumstances exist from which the owner could reasonably foresee that its customers have a risk of peril above and beyond the ordinary and that appropriate security measures should be taken. . . . The test for determining the foreseeability requirement for injuries to customers by the criminal acts of third parties occurring in a business' parking lot is determined to be the "totality of the circumstances" rule." The circumstances to be considered however, "must have a direct relationship to the harm incurred in regard to foreseeability. Prior incidents remain perhaps the most significant factor, but the precise area of the parking lot is not the only area which must be considered. If the parking lot is located in a known high crime area, that factor should be considered. For instance, one should not be able to open an all-night, poorly lit parking lot in a dangerous high crime area of an inner city with no security and have no legal foreseeability until after a substantial number of one's own patrons have fallen victim to violent crimes. Criminal activity in such circumstances is not only foreseeable but virtually inevitable. . . . It is only where the frequency and severity of criminal conduct substantially exceed the norm or where the totality of the circumstances indicates the risk is foreseeably high that a duty should be placed upon the owner of the premises to provide security. The duty to provide security is determined under the reasonable person standard. Thus, the duty to provide security and the level of such security must be reasonable--that includes the economic feasibility of the level of security. . . . The shopping center owner is not under a duty to provide such security as will prevent attacks on the patrons--such a duty would make the owner the insurer of his patrons' safety. Rather, if because of the totality of the circumstances the owner has a duty to take security precautions by virtue of the foreseeability of criminal conduct, such security measures must also be reasonable under the totality of the circumstances.

The court noted that the only similar incident to the victim's shooting was another shooting that occurred on another part of the campus two years earlier. No shooting had occurred in any of the previous 17 annual fireworks displays. The lawsuit alleged that there was a high crime rate in the neighborhoods surrounding the university, but this allegation was not substantiated. Further, the university hired more than 100 police officers and security personnel to oversee the event. None of these individuals had any prior knowledge that the assailant intended to shoot anyone.[327]

• An Ohio court ruled that a state university was not liable for the rape of a female student that occurred in a vacant classroom. The court noted that the university could be liable for the victim's injuries only if "a rape was reasonably foreseeable" and the university "breached a duty of ordinary care by failing to take measures to protect the victim from being attacked and raped by a stranger." The victim claimed that her rape was foreseeable for the following reasons: (1) the university police department is undermanned as there are only three to five officers on duty during each shift, and these officers must patrol a campus that is located in a high-risk crime area and that spans 85 acres and 38 buildings; (2) three to five officers per shift cannot adequately secure campus buildings; (3) the university failed to lock classrooms when they were not in use and failed to have a policy requiring classrooms to be locked when they were not in use; (4) the amount of violent crime at the university was underreported,

---

[327] Seibert v. Vic Regnier Builders, Inc., 856 P.2d 1332 (1993).

was not consistent with the requirements of the Clery Act (which requires colleges and universities to publish data on student safety, campus security policies, and campus crime statistics) and this underreporting conveyed a false sense of security to students and prospective students.

The court concluded that in deciding if a particular crime was reasonably foreseeable, there are three factors that must be considered: (1) The "totality of the circumstances test" must be considered, including "past experiences and such factors as the location of the business and the character of the business." (2) "A business is not an absolute insurer of the safety of its customers." (3) "Criminal behavior of third persons is not predictable to any particular degree of certainty. It would be unreasonable, therefore, to hold a party liable for acts that are for the most part unforeseeable. Thus, the totality of the circumstances must be somewhat overwhelming before a business will be held to be on notice of and therefore under the duty to protect against the criminal acts of others." The court observed:

> Foresight, not retrospect, is the standard of diligence. It is nearly always easy, after an accident has happened, to see how it could have been avoided. But negligence is not a matter to be judged after the occurrence. It is always a question of what reasonably prudent men under the same circumstances would or should, in the exercise of reasonable care, have anticipated. Reasonable anticipation is that expectation created in the mind of the ordinarily prudent and competent person as the consequence of his reaction to any given set of circumstances. If such expectation carries recognition that the given set of circumstances is suggestive of danger, then failure to take appropriate safety measures constitutes negligence. On the contrary, there is no duty to guard when there is no danger reasonably to be apprehended. Negligence is gauged by the ability to anticipate. Precaution is a duty only so far as there is reason for apprehension. Reasonable apprehension does not include anticipation of every conceivable injury. There is no duty to guard against remote and doubtful dangers. (Quoting Shearman and Redfield on Negligence).

The court noted that in the five years prior to the victim's rape, only one rape occurred on the university campus, and this rape occurred in a restroom in a building adjacent to the building where the victim was raped. It concluded: "Recognizing that the university was not an absolute insurer of the victim's safety and that criminal behavior by third persons is not predictable to any particular degree of certainty, we cannot conclude that a rape at [the university] nearly one and one-half years before the victim's rape is sufficient as a matter of law to give the university reason to know that she likely would be raped in a classroom while she studied at 9 a.m. in the morning for a final examination. We therefore cannot conclude in this case that the totality of the circumstances is somewhat overwhelming such that the requisite foreseeability was established to hold the university liable for breaching a duty of care toward the victim."[328]

• A Washington state court ruled that a city was not liable for the shooting death of a patron at a party held in a city-owned facility. The victim's parents claimed that the shooting was foreseeable as a result of the "well-established theory of criminal

---

[328] Kleisch v. Cleveland State University, 2006 WL 701047 (unpublished decision, Ohio App. 2006).

victimization called [the] Lifestyle-Exposure Theory." This theory states that when certain "circumstances present themselves, there is a risk of personal victimization which is three to four times greater than normal." These circumstances are: (1) Groups of people 15 to 24 years of age; (2) in public places; (3) with strangers; (4) with alcohol or drugs present; (5) with inadequate supervision. The court began its opinion by noting that "where no evidence is presented that the defendant knew of the dangerous propensities of the individual responsible for the crime, and there is no history of such crimes occurring on the premises, the courts have held the criminal conduct unforeseeable as a matter of law. On the other hand, where there is a history of similar violence on the premises or the defendant knew of the dangerous propensities of the individual responsible, foreseeability has been established, at least sufficient to create a jury question."

The court concluded that in this case the victim's parents presented no evidence that the city knew of the violent propensities of the assailant or that there had been similarly violent episodes at the facility in the past." Instead, they alleged that there were a number of "unruly, aggressive, vulgar young people" at the party and that fights had occurred. The court noted that there was no evidence demonstrating how many fights occurred, how long they lasted, whether the victim was involved, and, "most importantly, whether any of the fights involved the use or threatened use of deadly force." Evidence of "antisocial, unruly, or even hostile behavior is generally insufficient to establish that a defendant with a supervisory duty should reasonably have anticipated a more serious misdeed."

The court also dismissed the parents' reliance on the "Lifestyle-Exposure Theory," noting that a risk that is "three to four times greater than normal" means nothing "without knowing what the baseline risk is."[329]

• As a crowd of several hundred persons was leaving a cheerleading competition at a public high school an altercation broke out among some people in the crowd. Gunfire erupted and a woman in the crowd was struck in the leg by a bullet. The woman sued the school, claiming that it was negligent in failing to provide adequate security personnel at the cheerleading competition. Further, she claimed that the school knew of "the high frequency of violence, and the reputation for violence at the school." The school asserted that the assault was the first violent crime to have occurred at a cheerleading competition or at any other event held at the school. A trial court dismissed the lawsuit on the ground that the assault was not reasonably foreseeable, and the victim appealed. The court began its opinion by noting that "when an injury is caused by the intervening criminal act of a third party . . . liability depends upon a more heightened showing of foreseeability than would be required if the act was merely negligent. Foreseeability of the risk must be more precisely shown because of the extraordinary nature of criminal conduct." The court continued:

> The question is not whether defendant should have known that fights, or minor scuffles might erupt at this gathering of 500-600 people on school property in the absence of an adequate security presence, including at the least a police cruiser. Rather, the question is whether the school had a duty to guard against a reasonably foreseeable risk that a person attending the competition would decide to settle a dispute with another individual over an item of clothing by indiscriminately shooting at that person while in the midst of a crowd of spectators. While indiscriminate shootings occur with sickening regularity in our

---

[329] Wilbert v. Metropolitan Park Dist. of Tacoma, 950 P.2d 522 (Wash. App. 1998).

community, and some even more tragically occur at or near school property, this does not mean that the city can be found liable for all such shootings. While . . . the foreseeability calculus does not require plaintiff to prove that a previous shooting had occurred at the same school after a cheerleading competition to establish the school's increased awareness of the probable danger of a particular criminal act, the evidence must at least demonstrate that the school should have anticipated the prospect of violent criminal conduct.

The court concluded that the evidence in this case failed to prove that the school had "an increased awareness that some third party's unlawful use of a firearm would cause the victim's injuries." For example, the victim offered no evidence of any shooting incidents, assaults, or other gun-related violence at any previous cheerleading competition or any other event at the school. The school's principal "provided no information with respect to the seizure of firearms at the school, assaults committed by unauthorized school visitors, or the use of firearms around the school during the school day or during after school events."[330]

(2) failure to hire security guards

Can a church be liable for deaths or injuries caused by an armed assailant as a result of a failure to employ security guards or police officers? Most churches do not employ such persons. Does this make them liable for shooting rampages that occur on their premises? No court has addressed this question in a published decision. But, a few courts have addressed this question in cases involving other property owners, and these courts generally have concluded that property owners have no duty to post security guards unless the foreseeability of violent crime is very high as a result of the same kinds of factors associated with the "totality of circumstances" test summarized previously.

> "It is an easy matter to know whether a stairway is defective and what repairs will put it in order. . . . But how can one know what measures will protect against the thug, the narcotic addict, the degenerate, the psychopath and the psychotic?" *Noble v. Los Angeles Dodgers, Inc., 214 Cal.Rptr. 395 (1985).*

Case Studies

• *The California Supreme Court ruled that a shopping mall owner's failure to employ security guards did not make it liable for the rape of a mall employee who worked for a photo processing service located in a secluded area of the mall. The court concluded that a property owner's duty to provide protection from foreseeable third party crime "is*

---

[330] Bailey v. District of Columbia, 668 A.2d 817 (D.C. App. 1995).

determined in part by balancing the foreseeability of the harm against the burden of the duty to be imposed. In cases where the burden of preventing future harm is great, a high degree of foreseeability may be required. On the other hand, in cases where there are strong policy reasons for preventing the harm, or the harm can be prevented by simple means, a lesser degree of foreseeability may be required. . . . Or, as one court has accurately explained, duty in such circumstances is determined by a balancing of foreseeability of the criminal acts against the burdensomeness, vagueness, and efficacy of the proposed security measures."

The court then addressed the need to hire security guards:

While there may be circumstances where the hiring of security guards will be required to satisfy a landowner's duty of care, such action will rarely, if ever, be found to be a "minimal burden." The monetary costs of security guards is not insignificant. Moreover, the obligation to provide patrols adequate to deter criminal conduct is not well defined. No one really knows why people commit crime, hence no one really knows what is "adequate" deterrence in any given situation. Finally, the social costs of imposing a duty on landowners to hire private police forces are also not insignificant. For these reasons, we conclude that a high degree of foreseeability is required in order to find that the scope of a landlord's duty of care includes the hiring of security guards. We further conclude that the requisite degree of foreseeability rarely, if ever, can be proven in the absence of prior similar incidents of violent crime on the landowner's premises. To hold otherwise would be to impose an unfair burden upon landlords and, in effect, would force landlords to become the insurers of public safety, contrary to well established policy in this state.

The court suggested that "it is possible that some other circumstances such as immediate proximity to a substantially similar business establishment that has experienced violent crime on its premises could provide the requisite degree of foreseeability." But the court concluded that this possible exception was not met in this case: "Violent criminal assaults were not sufficiently foreseeable to impose a duty upon [the mall owner] to provide security guards. [It] did not have notice of prior similar incidents occurring on the premises."

The court acknowledged that previous assaults and robberies had occurred at the mall, but it concluded that these offenses "were not similar in nature to the violent assault that [the victim in this case] suffered," and were not "sufficiently compelling to establish the high degree of foreseeability necessary to impose a duty to provide security guards."

The court noted that some properties, such as a parking garage or all-night convenience stores, may be so "inherently dangerous" that the owner may have a duty to employ security guards even without evidence of prior serious crimes on or near the property. But, such a rule would not apply to the typical retail store.[331]

• The California Supreme Court ruled that "only when heightened foreseeability of third party criminal activity on the premises exists--shown by prior similar incidents or other indications of a reasonably foreseeable risk of violent criminal assaults in that location— does the scope of a business proprietor's duty include an obligation to provide guards to protect the safety of patrons.[332]

---

[331] Ann M. v. Pacific Plaza Shopping Center, 25 Cal.Rptr.2d 137 (Cal. 1993).
[332] Delgado v. Trax Bar & Grill, 36 Cal.4th 224 (Cal. 2005).

• In a case discussed previously, a gunman entered a McDonald's restaurant and started shooting customers and employees. Before being killed by a police sharpshooter, the gunman killed 21 people and wounded 11 others. Several victims sued McDonald's for wrongful death and personal injuries, claiming that McDonald's failed to provide adequate security personnel to protect customers from dangerous and known risks. A California appeals court ruled that the restaurant's failure to hire security guards did not make it liable for the gunman's rampage. The court noted that there was no proof that the use of a uniformed, licensed security guard would have acted as a deterrent and prevented the shootings or minimized the extent of the harm. It stressed that "no one really knows why people commit crime, hence no one really knows what is 'adequate' deterrence in any given situation. While bright lights may deter some, they will not deter all. Some persons cannot be deterred by anything short of impenetrable walls and armed guards." The court concluded:

> Under the circumstances here, it cannot be reasonably urged that had McDonald's provided an unarmed, uniformed licensed security guard, the massacre would have been prevented or its extent diminished. The record defies such a conclusion. Rather, it paints a portrait of a demented, mentally unbalanced man, bent on murder and self-destruction, who viewed the nearby McDonald's restaurant with his binoculars from his apartment, kissed his wife goodbye and stated he was going "hunting for humans". He set out to kill the most people possible and went to the restaurant, unconcerned with detection, dressed in camouflage fatigue pants and heavily armed. Upon entry into the restaurant, he immediately began firing his weapons indiscriminately at everything and everyone in sight, reloading his weapons periodically and walking up and down the aisles slaughtering those he found still alive. His only apparent motive was killing. He made no effort to rob the restaurant, made no demands for money, and made no effort to take hostages. His indiscriminate slaughter of human beings--the worst mass killing by a single assailant in recent American history--only ended when he believed all were dead and he was felled by a police sharp-shooter. . . . Any reasonable protective measure such as security cameras, alarms and unarmed security guards, might have deterred ordinary criminal conduct because of the potential of identification and capture, but could not reasonably be expected to deter or hinder a maniacal, suicidal assailant unconcerned with his own safety, bent on committing mass murder.[333]

• The Louisiana Supreme Court ruled that a Wal-Mart store was not liable for an armed robbery of a customer in its parking lot. The customer claimed that Wal-Mart was liable for the robbery since it failed to post a security guard in the parking lot. The court disagreed. It applied a balancing test to determine whether a business owes a duty to protect its customers from the criminal acts of third persons. This test weighs the foreseeability of the crime risk on defendant's property and the gravity of the risk to determine the existence and the extent of defendant's duty. More specifically, the court held: "The greater the foreseeability and gravity of the harm, the greater the duty of care that will be imposed on the business. A very high degree of foreseeability is required to give rise to a duty to post security guards, but a lower degree of foreseeability may support a duty to implement lesser security measures such as using surveillance cameras."

---

[333] Lopez v. McDonald's Corporation, 238 Cal.Rptr. 436 (Cal. App. 1987).

> The court noted that the foreseeability and gravity of the harm are to be determined by the facts and circumstances of the case. The most important factor to be considered "is the existence, frequency and similarity of prior incidents of crime on the premises, but the location, nature and condition of the property should also be taken into account. It is highly unlikely that a crime risk will be sufficiently foreseeable for the imposition of a duty to provide security guards if there have not been previous instances of crime on the business' premises."
>
> The court found that during the prior six and one-half years the parking lot had been the scene of three predatory offenses and that the area surrounding the store was considered "a high crime area." This, however, was not enough for the court to find that Wal-Mart had a duty to post security guards in the parking lot.[334]

> • A Louisiana court ruled that a grocery store's failure to hire a security guard did not make it liable for the shooting of a customer by an armed gunman. The court observed: "Although business owners are not the insurers of their patrons' safety, they do have a duty to implement reasonable measures to protect their patrons from criminal acts when those acts are foreseeable. Generally, however, there is no duty to protect patrons from the criminal acts of third persons. Therefore, this duty only arises under limited circumstances, when the criminal act in question was reasonably foreseeable to the owner of the business. . . . The greater the foreseeability and gravity of the harm, the greater the duty of care that will be imposed on the business. A very high degree of foreseeability is required to give rise to a duty to post security guards, but a lower degree of foreseeability may support a duty to implement lesser security measures such as using surveillance cameras." The court concluded that the shooting in this case was not sufficiently foreseeable to impose upon the store a duty to hire security guards: "What we do know is that in the five years prior to this incident, there were not any criminal offenses committed on the premises. It is also relevant to note that [the victim] was shot at 9:00 a.m., and plaintiff's own security expert testified that he did not see that as a high crime time of day. Accordingly, we find that even though the area surrounding the store may have been a high crime area, the foreseeability and gravity of harm at 9:00 a.m. was extremely minimal. . . . Therefore . . . the store owed no duty to provide security guards."[335]

These cases, and many others, suggest that a church has no legal duty to hire security guards except in cases of "heightened foreseeability of third party criminal activity on the premises" due to "prior similar incidents or other indications of a reasonably foreseeable risk of violent criminal assaults on church property." Hiring one or more security guards is an expensive practice that will be justified only by a high degree of foreseeability that a shooting or other violent criminal act will occur on church property.

(3) negligent selection of security guard or security service

If a church decides to hire security guards, can it be liable for deaths and injuries that they cause, or fail to prevent, on the ground that the church was

---

[334] Posecai v. Wal-Mart Stores, Inc., 752 So.2d 762 (La. 1999).
[335] Mackey v. Jong's Super Value, 940 So.2d 118 (La. App. 2006).

negligent in selecting the guards? To illustrate, assume that a woman is shot by an armed assailant on church property despite the fact that the church employs a security guard. The woman sues the church, claiming that the church was negligent in selecting its security guard. She points out that the guard was not a police officer, had no law enforcement training, was not licensed, and had only minimal training in handling a firearm. Is it possible for the church to be responsible for her injuries under these circumstances? While no court has addressed this question in a published decision involving a church, a few have addressed the issue in other contexts. The principal cases are summarized below.

Case Studies

• A California court observed: "A security guard is liable to an injured customer when the guard fails to act reasonably and that failure causes injury. The business, in turn, may be liable for failing to hire a competent security guard. Having assumed the duty to protect one's patrons while on the premises of a business establishment, the proprietor will be liable if the guard acts unreasonably. Moreover, the proprietor will be directly liable when he or she negligently hires or retains an incompetent employee or negligently trains or supervises the employee. Under these circumstances, the injured patron need not prove the proprietor had notice of prior similar acts."[336]

• A Texas court ruled that an off-duty police officer acting as a security guard for a department store was acting "within the scope of his employment as a police officer" rather than as a security guard for the store when he allegedly used excessive force in apprehending a customer who was suspected of engaging in credit card fraud in a transaction. The victim sued the store on several grounds, including the negligent hiring of the security guard. The court observed:

> The basis of responsibility for negligent hiring and retention is the employer's negligence in hiring or retaining an incompetent employee who the employer knew or, in the exercise of ordinary care, should have known was incompetent or unfit, and thereby creating an unreasonable risk of harm to others. Negligence in hiring requires that the employer's failure to investigate, screen, or supervise its [employees] caused the injuries the plaintiffs allege. An employer is not negligent when there is nothing in the employee's background that would cause a reasonable employer not to hire or retain the employee.

The court noted that when an off-duty police officer acting as a department store's security guard attempts to apprehend a criminal, he or she is acting as an on-duty police officer. Since the officer is no longer acting as a store employee, the store cannot be liable for negligent hiring or retention based on the officer's alleged acts performed as an on-duty police officer. Further, even if the police officer was acting as a store employee at the time of the arrest, "there is no evidence which supports a claim of negligent hiring or retention. [The police officer] was hired by the store as a security officer in 1998. The record reflects, at that time, he had no complaints on his record. In order to demonstrate a claim for negligent hiring, there must be evidence

---

[336] Mata v. Mata, 130 Cal.Rptr.2d 141 (Cal. App. 2003).

in an employee's record that would cause a reasonable employer not to hire the employee."[337]

• *The Texas Supreme Court ruled that a night club was not responsible on the basis of negligent hiring for injuries inflicted by its security guard on an individual who had been denied admittance. The individual was turned away because he was intoxicated. He claimed that the club's security guard slammed his head against a concrete wall, knocking him unconscious, and then struck him several times. The altercation resulted in multiple injuries to the victim, including a fractured skull. The victim sued the club, claiming that it had been negligent in hiring the security guard. Specifically, the guard argued that the club was negligent in hiring the security guard because it did not perform a background check, did not require a job application, and allowed a third party to hire him. A jury found the club liable for its security guard's actions, but this outcome was reversed on appeal by the state supreme court on the ground that "there was insufficient evidence to support the jury's finding that [the club] was negligent or malicious in hiring and retaining [the guard]." The court concluded:*

> *There is no evidence to support the jury's finding that the club's lack of a background check caused the altercation or the injuries. As to negligence in hiring, the evidence indicates that even if the club had investigated the security guard before hiring him, nothing would have been found that would cause a reasonable employer to not hire him. The evidence showed that the security guard violated a requirement in the applicable peace officer manual by accepting employment at the club, and that his primary employer had reprimanded him for the use of a profanity to a member of the public. This evidence is not sufficient to have put the club on notice that hiring him would create a risk of harm to the public, even if the club had done a background check. . . .*
>
> *Also, no evidence was presented that the guard was an incompetent or unfit security guard such that the club was negligent in retaining him after he was hired. The club hired him as a security guard to assist in protecting its property and patrons, a job specially suited to a trained peace officer. While [the victim] presented evidence that the club did not perform a background check or train the security guard, his status as a certified peace officer made him fit for this type of work, and there was no conflicting evidence that he was unfit for the security position prior to the incident in question.*

The court noted that the security guard was a commissioned peace officer, and had attended a law enforcement academy.[338]

Such cases demonstrate that a church may be liable on the basis of negligent hiring for injuries caused by, or not prevented by, a security guard if the church failed to exercise reasonable care in investigating the competency of the guard before hiring him or her. However, this risk can be reduced by exercising reasonable care in selecting a security guard. As will be noted later in this section, the exercise of reasonable care can best be demonstrated by hiring only uniformed, off-duty police officers as security guards.

---

[337] Ogg v. Dillard's, Inc. 2007 WL 3317480 (unpublished decision, Tex. App. 2007).

[338] Fifth Club, Inc. v. Ramirez, 196 S.W.3d 788 (Tex. 2006).

(4) liability for acts of security guards

Churches that hire security guards may be liable for deaths and injuries caused by the negligence of their guards. This is so even if a church did not have a legal duty to hire security guards because criminal acts on church property were not foreseeable. As one court has observed, "We do not hold that business owners owe any duty to the public to provide security services generally. We simply find that where a business owner undertakes to provide security services, he remains liable as though he directly employed the security personnel, regardless of whether they are technically employed by an independent entity." The court noted that "the majority of jurisdictions that have considered this issue have reached the same conclusion [and] have recognized the existence of this specific nondelegable duty, either explicitly or by imposing vicarious liability on a store for the intentional torts of independently contracted security guards regardless of the nature of the employment relationship between the store and the security agency."[339]

Case Study

• *A Pizza Hut restaurant employed an off-duty uniformed and armed police officer as a security guard. The restaurant was in a high-crime area and had been robbed or burglarized more than 20 times. Three armed robbers entered the restaurant while the security guard was sitting at a table obscured from view behind a partition, reading a book and visiting with an acquaintance. One of the robbers pointed a shotgun at the officer's face and ordered him not to move. The officer allegedly made a slight movement to his right, which caused the robber to fire his shotgun. The blast missed the officer, but killed one patron and wounded another. The family of the deceased victim sued Pizza Hut, claiming that the shooting was caused by the security guard's negligence. The Louisiana Supreme Court agreed that the shooting was due to the security guard's negligence, and that this negligence could be imputed to Pizza Hut. The court found the following acts to have been negligent: (1) the security guard failed to position himself where he was clearly visible to potential armed robbers; (2) the security guard was eating a salad at a table inside the restaurant while on duty; (3) the security guard made a slight movement when ordered by one of the robbers not to move. The court concluded: "A business which undertakes to hire a security guard to protect itself and its patrons is liable for physical harm which occurs because of negligence on the part of that guard."[340]*

---

[339] Simon v. Safeway, Inc., 2007 WL 4441194 (unpublished decision, Ariz. App. 2007).

[340] Harris v. Pizza Hut, 455 So.2d 1364 (La. 1984).

3. Risk Management

> "[W]hat protective measures should be pursued to protect against a mass murderous assault truly defy exact delineation, because how can one know which measures will be effective against a degenerate, a psychopath or a psychotic?" *Lopez v. McDonald's Corporation, 238 Cal.Rptr. 436 (Cal. App. 1987).*

Courts, public figures, and law enforcement officials have all acknowledged that no level of risk management can thwart a dedicated killer from shooting people on church premises. President Bill Clinton, following a 1999 shooting rampage in a Texas church that left 7 dead and 7 more wounded, noted that "there is nothing we can do to assure that this will never happen, but there is a lot more we can do to assure that it will happen more rarely." Even the most stringent precautions will not prevent such incidents. To illustrate, consider a church that uses metal detectors at each entrance, and armed guards. Will these measures prevent shooting incidents from happening? Not at all. They would not stop a dedicated assailant who is sufficiently armed.

If no level of risk management can prevent such incidents from happening, what should churches do? Church leaders should view risk management as achieving four attainable objectives:

• Reduce the risk that shootings and other criminal assaults will happen on church property. In the words of President Clinton, "there is nothing we can do to assure that this will never happen, but there is a lot more we can do to assure that it will happen more rarely."

• Contain the damage if an incident should occur, through an appropriate response.

• Ensure that the church's precautionary measures satisfy the applicable legal duty of care. As noted previously, most courts have ruled that the level of precaution a property owner should take is proportional to the foreseeability that a shooting or other violent criminal act will occur on the property. The very highest level of care will be required when multiple crimes have occurred in recent years on or near church property involving shootings or other assaultive acts, or when a church receives a direct threat that a shooting or assault will occur.

• Ensure that the church's precautionary measures are consistent with its moral values. Most churches place a high value on human life as a result of theological and biblical principles, and may wish to adopt precautionary measures that transcend those of local businesses unconstrained by those principles.

Several precautionary measures are described below.

(1) security guards

Churches should consider using security guards in some situations, including the following

(a) A legal duty to employ security guards may exist because the risk of shootings or other violent crimes on church property is highly foreseeable based on the following factors described above:

   • whether any criminal conduct previously occurred on or near the property;

   • how recently and how often similar crimes occurred;

   • how similar the previous crimes were to the conduct in question; and

   • what publicity was given the previous crimes to indicate that the church knew or should have known about them.

(b) The use of one or more security guards is deemed necessary to further a church's theological and biblical principles, whether or not legally required.

As noted above, a church that uses security guards may be liable for deaths and injuries caused by the negligence of their guards based on at least two potential grounds: (1) negligent hiring, and (2) a nondelegable duty to exercise reasonable care in the protection of the public when a security guard is employed, whether or not the church had a legal duty to employ a guard. These risks make it imperative for churches that elect to use security guards to select persons of demonstrable competence. Consider the following options:

a. one or more armed, uniformed off-duty police officers during worship services and other events involving multiple persons

A church's risk of liability for injuries caused by, or not prevented by, a security guard can be reduced by exercising reasonable care in selecting a security guard. The exercise of reasonable care can best be demonstrated by hiring only uniformed, off-duty police officers as security guards since such persons:

   • are thoroughly screened before being hired as police officers;

   • receive extensive training in dealing with volatile situations;

   • receive extensive training in the use of firearms;

   • receive continuing training in the use of firearms, and other job-related skills;

- according to some courts, become "on-duty" police officers even while otherwise acting as private security guards when responding to criminal activity, which has the effect of insulating their employer from liability based on negligent hiring or retention for their actions; and

- serve as a deterrent to crime because of their police uniform.

Churches considering the use of uniformed off-duty police officers should check with the local police department regarding the recruitment of such persons as security guards, and the number that are needed.

b. one or more uniformed, private security guards

Some churches that decide to employ security guards may opt for uniformed, private security guards who are hired directly by the church, or who work for a security firm that provides guards to the church pursuant to a contractual agreement. Sometimes, these persons are member of the church with nothing more than a permit to carry a concealed weapon. Churches will find it more difficult to defend against a negligent hiring claim when hiring security guards who are not police officers. But the risk can be reduced to some degree through various means, including the following:

- conduct a thorough criminal records check on the individual;

- obtain several references, ideally from other institutions where the person has served as a security guard;

- make sure that the guard is licensed under state law (if possible); and

- have the individual complete a detailed application documenting all prior experience as a security guard or police officer, along with a full description of all prior law enforcement and firearms training, and any licenses or certifications the person currently has as a security guard, police officer, or firearms trainer, under state or federal law.

According to the United States Department of Labor:

Most States require that guards be licensed. To be licensed as a guard, individuals must usually be at least 18 years old, pass a background check, and complete classroom training in such subjects as property rights, emergency procedures, and detention of suspected criminals. Drug testing often is required and may be random and ongoing.

Guards who carry weapons must be licensed by the appropriate government authority, and some receive further certification as special police officers, allowing them to make limited types of arrests while on duty. Armed guard positions have more stringent background checks and entry requirements than those of unarmed guards.

An increasing number of states are making ongoing training a legal requirement for retention of licensure. Guards may receive training in protection, public relations, report writing, crisis deterrence, first aid, and specialized training relevant to their particular assignment.

The American Society for Industrial Security International has written voluntary training guidelines that are intended to provide regulating bodies consistent minimum standards for the quality of security services. These guidelines recommend that security guards receive at least 48 hours of training within the first 100 days of employment. The guidelines also suggest that security guards be required to pass a written or performance examination covering topics such as sharing information with law enforcement, crime prevention, handling evidence, the use of force, court testimony, report writing, interpersonal and communication skills, and emergency response procedures. In addition, they recommend annual retraining and additional firearms training for armed officers. . . .

Obviously, security guards with little or no training, and who are not licensed under state law, present the greatest risk of liability to a church or other employer as a result of injuries they inflict while responding to a crime or otherwise performing their duties, or injuries they fail to prevent.

c. using church members legally authorized to carry a concealed weapon as non-uniformed security guards

Such persons generally offer the least risk reduction of any category of security guard if they have little or no law enforcement training, and are not licensed as security guards under state law. Further, they do not provide the possible deterrence that accompanies a uniform, even it is a uniform of a private security guard rather than a police officer.

d. ushers and greeters

While technically not security guards, properly trained ushers and greeters can serve a vital role in alerting the church's crisis response team, or local law enforcement, to suspicious behavior or acts of violence when they occur. Often, such persons may be the first responders. For this reason, it is important for them to carry cell phones.

(2) technology

Like security guards, crime-fighting technologies should be implemented as a result of either or both of the following grounds:

(a) A legal duty to install technological devices may exist because the risk of shootings or other violent crimes on church property is highly foreseeable based on the following factors described above:

- whether any criminal conduct previously occurred on or near the property;

- how recently and how often similar crimes occurred;

- how similar the previous crimes were to the conduct in question; and

- what publicity was given the previous crimes to indicate that the church knew or should have known about them.

(b) The use of one or more technological devices is deemed necessary to further a church's theological and biblical principles, whether or not legally required.

In evaluating the feasibility of various technologies to prevent or reduce the risk of shootings in public schools, the United States Department of Justice noted that the effectiveness, affordability, and acceptability of each technology must be considered. To illustrate, many church leaders would regard metal detectors at church entrances to be unacceptable, even if affordable and effective, because they are incompatible with the concept of "sanctuary" and are at odds with biblical assurances of providence and divine protection. For many smaller churches, such devices would be unaffordable.

Listed below are three different devices that often are used to prevent or reduce the risk of crime. In each case, church leaders should consider the device's effectiveness, affordability, and acceptability in evaluating its usefulness.

a. surveillance cameras

Surveillance cameras ordinarily cannot prevent shootings and other violent crimes on church property, but they can act as a deterrent to crime, provide a record of what happened, allow church staff to monitor the entire church campus from a single location, and expedite a call to the police in the event of suspicious behavior.

On the downside: (1) surveillance cameras are expensive, and this disadvantage is compounded when multiple cameras are employed; (2) someone must be tasked with the responsibility of continually checking the monitors, and this removes the person from performing more active surveillance by personally visiting areas where people congregate; (3) selecting the appropriate equipment requires technical knowledge; (4) ongoing maintenance and operational support are required; (5) some individuals will challenge the need for cameras in a church; (6) persons with knowledge of the installed video system's capabilities may not be deterred by them, and possibly could circumvent the system to their advantage or simply carry out their criminal acts in a different area of the church; and (7) cameras will not deter dedicated assailants, especially if they plan on killing themselves at the end of their crime spree.

Effectiveness of Security Cameras

"Experiments were run at Sandia National Laboratories 20 years ago for the U.S. Department of Energy to test the effectiveness of an individual whose task was to sit in front of a video monitors for several hours a day and watch for particular events. These studies demonstrated that such a task, even when assigned to a person who is dedicated and well-intentioned, will not support an effective security system. After only 20 minutes of watching and evaluating monitor screens, the attention of most individuals has degenerated to well below acceptable levels. Monitoring video screens is both boring and mesmerizing. There is no intellectually engaging stimuli, such as when watching a television program. This is particularly true if a staff member is asked to watch multiple monitors, with scenes of [persons] milling about in various hallways, in an attempt to watch for security incidents." [341]

b. metal detectors

Most church leaders, even in high crime areas, would consider the use of metal detectors at church entrances to be so offensive to congregational members and visitors, and so fundamentally incompatible with the nature of the church as a sanctuary, that their use would be unthinkable. As noted above, risk management technologies must be evaluated in terms of their effectiveness, affordability, and acceptability. Even if metal detectors at church entrances would be an effective deterrent to violent crime, and affordable, they would be considered unacceptable by most church members. This would especially be so for churches in low crime areas, and with no history of shootings or other violent crimes on or near church property. In summary, the use of metal detectors at church entrances would be an extraordinary measure justified by only a high foreseeability of violent crime. Few churches, even in high crime areas, utilize these devices.

Here are some points to note about metal detectors:

• Metal detectors work very well. They are considered a mature technology and can accurately detect the presence of most types of firearms and knives.

• However, metal detectors work very poorly if the user is not aware of their limitations before beginning a weapon detection program and is not prepared for the amount of trained and motivated manpower required to operate these devices successfully.

• When a questionable item or material is detected by such a device, the detector produces an alarm signal; this signal can be audible, visible (lights), or both. Unfortunately, a metal detector alone cannot distinguish between a gun and a large metal belt buckle. This shortcoming is what makes weapon detection programs impractical in many contexts. Trained employees are needed to make these determinations.

---

[341] Department of Justice, Research Report: The Appropriate and Effective Use of Security Technologies in U.S. Schools.

• Metal detectors are usually not effective when used on purses, bookbags, briefcases, or suitcases. There is usually a large number of different objects or materials located in or as part of the composition of these carried items that would cause an alarm.

• The difficulty in interpreting the results of metal detector scans will require many persons to be pulled aside, as at an airport, for more thorough screening, including pat downs. The end result will be clogged lines of parishioners, shoes in hand, impatiently waiting to enter their church. One can easily imagine the firestorm this would elicit.

• Walk-through metal detectors are expensive. An additional cost would be the use of trained operators.

• A greater problem is the churches usually have multiple entry points. Few churches can afford to have multiple entry setups with complete metal detection equipment and trained operators. The cost of the equipment would be quite high, but not nearly as prohibitive as the manpower to run these multiple systems.

• Metal detectors would not stop a dedicated and armed assailant, who could overpower the screeners.

• Hand-held scanners are available, but generally are used as a supplement to portal metal detectors. As in airports procedures, the hand-held detectors allow the security staff to more accurately locate the source of an alarm on a person's body, after he or she has already walked through a portal system and triggered an alarm.

Pitfalls of Metal Detectors

"The initial purchase price of a portal metal detector is almost insignificant compared with the ongoing personnel costs to operate the equipment in a complete weapon detection program. An excellent example that illustrates this fact is the successful weapon detection program run by the New York City (NYC) Board of Education in about 50 of its inner-city high schools. For just one of its schools with about 2,000 students, the weapon detection program requires 9 security officers for approximately 2 hours each morning. Two officers run the two initial portal metal detectors, two officers run the baggage x-ray machines, one officer runs the secondary portal metal detector for students who fail the initial detector, two officers (a male and a female) operate the hand scanners on students who fail the secondary metal detector, and two officers keep the students flowing smoothly and quickly through the system, such that nobody is able to bypass any part of the system. It should be noted that the only way these schools are able to avoid huge waiting lines, even with this much equipment and this many officers, and still get everybody to class on time is by a complete restructuring of their class periods. There is a significant staggering of first period start times so that the students arrive over a 90-minute period." [342]

---

[342] *Id.*

c. entry control technologies

There are four principal ways that places of public accommodation can permit or deny access. The first and most common approach is manpower intensive, and the remaining three employ technology devices. These four approaches are:

- A security guard controls entry; ID cards or other means of identification may be checked.

- Electronic devices, such as a card reader, check special ID cards or badges issued to persons whose access is permitted. Viable card technologies for schools include bar codes or magnetic strips for card-swipe readers (such as those used for most credit cards) or passive or active radio frequency (RF) cards for proximity readers, which can validate a card several inches to several feet away (depending on the cost of the system).

- A PIN number is issued to persons whose access is permitted, and such persons enter the number on a keypad to gain admittance.

- A biometric device for feature recognition.

Such measures, like the use of metal detectors at church entrances, would not stop an armed and dedicated assailant. In addition, they would not be acceptable to most congregations since:

- They would exclude visitors from attending church.

- They would not accommodate members who forget their badge or card, or forget their PIN number. This could happen to any member, but the elderly would be most vulnerable to unintended exclusion.

- Card readers do not read cards that have become demagnetized.

- In the case of keypads and card readers, there is no way to ascertain that only a single authorized person is entering, since unauthorized persons could "tailgate" (follow an authorized person through the checkpoint).

- Cards and badges can be stolen and used by unauthorized persons.

- The cost of a card or badge reader, or keypad system, can be substantial, especially if used at more than one entry.

- Keypads and card readers are prone to malfunction. The prospect of unhappy church members standing outside in the rain, unable to enter their church because of a machine malfunction, is an unpleasant but virtually certain scenario.

Some churches use keypads or card readers during the week to restrict access to church employees.

(3) signage

Conspicuous signs at church entrances may serve many purposes. Their value to security should not be underestimated. Signs are not overly expensive, but the price of not having one can sometimes be substantial. Consider the following:

• Signs that inform persons entering a building that certain security measures are in place can provide a frontline deterrent. Without any other knowledge, an outsider faced with the choice of committing an assault or other violent crime in a church with security warning signs or one with no signs or other obvious indications of self-defense will often choose the latter.

• A church's potential liability can be reduced through the use of signs. A piece of information that can be important to include on a warning sign is whether cameras are not being monitored. Some victims of assaults in a public building have filed successful lawsuits, claiming that they did nothing to defend themselves because they were under the impression that, because a video camera was aimed directly at them, help would surely arrive soon. This is a common assumption. They did not realize that the camera was not being monitored. Sample wording for a school sign regarding this particular issue could be: WARNING: This facility employs video surveillance equipment for security purposes. This equipment may or may not be monitored at any time.

(4) other measures

Unfortunately, recent tragedies in the United States have demonstrated the need for churches to be prepared to respond to shootings and other violent crimes. The United States Department of Justice has prepared the following recommendations for schools to help reduce the risk of violent crime (the word "church" is substituted for "school"). *Department of Justice, Research Report: The Appropriate and Effective Use of Security Technologies in U.S. Schools.*

• Every church needs a well-thought-out, annually updated crisis plan, with regular training for all those who might be involved.

• The crisis plan needs to make assignments of who is in charge during different types of emergencies; who is the alternate in charge; who is called first, by whom, from where, and using what; whether persons are relocated and how; what type of statement is made to the press and by whom; and who is in charge when emergency teams (fire, police, and so forth) arrive on the scene. These are only a few of the specifications called for.

• In the best of all possible situations, a predetermined team will immediately be mobilized upon the occurrence of a serious situation. Team members will know who to look to for decisions and then proceed automatically in their roles for the particular plan chosen to be implemented.

• Crisis team members should wear distinctive clothing, and be located in places of high visibility, so they be contacted in the event of a crisis.

• Crisis team members should immediately contact local law enforcement when a crisis is reported, either on a cell phone or 2-way radio. All crisis team members should have one or both of these devices with them at all times while on church premises.

• Consider the use of "duress alarms" that anyone can activate to report a crisis. These can activate an audible alarm, or an inaudible alarm that is detected only by crisis team members.

• Be sure to have your crisis plan reviewed by local law enforcement professionals; your insurance agent; and an attorney.

Conclusions

Listed below are several conclusions, based on the material presented in this section:

• Church shootings, and other violent crimes on church premises, are rare.

• The law imposes upon any place of public accommodation, including a church, a duty to protect occupants against foreseeable criminal acts. The level of protection is directly proportional to the degree of foreseeability. Many courts assess foreseeability on the basis of the following factors: (1) whether any criminal conduct previously occurred on or near the property; (2) how recently and how often similar crimes occurred; (3) how similar the previous crimes were to the conduct in question; and (4) what publicity was given the previous crimes to indicate that the church knew or should have known about them. If shootings or other violent crimes on church property are highly foreseeable based on these factors, then a church has a heightened duty to implement measures to protect occupants from such acts.

• Many church leaders and congregations, guided and informed by their theological values, feel compelled to take steps to protect human life from acts of violence whether or not they have a legal duty to do so.

• In evaluating which measures to implement in order to discharge a legal or moral duty to protect occupants, church leaders should consider the affordability, effectiveness, and acceptability of a measure before implementing it.

• Church leaders should consult with local law enforcement professionals, the church insurance agent, and legal counsel, in making decisions regarding which protective measures to implement. These same persons should also review the church's crisis response plan.

• Contact other churches and other places of public accommodation in your community to see what measures they have enacted to protect occupants against shootings and other violent crimes. Examples include schools, malls, libraries, restaurants, stores, sports facilities, theatres, and concert halls. This research will help church leaders ascertain the "community standard," which is an important consideration in deciding if a property owner was negligent.

• Note that even the most stringent protective measures would have prevented few if any of the 15 shooting incidents on church property summarized in this section. In fact, in some of these cases, the church had implemented what seemed to be reasonable precautionary measures. However, no measures will foil an armed and dedicated assailant, especially if that person plans on taking his or her own life.

• While it is not possible for churches to prevent acts of violence on their premises, it is possible to deter such acts in some cases, and to contain the damage and destruction when an incident erupts.

Church Parking Lots

This section has addressed shootings and other violent crimes inside churches. Criminal acts also may occur in church parking lots. While these may include assaults, shootings, abductions, and rapes, they more often involve vandalism and property offenses. As with criminal acts occurring in church buildings, a church's legal duty to implement risk-reducing measurers in the parking lot will be based on the foreseeability that criminal acts will occur there. Churches have used some or all of the following measures to address this risk:

(1) Provide adequate illumination of the parking lot.

(2) Designate persons who will accompany members to their car upon request. Be sure that this option is communicated to the congregation.

(3) Install one or more wide-angle video cameras on the church roof to monitor parking areas.

(4) Have a uniformed security guard, or off-duty police officer, monitor the parking lot.

For more suggestions, church leaders should contact local law enforcement officials and the church's insurance agent.

Skate Ramps

§ 7-20.5

Key point 7-20.5. *Some churches have installed skate ramps on their property as a means of outreach to the community. Skate ramps involve significant legal risks that must be recognized and managed.*

Church leaders should consider the following points before installing a skateboard ramp on church property:

1. **A high-risk activity.** Skateboarding is inherently dangerous. While most injuries are scrapes and bruises, more serious injuries including brain injuries and death sometimes occur. The risk is elevated because of

the tendency of skateboarders to mimic stunts they see on television. Some injuries occur to bystanders who are struck by flying skateboards. The U.S. Consumer Product Safety Commission reported that 104,000 persons were treated in hospital emergency rooms in a recent year due to skateboard-related injuries. Most injuries were sustained by minors who often lack the balance and fine motor skills required for the safe operation of a skateboard.

2. **City ordinances.** Many cities have enacted ordinances addressing skateboarding on private property that is open to the public (i.e., parking lots). It is important to know if your community has enacted such legislation, since these laws will directly address your question. The typical ordinance specifies that skateboarding is prohibited on private property that is open to the public so long as the property owner posts one or more signs that provide reasonable notice to the public that skateboarding is not permitted. The size and content of such signs is usually prescribed by the ordinance. Many of these ordinances include roller blades, roller skates, and other devices. Violators generally are punished with confiscation of the offending device plus a small fine. Fines may increase with subsequent violations.

3. **State laws.** Some states have enacted laws that address skateboarding. To illustrate, the New York legislature enacted a law in 2004 requiring minors to wear helmets while skateboarding. Such legislation is based on the dramatic reduction in serious injuries among skateboarders who wear helmets. It is important for church leaders to be familiar with any state requirements, especially if they operate a skateboarding program.

4. **Unsupervised ramps.** Some churches construct skateboard ramps as a means of reaching out to minors, whether members of the church or not. Such facilities may be unsupervised, or supervised. To illustrate, many cities operate unsupervised skateboard parks that contain notices informing the public that the facility is unsupervised, that persons use it at their own risk, and that users must comply with enumerated safety requirements which typically include the following: (1) the use of helmets and knee and elbow pads; (2) no night-time use; (3) no modifications to the facility; (4) no motorized devices or other wheeled devices are allowed; (5) all users must inspect the ramps prior to use; and (6) a minimum age. Obviously, unsupervised skateboard ramps expose a church to some risk of liability, especially for injuries to minors who, according to some courts, cannot "assume" risks.

5. **Supervised ramps.** Some churches construct skateboard ramps as part of a supervised program. Users may include minors or adults, and church members or nonmembers. The risk of liability for supervised ramps is often managed by adopting various precautions, including some or all of the following: (1) The same precautions mentioned under "unsupervised ramps." (2) All adult users sign an assumption of risk form. (3) All

minors are required to provide a document signed by a parent that consents to their use of the ramp and authorizes emergency medical treatment in the event that a parent or guardian cannot be reached. Contact information for the parents or guardians should be provided on the form. Some churches incorporate a liability release in the form, but such releases often are ineffective in the case of minors.

Note that a church's liability for injuries to skateboarders occurring during a supervised program will be based on negligent supervision. Be sure that you are providing adequate supervision. Check with other operators of skateboard ramps to see how they are supervising their activities.

6. Insurance. Check to be sure that the risks associated with skateboard ramps are covered by the church's insurance policy. Your insurer may have additional recommendation addressing risk management.

7. Other charities. Check with other churches and charities that use skate ramps to find out what they are doing to manage the risks. Adopt procedures and precautions that you consider helpful.

8. Legal review. Given the high level of risk, a church should not construct and operate a skateboarding facility without the prior review and approval of legal counsel.

Sound Rooms

§ 7-20.6

Key point 7-20.6. *Many churches have installed sound rooms on their property to centralize and enhance to audio quality of worship services and special events. Sound rooms involve unique legal risks that must be recognized and managed.*

Many churches have sound rooms in which a volunteer or employee operates and controls sound equipment during religious services and other events. Such rooms are often enclosed, and are magnets for minors who are attracted to the technical equipment. A number of cases of child molestation have occurred in church sound rooms. Often, the sound technician invites minors to "assist" him in operating the equipment, and arranges "training" at times when the room is isolated and unsupervised. It is a perfect arrangement for a child molester.

In a case in Georgia, a church choir director also operated the church's audiovisual equipment during various events. He sexually molested two minors who were assisting him in the sound room. The offender was charged with aggravated child molestation, and was convicted. A state appeals court concluded that there was ample evidence for conviction, but ordered a new trial due to ineffective trial counsel.[343]

---

[343] Johnson v. State, 643 S.E.2d 556 (Ga. App. 2007).

This case demonstrates the risk posed by sound rooms. Church leaders should recognize this risk, and take steps to manage it. Here are ten precautions to consider:

(1) Do a thorough background check on any persons who have access to the sound room.

(2) Prohibit any "training" of minors in the sound room at any time, unless there are two prescreened adults present at all times. Risk is reduced even more if all training of minors is prohibited, even with two adults present.

(3) Do not let minors "assist" sound technicians in the sound room unless there are two prescreened adults present at all times. Risk is reduced even more if minors are prohibited from helping in the sound room, even with two adults present.

(4) "Training" of minors in the sound room during times when few if any persons are present at the church should be strictly forbidden.

(5) Display a large and conspicuous summary of your restrictions in the sound room.

(6) Any sound technician who violates any of your restrictions should immediately be relieved of all responsibilities in the sound room.

(7) The sound room should be locked except when needed for church use (services and other events, repairs, installation of new equipment, etc.).

(8) Check with a local attorney for additional recommendations.

(9) Check with your insurance agent for additional recommendations.

(10) Check with other churches and charities in your area to see what kind of restrictions they have implemented.

Embezzlement
§ 7-21

Key point 7-21. *Embezzlement refers to the wrongful conversion of funds that are lawfully in one's possession. Embezzlement is a common occurrence in churches because of weak internal controls.*

1. In General

As hard as it may be to believe, embezzlement is a relatively common occurrence in churches. As a result, it is important for church leaders to take this risk seriously.

Why Church Leaders Should Take the Risk of Embezzlement Seriously
• **Removing temptation.** Churches that take steps to prevent embezzlement remove a source of possible temptation from church employees and volunteers who work with money.
• **Protecting reputations.** By taking steps to prevent embezzlement, a church protects the reputation of innocent employees and volunteers who otherwise might be suspected of financial wrongdoing when financial irregularities occur.
• **Avoiding confrontations.** By taking steps to prevent embezzlement, a church avoids the unpleasant task of confronting individuals who are suspected of embezzlement.
• **Avoiding church division.** By taking steps to prevent embezzlement, a church avoids the risk of congregational division that often is associated with cases of embezzlement—with some members wanting to show mercy to the offender and others demanding justice.
• **Avoiding the need to inform donors.** By taking steps to prevent embezzlement, a church reduces the risk of having to tell donors that some of their contributions have been misappropriated by a church employee or volunteer.
• **Protecting the reputation of church leaders.** By taking steps to prevent embezzlement, a church reduces the damage to the reputation and stature of its leaders who otherwise may be blamed for allowing embezzlement to occur.
• **Preserving accountability.** Churches that take steps to prevent embezzlement help to create a "culture of accountability" with regard to church funds.

2. Definition of Embezzlement

The definition of embezzlement varies slightly from state to state, but in general it refers to the wrongful conversion of property that is lawfully in your possession. The idea is that someone has legal control or custody of property or funds, and then decides to convert the property or funds to his or her own personal use.

Most people who embezzle funds insist that they intended to pay the money back and were simply "borrowing" the funds temporarily. An intent to pay back embezzled funds is not a defense to the crime of embezzlement. Most church employees who embezzle funds plan on repaying the church fully before anyone suspects what has happened. One can only imagine how many such schemes actually work without anyone knowing about it. The courts are not persuaded by the claims of embezzlers that they intended to fully pay back the funds they misappropriated. The crime is complete when the embezzler misappropriates the church's funds to his or her own personal use. As one court has noted:

The act of embezzlement is complete the moment the official converts the money to his own use even though he then has the intent to restore it. Few embezzlements are committed except with the full belief upon the part of the guilty person that he can and will restore the property before the day of accounting occurs. There is where the danger lies and the statute prohibiting embezzlement is passed in order to protect the public against such venturesome enterprises by people who have money in their control.

In short, it does not matter that someone intended to pay back embezzled funds. This intent in no way justifies or excuses the crime. The crime is complete when the funds are converted to one's own use--whether or not there was an intent to pay them back.

What if the embezzled funds are returned? The crime of embezzlement has occurred even if the embezzled funds in fact are paid back. Of course, it may be less likely that a prosecutor will prosecute a case under these circumstances. And even if the embezzler is prosecuted, this evidence may lessen the punishment. But the courts have consistently ruled that an actual return of embezzled funds does not purge the offense of its criminal nature or absolve the embezzler from punishment.

Key point. *Even if an embezzler is caught or confesses, and then agrees to "pay back" the embezzled funds, church officials seldom know if all embezzled funds are being returned. They are relying almost entirely on the word of a thief.*

3. Why Churches Are Vulnerable

Many churches refuse to adopt measures to reduce the risk of embezzlement out of a fear that such measures will reflect a lack of trust in those persons who handle church funds.

• **Examples** *Tom has counted the church offering at his church for 25 years. The church board has discussed this arrangement several times, but fails to stop it out of a fear of offending Tom.*

4. How Embezzlement Occurs

Let's look at a few cases of actual embezzlement of church funds to see how it can occur.

• *An usher collected offerings each week in the church balcony, and pocketed all loose bills while carrying the offering plates down a stairway to the main floor. Church officials later estimated that he embezzled several thousands of dollars over a number of years, before being caught.*

• *The same two persons counted church offerings for many years. Each week they removed all loose coins and currency (not in offering envelopes) and split it between them. This practice went on for several years, and church officials later estimated that the two had embezzled several tens of thousands of dollars.*

• *A church left its Sunday offering, along with the official count, in a safe in the church office until Monday. On Monday morning a church employee deposited the offering. The employee ignored the official counts, and deposited the offering less loose coins and currency (which she retained). The deposits were never checked against the offering counts.*

• *A church child care director embezzled church funds by issuing herself paychecks for the gross amount of her pay (before deductions for tax withholding). The church withheld taxes and paid them to the government, but her paychecks reflected the gross amount of her pay.*

• *A pastor had the sole authority to write checks on the church's checking account. He used church funds to pay for several personal expenses, amounting to thousands of dollars each year, until his actions were discovered.*

• *A church bookkeeper embezzled several thousand dollars by issuing checks to a fictitious company. He opened an account in the name of a fictitious company, issued church checks to the company for services that were never performed, and then deposited the checks in the fictitious company's account. He later withdrew the funds and purchased two automobiles which he gave to a friend. A court ruled that the friend had to give the cars back to the church, since they had been purchased with embezzled church funds. The point here, as noted by the court, is that one who acquires property that was purchased with embezzled church funds may be required to transfer the property to the church.*

• *A church bookkeeper's responsibilities included managing the church's bank account, maintaining financial records, and handling the church's finances. A few years after she started working at the church, she began to misappropriate church funds by issuing unauthorized checks to herself, her personal creditors, and other individuals. According to the church's investigation, she embezzled nearly $560,000 over an eight-year period. The embezzlement was eventually discovered, and the bookkeeper was arrested and charged with grand theft. She pled guilty to misappropriating the funds and was convicted of grand theft and sentenced to a ten-year prison term.*[344]

• *A minister received an unauthorized kickback of 5% of all funds paid by a church to a contractor who had been hired to build a new church facility. The minister received over $80,000 from this arrangement, in exchange for which he persuaded the church to use the contractor. The minister's claim that the $80,000 represented a legal and nontaxable "love offering" was rejected by a federal court that found the minister guilty of several felony counts. This arrangement was not disclosed to the church board, and obviously amounted to an unauthorized diversion of church funds back to the minister.*

---

[344] Magpusao v. Magpusao, 265 B.R. 492 (M.D. Fla. 2001).

• A volunteer church treasurer began using church funds to pay a number of personal debts, including his mortgage, his cell phone bill, a car loan, and other personal expenses. On several occasions, he made the checks payable to himself and indicated "payroll" on the checks. After the end of his two-year term as treasurer, his successor discovered the discrepancies in the church's accounts. It was later determined that 142 checks, worth $82,130, had been "written outside the scope" of the former treasurer's authority and for his personal benefit. The church informed the police, and the former treasurer was charged with five separate counts of embezzlement.[345]

• A church accountant embezzled $212,000 in church funds. This person's scheme was to divert to his own use several designated offerings, and to inflate the cost of equipment that he paid for with his own funds and that the church later reimbursed at the inflated amounts. The interesting aspect of this case was that the accountant was not only found guilty of embezzlement, but he was also convicted for tax evasion because he had failed to report any of the embezzled money as taxable income, and was sentenced to prison.

• A court ruled that an insurance company that paid out $26,000 to a charity because of an act of embezzlement could sue the embezzler for the full amount that it paid. This is an important case, for it demonstrates that a church employee who embezzles church funds may be sued by the church insurance company if it pays out a claim based on the embezzlement. In other words, the fact that the church decides not to sue the embezzler does not mean that the person will be free from any personal liability. If the church has insurance to cover the loss, the insurance company can go after the embezzler for a full recovery of the amount that it paid out on account of the embezzlement.

• Two deacons were responsible for collecting offerings from church members, depositing the funds into the church's bank account, and paying for authorized maintenance and repairs to the church building and facilities. Both deacons were authorized to sign checks individually, without the safeguard of requiring two signatories. They were not, however, authorized to make expenditures without the approval of the members, which was determined at meetings held after church services. Over the course of six months, one of the deacons (the "defendant") wrote checks totaling $1,600 to himself, with no documentation showing that he used the funds to pay for expenditures authorized by the congregation. When the other deacon became aware of the defendant's behavior, he notified law enforcement officials. An investigation was initiated that resulted in the indictment of the defendant for embezzlement. The jury found him guilty, and he was sentenced to a ten-year term of imprisonment and ordered to pay restitution in the amount of $2,255.[346]

• A church administrator embezzled over $350,000 from his church. He wrote unauthorized checks to himself and others from the church's accounts, and used the church's credit card on over 300 occasions to purchase personal items. Police officers were called and he made a full confession. The church secured a $1 million civil judgment against him. He was prosecuted and convicted on four felony counts

---

[345] Bragg v. Commonwealth, 593 S.E.2d 558 (Va. App. 2004).

[346] Coleman v. State, 947 So.2d 878 (Miss. 2006) (the verdict was reversed on appeal due to a technicality).

including forgery and theft, and was sentenced to 32 years in prison based on "aggravated circumstances" (the large amount of money that had been stolen, the care and planning that went into the crimes and their concealment, the fact that a great number of checks were stolen and unauthorized credit card charges made, and breach of trust). Several years earlier, the administrator embezzled a large amount from a prior church employer. However, that church chose not to initiate criminal charges, believing that he had learned his lesson.[347]

5. Reducing the Risk of Embezzlement

Can the risk of embezzlement be reduced? If so, how? The good news is that there are number of steps that church leaders can take to reduce this risk, and most of them are quite simple. Consider the following:

1. **Implement an effective system of internal control.** The first and most effective deterrent to embezzlement is a strong system of "internal control." Internal control is an accounting term that refers to policies and procedures adopted by an organization to safeguard its assets and promote the accuracy of its financial records. What procedures has your church adopted to insure that cash receipts are properly recorded and deposited, and that only those cash disbursements that are properly authorized are made? These are the kinds of questions that are addressed by a church's system of internal control. A table in this chapter addresses a number of common weaknesses in church internal control that increase the risk of embezzlement. The table provides helpful suggestions for responding to these weaknesses.

Key point. The most important point to emphasize is "division of responsibilities." The more that tasks and responsibilities are shared or divided, the less risk there will be of embezzlement.

Key point. Many churches refuse to implement basic principles of internal control out of a fear of "offending" persons who may feel that they are being suspected of misconduct. The issue here is not one of hurt feelings, but accountability. The church, more than any other institution in society, should set the standard for financial accountability. After all, its programs and activities are rooted in religion, and it is funded entirely with donations from persons who rightfully assume that their contributions are being used for religious purposes. The church has a high responsibility to promote financial accountability. This duty is simply not met when the practices described above are followed.

2. **Screen persons with financial responsibility.** Some churches screen bookkeepers, accountants, and other employees who will have access to funds or be involved in financial decisions. Screening can consist

---

[347] Kemp v. State, 887 N.E.2d 102 (Ind. App. 2008). A state appeals court, calling the offenses "undeniably despicable," reduced the sentence from 32 to 16 years based on the "mitigating factors" of no prior criminal record and a full confession.

of obtaining references from employers, prior employers, and other churches or charities with which the person has been employed or associated.

3. **Annual audits.** A church can reduce the risk of embezzlement by having an annual audit of its financial records by a CPA firm. An audit accomplishes three important functions:

• An audit promotes an environment of accountability in which opportunities for embezzlement (and therefore the risk of embezzlement) are reduced.

• The CPA (or CPAs) who conducts the audit will provide the church leadership with a "management letter" that points out weaknesses and inefficiencies in the church's accounting and financial procedures. This information is invaluable to church leaders.

• An audit contributes to the integrity and reputation of church leaders and staff members who handle funds.

Key point. *Don't confuse an audit with a more limited engagement that CPAs will perform, such as a "compilation."*

Key point. *Audits can be expensive, and this will be a very relevant consideration for smaller churches. Of course, the time involved in performing an audit for a smaller church will be limited, which will result in a lower fee. Churches can control the cost of an audit by obtaining bids. Also, by staying with the same CPA firm, most churches will realize a savings in the second and succeeding years since the CPA will not have to spend time becoming familiar with the church's financial and accounting procedures.*

Key point. *Smaller churches that cannot afford a full audit may want to consider two other options: (1) Hire a CPA to conduct a review, which is a simpler and less expensive procedure. If the review detects irregularities, a full audit may be considered worth the price. (2) Create an internal audit committee if there are accountants or business leaders within the church who have the ability to review accounting procedures and practices and look for weaknesses. These people often are very familiar with sound internal control policies, and will quickly correct weaknesses in the church's financial operations. An added bonus--such a committee will serve as a deterrent to those who might otherwise be tempted to embezzle church funds.*

4. **Bonding of persons who handle funds.** Churches can address the risk of embezzlement by bonding the church treasurer and any bookkeeper or accountant that is on staff. You can also purchase a blanket policy to cover all employees and officers. It is important to note that insurance policies vary. Some require that the embezzler be convicted before it will pay a claim, while others do not. The period of time covered by the policy will also vary. These are important points to be discussed by your church board in consultation with your insurance agent.

Key point. *Insurance is not a substitute for implementing a sound system of internal control.*

Table 7-1 How Embezzlement Occurs: Common Examples of Poor Internal Control		
example of poor internal control	**how embezzlement may occur**	**preventive action**
(1) One person counts church offerings.	This person may remove cash, especially if not in an offering envelope.	Have more than one person count each offering. The more persons that are involved, the lower the risk of embezzlement.
(2) There is not regular turnover or rotation among the persons who count church offerings.	The same two persons count church offerings every week. After a number of years, they agree to remove cash and divide it between them.	A pool of counters should be identified, and each offering should be counted by a randomly selected number of persons from this pool.
(3) One person collects the offerings.	An usher collects offerings in the church balcony during each service, and while carrying offerings down a stairway to a counting room he pockets all loose bills.	There should be at least two persons who collect the offering in the balcony, and they should together carry the offering down the stairs to the counting room. Further, these persons should be rotated.
(4) Offering counts are submitted to the person who deposits the offering.	The counters provide the individual who deposits the offering with a count. This individual disregards the count, withholds several bills unaccompanied by offering envelopes, and then deposits the lower amount.	Different persons should count and deposit church offerings. A person who neither counts offerings nor deposits them with a bank should be assigned the responsibility of reconciling offering counts with the bank deposit slips.
(5) Offering counts and bank deposit slips are not regularly reconciled.	A church only assigns an employee to reconcile the first offering of each month with a bank deposit slip. The person who deposits offerings is aware of this practice, and embezzles loose cash before depositing offerings from the remaining services of each month.	Offering counts and bank deposit slips should be reconciled for every service. Or, reconcile offering counts with monthly bank statements.

Table 7-1 How Embezzlement Occurs: Common Examples of Poor Internal Control		
example of poor internal control	how embezzlement may occur	preventive action
(6) Only one signature is needed to write a check.	A church employee is given sole signature authority on the church's checking account. The employee pays for a number of personal expenses with this checking account.	At least two signatures should be required for all checks above a nominal amount.
(7) Members who contribute coins and currency (not checks) do not use offering envelopes.	This is one of the major causes of embezzlement. Persons who embezzle church funds often restrict their activities to cash that was not contributed in an offering envelope. Embezzlers assume that it will be more difficult to detect their behavior under these circumstances, since the church cannot provide these donors with a receipt for their contributions (that will reveal discrepancies).	Churches should provide offering envelopes to all members for each week, and also place them in church pews for easy access. Members should be encouraged periodically to use offering envelopes. While they are not required to substantiate charitable contributions, they do reduce the risk of embezzlement. Also, offering counts should note (as a subtotal) loose cash unaccompanied by offering envelopes. This practice will reveal fluctuations that may indicate embezzlement, and will serve as a deterrent.
(8) Contribution receipts are not issued to members, or they are issued but members are not encouraged to report discrepancies to the church board.	A church does not provide members with receipts of their contributions. A church employee embezzles cash (whether or not accompanied by an offering envelope), knowing that the risk of discovery is remote. The same risk exists if a church issues contribution receipts but does not actively encourage members to verify the accuracy of these receipts.	Churches should issue a contribution receipt to each donor, and encourage donors to immediately call to the attention of church leaders any discrepancies between their own records and the amount reflected on the church receipt. Discrepancies should not be reported to the person who prepares contribution receipts.

Table 7-1 How Embezzlement Occurs: Common Examples of Poor Internal Control		
example of poor internal control	how embezzlement may occur	preventive action
(9) Offerings are not deposited immediately.	When offerings are not promptly deposited, the risk of embezzlement increases since funds are accessible longer. Further, some persons may claim they "reimbursed" themselves out of church funds for unauthorized expenses.	Offerings should be deposited promptly with a bank.
(10) Monthly bank statements are not reviewed by someone having no responsibility for handling cash.	A church bookkeeper writes a check to a fictitious company, then cashes it. The bookkeeper is responsible for reconciling bank statements, and does not disclose the embezzlement.	Monthly bank statements should be reviewed by a church official or employee having no responsibility for handling cash or writing checks (ideally, the statements should be sent to this person's residence). This form of embezzlement also can be avoided by requiring two signatures on all checks.
(11) Reimbursing employees for travel expenses or purchases of church equipment or supplies without requiring adequate substantiation.	A church employee claims to have purchased equipment for church use, and is reimbursed without substantiation. In fact, the purchase was solely for personal use.	Do not reimburse any employee's purchase of church supplies or equipment without first obtaining proof that the purchase was duly authorized; also insist on seeing a receipt documenting what was purchased and its price.

6. Responding to Allegations of Embezzlement

Sometimes a person who has embezzled church funds will voluntarily confess—usually out of a fear that he or she is about to be "caught." But in many cases the embezzler does not confess—at least initially. Discrepancies or irregularities may occur which cause church leaders to suspect this person. Consider the following examples.

• **Examples.** *The same person has counted church offerings for many years. The pastor inadvertently notices that offerings are always higher when this person is absent (due to illness, business, or vacation).*

• *Church officials noticed that a church bookkeeper was living a higher standard of living than was realistic given her income. Among other things, she purchased an expensive home and a luxury car.*

• *Church offerings have remained constant, or increased slightly, despite the fact that attendance has increased.*

• *A church treasurer notices that a church official with sole signature authority on the church checking account has purchased a number of expensive items from unknown companies without any documentation to prove what was purchased and why.*

Church leaders often are unsure how to address suspected cases of embezzlement. The suspected embezzler is almost always a trusted member or employee, and church leaders are reluctant to accuse such a person without irrefutable evidence that he or she is guilty. Seldom does such evidence exist. The pastor may confront the person about the suspicion, but in many cases the individual will deny any wrongdoing—even if guilty. This compounds the frustration of church officials, who do not know how to proceed.

Here is a checklist of steps that church leaders can take to help resolve such difficult cases:

1. *Confront the suspected embezzler.* The pastor and at least one other church leader should confront the suspected embezzler. Inform the person that the church has evidence indicating that he or she has embezzled church funds. Seek a confession. Inform the person that if no one confesses, the church will be forced to call in a CPA firm to confirm that embezzlement has occurred, and to identify the probable embezzler.

▶ *Embezzlement is a criminal offense. Depending on the amount of funds or property taken, it may be a felony that can result in a sentence in the state penitentiary. This obviously would have a devastating impact on the embezzler, and his or her family. If the evidence clearly indicates that a particular member or employee has embezzled church funds, but this person denies any wrongdoing, inform him or her that the church may be forced to turn the matter over to the police for investigation and prosecution.*

▶ *Embezzlers never report their illegally obtained "income" on their tax returns. Nor do they suspect that failure to do so may subject them to criminal tax evasion charges! In fact, in some cases it is actually more likely that the IRS will prosecute the embezzler for tax evasion than the local prosecutor will prosecute for the crime of embezzlement. If the evidence clearly indicates that a particular member or employee has embezzled church funds, but this person denies any wrongdoing, inform him or her that the church may be forced to turn the matter over to the IRS for investigation and possible prosecution.*

2. *Have a local CPA conduct an audit to establish that embezzlement has occurred, and provide an estimate of how much was embezzled.* If the suspected embezzler denies any wrongdoing (or if embezzlement is suspected but it is not clear who is guilty), church leaders should consider hiring a local CPA firm to look for evidence of embezzlement. There is a good possibility that the embezzlement will be detected, and that the perpetrator will be identified.

▶ *CPAs can also help the church establish a strong system of internal control to reduce the risk of embezzlement in the future.*

Many church leaders have found that turning the investigation over to a CPA firm is much more acceptable than conducting the investigation internally. The CPA firm is completely objective, and ordinarily will not know the suspected embezzler. Further, few church members will object to the church hiring a CPA firm to detect wrongdoing and help establish a sound system of internal control.

3. *Contacting the police or local prosecutor.* If the suspected embezzler does not confess, or if embezzlement is suspected but it is not clear who is guilty, church leaders must consider turning the matter over to the police or local prosecutor. This is a very difficult decision, since it may result in the prosecution and incarceration of a member of the congregation.

4. *The embezzler confesses.* In some cases the embezzler eventually confesses. Often, this is to prevent the church from turning the case over to the IRS or the police, or to a CPA firm. Embezzlers believe they will receive "better treatment" from their own church than from the government. In many cases they are correct. It often is astonishing how quickly church members will rally in support of the embezzler once he or she confesses—no matter how much money was stolen from the church. This is especially true when the embezzler used the embezzled funds for a "noble" purpose, such as medical bills for a sick child. Many church members demand that the embezzler be forgiven. They are shocked and repulsed by the suggestion that the embezzler—their friend and fellow church member—be turned over to the IRS or the police! But is it this simple? Should church leaders join in the outpouring of sympathy? Should the matter be dropped once the embezzler confesses?

These are questions that each church will have to answer for itself, depending on the circumstances of each case. *Before forgiving the embezzler and dropping the matter, church leaders should consider the following points:*

(1) *A serious crime has been committed, and the embezzler has breached a sacred trust.* The church should insist, at a minimum, that the embezzler must:

- disclose how much money was embezzled

- make full restitution by paying back all embezzled funds within a specified period of time, and

- immediately and permanently be removed from any position within the church involving access to church funds

▶ *Closely scrutinize and question the amount of funds the embezzler claims to have taken. Remember, you are relying on the word of an admitted thief. Is it a realistic amount? Is it consistent with the irregularities or discrepancies that caused church leaders to suspect embezzlement in the first place? If in doubt, consider hiring a local CPA to review the amount the embezzler claims to have stolen.*

(2) *In many cases the embezzler will insist that he or she is not able to pay back the embezzled funds.* The embezzled funds already have been spent. This presents church leaders with a difficult decision, since the embezzler has received unreported taxable income from the church. The embezzler should be informed that the embezzled funds must either be returned within a specified time, or a promissory note must be signed promising to pay back the embezzled funds within a specified period of time. The embezzler should be informed that failure to agree to either alternative will force the church to issue him or her a 1099 (or a corrected W-2 if the embezzler is an employee) reporting the embezzled funds as taxable income. Failure to do so will subject the church to a potential penalty (up to $10,000) for aiding and abetting in the substantial understatement of taxable income under section 6701 of the tax code.

▶ *An embezzler's biggest problem ordinarily will not be with the church or even with the local prosecutor. It will be with the IRS for failure to report taxable income. There are only two ways to avoid trouble with the IRS: (1) the embezzler pays back the embezzled funds, or (2) the church reports the embezzled funds as taxable income on a 1099 or corrected W-2.*

(3) *Church leaders must also remember that they owe a fiduciary obligation to the church and that they are stewards of the church's resources.* Viewing the offender with mercy does not necessarily mean that the debt must be forgiven and a criminal act ignored. Churches are public charities that exist to serve religious purposes, and they are funded entirely out of charitable contributions from persons who justifiably assume that their contributions will be used to further the church's mission. These purposes may not be served when a church forgives and ignores cases of embezzlement.

▶ *The federal Employee Polygraph Protection Act prohibits most employers from requiring or even suggesting that an employee submit to a polygraph exam. Employers also are prevented from dismissing or disciplining an employee for refusing to take a polygraph exam. There is an exception that may apply in some cases—an employer may require that an employee take a polygraph exam if the employee is suspected of a specific act of theft or other economic loss and the employer has reported the matter to the police. However, the employer must follow very strict requirements to avoid liability. A church should never suggest or require that an employee submit to a polygraph exam, even in cases of suspected embezzlement, without first contacting a local attorney for legal advice.*

7. The Consequences of Embezzlement

Persons who embezzle church funds face a number of consequences. Some of them may come as unpleasant surprises. Here are four of them.

• **Felony conviction.** Embezzling church funds is a felony in most states, and conviction can lead to a term in a state penitentiary. The definition of embezzlement varies slightly from state to state, but in general it refers to the wrongful conversion of property that is lawfully in your possession. The idea is that someone has legal control or custody of property or funds, and then decides to convert the property or funds to his or her own personal use.

Key point. *It does not matter that the embezzler intended to pay back the embezzled funds. This intent in no way justifies or excuses the crime. The crime is complete when the funds are converted to one's own use—whether or not there was an intent to pay them back.*

Key point. *Sometimes an embezzler, when caught, will agree to pay back embezzled funds. This does not alter the fact that the crime of embezzlement has occurred. Of course, it may be less likely that a prosecutor will prosecute the case under these circumstances. And even if the embezzler is prosecuted, this evidence may lessen the punishment. But the courts have consistently ruled that an actual return of embezzled property does not purge the offense of its criminal nature or absolve the embezzler from punishment for his or her wrongdoing. Also, note that church officials seldom know if all embezzled funds are being returned. They are relying almost entirely on the word of the thief.*

• **Tax evasion.** In many cases the embezzler's biggest concern is not the possibility of being prosecuted for the crime of embezzlement. Rather, it is the possibility of being prosecuted by the IRS for tax evasion. Embezzlers never report their illegally obtained "income" on their tax returns. Nor do they suspect that failure to do so may subject them to criminal tax evasion charges. In fact, in some cases it is actually more likely that the IRS will prosecute the embezzler for tax evasion than the local prosecutor will prosecute for the crime of embezzlement.

Example. *A church accountant embezzled $212,000 in church funds. His scheme was to divert to his own use several designated offerings, and to inflate the cost of* equipment that he paid for with his own funds and that the church later reimbursed at the inflated amounts. The accountant not only was found guilty of embezzlement, but he was also convicted of tax evasion because he had failed to report any of the embezzled money as taxable income. He was sentenced to a 2-year prison term, followed by 2 years of probation.

- **Recovery of property purchased with embezzled funds.** Here's a real shocker— persons who receive property purchased by the embezzler with embezzled funds may be required to return the property to the church!

Example. A church bookkeeper embezzled several thousand dollars by issuing checks to a fictitious company. He opened an account in the name of a fictitious company, issued church checks to the company for services that were never performed, and then deposited the checks in the fictitious company's account. He later withdrew the funds and purchased two automobiles which he gave to a friend. A court ruled that the friend had to give the cars back to the church, since they had been purchased with embezzled church funds. The point here, as noted by the court, is that one who acquires property with embezzled church funds may be required to transfer the property to the church.

- **Insurance company lawsuits.** As if the three consequences summarized above are not enough, embezzlers face an additional consequence—they may be sued by an insurance company that pays a claim based on the embezzlement. Many churches purchase insurance to cover financial losses due to theft or embezzlement. Insurance companies that pay out claims based on such losses are free to sue the persons responsible.

Example. A court ruled that an insurance company that paid out $26,000 to a charity because of an act of embezzlement could sue the embezzler for the full amount that it paid. Such cases illustrate an important point—a church employee or volunteer who embezzles church funds may be sued by the church insurance company if it pays out a claim based on the embezzlement.

8. Confidentiality and Privileged Communications

Sometimes ministers learn of embezzlement through a confession by the embezzler in the course of confidential counseling. This presents the minister with a dilemma—either protect the confidentiality of the confession and refuse to disclose it, or ignore confidentiality and disclose the confession. This dilemma is compounded by the fact that some ministers have been sued for disclosing confidential information without the consent of the other person. Embezzlers may claim that they confessed their crime to their minister in confidence and in the course of spiritual counseling, with no thought that the minister would disclose the information to others.

▶ *Ministers who disclose confidential information without permission risk being sued for breaching their duty of confidentiality. When an employee or volunteer approaches a minister and confesses to embezzling church funds, there normally will be an expectation that the minister will keep that information in confidence. There is no sign above the minister's desk that says, "Warning: confessions of criminal activity will be promptly shared with the board or with the civil authorities."[348] Ministers who violate this expectation need to understand that they face potential legal liability for doing so—unless they have the employee's permission, in writing.*

Ministers who receive a confidential confession of embezzlement from a church employee or volunteer should not disclose this information to others, including the church board, without the person's written permission. If the embezzler does not consent to the disclosure of the confession, and refuses to meet with the board, the minister should not disclose the information to any other person. Disclosure under these circumstances could result in a lawsuit being brought against the minister and church.

Does this mean that the minister should drop the matter? Not necessarily. The minister is free to gather independent evidence that embezzlement occurred, so long as this is done without disclosing the confession. For example, the minister could persuade the church board to hire a CPA to conduct an audit of the church's financial records. Such a procedure may reveal that embezzlement has occurred. The minister also should attempt to persuade the embezzler to confess to the board.

Key point. *Closely related to the concept of confidentiality is the clergy-penitent privilege. Ministers cannot be compelled to disclose in court the contents of confidential communications shared with them in the course of spiritual counseling.*

Example. *Late one night, a church treasurer arranged a meeting with her priest after informing him that she "had done something almost as bad as murder." The treasurer, after requesting that their conversation be kept confidential, informed the priest that she had embezzled $30,000 in church funds. The priest, with the permission of the treasurer, sought the assistance of the church board. The board decided that the embezzlement had to be reported to the local police. The treasurer was later prosecuted for embezzling church funds, and she was convicted and sentenced to 4 months in jail despite the fact that she fully repaid the church prior to her trial. She appealed her conviction on the ground that it had been based on her confidential statements to the priest which, in her opinion, were "penitential communications" that were privileged against disclosure in court. The appeals court concluded that the statements made by the church treasurer to the priest were not privileged since they involved a "problem-solving entreaty" by the treasurer rather than "a request to make a true confession seeking forgiveness or absolution—the very essence of the spiritual relationship privileged under the statute." That is, the treasurer sought out the priest not for spiritual counseling, but to disclose her embezzlement and to seek his counsel on how to correct the problem. The court also emphasized that the treasurer had "released" the priest from his assurance of confidentiality by consenting to his disclosure of the facts of the case to the church board members.*

---

[348] *See* Lightman v. Flaum, 687 N.Y.S.2d 562 (Sup. 1999), in which the court observed: "It is beyond peradventure that, when one seeks the solace and spiritual advice and guidance of a member of the clergy, whether it be a priest, rabbi or minister, on such sensitive, personal matters as those involved in our case, this is not done as a prelude to an announcement from the pulpit."

9. Informing the Congregation

Church leaders often refuse to disclose to the congregation any information about an incident of embezzlement for fear of being sued for defamation. This concern is understandable. However, serious problems can occur when the pastor or church board dismisses a long-term employee or volunteer for embezzlement and nothing is disclosed to the membership. Church leaders under these circumstances often are accused of acting arbitrarily, and there is a demand for an explanation. Refusal to respond to such demands may place the church leadership in an even worse light.

There is a possible answer to this dilemma. Many states recognize the concept of "qualified privilege." This means that statements made to others concerning a matter of common interest cannot be defamatory unless made with malice. Statements are made with malice if they are made with a knowledge that they are false, or with a reckless disregard as to their truth or falsity. In the church context, this privilege protects statements made by members to other members concerning matters of common interest. Such communications cannot be defamatory unless malice is proven. Church leaders who decide to disclose why an embezzler was dismissed can reduce the legal risk to the church and themselves by following a few basic precautions:

- Only share information with active voting members of the church—at a membership meeting or by letter. The qualified privilege does not apply if the communication is made to non-members.

- Adopt procedures that will confirm that no non-member received the information.

- Limit your remarks to factual information and do not express opinions.

- Prepare in advance a written statement that is communicated with members, and that is approved in advance by an attorney.

Key point. *In some cases, it is helpful to obtain a signed confession from an individual who has been found guilty or who has confessed. If the individual consents to the communication of the confession to church members, then you can quote from the confession in a letter that is sent to members of the congregation, or in a membership meeting. Be sure that this consent is in writing.*

Key point. *One court ruled that a church could be sued for defamation for sharing suspicions regarding a church treasurer's embezzlement with members in a congregational meeting. The court concluded that the treasurer should have been investigated and dismissed by the board, without informing the congregation. While no other court has reached a similar conclusion, this case suggests that church leaders should disclose cases of embezzlement to the church membership only if (1) absolutely necessary (for example, to reduce congregational unrest), and (2) an attorney is involved in making this decision.*

10. Avoiding false accusations

In some cases it is not certain that embezzlement has occurred, or that a particular individual is guilty. A church must be careful in how it proceeds in these cases to avoid possible liability for defamation or emotional distress.

Example. *A church's senior pastor believed that certain members of the church board (including the chairman) had diverted $94,000 of church funds earmarked for a remodeling project to other uses. He expressed his concerns at meetings of the church board, and to the entire congregation at a special business meeting. He informed the congregation that he wanted an "accounting" of the funds to determine if they had been used improperly, and he insisted that the board chairman resign his position. The chairman claimed that the pastor's acts amounted to a "false accusation" that he and other board members had embezzled church funds. The pastor retained an attorney who wrote the board chairman a letter demanding that he "immediately cease and desist from [his] unlawful threats, harassment, blackmail and extortion of the pastor." The attorney's letter continued:*

> *It is a disgrace that a man who holds himself out to be a Christian engages in such conduct. You are upset that the pastor has requested an accounting of the church monies which you have controlled for years and, rather than provide the information, you have launched a personal attack on him. The only conclusion one can reach from such behavior is that you have, in fact, embezzled money from the church. The pastor has referred this matter to the appropriate church board as well as governing bodies. We are confident that they will pursue actions against you to recover all church property.*

> *The deposed board chairman sued the church for defamation. A trial court dismissed the lawsuit and a state appeals court affirmed the trial court's ruling. It noted that the pastor's expressing concerns about the use of designated church funds was not defamatory, and the attorney's letter that accused the board chairman of "embezzlement" was not defamatory since it was protected by the "litigation privilege" (good faith statements made in contemplation of litigation generally cannot be defamatory). Miller v. Second Baptist Church, 2004 WL 1161653 (Cal. App. 2004).*[349]

Example. *A church convened a special business meeting at which the church treasurer was accused of embezzling church funds. Following this meeting the treasurer was shunned by church members who viewed her as guilty. This case is tragic, since the treasurer had been a long and devoted member of the church. Her life was ruined by the allegation, and she had to leave the church. It was later proven that she was completely innocent. She later filed a lawsuit, accusing the pastor and members of the church board of defamation. A court agreed with her, and awarded her a substantial verdict. The court pointed out that the accusation of embezzlement was based on flimsy evidence and could have easily been refuted with any reasonable investigation. The court concluded that church leaders are liable for defamation if they charge a church worker with embezzlement without first conducting a good faith investigation. The court also pointed out that the charges should not have been disclosed to the congregation, but rather should have been discussed among the church board and a decision made at that level on whether or not to dismiss the treasurer.*

---

[349] Miller v. Second Baptist Church, 2004 WL 1161653 (unpublished decision, Cal. App. 2004).

This case provides church leaders with very helpful guidance in handling suspicions of embezzlement. Do not rush to judgment. Conduct a deliberate and competent investigation, and let the church board resolve the issue without involving or informing the congregation, if possible. In some cases, congregational outrage may occur following the dismissal of an embezzler by the pastor or church board, especially if nothing is communicated to the congregation about the basis for the action. In these cases the board may decide that the membership must be informed. If so, refer to the above discussion on "informing the congregation."

10. The Employee Polygraph Protection Act

The federal Employee Polygraph Protection Act (EPPA) prohibits employers from requiring or requesting any employee or job applicant to take a lie detector test, or from discharging, disciplining, or discriminating against an employee or prospective employee for refusing to take a test or for exercising other rights under the Act.

However, the Act contains limited exemptions where polygraph tests (but no other lie detector tests) may be administered, subject to certain restrictions. One exception allows employers to ask employees to submit to a polygraph exam if they are suspected of theft and there is an ongoing investigation. Here are the details of this exception:

[This Act] shall not prohibit an employer from requesting an employee to submit to a polygraph test if—

(1) the test is administered in connection with an ongoing investigation involving economic loss or injury to the employer's business, such as theft, embezzlement, misappropriation, or an act of unlawful industrial espionage or sabotage;

(2) the employee had access to the property that is the subject of the investigation;

(3) the employer had a reasonable suspicion that the employee was involved in the incident or activity under investigation; and

(4) the employer executes a statement, provided to the examinee before the test, that—(A) sets forth with particularity the specific incident or activity being investigated and the basis for testing particular employees, (B) is signed by a person (other than a polygraph examiner) authorized to legally bind the employer, (C) is retained by the employer for at least 3 years, and (D) contains at a minimum—(i) an identification of the specific economic loss or injury to the business of the employer, (ii) a statement indicating that the employee had access to the property that is the subject of the investigation, and (iii) a statement describing the basis of the employer's reasonable suspicion that the employee was involved in the incident or activity under investigation.[350]

---

[350] 29 U.S.C. § 2006(d).

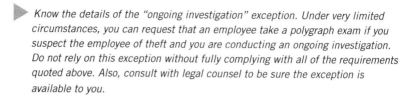 *Know the details of the "ongoing investigation" exception. Under very limited circumstances, you can request that an employee take a polygraph exam if you suspect the employee of theft and you are conducting an ongoing investigation. Do not rely on this exception without fully complying with all of the requirements quoted above. Also, consult with legal counsel to be sure the exception is available to you.*

Examples

• *A church board suspects the church's volunteer treasurer of embezzling several thousands of dollars of church funds. The treasurer is called into a board meeting, and is told "you can clear your name if you submit to a polygraph exam." Does this conduct violate the Employee Polygraph Protection Act? Possibly not. The Act only protects "employees," and so a volunteer treasurer presumably would not be covered. However, if the treasurer receives any compensation whatever for her services, or is a "prospective employee," then the Act would apply. Because of the possibility that volunteer workers may in some cases be deemed "employees," you should not suggest or request that they take a polygraph exam without the advice of legal counsel.*

• *Same facts as the previous example, except that the church suspects a full-time secretary of embezzlement. Can it suggest that the secretary take a polygraph exam? Only if all the requirements of the "ongoing investigation" exception apply. These include: (1) the test is administered in connection with an ongoing investigation involving economic loss or injury to the employer's business, such as theft or embezzlement; (2) the employee had access to the property that is the subject of the investigation; (3) the employer had a reasonable suspicion that the employee was involved in the incident or activity under investigation; and (4) the employer executes a statement, provided to the examinee before the test, that—(A) sets forth with particularity the specific incident or activity being investigated and the basis for testing particular employees, (B) is signed by a person (other than a polygraph examiner) authorized to legally bind the employer, (C) is retained by the employer for at least 3 years, and (D) contains at a minimum—(i) an identification of the specific economic loss or injury to the business of the employer, (ii) a statement indicating that the employee had access to the property that is the subject of the investigation, and (iii) a statement describing the basis of the employer's reasonable suspicion that the employee was involved in the incident or activity under investigation.*

The EPPA provides that an employer that violates the Act is liable to the employee or prospective employee for "such relief as may be appropriate, including, but not limited to, employment, reinstatement, promotion, and the payment of lost wages and benefits." A court may also award damages based on "emotional distress," and punitive damages.

Key point. *Damages awarded for violating the Employee Polygraph Protection Act may not be covered under a church's liability insurance policy. This is another reason for church leaders to assume that the Act applies to their church, and to interpret its provisions prudently.*

Instructional Aids to Chapter 7

Key Terms

accessory use

adverse possession

building code

compulsory deference rule

condemnation

congregational

constructive trust

disaffiliation

embezzlement

eminent domain

Employee Polygraph Protection Act

hierarchical

implied trust doctrine

invitees, licensees, and trespassers

just compensation

landmarking

materialmen's liens

neutral principles of law

nuisance

polity

premises liability

qualified privilege

Religious Land Use and Institutionalized Persons Act

Residential Lead-Based Paint Hazard Reduction Act

restrictive covenants

resulting trust

reversion clauses

special use permit

Watson v. Jones

Learning Objectives

- Understand the difference between hierarchical and congregational churches.

- Explain the compulsory deference rule.

- Explain the neutral principles of law approach to resolving church property disputes.

- Describe how the courts resolve property disputes involving congregational churches.

- Describe how the courts resolve property disputes involving hierarchical churches.

- Identify several methods of resolving potential property disputes internally without the need for civil court intervention.

- Have a basic understanding of zoning laws, and their application to churches.

- Be familiar with the Religious Land Use and Institutionalized Persons Act, and its application to churches.

- Explain eminent domain, and understand its relevance to churches.

- Explain landmarking, and understand its relevance to churches.

- Explain restrictive covenants, and understand their relevance to churches.

- Explain reversionary clauses in deeds, and understand their relevance to churches.

- Explain materialmen's liens, and understand their relevance to churches.

- Explain adverse possession, and understand its relevance to churches.

- Define premises liability, and understand its application to church property and activities.

- Be able to define embezzlement, explain how it occurs, and describe ways to prevent it.

Short-Answer Questions

1. A church is an independent church that was started several years ago by Pastor Steve. The church charter recites the church's doctrinal positions, including the infallibility of the Bible. Pastor Steve left the church two years ago. The pastoral change resulted in a significant change in the church's membership. Many new persons began attending the church, while many long-term members left. This year, a majority of the church congregation voted to amend the charter to remove the doctrinal position of Biblical inerrancy. A minority of members protested. A schism resulted. Which faction is entitled to the church property?

2. An elderly church member dies several years ago, leaving a will in which she gave $500,000 of her estate to her local church "to be used exclusively for the construction of a new sanctuary for so long as the church remains affiliated with [a named denomination], and, in the event the church ever disaffiliates from [the denomination], then to said denomination." The member's church constructed a new sanctuary. This year, a new minister convinces a majority of church members to vote to disaffiliate from the denomination. A minority of members claim that the majority is no longer entitled to keep the church property. The majority disagrees. What is the most likely outcome of this case?

3. A church amends its bylaws to read, in part: "In the event that the church shall ever disaffiliate from [a named denomination], its properties shall immediately revert to said denomination." A controversy within the church leads to a division of the congregation. A majority of the members vote to disaffiliate from the denomination. Immediately after taking the vote to disaffiliate, the church membership votes to amend the bylaws by deleting the reverter clause quoted above. A minority of members contend that the property now belongs to the denomination. What is the most likely outcome of this case?

4. The *deed* to a church's property vests title in the church for so long as it is affiliated with its parent denomination, and if it ceases to be so affiliated, then title reverts to the denomination. The *church bylaws* specify that if the church ever disaffiliates from its parent denomination, then title to all church property immediately reverts to the denomination. The *bylaws of the denomination* specify that the property of any church that "departs from the stated doctrines" of the denomination shall revert to the denomination. A majority of the church's

members vote to disaffiliate from the parent denomination. They also (1) vote to amend the bylaws by deleting the reverter clause, and (2) authorize the church board to deed the church property back to the church without a reverter clause. A minority of members claim that the denomination's bylaw provision requires that all church property revert to the denomination. The church disagrees. What is the most likely outcome of this case?

5. A majority of the members of a local church vote to disaffiliate from a parent denomination. The denomination has an ecclesiastical tribunal that rules that title to all church property now belongs to the denomination. The church ignores this ruling on the ground that it is no longer affiliated with the denomination and therefore is not subject to its rulings. Who owns the property?

6. Give four examples of "neutral principles of law."

7. Explain the "compulsory deference rule."

8. Explain the difference between a hierarchical and a congregational church.

9. The membership of a small church gradually departs from several of the original doctrinal positions of the church. Only one member is left who adheres to the original doctrines. This member claims that title to the church's property is legally vested in himself, and not in the majority. Do you agree? Explain.

10. A denomination's bylaws contain a provision specifying that the property of a local church reverts to the denomination in the event the church "deviates from the doctrines" of the denomination. Is such a clause an effective way for the denomination to maintain control over the property? Why or why not?

11. A denomination's bylaws contain a provision specifying that the property of a local church reverts to the denomination in the event the church "disaffiliates from" the denomination. Is such a clause an effective way for the denomination to maintain control over the property? Why or why not?

12. A church adopts a bylaw provision stating that the church is affiliated with a particular denomination. This provision further states that it is "not amendable." Would such a clause be legally enforceable?

13. A church adopts a bylaw provision stating that the church is affiliated with a particular denomination. This provision further states that it is amendable only by a 100% vote of all active members. Would such a clause be legally enforceable?

14. A local congregational church splits, and a minority of members who continue to adhere to the original doctrine of the church are expelled from the property. They form their own church and purchase a church building. They want

to take whatever steps as are necessary to ensure that those members adhering to the original doctrine of the church will never be ousted from the property. What steps would you recommend?

15. Same facts as question 14, except that the church is hierarchical in structure.

16. A denomination purchases a church building for a mission church. What steps could the denomination take to ensure that title to the property will remain with those members who desire to remain affiliated with it?

17. A national church denomination adopts a bylaw amendment specifying that the properties of affiliated churches are thereafter held "in trust" for the denomination. An affiliated church votes to withdraw from the denomination. Is the affiliated church entitled to retain its property, or will it revert to the denomination?

18. A denominational agency purchases land for a new church, pays for the construction of a church building, and installs a pastor. Several years later, the church votes to disaffiliate from the denomination. What legal principle could the denomination assert to acquire control of the church property?

19. A church purchases a tract of undeveloped land in order to construct a new facility. It learns that it is required by the local zoning ordinance to obtain a special use permit before it can begin construction. The church insists that the special use permit requirement violates its First Amendment right to freely exercise its religion. Assess the validity of the church's claim.

20. A city council believes that the city has enough churches, so it enacts an ordinance banning any new churches. Assess the constitutional validity of such a ordinance.

21. A church's present facility has become too crowded, and the church decides to purchase an undeveloped lot in a residential zone of the city as a site for a new building. Neighboring landowners oppose construction on the ground that a church would increase traffic congestion, create additional hazards for children playing in the street, cause additional pollution and noise, and depreciate property values in the neighborhood. Will a civil court prohibit the church from constructing a new facility in the residential zone on the basis of the neighbors' arguments? Explain.

22. Can a city exclude a church from building a new facility anywhere within areas of town that are zoned for residential use? Explain.

23. A church wants to open a private elementary school and a child care

facility on its property. It is located in an area zoned for residential and church uses. Will the elementary and nursery schools be permitted uses? Explain.

24. A church is designated as a "landmark" by a local board. As a result, the church is not able to expand its present facilities. The church sues the city, claiming that this restriction violates the First Amendment guaranty of religious freedom. Will the church prevail? Is there an argument the church could make that would increase its chances of winning?

25. A state office informs a church that the construction of new highway will make it necessary to demolish the church. Is the church entitled to compensation from the state? If so, in what amount?

26. A city announces that it will use the power of eminent domain to take a church's property so that it can be demolished and replaced by a commercial building that will pay property taxes. What, if any, legal defenses would the church have in such a case?

27. Identify at least two reasons why it is important for church leaders to be familiar with the wording in deeds to church property.

28. What is a materialman's lien? How is it created? Give an example of how such a lien may be imposed on church property. What is the legal effect of such a lien?

29. Briefly describe the protections provided by the Religious Land Use and Institutionalized Persons Act.

30. A city ordinance prohibits churches and all other charitable organizations from locating in residential areas without obtaining a special use permit from city officials. A church applies for a permit, and a hearing is conducted at which several neighboring homeowners complain that their property valuations will decline if a church is allowed in their neighborhood. The church's application for a permit is denied. The church sues the city, claiming that its rights under RLUIPA have been violated. What is the most likely outcome of this case?

31. Same facts as example 30, except that the city ordinance only required religious organizations to apply for a special use permit in order to use property in residential areas for religious purposes. Several other charitable organizations are not required to obtain such a permit. Will the city' actions violate RLUIPA? The First Amendment? Explain.

32. Does a city have the legal authority to restrict the size of church signs? Explain.

33. Summarize the application of the Residential Lead-Based Paint Hazard

Reduction Act to churches.

34. A church purchased a home in 1960 to use as a parsonage. The church's senior pastor moves out of the parsonage this year and purchases a home. The church decides to retain the parsonage, and later the parsonage is leased to a family with two young children. Church leaders are not familiar with the Residential Lead-Based Paint Hazard Reduction Act, and do not comply with any of its provisions. After living in the parsonage for several months the lessees' children begin to exhibit serious neurological problems. A physician diagnoses the condition as lead poisoning, and it is later determined that the children have been eating lead-based paint in the parsonage. The parents sue the church on the basis of the Residential Lead-Based Paint Hazard Reduction Act. What is the most likely outcome of this lawsuit? If a court concludes that each child's injuries amount to $1 million, what is the total liability of the church?

35. Same facts as the previous example, except that the parsonage was constructed in 1980, and acquired by the church in 1983.

36. A church purchased a home in 1970 to use as a parsonage. This year the senior pastor moves out of the parsonage, and the church allows its youth pastor to move in. The youth pastor has three minor children. Is this transaction subject to the Residential Lead-Based Paint Hazard Reduction Act? Explain.

37. A church leases a portion of its premises to another congregation on Sunday afternoons. The other congregation conducts religious services, and education classes for adults and children. While the church is leasing its premises to the other congregation, is it subject to the provisions of the Residential Lead-Based Paint Hazard Reduction Act? Explain.

38. A church purchases three homes next to its parking lot, to accommodate future expansion. The homes were each constructed in the 1950s. The church rents the homes. Are these rental arrangements subject to the Residential Lead-Based Paint Hazard Reduction Act?

39. What is "just compensation" in the context of eminent domain?

40. A church chooses not to rent its facility to religious groups that are not Christian. Has it violated the federal Fair Housing Act? Explain.

41. Define the terms invitee, licensee, and trespasser, and summarize the duty of care that a landowner owes to each category.

42. An armed assailant enters a church during a worship service, and shoots three persons in the church lobby. Is the church legally responsible to the victims? What factors would a court consider in resolving this question?

43. Under what circumstances might a church have a legal duty to employ

armed police officers or security guards on its premises during worship services?

44. What legal risks would be associated with a church's decision to employ armed security guards on its premises?

45. A church decides to manage the risk of shootings on its premises by installing metal detectors at its two primary entrances. Evaluate the pros and cons of the church's decision.

46. A church decides to manage the risk of shootings on its premises by installing video cameras in the main lobby of the church as well as in a few hallways. Evaluate the pros and cons of the church's decision.

47. A church member stumbles on a puddle of water on a tile floor in a church basement prior to a morning worship service.

> a. On the basis of what legal theory would the church most likely be responsible for the victim's injuries?
>
> b. What defenses are available to the church?
>
> c. Would such a risk be covered under a standard general liability insurance policy? If so, would the church have to pay for its own legal defense? Explain.

48. On a Saturday afternoon, several neighborhood children are playing on recreational equipment on a church's property. No church employee or member is present. One of the children is injured when she falls off of one piece of equipment. She sues the church.

> a. On the basis of what legal theory would the church most likely be responsible for the victim's injuries?
>
> b. What defenses are available to the church?

49. What steps could a church take to manage the risks associated with the construction of a skate ramp on its property?

50. What legal risks are associated with sound rooms in churches? What steps can churches take to manage these risks?

51. Define embezzlement.

52. A church bookkeeper embezzles $10,000 in church funds, but plans on

reimbursing the church as soon as she is able to do so. Is this intent to make full restitution an effective defense to a charge of embezzlement? Explain.

53. List three ways that embezzlement of church funds can occur.

54. List at least five steps that a church can take to reduce the risk of embezzlement.

55. Why might the IRS be interested in learning about the embezzlement of church funds?

56. A church treasurer confesses to the pastor that he has embezzled $50,000 in church funds. Which of the following actions may expose the church to legal liability:

    a. The pastor immediately informs the board.

    b. The board notifies the police.

    c. The treasurer is prosecuted and convicted, and sentenced to prison.

    d. The pastor informs the congregation following a worship service.

57. What are "internal controls"? Identify three internal controls.

58. A church treasurer confesses to the pastor that she has embezzled $10,000 in church funds. She agrees to pay back the full amount, and resigns from her position. Answer the following questions:

    a. Has the crime of embezzlement been committed if the treasurer in fact pays back the full $10,000?

    b. Should the pastor inform the police or local prosecutor?

    c. Several members of the congregation ask the pastor why the treasurer has been removed. Should the pastor disclose the reason to the congregation? If so, how?

59. How might a pastor or church board manage the risk associated with informing the congregation concerning the embezzlement of church funds?

Essay Problems

1. The Supreme Court has ruled that the courts are free to disregard the rulings of the ecclesiastical tribunals of religious denominations in church property disputes when no question of religious doctrine or polity is involved. For example, courts are now free to apply the "neutral principles of law" approach in resolving church property disputes even if this produces a result contrary to the ruling of a religious denomination, so long as no question of religious doctrine or polity is involved. Do you believe that the Supreme Court has given the civil courts too much authority in this context? Should the courts always be compelled to defer to the ruling of religious denominations? Explain.

2. In 1969, the Supreme Court ruled that the courts no longer can resolve church property disputes on the basis of religious doctrine. Do you agree with this decision? Do you believe that the courts should have the authority to resolve church property disputes in those cases not involving religious doctrine? Explain.

3. A church treasurer confesses to embezzlement, pays back the embezzled funds, and resigns. Should the church turn the matter over to the local prosecutor? What considerations would be relevant in reaching a decision?

INDEX